The history of the city

LEONARDO BENEVOLO
The history of the city

Translated by Geoffrey Culverwell

SCOLAR PRESS
London 1980

Storia della Città published in Italy 1975 by Editori Laterza, Rome
Copyright © Editori Laterza, 1975

First published in Great Britain 1980 by Scolar Press,
90/91 Great Russell Street, London WC1B 3PY
Scolar Press is an imprint of Bemrose UK Limited
This translation copyright © Scolar Press, 1980

British Library Cataloguing in Publication Data
Benevolo, Leonardo
    The history of the city.
    1. Cities and towns – History
    I. Title
    301.36'3'09   HT111
    ISBN 0 85967 534 3

Designed by Thumb Design Partnership London
Phototypeset in V.I.P. Garamond by
Western Printing Services Ltd, Bristol, England
Printed in U.S.A.

Contents

		Introduction	5
Chapter	1	The prehistoric background and the origins of the city	7
Chapter	2	The free city in Greece	55
Chapter	3	Rome: city and worldwide empire	135
Chapter	4	The formation of the medieval environment	253
Chapter	5	The cities of Islam	259
Chapter	6	European cities in the Middle Ages	287
Chapter	7	Renaissance art	501
Chapter	8	Italian cities during the Renaissance	535
Chapter	9	European colonisation	605
Chapter	10	The capitals of baroque Europe	653
Chapter	11	The setting of the Industrial Revolution	733
Chapter	12	The 'post-liberal' city	765
Chapter	13	The modern city	841
Chapter	14	The situation today	897
		Index of names	1009

Introduction

This book, which provides a basic history of the man-made environment, is in the form of a short written text combined with a large number of illustrations. A great deal of the material included in it is based on the drawing course devised for the Liceo Scientificato* (published by Editori Laterza), itself an attempt to provide a basic environmental education to those pupils who have not yet decided on their future career. The curriculum in Italian schools is such that this type of course can only be attempted in the Liceo Scientificato, where it can be taught in the context of the one traditional subject — drawing — which lies midway between Arts and Sciences, the two disparate alternatives open for study in other types of school. Yet this basic education is needed in order to be able to understand properly the historical reasons for the particular environment in which each of us finds ourselves. Everyone should learn how to interpret and describe the material world without resorting to high-flown rhetoric, so that it can be discussed and modified and not just accepted without thinking.

It has therefore been decided to turn the history textbooks that form part of the drawing course — covering classical antiquity, the Middle Ages and the modern and contemporary periods — into a single volume aimed at a wider non-specialist readership. No longer being subject to the limitations inherent in an academic course, the original material has been expanded and includes data on earlier and more remote cities and thereby gives a more extensive and comprehensive picture of urban development in various

parts of the world.

Despite these additions the book still has a single theme — the emergence and transformation of the urban environment in Europe and the Near East. Developments in other areas (the Far East, Africa and the Americas) are referred to only when they relate to events in Europe; the book describes the cities which existed prior to the advent of Europeans, and also those built in the post-colonial era when Europe was the dominant force in the world.

The choice of the city as the classic, indeed the definitive, example of man-made environment is justified with regard to Europe, since it was there that the idea first emerged of the city as an integral and self-contained settlement, containing within itself other lesser settlements — living quarters, buildings and so on — which either form a part of the whole or act as incomplete models of it. Yet cities still remain specifically historical creations. They have not always existed; they began at a certain period in the evolution of society and can equally be ended or radically transformed at another. They came into being not as a result of any natural necessity, but as the result of an historical need, and they will continue only for as long as this need persists.

It is for this reason that the origins of the city in the ancient world need to be explained, as does its future in the modern world, so far as this is possible. In order to do this, the major changes in productive organisation that have transformed everyday life and on each occasion led to a sharp rise in population are briefly charted.

* Italian secondary schools specialising in scientific subjects.

1. Man appeared on earth some 500,000 years ago, and for a very long time (a period corresponding to the geological Pleistocene period) he lived by food-gathering, seeking shelter in the natural environment without making any deep or lasting changes to it. Archaeologists call this the Palaeolithic (Old Stone) Age, and it covers more than 95 per cent of man's history. There are even some societies in the modern world, isolated by jungle and desert, that have still not progressed beyond the Palaeolithic stage.

2. About 10,000 years ago, after the glaciers had melted — an event that marked the last major change in the natural environment of the world and its transition from the Pleistocene to the Holocene era — the inhabitants of the temperate zones learned to produce their own food by growing crops and rearing cattle. They also organised permanent settlements near their places of work, and these became the first villages. This era is known as the Neolithic (New Stone) Age, and for many people it lasted right up until their first encounter with Europeans; the Maoris of New Zealand, for example, remained at this stage until the beginning of the nineteenth century.

3. About 5,000 years ago, on the alluvial plains of the Near East, a few of these villages were transformed into cities. The food-producers were persuaded or forced to produce a surplus so as to support a population of specialists such as craftsmen, merchants, soldiers and priests, who lived in a more complex settlement, the city, and from there controlled the surrounding countryside. This reorganisation of society made the invention of writing a necessity, and it was this innovation that marked the end of prehistory and the advent of civilisation and written history. From this period on, every historical event depended on the quantity and distribution of the surplus product.

Scholars make a distinction between the Bronze Age and the Iron Age. During the former, rare and expensive metals were used to manufacture tools and weapons, thus restricting their possession to members of a small ruling class who monopolised the whole of the available surplus and, because of their limited numbers, also prevented any growth in population or production. During the latter period, however, which began in about 1200 BC, the widespread availability of cheaper metal utensils and the introduction of coinage and the alphabet enabled the ruling class to expand and allow for a new growth in population. The Graeco-Roman civilisation developed this type of organisation over a large self-contained economic zone — the Mediterranean basin — but it also enslaved and impoverished those directly responsible for production, a trend that resulted in its gradual economic collapse from the fourth century AD onwards.

4. Other historical developments, such as the change from a feudal to a bourgeois society, paved the way for the next major historical upheaval: the use of mechanisation and automation to produce the increased output which characterises modern industrial society. This growing and seemingly limitless surplus need not necessarily be restricted to members of the ruling class; it could well be distributed amongst the majority or even, theoretically, amongst the entire population, which, freed from economic restraints, could increase in number until it reached or even surpassed the limits imposed by the natural environment. In this new industrial world there is still a great contrast between the urban centres (the domain of the ruling classes) and the rural areas (the domain of the subordinate classes), but this dichotomy is no longer inevitable and could well be overcome. This possibility leads to ideas of a new, self-contained settlement like the ancient city (and therefore still called 'a city'), which would embrace all areas of habitation: the modern city, in fact.

In this historical survey a comprehensive examination will be made of the changes that have occurred in the physical environment, an area which is influenced by all the other aspects of civilisation and in turn influences them itself, taking into account the way in which the monuments of the past have hindered these changes and the buildings of the modern era have hastened them.

1
The prehistoric background and the origins of the city

We have only a rough idea of what the world was like in which tens of thousands of generations of Neolithic men lived. It was during this period that the last major geological changes were shaping the natural environment which today, given the briefness of our historical perspective, seems so fixed and unchanging. The man-made environment was merely a superficial modification of that vast and hostile natural environment. Man's refuge was a natural hollow or a shelter made of skins draped over a crude wooden framework. With no evidence to go on, early illustrators tried to visualise what the life of these primitive men was like (Fig. 2).

By excavating and studying the material traces left by primitive man modern archaeologists have given us a picture which, although more realistic, is at the same time more confused. Archaeological evidence of the earliest settlements consists mainly of the refuse of human activity — remains of food, fragments discarded during the processing of stone and wood, and finished articles that were used and then later abandoned or buried. The distribution of these objects round the nucleus of the hearth — the classic pointer to the presence of men who had learned to use fire — implies a self-contained entity that could be called a primitive dwelling, even though we cannot detect a clearly recognisable shape in it (Figs 1, 2, 4).

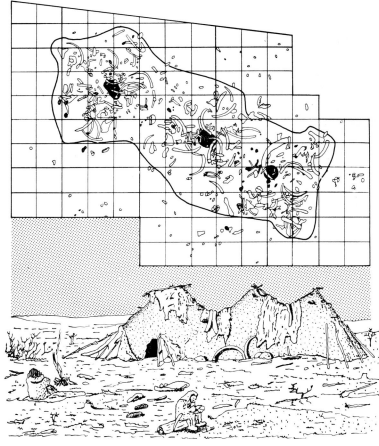

Fig. 1   Late Palaeolithic dwelling in the Ukraine.

Fig. 2   The life of primitive man, as seen in an illustration from a treatise by Vitruvius, published in France in 1547.

Figs 3–4   Remains of Palaeolithic camps in Ahrensburg-Holstein in northern Germany. They include a winter camp and a summer camp.

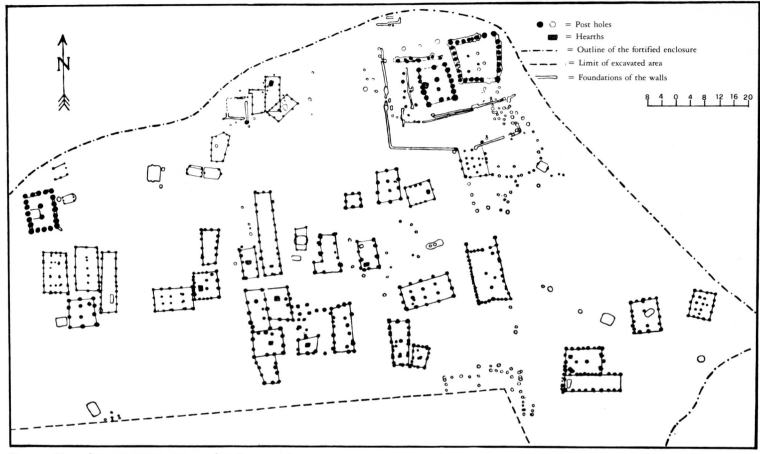

Fig. 5   Plan of the Neolithic village of Hallstatt in Germany.

Neolithic settlements were not sited in a purely natural environment, but in a part of nature transformed according to a human plan. It included cultivated land where food could be produced rather than merely gathered, shelters for people and for domestic animals, stores of food for a whole season or even longer, the equipment needed for crop-growing, cattle-rearing, defence, decoration and worship. We can reconstruct this environment reasonably accurately, because archaeologists have excavated many of these settlements, some of them built on a large scale and others following a recognisable pattern. We are able to fill in the missing sections and reconstruct the plan on which they were based (Figs 5–12). Ethnologists are also studying present-day societies that have preserved a Neolithic economic and social system, and whose villages are comparable to those of the past. They belong to a distinctive historical tradition that has survived into modern times, but which is destined to disappear as the world grows increasingly smaller (Figs 13–16).

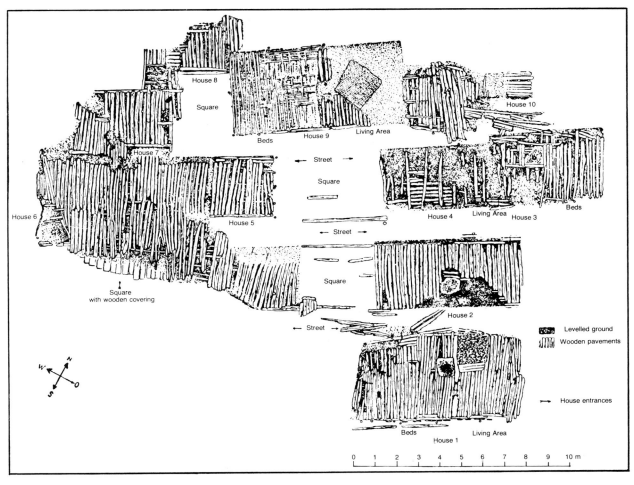

House 8

Square

Beds

House 7

House 9

Living Area

House 10

← Street →

Square

House 6

House 5

House 4

Living Area

House 3

Beds

← Street →

Square

Square
with wooden covering

House 2

← Street →

Levelled ground

Wooden pavements

House entrances

Beds

Living Area

House 1

0 1 2 3 4 5 6 7 8 9 10 m

Figs 6–7 Plan and reconstruction of the Neolithic village of Aichbühl in Federseemoor in Germany (*c.* 2000 BC).

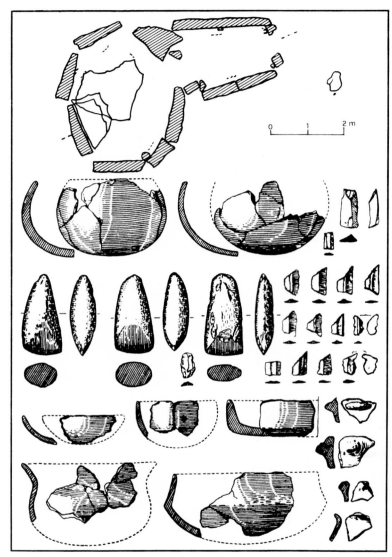

Figs 9–10   Two rock inscriptions of the pre-Roman period in the Val Camonica, with shapes representing wooden houses.

Fig. 8   Plan of a Neolithic tomb at Alemtejo in Spain with its grave goods — vases and cutting tools, shown one-fifth actual size; flint objects, shown two-fifths actual size (*c.* 1500 BC).

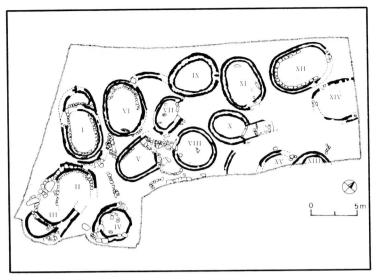

Fig. 11　Foundations of Neolithic oval huts at San Giovenale near Rome.

Fig. 12　Plan of the village of Montagnola on Filicudi, one of the Aeolian (or Lipari) Islands (*c.* 1500 BC).

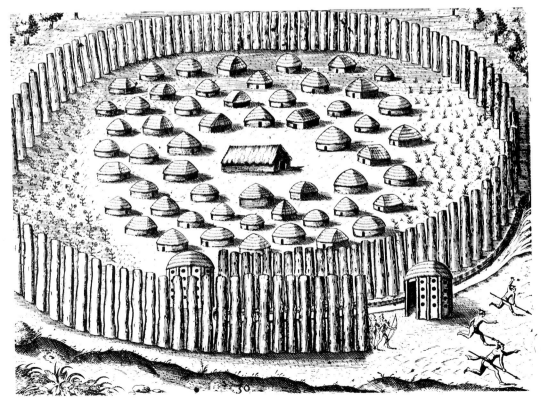

Fig. 13　An engraving by Theodore de Bry of an Indian village in Florida (*c.* 1590 AD).

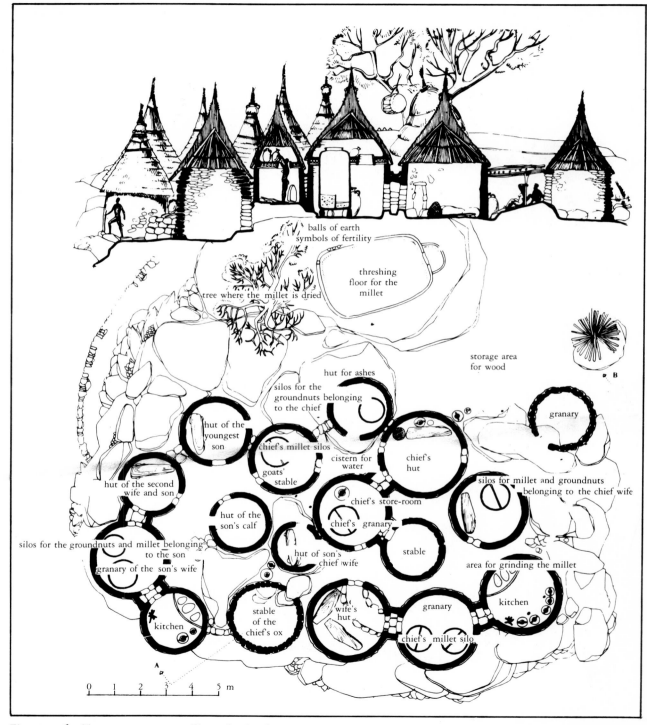

balls of earth
symbols of fertility

threshing
floor for the
millet

tree where the millet is dried

storage area
for wood

hut for ashes

silos for the
groundnuts belonging
to the chief

hut of the
youngest
son

chief's millet silos

cistern for
water

chief's
hut

granary

hut of the second
wife and son

goats'
stable

silos for millet and groundnuts
belonging to the chief wife

chief's store-room

hut of the
son's calf

chief's granary

silos for the groundnuts and millet belonging
to the son

hut of son's
chief wife

stable

area for grinding the millet

granary of the son's wife

kitchen

stable
of the
chief's ox

wife's
hut

granary

kitchen

chief's millet silo

0 1 2 3 4 5 m

Figs 14–16 Two contemporary villages in the Cameroons.

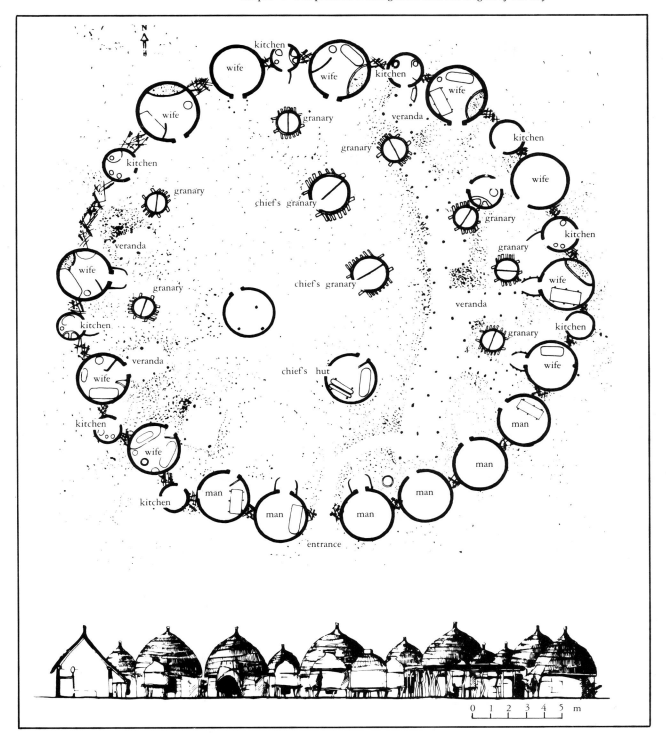

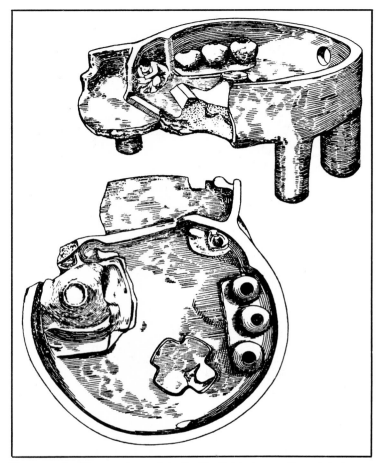

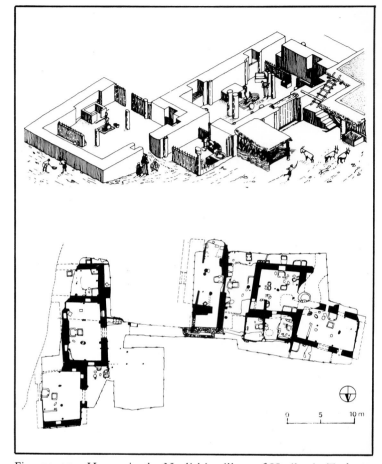

Figs 17–18   Terracotta model of a Neolithic hut at Popudnia in the Ukraine, showing the porch, the oven, grain jars, a cruciform platform and a millstone (*c.* 2000 BC).

Figs 19–20   Houses in the Neolithic village of Hacilar in Turkey, *c.* 5000 BC. Each house consists of a large room, supported by wooden columns and divided by lightweight partitions. The room on the right leads to an upper storey, possibly intended as an attic or veranda.

The city — a fully-fledged place of settlement, the aloof and privileged seat of authority — had its roots in the village tradition, but it was not merely an enlarged village. It developed when certain categories of work were no longer carried out by the people who worked the land, but by others who were freed from this obligation and who were supported by the surplus produced by the cultivators.

This phenomenon resulted in the birth of two distinct social classes — the ruling élite and the subordinates. At the same time it became possible to develop specialised indus-

tries and services, and agricultural production could be increased by the use of the products of these specialised craftsmen. Society was now capable of developing and also planning its own development.

The city, the hub of this development, was not only larger than the village; it also evolved much faster, and thereby altered the whole tempo of civilised history. The slow changes in the countryside (where the surplus was produced) shows how infrequently the economic structure changed, while the rapid changes in the city (where the surplus was distributed) bear witness to the way in which the composition and activities of the ruling class were constantly altering in a way that affected the whole of society. The adventure of civilisation had begun, and with it an era of continuous reassessment and change.

The evidence at present available suggests that this decisive leap forward (or 'the urban revolution', as it has been called) began in the vast, crescent-shaped plain that stretches from the Mediterranean to the Persian Gulf, lying between the deserts of Africa and Arabia and the mountains to the north. When the climate changed at the end of the Ice Age this area was covered by a wide variety of vegetation, sparser than the northern forest but much lusher than the southern desert (Fig. 21). This plain could be cultivated only where there was a source of water, whether from a river or natural spring or a man-made irrigation channel. A large number of fruit-bearing trees or plants grew there (olive and fig trees, vines and date palms), while the rivers and seas meant that the land was easily accessible, a fact which encouraged trade and intercommunication. Also, as the skies were almost always clear, the movements of the stars could be charted at night and the measuring of time made easier.

In this region a small number of Neolithic societies, whose members were already familiar with the cultivation of cereal crops, metalworking, the wheel, ox-drawn carts, pack-mules and both rowing and sailing boats, found an environment which, although not easy to work, was capable of producing a much greater yield if labour was organised on a communal basis.

The rich, moist soil provided ideal conditions for both cereal crops and fruit trees, and the area under cultivation could be further extended by means of land reclamation and irrigation. Some of the food produced could also be stored and used for trade or to enable the settlements to embark on large-scale community projects. This was the beginning of the new economic spiral: increased agricultural production resulted in a surplus to be stored in the city, and successive increases in population and in output ensured the city's technical and military hegemony over the countryside.

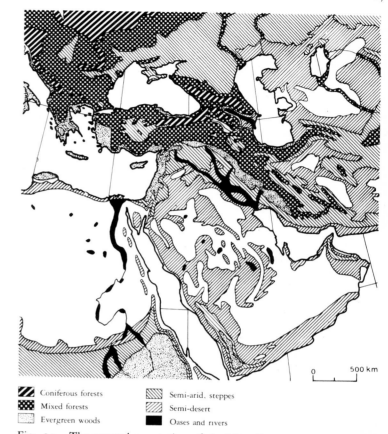

▨ Coniferous forests	▨ Semi-arid, steppes
▨ Mixed forests	▨ Semi-desert
░ Evergreen woods	■ Oases and rivers

Fig. 21 The natural vegetation of the Near East at the end of the Ice Age and prior to human cultivation. The fertile strips along the banks of the Nile, the Tigris and the Euphrates became the site of the first urban civilisations during the fourth millennium BC.

0 ___ 500 km

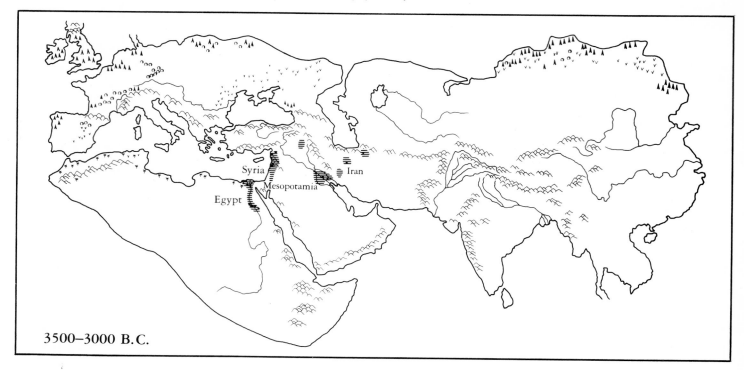

3500–3000 B.C.

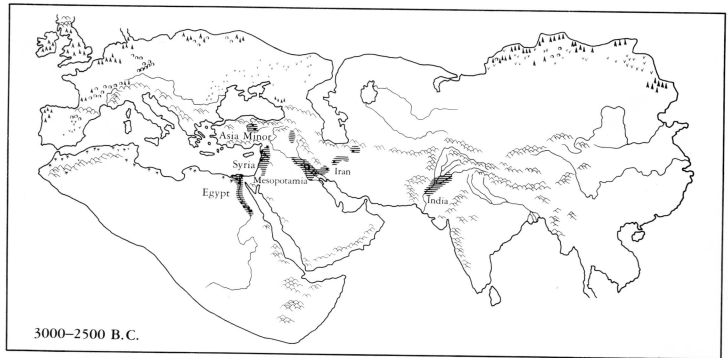

3000–2500 B.C.

Figs 22–5   The development of urban civilisation between 3500 and 1500 BC.

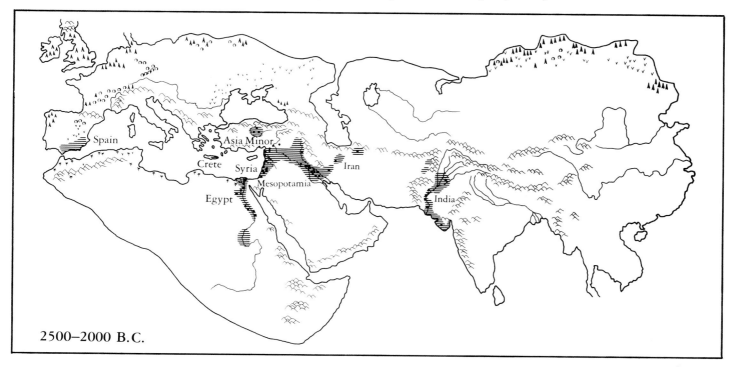

2500–2000 B.C.

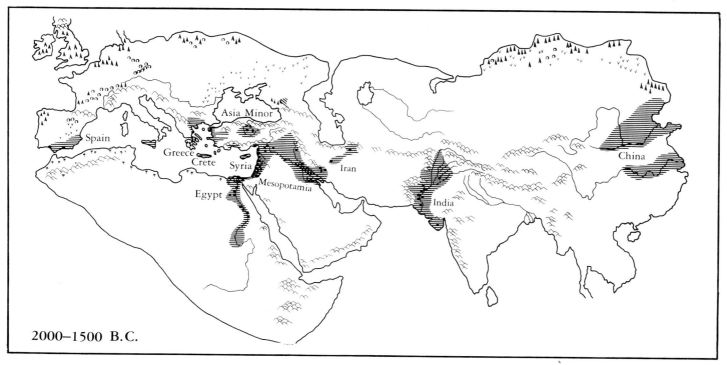

2000–1500 B.C.

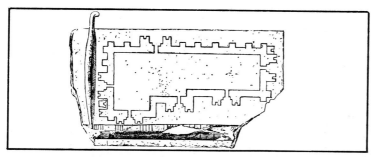

Fig. 26   A Sumerian city. Detail from a statue of Gudea, from Tello (*c.* 2000 BC).

In Mesopotamia (the name given to the alluvial plain lying between the Tigris and the Euphrates) the surplus was controlled by the governors of the cities in their capacity as representatives of the local deities. They exacted a percentage of the produce from the community's land as tribute, and received a major part of the booty of war, controlling the wealth of the community by administering the food supply of the whole population, by arranging for the manufacture or import of the stone and metal tools needed for war and for everyday use, and by maintaining the statistical information required to ensure the smooth running of the community. This organisational set-up left its traces on the natural environment in many ways. There were canals which were used to irrigate the land and to transport raw materials and finished products, walls that served to mark the boundaries of the cities and to protect them in case of attack by enemies, storehouses containing large numbers of clay tablets covered in cuneiform writing, and temples, terraces and stepped pyramids (ziggurats). These buildings, like the houses of the common people, were made of the same clay and bricks used in the Near East to this day. The elements have destroyed them, but the earth has preserved the traces of man's work in a series of layers piled one on top of the other in strict chronological order, and it is there that the priceless clay tablets with their cuneiform writing have been discovered. The tablets that date from after 3000 BC can be deciphered with certainty, and it is from these that archaeologists have been able to reconstruct, step by step, the formation and daily life of mankind's earliest cities from the fourth millennium onwards.

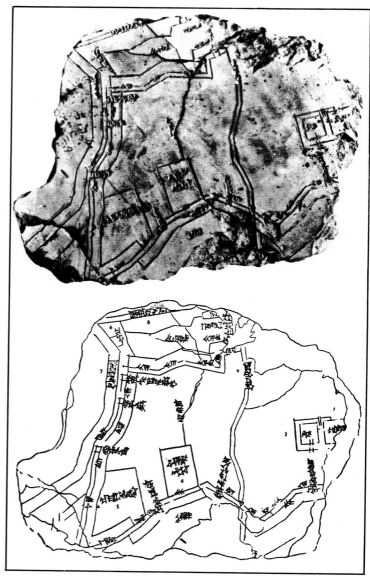

Figs 27–8   A Sumerian tablet showing the plan of the city of Nippur (*c.* 1500 BC).

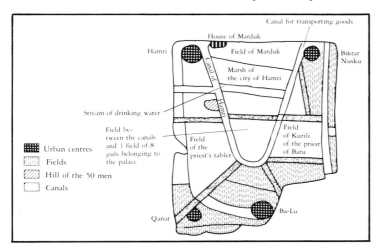

Fig. 29 Another tablet found at Nippur, showing the layout of part of the territory.

By the beginning of the third millennium BC, the Sumerian cities had grown considerably in size, their inhabitants being numbered in tens of thousands; Ur (Figs 31–8), for example, covered an area of approximately 100 hectares. These cities were surrounded by either a wall or a ditch, defensive measures which for the first time also provided a barrier between the natural environment and the artificially-enclosed urban area. The surrounding countryside was itself subjected to man-made changes: instead of marshes and areas of desert there were now fields, meadows and orchards, divided up by a network of irrigation canals (Fig. 29). In the cities the temples were distinguished from the ordinary dwelling-houses by their greater size and elevation. In fact, apart from the sanctuary and the observatory tower (ziggurat), they also contained workshops, storehouses, and shops where various categories of specialised craftsmen lived and worked.

Fig. 30 Statue of a Sumerian dignitary, from Tell Asmar.

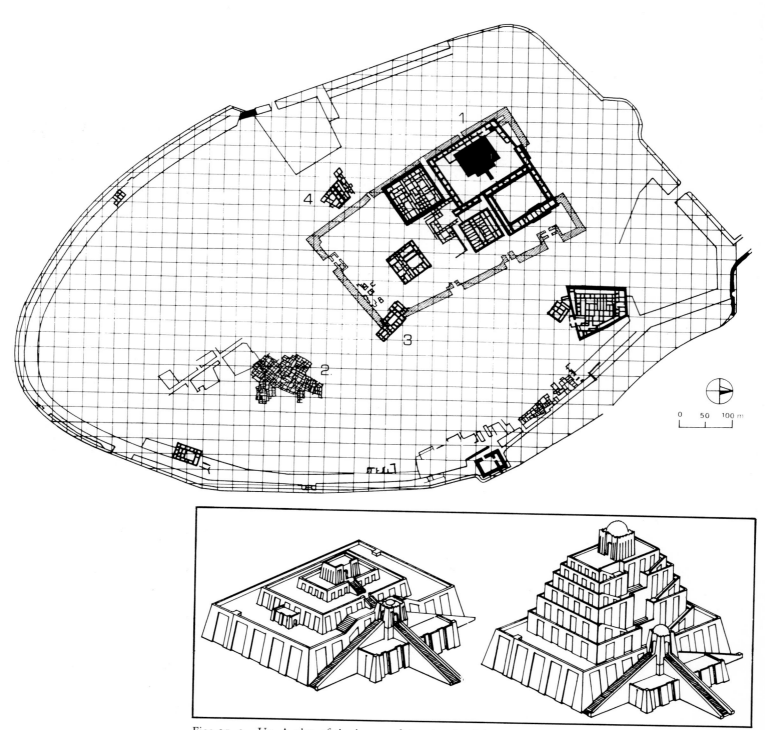

Figs 31–3   Ur. A plan of the layout of the city. Models showing the development of the ziggurat, (1) in plan above, in two successive eras.

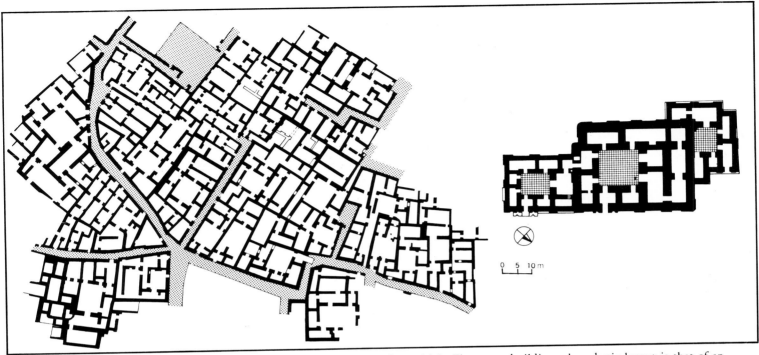

Figs 34–5   Plans, on the same scale, of Area (2) and of the royal mausoleum (3) in Fig. 31, a building whose basic layout is that of an enlarged house.

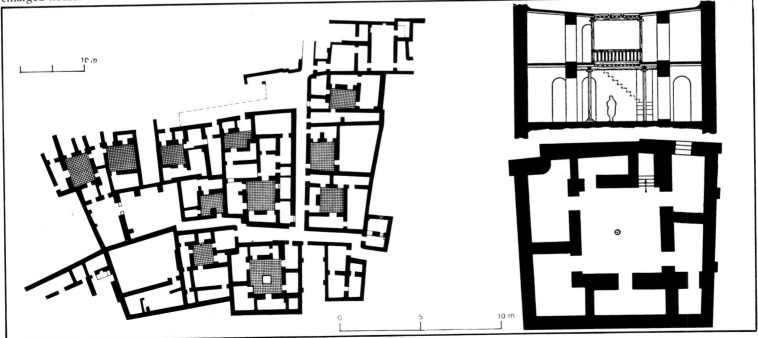

Figs 36–8   A plan of Area (4) in Fig. 31. Plan and cross-section of the house seen in the lower half of the plan of Area (4).

Fig. 39   The manufacture of clay bricks, which are mixed with straw and then baked in the sun. These bricks, of a type widely used in the Near East from earliest times, and still in use today, are built up into walls and then covered with a further layer of clay. Their main advantage is that they can be made into a variety of shapes, but they are vulnerable to the effects of rain, and buildings made from them need continual upkeep.

At this stage the urban area had already been divided into privately-owned units, whereas the countryside was administered in common on behalf of the local deities. At Lagash the countryside was split up between some twenty deities, one of whom, Bau, owned approximately 3,250 hectares. Three-quarters of this land was divided into individual family plots, while the remaining quarter was cultivated either by paid workers, by tenants (who paid a tribute of between a seventh and an eighth part of its yield) or by the unpaid labour of the other inhabitants. Apart from a number of officials, scribes and priests, the temple also

Fig. 40   Photograph of a modern-day village near Shiraz in Iran, whose buildings are constructed from the clay bricks shown in Fig. 39. The materials are the same as were used at Ur and the other ancient cities discussed in this chapter.

employed twenty-one bakers assisted by twenty-seven slaves, twenty-five brewers and their six slaves, a smith, forty women skilled in the preparation of wool, and a variety of other women who spun and wove the cloth.

Until the middle of the third millennium the cities of Mesopotamia formed a number of separate and independent states, continually struggling to increase their share of the rich alluvial plain bounded by the two rivers, an area that by now had been totally colonised. These conflicts had a detrimental effect on economic development and only ceased when the head of a particular city became powerful enough

Figs 41–2   Ur. Cross-section of a tomb, and gold jewellery found in a burial place.

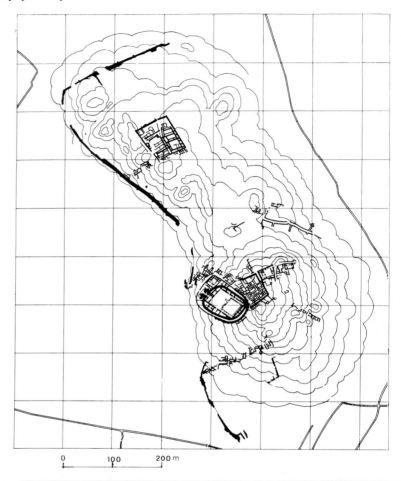

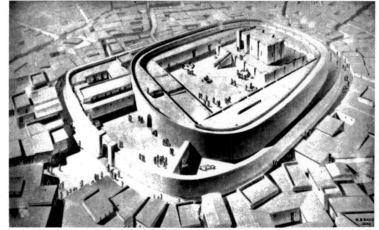

Figs 43–4   The city of Hafaga and its main temple.

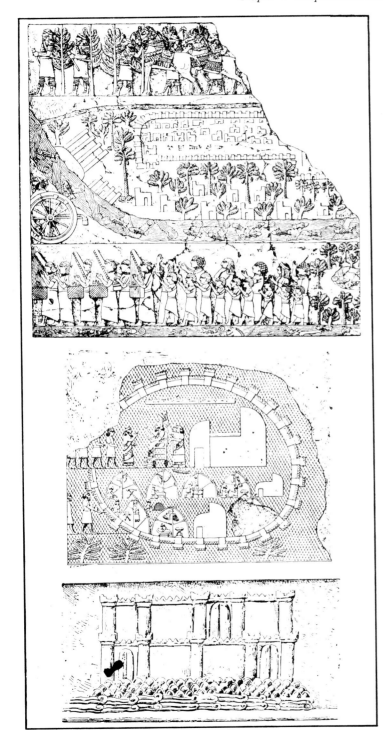

Figs 45–6   Assyrian bas-reliefs showing scenes of city life.

Fig. 47   Aerial view of the city of Arbela in Mesopotamia, a site that has been continuously inhabited for 5,000 years.

Fig. 48   Bronze head of an Assyrian king, possibly Sargon I, found at Nineveh (*c.* 2500 BC).

to impose his authority on the whole region. The first man to establish a stable empire was the Akkadian king, Sargon, whose empire, founded towards the middle of the third millennium, lasted for roughly a hundred years. Later on, his achievement was emulated by the Sumerian kings of Ur, by the Babylonian king, Hammurabi, and the kings of Persia and Assyria. The physical effects of these periods of domination were as follows:

1. The foundation of new residential cities, in which the main source of power lay in the royal palace rather than the temple. Examples of this are the city-palaces of the Persian kings at Pasargadae and Persepolis, and the earlier city-palace of Sargon II near Nineveh (Figs 49–55).

2. The growth of certain cities such as Babylon and Nineveh, each of which became the capital of an empire, the hub of political power and the commercial and administrative centre of a greatly enlarged world. They were the first cities to reach dimensions comparable to those of a modern metropolis, and have for a long time been regarded as the first examples of large urban conglomerations, and consequently also as the first places to experience the advantages and drawbacks of crowded city life.

Babylon, the capital of King Hammurabi, which was laid out in about 2000 BC, was in the shape of a rectangle measuring 2,500 metres by 1,500 metres, divided into two unequal halves by the River Euphrates (Figs 58–63). The city itself, which was walled, covered an area of some 400 hectares, while another wall, further out, enclosed an area almost twice as large. All the buildings within the inner wall, and not just the temples and palaces, were laid out in a strictly geometrical pattern with streets that were straight and of uniform width, and walls that intersected at right angles. In this way the distinction between public buildings and those inhabited by the ordinary people was erased: the city became composed of a series of different quarters, the outer ones being accessible to everyone and the innermost ones being reserved for the kings and the priests. It was these last who were in communication with the gods, as can be seen in sculpture of the time, and for this reason it was they who had control over all things temporal. Private houses, such as the one illustrated on page 32, were miniature versions of the temples and palaces, complete with inner courtyards and stepped walls.

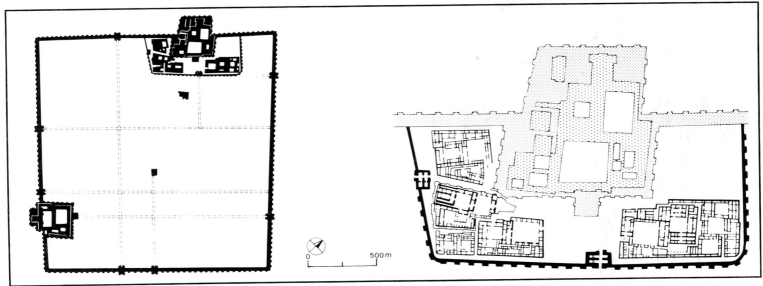

Figs 49–50   Khorsabad, the new city founded by Sargon II near Nineveh (721–705 BC). General layout and plan of the citadel showing the houses of the nobility round the royal palace.

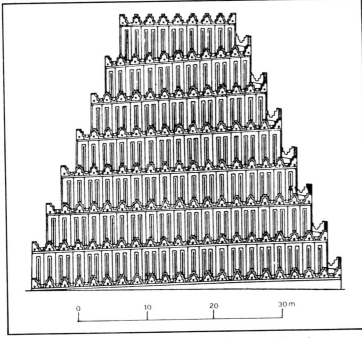

Fig. 51   The ziggurat that formed part of Sargon II's palace complex.

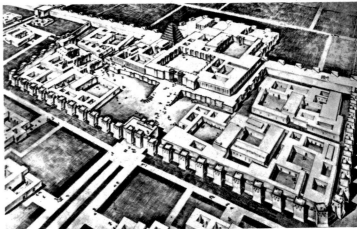

Fig. 52   Aerial view of the citadel of Khorsabad.

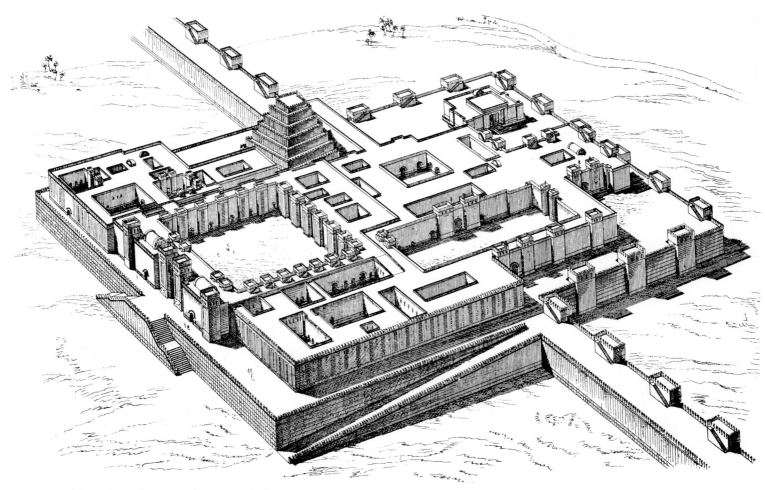

Figs 53–5   The palace of Sargon II at Khorsabad. A bird's eye view of the royal buildings (late nineteenth-century drawing). Diagram of the general layout. View from the top of the ziggurat.

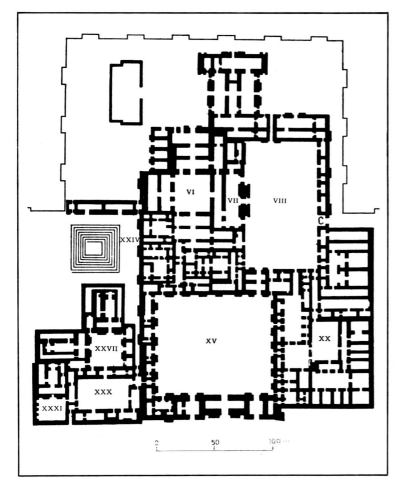

Fig. 56 Bas-relief from the palace at Khorsabad showing the capture of a city by Sargon II.

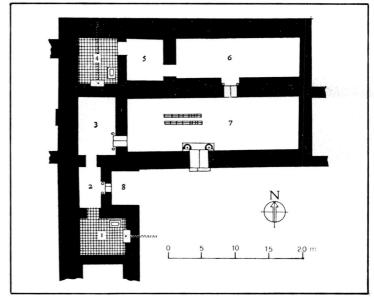

Fig. 57 Diagram of the private apartments in the Assyrian palace at Arslan Tash in Syria:

1, 2, 3. Main bedroom, with dressing room and bathroom.
4, 5, 6. Secondary bedroom, with dressing room and bathroom.
7. Combined reception and living-room.
8. Watchman's post.

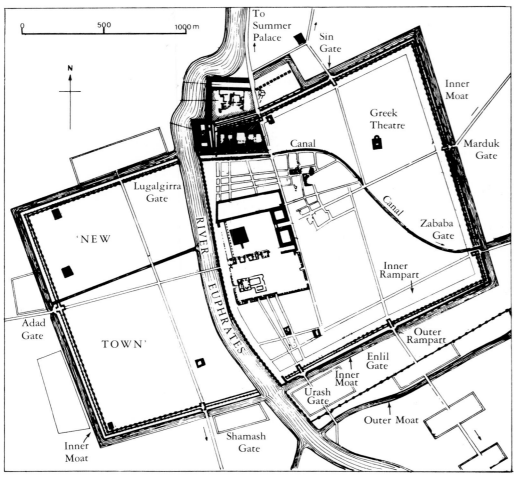

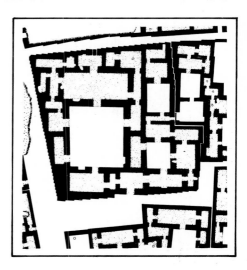

Figs 58–61   Babylon. Plan of the central section. View of the fortress (the so-called hanging gardens). Plan and view of a house next to the temple of Ishtar.

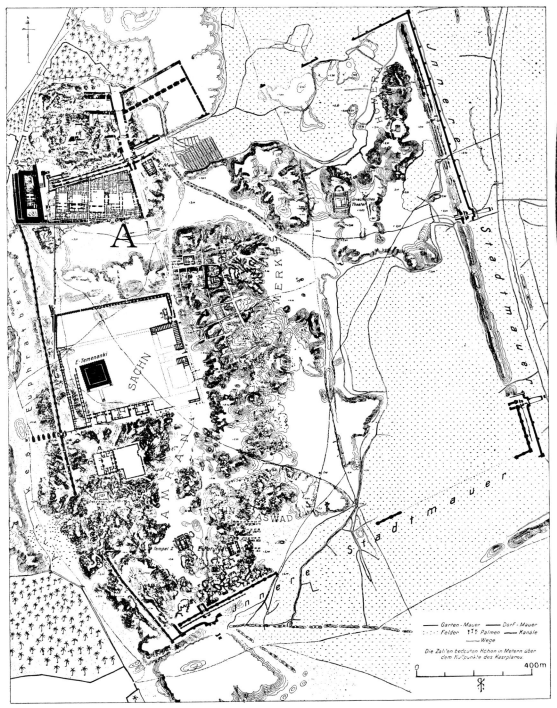

Fig. 62 Babylon. The stele of Mardukapaliddina (714 BC), records the granting of land by the Assyrian kings to a Babylonian vassal.

Fig. 63 Babylon. Plan of excavations in the eastern part of the city. The site of the fortress and of the house next to the temple of Ishtar are marked by the letters A and B.

1. Site of the earliest settlement (*c.* 1900 BC).
2. Temple of the god Hatti and the goddess Arinna (*c.* 1200 BC).
3. Main citadel (1300–1200 BC).
4. Hitherto unexcavated southern citadel (1200 BC).
5. Fortress (1200 BC).
6. Royal gate (1400 BC).
7–10. Temples (*c.* 1200 BC).
11. Sphinx gate (1400 BC).
12. Lion gate (1400 BC).
13. New fortress (1200 BC).
14. Yellow fortress (1200 BC).

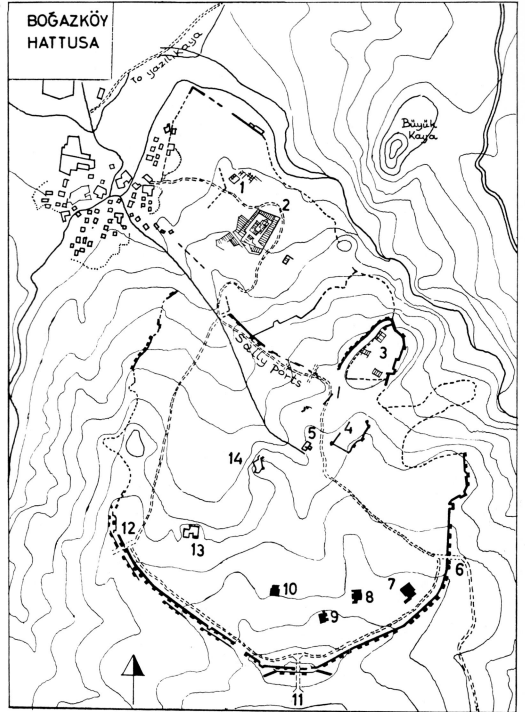

Figs 64–5   Plan of the city of Hattusa, capital of the Hittite kingdom and of the main temple.

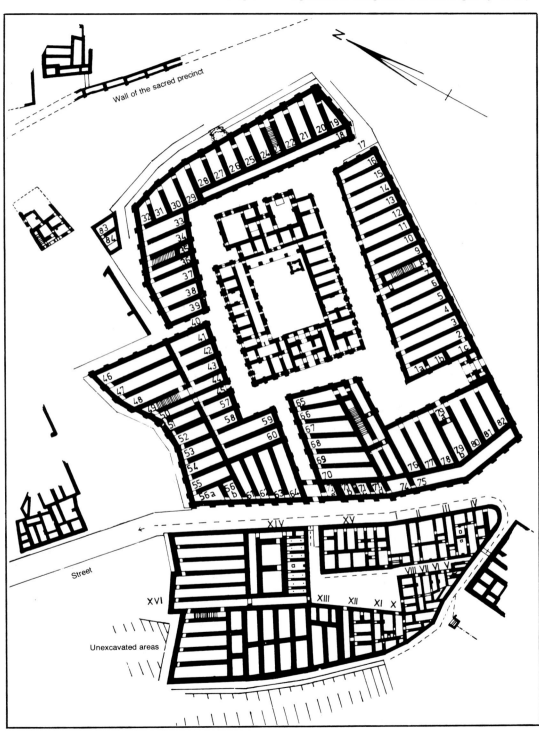

Wall of the sacred precinct

N

Street

Unexcavated areas

The rooms numbered from 1 to 84 (in the area around the central sanctuary) were used for storing merchandise and the temple treasure. To the south of the temple a number of buildings have been excavated which form part of the main town. They consist of sixteen units (indicated by Roman numerals) grouped round a central courtyard; they were possibly living quarters or workshops for the people employed by the temple. This workforce (according to a tablet found in Unit XIV) comprised eighteen priests, twenty-nine musicians, nineteen scribes for writing on clay tablets, thirty-three scribes for writing on wood, thirty-five seers, and ten singers.

Fig. 66 The pyramids of Gizeh tower over the surrounding desert.

Fig. 67 The Egyptian hieroglyph for 'city'.

The origins of Egyptian urban civilisation cannot be studied in the same way as those of Mesopotamia, since the earliest settlements there were destroyed by the annual floodings of the Nile. Even the most recent examples of large cities, such as Memphis and Thebes, are remarkable for their stone monuments, their tombs and their temples, and not for their houses and palaces, which have long since disappeared under modern fields and settlements.

Archaeological documentation has revealed Egyptian civilisation at a stage when it was already fully developed following the unification of the Upper and Lower Kingdoms at the end of the fourth millennium. Evidence found in the earliest tombs shows how the kings at the time had conquered already existing communities and assumed the powers of the local deities. Unlike the rulers of Sumer, who were the representatives of the gods, the Egyptian kings were themselves divine, and it was they who were responsible for ensuring a good harvest and, most particularly, for making sure that the waters of the Nile flooded at the right time each year. Consequently, the pharaoh became the most powerful figure in the land and received a far greater amount of tribute than that enjoyed by the Mesopotamian priesthood. He used this surplus to build public works, cities, and temples for local and national gods, but especially for the erection of his own monumental tomb, a symbol of his immortality which, along with the preservation of his body, guaranteed the survival of his power for the good of the community.

During the third millennium, as Egypt became more and more densely populated and increasingly wealthy, these tombs became correspondingly more and more grandiose, even though their external appearance still retained the

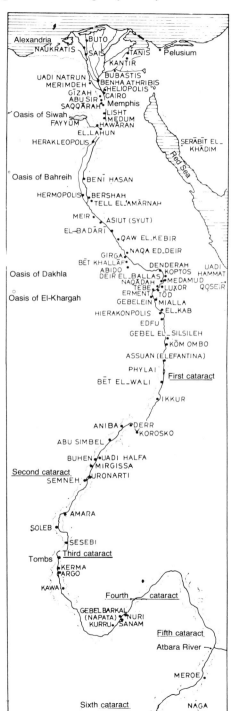

Fig. 68
Map of ancient Egypt.

Figs 69–70   The pyramids of Gizeh seen from the air.
Nineteenth-century drawing of a conjectural reconstruction.

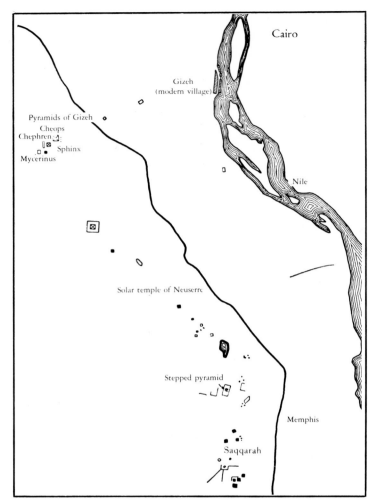

Fig. 71   Map of the area around Memphis.

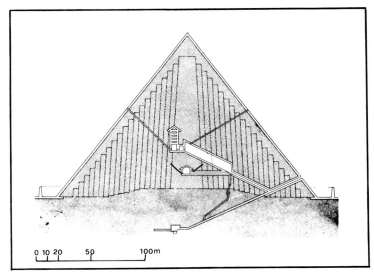

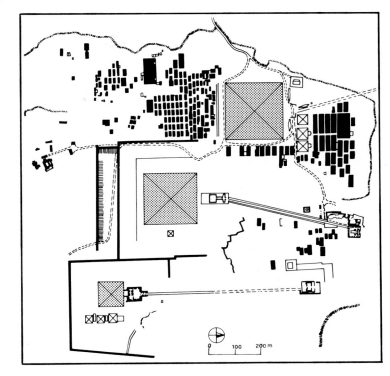

Figs 72–3   Cross-section of the Great Pyramid of Cheops. Plan of the Gizeh complex; the pyramids of Cheops, Chephren, and Mycerinus are represented by the shaded squares, while the lesser buildings are shown in black.

simple pyramid shape. The greatest of these pyramids, that of Cheops, dating from the Fourth Dynasty, measures 225 metres along each side and reaches a height of almost 150 metres. It is one of mankind's most impressive monuments and, according to a tradition handed down by Herodotus, it involved the work of 100,000 men over a period of twenty years, an estimate that modern scholars regard as perfectly feasible. Where else would it be possible to erect such an enormous monument except in the populous regions of the Lower Nile?

We know that Menes, the first pharaoh, founded the city of Memphis near the head of the Nile delta and surrounded it by 'a white wall'. The temple of the local deity, Ptah, is not to be found within the city but 'south of the wall', while on the outskirts, on the fringes of the desert, are the pyramids of the kings of the first four Dynasties (Figs 69–74) and the sun-temples of the Fifth (Figs 77–8). The original layout of the settlement remains a mystery, and it is not easy to visualise the relationship between the colossal monuments and the houses of the living, though it was certainly very different from the city/temple relationship of Mesopotamia.

In Egypt, particularly during the early years, we can find no connection between the buildings of the living and those of the dead; in fact, there is a sharply delineated contrast between the two. The ancient Egyptians' monuments do not stand at the centre of their cities; they form their own kind of self-contained city, a sacred and everlasting memorial dwarfing the transitory abodes of mere mortals. The holy city is built of stone so that it will survive the ravages of time. It is composed of simple geometrical shapes — prisms, pyramids, obelisks — or with gigantic

Fig. 74   View of one corner of the Great Pyramid of Cheops.

Fig. 75   Monumental head of a pharaoh of the Third Dynasty (*c.* 2750 BC).

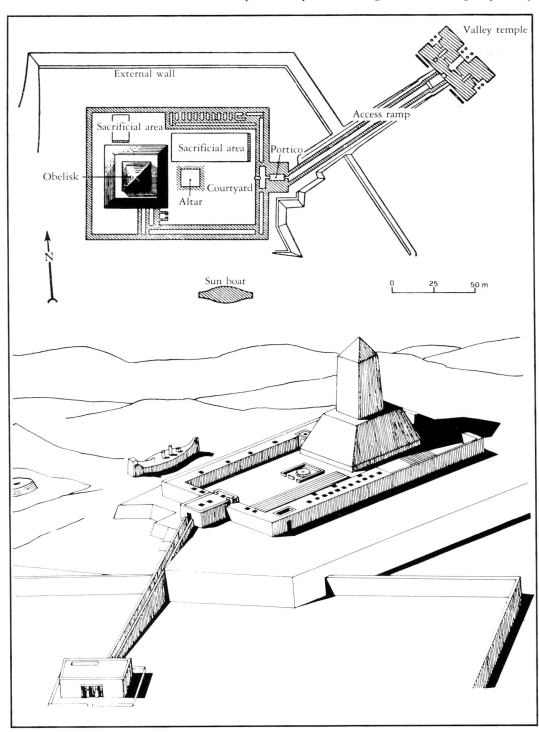

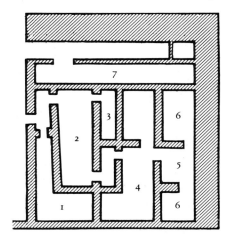

Fig. 76 Plan of a house of the Fourth Dynasty at Gizeh (*c*. 2600 BC).

1. Entrance.
2. Courtyard.
3. Larder.
4. Living-room.
5. Hall.
6. Bedroom.
7. Storeroom.

Figs 77–8 The sun temple of Horus at Abusir from the Fifth Dynasty (*c*. 2500 BC): plan and conjectural reconstruction.

Fig. 79   Model of a transport boat, discovered in a tomb of the Twelfth Dynasty (*c.* 1800 BC).

statues like the Sphinx which, by virtue of the superhuman scale on which they were constructed, have more in common with the works of Nature. It is a city for the dead, who rest there surrounded by everything they will need for the endless hereafter; but it is designed to be seen from afar, as a background for the city of the living. There, by contrast, everything is made of mud bricks, including the palaces of the pharaohs; it is just a temporary resting place, somewhere that will be occupied for only a short time and will soon fall into decay. One important section of the population — the men involved in the building of the pyramids and temples and their families — must have lived in the encampments archaeologists have unearthed near all the great monuments and which were abandoned as soon as the work was completed (Figs 80, 82–5).

In other respects, the holy city — the only one we are able to study and examine nowadays — is a faithful copy of its mortal counterpart in which all the people and utensils of everyday life were reproduced and consigned to posterity. There are beautifully-made carvings that provide realistic portrayals of the faces of the dead, freezing them forever in an effort to halt the transience of life (Figs 75, 81).

This attempt to construct a flawless and incorruptible facsimile of human life — to accumulate possessions for the

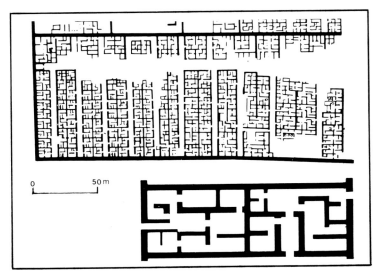

Fig. 80   The village of El Lahun, built in about 1800 BC by Sesostris II for workmen involved in building a pyramid. Plan of the settlement and of a typical dwelling.

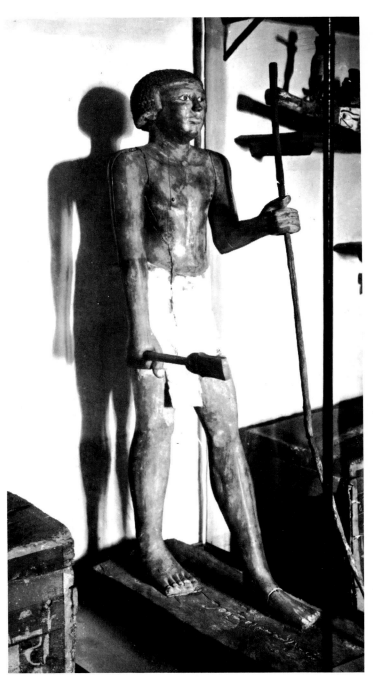

Fig. 81   Wooden funerary statue from the Twelfth Dynasty (*c.* 1800 BC).

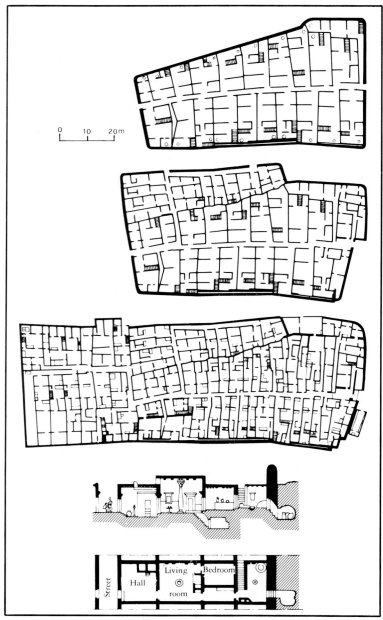

Figs 82–5   The village of Deir-el-Medina, built by Tutmosis I in about 1400 BC for those working in the Valley of the Kings near Thebes, and later enlarged. Plans of its layout and designs of typical houses.

Fig. 86   Bas-relief from the Middle Kingdom, showing a colossus being transported on a vast kind of sledge.

hereafter rather than for life itself — could not always be carried out with the same degree of lavishness. In the middle of the third millennium the Egyptian economy, which until then had been geared towards the after-life, underwent a severe crisis, and when, during the Middle Kingdom (second millennium BC), it was finally reorganised, the contrast between the two worlds became less marked and the two cities tended to merge into one.

Thebes, the capital of the Middle Kingdom, is still divided into two sections, with the inhabited part on the right bank of the Nile and the necropolis on the left (Fig. 87), but now the most imposing buildings are the temples constructed in the city of the living: Karnak and Luxor (Figs 88–92). The tombs are hidden in the rock (Figs 93–4), and all that is visible are the entrance temples which are similar to those already mentioned (Figs 101, 103). Between these two massive buildings we must visualise houses and sub-urbs, in which lived a far more varied society and amongst whom the wealth was much more widely distributed. At the top of the social hierarchy was the pharaoh, whose power is revealed by his ability to select the choicest and most luxurious artefacts for his palaces or his tomb. The clothing, jewellery and furnishings found in the royal tombs are of the highest quality of workmanship and seem to have been chosen from a wide variety of merchandise readily available at the time.

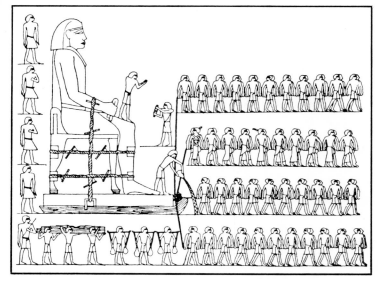

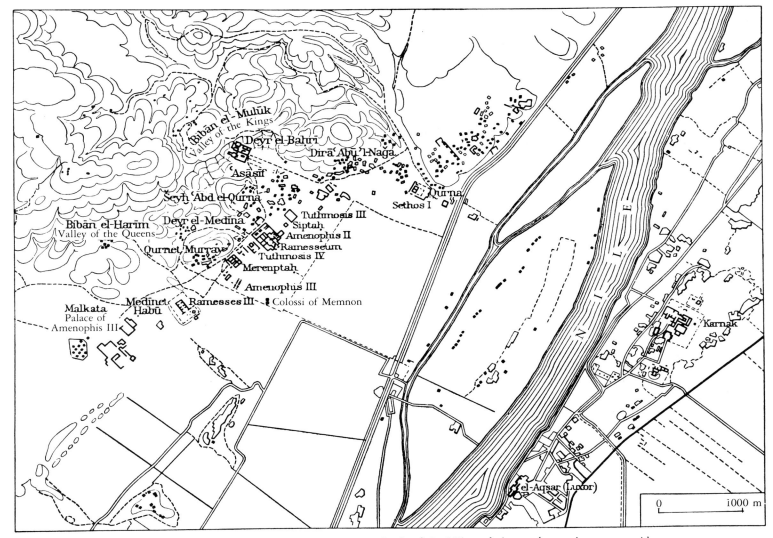

Fig. 87   A general plan of Thebes, showing the temples on the east bank of the Nile and the tombs on the western side.

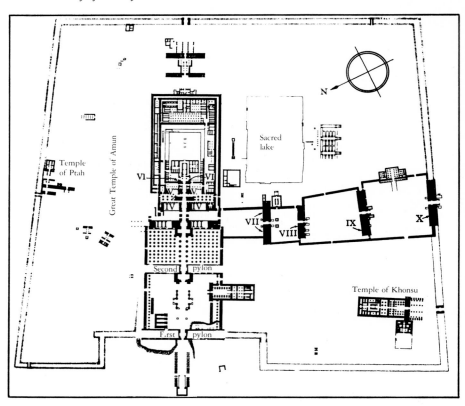

Figs 88–90   The temples of Karnak at Thebes: plan of
the general layout, diagram and side-view of the temple
of Khonsu. The Roman numerals represent the ten pairs
of pylons.

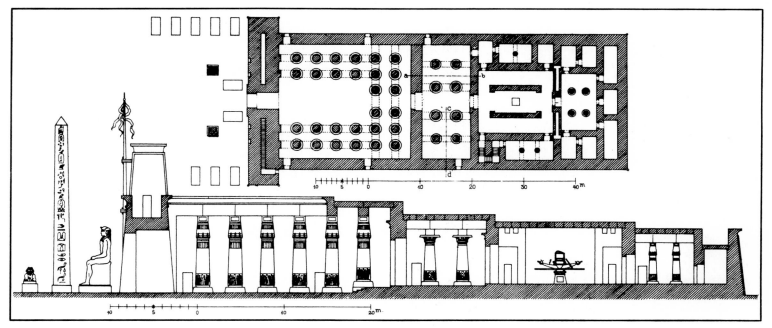

Figs 91–2 Details of the great pillared hall of the temple of
Amun at Karnak, situated between the second and third pylon.

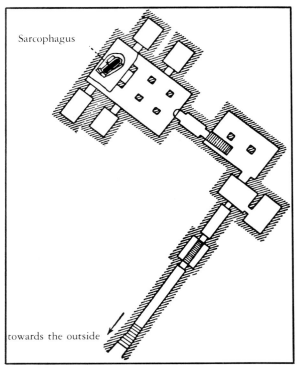

Figs 93–4   Plan of the tomb of Amenhotep II
(*c.* 1380 BC) in the Valley of the Kings. Detail of one
of the wall paintings showing the pharaoh with the
goddess Hathor.

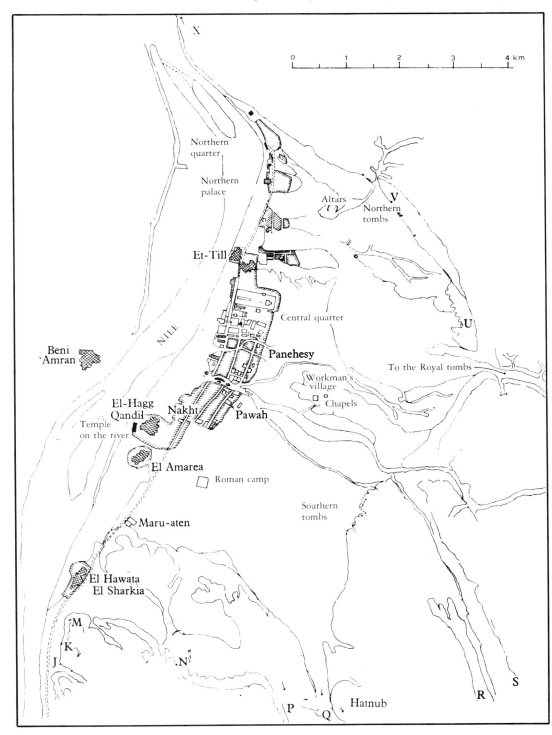

Fig. 95 A statue of Amenhotep IV (Akhenaten) in which the royal personage is portrayed with an unusual degree of realism.

Fig. 96 A plan of Tell-el-Amarna, the new capital founded by Amenhotep IV (*c.* 1370–1350 BC) and abandoned shortly after. It has been possible to excavate and study this city in more detail than any other ancient Egyptian city, and the close relationship between palaces, temples and houses presents the modern student with a much more familiar layout.

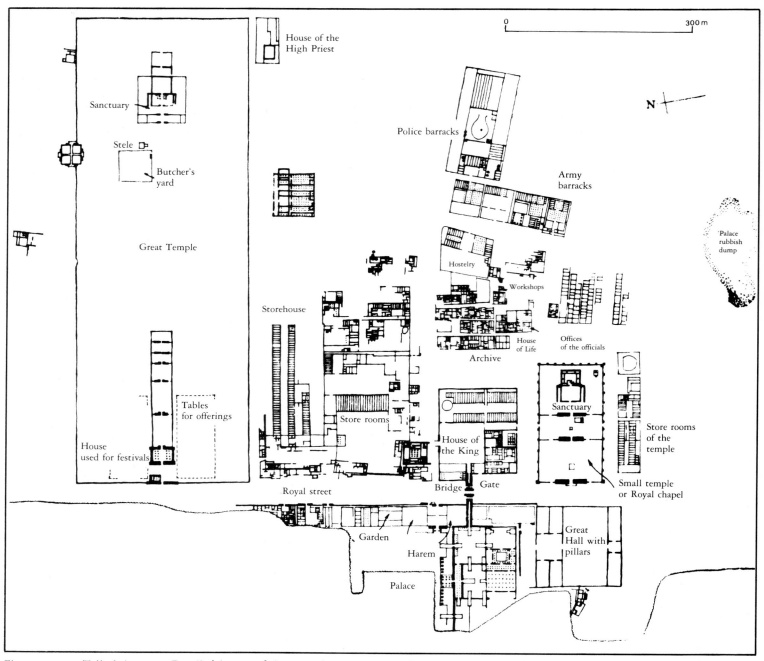

House of the
High Priest

Sanctuary

Stele

Butcher's
yard

Great Temple

Tables
for offerings

House
used for festivals

Royal street

Storehouse

Store rooms

House of
the King

Bridge   Gate

Police barracks

Army
barracks

Hostelry

Workshops

House
of Life

Archive

Offices
of the officials

Sanctuary

Store rooms
of the
temple

Small temple
or Royal chapel

'Palace
rubbish
dump

Garden

Harem

Palace

Great
Hall with
pillars

0   300 m

N

Figs 97–100   Tell-el-Amarna. Detailed layout of the central quarter. Plan of the palace alongside the royal road. View of the bridge
joining the palace with the king's house. Plan of the house belonging to the official Nakht.

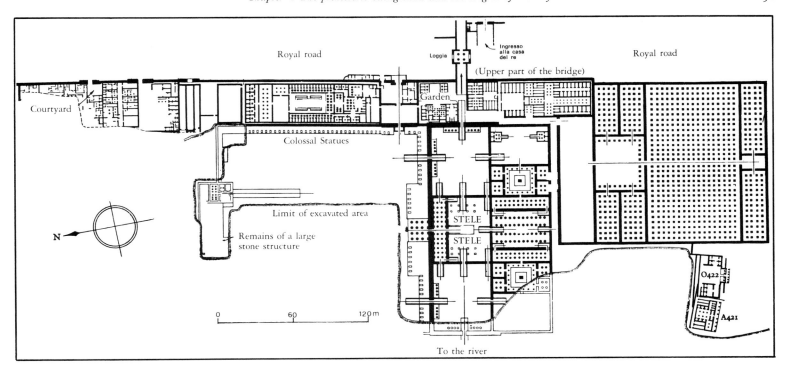

Royal road

Royal road

Loggia

Ingresso
alla casa
del re

(Upper part of the bridge)

Garden

Courtyard

Colossal Statues

N

Limit of excavated area

STELE

Remains of a large
stone structure

STELE

O422

A421

0   60   120 m

To the river

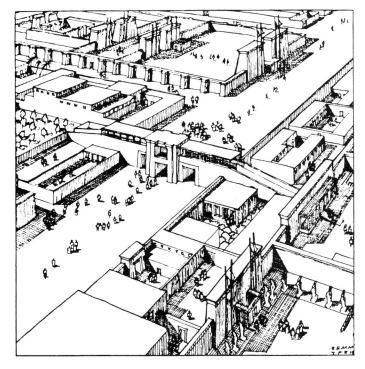

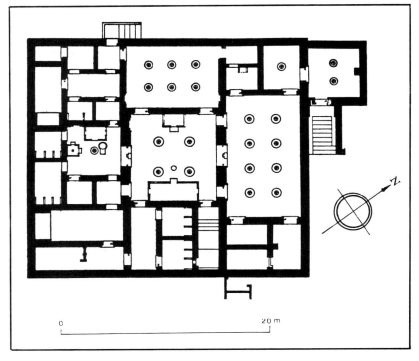

0   20 m

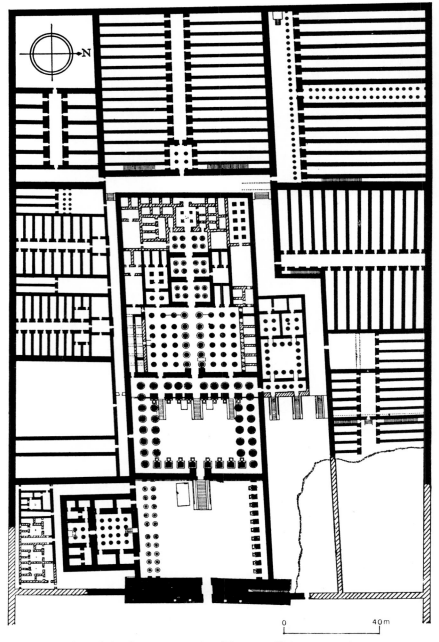

Fig. 101   Plan of the funerary temple of Rameses II (*c.* 1300 BC).

Fig. 102   The god Osiris in a wall painting from the tomb of the pharaoh
Horemheb (*c.* 1200 BC).

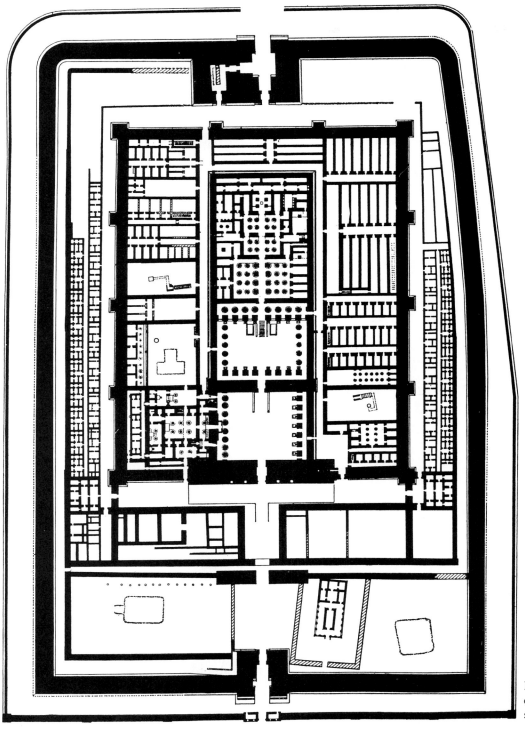

Fig. 103　Plan of the funerary temple of Rameses III (*c.* 1200 BC) on the same scale as Fig. 101.

Fig. 104   Statue of the pharaoh
Rameses II (*c.* 1250 BC).

2
The free city in Greece

During the Bronze Age the Greek peninsula lay on the periphery of the civilised world. The mountainous and fragmented nature of the terrain did not lend itself to the formation of a single unified state, and it remained split up into a large number of small independent principalities. Each principality was governed by its own warrior family who controlled a small area of territory with access to the sea from a fortress situated on higher ground.

These states owed their relative prosperity to the intensive maritime trade of the second millennium and to the various industries that they developed. The treasures discovered in the royal tombs at Mycenae and Tiryns show the modest extent of the surplus accumulated by a narrow-based ruling class. The collapse of the Bronze Age economy, however, and the invasions of barbarians from the north at the beginning of the Iron Age brought their civilisation to an end, forcing the cities to revert for several centuries to a near-Neolithic self-sufficiency.

Their subsequent evolution was directly influenced by the innovations of the new economic system (iron, the alphabet and coinage), while their geographical position, which favoured maritime trade, and the fact that many of their institutions had not survived from the Bronze Age, allowed them to develop a new form of government. The princely city became the *polis*, controlled by either an aristocracy or a democracy, and the old hierarchial economy became transformed into a new monetary economy. From the third century onwards this system spread throughout

Fig. 105   An archaic Greek sculpture in the National Museum in Athens.

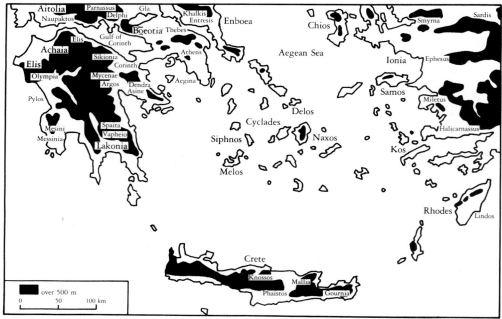

Fig. 106   The Aegean world.

the Eastern Mediterranean area and it was in this environment that a new culture developed which still forms the basis of our intellectual traditions today.

At this point it becomes necessary to give a brief outline of the way in which the *polis* or city-state was organised, especially in view of the extraordinary effect it had on literature, science and art.

Originally the city-state started as an area of high ground on which the inhabitants of the countryside would take refuge in case of attack, but later it spread out and was generally surrounded by a protective wall. It was at this point that a distinction began to be made between the upper city, or *acropolis*, where the inhabitants could seek a final refuge and where the temples of the gods were situated, and the lower city, or *astu*, in which commerce and the business of civil administration were conducted. Nevertheless, they both formed part of a single entity, because the city community acted as sole administrator, whatever political system it subscribed to.

The various bodies needed to uphold this administration were as follows:

1. The common hearth, dedicated to the guardian deity of the city, where sacrifices and ritual feasting took place and foreign guests were received. Originally it was the hearth of the royal palace, but it subsequently became a symbolic place, situated next to the building in which the highest ranking officials of the city resided; these officials were called *prytaneis* by the Greeks and the building became known as the *prytaneion*. It comprised an altar with a trench full of glowing embers, a kitchen and one or more banqueting halls. The fire had to be always kept alight, and when emigrants left to found a colony overseas they took with them fire from the hearth of their home-city to burn in the *prytaneion* of their new settlement.

2. The council of nobles or officials, which represented the citizenry, was known as the *boule*. This body sent representatives to the *prytaneion* and met in a covered hall known as the *bouleuterion*.

3. The assembly of citizens, or agora, who met to listen to the decisions of their rulers or to debate. They normally met in the market place (also known as the agora), but in larger cities there was an open area set aside specifically for the purpose: in Athens, for example, it was known as the Pnyx. In the cities ruled by a democracy the *prytaneion*

Fig. 107 A coin from the city of Naxos, bearing the likenesses of Dionysos and Silenos.

and the *bouleuterion* were to be found near the agora.

Every city possessed a certain amount of territory from which it obtained its food supply, and although these secondary settlements possessed their own assemblies and also enjoyed a certain degree of independence, they were bound to the central *prytaneion* and *bouleuterion* in the capital city. Mountains formed the natural boundaries of these territories, which almost always included a port situated some distance away from the main city. Even though the sea provided the main route of communication with the outside world, the cities were generally sited inland to avoid the depredations of pirates.

The surrounding territory could be extended either by means of conquest or by alliances with neighbouring cities. Sparta, for example, ended up by controlling almost half of the Peloponnese (an area of some 8,400 square kilometres), while Athens held sway over Attica and the island of Salamis, a total of 2,650 square kilometres. Of the Greek colonies in Italy, Syracuse ultimately possessed a territory of 4,700 square kilometres, and Agrigentum an area of 4,300 square kilometres. Other cities, however, possessed far less land, and some of them had very little territory indeed; Thebes had roughly 1,000 square kilometres, and Corinth a mere 880. Some of the smaller islands had only a single city; Aegina, for instance, had 85 square kilometres, and Naxos and Samos approximately 450. Of the larger islands, only Rhodes (1,460 sq. km.) succeeded in unifying its three cities at the end of the fifth century, whereas Lesbos (1,740 sq. km.) was divided among five cities, and Crete (8,600 sq. km.) comprised more than fifty.

The population of Greek cities (excluding slaves and foreigners) was constantly being reduced, not only because of a lack of resources but also because of a conscious political decision: every time the population exceeded a certain figure an expedition would be organised to set up some distant colony. Athens had some 40,000 inhabitants during the time of Pericles, and only three other cities, Syracuse, Agrigentum and Argos, possessed more than 20,000. During the fifth century Syracuse reached a total of approximately 50,000 inhabitants by forcibly containing the populations of the cities it had conquered (Fig. 207). There were only fifteen cities with a population of about 10,000, the number which was considered appropriate for a large city and which theorists advised against exceeding. Even Sparta at the time of the Persian wars had approximately 8,000 inhabitants, while the rich and famous island city of Aegina had a mere 2,000.

This self-imposed limit was not regarded as being in any way restrictive; it was a necessary pre-condition for the orderly development of civil life. The population had to be large enough to enable an army to be raised, but not so large as to impede the smooth running of the assembly; that is, it had to be small enough for the citizens to be able to have some knowledge of each other and so choose their magistrates. If the population fell below a certain level there was the fear of a lack of manpower developing, while if the city grew too much it would cease to be an orderly community and become an ungovernable and unwieldy mass. The vital difference between the Greeks and the barbarians of the East was that the former owed their existence to a well-ordered workforce who lived in carefully planned cities, whereas the latter relied on vast hordes of slaves. The Greeks were conscious of the fact that they shared a common civilisation with their fellow-Greeks, but they did not have any desire for political union because they knew that their superiority depended precisely on the concept of the *polis*, in which the collective freedoms of society could be achieved. Individual liberty could also exist, but that was not indispensable.

The fatherland, as the word suggests, was the common heritage of people descended from the same ancestry, from the same father. Patriotism was such an intensely-felt emotion because the object of its devotion was so limited and so concrete:

Fig. 108   A sculpture from the fifth century BC in the National Museum in Athens.

Fig. 109   The Temple of Neptune at Paestum (fifth century BC).

A small territory, backing on to a mountain, crossed by a stream, hollowed out by a bay; a few kilometres away, higher ground acts as a boundary. All a man has to do is to go up on to the acropolis to be able to encompass the whole area in a single, sweeping glance. This is the sacred earth of the fatherland: the family ground, the tombs of his ancestors, the fields whose owners he knows, the mountain into which he goes to collect wood, where the flocks are taken to pasture or where honey is collected, the temples in which he attends sacrifices, the acropolis to which the processions lead. The city, even the smallest one, is the thing for which Hector died, for which the Spartans considered it an honour to fall in the front line, whose paean the combatants at Salamis sang as they boarded the enemy's ships, and for which Socrates drank hemlock rather than disobey its laws.

(G. Glotz, Introduction to *La città greca*, Turin 1955.)

Let us then analyse this new concept of the city, whose mainstay was the idea of civilised co-existence, an ideal that is revealed by four factors:

1. The city was a single, united entity, in which there were no restricted or independent areas. It could be surrounded by walls, but not subdivided into secondary zones, as was the case with the Near Eastern cities we have already looked at. The houses in which people lived were all built on the same lines; they varied only in size, not in architectural style. They were spread throughout the city and no quarters were reserved exclusively for members of a certain class or a certain family.

There were certain specific areas (the agora and the *theatron*) in which the majority, if not the whole, of the population could meet and assert their rights as a single community.

2. The city was divided into three zones: the private areas, which were set aside for the inhabitants' houses; the sacred areas, which contained the temples of the gods; and the public areas, used for political meetings, sport, commerce and theatre. The state, which embodied the will of the people, was directly responsible for the public areas and also had a say in what happened in the private and sacred areas; but it was the difference in function between these three areas that was far more important than any other difference, whether real or traditional. Visually, the temples outshone all the other buildings in the city mainly because of their quality rather than their size. They were situated in a dominant position, distanced from the other buildings, and designed on very austere and simple lines, following architectural styles, such as the Doric and Ionic orders, that had been perfected over a number of years. Their method of construction was consciously uncomplicated, with stone walls and columns holding up the architraves and cross-beams (Fig. 111), so that technical necessity would affect the overall form as little as possible. More complicated architectural features such as vaulting (Fig. 110) were reserved for buildings of lesser importance.

3. The city was an artificial organism inserted into the natural environment, to which it was attached by a very tenuous link. It respected the natural lines of the countryside, which in many respects it made little effort to change. This was interpreted and complemented architecturally, with the perfect symmetry of the temples, enhanced by the serried rows of columns, and balanced by the irregu-

Fig. 110   The vaulted roof of the passageway leading into the stadium at Olympia.

larity of the surrounding complex of buildings that in turn gradually melted into the natural disorder of the countryside (Figs 113–20). The extent of this balance between art and nature gives every city its own highly individual character.

4. The city was basically a living organism, but at a given time it could reach a point of stabilisation, a state that its inhabitants preferred not to destroy by partial modifications. Any growth in its population did not produce a gradual spread in its land area; either it led to the construction of another complex of buildings, as large as or greater than the original, a practice that resulted in a distinction being made between the old city (*palaiopolis*) and the new city (*neapolis*) (see Fig. 179), or it led to the founding of a colony in some distant region overseas.

It is for these qualities — unity, a lack of rigidity, the maintenance of a balance with nature, stability of growth — that the Greek city has always been, and will remain, a valid model for all other urban developments. It succeeded in achieving a precise and lasting realisation of the theory of human co-existence.

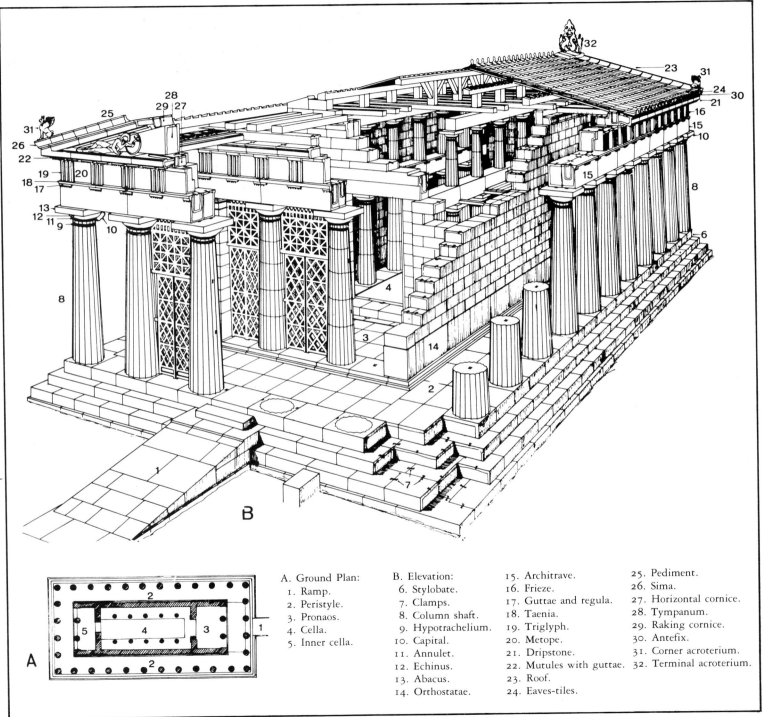

A. Ground Plan:
 1. Ramp.
 2. Peristyle.
 3. Pronaos.
 4. Cella.
 5. Inner cella.

B. Elevation:
 6. Stylobate.
 7. Clamps.
 8. Column shaft.
 9. Hypotrachelium.
 10. Capital.
 11. Annulet.
 12. Echinus.
 13. Abacus.
 14. Orthostatae.

15. Architrave.
16. Frieze.
17. Guttae and regula.
18. Taenia.
19. Triglyph.
20. Metope.
21. Dripstone.
22. Mutules with guttae.
23. Roof.
24. Eaves-tiles.

25. Pediment.
26. Sima.
27. Horizontal cornice.
28. Tympanum.
29. Raking cornice.
30. Antefix.
31. Corner acroterium.
32. Terminal acroterium.

Figs 111–12   The architraval structure of a Greek Doric temple from the fifth century BC. Each secondary architectural feature has its own name and its own established form.

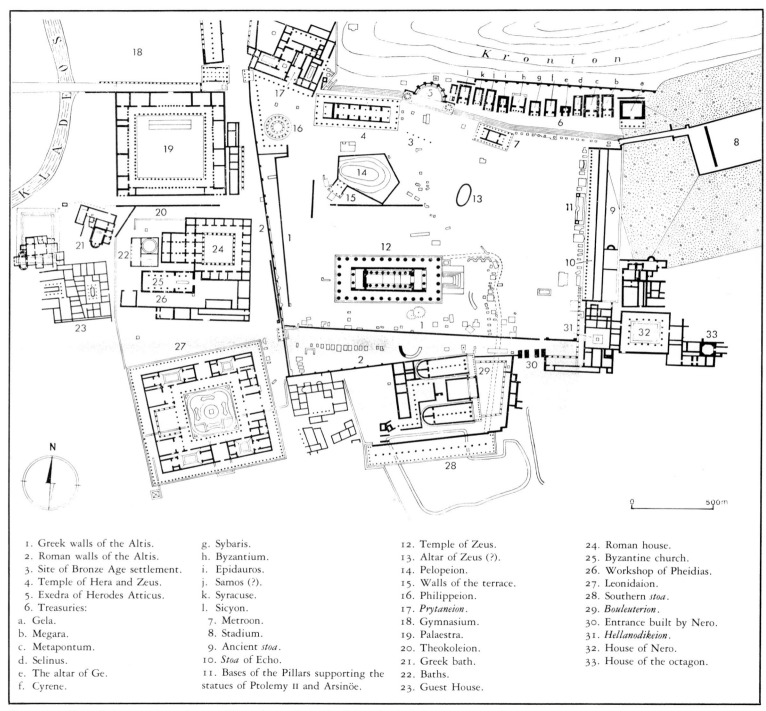

Fig. 113   Plan of the sacred precinct at Olympia, at the end of the Classical Age.

1. Greek walls of the Altis.
2. Roman walls of the Altis.
3. Site of Bronze Age settlement.
4. Temple of Hera and Zeus.
5. Exedra of Herodes Atticus.
6. Treasuries:
a. Gela.
b. Megara.
c. Metapontum.
d. Selinus.
e. The altar of Ge.
f. Cyrene.

g. Sybaris.
h. Byzantium.
i. Epidauros.
j. Samos (?).
k. Syracuse.
l. Sicyon.
7. Metroon.
8. Stadium.
9. Ancient *stoa*.
10. *Stoa* of Echo.
11. Bases of the Pillars supporting the statues of Ptolemy II and Arsinöe.

12. Temple of Zeus.
13. Altar of Zeus (?).
14. Pelopeion.
15. Walls of the terrace.
16. Philippeion.
17. *Prytaneion*.
18. Gymnasium.
19. Palaestra.
20. Theokoleion.
21. Greek bath.
22. Baths.
23. Guest House.

24. Roman house.
25. Byzantine church.
26. Workshop of Pheidias.
27. Leonidaion.
28. Southern *stoa*.
29. *Bouleuterion*.
30. Entrance built by Nero.
31. *Hellanodikeion*.
32. House of Nero.
33. House of the octagon.

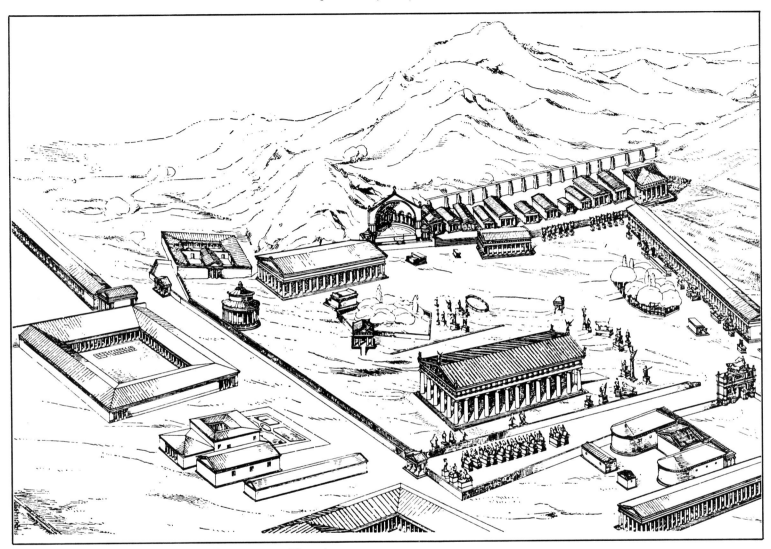

Fig. 114   Reconstruction of the sacred precincts at Olympia.

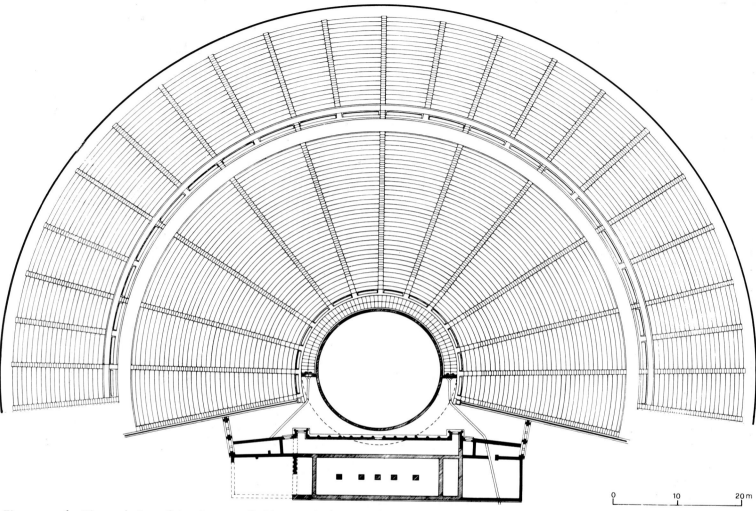

0   10   20 m

Figs 115–16   Plan and view of the theatre at Epidauros, the best
preserved of all Greek amphitheatres.

1. Enclosing wall.
2. Sacred way.
3. The Corcyran bull.
4. Treasury of the Arcadians.
5. Statue of Philopoimen.
6. Exedra.
7. Votive offering for the Battle of Marathon; votive offering of the Argive kings.
8. Seven against Thebes.
9. Horse.
10. The *Epigonoi*.
11. Monument of the kings of Argos.
12. Treasury (*thesauros*) of the Tarentines.
13. of the Sicyonians.
14. of Siphnos.
15. of Thebes.
16. of Potidaea.
17. of Athens.
18. of Syracuse.
19. of Aeolia.
20. of Cnidos.
21. *Bouleuterion*.
22. The Boetians' base.
23. The Sibyl's rock.
24. The *temenos* of Ge.
25. The Asklepeion or *temenos* of the Muses.
26. The Naxian Sphinx.
27. Rock of Latona.
28. Porch of the Athenians.
29. *Thesauros* of Corinth.
30. *Thesauros* of Cyrene.
31. *Prytaneion*.
32. Polygonal wall and terracing.
33. Votive offering of the Messenians.
34. Monument of Aemilius Paulus.
35. Tripod of Plataea.
36. Rhodian chariot.
37. Altar of Chios.
38. Temple of Apollo.
39. Monument of Eumenes.
40. Votive offering of Corcyra (Corfu).
41. *Thesauros*(?).
42. Hunting monument of Alexander.
43. Retaining wall.
44. Monument of Prusias.
45. Monument of Aristaineta.
46. Votive offering of Phocaea.
47. Votive offering of Syracuse.
48. *Thesauros* of Acanthos.
49. Statue of Attalos.
50. Statue of Eumenes.
51. *Stoa* of Attalos.
52. *Temenos* of Neoptolemos.
53. Monument of Daochos.
54. Covered walk.
55. *Temenos* of Poseidon.
56. *Temenos* of Dionysis.
57. Theatre.
58. Theatre portico.
59. *Lesche* of the Cnidians.

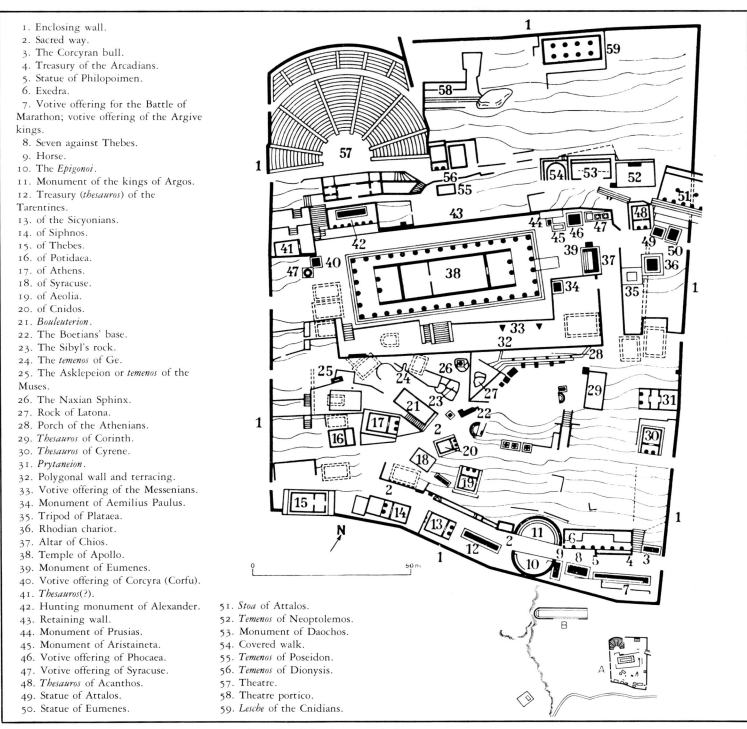

Figs 117–18   Delphi. Plan of the Sanctuary of Apollo (A in the general plan).

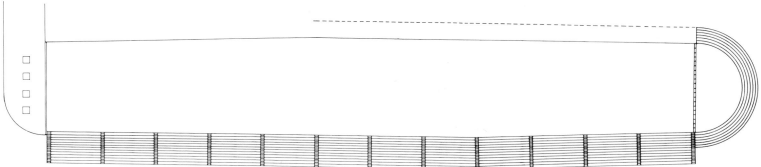

Figs 119–20   View and plan of the stadium at Delphi. The track measures 192 metres from the starting line to the finishing line, a distance equivalent to the Greek measure, the *stadion*.

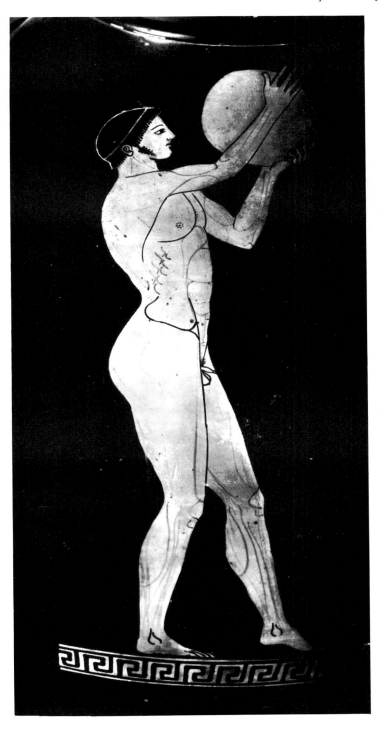

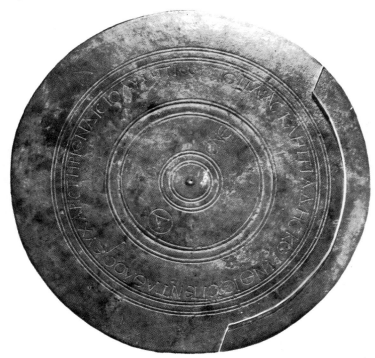

Figs 121–2   A bronze discus preserved in the museum at Olympia, measuring 22 cm in diameter and weighing roughly 2 kg. A discus thrower pictured on the side of an Attic amphora dating from the beginning of the fifth century BC.

Fig. 123   A drawing by Le Corbusier of the site of Athens.

Fig. 124   The silver didrachma, an Athenian coin, showing the head of Athena and her emblem, the owl.

Let us now turn to Athens, the most illustrious city of ancient Greece.

Athens is situated in the central plain of Attica, an area surrounded by a series of mountains — to the west, Aigaleos, to the north, Parnis, and to the east, Hymettus and Pentelikon — and bounded in the south by a jagged coastline. There are, however, broad valleys between the mountains to facilitate communications with other parts of the region, and the sea gives easy access to the neighbouring islands of Aegina and Salamis, and to the Cyclades that lie beyond.

The plain is traversed by two small rivers, the Kephisos and the Ilisos, between which there are a number of areas of high ground: Lycabettos, the Acropolis, the Areopagus, the hill of the Nymphs, the Pnyx, the Mouseion. The Acropolis, 156 metres above sea level, is the only one that offers a sure place of refuge because of the steepness of its sides and the broadness of its plateau. It became the site of the earliest settlement and remained the visual and administrative centre of the subsequent metropolis, which Herodotus calls a 'wheel-shaped city'.

The great city of Athens was formed when the inhabitants of the lesser settlements in Attica were either persuaded or forced — traditionally by Theseus — to move into the area surrounding the Acropolis. The centre of this new settlement was the slightly raised area of ground to the north of the Acropolis and the Areopagus, where the Agora developed. The law courts were situated on the Areopagus hill, while certain important sanctuaries, such as those of Dionysos and Olympian Zeus, were on the southern side, which, being the most favoured slope, was probably the site of the settlement's first expansion. In this way there developed a separate and distinct complex in which every natural and traditional feature was utilised for a specific purpose. The city, on the other hand, existed purely in order to provide a single environment for a multitude of different activities: it acted not only as a political, commercial and religious centre, but also as a place of refuge for a population that was, for the most part, scattered throughout the surrounding territory.

Every activity of the citizenry had its own special building, and the Athenians gradually became more and more proficient at designing monumental civic architecture. During the seventh century they built a large temple in the middle of the Acropolis, which had become a sacred area. Following the institution of the Panathenaïc festivals in 556 BC, a sacred way was inaugurated which led from the Dipylon gate to the western entrance of the Acropolis and crossed the Agora diagonally. Pisistratus and his successors built the first city walls (embracing an area of 60 hectares),

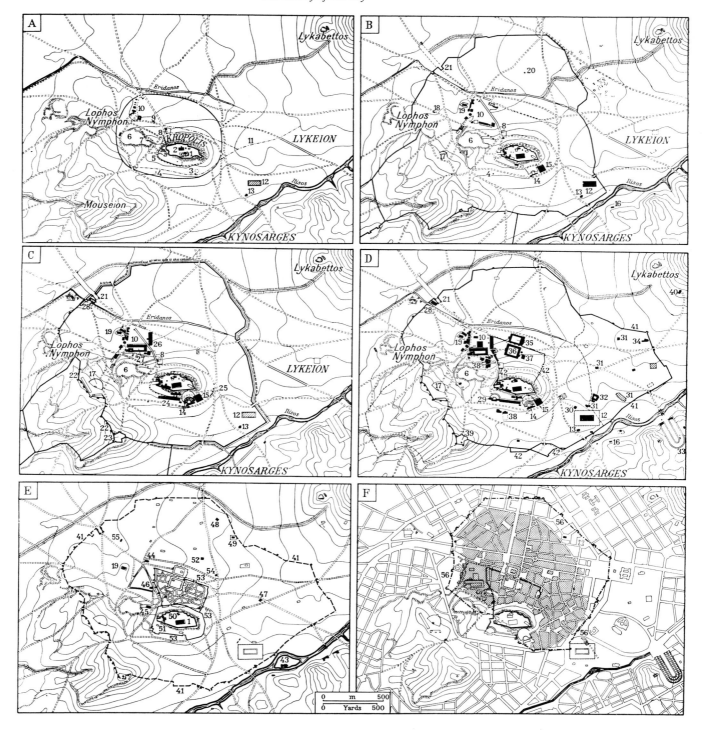

A. Classical era, showing the supposed outline of the sixth-century walls.
B. Classical era, showing the outline of the walls of Themistocles.
C. Hellenistic era, showing the *diateichisma* (wall of enclosure built after the demolition of the Long Walls between Athens and Piraeus).
D. Roman Era, showing the enlargement of Hadrian's wall and the inner walls of late antiquity.

E. Medieval era, showing the remains of the old walls and those built by the Franks (the so-called Wall of Valerian), enclosing the medieval district (53).
F. Modern era, showing the Turkish walls, built after the fifth century (56), and the development of the city up until the nineteenth century (the dotted area superimposed on the modern layout).

Individual monuments, which recur in different maps:
1. Parthenon, later the Church of Panagia Theotokos Atheniotissa (during the fifth and sixth centuries).
2. Temple of Athena Polias.
3. Sanctuary of Dionysos.
4. Sanctuary of the Nymphs.
5. Enneapylon.
6. Areopagus.
7. Semnai.
8. Eleusinion.
9. Enneakrounos.
10. Agora.
11. Aqueduct of Pisistratus.
12. Olympieion.
13. Pythion.
14. Theatre of Dionysos.
15. Odeon of Pericles.
16. Temple of Demeter and Kore.
17. Pnyx.
18. Temple of Artemis.

19. Hephaisteion, later Church of St George (during the fifth and sixth centuries).
20. Altar of Zeus and Athena Phratria.
21. Dipylon.
22. *Diateichisma* from the early Hellenistic period.
23. Praesidium of the Macedonians.
24. *Stoa* of Eumenes.
25. The Choregic monument of Lysicrates.
26. *Stoa* of Attalus.
27. Commercial agora.
28. Pompeion.
29. Odeon of Herodes Atticus.
30. Gate leading to Hadrian's Arch.
31. Baths.
32. Gymnasium.
33. Stadium.
34. Villa.
35. Library of Hadrian.
36. Roman agora.
37. Agoranomion and Tower of the Winds.

38. School.
39. Monument of Antiochus Philopappos.
40. Hydraulic cistern of the era of Hadrian.
41. Hadrian's Wall.
42. Walls of late antiquity.
43. Basilica of Bishop Leonidas.
44. St Philip.
45. St Dionysius the Areopagite.
46. Holy Apostles.
47. Sotira Likodimou.
48. St Theodore.
49. St George.
50. Aya Triada (formerly Erechtheion).
51. Holy Angels (formerly Propylaea).
52. Kapnikarea.
53. Frankish walls.
54. Panagia Gorgoepikoos (Little Cathedral — now St Eleutherios).
55. Holy Angels.
56. Turkish walls.

Fig. 125   The development of Athens over six successive eras.

the first monumental buildings round the Agora, the aqueduct that carried water from the Ilisos to the city, and laid the foundations of the Theatre of Dionysos on the southern slopes of the Acropolis. During the time of Cleisthenes the Pnyx became the regular meeting place for the assembly, the *bouleuterion* was set up in the Agora, and, on a site parallel to that of the temple which already stood on the Acropolis, work began on a second monumental temple, later to be incorporated into Pericles' Parthenon.

In 479 BC, Athens, by that time a prosperous and well-endowed city, was destroyed by the invading Persians. Immediately afterwards, Themistocles had a new and more extensive wall built, which embraced an area of approximately 250 hectares, as well as reconstructing the buildings in the Agora and establishing Piraeus as a military and commercial port. Under Pericles the Acropolis was almost completely redone: the Parthenon was erected (447–438

BC), as were the Propylaea (437–432 BC), the Temple of Athene Nike (c. 430–420 BC) and the Erechtheion (421–405 BC). The city expanded beyond the walls of Themistocles and began to grow into a much more complex territorial entity; the rectilinear road — the *dromos* — leading from the Dipylon Gate to the Academy was laid out, and the walls joining the city to Piraeus were erected according to the strictly geometrical plans drawn up by Hippodamus. The walls built by Themistocles were altered by Cleon in order to strengthen the defences in the western part of the city, and the finishing touches were put to the Theatre of Dionysos, where the whole population of Athens could gather to hear the tragedies of Aeschylus, Sophocles and Euripides and the comedies of Aristophanes (Figs 145–7).

This process of self-improvement, which lasted for as long as Athens remained free and powerful, was not the

Fig. 126   Athens, the top of the Areopagus Hill.

result of any fixed forward planning policy; it was just a series of projects that slowly but surely gave the city its orderly appearance, and which also blended sympathetically into the natural environment. The city also possessed an extraordinary unity which derived from the cohesiveness and the sense of responsibility of all those who had participated in its development, whether rulers, planners or manual workers. Today we are grown used to differentiating between architecture, sculpture, painting and ornament, but in Athens it was impossible to draw such distinctions.

Even in the heart of the city, neither the streets nor the walls nor the monumental buildings succeeded in concealing the natural contours of the terrain; outcrops of rock and steep natural terraces were left untouched in many places, or cut away and levelled off in a way that respected their natural proportions (Figs 126–7). Buildings from past ages that had fallen into disrepair were often preserved and incorporated into later ones, and in this way nature and history were both kept alive in the new environment of the city. They formed the background for such innovations as statues which were as large as buildings (the massive bronze Athena Promakos, for example, whose metallic gleam could be seen by those far out at sea) and buildings, both large and small, that were made of Pentelic marble and finished with the same care as sculptures, as well as being coloured like paintings.

Fig. 127   Athens, view of the Acropolis from Pnyx.

In the monuments of the Acropolis (Figs 128–44) it is impossible to tell where architecture ends and ornament begins; the columns, capitals, bases and cornices are a series of identical and complicated sculptural works (Fig. 143), while the friezes and the statues in the pediments form completely different configurations, but are made of the same materials and worked with the same degree of artistry. In one instance (the Caryatid portico of the Erechtheion) six identical statues take the place of six pillars (Fig. 144). All these carvings were made in a workshop and then later placed *in situ*, which is why the technical precision and the marginal differences in dimension (tolerance, as it is known nowadays) are equal in both cases. The trunks of the columns, the components of the cornices, the stones in the walls and the roofing slabs (both of which were of marble, as were the beams) fit together with minute precision (Fig. 140). In the shrine of the Parthenon there was also the temple's holiest statue, a great carved wooden figure of Athena Parthenos by Phidias, covered in gold and ivory and worked with a goldsmith's precision.

Thus man's presence in the natural environment came to be noted for its quality rather than its quantity; the city, like the political city-state organisation, was a construction on a human scale, surrounded and dominated by the vastness of nature. Man, by using his skills, was able to improve this construction and tried to emulate the perfection of nature by imposing the same close relationship between individual elements and the whole. The monumental com-

Fig. 128   Athens, view of the Acropolis from the west.

plex of the Acropolis can be seen from every part of the city, and the simple and rational designs of the temples are also visible at great distances. It is only at closer quarters that the secondary elements of design become apparent — the repeated architectural features, such as columns, bases and capitals, and the smaller sculptural details, which were picked out in colour. The whole ensemble is composed of a mass of interrelating shapes, varying in scale from the massive to the minute.

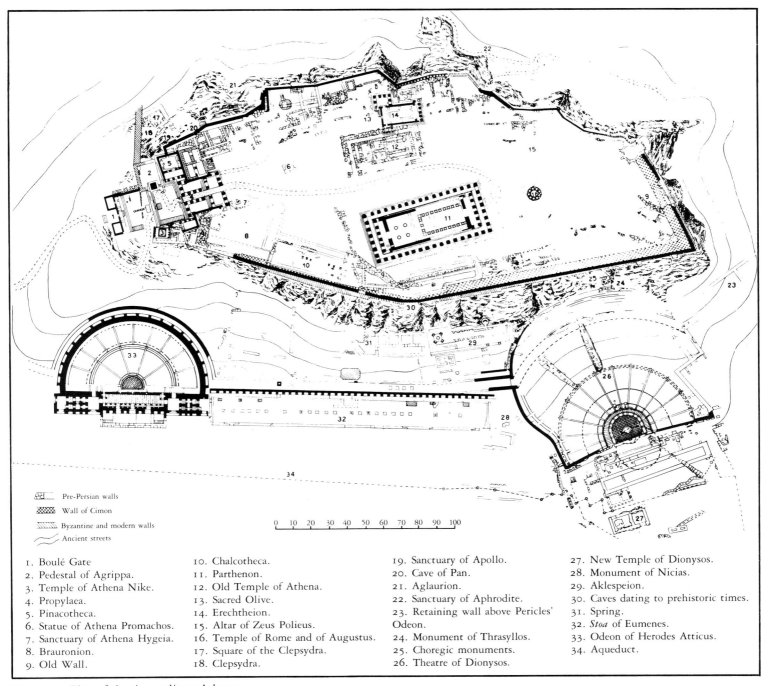

0 10 20 30 40 50 60 70 80 90 100

1. Boulé Gate
2. Pedestal of Agrippa.
3. Temple of Athena Nike.
4. Propylaea.
5. Pinacotheca.
6. Statue of Athena Promachos.
7. Sanctuary of Athena Hygeia.
8. Brauronion.
9. Old Wall.

10. Chalcotheca.
11. Parthenon.
12. Old Temple of Athena.
13. Sacred Olive.
14. Erechtheion.
15. Altar of Zeus Polieus.
16. Temple of Rome and of Augustus.
17. Square of the Clepsydra.
18. Clepsydra.

19. Sanctuary of Apollo.
20. Cave of Pan.
21. Aglaurion.
22. Sanctuary of Aphrodite.
23. Retaining wall above Pericles' Odeon.
24. Monument of Thrasyllos.
25. Choregic monuments.
26. Theatre of Dionysos.

27. New Temple of Dionysos.
28. Monument of Nicias.
29. Aklespeion.
30. Caves dating to prehistoric times.
31. Spring.
32. *Stoa* of Eumenes.
33. Odeon of Herodes Atticus.
34. Aqueduct.

Fig. 129   Plan of the Acropolis at Athens.

Fig. 130   Tourists visiting the ruins of the Parthenon.

Fig. 131   Ruins of the Propylaea.

Fig. 132   Ruins of the Erechtheion.

1. Rear porch.
2. Parthenon.
3. Statue of Athena Parthenos.
4. Anterior porch.

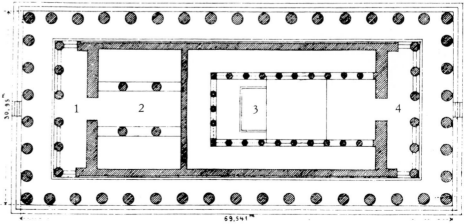

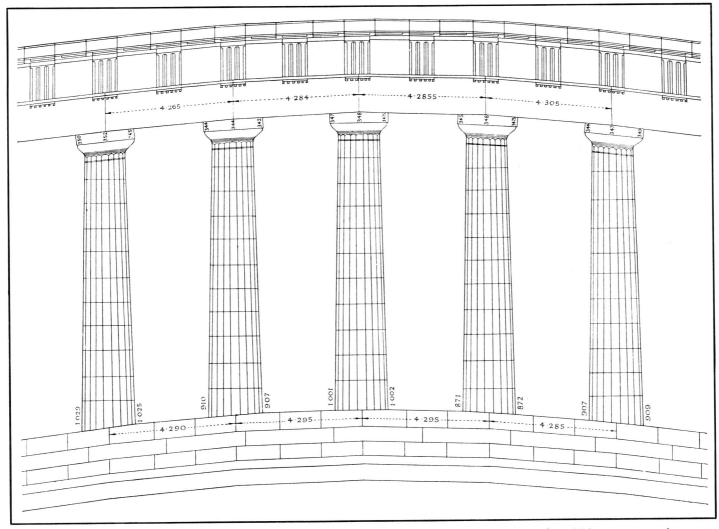

Figs 133–5 Eastern façade and plan of the Parthenon. Diagram showing a section of the northern side, which exaggerates the way the colonnade was misshaped to achieve a better optical effect.

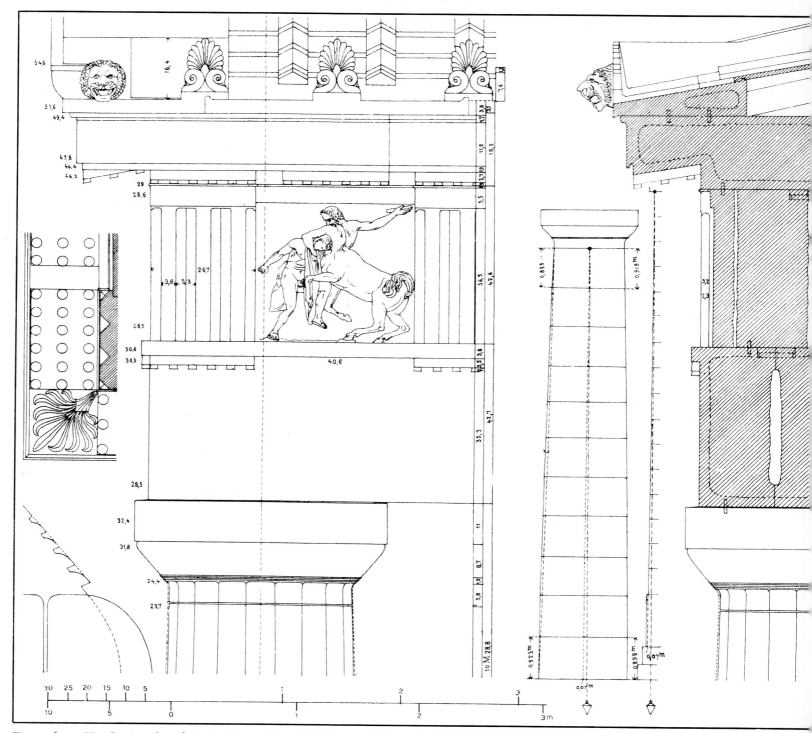

Figs 136–7   The Doric order of the Parthenon. Detailed diagrams of the capital and pediment. View of a pillar near the north-eastern corner.

Fig. 138   The marbles from the eastern pediment of the Parthenon, now in the British Museum.

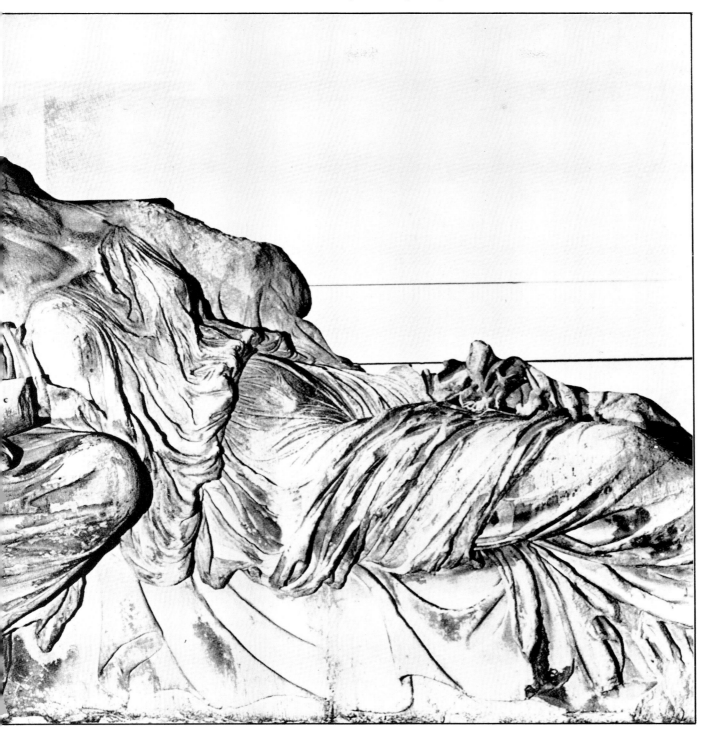

Fig. 139   The base of one of the
Parthenon's pillars.

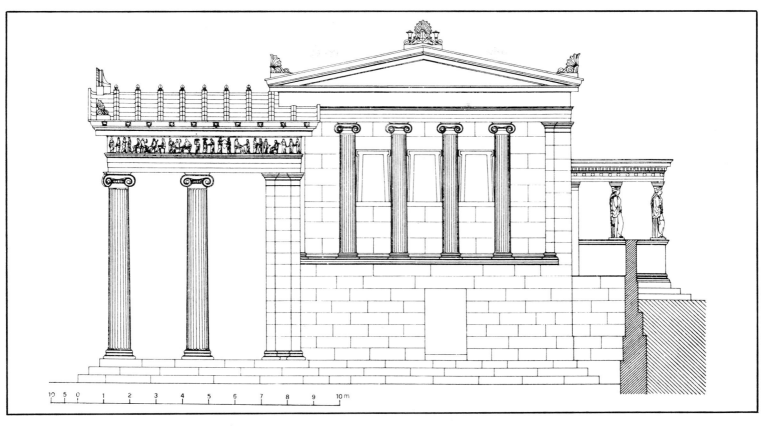

Figs 140–1   Western view of the Erechtheion. Reconstruction of the Acropolis (the Erechtheion is on the left, the Parthenon on the right).

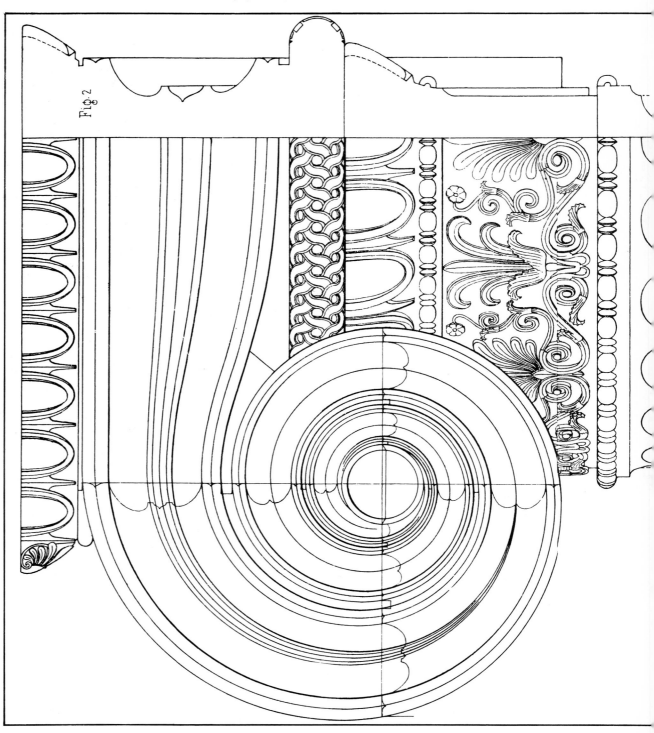

Fig 2

Figs 142–3   Diagrams of
a capital from the northern
portico of the Erechtheion,
reduced to a quarter of the
actual size.

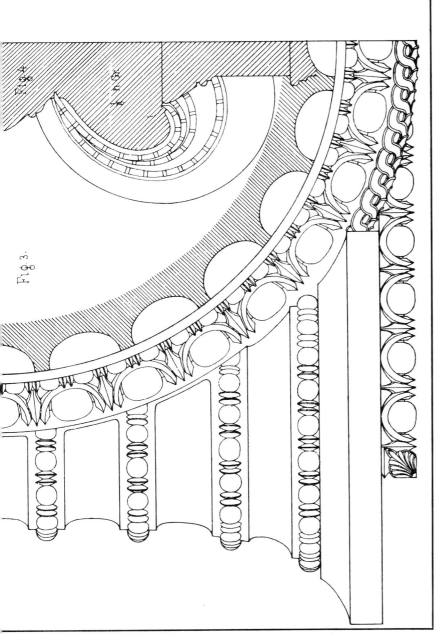

Fig. 144   One of the Caryatids supporting the southern portico of the Erechtheion.

Figs 145–7   The Theatre of Dionysos
at Athens. A photograph of two
admission tokens, now in the
Numismatic Museum in Athens, two
modern views, and the overall plan.

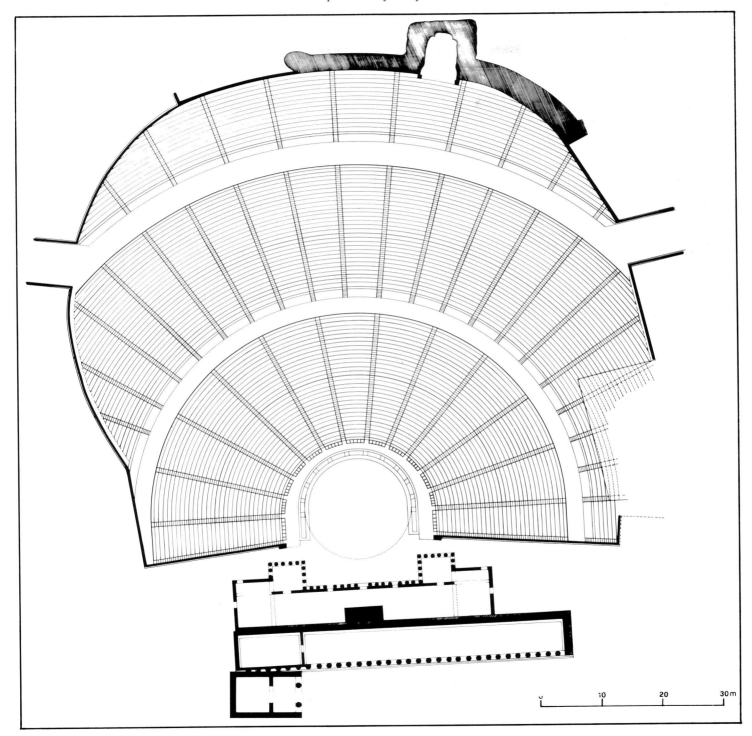

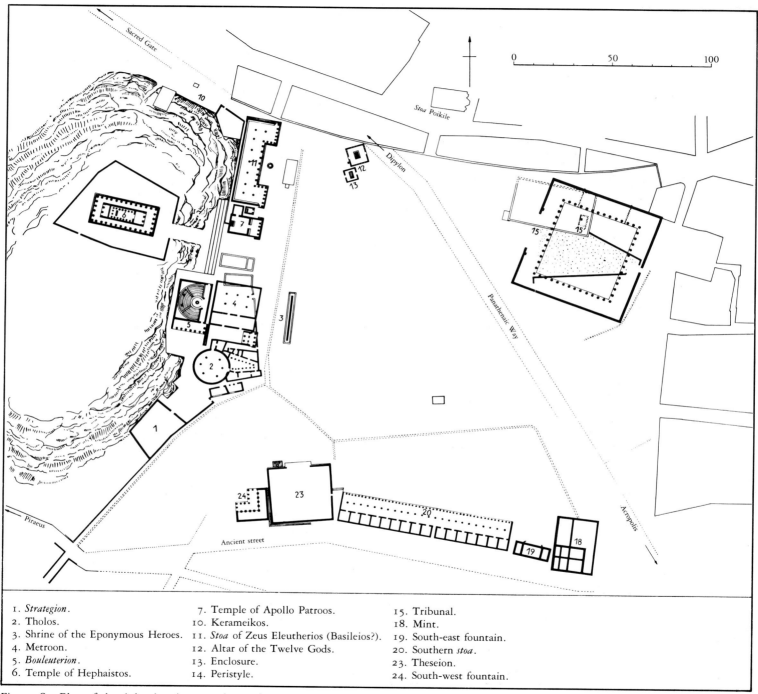

1. *Strategion*.
2. Tholos.
3. Shrine of the Eponymous Heroes.
4. Metroon.
5. *Bouleuterion*.
6. Temple of Hephaistos.

7. Temple of Apollo Patroos.
10. Kerameikos.
11. *Stoa* of Zeus Eleutherios (Basileios?).
12. Altar of the Twelve Gods.
13. Enclosure.
14. Peristyle.

15. Tribunal.
18. Mint.
19. South-east fountain.
20. Southern *stoa*.
23. Theseion.
24. South-west fountain.

Fig. 148   Plan of the Athenian Agora as it was in 300 BC.

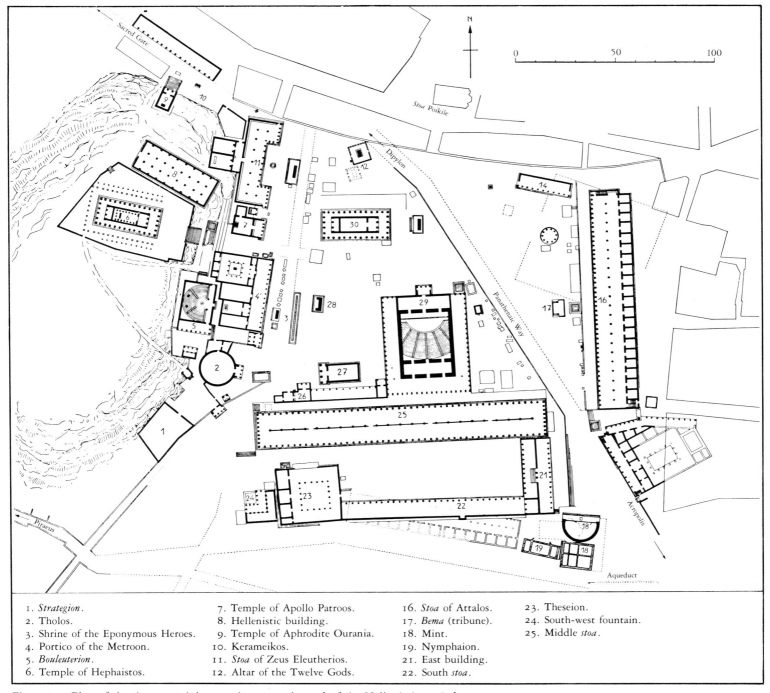

1. *Strategion*.
2. Tholos.
3. Shrine of the Eponymous Heroes.
4. Portico of the Metroon.
5. *Bouleuterion*.
6. Temple of Hephaistos.
7. Temple of Apollo Patroos.
8. Hellenistic building.
9. Temple of Aphrodite Ourania.
10. Kerameikos.
11. *Stoa* of Zeus Eleutherios.
12. Altar of the Twelve Gods.
16. *Stoa* of Attalos.
17. *Bema* (tribune).
18. Mint.
19. Nymphaion.
21. East building.
22. South *stoa*.
23. Theseion.
24. South-west fountain.
25. Middle *stoa*.

Fig. 149   Plan of the Agora at Athens as it was at the end of the Hellenistic period.

Fig. 150   View of the Athenian
Agora during the Roman period.

A Acropolis.
S *Stoa* (colonnade).
O Odeon.
T Temples.
C *Bouleuterion*.

Fig. 151   Two *ostraka*, pieces of earthenware used for the vote
of exile (*ostrakismos*) against Themistocles and Aristides.

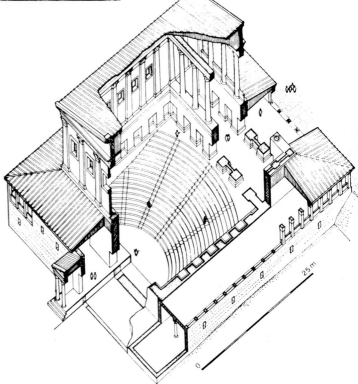

Fig. 152   Diagram of the Odeon of Agrippa (*c*. 15 BC).

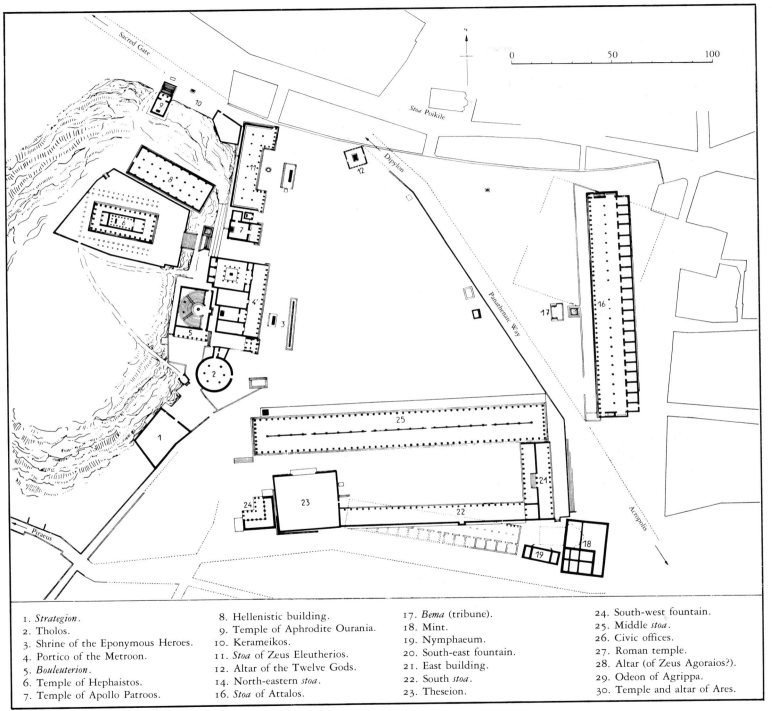

Fig. 153   Plan of the Athenian Agora during the Roman period.

1. *Strategion*.
2. Tholos.
3. Shrine of the Eponymous Heroes.
4. Portico of the Metroon.
5. *Bouleuterion*.
6. Temple of Hephaistos.
7. Temple of Apollo Patroos.
8. Hellenistic building.
9. Temple of Aphrodite Ourania.
10. Kerameikos.
11. *Stoa* of Zeus Eleutherios.
12. Altar of the Twelve Gods.
14. North-eastern *stoa*.
16. *Stoa* of Attalos.
17. *Bema* (tribune).
18. Mint.
19. Nymphaeum.
20. South-east fountain.
21. East building.
22. South *stoa*.
23. Theseion.
24. South-west fountain.
25. Middle *stoa*.
26. Civic offices.
27. Roman temple.
28. Altar (of Zeus Agoraios?).
29. Odeon of Agrippa.
30. Temple and altar of Ares.

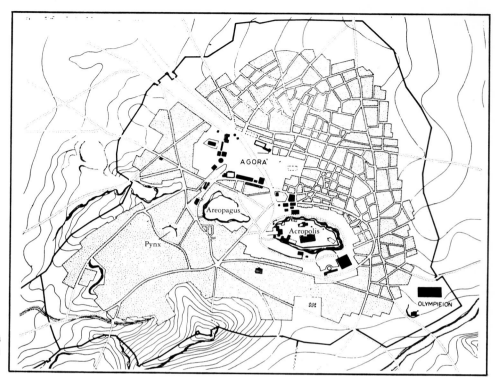

Fig. 154   Rough plan of Athens
during the time of Pericles; the
residential quarters (dotted areas) can
be seen spread out around the public
buildings (black areas).

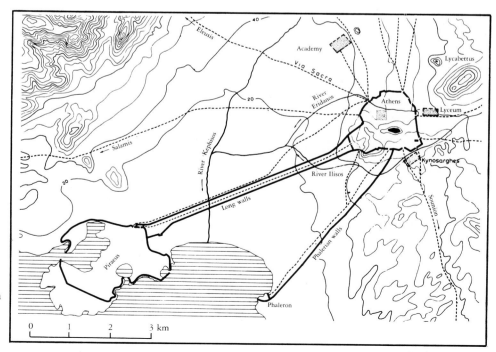

Fig. 155   Athens during the fifth
century BC, with the long walls
joining the city to the harbour at
Piraeus.

We have to try to visualise the city's residential quarters, which were built in the districts surrounding the Acropolis and the other public areas (Figs 154, 157). The streets discovered by archaeologists so far do not seem to follow any regular pattern, except for the rectilinear *dromos* that runs from the Agora to the Dipylon Gate, while the houses, which were certainly modest, have disappeared leaving little trace. If we examine the houses which have been excavated at Delos in the area round the theatre (Figs 158–60) and which date from the same period, we can get an idea of the ones at Athens. The simplicity of these houses results from the fact that their occupants did not spend much time at home. The greater part of the day was spent in the public areas, which were laid out according to decisions taken by the community assembly. The monuments scattered throughout every district are a continual reminder of how the city was, quite literally, the common property of its citizens.

Fig. 156   The structure of a marble wall on the Acropolis at Athens.

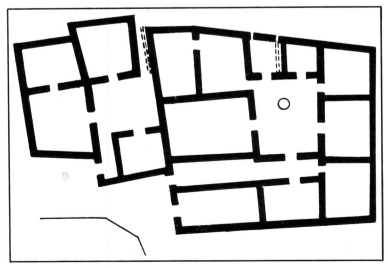

Fig. 157   Plans of two Athenian houses of the fifth century BC.

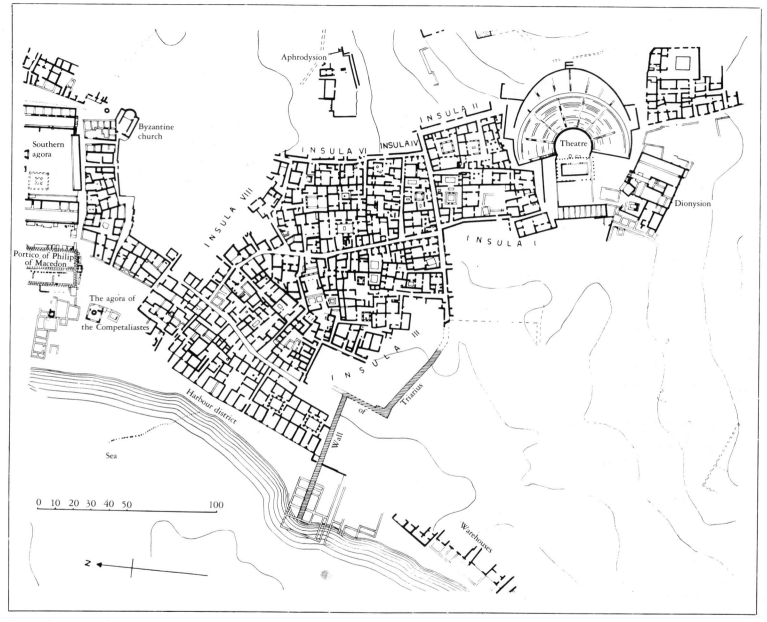

Fig. 158   The harbour area at Delos. The houses excavated date from the third and second centuries BC and correspond to a type that spread throughout Greek cities from the fourth century onwards. Demosthenes wrote that the first houses with a pillared courtyard were built on the outskirts of Athens towards the middle of the fourth century.

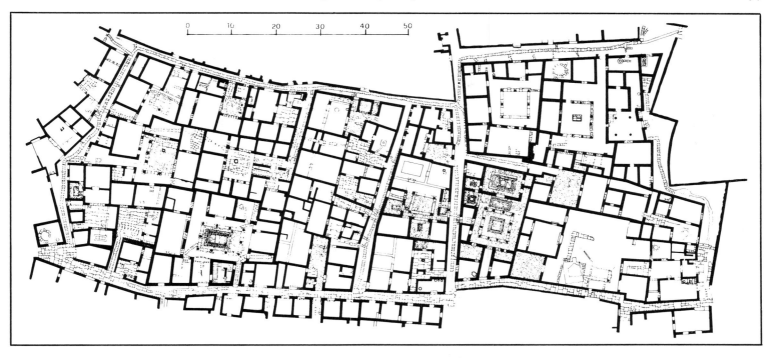

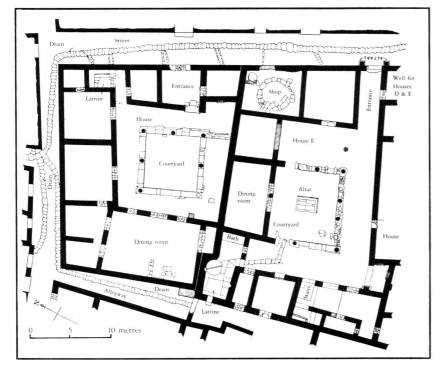

Figs 159–60 *Insulae* I, II, IV, and VI at Delos, and two houses from *insula* II.

Figs 161–4   Four kitchen utensils made of terracotta: a pot with brazier, a grill, an oven, a tureen.

The everyday utensils preserved in the Agora Museum in Athens give an idea of the simplicity of life in the city of Pericles and Phidias (Figs 161–9). The wealth of Athens went towards public rather than private consumption, which explains the scarcity and the utilitarian nature of the inhabitants' household effects.

In later years Athens spread eastwards to the plain beyond the Olympieion (the Temple of Olympian Zeus) and the Acropolis became its exact centre, which it continued to be, despite numerous Hellenistic and Roman additions to the city. These additions included such things as the two new porticoes in the Agora, the Portico of Eumenes at the

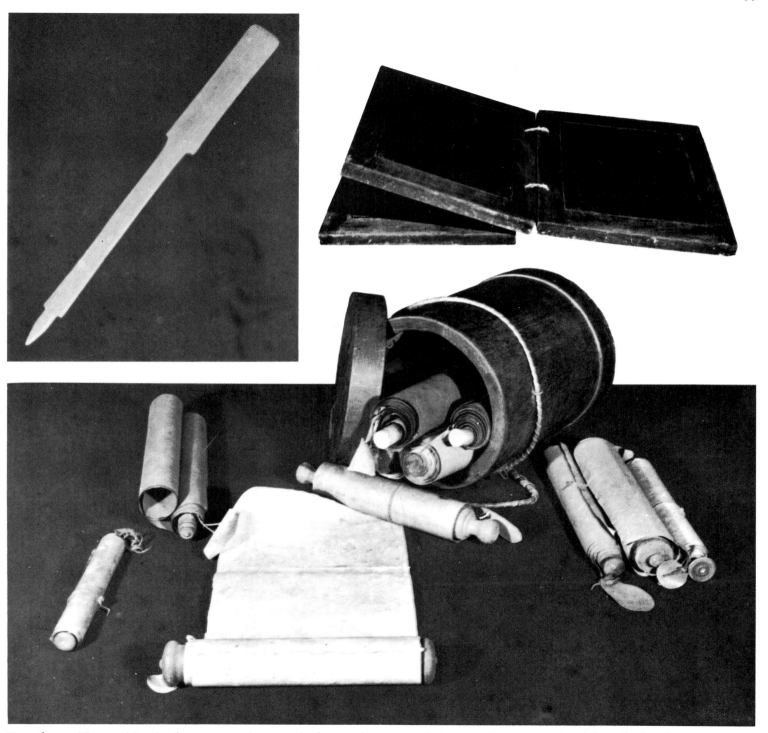

Figs 165–7   Three writing implements: a stylus, waxed tablets and papyrus rolls in a wooden container (used from the fourth century onwards).

south of the Acropolis, the new Roman Agora, the Odeon of Agrippa, the Odeon of Herodes Atticus, Hadrian's Library, and, finally, the so-called city of Hadrian, the name given to the eastern extension of Athens, which included the new Olympieion, the palaestra and the baths (Fig. 170).

At the end of the classical era the great city of Athens fell into decay, and the inhabited area became restricted to a small central zone around the Acropolis and the Roman Agora. The city remained a minor provincial township until 1827, the year in which the Turks were finally expelled (Figs 171–2). In 1834 Athens was chosen as the modern Greek capital, from which time it began to expand at an uncontrolled rate, with only the Acropolis, the hills to the south-west and Mount Lycabettus being left untouched; it

spread as far as Piraeus and now covers the whole area between the foot of the mountains and the sea.

The Acropolis, the Agora and the main groups of monuments have now become archaeological zones, in which excavations continue. It has even been recently proposed to free a great part of the ancient city by demolishing the old quarters that lie to the north of the Acropolis. It is easy to get an idea of what ancient Athens looked like by visiting the ruins and the museums, but the temples of the Acropolis, which are still plainly visible from all parts of the city, are living proof that Athens was indeed one of the most important milestones in the history of mankind, even though they stand forlornly in the middle of a sad and chaotic Third World city, which has nothing in common with its ancient counterpart except a name (Figs 174–7).

Figs 168–9   Knucklebones (from goats' feet) and dice, used for games. An *amis* (a terracotta receptable used instead of a latrine).

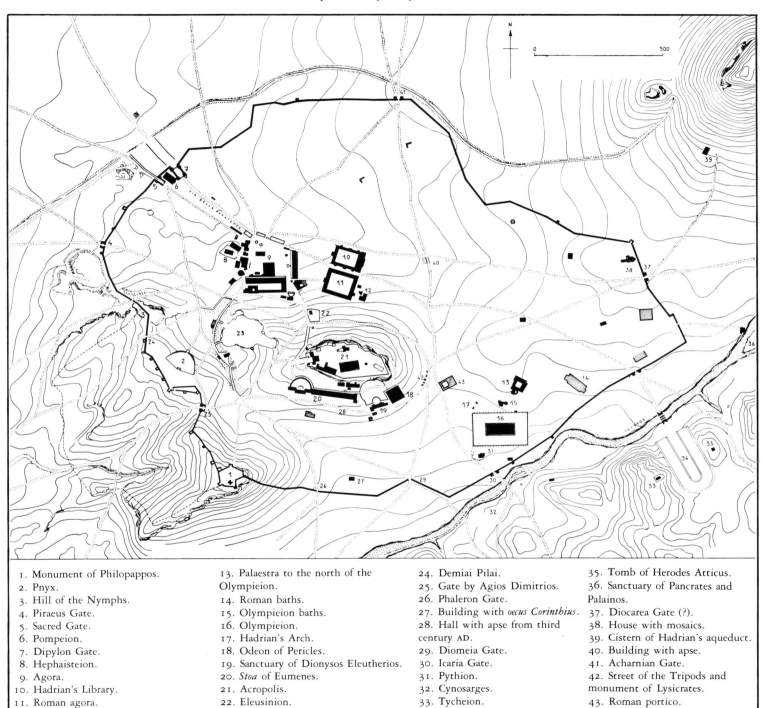

1. Monument of Philopappos.
2. Pnyx.
3. Hill of the Nymphs.
4. Piraeus Gate.
5. Sacred Gate.
6. Pompeion.
7. Dipylon Gate.
8. Hephaisteion.
9. Agora.
10. Hadrian's Library.
11. Roman agora.
12. *Agoranomion* and Tower of the Winds.
13. Palaestra to the north of the Olympieion.
14. Roman baths.
15. Olympieion baths.
16. Olympieion.
17. Hadrian's Arch.
18. Odeon of Pericles.
19. Sanctuary of Dionysos Eleutherios.
20. *Stoa* of Eumenes.
21. Acropolis.
22. Eleusinion.
23. Areopagus.
24. Demiai Pilai.
25. Gate by Agios Dimitrios.
26. Phaleron Gate.
27. Building with *oecus Corinthius*.
28. Hall with apse from third century AD.
29. Diomeia Gate.
30. Icaria Gate.
31. Pythion.
32. Cynosarges.
33. Tycheion.
34. Stadium.
35. Tomb of Herodes Atticus.
36. Sanctuary of Pancrates and Palainos.
37. Diocarea Gate (?).
38. House with mosaics.
39. Cistern of Hadrian's aqueduct.
40. Building with apse.
41. Acharnian Gate.
42. Street of the Tripods and monument of Lysicrates.
43. Roman portico.

Fig. 170 Plan of Athens at the end of the classical era.

Figs 171–2   Plan of Athens at the end of the
period of Turkish domination, on the same scale as
the preceding plan, and a view of the city in 1835,
the year of the foundation of the modern Greek
State.

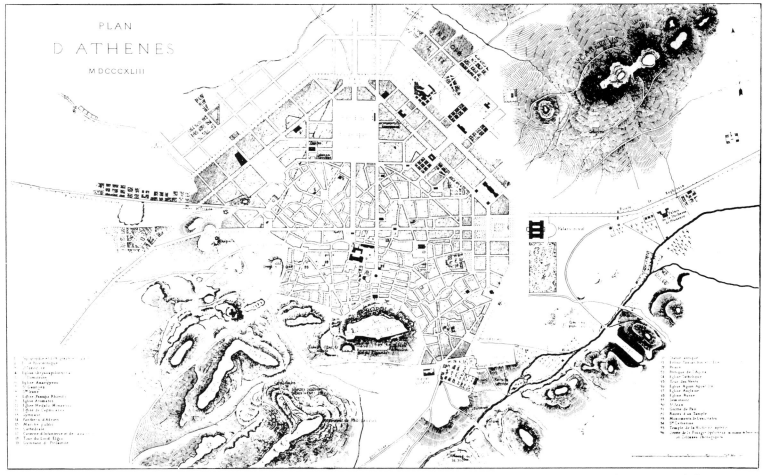

Fig. 173   Map of the new Athens in 1842, following work by the town-planner Leone von Klenze. The city still spreads northwards from the Acropolis.

Fig. 174   The Stadium of Herodes Atticus at Athens, which was reconstructed for the first modern Olympic Games.

Fig. 175   The cityscape of modern Athens; in the background can be seen the Acropolis and Mount Lycabettus.

Figs 176–7 The monuments of the Acropolis in their contemporary setting. Above, the Propylaea, the Parthenon, the Odeon of Herodes Atticus and, in the background, Mount Lycabettus. Below, the Parthenon, the Erechtheion and, beyond, the Hill of the Pnyx.

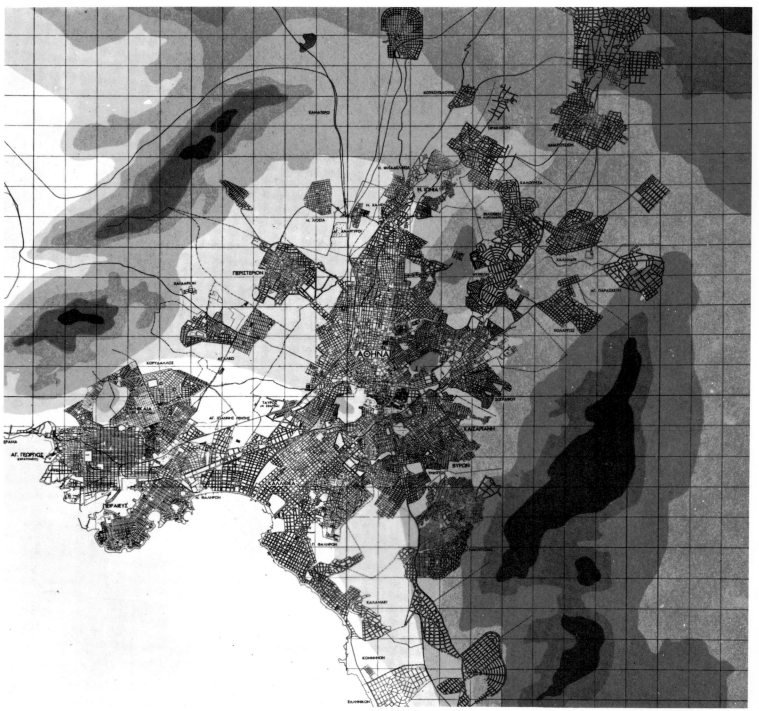

Fig. 178   Map of modern Athens, made in 1950; the population has since doubled. Cf. Fig. 155.

Hippodamus of Miletus is remembered by Aristotle as
being the author of a political theory: 'His system was for a
city with a population of ten thousand, divided into three
classes; for he made one class of artisans, one of farmers, and
the third the class that fought for the state in war and was
the armed class. He divided the land into three parts, one
sacred, one public and one private.' (*Politics*, II, 1267 b.) He
was also the man who invented the division of cities into
blocks, and, apart from having laid out Piraeus, he may also
have been responsible for planning Miletus and Rhodes.

These cities, and others founded in both the Western
and Eastern Mediterranean, such as Olynthus, Agrigentum, Paestum, Naples (Neapolis) and Pompeii, were laid
out according to a geometrical plan. This plan governed
everything from the scale of individual buildings to the
scale of the city as a whole, just like in the ancient Bronze
Age cities of the Near East (Babylon, for example, which we
dealt with on pages 28, 32 and 33). Although it was a new
rule, and one which allowed for no compromise, it also
strengthened and formalised the structural characteristics of
the Greek city.

The streets ran in straight lines, with a few main ones
(using length as the criterion), which divided the city into a
series of strips, and a larger number of secondary streets,
which crossed the former at right angles. None of them had
any pretensions to grandeur, being of modest dimensions:
the main streets were between 5 and 10 metres wide, while
the secondary ones measured between 3 and 5 metres across.
The result was a grid of uniformly rectangular blocks
(*insulae*), which varied in certain cases in order to fit in with
the local terrain. A lesser block — the distance between two
secondary streets — would be large enough to accommodate
one or two individual houses (often 30 to 35 metres), while a
larger one — the distance between two main streets — was
designed to provide enough space for an uninterrupted line
of houses (from 50 up to 300 metres). The special civil and
religious precincts did not occupy space outside the scope of
this geometrical plan; they formed part of the grid and often
took up an area equivalent to one or more blocks, which
explains why the main streets did not enter them, but ran
alongside. The city boundaries did not follow a regular
pattern, and neither did the building groups when they

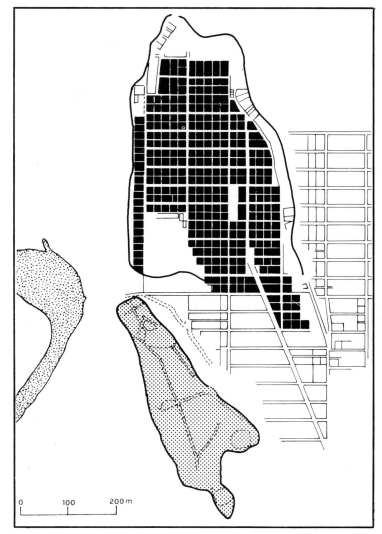

Fig. 179   Plan of Olynthus, following its expansion by
Hippodamus (432 BC). The dotted area in the foreground shows the
original nucleus (the *palaiopolis*).

encountered such natural obstacles as mountains or coasts.
The city walls were also equally flexible: they did not
necessarily follow the pattern of the buildings, but encircled
easily defendable areas of high ground, even if these were
situated some distance away from the inhabited areas,
which explains their irregular outline.

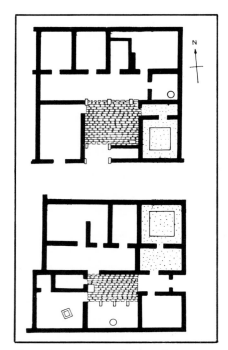

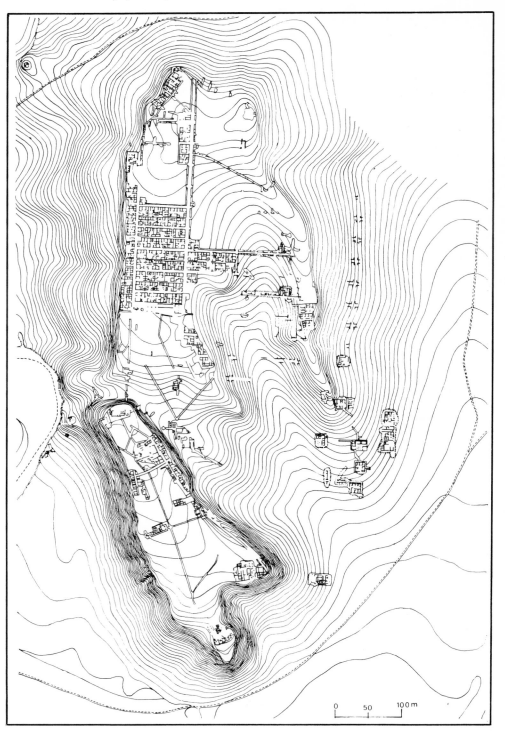

Figs 180–1 General plan of the
excavations at Olynthus; above, the
ground plan of two houses that typify
the Hippodamian expansion.

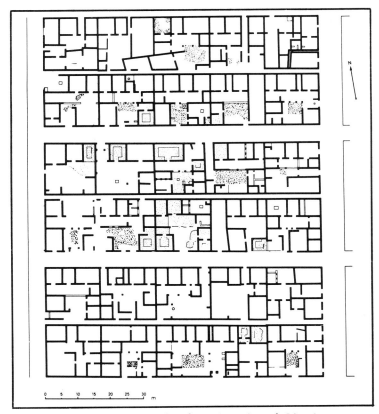

Fig. 182   Three blocks (*insulae*) from the enlarged Olynthus,
measuring 120 × 300 feet (*c.* 35 × 90 metres).

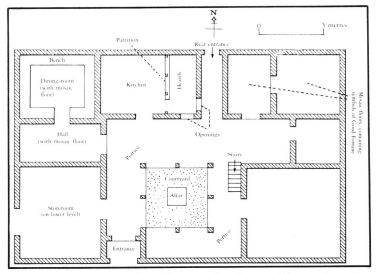

Fig. 183   The 'House of Good Fortune', a large residence situated
on the periphery of the new city.

The immutability of this grid, which was determined
by the needs of the houses and not by the exceptional
demands imposed by temples and palaces, strengthened the
unified nature of the city, as well as confirming the way in
which all parts of the city, whether private or public, were
subject to a common law, imposed by the public will. The
fact that the distance between the rectangular blocks could
be varied at will meant that every city was unique, and not
tied to a single prototype. Also, the irregularity of the
boundaries and the way in which the walls did not follow
the outline of the inhabited areas meant that a balance was
maintained between the natural and man-made environment, thereby lessening the overall contrast between the
city and the surrounding countryside (Figs 180–205).

In this way, regularity was not taken to such a pitch that
the relationship between man and nature was compromised;
it allowed the city to develop in a controlled way, even when
it had achieved a considerable size, and it allowed for a
certain degree of added growth in a city that had already
been formed. It was this last possibility that was widely
exploited during the Hellenistic era.

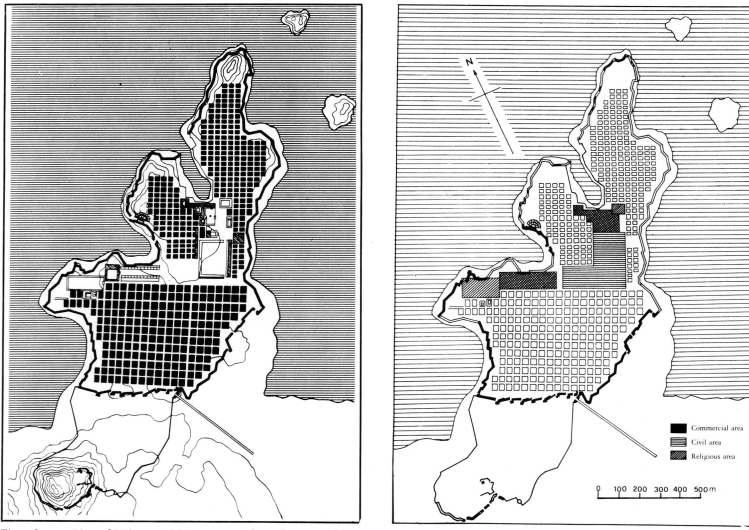

Figs 184–5   Plan of Miletus, which was carried out by Hippodamus in the fifth century BC after the Persian Wars. The blocks measure 100 × 175 feet (*c.* 30 × 52 metres). The diagram on the right shows the city's zonal division.

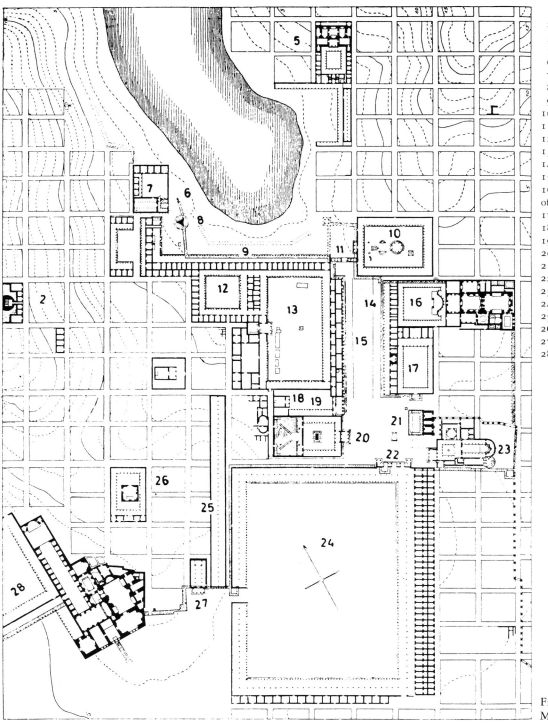

1. Theatre.
2. *Heroum* (a monumental tomb).
3–4. Two lion statues.
5. Roman baths.
6. Small harbour monument.
7. Synagogue.
8. Large harbour monument.
9. Harbour portico.
10. *Delphinion* (sanctuary of Apollo).
11. Harbour gate.
12. Small market.
13. Northern agora.
14. Ionic portico.
15. Processional road.
16. Baths of Capitus (Roman governor of the first century AD).
17. Gymnasium.
18. Temple of Asklepeion.
19. Sanctuary of the Imperial cult (?).
20. *Bouleuterion*.
21. Nymphaeum.
22. Northern gate.
23. Christian Church (fifth century AD).
24. Southern agora.
25. Storehouses.
26. Roman *Heroum*.
27. Temple of Serapis.
28. Baths of Faustina.

Fig. 186 Plan of the city centre of Miletus.

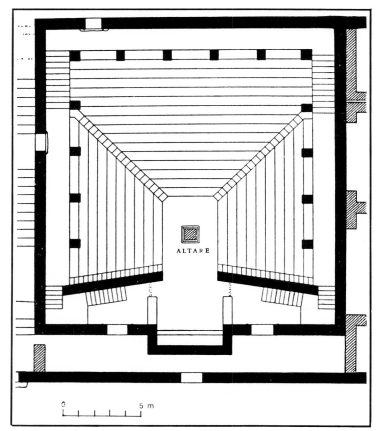

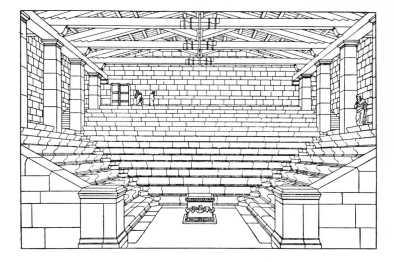

Figs 187–90 Priene (founded in about 350 BC). Plan and reconstruction of the *ekklesiasterion*, a large meeting hall with seating for between 600 and 700 people, where the assembly may have met under cover. Overall plan with the residential blocks shown in black and the public buildings drawn in outline. Facing: a general map of the excavations. Priene had about 4,000 inhabitants, and its theatre held 6,000 people.

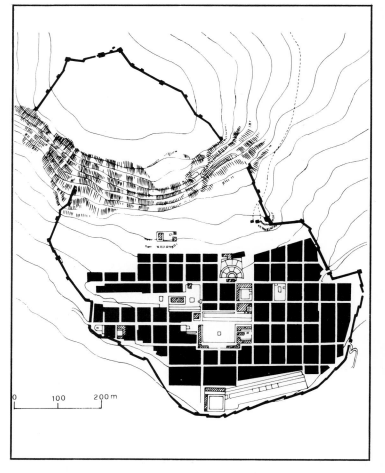

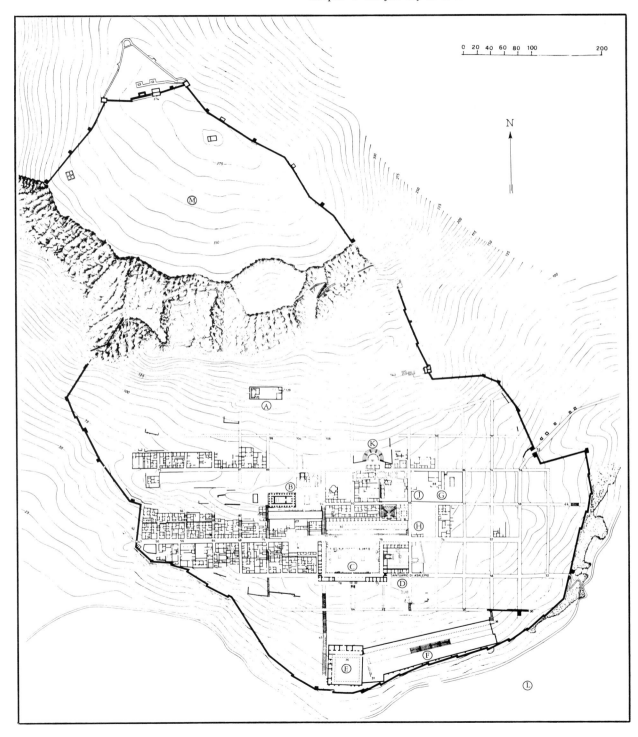

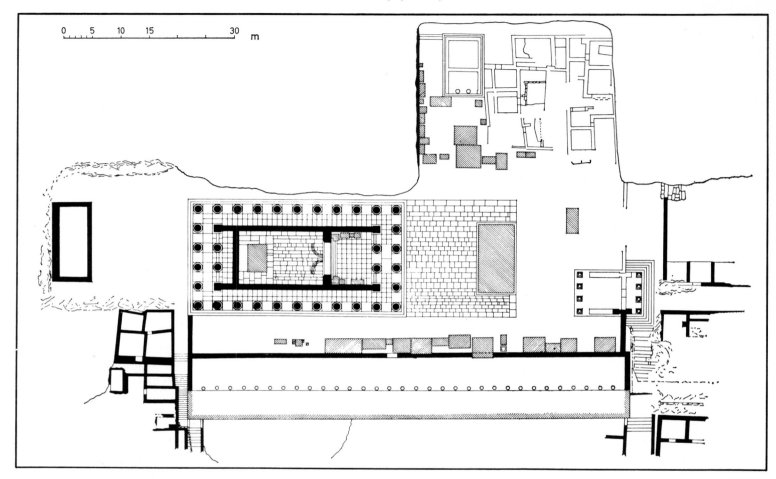

Figs 191–3   Plans of the two main public areas in
Priene (the sanctuary of Athena and the agora), and of
two typical houses, with both diagrams on the same
scale. The dimensional relationship between all Priene's
buildings, both private and public, form the basis of the
city's general design.

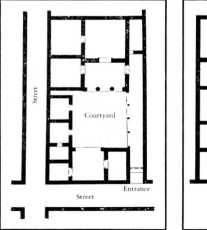

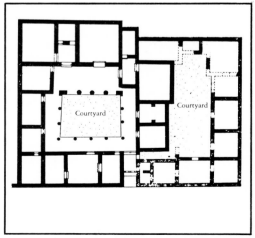

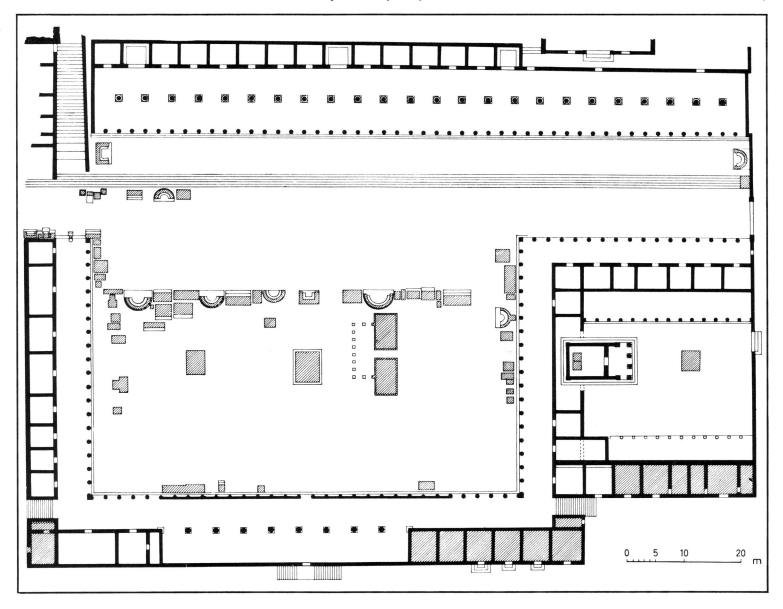

Fig. 194   Aerial view of Priene.

A. Agora.
B. Temple of Asklepios.
C. *Prytaneion*.
D. *Ekklesiasterion*.
E. Gymnasium.
F. Theatre.

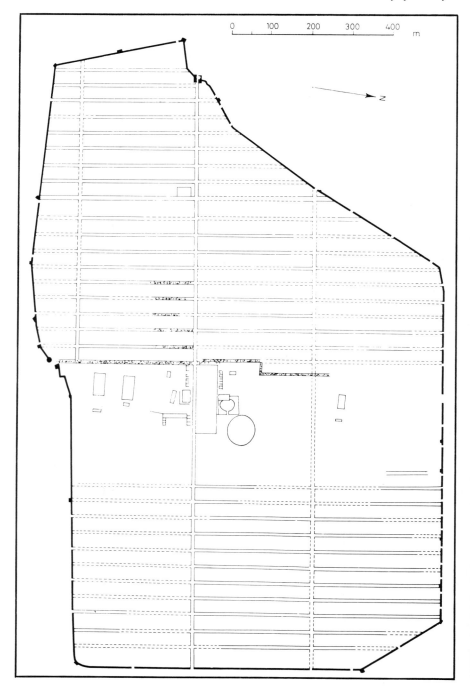

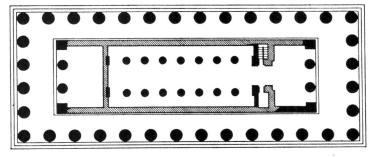

Figs 195–8 General plan of Paestum — each block measures 120 × 1,000 feet (*c.* 35 × 300 metres) — and the Temple of Neptune, situated in the central sacred area.

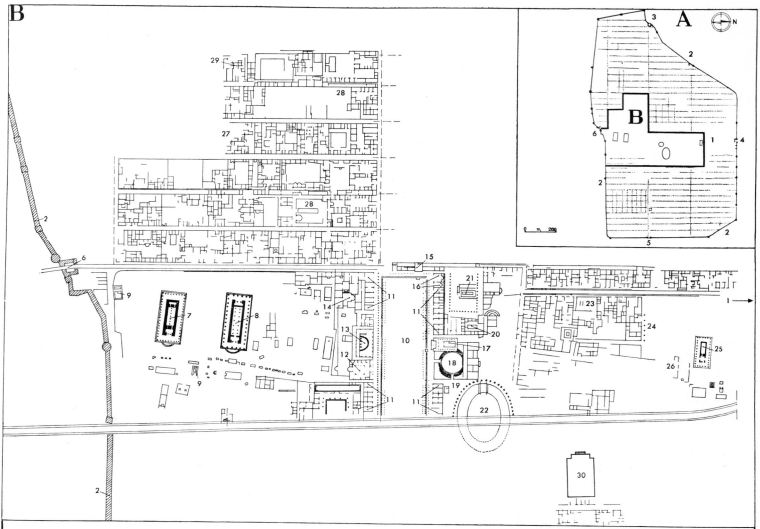

A. General plan of the ancient city, showing the walls and the outline of the street network and traces of buildings revealed by aerial photography.
B. Plan of the sector containing the Greek sanctuary (corresponding to the white area in Map A). Principal monuments and complexes:
  1. Area of Neolithic necropolis.
  2. Wall.
  3. Sea Gate.
  4. Golden Gate.
  5. Sirena Gate.
  6. Giustizia Gate.

  7. Basilica with altar in front.
  8. Temple of Poseidon with Greek and Roman altars in front.
  9. Small temple.
  10. Forum.
  11. *Tabernae*.
  12. *Macellum*.
  13. Exedra.
  14. Baths of Venneianus.
  15. Shrine of the Lares.
  16. Roman sacellum.
  17. Italic temple.
  18. Greek theatre.
  19. *Aerarium*.

  20. Greek gymnasium.
  21. Roman palaestra with swimming bath below.
  22. Amphitheatre.
  23. Sacellum with *temenos*.
  24. Roman arcade.
  25. Athenaeion (Temple of Ceres) with altar in front and votive pillars.
  26. Archaic shrine.
  27. Residential quarters.
  28. Baths.
  29. Pottery.
  30. Modern museum.

Figs 199–200   Plan and aerial view of the centre of Paestum showing the extent of the excavations so far.

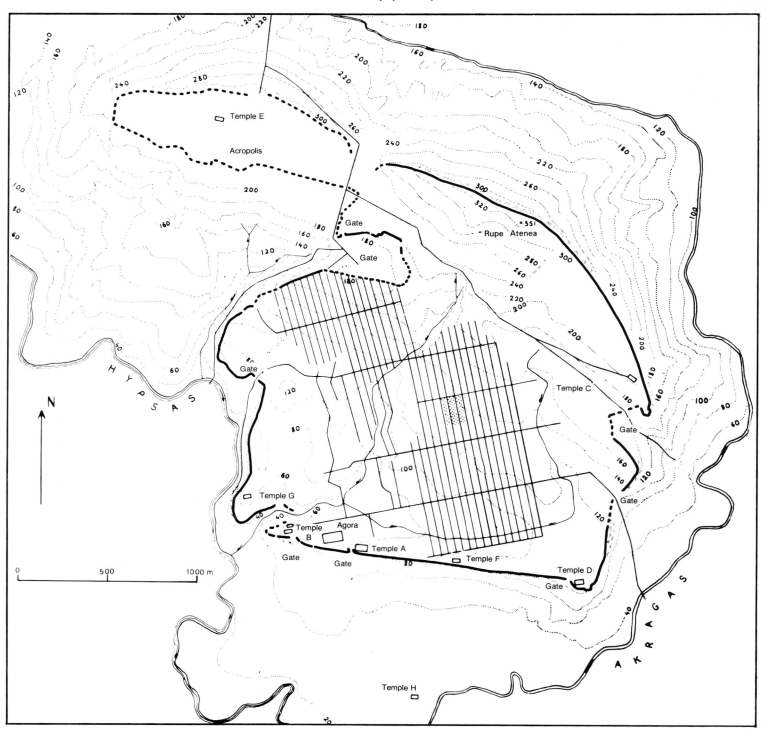

Figs 201–2   General plan of Agrigentum and of the excavated area at the centre of the city (the dotted area in Fig. 201). The blocks measure 120 × 1000 feet (*c*. 35 × 300 metres), as at Paestum.

Figs 203–4 Agrigentum. Aerial view of temple A. View from temple B towards the city and the acropolis, where the modern town is sited; in the lower part of the photograph, lying on the ground, can be seen one of the Caryatids from the temple.

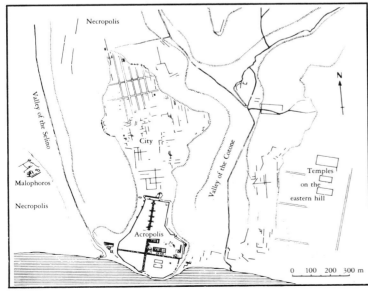

Figs 205–6 (left and overleaf). Selinunte. Plan of the excavations and aerial view of the temples on the eastern hill (the nearer one has been re-erected by archaeologists). The blocks have a constant width of 100 feet (*c.* 30 metres).

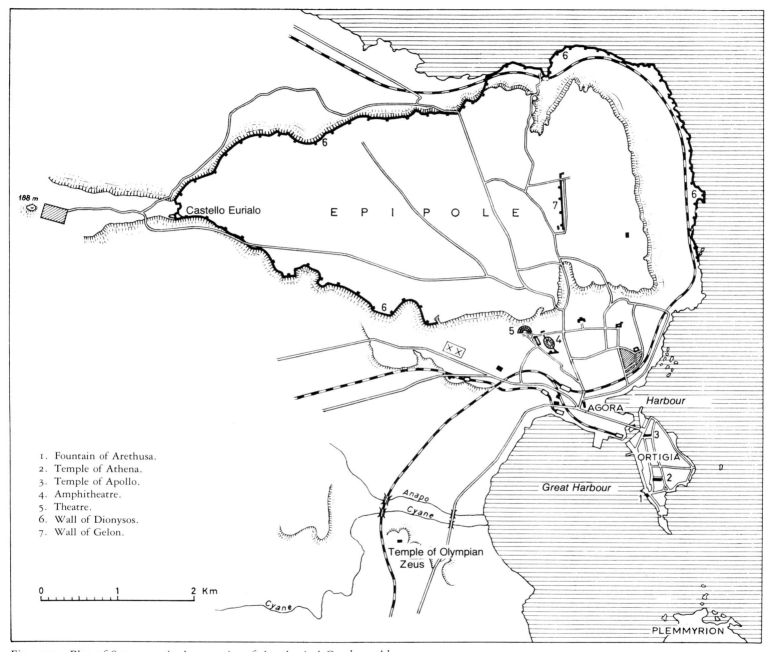

188 m

Castello Eurialo

E P I P O L E

1. Fountain of Arethusa.
2. Temple of Athena.
3. Temple of Apollo.
4. Amphitheatre.
5. Theatre.
6. Wall of Dionysos.
7. Wall of Gelon.

Harbour

AGORA

ORTIGIA

Great Harbour

Anapo

Cyane

Temple of Olympian
Zeus

0   1   2 Km

Cyane

PLEMMYRION

Fig. 207   Plan of Syracuse, the largest city of the classical Greek world.

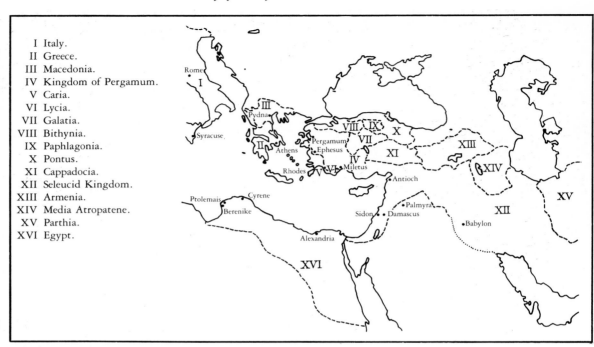

I Italy.
II Greece.
III Macedonia.
IV Kingdom of Pergamum.
V Caria.
VI Lycia.
VII Galatia.
VIII Bithynia.
IX Paphlagonia.
X Pontus.
XI Cappadocia.
XII Seleucid Kingdom.
XIII Armenia.
XIV Media Atropatene.
XV Parthia.
XVI Egypt.

Fig. 208   The Hellenistic world at the close of the third century BC.

It should be borne in mind that, as the Greek city was a physical expression of the society which it contained, the independence of the city-state and its controlled development were vital pre-conditions for the maintenance of its ethical values. When Greece was united under Philip of Macedon, the autonomous equilibrium of the various city communities and also that of their surroundings ended. The different skills that had been perfected by the Greeks — science, philosophy, economics, architecture, town planning — were now ready to be spread throughout the civilised world and to confront the differing traditions of the West and East.

Alexander and his successors were not only in a position to set up colonies as large as the cities which had founded them, but also to establish great metropoles comparable in every respect to the ancient Near Eastern capitals. The geometrical schema suggested by Hippodamus succeeded in achieving a rational distribution of all the disparate elements contained in a single city, and the resulting ensemble was at the same time both orderly and bustling, with an atmosphere similar in many respects to that of a modern city.

Fig. 209   A Hellenistic sculpture: the head of Laocöon in the Vatican Museum.

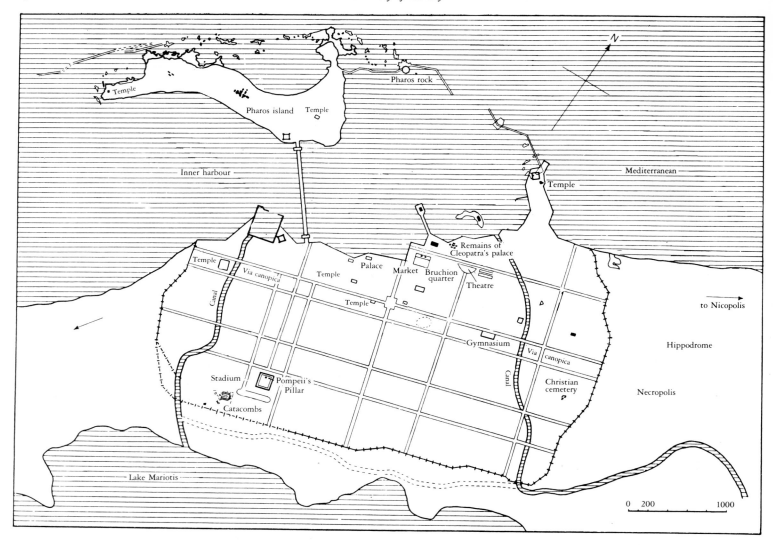

Figs 210–11   Plan of ancient
Alexandria and of the modern city.

1. Catacombs.
2. Palace of Ras-el-Tin.
3, 4, 6. Mosques.
5. Fortress.
7. Graeco-Roman Museum.
8. Fine Arts Museum.

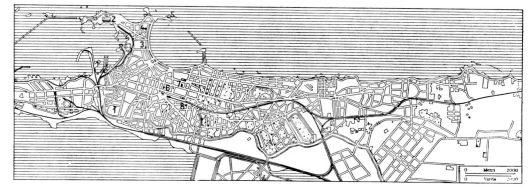

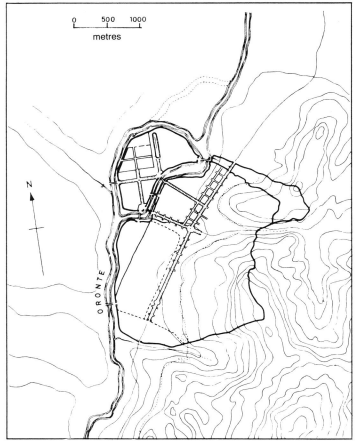

Fig. 212   Plan of Antioch, on the same scale as that of Alexandria.

Figs 213–14   Pergamum, plan and cross section of city.

6. Stadium.
7. Gurnellia.
8. Acropolis.
9. Altar.
10. Terrace of Demeter.
11. Gymnasium.
12. Lower agora.
13. Gateway of Eumenes.
14. Kizil Avlu (the Red Hall).

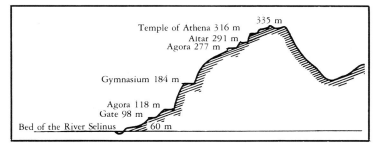

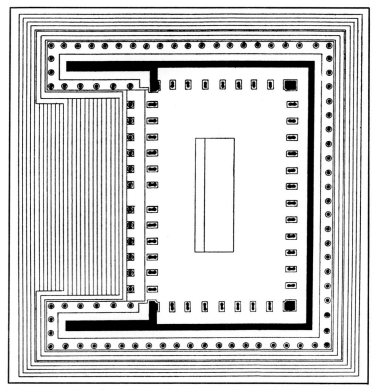

Fig. 215   Plan of the Altar of Zeus in the upper city (see Fig. 217, no. 20).

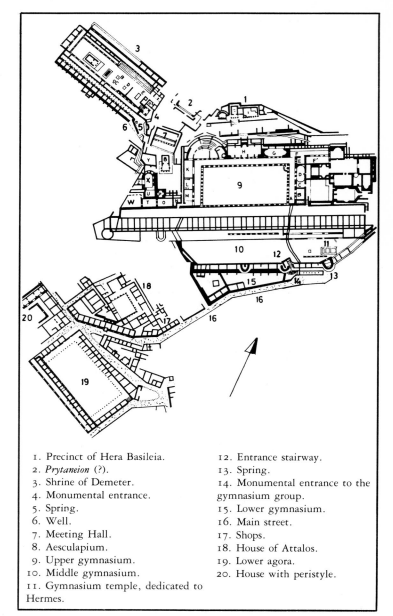

1. Precinct of Hera Basileia.
2. *Prytaneion* (?).
3. Shrine of Demeter.
4. Monumental entrance.
5. Spring.
6. Well.
7. Meeting Hall.
8. Aesculapium.
9. Upper gymnasium.
10. Middle gymnasium.
11. Gymnasium temple, dedicated to Hermes.
12. Entrance stairway.
13. Spring.
14. Monumental entrance to the gymnasium group.
15. Lower gymnasium.
16. Main street.
17. Shops.
18. House of Attalos.
19. Lower agora.
20. House with peristyle.

Fig. 216   Plan of the city of Pergamum.

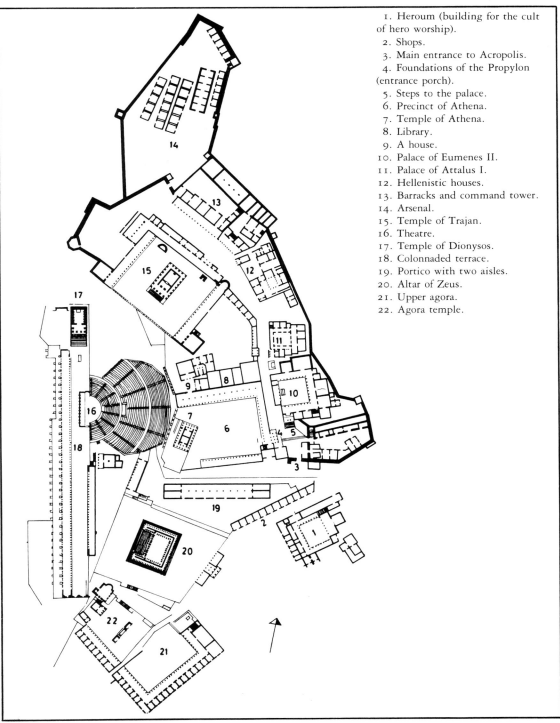

1. Heroum (building for the cult of hero worship).
2. Shops.
3. Main entrance to Acropolis.
4. Foundations of the Propylon (entrance porch).
5. Steps to the palace.
6. Precinct of Athena.
7. Temple of Athena.
8. Library.
9. A house.
10. Palace of Eumenes II.
11. Palace of Attalus I.
12. Hellenistic houses.
13. Barracks and command tower.
14. Arsenal.
15. Temple of Trajan.
16. Theatre.
17. Temple of Dionysos.
18. Colonnaded terrace.
19. Portico with two aisles.
20. Altar of Zeus.
21. Upper agora.
22. Agora temple.

Fig. 217   Plan of the upper city (acropolis) of Pergamum.

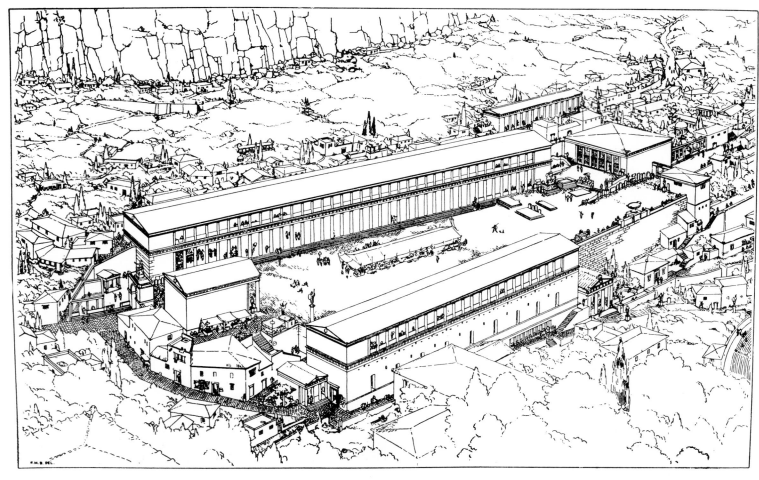

Fig. 218 Reconstruction and plan of
the Hellenistic agora at Assos.

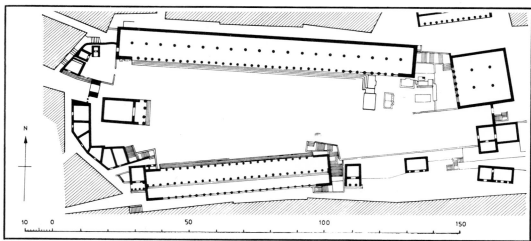

3
Rome: city and worldwide empire

There are several factors that should be borne in mind when dealing with the Roman State and its success in achieving the political unification of the whole Mediterranean world.

1. The original background to the growth of Roman power; that is to say, the Etruscan civilisation, which between the seventh and sixth centuries BC spread through Italy from the Po Valley to Campania.

2. The extraordinary development of Rome itself, which began as a small and insignificant town sandwiched between the Etruscan dominions and territory colonised by the Greeks, and finally ended up as a city *par excellence* and capital of a vast empire.

3. The colonising methods used by the Romans throughout their empire, three main aspects of which — those concerned with actual physical changes to the environment — we shall deal with here. They were as follows:

    (a) The creation of infrastructures, such as bridges, roads, lines of fortification and aqueducts.

    (b) The division of agricultural land into farmed units.

    (c) The foundation of new cities.

4. The decentralisation of political office during the latter days of the Empire, a process that resulted in the setting up of regional capitals like Constantinople, which remained capital of the Eastern Empire for a thousand years after the eclipse of Rome itself.

Constantinople later became Istanbul, capital of the Ottoman Empire, and it continues to be one of the principal cities of the Western world.

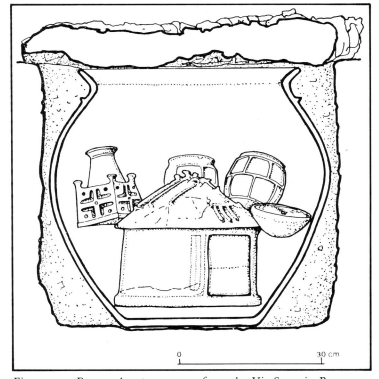

Fig. 219.   Bronze Age *pozzo* grave from the Via Sacra in Rome.

Fig. 220 Italy prior to the
Roman conquest.

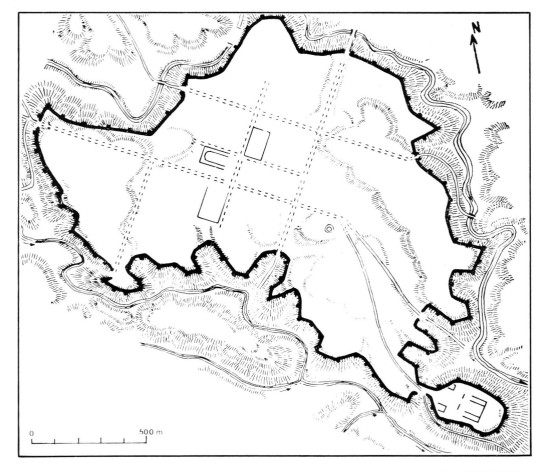

Fig. 221 Plan of the city of Veii, showing the Etruscan wall; the regular internal layout dates from Roman times.

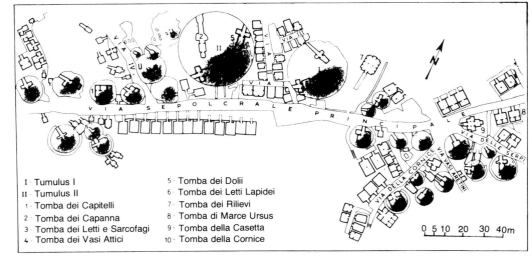

I · Tumulus I
II · Tumulus II
1 · Tomba dei Capitelli
2 · Tomba dei Capanna
3 · Tomba dei Letti e Sarcofagi
4 · Tomba dei Vasi Attici

5 · Tomba dei Dolii
6 · Tomba dei Letti Lapidei
7 · Tomba dei Rilievi
8 · Tomba di Marce Ursus
9 · Tomba della Casetta
10 · Tomba della Cornice

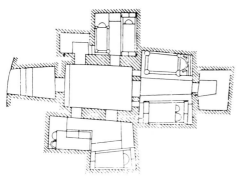

Figs 222–3 Plans of the necropolis at Cerveteri and of the Tomba della Casetta (9).

Fig. 224   An Etruscan carving from a tomb in the necropolis at Volsinii.

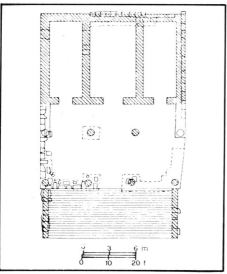

Fig. 225   An Etruscan funerary urn in the shape of a house from the archaeological museum in Florence.

Figs 226–7   Plan of the Etruscan temple at Orvieto, and a model of the first Temple of Jupiter on the Capitoline Hill in Rome.

The Etruscan civilisation first emerged in Italy during the Iron Age (from the ninth century BC onwards), on the Tyrrhenian coast between the Arno and the Tiber. Then, during the seventh and sixth centuries BC, it spread northwards to the Po valley and southwards to Campania, finally coming into contact with the Greek colonies in southern Italy. As a result of its overseas trading activities, it also came into contact with other Mediterranean civilisations, whose influences it absorbed.

In Etruria, as in Greece, there were a number of city-states, normally governed by an aristocratic regime, which were united in a religious league centred on Bolsena. The main cities — Volterra, Arezzo, Cortuna, Chiusi, Perugia, Vetulonia, Tarquinia, Vulci, Cerveteri, Veii — were sited on easily defensible areas of high ground, but were radically changed by the Romans. The only purely Etruscan elements that have survived are the irregularly contoured walls (Fig. 221) and a few isolated monuments, but thanks to an account written by Vitruvius at the time of Augustus, we do know what Etruscan temples looked like. They were fairly simple constructions of stone and wood, overlaid with rich terracotta decoration, and it is probable that the earliest temples built on the Capitoline Hill in Rome would have been similarly designed (Figs 226–7).

Ancient writers have credited the Etruscans with having invented the procedures for founding a city which the Romans subsequently adopted. These involved, first, the *inauguratio* (consulting the gods before beginning work), secondly, the *limitatio* (tracing the external perimeter and the internal limits of the city) and, thirdly, the *consacratio* (celebrating the newly founded city with sacrifices). The Etruscan cities, however, did not follow the same geometrical plan as Roman ones.

Excavations round the Etruscans' cities have revealed a large number of underground tombs, some of which still possess their full complement of funerary furniture (paintings, sculptures and everyday utensils) that provide us with a startlingly fresh insight into the everyday lives of these people (Figs 222–5).

On the fringe of Etruria the city of Rome slowly developed: a small settlement that gradually grew into the most powerful force in the Mediterranean world. Rome was not the chosen capital: that role was forced on it by the fact that its Empire was the product of a city-state which had spread and spread. For this same reason the city grew as its territory increased, but it still retained many characteristics that betrayed its village origins. It was, in fact, a village that grew, little by little, into a world centre. When the political unity of the Empire became a *fait accompli*, the Emperor Caracalla, in 212 AD, granted Roman citizenship to the whole imperial population. The city (*urbs*) was now a vast territorial unit. It drew people and products from its own world, a world that was united, governed, surrounded by walls and crossed by roads just like an ordinary city.

Ovid, in *Fasti* II, 683–4, expresses the thought that 'To other peoples a special part of the earth has been assigned, but for the Romans the limit of their city is the limit of the world.'

The glory of Rome, the world city — established in the Augustan Age and celebrated in verse by Horace, Virgil and Ovid — has lived on in the annals of history, and, as the seat of the Papacy, it has become the spiritual home for millions. Rome remained the centre of the world ('All roads lead to Rome') even during the Middle Ages, when it was little more than an impoverished village, and in modern times it still exerts a powerful pull despite its secondary status. Although it was only during the imperial era that the cultural myth coincided with reality, the remains of the ancient capital continue to dominate the landscape and mood of the city.

In our examination of the way in which the city evolved, from its earliest origins to the days of the late Empire, we will pause to describe its layout during its period of maximum expansion in the second and third centuries AD. We will then make a brief comparison between ancient and modern Rome, returning to the other phases of its historical development in later chapters.

As is always the case, the city's origins were influenced by the nature of its physical environment, but the site chosen, on the lower reaches of the Tiber, does not appear to differ very greatly from other possible sites in the vicinity, and the city's primary characteristics seem relatively unimportant when compared to the significance of later development.

The Tiber after a very sharp bend, divides into two, leaving an island (the modern Isola Tiberina) in the middle,

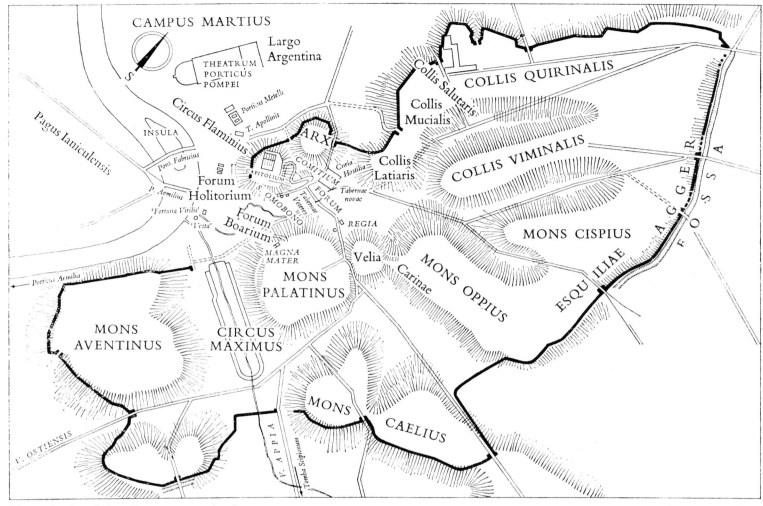

Fig. 228   Republican Rome, on a scale of 1:20,000.

and here it becomes much easier to cross, either by fording or by means of a ferry. On the left bank there is a series of hills whose steep slopes reach down almost to the riverside. The Etruscans, who occupied the right bank, had a vested interest in keeping this crossing clear so as to maintain access to their possessions in Campania. Because of this traffic, a fair and a market grew up there (later to be incorporated in the city as the Forum Boarium and the Forum Holitorium), while the adjacent hills became the site of the first fortified villages, intended to protect the river crossing.

It has been suggested that the earliest inhabited area was at the top of the Palatine Hill, the only one to have steep and easily defensible sides (unlike the Quirinal, the Caelian and so on) and also the only one to have enough space at its summit for a village. Later on a city was founded that included all seven of the traditional hills and was divided into four parts:

Suburbana, centred on the Caelian Hill;

Esquilina, surrounding the Esquiline Hill, Mons Oppius and Mons Cispius;

Collina, around the Viminal and Quirinal Hills;

Palatina, named after the Palatine Hill, which it included.

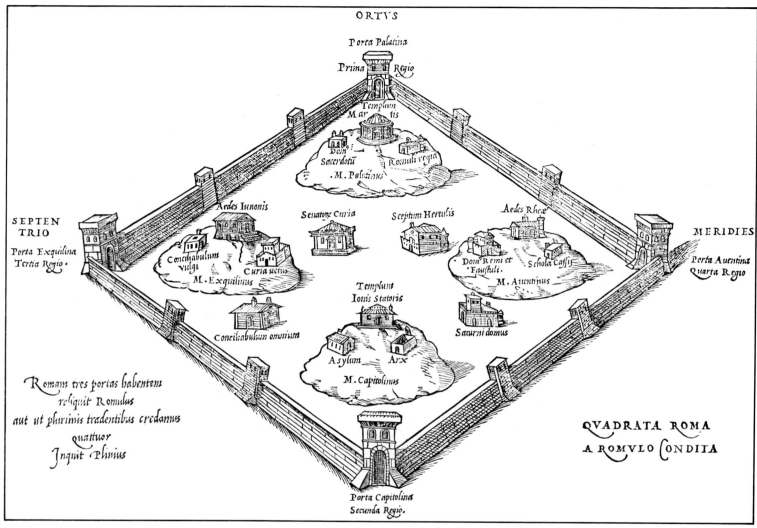

Fig. 229   Rome, a city built in a perfect square; an engraving from 1527.

The central valley between the four districts was drained by digging the Cloaca Maxima, and on this land was built a new commercial area known as the Forum Romanum. The Capitoline Hill, which fulfilled the function of an *acropolis*, and the Aventine Hill, which at a later date (456 BC) was granted to the *plebs* during their struggle with the patricians, both remained outside the city proper. From the writings of Varro we know the approximate limits of this 'Rome of the four regions', which was probably surrounded by a wall. Its internal area, some 285 hectares, made it the largest city in mainland Italy at the time.

During the Gallic invasion of 378 BC the whole city was occupied and burnt, with the exception of the Capitol. Immediately afterwards it was rebuilt (without correcting its asymmetrical outline) and protected by the addition of a wall of stone blocks, named after Servius Tullius who, according to legend, had founded the city. This wall encompassed the Aventine Hill, the Capitoline Hill and part of the high ground to the north of the Quirinal, a total of 426 hectares in all, a greater area than that occupied by

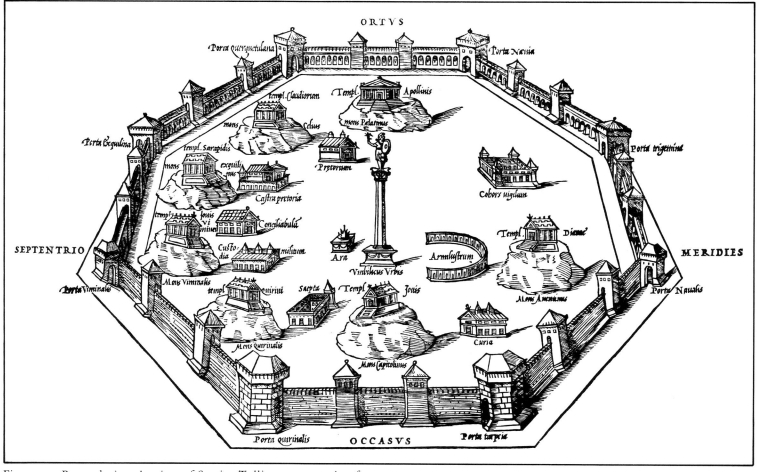

Fig. 230   Rome during the time of Servius Tullius; an engraving from 1527.

Athens during the same period. Thus, from the fourth century onwards, Rome had acquired all the trappings of a major city. In 329 work began on transforming the valley between the Palatine and Aventine Hills into the Circus Maximus, while in 312 the first aqueduct (Aqua Claudia) was constructed to provide water for the upper levels of the city. Also, buildings began to rise on the large tract of flat land that lies between the hills and the bend in the river, where the area reserved for use by the army was situated (the Campus Martius): the Circus Flaminius (221 BC), the Porticus Metellianus (149 BC), and the Theatrum Pompei (c. 50 BC). The Forum was established and was surrounded with basilicas so that the citizens could conduct their business

under cover. The earliest was the Basilica Porcia (184 BC), but all of the basilicas from this period have since been destroyed, with the exception of the Basilica Aemilia, which was built in 179 BC. Elsewhere, on the Capitoline Hill for example, large numbers of temples were built, while the banks of the river beneath the Aventine Hill were transformed into an Emporium (Fig. 228).

Passing from the republican to the imperial era, the buildings in Rome became more and more grandiose, until they finally came into conflict with the city's existing layout. In order to make more space, work began on the demolition of the older buildings.

Julius Caesar enlarged the Forum by the addition of the

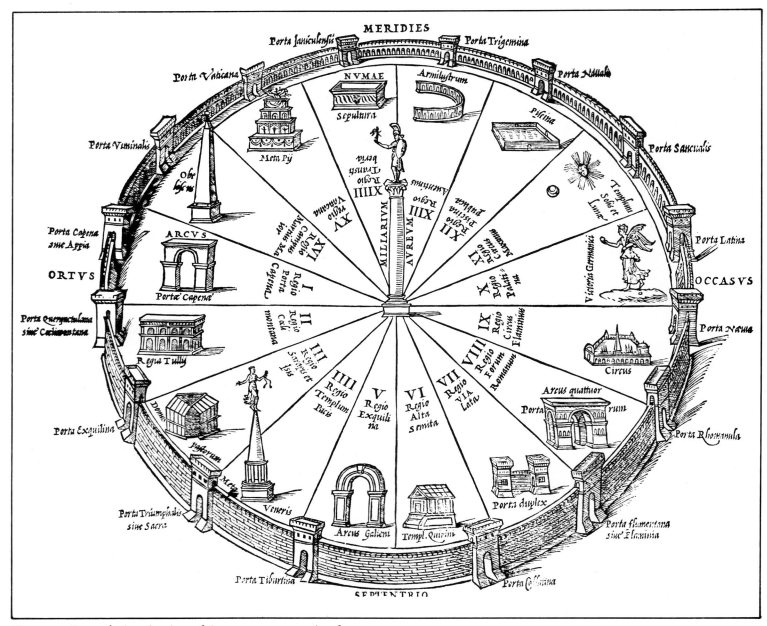

Fig. 231   Rome during the time of Augustus; an engraving from 1527.

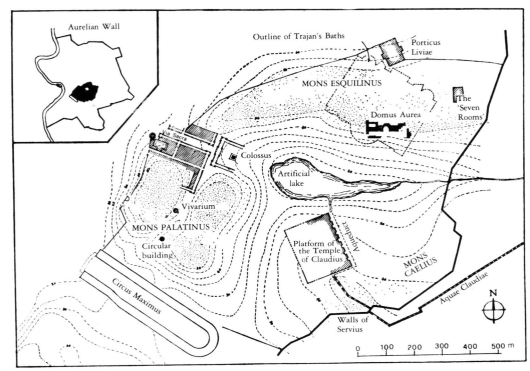

Fig. 232 Plan of Nero's Domus Aurea and its park.

Basilica Julia and by the construction of the new Forum Caesaris to the north of the existing one. He made space for this new forum by buying an area of land at the foot of the Capitoline Hill for 100 million *sestertii* and demolishing the buildings that stood on it. There was also a scheme, which was never carried out, to divert the waters of the Tiber to flow round the foot of the hills on the right-hand bank, thereby linking the Campus Martius to the Campus Vaticanus and enabling the city to spread freely over the western plain.

Augustus covered the Campus Martius with a whole series of buildings — the Theatre of Marcellus, Agrippa's Baths, the Ara Pacis, his own mausoleum and the Pantheon — and built the Forum Augusti next to the Forum Caesaris. He also began work on the Imperial Palace on the Palatine Hill, as well as erecting a number of temples, reorganising the aqueduct system, reinforcing the river banks and dividing the city up into fourteen new regions. In addition to all the building in the public sector, there was also an increase in private construction, which, due to the shortage of land, took the form of the erection of multi-storeyed

insulae, in which the poorest sections of the population were housed. By about 5 BC the inhabitants of Rome totalled 500,000.

Augustus's successors extended the palace on the Palatine Hill, established a permanent camp for the Praetorian Guard (the Castra Praetoria) and continued his reorganisation programme in a somewhat haphazard way. Following the fire in 64 AD, Nero gained an opportunity to make radical changes to the city: he built himself an extraordinary residence, the Domus Aurea, which occupied a vast area of land between the Palatine, Caelian and Esquiline Hills, and was situated in a park filled with buildings (Fig. 232). He also supervised the reconstruction of the devastated areas on carefully calculated lines, even though he had to work within the framework of the existing urban pattern.

Tacitus, who describes this reconstruction (XV, 43), gives us an idea of conditions in the city during this period:

In Rome . . . construction was not . . . without plan or demarcation. Street-fronts were of regulated dimensions and alignment, streets were

Fig. 233　Portrait bust of Scipio Africanus.

broad, and houses spacious. Their height was restricted, and their frontages protected by colonnades. Nero undertook to erect these at his own expense, and also to clear debris from building sites before transferring them to their owners. He announced bonuses, in proportion to rank and resources, for the completion of houses and blocks before a given date. Rubbish was to be dumped in the Ostian marshes by cornships returning down the Tiber. A fixed proportion of every building had to be massive, untimbered stone from Gabii or Alba (these stones being fireproof). Furthermore, guards were to ensure a more abundant and extensive public water-supply, hitherto diminished by irregular private enterprise. . . . semi-detached houses were forbidden — they must have their own own walls. These measures were welcomed for their practicality, and they beautified the new city. Some, however, believed that the old town's configuration had been healthier, since its narrow streets and high houses had provided protection against the burning sun, whereas now the shadowless open spaces radiated a fiercer heat.

The Flavian emperors continued with the renovations started by Nero. Vespasian had the Domus Aurea destroyed and, in the section of the park where the artificial lake had been, began to build the city's great amphitheatre, the Colosseum (Figs 255–8). At the same time he constructed the new Forum Vespasiani between the Colosseum and the old Forums. Domitian further extended the palace on the Palatine Hill so that it covered almost the whole of the hill, and embarked on a series of improvements to the Campus Martius, which had been damaged by a fire in 80 AD. He also erected a group of monumental buildings around a new stadium (later to become the Piazza Navona).

Trajan ordered the demolition of the *sella* that lay between the Quirinal and Capitoline Hills, separating the monumental areas of the Forums and the Campus Martius, and built a new city centre on the site, which comprised the great Forum Traiani and the market on the slopes of the Quirinal Hill. On the Mons Oppius he erected the great Thermae Traianae, and had the House of the Vestal Virgins rebuilt near the Forum. His successor, the Emperor Hadrian, not only rebuilt Augustus' Pantheon (Figs 262–3), but also completed the Templum Veneris et Romae opposite the Colosseum, and built a mausoleum for himself on the far bank of the Tiber and joined it to the main part of the city by the Pons Aelius.

At this moment, when the Empire was at its most prosperous, Rome reached its point of maximum develop-

ment, while still retaining a carefully planned and coherent physical appearance (Fig. 236). The vast public buildings, erected with the help of the best architects and artists of the Empire, maintained the same respect for the balance between architectural form and decorative refinement that the Greeks had practised. In some commemorative monuments, such as Augustus' Ara Pacis, the triumphal arches, the celebratory columns of Trajan and Antoninus Pius (Figs 247–53, 260), the main focus was on the decorative friezes, which presented accounts of specific historical events, with each individual series being complete in itself. The city, however, which provided the setting for these self-contained and unrelated structures, lacked both their sense of balance and their feeling of completeness: it sprawled over a large area of land, concealing the natural features of the environment and pushing the countryside far into the distance.

Successive emperors further embellished the urban area with a variety of additions. The Severi put the finishing touches to the palace on the Palatine Hill, completing the sides facing the Circus Maximus and the Caelian Hill, and constructed Caracalla's Baths (285–305 AD), and the baths and basilica of Constantine.

In these last works, the classical balance between architectural form and decorative detail was broken. Although the great vaulted roofs of some of the buildings were the product of increasingly advanced technical skills, less and less attention was paid to the old architectural disciplines and decorative sculpture became altogether coarser and cruder; occasionally it was just a piece taken from some other more ancient monument, as in Constantine's Arch (Fig. 266). Carving and painted adornment developed into separate elements, unrelated to the overall architectural effect, and the coherence and formal unity of the Greeks disappeared completely.

After Constantine, who moved the imperial capital to Byzantium, no other great public works were undertaken in Rome, but the last emperors did publish a series of edicts designed to ensure the conservation of the monuments that already existed in the city. Honorius doubled the height of the Aurelian Walls, which remained capable of defending Rome during times of siege right up to modern times. Meanwhile Christian churches were springing up on the

Figs 234–5   The monumental centre of Rome, as it is now and as seen in a model reconstruction made in 1939. In the foreground: the Circus Maximus, the Palatine Hill (to which Claudius' aqueduct led) and the Colosseum. In the background: the Forums, the Capitol and the Campus Martius.

fringes of the city, Christianity having been recognised officially in 313 AD.

Up until the second century AD Rome was an open city, continually growing and spreading over a larger and larger area, never needing a defensive wall. The fourteen Augustan regions continued to form the basis of its administrative organisation, but their external boundaries were constantly changing. For taxation purposes the boundary was reckoned to extend to a distance of 1,000 feet beyond the last buildings, a line that encompassed, at the time of the city's greatest development, an area of some 2,000 hectares. The Aurelian Walls protected only the very heart of Rome (1,386 hectares), just as the ones built around cities in Gaul against the Germans provided protection for a limited central area. The surrounding countryside was occupied by large numbers of suburban villas (Figs 267–70), of which the Emperor Hadrian's villa near Tivoli is an example, while the roads were flanked by tombs, temples and military and sporting establishments, whose remains can still be seen along the Via Appia outside Rome.

ROME.
Plan of the ancient city:
GATES
1. Porta Sanqualis.
2. Porta Quirinalis.
3. Porta Collina.
4. Porta Viminalis.
5. Porta Esquilina.
6. Porta Caelimontana.
7. Porta Querquetulana.
8. Porta Capena.
9. Porta Naevia.
10. Porta Raudusculana.
11. Porta Lavernalis.
12. Porta Trigemina.

MONUMENTS WITHIN THE
INNER WALLS:
13. Templum Iovis.
14. Arx.
15. Fortunae et Matris Matutae.
16. Ara Maxima.
17. Circus Maximus.
18. Templum Cereris.
19. Templum Lunae.
20. Templum Minervae.
21. Templum Iunonis Reginae.
22. Thermae Decianae.
23. Templum Dianae.
24. Domus et thermae Surae.
25. Templum Bonae Deae.
26. Septizonium Severi.
27. Templum Divi Claudii.
28. Arcus Constantini.
29. Amphitheatrum.
30. Ludus Magnus.
31. Thermae Titianae.
32. Thermae Traianae.
33. Horti Maecenatis and Auditorium.
34. Arcus Gallieno.
35. Templum Iunonis Lucinae.
36. Thermae Diocletiani.
37. Templum Fortunae.
38. Thermae Constantinianae.

GATES IN THE OUTER WALLS:
39. Porta Flaminia.
40. Porta Pinciana.
41. Porta Nomentuana.
42. Porta Tiburtina.

43. Porta Asinaria.
44. Porta Metronia.
45. Porta Latina.
46. Porta Appia.
47. Porta Ardeatina.
48. Porta Ostiensis.
49. Porta Portuensis.
50. Porta Aurelia.
51. Porta Septimiana.

MONUMENTS CONTAINED
BETWEEN THE TWO WALLS:
52. Porticus Aemilia.
53. Horrea Galbiana.
54. Horrea Lolliana.
55. Sepulcrum Scipionum.
56. Thermae Antoninianae.
57. Domus Lateranorum.

58. Ludus.
59. Thermae Helenae.
60. Horti Lamiani.
61. Nymphaeum.
62. Campus Cohortium Praetoriarum.
63. Castra Praetoria.
64. Templum Veneris Erucinae.
65. Mausoleum Augusti.
66. Ara Pacis.
67. Solarium.
68. Templum Solis Aureliani (?).
69. Templum Divi Hadriani.
70. Iseum.
71. Saepta.
72. Thermae Agrippae.
73. Pantheon.
74. Thermae Neronianae.
75. Stadium.
76. Theatrum Pompei.

77. Porticus Pompeiana.
78. Circus Flaminius.
79. Theatrum Balbi.
80. Porticus Octaviae.
81. Theatrum Marcelli.
82. Mausoleum Hadriani.
83. Circus Gaii et Neronis.

BRIDGES:
84. Pons Aelius.
85. Pons Neronianus.
86. Pons Agrippae.
87. Pons Aurelius.
88. Pons Fabricius.
89. Pons Cestius.
90. Pons Aemilius.
91. Pons Sublicius.
92. Pons Probi (Theodosii).

Fig. 236   Map of imperial Rome.

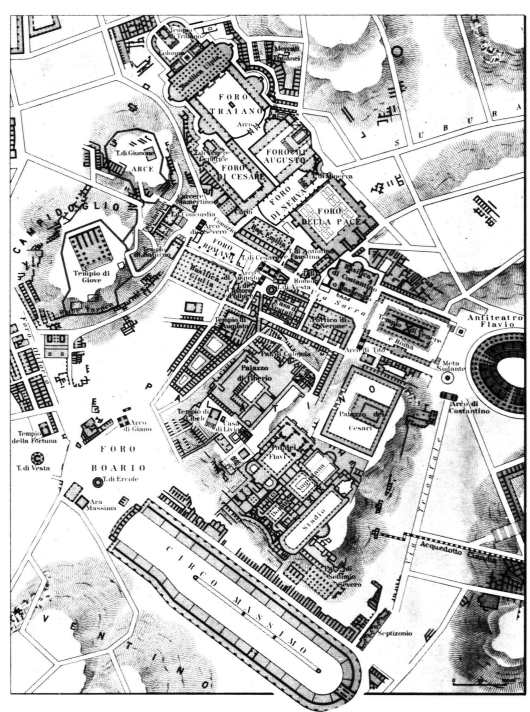

Fig. 237 The monumental centre of the city (cf. Figs 234, 235).

Figs 238–9   Two views of the ruins in the Forum at Rome, looking towards the south-east and the north-west.

Figs 240–1   The archaeological zone in the centre
of modern Rome; the broad roads cutting through
it were built during the Fascist era.

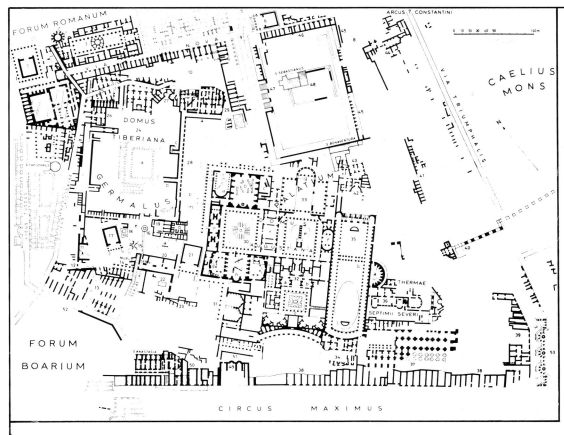

28. Cryptoporticus built by Nero.
    a. side wing.
    b. wing added by the Flavian emperors.
29. Buildings from Domitian's time.
30. Palace of the Flavian Emperors.
    a. basilica.
    b. court of honour.
    c. *Lararium*.
    d. peristyle.
    e. springs and baths.
    f. *tablinum*.
    g–h. fountains.
    i. rear portico.
31. Libraries.
32. Domus Augustana. Lower floor:
    a–b. *tablinum*.
    c. *Lararium*.
    d. peristyle.
33. Domus Augustana. Upper floor:
    e. peristyle and *aediculae*.
    f. Nymphaeum.
    g. *exedra*.
34. Imperial box on the Circus Maximus.
35. Stadium or Hippodrome:
    a. *exedra*.
    b. entrance wide enough for carriages.
36. Thermae Septimii Severi.
37. Substructures of Septimius Severus.
38. *Tabernae* opposite the Circus Maximus.
39. *Insulae* and substructures.
40. Arches of the aqua Claudia.
41. Houses from imperial times.
42. Nymphaeum of the Canopic type.
43. Underground water cisterns.
44. Houses from imperial times.
45–6. Massive substructural walls.
47. Pentapylum Elagabali.
48. Aedes Caesarum.
49. School of public heralds.
50. Workshops buried underneath S. Anastasia.
51. Paedagogium.
52. Lupercal.
53. Septizonium Severi.

ROME.

Plan of the imperial buildings on the Palatine Hill:

1. Aedes Castoris.
2. Aedes Vestae.
3. Atrium Vestae.
4. Vestibulum Domus Aureae.
5. Arcus Titi.
6. Aedes Iovis Statoris.
7. Arcus Constantini.
8. Capita Bubula.
9. Porta Mugonia.
10. Aedes Victoriae.

11. Murus 'Romuli'.
12. *Insulae* from the imperial era.
13. Ara dei ignoti.
14. Tomb and *sacelli* from archaic period.
15. Cistern and wall from archaic period.
16. Cistern with *tholus*.
17. Templum Matris Magnae.
18. Auguratorium.
19. Domus Augustana (Domus Liviae).
    a. peristyle,
    b. cistern and portico.
20. 'Locus editus atque singularis'.
21. Aedes Apollonis.

22. Foundations of unknown building.
23. Houses from the Republican era.
24. Domus Tiberiana.
    a. buried central atrium.
    b–c. stairways leading to false portico.
    d. vivarium.
    e. guardrooms.
    f. stairs leading directly to the *clivus Victoriae*.
25. Substructures along the *clivus Victoriae*.
26. Remains of Caligula's palace.
27. Remains of the Domus Commodiana.

Fig. 242   Plan of the buildings excavated on the Palatine Hill.

Fig. 243   The Campus Martius area, in a relief model made in 1939; in the centre is the Pantheon, on the left, a part of Domitian's stadium (which corresponds to the modern Piazza Navona), while the monumental centre can be seen in the background.

Fig. 244 The Forum zone; in the foreground is the Capitol, on the right, the Palatine Hill, and in the background, the Colosseum and Trajan's Baths.

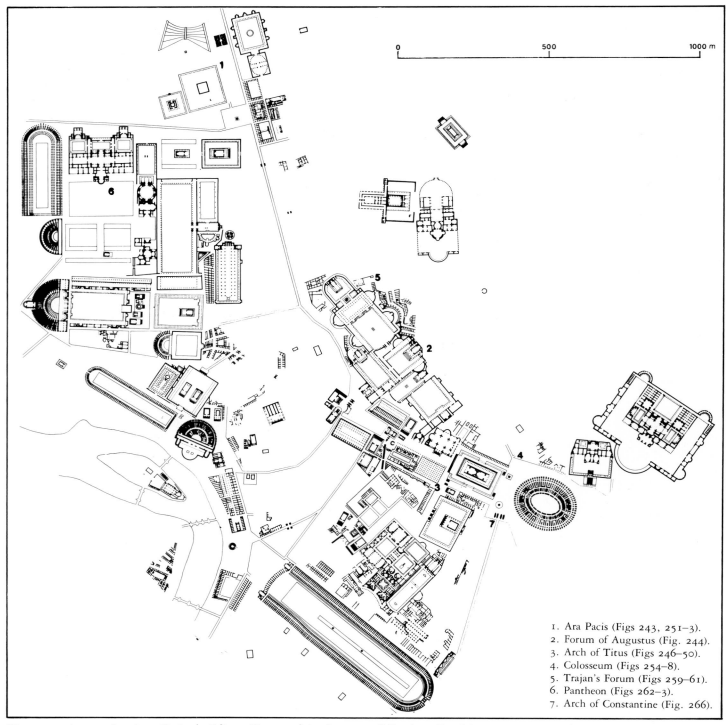

0   500   1000 m

1. Ara Pacis (Figs 243, 251–3).
2. Forum of Augustus (Fig. 244).
3. Arch of Titus (Figs 246–50).
4. Colosseum (Figs 254–8).
5. Trajan's Forum (Figs 259–61).
6. Pantheon (Figs 262–3).
7. Arch of Constantine (Fig. 266).

Fig. 245   A map showing all the buildings illustrated in the pages following, listed in chronological order.

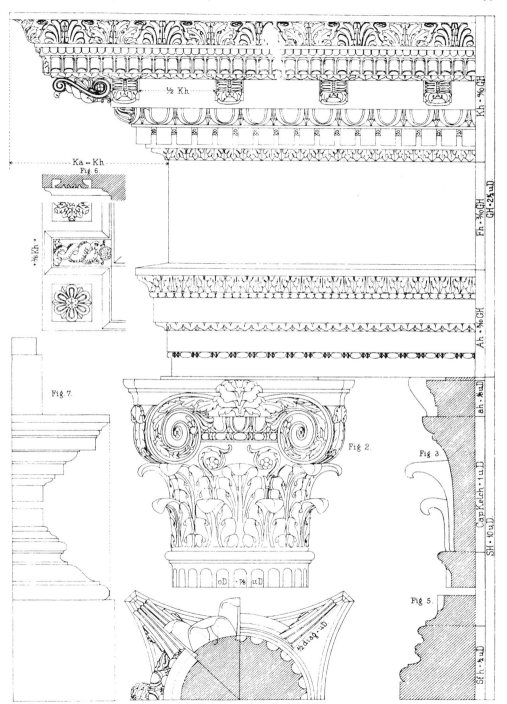

Figs 246–8   The Arch of Titus.
View, diagram, and a drawing of its
architectural order on a scale of 1:25.

Figs 249–50 The two reliefs on the inside of the Arch of Titus, which show the emperor's triumph following the conquest of Jerusalem in 70 AD; on the left, the trophies taken from the temple, and on the right, the emperor's chariot.

Figs 251-3 Two marble reliefs from the Ara Pacis of Augustus, showing a procession of officials, and a coin from the reign of Nero, which depicts the monument.

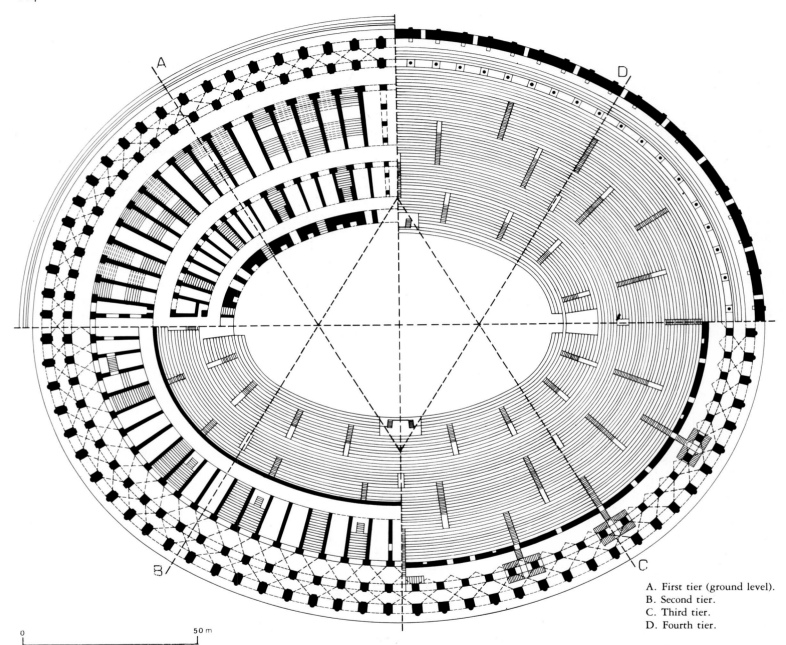

A. First tier (ground level).
B. Second tier.
C. Third tier.
D. Fourth tier.

0   50 m

Fig. 254   Plan of the Colosseum (72–80 AD).

Figs 255–7 The Colosseum. A coin of Gordianus II, showing games taking place in the arena. The exterior of the Colosseum, as it is now, and as it was, according to a model made in 1939.

Fig. 258   The ruins of the Colosseum, as seen from the campanile of S. Francesca Romana at the beginning of the century.

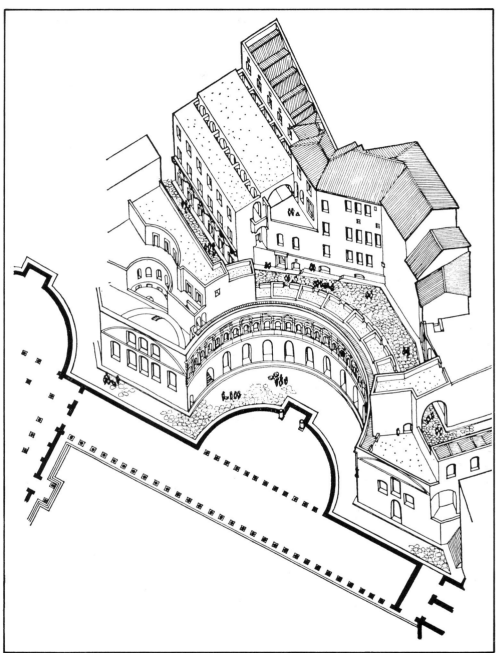

Figs 259–60 Trajan's Forum: the buildings on different levels at
the foot of the Esquiline Hill with the markets built by the
Emperor; Trajan's Column (*c.* 100–12 AD).

Fig. 264   A fragment of the *forma urbis*, a marble plan of Rome, carved between 203 and 211 AD during the time of the Severi.

Fig. 265   An inscription of Septimius Severus, now in the Lateran Museum.

Fig. 266   Constantine's Triumphal Arch (315 AD).

Figs 267–8 One of the great villas near Rome: the Villa dei Sette Bassi, next to the Via Latina (*c.* 140–60 AD), with its large terraced gardens.

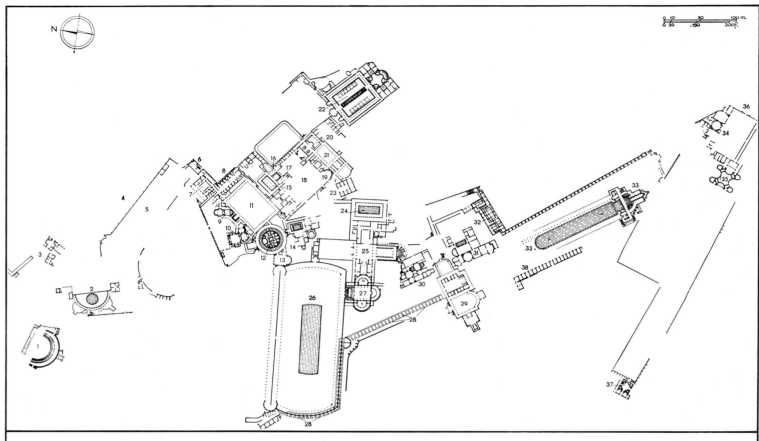

1. Greek theatre.	11. Courtyard of the Libraries.	21. Room with Doric pilasters.	31. Small Baths.
2. Nymphaeum, supposed *tempietto* of Venus.	12. Island Nymphaeum (*theatrum maritimum*).	22. Golden square.	32. *Praetorium*.
3. *Palaestra*.	13. Philosophers' Hall.	23. Guards' quarters.	33. Canopus.
4. Valley of Tempe.	14. Baths with *Heliocaminus*.	24. Four-sided portico with *piscina*.	34. Entrance-court of Academy.
5. Terrace of Tempe.	15. Cryptoporticus.	25. Nymphaeum, once thought to be a stadium.	35. Pavilion of the Academy.
6. Pavilion of Tempe.	16. Room with three aisles.	26. Poikile.	36. Odeon.
7. Imperial *triclinium*.	17. Private library.	27. Building with three *exedras*.	37. Tower of Roccabruna.
8. Guest rooms.	18. Palace peristyle.	28. The Hundred Small Rooms.	38. Museum.
9. Latin Library.	19. Summer *triclinium*.	29. *Vestibulum*.	
10. Greek Library.	20. Palace Nymphaeum.	30. Great Baths.	

Fig. 269   Hadrian's Villa near Tivoli, the greatest of the suburban villas (*c.* 125–35 AD).

Fig. 270   Aerial view of Hadrian's Villa near Tivoli.

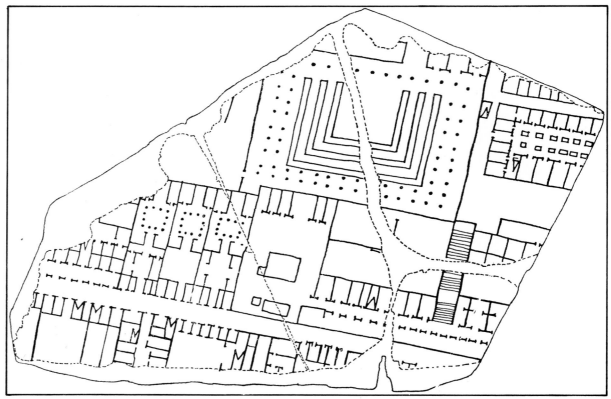

Fig. 271   A fragment of the *forma urbis*, in which three adjoining *domus* can be seen on the left.

Until the third century AD the city housed between 700,000 and 1,000,000 inhabitants, the greatest concentration of humanity ever known in the western world. We have to try and visualise the vast numbers of houses clustering round the public monuments, and seek to analyse the complex way in which this great urban conglomeration functioned.

The census returns for the end of the third century give us the following statistics: 1,790 *domus* and 44,300 *insulae*. The *domus* (Fig. 271) were the characteristic single family houses of Mediterranean cities, built on one or two storeys and facing inwards rather than outwards. They were composed of a number of rooms, each of which had its own specific use, grouped round an *atrium* and a *peristylium*, and they covered an area of 800 to 1,000 square metres, like the famous ones at Pompeii and Herculaneum (Figs 276–96). They were the exclusive domain of rich families who could afford to pay for the land on which they stood. The *insulae*

(Fig. 274) were residential blocks on several floors, designed for multiple occupation and covering an area of 300–400 square metres. They consisted of a number of equal-sized rooms facing outwards with windows and balconies, with the ground floors being occupied either by shops (*tabernae*) or more luxurious residences (also called *domus*), and the upper ones divided into apartments (*cenacula*) of varying sizes for the middle and lower classes. Excavations at Ostia give a good idea of what these *insulae* were like (Figs 307–10).

They first began to spring up towards the fourth century BC to provide shelter within the Servian Walls for a growing population, and gradually became higher and higher until Augustus imposed a height limit of 21 metres (six to seven storeys), which was later reduced by Trajan to 18 metres (five to six storeys). Because their walls were never more than 45 cm. thick, and because they were built around a wooden framework, they frequently collapsed. The *cenacula* had no running water, which only reached the ground floors, nor did they possess their own lavatories. The inhabitants emptied their pots into a communal receptacle — the *dolium* — which was kept on the landing, or, as many writers testify, they threw the contents straight out of their windows on to the street below. There was no form of heating and no chimney pipes (to cook or keep themselves warm the inhabitants used portable braziers, heightening the risk of fire), and the windows had no panes, merely curtains or wooden shutters that excluded both air and light. Despite all these drawbacks, rents in the capital were very high. During the time of Caesar, a *domus* cost 30,000 sestertii a year, and for the worst *cenaculum* one had to pay at least 2,000 sestertii, the same amount as it would have cost to buy a farm in the provinces. Residential accommodation was built by private entrepreneurs, who were guilty of widespread speculation in both land and housing, a practice which everyone bemoaned from the republican era on. Although the state imposed various rules and regulations, it never succeeded in easing the plight of the vast majority of its citizens. By contrast, the state did intervene adequately to ensure the setting up and smooth running of the city's public services.

Figs 272–5 Two items of furniture from a *cenaculum*: a lantern, a portable stove, and fragments of the *forma urbis* with plans of *insulae*.

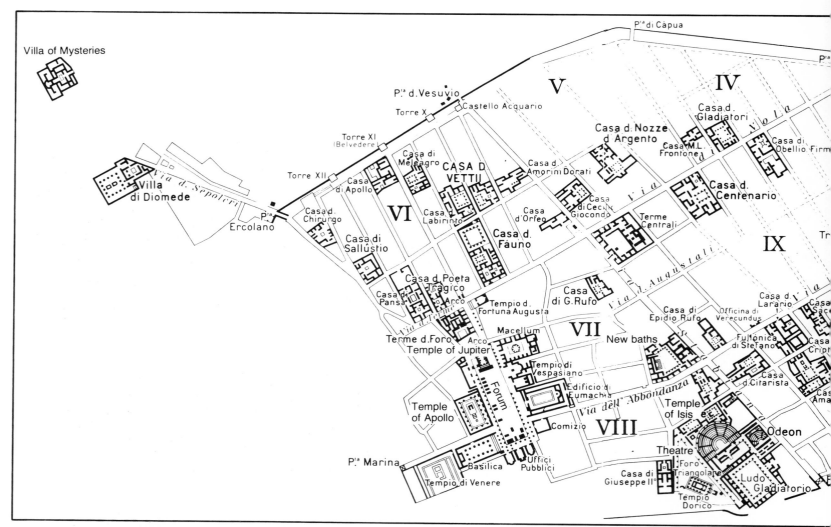

Figs 276–80   Plans of Pompeii, showing the principal buildings unearthed before 1958. The city, which consists of an ancient centre (the area of dark shading in the small map) and a fifth-century BC Hippodamian addition, was destroyed in 79 BC by Mount Vesuvius, which erupted and buried it under a layer of volcanic ash. Excavations, which began in 1748, have revealed buildings and utensils that give a precise idea of the inhabitants' lives at the moment of destruction.
Right: a view of the excavations from the Vesuvian Gate, and the imprint of two bodies found in the House of the False Portico.

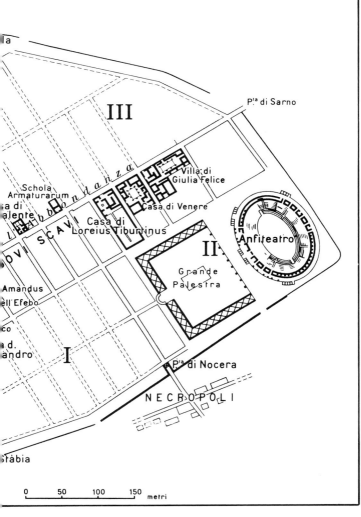

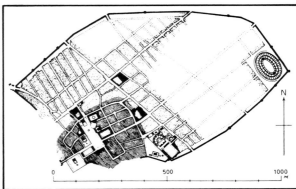

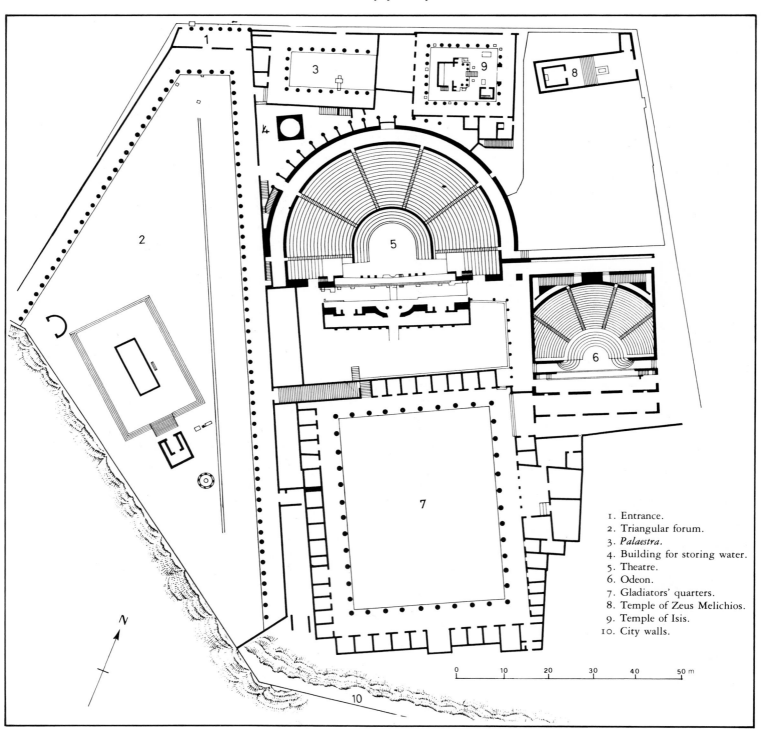

1. Entrance.
2. Triangular forum.
3. *Palaestra*.
4. Building for storing water.
5. Theatre.
6. Odeon.
7. Gladiators' quarters.
8. Temple of Zeus Melichios.
9. Temple of Isis.
10. City walls.

N

0   10   20   30   40   50 m

Figs 281–2   Pompeii: Plan of the triangular forum, with the theatre and odeon. Aerial view: in the foreground, the triangular forum and the modern service buildings of the archaeological zone.

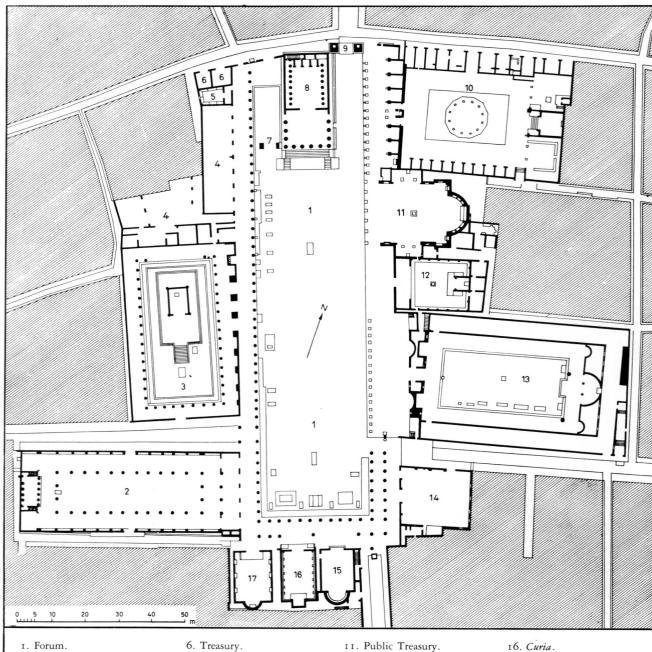

0 5 10 20 30 40 50
m

1. Forum.
2. Basilica.
3. Temple of Apollo.
4. Market.
5. *Forica* (public latrines).

6. Treasury.
7. Arch.
8. *Capitolium*.
9. Arch of Tiberius.
10. *Macellum*.

11. Public Treasury.
12. Temple of Vespasian.
13. Building of Eumachia.
14. *Comitium*.
15. Building of the *Duumviri*.

16. *Curia*.
17. Building of the *Aediles*.

Figs 283–4   Pompeii. Plan of the main forum, and a view looking towards Vesuvius.

Fig. 285   Pompeii. A part of the Street of Abundance.

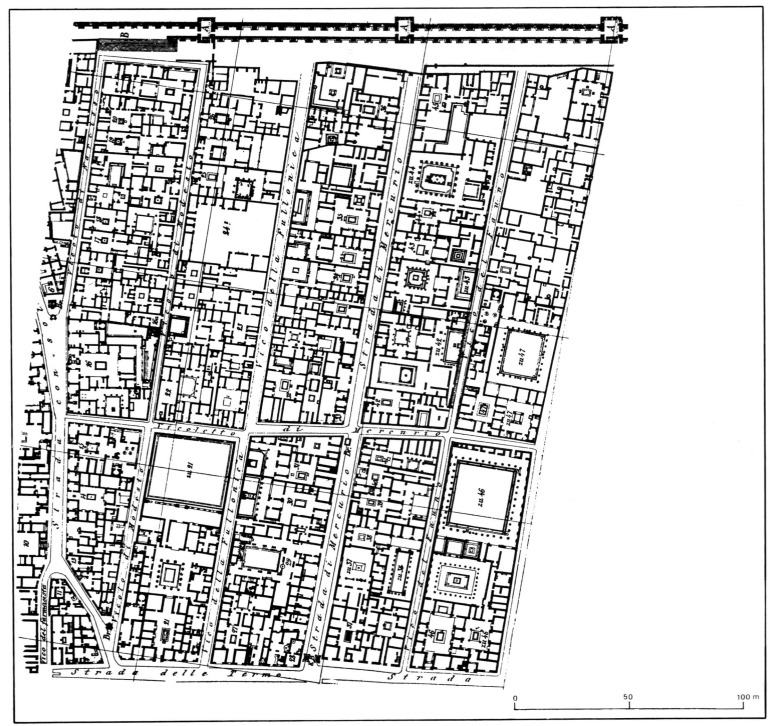

Fig. 286 An area of Pompeii, directly to the north of the main forum (cf. Fig. 277).

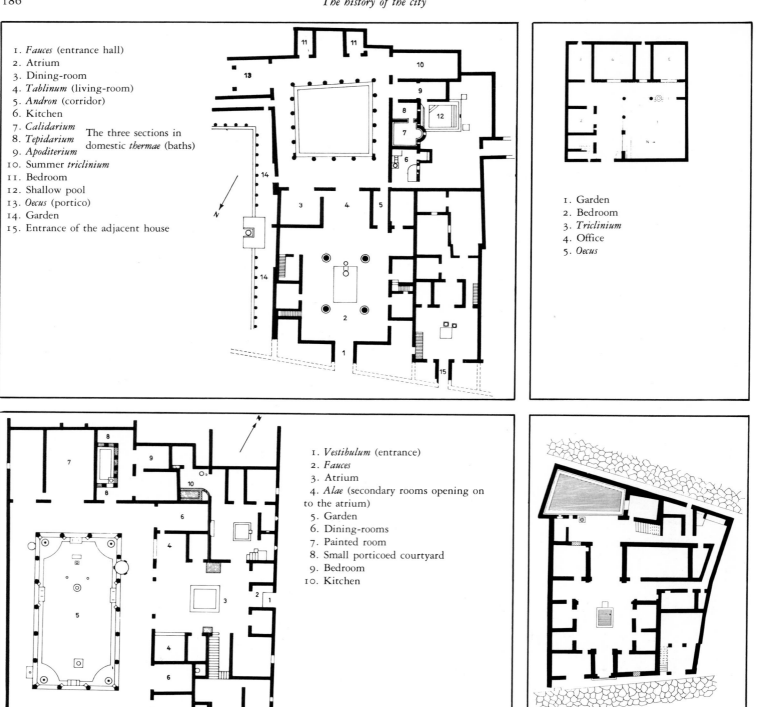

1. *Fauces* (entrance hall)
2. Atrium
3. Dining-room
4. *Tablinum* (living-room)
5. *Andron* (corridor)
6. Kitchen
7. *Calidarium*   The three sections in
8. *Tepidarium*   domestic *thermae* (baths)
9. *Apoditerium*
10. Summer *triclinium*
11. Bedroom
12. Shallow pool
13. *Oecus* (portico)
14. Garden
15. Entrance of the adjacent house

1. Garden
2. Bedroom
3. *Triclinium*
4. Office
5. *Oecus*

1. *Vestibulum* (entrance)
2. *Fauces*
3. Atrium
4. *Alae* (secondary rooms opening on
to the atrium)
5. Garden
6. Dining-rooms
7. Painted room
8. Small porticoed courtyard
9. Bedroom
10. Kitchen

Figs 287–90   Plans of four houses at Pompeii; left, the House of the Silver Wedding and the House of the Vetii, right, the House of Pinarius Ceriale and the House of the Surgeon.

Fig. 291 A Pompeiian fresco preserved in the National Museum in Naples.

Fig. 292   The atrium of the House of Menander.

Fig. 293   The summer *triclinium* of the House of Caius.

Fig. 294   The *prelum* in the winery at the Villa dei Misteri.

THERMAE
M. CRASSI FRUGII
AQUA . MARINA . ET . BALN .
AQUA . DULCI . JANUARIUS . L .

IN . PRAEDIS .
C . LEGIANNI . VERI
BALNEUM . MORE . URBICO . LAVAT .
OMNIA . COMMODA . PRAESTANTUR .

IN PRAEDIS . JULIAE . S . P . F . FELICIS
LOCANTUR
BALNEUM . VENEREUM . ET .
NONGENTUM . PERGULAE
CENACULA . EX . IDIBUS . AUG .
PRIORIS . IN . IDUS . AUG .
SEXTAS . ANNOS . CONTINUOS .
QUINQUE .
S . Q . D . L . E . N . C .

Fig. 295   Three inscriptions bearing advertisements for the public baths at Pompeii.

HERCULANEUM.
General plan of the excavations.

1. House of the Genius.	12. House of the Stags.	25. Baths.
2. House of Argus.	13. Sacred area.	26. House of Galba.
3. House of Aristides.	14. Altar of M. Nonius Balbus.	27. Suburban Baths.
4. House of the Wooden Partition.	15. House of the Bicentenary.	28. House of the Gem.
5. House of the Skeleton.	16. House of the Mosaic of Neptune	29. House of the Relief of Telephus.
6. House of the Bronze Herma.	and Amphitrite.	30. Entrance hall of the *Palaestra*.
7. House of the Inn.	17. House of the Corinthian Atrium.	31. *Palaestra*.
8. *Sacella*.	18. House of the Furniture.	32. *Piscina*.
9. House of the Alcove.	19. House of the Sacellum.	33. *Natatio*.
10. House of the Cloth.	20. House of the Loom.	34. Aula with apse.
11. House of the Atrium with a Mosaic.	21. House of the Samnite.	35. Upper aula.
	22. House of the Grand Portal.	
	23. House of the Black Salon.	
	24. House of the two Atriums.	

Fig. 296   Ground plan of Herculaneum, which was buried by the same eruption as Pompeii in 79 AD.

The street system was the worst of the public works; it developed into an 85 kilometre network of winding thoroughfares, almost invariably on the narrow side. There were *itinera*, which were solely for the use of pedestrians, *actus*, which were broad enough to take one cart at a time, and *viae*, which could accommodate two carts side by side. There were only two *viae* in the centre of the city — the Via Sacra and the Via Nova, which ran along the sides of the Forum — and some twenty in the outskirts, such as the Via Appia, Via Flaminia, Via Ostiensis, Via Latina, Via Labicana. All were supposed to have a maximum width of 4.80 metres, according to the Twelve Tables, but some were as wide as 6.50 metres. In the rest of the city the law stated that the streets should be at least 2.90 metres wide, so that the houses on either side could have balconies on the upper floors. This network, which had been planned when Rome was still relatively small, became inadequate for a metropolis of a million inhabitants, especially as there was no public street cleaning service or lighting programme. Caesar, however, published an edict that made street cleaning the responsibility of local residents, and also forbade the use of streets by carts between the hours of sunrise and sunset, except for those involved in construction work. The result of this was that the city became extremely noisy at night-time.

The sewers, started in the sixth century BC, were continually extended and enlarged. In some places they were wide enough to accommodate two hay waggons side by side, and Agrippa was able to make a tour of inspection by boat. Their function was to carry away rainwater, the overflow from the aqueducts and the waste products from public buildings and from some of the *domus* at ground level. Many other buildings, which were sited too far away from the drains, put their waste into cesspools or garbage heaps, neither of which were ever totally eliminated.

There were thirteen aqueducts, which carried more than a thousand million cubic metres of water every day to Rome

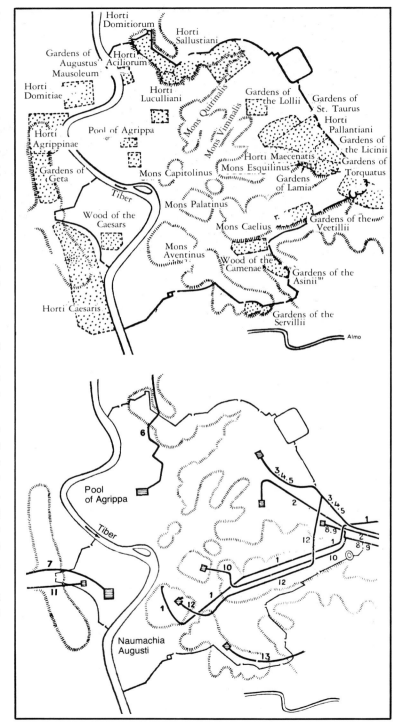

Figs 297–8   The gardens and aqueducts of Rome.

1. Aqua Appia	5. Aqua Julia	8. Aqua Claudia	11. Aqua Traiana
2. Anio Vetus	6. Aqua Virgo	9. Anio Novus	12. Aquae Marciae
3. Aqua Marcia	7. Aqua Alsietina	10. Arcus Neroniani	13. Aqua Antoniana
4. Aqua Tepula			

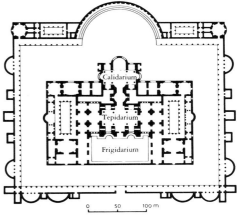

Figs 299–300 Diocletian's Baths in Rome (Fig. 236, no. 36): plan, and view of the ruins as they are today.

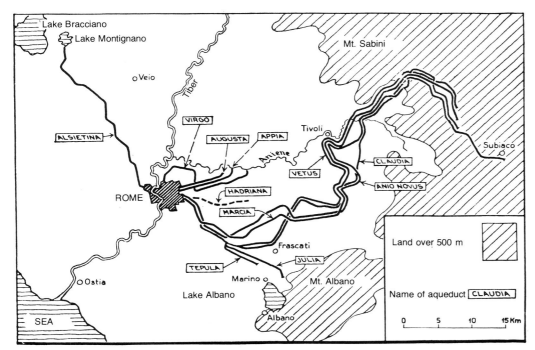

Fig. 301 Map showing the aqueducts of imperial Rome.

from the neighbouring mountains, and during the Republic this water was reserved for public use; only the surplus from the fountains (*aqua caduca*) was allowed to be used by private individuals. Later on, during imperial times, some citizens were granted a concession, either freely or on payment, for a fixed amount of water for the ground floors of their *domus*. The remainder was assigned to the public domain, for use in the fountains, latrines and the great baths that served vast areas of the city. It was this huge and easily accessible network of public hygiene services that compensated for the lack of sanitation in the majority of private houses (Figs 297–301).

The state was largely responsible for providing the population with food and entertainment, both of which came to be regarded as public services by the citizens of Rome. Approximately 150,000 people were fed at public expense, and during public holidays (182 days a year) all entertainments were free.

The city's food supply was brought by sea to the mouth of the Tiber, where the large port of Ostia (Figs 302–10) was built. From there it was taken in smaller craft to Rome, where an impressive system of unloading points and store-houses (*horrea*) had been constructed just before the Isola Tiberina. The hill known as Monte Testaccio (Figs 311–12) is composed solely of the remains of earthenware storage jars discarded after use.

The Romans constructed circuses to hold their spec-tacles and the most important, the Circus Maximus, occupied the entire valley between the Palatine and Aven-tine Hills and could hold approximately 250,000 people. They also built theatres, such as the Theatrum Marcelli, the Theatrum Balbi and the Theatrum Pompei, whose seating capacity varied between 10,000 and 25,000, and amphitheatres for the gladitorial games (the Colosseum with seats for 50,000 people, and the Amphitheatrum Castrense). In addition, there were special places where mock sea battles were held (*naumachiae*), like the ones built by Augustus and Trajan on the right hand bank of the Tiber. These have since disappeared.

The size and number of these buildings demonstrate the vastness of the resources at the authorities' disposal, in terms of money, materials and slave labour, which was

drawn from all parts of the Empire. Its political supremacy attracted ever increasing numbers of people to Rome, but it also furnished the means to make the city function properly. However, this great concentration of people did present a number of problems (how to provide enough housing, how to prevent the streets becoming completely clogged with traffic and people, how to dispose of all the rubbish, how to get enough food and water, and even how to keep everyone entertained), and all technical means available were brought into action. But ancient technology did not progress con-tinually like its modern counterpart and, as a result, the city reached a certain stage in its development and then ground to a halt.

Naturally enough, the ability to keep the city function-ing depended on the political stability of the Empire. And so, when the Empire began to run into difficulties, the failure of goods to arrive by sea at Ostia forced a large part of the population to move from the city to the countryside. The collapse of the aqueducts (either from lack of mainten-ance or as a result of damage inflicted by invaders) made the upper areas, the old nucleus of Rome, uninhabitable, and compelled the people to take up residence in the flat land on either side of the Tiber (the Campus Martius and modern-day Trastevere), where water could be obtained from the river or from wells.

Thus began the transformation of ancient Rome into modern Rome. The modern city began life as an emergency town in the empty spaces of the ancient capital, huddled amongst the majestic ruins of the past (the Theatrum Mar-celli, the Pantheon, the Theatrum Pompei, the mausoleum of Augustus and Domitian's stadium), all of which towered over its houses. The old city centre with its great monu-ments (the Forum, the Capitol, the Palatine Hill and the Colosseum) stood on the edge of the new town, because it had been founded on the hilly site of the first inhabited settlement. The great baths, that had been designed to serve the most densely-populated districts (those of Caracalla and Diocletian), and the great Christian basilicas, built on the edges of the city during the fourth century AD (San Paolo, San Lorenzo, San Giovanni, Santa Maria Maggiore), found themselves in the midst of desolation, while the Aurelian Wall wound its way through the hills, surrounded by fields.

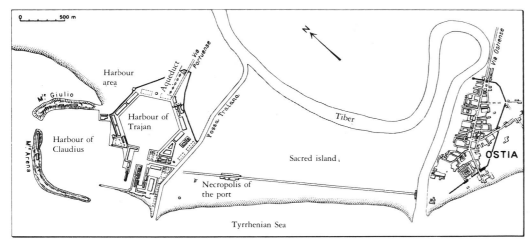

Fig. 302 The harbour system of ancient Rome, at the mouth of the Tiber; the modern Fiumicino was the canal that joined the two man-made harbours to the Tiber.

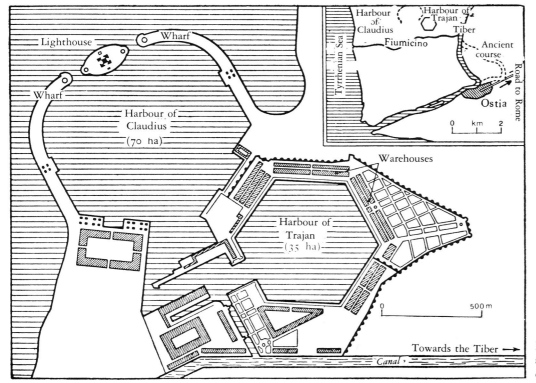

Fig. 303 The harbours of Claudius and Trajan, showing the surrounding complex of storehouses.

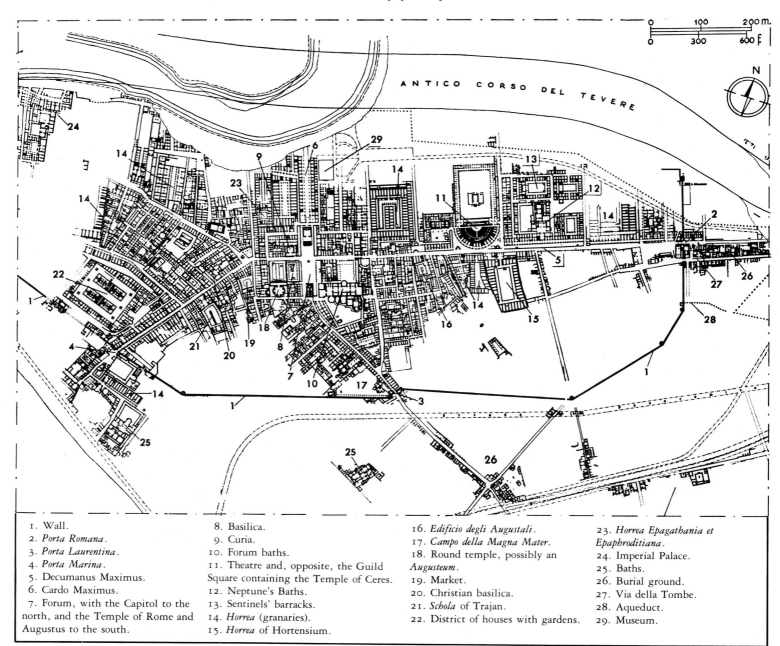

Fig. 304   Map of ancient Ostia.

1. Wall.
2. *Porta Romana*.
3. *Porta Laurentina*.
4. *Porta Marina*.
5. Decumanus Maximus.
6. Cardo Maximus.
7. Forum, with the Capitol to the north, and the Temple of Rome and Augustus to the south.

8. Basilica.
9. Curia.
10. Forum baths.
11. Theatre and, opposite, the Guild Square containing the Temple of Ceres.
12. Neptune's Baths.
13. Sentinels' barracks.
14. *Horrea* (granaries).
15. *Horrea* of Hortensium.

16. *Edificio degli Augustali*.
17. *Campo della Magna Mater*.
18. Round temple, possibly an *Augusteum*.
19. Market.
20. Christian basilica.
21. *Schola* of Trajan.
22. District of houses with gardens.

23. *Horrea Epagathania et Epaphroditiana*.
24. Imperial Palace.
25. Baths.
26. Burial ground.
27. Via della Tombe.
28. Aqueduct.
29. Museum.

Fig. 305   Aerial view of Ostia.

Fig. 306   Ostia. Aerial view of the central part of the city, crossed by the Decumanus Maximus; in the foreground, the theatre.

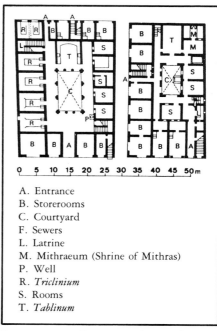

A. Entrance
B. Storerooms
C. Courtyard
F. Sewers
L. Latrine
M. Mithraeum (Shrine of Mithras)
P. Well
R. *Triclinium*
S. Rooms
T. *Tablinum*

Figs 307–10 Reconstructions and plans of some of the *insulae* at Ostia.

Figs 311–12   The area of Rome, down-river from the Isola Tiberina, where the barges were unloaded, showing the groups of public warehouses. The accumulated debris from all the discarded storage jars produced the Monte Testaccio, here seen in a relief model from the mid-nineteenth century.

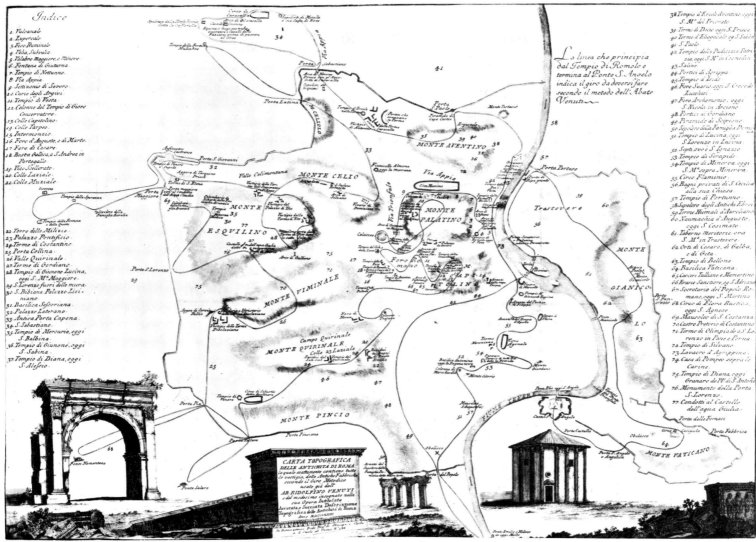

Fig. 313   A map of 1723, designed for visitors to the monuments of ancient Rome.

Between the early Middle Ages and 1870 Rome was transformed and enriched by many beautiful buildings, but it still continued to be a city of minor importance, covering a fraction of the territory once occupied by the capital of the ancient world. The relationship between this living city and the ubiquitous ghost of its predecessor had a decisive effect on its character, as well as attracting visitors from all over the known world. Modern Rome, however, could never become a continuation of classical Rome, despite artists of the Renaissance and the ambitions of the Papacy from Sixtus IV to Clement VIII. Reality did not substantiate the myth of the Eternal City, created by the writers of antiquity and revived periodically for rhetorical or political reasons. Instead, Rome remained a living proof of the transience of worldly glories, the ravages of time, the fickleness of Fortune, just as Goethe, Leopardi, Stendhal and so many other visitors during the eighteenth and nineteenth centuries had seen (Figs 313–22).

Fig. 314 Monuments and everyday life: the coal merchant's and saddler's shops in the vaults of the Theatrum Marcelli, before the demolitions of the Fascist era.

This view of Rome, the reasons for which were very obvious up to a hundred years ago, has to be analysed more carefully nowadays, as all the features of the traditional setting (the Papal city, the ruins of the ancient city and the areas of desolation surrounding them) have since been overrun and disfigured by the enormous development of the contemporary city (Fig. 315). We shall return later to discuss the character of modern-day Rome and the reasons why it has developed in the way it has, but for the moment suffice it to say that the districts built during the last hundred years (the nineteenth-century building within the Aurelian Walls and on the Esquiline and Aventine Hills, and the ten kilometre-deep strip outside the walls that has been built over during modern times) are totally unrelated to the continuity of the city's history from its earliest origins to 1870. The ruins of the ancient city and the remains of the Papal city — the historical centre and the villas — still stand in the midst of a wasteland, but one inhabited by more than three million people and filled with cars and ten-storey houses.

The traditional progression from countryside to ruins to inhabited areas can still be experienced by entering Rome from the Via Appia Antica, which has been miraculously left relatively untouched. Following the thin strip of Roman road, one arrives at the Porta S. Sebastiano, where the compact stonework of the Aurelian Walls is still clearly visible (one should ignore the walls of the houses in the neighbouring residential districts to the east and west). Entering the city and leaving Caracalla's Baths on the left, one reaches the Porta Capena, to be confronted by the Imperial Palace situated on the Palatine Hill. On the left is the Circus Maximus, while to the right stands the Arch of Constantine and the Via Triumphalis, which leads to the Colosseum. The ancient centre of Rome — the Palatine Hill, the Forums, the Capitol, and parts of the Caelian Hill and the Mons Oppius — is now an archaeological zone, which has been excavated and fenced off and provides a welcome oasis of calm in the middle of the city, even though it is broken by a number of main roads. The other major buildings of antiquity — the Pantheon and the Castel S. Angelo (Hadrian's Mausoleum) — have either been incorporated into the city or form other small archaeological enclaves, like the temples of Largo Argentina, Diocletian's

Baths, the Mausoleum of Augustus and the Theatrum Marcelli. The Aurelian Walls are now surrounded by modern buildings on both sides, while the roads built alongside them send traffic speeding around the perimeter.

In order for the Empire to function smoothly a number of modifications had to be made to the natural terrain, and these are remarkable for their vast scale rather than for any technical innovations. Goethe, who came across these man-made works — bridges, roads and aqueducts — during his travels in Italy, likened them to 'a second nature, working for civilisation', and they are indeed similar to the works of nature in their simplicity, their size and the way in which they repeat the same basic elements. The Romans used construction techniques from the Hellenistic world,

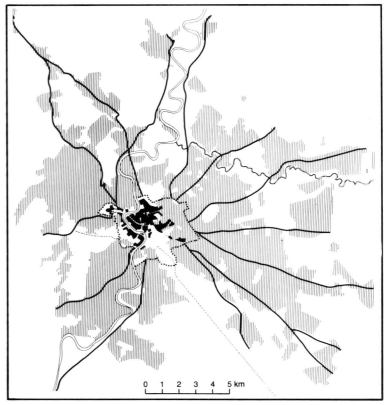

Fig. 315 Modern Rome. In the centre, the historic city enclosed by the Aurelian Walls; in the surrounding areas, the modern districts built along the *viae consulares*.

Fig. 316   A Roman road at Paestum.

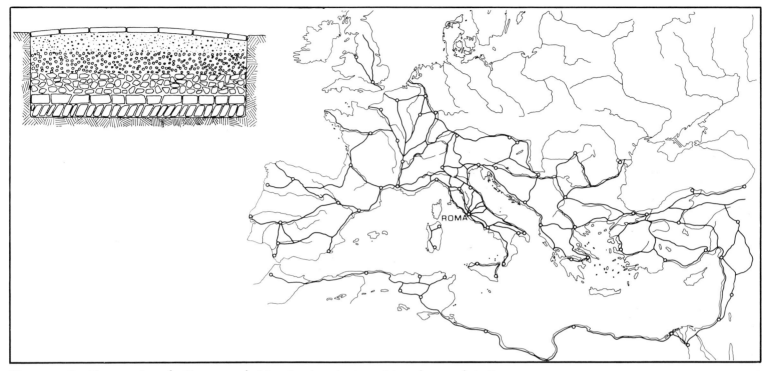

Figs 317–18   Cross-section of a Roman road. Map showing the imperial road network in Europe.

which they had come into contact with in southern Italy, and in 302 BC work started on the first important road and the first aqueduct (the Via Appia and the Aqua Appia). Having decided to adopt these techniques, the Romans were able to spread them throughout their empire.

ROADS AND BRIDGES

The building of roads increased as new provinces were added to the Empire. They were first used by the armies, then as trade routes, and finally as a means of speeding up administrative communication.

The roads were laid on a foundation of broken stones (*rudus*) covered by layers of gravel, which became progressively finer near the surface, and topped by a pavement of many-sided flat stones (*gremium* — Fig. 317). The width was limited to between 4 and 6 metres, enough space to allow the passage of pedestrians (*iter*) and carts (*actus*), but in the case of curves and inclines, the main preoccupation was

to ensure that journeys were as straightforward and as quick as possible. Where there were no natural obstacles, the roads ran in dead straight lines, even for extremely long distances; the Via Appia, for example, runs in a straight line for 60 kilometres along the Pontine Marshes. In places where the surface was uneven, the rocks were hacked away so as to enable the road to run as smoothly and as directly as possible, like at Montagna Spaccata, for example, between Pozzuoli and Capua, or the Passo del Furlo, where the Via Flaminia crosses the Apennines, or the 40 metre-deep cutting which enables the Via Appia to pass through the Pisco Montano di Terracina between the *acropolis* and the sea. The Romans even built tunnels, such as the Grotta della Pace, which joined Lake Avernus to Cumae and was 900 metres long and illuminated by light wells.

In order to cross the rivers that lay in the way of the roads, numerous bridges were constructed, either of wood or stone. Many of these are still in use: for example, the five in Rome — the Ponte Milvio (Fig. 320), the Ponte Elio, the

Figs 319–20   The Via Appia near Rome, flanked by tombs: The Ponte Milvio crossing the Tiber at the start of the Via Flaminia.

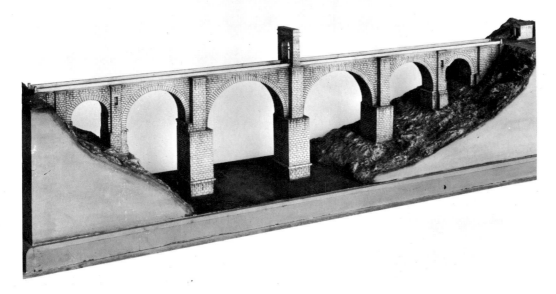

Fig. 321 Model of the Roman bridge across the Tagus at Alcantara, dedicated to Trajan.

Ponte Sisto and the two on the Isola Tiberina — the two which cross the Flaminia at Narni and Rimini, the one at Ascoli over the Tronto, and the Ponte di Pietra at Verona. Their width was always restricted to a maximum of between 7 and 8 metres, but their length could be considerable (the bridge at Mérida in Spain has 60 arches and is almost 800 metres long), and in the bridge over the Tagus at Alcantara (Fig. 321) the arches have a span of 35 metres.

From the time of Augustus onwards, the Roman network of roads was used for a regular postal system (*cursus publicus*), with secondary stations (*mutationes*), where the riders changed their horses, and principal stations (*mansiones*) spaced a day's journey apart from each other, with six or seven intermediate *mutationes*, where the riders spent the night. The *cursus*, which employed couriers on horses (*speculatores*) or carts, if goods had to be transported, was reserved for the use of public officials, but private individuals could provide their own postal system by using *tabellari*, who travelled by foot or on horseback.

AQUEDUCTS

Aqueducts too, like the roads, were treated as public services. They were built by the state or the local administration for public use; private consumption was of secondary importance.

Fig. 322   An aqueduct in the midst of the Roman countryside.

Fig. 323   The Roman aqueduct at Segovia, called 'The Devil's Bridge'.

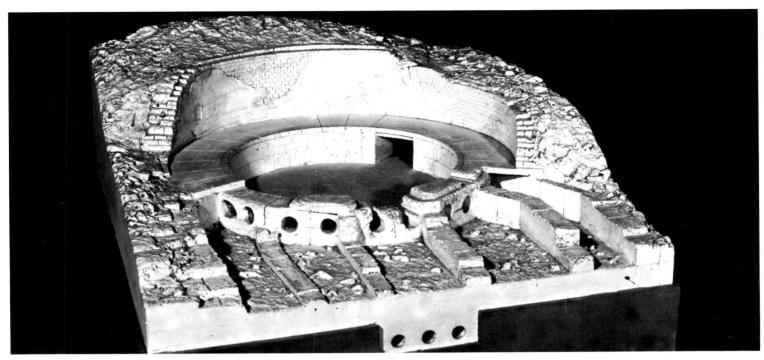

Fig. 324   The distribution *castellum* for the aqueduct at Nîmes; a model made in 1939.

The Romans preferred to use spring water or filtered river water; they channelled it into a rectangular conduit (*specus*) coated with a plaster of powdered brick (*opus signinum*), which, although covered, was accessible for inspection and also allowed fresh air to reach the water. The gradient was kept as constant as possible (from 10 to 0.2 per thousand, depending on the characteristics of each aqueduct) so as to enable the water to flow freely (Fig. 326), even though the Romans, like the Greeks, understood the siphon principle and made very skilful use of it in certain cases. In the Alatri aqueduct, built in 134 BC, a pressure of ten atmospheres was achieved and high resistance pipes were used, while in the aqueduct at Lyons there is a triple siphon with lead pipes. They preferred, however, for the water to arrive in the cities at a low rate of pressure, so as not to place too great a strain on the distribution pipes. It is for this reason that their aqueducts were raised on one or more series of arches when crossing a valley.

Along the sides of the aqueducts, and also at the point of arrival, there were reservoirs (*piscinae limariae*), in which the water deposited its impurities before being decanted into distribution cisterns (*castella* — Fig. 324). There it was measured as it passed through the bronze *calices* on its way into the city's pipes, which consisted of ten foot-long sections of lead tubing (*fistulae*). In certain circumstances there were much larger reservoirs; Misenum, for example, an important military port, had one called the Piscina Mirabilis, with a capacity of 12,600 cubic metres.

Sometimes the structures that the Romans built in the provinces — like the aqueducts at Tarragona and Segovia in Spain and at Nîmes in France (Figs 323, 327–8), all of which have more than one tier of arches — seem to be the product of a desire to leave monumental reminders of their presence, rather than the consequence of any technical constraints. In fact, during the Middle Ages, when the erection of such structures had become impossible, the people called them 'Devil's bridges' and regarded them as being the works of some supernatural force.

Fig. 325   The ruins of the aqueduct of Claudius: at the top can be
seen the water conduit.

Fig. 326   Cross-section of the conduit in the Anio Vetus aqueduct
at Rome.

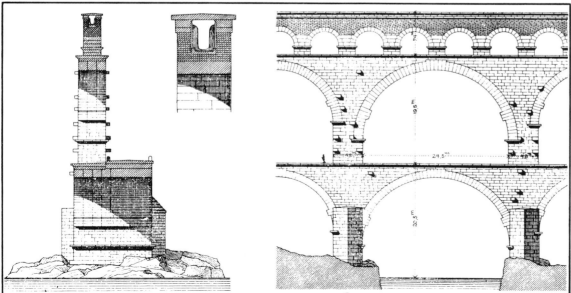

Figs 327–8 The Pont du Gard at Nîmes in southern France: perspective; side and sectional views.

LINES OF FORTIFICATION

At the farthest edges of the Empire, where the Romans had called a halt to their conquests, they consolidated the frontiers by building a *limes*, which was a defensive system occupying a strip of land whose depth varied from frontier to frontier.

To give the army greater manoeuvrability, the essential component of these *limites* was a road, which would run through clearings in wooded areas and, in marshy areas, be raised above ground level. They were also reinforced with a *fossatum* (an artificial trench dug when there was no natural defence such as a river) and a *vallum* (a solid wall of wood, earth or stone). Nearby, or sometimes actually forming part of them, were the military installations: the camps (*castra*), the lesser forts (*castella*) and the fortified strongholds (*burgi* and *turres*). Further back into the hinterland lay the *oppida* or fortified towns, which also formed part of the defensive system.

The two most important *limites* lay in the northern reaches of the Empire: the German *limes* (Fig. 331) built beyond the Rhine and the Danube by Tiberius, Germanicus and Domitian, which was more like a strategic highway running along an open frontier than a defensive measure, and Hadrian's Wall (Fig. 329), which separated England from the Scots and took the form of a line of garrison fortresses. The former is more than 500 kilometres long, while the latter measures some 110. In many respects they can be regarded as complementary adjuncts to the natural frontiers formed by the sea, the Rhine and the Danube, thereby confirming the analogy of the Empire with the city. The Empire also had its roads, its walls and its public services, just like the city; the only difference was that one was on a much vaster scale than the other.

Fig. 329   Roman public works in Britain: roads, canals, cities and Hadrian's wall.

Fig. 330   The tribunal palace in the encampment of Xanten (Castra Vetera) in Germany.

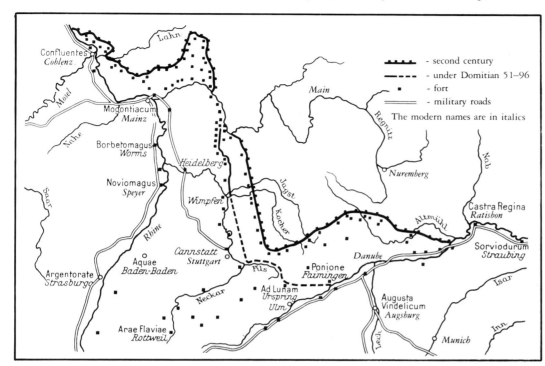

Fig. 331　The Roman *limes* in Germany, between the Rhine and the Danube.

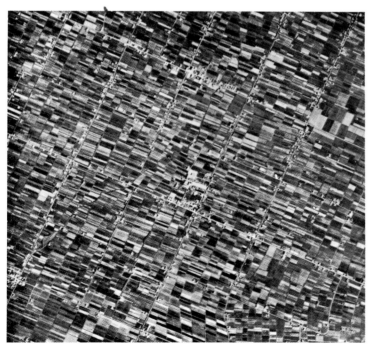

Figs 332–3　Reminders of Roman colonisation in the landscape of today: the *centuriatio* in the Emilian countryside, and the *limes* near Welzheim in Würtemberg.

THE COLONISATION OF AGRICULTURAL LAND

The straight lines of the main roads acted as reference lines for the division of arable land (the *centuriatio*), where they had been assigned to Roman or Latin colonists sent into conquered territory.

The *centuriatio* was based on a grid of secondary roads (also known as *limites*); the *decumani*, which ran parallel to the longest side of the territory or the main road, and the *cardines*, which were shorter and ran at right angles to the *decumani*. They were 20 *actus* apart (the *actus* being a unit of agrarian measure equal to about 35 metres), that is to say approximately 700 metres, and they divided the land into squares called *centuriae*, each of which covered an area of 200 *iogeri* (*c.* 50 hectares). These could be granted to a single owner, or to any number of different owners; in one instance, in the colony of Terracina which was founded in 329 BC, they were divided between 100 owners.

The measuring operation was carried out by special technicians, called *agrimensori* or *gromatici*, with an implement called a *groma* (Fig. 334). Ancient writers connected the work with the Etruscan science of augury, and with the division of the heavens according to the direction of the cardinal points. However, the orientation of the *decumani* and the *cardines* did not normally follow the cardinal points of the compass; they were planned so as to exploit the natural lay of the land as much as possible. Once an area had been divided, a plan of the scheme was made in bronze, with one copy being kept in the headquarters of the colony and another being sent to Rome.

The *limites*, as we have already noted, were both cadastral boundaries and public thoroughfares, and due to this dual function they formed an impressive network of secondary roads, which the ancient world had never seen before. It also ensured total penetration by the Roman agrarian, economic and administrative systems.

The chessboard effect of the Roman *centuriatio* is still clearly visible in many of the plains of the Empire, notably in northern Italy (Emilia and Veneto), around Florence, in the Capuan plain, in Tunisia and in southern France (Figs 332, 336–7). Property boundaries, roads and canals have continued to follow its outline, even after the old agricultural system has disappeared.

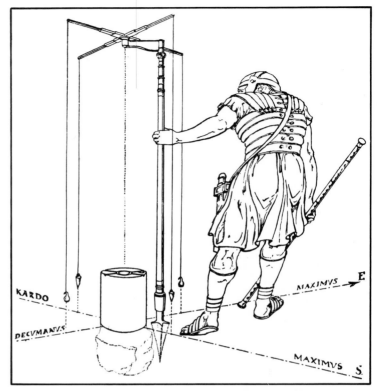

Fig. 334   The *groma*, which was used to trace the perpendicular alignment of the *centuriatio* and also in the planning of cities. It was made of four small strips of wood, roughly 45 cm long, from which hung four plumb-lines; the central stake, to which the pieces of wood were attached, was driven into the ground in such a way that the centre was vertically over the circle carved in the marker stone.

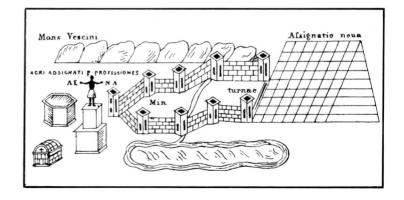

Fig. 335   The *centuriatio* of Minturno, as it is shown in the book of the *Gromatici veteres*.

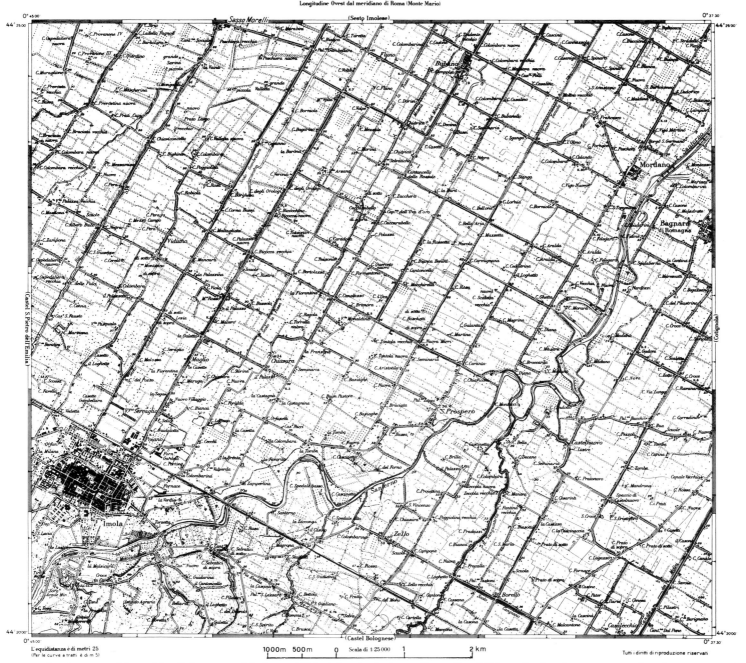

Fig. 336   Area no. 88 11 SO of the map of Italy, published by the Istituto Geografico Militare (scale of 1:25,000, reduced to 1:50,000). The *centuriatio* of the countryside to the north of Imola can be clearly seen.

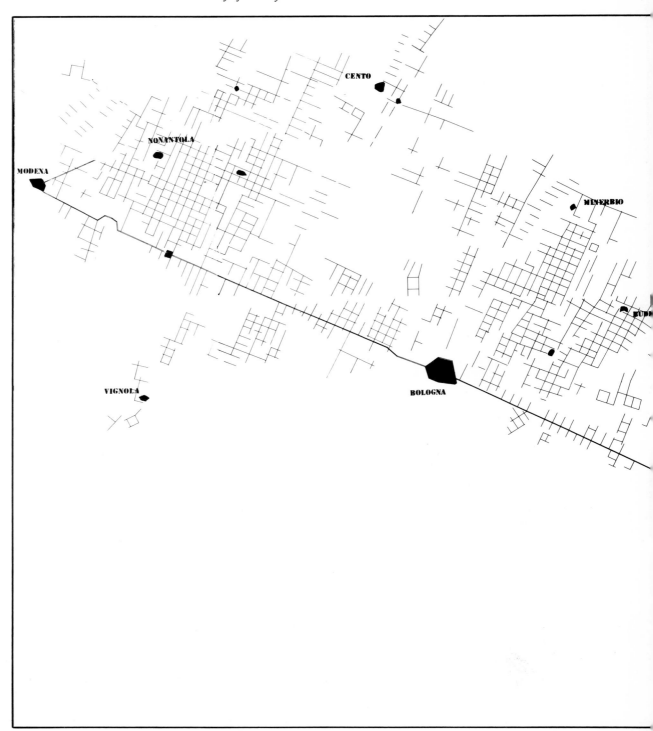

Fig. 337   The *centuriatio* outline which still survives in Emilia.

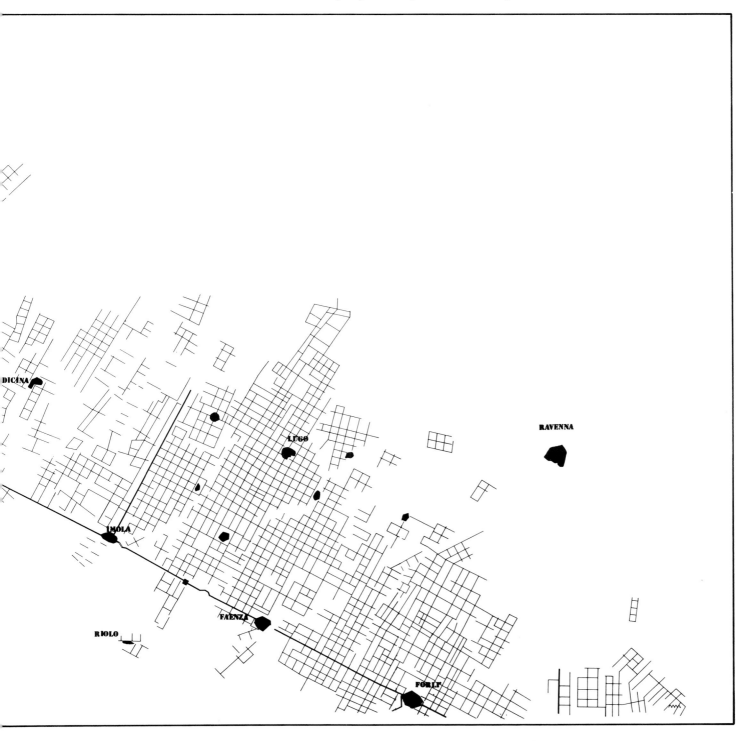

Figs 338–41 An old Roman farmhouse: the rustic Villa di Boscoreale in Campagnia. A plan of its layout, two views of a three-dimensional model and an example of an agricultural cart (*plaustrum*), preserved in a museum in Rome.

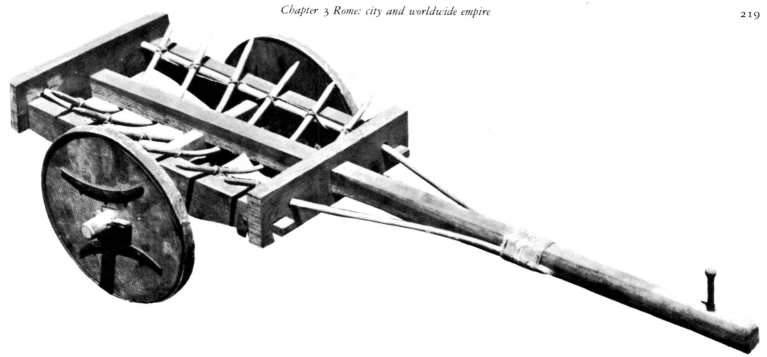

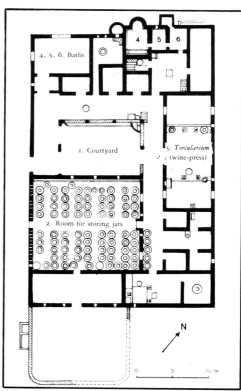

4, 5, 6. Baths

4 5 6

1. Courtyard

3. *Torcularium*
   (wine-press)

2. Room for storing jars

N

0   5   10 m

THE NEW CITIES

In the *centuriatio* layout there were two principal axes, the *decumanus maximus* and the *cardo maximus*, which were wider than the other *decumani* and *cardines* and crossed at a point that was considered to be the ideal centre of the colony. Ancient writers considered it particularly propitious when the two territorial axes coincided with the two axes of the city, so that the roads leading out into the country from the city were a continuation of those within the city.

Roman military encampments were also laid out in the same way (Fig. 345), and we know that many of these camps subsequently grew into cities, and that the colonists sent into the *centuriationes* were often military veterans. However, other cities and colonies were of purely civilian origin, and some were founded before the Romans had established the rules for laying out encampments. Thus all the Roman cities that are laid out along geometrical lines, whether of military or civilian origin, can be regarded as being the product of an urban application of the *centuriatio* system — a simplified and standardised extension of the Hippodamian ideal practised in the Hellenistic world.

The difference in scale between the urban and territorial grids meant that they came to be regarded as two distinct concepts (in classical culture, major differences in size always develop into qualitative differences). Sometimes cities were founded at the same time as the countryside was being divided up, with the result that the axes of their two road systems coincided, whilst in other cases the two events took place separately, which in some instances meant that the two systems had different orientations. In sloping terrain the *decumani* were arranged horizontally, and the *cardines* followed the line of the steepest inclines. When there was a river or some other stretch of water, such as the sea, the *decumani* would run parallel to the edge, with the *cardines* running at right angles to them.

Naturally the urban grid was more flexible and more variable than its territorial counterpart. The blocks of buildings, which were square or rectangular verging on the square, measured between 70 × 70 and 150 × 150 metres,

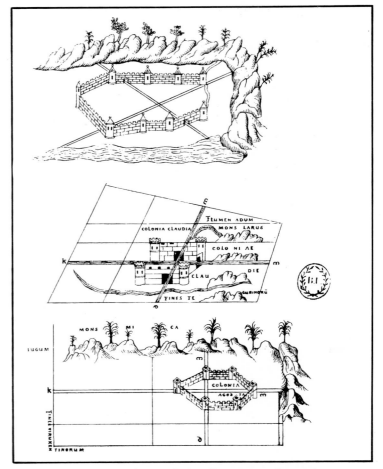

Fig. 342 Examples of cities designed on two orthogonal axes, from an illustration in the book of *Gromatici veteres*.

but the regularity of the grid was often interrupted by curved streets, especially where the latter had to correlate with a bridge that could only be built in a certain spot. It was also possible for one or more of the central blocks to be either modified or completely omitted to make way for the forum or other public buildings. The perimeter, protected by defensive walls, was normally of rectangular shape and enveloped by a solid block of buildings, while the

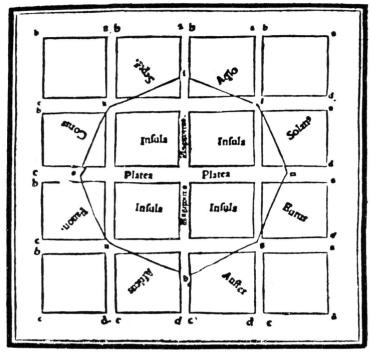

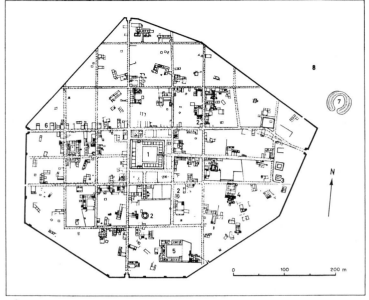

1. Forum.
2. Temples.
3. Sacred area.
4. Baths.
5. Barracks.
6. Storehouses.
7. Amphitheatre.
8. Temple (?).

Figs 343–4 The chessboard design of a Roman city, as seen in Vitruvius' treatise (from an illustration of 1536), and an actual example: Silchester in England.

amphitheatre was situated on the periphery of the town, either immediately inside or immediately outside the walls.

The cities founded by the Romans varied in size from 12 to 200 hectares or more. After Rome, the largest town in Italy was Capua, which covered an area of 180 hectares. Other new cities included:

Milan	133 hectares	Aosta	41 hectares
Bologna	83 hectares	Rimini	34 hectares
Turin	47 hectares	Florence	22 hectares
Verona	45 hectares	Pola	16 hectares

Outside Italy there were even bigger new cities:

Leptis Magna	400 hectares	London and Lyons	140 hectares
Trier	285 hectares	Cologne	100 hectares
Nîmes	220 hectares	Cadiz	80 hectares
Vienna	200 hectares	Paris	55 hectares

The population density varied from 200 to 500 people per hectare. And so a medium-sized Italian city like Turin, Verona or Aosta could have 20,000 inhabitants, while Milan, London and Lyons had 50,000 inhabitants, and Leptis Magna, 100,000. These figures are far less than those for the great pre-Roman cities of the Eastern Mediterranean; Alexandria, its economic capital, covered some 900 hectares and possessed a population of between 500,000 and 1,000,000, a figure not far removed from the million people boasted by imperial Rome. Carthage, with a surface area of 305 hectares, had 2–300,000 inhabitants, and Antioch was also roughly the same size.

The Romans founded a great number of cities in Italy and the western parts of the Empire, and these cities continued to function as fortified strongholds or as rallying points for the local populations even after the Empire had fallen. It is for this reason that almost all the important cities in Italy, as well as many of the principal ones elsewhere in Europe — Paris, London, Vienna, Cologne — have grown up on the site of a Roman city and still bear traces of the grid-system of *decumani* and *cardines* in their centres (Figs 347–8).

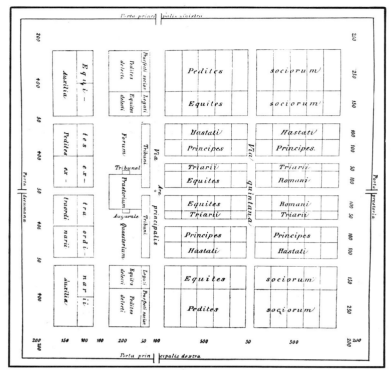

Fig. 345   The Roman military encampment, as described by
Polybius.

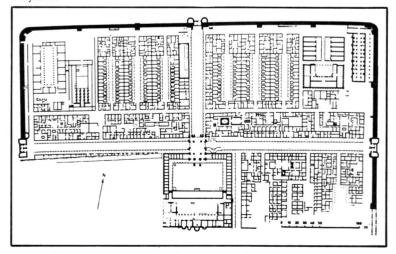

Fig. 346   The northern part of the camp of Lambaesis in Africa.

Figs 347–8   Two Roman camps along the Danube, both of which
have become the nucleus of important cities: Ratisbon and Vienna.

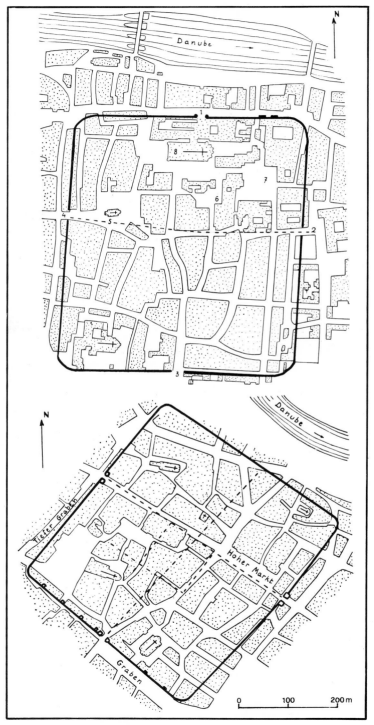

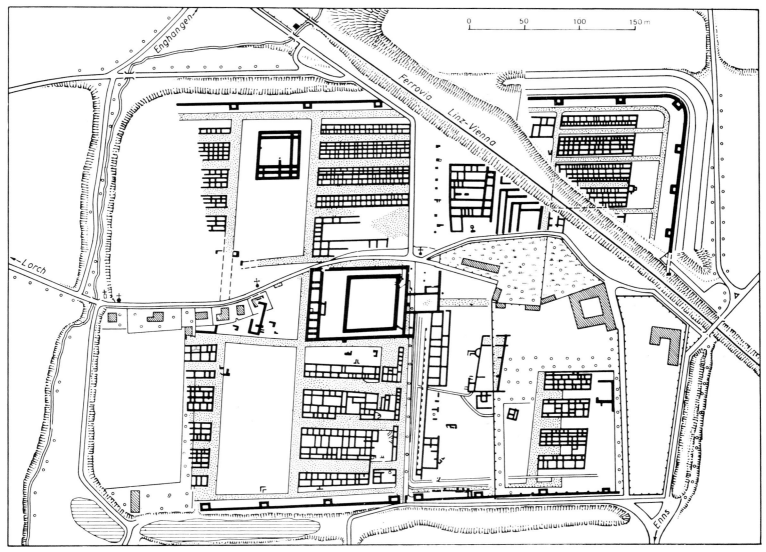

Fig. 349   The Roman camp of Lauriacum in Austria (third century AD), which is now in the middle of a stretch of countryside crossed by the Vienna–Linz railway line.

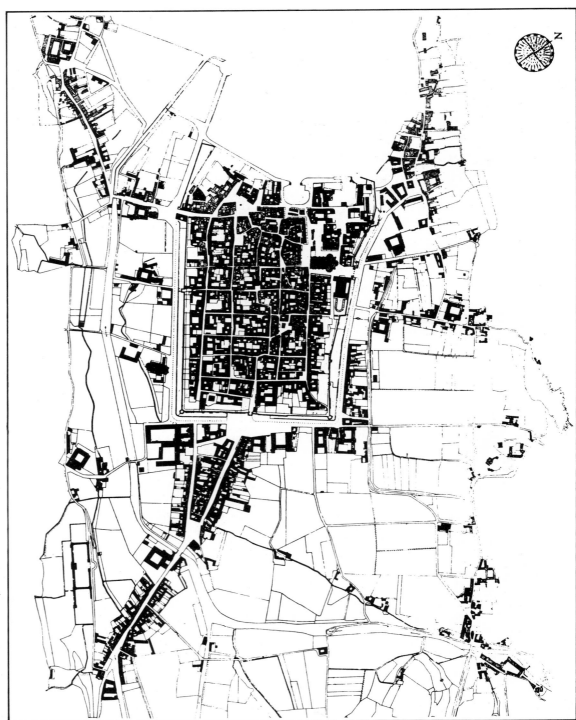

Figs 350–1 Cadastral plan of 1858
and aerial view of the city of Como;
the outline of the original Roman
encampment, which formed the
nucleus of the modern city, can be
clearly seen.

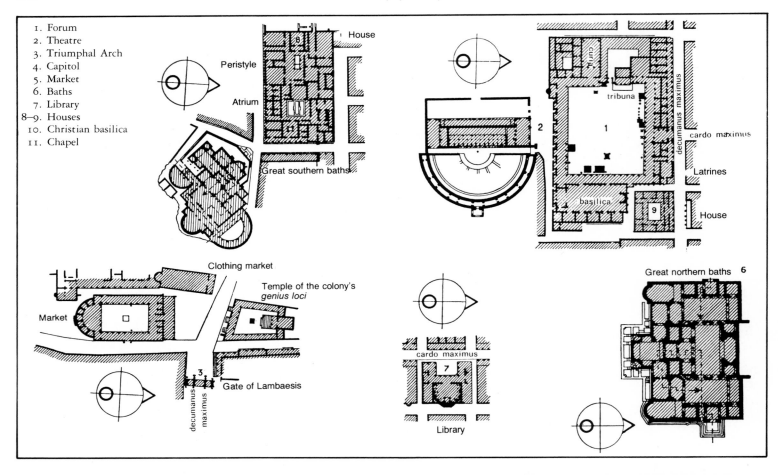

1. Forum
2. Theatre
3. Triumphal Arch
4. Capitol
5. Market
6. Baths
7. Library
8–9. Houses
10. Christian basilica
11. Chapel

House
Peristyle
Atrium
Great southern baths
curia
tribuna
decumanus maximus
cardo maximus
Latrines
basilica
House
2
1
9

Clothing market
Market
Temple of the colony's *genius loci*
3
decumanus maximus
Gate of Lambaesis
cardo maximus
7
Library
Great northern baths   6

Figs 352–8   Timgad in Algeria, a Roman city abandoned in the seventh century and almost completely excavated; plans and aerial view.

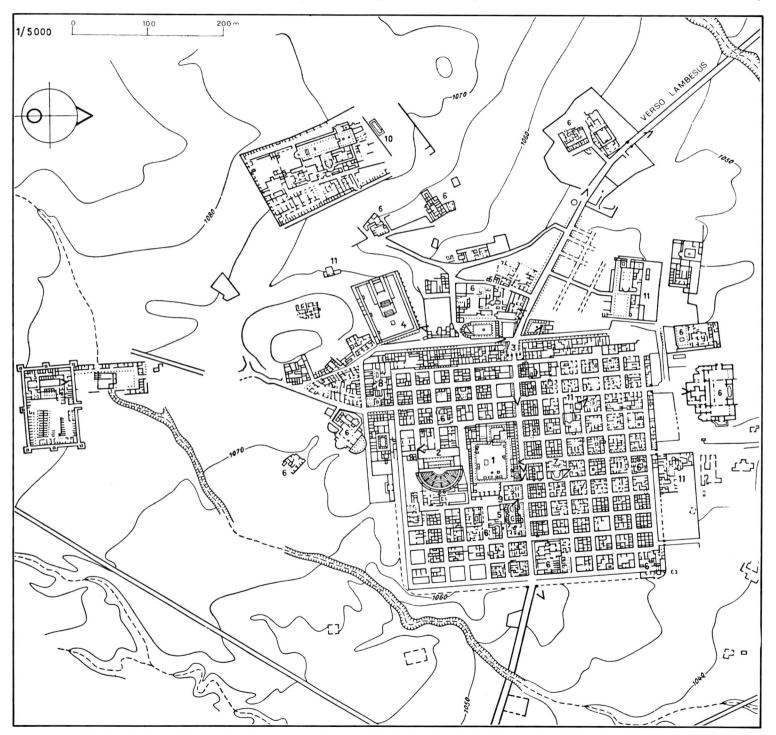

VERSO LAMBESUS

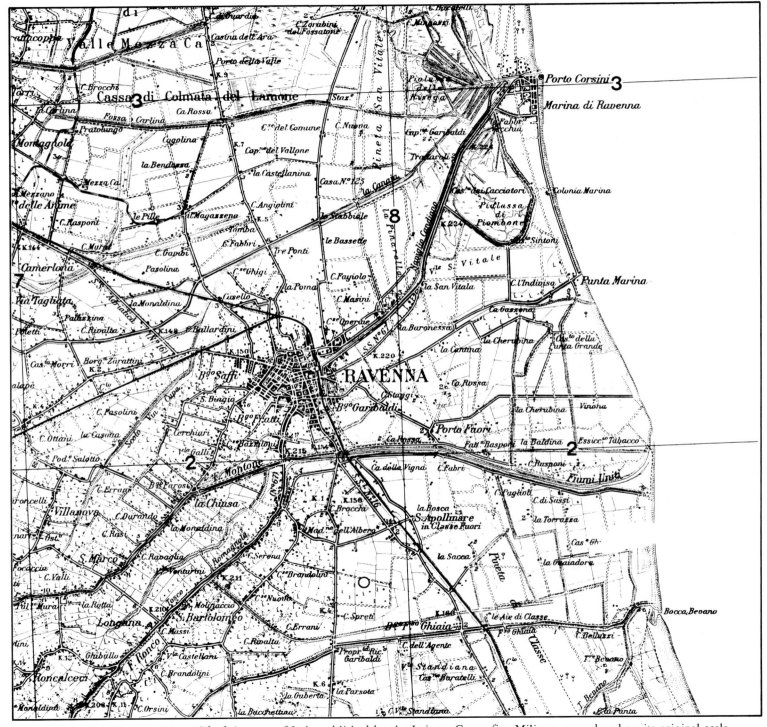

Fig. 364   Modern Ravenna (sheet 86 of the map of Italy published by the Istituto Geografico Militare, reproduced on its original scale of 1:100,000). Ancient Ravenna was situated on the sea, which is now some 8 kilometres away, and the whole area to the south-west was taken up by a lagoon.

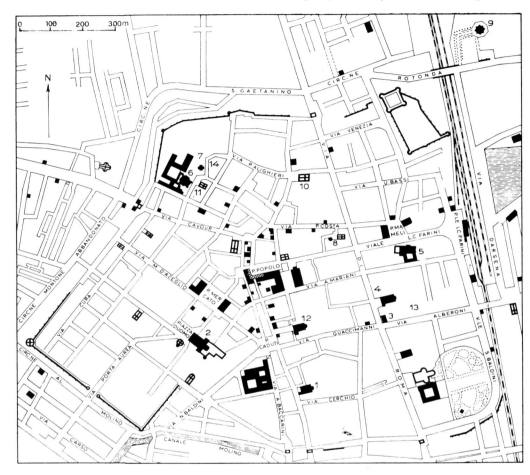

Fig. 365   Plan of Ravenna, showing the monuments of Antiquity.

1. Basilica of St Agatha.
2. Cathedral and archbishop's chapel.
3. Church of San Salvatore.
4. Basilica of San Apollinare Nuovo.
5. Basilica of St John the Evangelist.
6. Basilica of San Vitale.
7. Mausoleum of Galla Placidia.
8. Baptistry of the Arians.
9. Mausoleum of Theodoric.
10. St John the Baptist.
11. Santa Maria Maggiore.
12. St Francis.
13. So-called Palace of Theodoric.
14. Santa Croce.

Ravenna was a Roman city of secondary importance, situated amongst the marshes of Romagna. Augustus built the military port of Classe some three kilometres away, at the point where the waters of the lagoon were deepest. This meant that the city, already fortified on its inland side, was now connected by sea to the whole of the Mediterranean world. Because of this, Honorius chose it as capital of the Western Empire in 402 AD, and it subsequently became capital of the Ostrogoth kingdom and of the Byzantine provinces in Italy; it was during this period (from the fourth to the sixth century AD) that the city reached its zenith. Its walls survived up until the end of the nineteenth century (Figs 364–5), but the imperial and royal palaces have disappeared; only the churches are left — S. Apollinare in Classe,

S. Apollinare Nuovo, S. Vitale, and the two baptistries — forming the most important group of buildings from late antiquity in all Italy. Their exteriors are unadorned, but inside they are covered with the most beautiful polychrome marble and mosaic decoration, which spreads over the whole interior and transforms all the architectural elements (Fig. 369). Ravenna's fortunes were tied to those of Byzantine rule in Italy, and it subsequently found itself isolated from the mainstream of history, becoming, under Papal governorship, a quiet provincial city, famous only for the memory of its glorious history. Nowadays it is a booming industrial centre, and modern buildings are encroaching on the old marshes and surrounding the fragile monuments of the past.

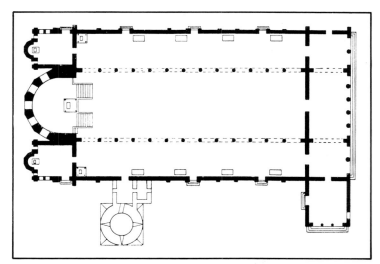

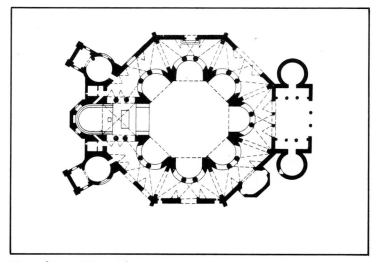

Fig. 366   Plan of the Church of San Apollinare in Classe at Ravenna, consecrated in 549 AD; the building in white is the round campanile, added during the tenth century (scale 1:800).

Figs 367–9   Views of the exterior and interior of the Church of San Vitale in Ravenna, consecrated in 347 AD; plan of its overall layout (scale 1:800).

Fig. 370   A capital in the Church of San Apollinare in Classe.

Figs 371–2   The imperial palace and the port of Classe, as depicted in the mosaics of San Apollinare Nuovo in Ravenna.

Byzantium was already one of the richest and most populous colonial Greek cities, favoured by its exceptional situation on a promontory overlooking the straits of the Bosphorus between the Black Sea and the Mediterranean. Constantine transformed it between 326 and 330 AD, dividing it into fourteen regions, like Rome, and constructing a new set of walls that enclosed four times as much land as before. In 414 AD Theodosius enlarged it even more by building another wall further inland; this meant that Constantinople now covered some 1,400 hectares (almost the same as the area in Rome surrounded by the Aurelian Walls) and had a population of roughly half a million inhabitants (Fig. 374).

The Walls of Theodosius acted as the definitive boundary mark for the city wall until modern times. Inside them, however, the transformation continued: in the old city centre, Constantine built an acropolis, an imperial palace and a hippodrome (like the Capitol, the Palatine Palace and the Circus Maximus in Rome), and constructed a forum between the old and new cities, while Theodosius built a new forum in the middle of the most populated area, and extended the port. Following the fire in 532 AD, Justinian rebuilt the palace and also completed, nearby, the great Church of Santa Sophia, a building that synthesised for the first time the artistic experiences of the whole Mediterranean world (Figs 375–81, 383–4). Its system of vaulted roofs and the way in which it was embellished with such precious materials as marble, glass mosaic and metal, created a new form of harmony that differed radically from the classical idea, but which inspired Byzantine, Arab and Persian architecture, and still survives in the Middle East today. In the outer reaches of the city, on the site of Constantine's tomb, Justinian built another famous church, that of the Holy Apostles, which served as the model for St Mark's Cathedral in Venice, but it has since been destroyed.

As far as we can tell, the city grew up round these monuments in the same dense and disorderly way as in Rome. A law passed in 476 AD laid down that all new roads should be at least 3.50 metres wide; few roads (two which

Figs 373–4 Constantinople: a personification of the city on a coin of Constantius II, and a plan of the fourteen regions into which it was divided.

ran along the shoreline and one that ran down the back of the promontory, forking like a Y) were wider or more imposing than that. The city's water supply arrived via a number of aqueducts (most of them subterranean, as a precaution against enemy attack), and was stored in vast covered or underground cisterns.

Constantinople continued to be the capital of the Eastern Empire until the fifteenth century. The Crusaders who sacked the city in 1204 were astonished to see a metropolis that was larger and richer than almost any city in Europe. The Ottomans finally captured it in 1435, when Constantinople became Istanbul, the capital of their empire, and today it is still one of the most important cities of the Middle Eastern world.

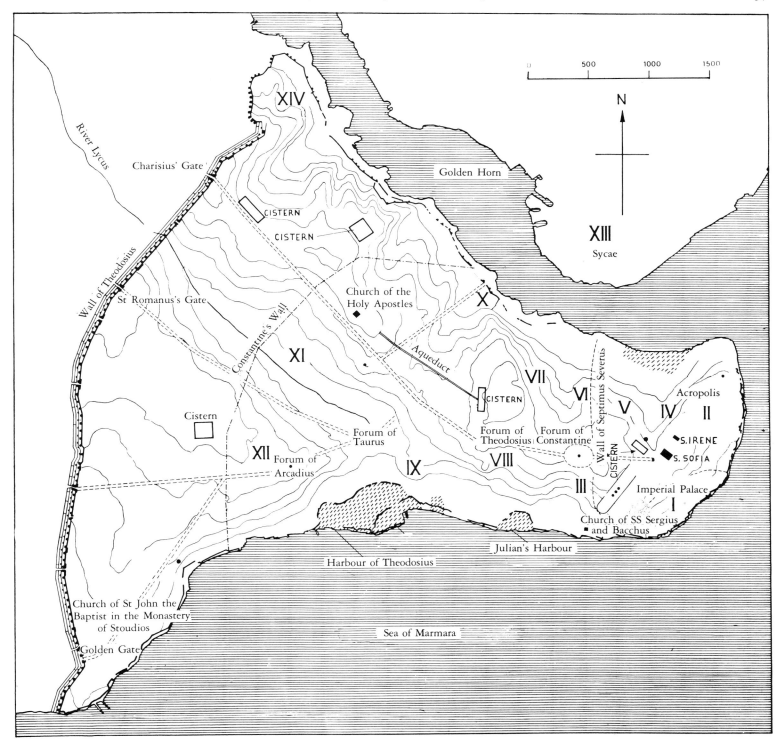

River Lycus

Charisius' Gate

CISTERN

CISTERN

Golden Horn

XIV

N

0   500   1000   1500

XIII

Sycae

Wall of Theodosius

St Romanus's Gate

Church of the
Holy Apostles

X

Constantine's Wall

Aqueduct

XI

CISTERN

VII

Acropolis

Wall of Septimus Severus

VI

V

IV

II

Cistern

Forum of
Taurus

Forum of
Theodosius

Forum of
Constantine

S. IRENE

CISTERN

S. SOFIA

XII

Forum of
Arcadius

IX

VIII

III

Imperial Palace

I

Church of SS Sergius
and Bacchus

Julian's Harbour

Harbour of Theodosius

Church of St John the
Baptist in the Monastery
of Stoudios

Golden Gate

Sea of Marmara

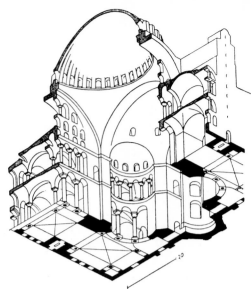

Figs 375–9   The Church of Santa Sophia in Constantinople (*c.* 525–27 AD): ground plan on a scale of 1:800 (the same as Figs 366, 369), cross-section, exterior view and sectional view of interior. The white areas represent later additions.

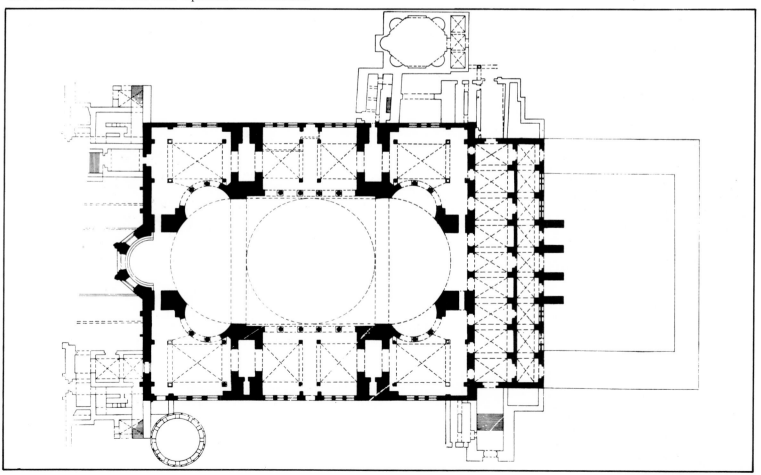

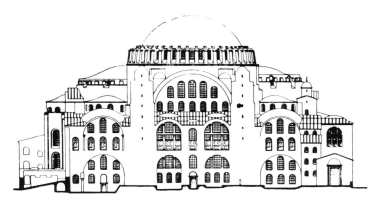

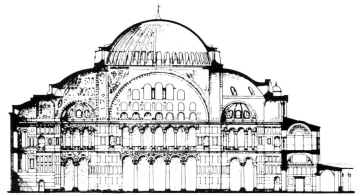

Figs 380–1   The dome of Santa Sophia, which collapsed in 558 and was rebuilt in 562 AD.

Fig. 382   A Byzantine emperor, from the *Cosmographia* of Sebastian Münster (1543).

Figs 383–4   A detail of the interior of Santa Sophia in Constantinople, and a lithograph of 1852, showing the church after its conversion into a mosque.

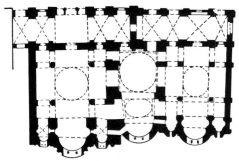

Figs 385–7   The religious buildings
of the Pantocrator, built during the
twelfth century; ground plan, rear
view and cross-section (scale 1:800).

Fig. 388   The Pantocrator buildings as they are today, situated in the centre of a run-down area of Istanbul.

Figs 389–90   Two views of Constantinople towards the end of the Empire, from the *Cronaca mondiale* of Schedel (1493).

Figs 393–4   The Sülemaniye Mosque, the most important monument erected by the Ottomans in their capital (1550–7).

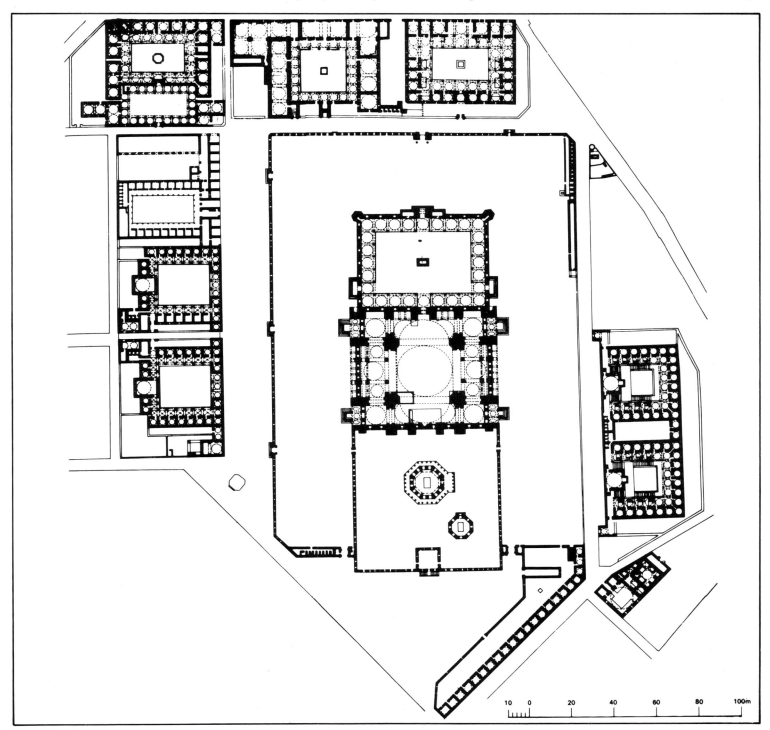

Fig. 395   An engraving (1705), showing Constantinople situated beyond the Dardanelles and the Sea of Marmara.

4
The formation of the medieval environment

The north-western areas of the former Roman Empire — Gaul, Italy, Germany and Britain — had all been occupied by barbarians since the fifth century, and, with the threat of an Arab advance from the seventh century onwards, they found themselves isolated on the edge of the ancient civilised world, their cities in a decline that often proved irreversible. After the turn of the eleventh century, this area, which later became the Europe of today, was the scene of a revival in civil and economic life, and the cities once more began to grow. This area was distinguished, however, from the rest of the Mediterranean in that the post-Roman decline broke the continuity of their development.

In many cases the new towns and cities were founded on the remains of the old ones, but with a different social character and a different architectural layout, which links them directly to the modern cities of today. All that remained of the old Roman cities were ruins, which, although they were studied and visited, did not make any practical contribution to their new surroundings. On the other hand, medieval cities — even those like Viterbo, Siena, Chartres, Gubbio and Bruges, which have remained essentially unchanged — are still lived in and still retain their original characteristics. Some have grown into full-scale metropoles (Paris and London, for example), and the original medieval zone has been reduced to a small central nucleus; yet it is surprising how some medieval elements still exercise an influence on the much larger contemporary city. Paris, for instance, is still basically divided into three parts — the Île de la Cité, the *ville* on the right bank of the Seine, and the *université* on the left — while London has retained the City, the old medieval centre that now functions as its economic and commercial heart.

It is this continuing link between Middle Ages and the present day that makes the study of medieval towns and cities such an interesting, and difficult, subject. What should be studied is not a dead city but a city that has partly survived within a modern urban complex. Whereas a dead city, such as Pompeii, Ostia, Timgad or Priene, can be excavated and rebuilt with great precision, thanks to the specialised science of archaeology, which has been developed for that purpose over the last two hundred years, a living city such as Siena or San Gimignano cannot be cleared to make way for scientific research. Houses have been endlessly altered to suit the various needs of their inhabitants over the centuries, and nobody ever thought (except perhaps in the immediate past) of making a precise study of the buildings and streets in different towns. Often it is only the monuments (palaces, cathedrals) that people are aware of; during the last century entire medieval quarters have been demolished without anyone even bothering to take photographs or make drawings.

We therefore have to make use of more restricted and less certain documentation, but this can be compensated for by direct experience: for example, it is possible to walk through the Piazza del Campo in Siena, round Chartres Cathedral, down the streets of Perugia, Assisi or Orvieto and meet the descendants of the medieval inhabitants, who sometimes still live in the same houses and work in the same

Fig. 396   An area of the medieval countryside, with a farm and a fortified stronghold, as seen in a painting of the School of Ambrogio Lorenzetti in the Accademia di Belle Arti, Siena.

workshops as their ancestors.

The most obvious effect of the economic and political crisis that gripped Europe following the collapse of the Roman Empire was the decay of the cities and the dispersal of their inhabitants into the countryside, where they were able to live off the land.

The countryside was divided into large estates (5,000 hectares on average, but sometimes even larger), which contained hundreds of farms. At the centre was the owner's usual place of residence — a cathedral, an abbey, a castle — but the estates often spread far beyond the buildings' immediate surroundings, and each section would be controlled from the local manor (in France this was called a *cour*, in Italy, a *corte*, and in Germany, a *Hof*). It was round this building that the grainstores, the stables and the houses of the landowner's vassals and his personal administrator were sited. The land controlled by the manor was divided into three parts: the seigneur's private domain, the farming land

Figs 397–400 A coin of Charlemagne (double life-size). A capital from the ninth-century abbey of Fulda in Germany. A ground plan of Charlemagne's Palatine Chapel at Aachen (Aix-la-Chapelle), on a scale of 1:800; the original walls are outlined in black, while later additions are in white (cf. Fig. 369, which shows the Church of San Vitale in Ravenna).

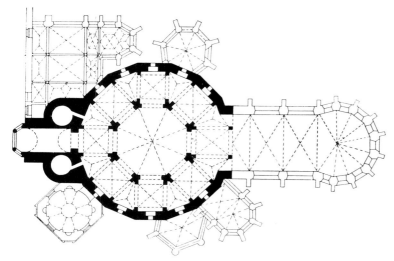

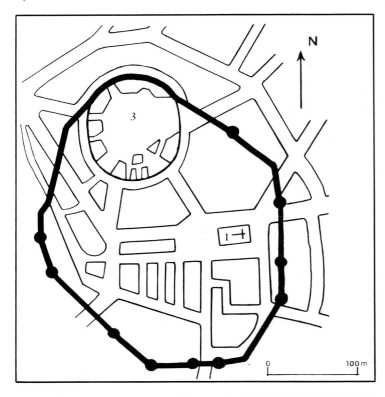

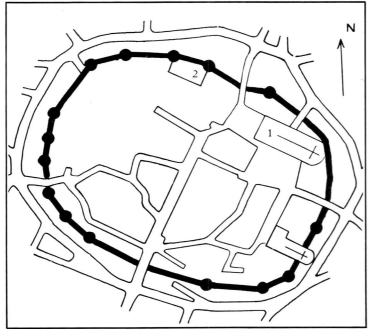

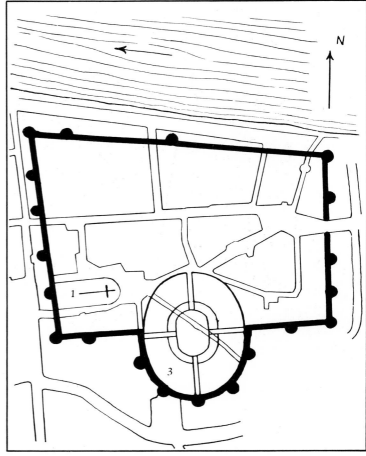

Figs 401–3   City walls of the third and fourth centuries AD in France: Périgueux, Senlis and Tours. They protected the central nucleus of the city, which contained the cathedral (1), the castle (2) and, in some cases, the amphitheatre (3).

shared by the serfs and the common land (woods, meadows and marshes), where everyone had the right to graze their livestock, gather wood and pick wild fruits and berries.

In this rural society, which formed the basis of feudal society, cities played a very secondary role: they no longer functioned as administrative centres, and they became less and less important as trading and manufacturing centres. The old Roman buildings which were still standing became places of refuge, and the great public monuments of antiquity (the baths, theatres and amphitheatres) were often transformed into fortresses. City walls were either fully

Fig. 404 The medieval city built in the amphitheatre at Arles.

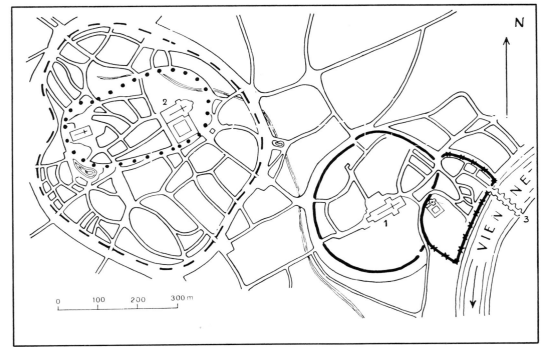

Fig. 405 The formation of the city of Limoges: the city founded in the fourth century around the cathedral (1); the suburb that grew up around the church of St Martial (2), with the tenth-century ramparts marked by a dotted line and the thirteenth-century ones by a series of dashes; to the east of the city, the suburb with a bridge over the river Vienne (3).

maintained or reduced so as to protect a very limited part of the city and surround only the most important strongholds. Churches were often built outside the walls near the tombs of the saints, who, according to Roman law, could not be buried within the city, and even the earliest episcopal residences were built outside the city walls (Figs 401–5).

At the same time as the jurisdictional differences between the city and the country were disappearing, the actual physical differences between the two were also being eroded. There was a great similarity between the way in which small, impoverished urban communities continued to exist in the middle of Roman cities that had become far too large for them, and the way in which villages sprang up in the countryside on sites that were naturally favoured, such as the point where two rivers meet or the top of a hill.

In both cases the most remarkable feature of the buildings is their spontaneity, their individuality and their infinite variety. These characteristics resulted not only from a lack of resources, a scarcity of skilled artisans, the absence of any organised artistic culture and the pressing need for defence and survival, but also from a new spirit of freedom and confidence. The new settlements fitted easily into the natural environment of the countryside and the man-made environment of the ruined cities; they did not follow any preconceived plan, and they adapted as well to the uneven contours of the terrain as to the regular patterns of Roman building. The final result was that they eradicated the difference between nature and geometry by gradually breaking down the linear precision of the ancient buildings and roads with small additions and variations, and by shaping the formless elements of the countryside by emphasising the outlines of hills, inlets and rivers.

The monumental buildings of the period also share the same characteristics, in that they were freely adapted from Roman and Byzantine models, and many works of figurative art seem coarse because the people who made them were not concerned with the traditional criteria of aesthetic perfection or visual pleasure (Figs 397–8, 406).

And so one of the fundamental characteristics of the urban scene was established: one that was to survive even subsequent developments.

Fig. 406   Twelfth-century ivory statuette of the Madonna and Child (Museo Nazionale, Florence).

5
The cities of Islam

While medieval culture and civilisation were still developing in Europe, in the Mediterranean world Islamic civilisation was already firmly established.

The Arabs had overrun almost all the coastal areas of the southern Mediterranean by the end of the seventh century. The first regions they encountered were the urbanised ones of the Hellenistic East, whose cities (Alexandria, Antioch, Damascus, Jerusalem) they took over and adapted for their own purposes; Damascus, for example, became the first capital of the Ummayad Caliphate (660–750 AD), and a mosque was erected in the city's sacred area (Figs 407–9).

When they subsequently made further conquests in the East and the West, the Arabs built their own cities: Kairouan, founded in Tunisia in 670, Shiraz in Persia in 674, Baghdad — the new capital of the Abbasid caliphs — in Mesopotamia in 762, Fez in Morocco in 808, and Cairo in Egypt in 969. When they crossed over into Spain (711 AD) and Sicily (827 AD), they chose Cordoba and Palermo as the respective capitals, both of which were transformed from cities of secondary importance into major centres of population with inhabitants numbered in hundreds of thousands.

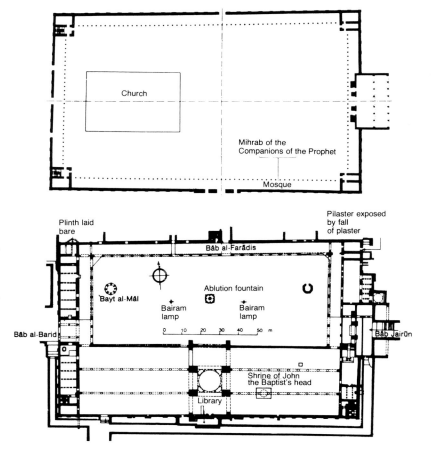

Figs 407–8   The Great Mosque in Damascus: the original site, which contained both the mosque and a church, and the sanctuary built after 705 AD.

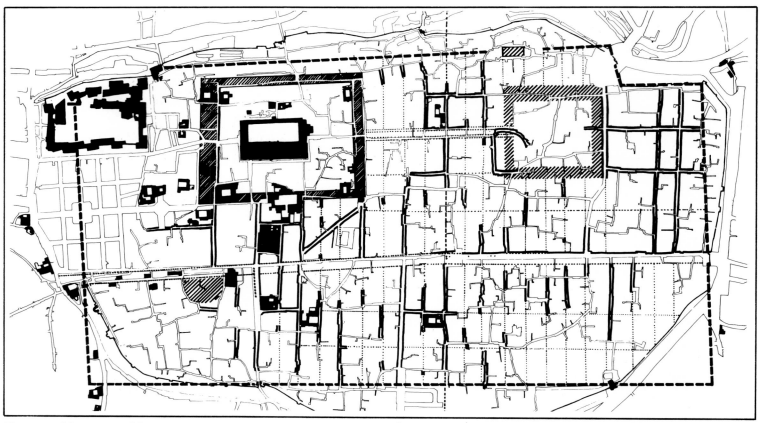

Fig. 409   The centre of Damascus, with the Great Mosque; the outline of the Arab city overlays the Hippodamian scheme of the Hellenistic city, destroying its geometricality. The monuments of the Arab city are in black, while those of the Hellenistic city are represented by the hatched areas.

The cities founded or transformed by the Arabs stretch from the Atlantic Ocean to the Indian sub-continent, and they share today the same similarities of composition as when they were first conceived. They retained one of the fundamental characteristics of the ancient city, which we have already discussed: namely, the way in which all the structural elements — the houses, the palaces, the public buildings — form a series of separate, inward-looking precincts. The squares (forums, agoras, market places) represented the largest enclosed areas, and did not form part of the system of streets, which were merely passageways scarcely large enough for pedestrians and carts to negotiate (the large porticoed streets of the Hellenistic cities were exceptional constructions, comparable to elongated squares). Apart from this inherited characteristic, there were certain radical differences between the cities of Islam and their predecessors.

1. The simplicity of their new cultural code, contained in the pages of the Koran, resulted in a reduction in social activity. Because of this, the Arab cities lacked the complexity of their Roman and Hellenistic counterparts: they had no forums, basilicas, theatres, amphitheatres, stadiums or gymnasiums, only private dwellings (ordinary houses, or palaces) and two categories of public building:

  (a) Baths for personal ablutions, the equivalent of the ancient *thermae*;

  (b) Mosques, for public worship, which had no classical counterpart. They were unlike either pagan temples (buildings that were closed to the public, and could only be looked at from the outside) or Christian churches (enclosed buildings, in which the faithful participated in a collective ceremony), and were composed of porticoed courtyards, with one portico that was deeper than the others and divided by a large number of rows of pillars, where the faithful gathered to pray either singly or in groups.

2. The widespread regimentation of the Hellenistic and Roman cities was abandoned, and there was not even a municipal administration to enforce the rules. Islam emphasised the private and secret nature of family life. The houses were almost invariably built on one level, and the cities grew into conglomerations of houses, whose exteriors gave no hint of their shape or their importance. The streets

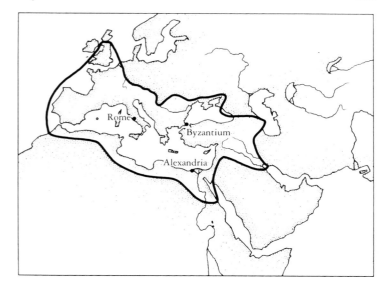

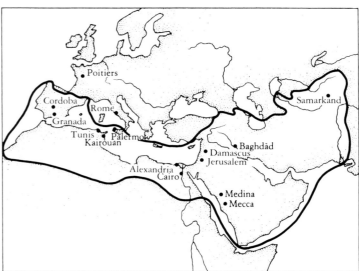

Figs 410–11 The Roman Empire, which embraced the whole Mediterranean area, and the territory conquered by the Arabs which divided the Mediterranean into two parts.

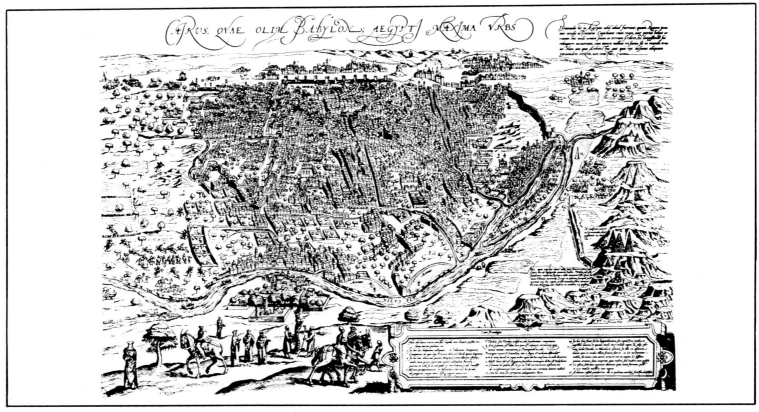

Fig. 412   Ancient view of Cairo, looking northwards. On the western bank of the Nile can be seen the Pyramids.

were narrow (7 feet wide) and formed a labyrinth of twisting alleyways which were often covered. These led to the doors of the houses, but did not give any real idea of the overall nature or dimensions of the quarter. Another feature was that the merchants' shops were not grouped in a square, but lined up along a series of streets, either covered or uncovered, which formed the bazaar, and the contrast between this irregularity and the strict geometricality of the great open courtyards in front of the mosques, made the latter seem even more impressive.

3. The cities became increasingly compact, enclosed by one or two walls which divided them up into various areas, the innermost one being called the *medina*. Each ethnic or religious group had its own quarter, and the local ruler would live in an outlying area (the *makhzan*) which was protected from any riots or unrest. The entrance gate (the *bab*) was often a monumental and intricate structure, with an outer gate, one or more intermediary courtyards, and an inner gate, and it acted as a meeting place for people entering and leaving the city. In fact, the inner gate led

Fig. 413   The Casbah in Algiers, as seen in a relief model made by the French in 1830, the year in which they conquered the country.

straight into the street system, whose narrowness precluded such gatherings.

4. The *Hadith* (or Traditions of the Prophet) prohibited the representation of the human form and this halted the development of figurative arts in the classical sense; instead, a system of abstract decoration was developed, based on geometrical figures and the Arabic script, and closely integrated with their architecture. These decorative motifs spread throughout the Islamic world, with remarkably few variations (Figs 450–1).

As a result of these characteristics, the cities of Islam bore a greater resemblance to the pre-Hellenistic cities of the East (Ur, for example, the first city illustrated in this book). The Muslims interrupted the colonisation of the Near East by the Greeks and Romans and gave new life to the much more ancient civilisations that had started in the area some four thousand years earlier. Between the eighth and twelfth centuries this region became, once more, the civilised heart of the ancient continent that lies at the crossroads of Asia, Europe and Africa.

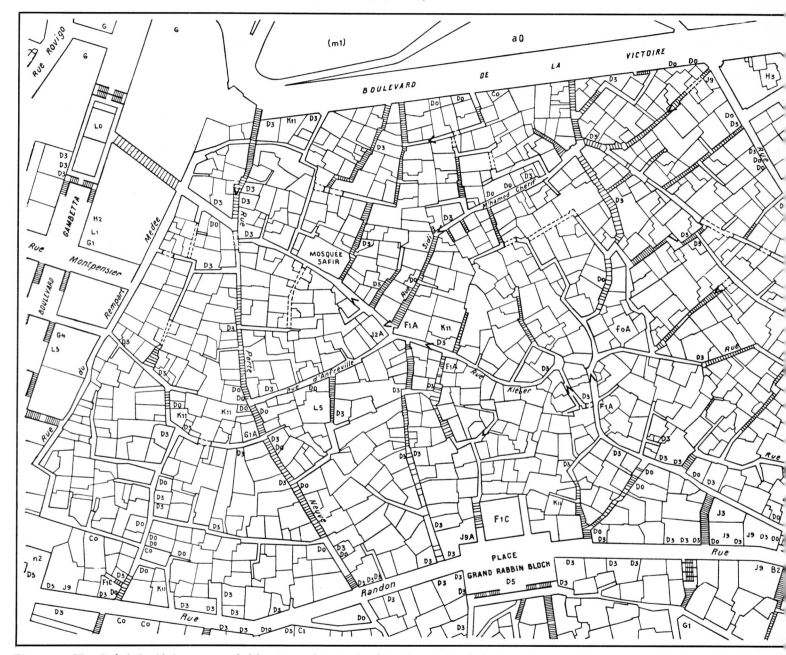

Fig. 414   The Casbah in Algiers surrounded by the modern roads of the Europeanised city.

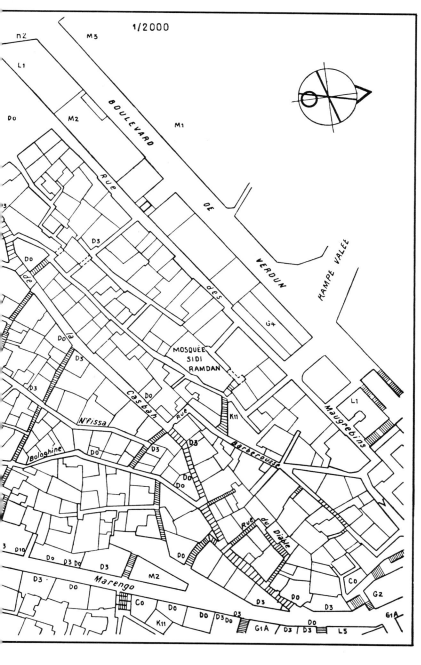

1/2000

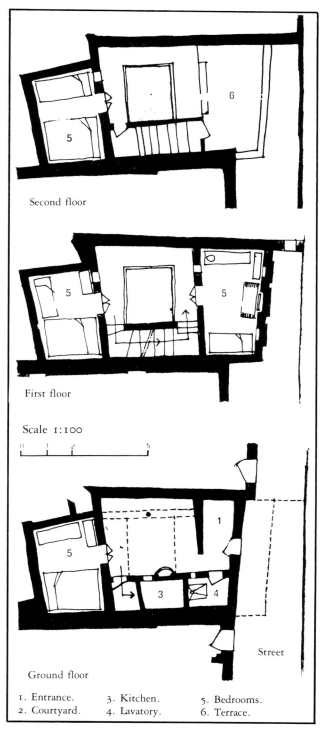

Second floor

First floor

Scale 1:100

0   1   2   5

Ground floor

Figs 415-17   Plans of a house in the Casbah (5 rue Kherredin):

1. Entrance.   3. Kitchen.   5. Bedrooms.
2. Courtyard.   4. Lavatory.   6. Terrace.

Fig. 418   Aerial view of the townscape of Tripoli; each house has its own private courtyard, whether large or small, on to which it faces.

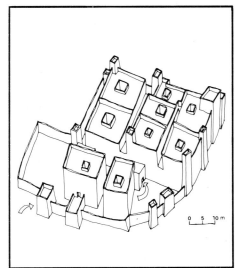

Figs 419–20   The central courtyard becomes narrow and deep in isolated buildings such as the Moroccan *Ksar*.

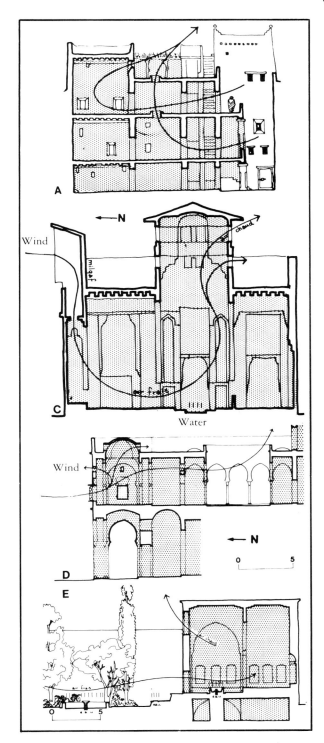

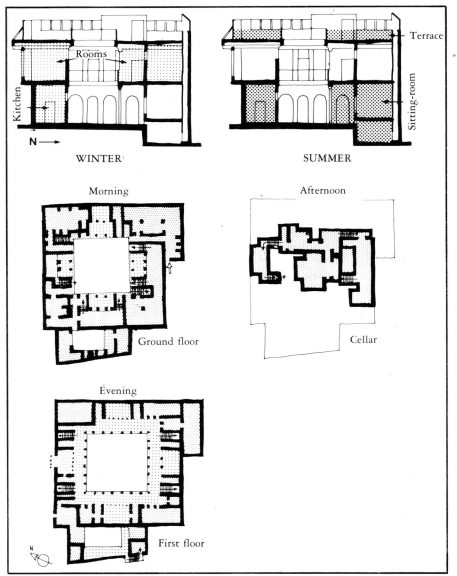

Figs 421–5   The rooms are distributed round the courtyard so as to allow them to be used for different purposes, depending on the time of the day or the season of the year; these particular drawings are of a house in Baghdad.

Figs 426–9   The arrangements of courtyards, rooms and covered porticoes on different levels allows the air to circulate and counteract the effects of the heat; the examples shown here are typical of the houses found near areas of desert from Morocco to Afghanistan.

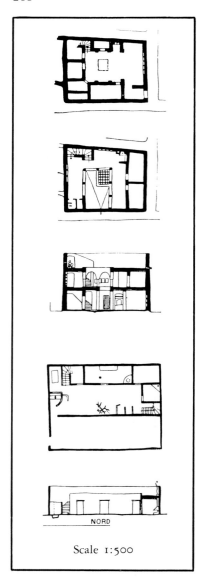

Scale 1:500

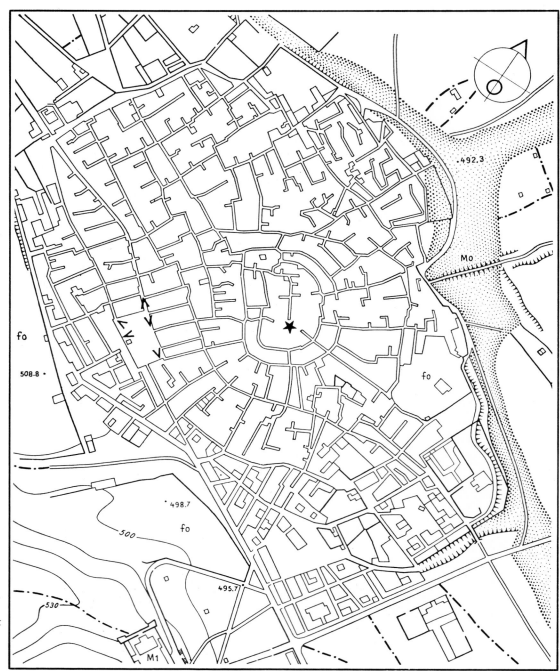

Figs 430–6   The city of Ghardaia in
Algeria, founded in 1035: plan;
drawings of two types of houses, on
two floors and on one; aerial view. At
the centre of the plan, in the place
marked by a star, there is a mosque
with a tall minaret.

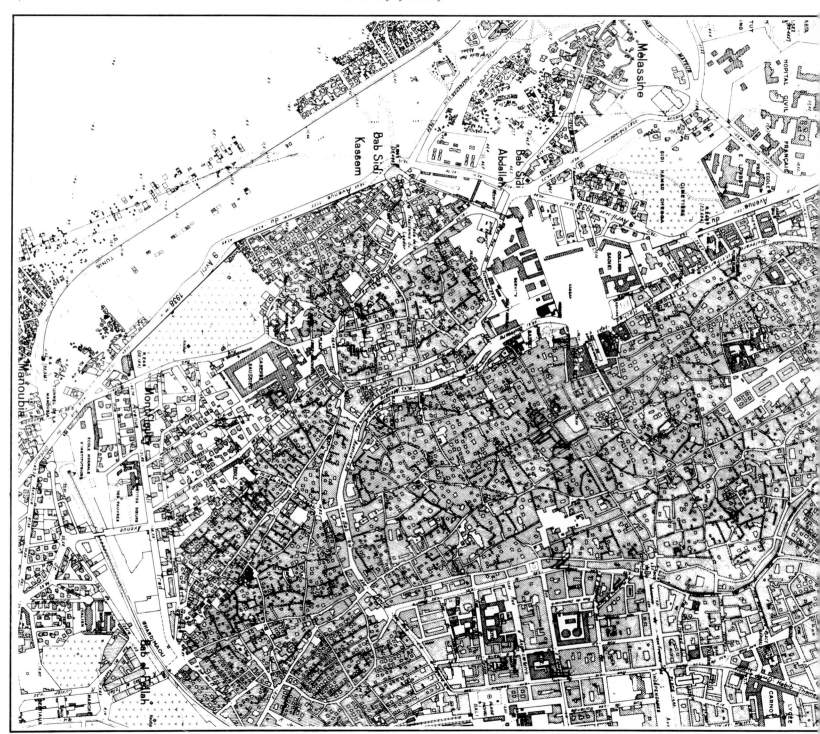

Fig. 437   Plan of the Arab city of Tunis, surrounded by the areas inhabited by French settlers (scale 1:100,000).

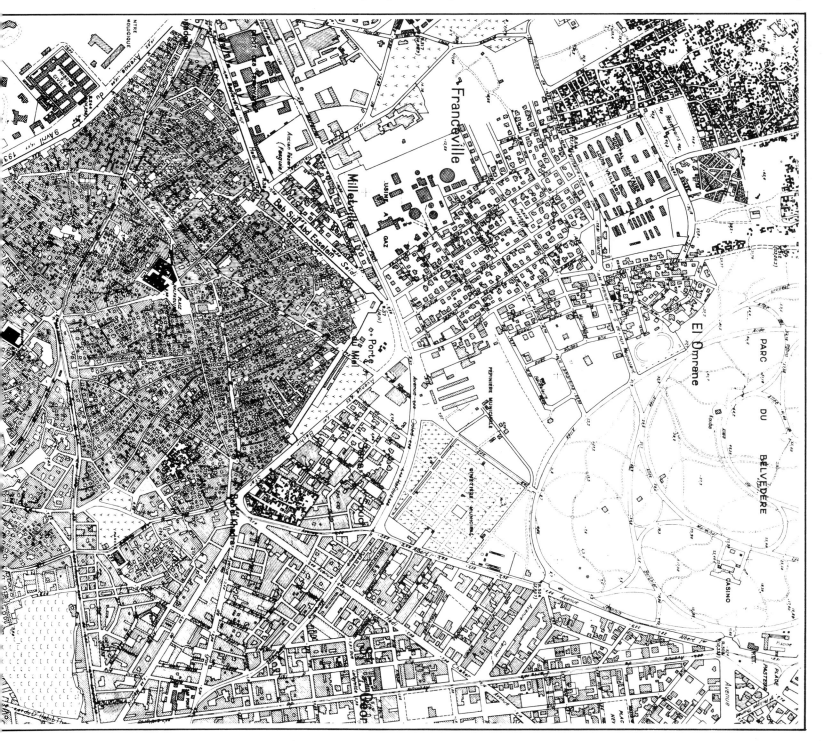

During this period, the Arab cities became the largest and richest in the world. Baghdad, which was founded in 762 according to a very ambitious circular urban plan, with a diameter of more than $2\frac{1}{2}$ kilometres, had more than a million inhabitants and was for a long time the main cultural and commercial centre of the world. In 1258 it was destroyed by the Mongols, and, although it was rebuilt on the same site, the original circular plan was not adhered to. The capitals of the peripheral states in the West and the East were only a little less grandiose and impressive. Cordoba, in Spain (Figs 440–3), and Palermo, in Sicily (Figs 452–3), had hundreds of thousands of inhabitants, who lived in vast areas full of gardens and orchards, but both cities went into a rapid decline following their reconquest by the Christians. The capitals of the eastern states, however, Isfahan and Shiraz in Persia, and Agra and Delhi in India, retained their importance and their large populations right up into modern times. During the sixteenth, seventeenth and eighteenth centuries they were remodelled architecturally, as well as being laid out on different lines in accordance with the new fashion for large-scale geometricality, rather in the same way that the baroque capitals of Europe were redesigned.

Isfahan (Figs 454–8) was chosen as the new capital of Persia by Shah Abbas I (1599–1627). The old medieval city, centred on the Friday Mosque, was expanded westwards and southwards by means of a series of symmetrical constructions: the great Meidan-i-Shah square, the royal mosque, a rectilinear avenue surrounded by gardens, and two covered bridges. These new landmarks stood out in the cityscape, not because of their great size, but because of their strict geometrical shapes: a powerful expression of man's ability to control the environment, as at Versailles.

European travellers, ranging from the Crusaders who overran the Arab cities of the eastern Mediterranean to the merchants and ambassadors who visited the farthest flung courts of the East up until the eighteenth century, all marvelled at these magnificent cities, which fired the imagination of Europe and became the source of endless stories.

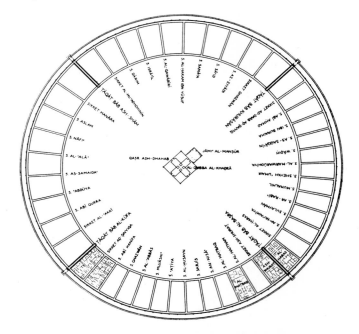

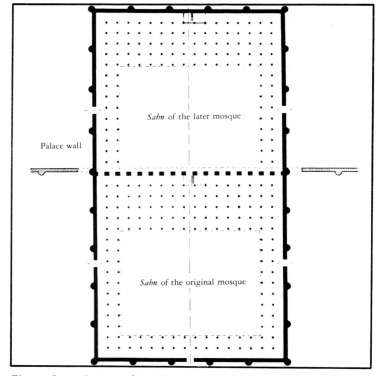

Figs 438–9   Layout of the circular city of Baghdad, planned and initiated by the Caliph al-Mansur in 762 AD. Plan of the Great Mosque in Baghdad.

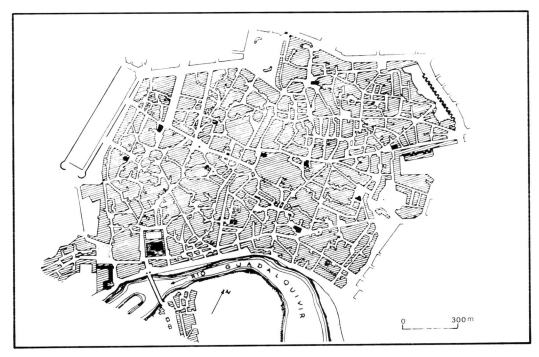

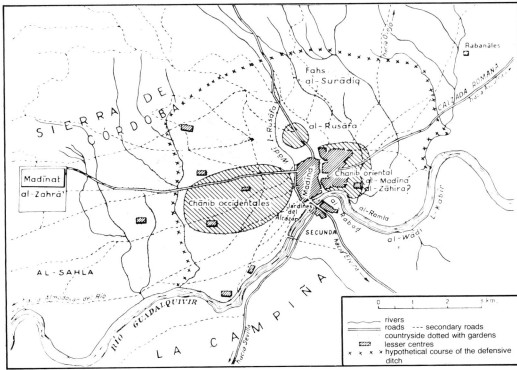

Figs 440–1 Cordoba, capital of the Moorish Kingdom in Spain: plan of the central nucleus. General layout: outside the city is the great palace of Madinat-al-Zahra, residence of the Caliph Abd-al-Rahman.

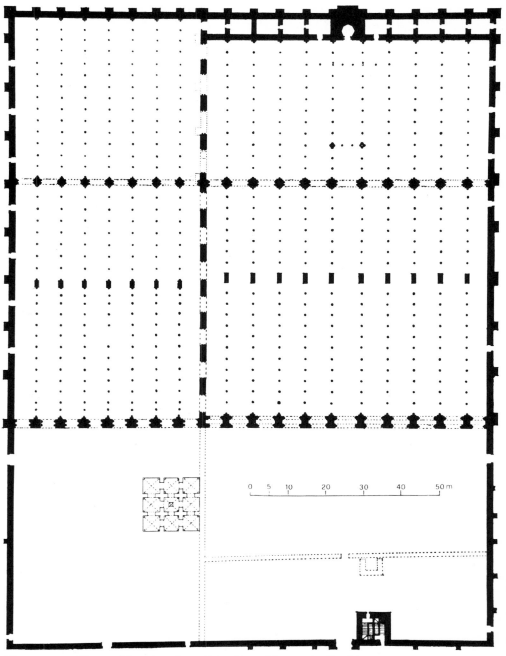

Figs 442–3   Plan and interior view of the Great Mosque in Cordoba.

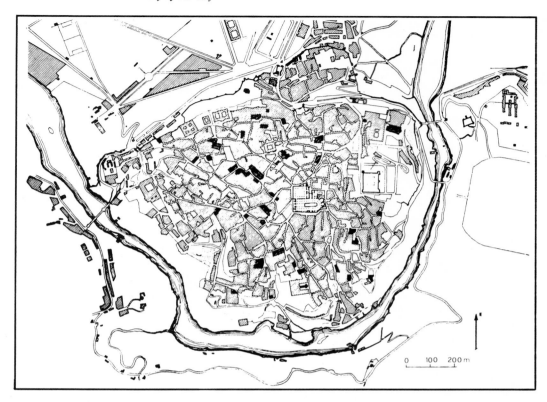

Figs 444–5   Plan and view of the Spanish city of Toledo, founded by the Moors; the cathedral stands on the site of the former mosque.

Fig. 446   The houses of the Moorish quarter in Seville, seen from the tower of the cathedral.

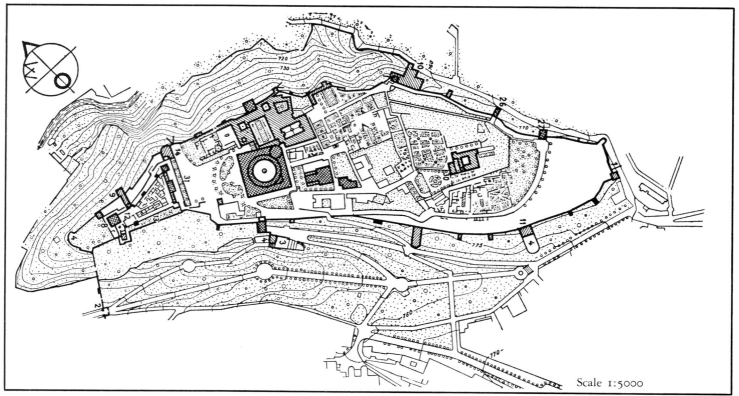

Scale 1:5000

Figs 447–8   View of the city of Granada, in Spain, and a plan of the citadel containing the palace of the Moorish kings (the Alhambra).

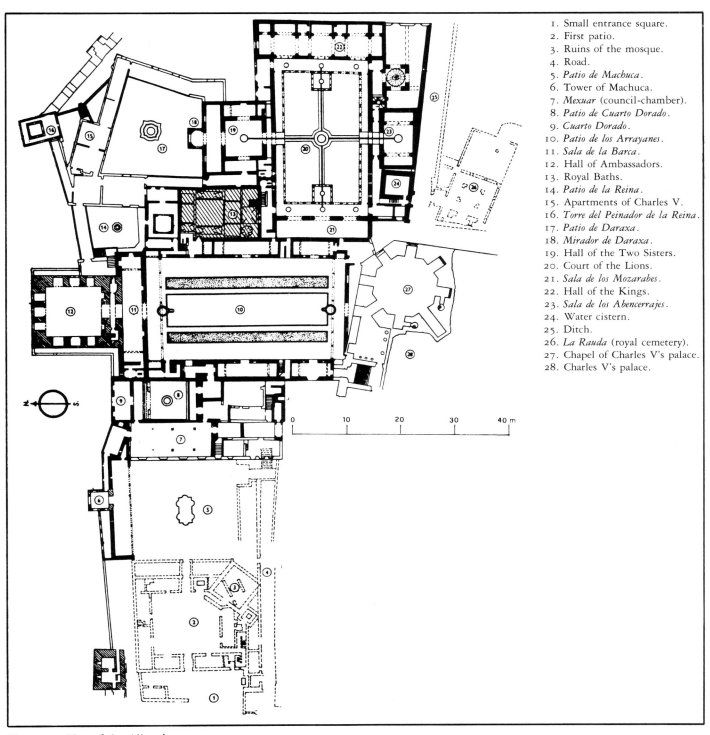

1. Small entrance square.
2. First patio.
3. Ruins of the mosque.
4. Road.
5. *Patio de Machuca*.
6. Tower of Machuca.
7. *Mexuar* (council-chamber).
8. *Patio de Cuarto Dorado*.
9. *Cuarto Dorado*.
10. *Patio de los Arrayanes*.
11. *Sala de la Barca*.
12. Hall of Ambassadors.
13. Royal Baths.
14. *Patio de la Reina*.
15. Apartments of Charles V.
16. *Torre del Peinador de la Reina*.
17. *Patio de Daraxa*.
18. *Mirador de Daraxa*.
19. Hall of the Two Sisters.
20. Court of the Lions.
21. *Sala de los Mozarabes*.
22. Hall of the Kings.
23. *Sala de los Abencerrajes*.
24. Water cistern.
25. Ditch.
26. *La Rauda* (royal cemetery).
27. Chapel of Charles V's palace.
28. Charles V's palace.

Fig. 449   Plan of the Alhambra.

Figs 450–1   Decorations in carved stone and in inlaid tile-work from the Alhambra palace.

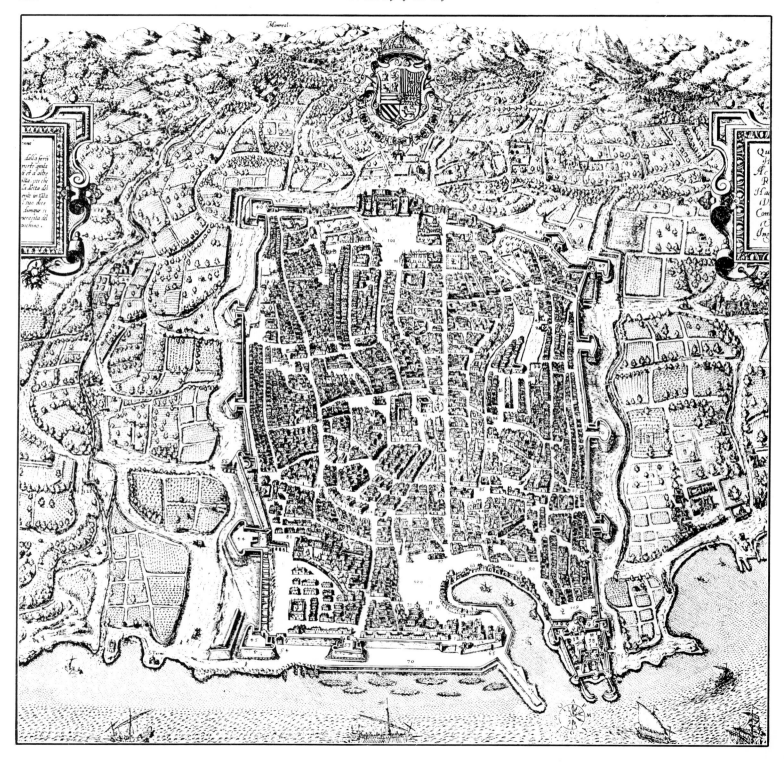

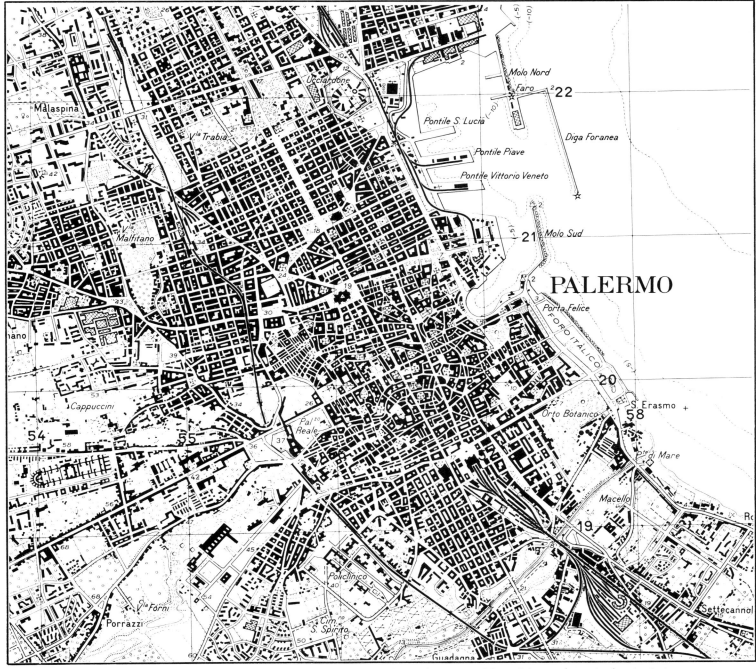

Figs 452–3   Palermo. Bird's eye view of the city, from the end of the sixteenth century. Map of the modern city by the Istituto Geografico Militare (scale 1:25,000). The winding streets of the Arab town can be clearly seen, cut across by the straight Spanish streets and surrounded by the square blocks of the modern quarters.

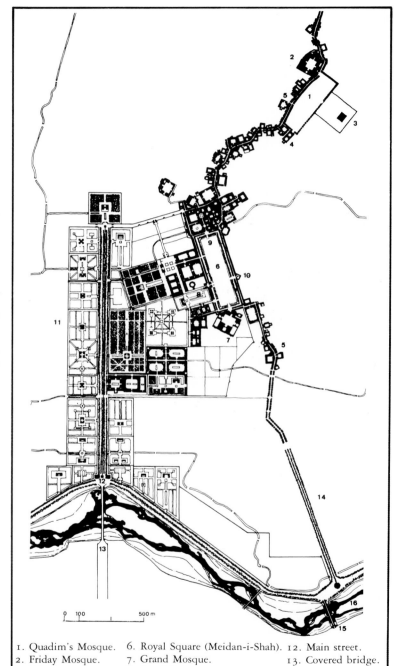

Figs 454–6   Isfahan: general view; plan of the alterations made by Shah Abbas I at the beginning of the seventeenth century; view of the Meidan-i-Shah and the Grand Mosque. (Eighteenth-century European engravings.)

1. Quadim's Mosque.	6. Royal Square (Meidan-i-Shah).	12. Main street.
2. Friday Mosque.	7. Grand Mosque.	13. Covered bridge.
3. Palace.	8. Royal Palace.	14. Secondary street.
4. Ali's Mosque.	9. Bazaar Gate.	15. Covered bridge.
5. Bazaar.	10. Sheikh Luftallah's Mosque.	16. River Zaindeh.
	11. Vizier's gardens.	

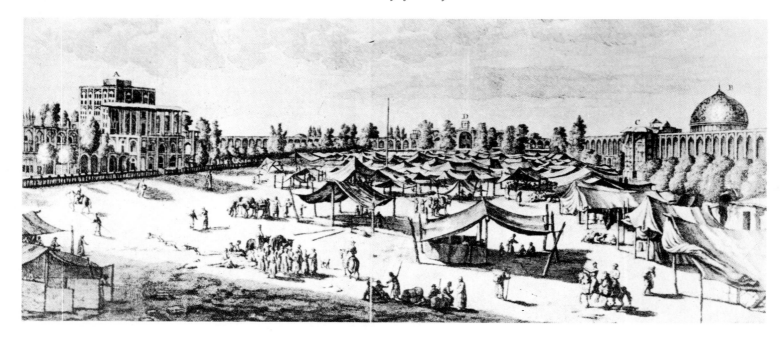

Figs 457–8   The Meidan-i-Shah and one of Isfahan's covered bridges. (Eighteenth-century European engravings.)

6
European cities in the Middle Ages

At the end of the tenth century Europe began to undergo an economic renaissance. The population increased (from approximately 22 million in 950 to some 55 million in 1350), agricultural output rose, and industry and commerce once more began to play an important economic role.

Historians have revealed a number of interrelated reasons for this phenomenon:

the settlement of the last invaders, the Arabs, Vikings and Hungarians;
new techniques in agriculture: the triennial rotation of fields, improved methods of yoking horses and oxen, the spread of water mills;
the influence of the maritime cities (Venice, Genoa, Pisa, Amalfi), which had retained their international trading activities in the Mediterranean and now began to stimulate the development of other cities as commercial cities.

This transformation radically altered the nature of urban and rural settlements, both of which we will deal with separately in the next two sections.

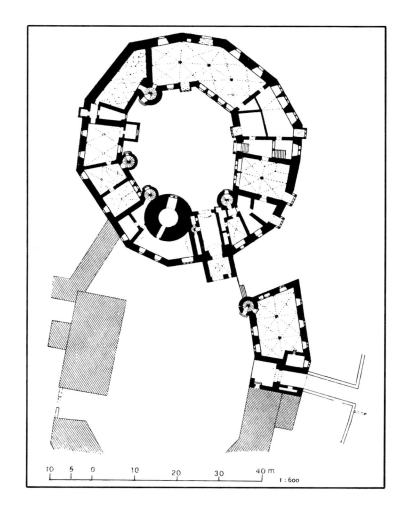

Fig. 459 Plan of the castle of Budingen in Germany. The ring shape, adopted for defensive reasons, became the original model for medieval cities.

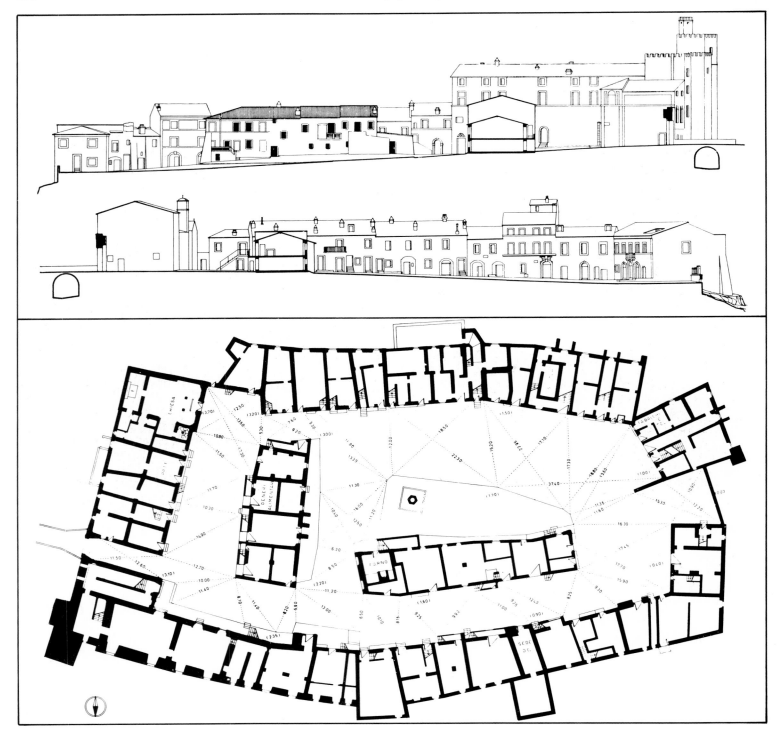

Figs 460–3   Sections, plan and internal view of San Vittorino near Rome: a village built during the early Middle Ages, whose layout
has remained virtually unchanged, despite the fact that the houses have been renewed on several occasions. Even today, the only entrance
is by means of a stone bridge that crosses the moat in the eastern corner (left on the plan) and which was originally a drawbridge. There
is even still an exit for use in emergencies (above left, next to the façade of the church), which leads to a path down the ravine to the
south of the village.

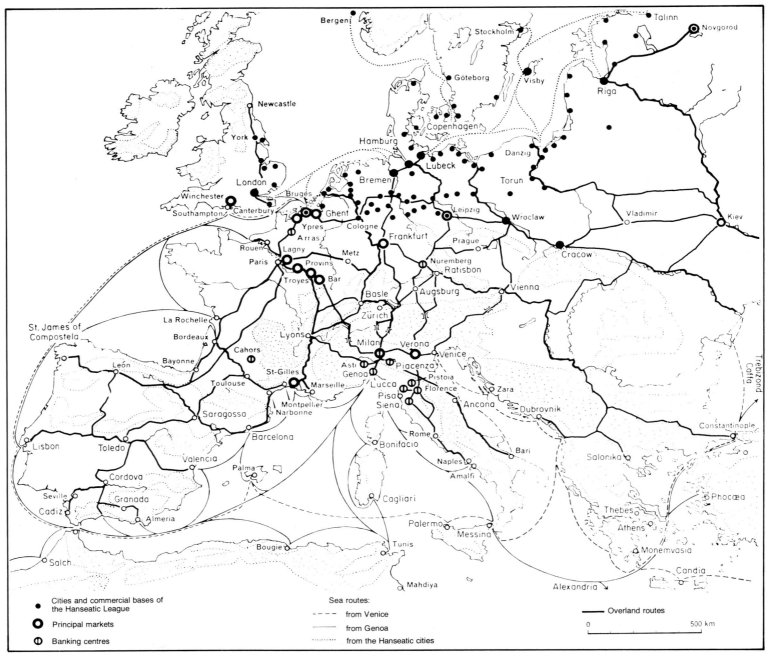

Fig. 464   Map of early medieval Europe; the dotted areas represent mountainous country.

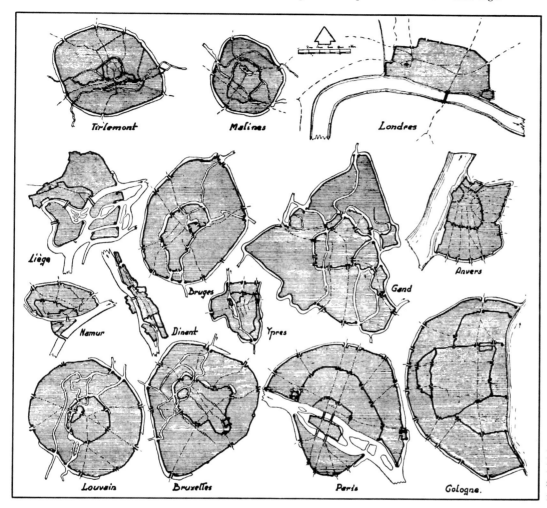

Tirlemont

Malines

Londres

Liège

Namur

Dinant

Bruges

Ypres

Gand

Anvers

Louvain

Bruxelles

Paris

Cologne.

Fig. 465   Seal of the merchants of the Hanseatic League in Novgorod.

Fig. 466   Plans of fourteen northern European cities, showing the succession of walls built up until the fourteenth century.

1. *The development of the city-state*

Some of the new population, unable to find work in the country, gathered in the cities, which explains the growth in the number of artisans and traders who lived on the fringes of the feudal organisation.

The fortified cities of the early Middle Ages, sometimes called burgs (from the medieval latin *burgus*), were too small to accommodate this increased population. As a result, new settlements sprang up outside the city gates, called suburbs, which soon became larger than the original urban nucleus. It became necessary, therefore, to build new walls to protect these suburbs and the other establishments (churches, abbeys, castles) that had grown up outside the old city, and this process of expansion often continued until some cities possessed several sets of walls.

The traders and artisans who inhabited these cities — the burgesses (*bourgeois*) — were in the majority from the very beginning. They therefore began to try and free themselves from the feudal political system and obtain conditions that would favour their own economic activities: freedom of the individual, judicial autonomy, administrative independence, and personal taxation proportionally related to income, the revenue from which could be used to finance works in the public interest (particularly defensive measures, such as walls and armaments).

This new movement, which originally started out as an association of private individuals, subsequently came into conflict with the bishops and feudal princes and grew into an organised political force. This was the origin of the Italian *comune*, a state with its own legislature, which had the power to overrule both groups and individuals, but which still respected their economic privileges.

The instruments of city government were as follows:

1. A main council, composed of representatives from the most important families;
2. A secondary council, which functioned as an executive body;
3. A certain number of magistrates, who were either elected or chosen by lot: in France they were called *jures*, in Italy *consoli*, in Flanders *échevins*.

These bodies were opposed by other associations that represented special sections of the community: the trade corporations, for example, known in England as guilds and in Italy and Germany as *arti* and *Zünfte* respectively, and the representatives of the soldiery, who elected their own magistrate, known in Italy as *il capitano del popolo*. In addition to the civil authorities, there were also the Church authorities, represented by the bishops and the monastic orders, who also had their seat in the city. In some parts of Italy there were also a chief magistrate, called the *podestà*, whose function was to arbitrate in case of political disagreement between the administration and the citizenry.

The medieval city-state depended on the countryside for its food supply and it always controlled a large area of land, the size of which varied according to the needs of the city.

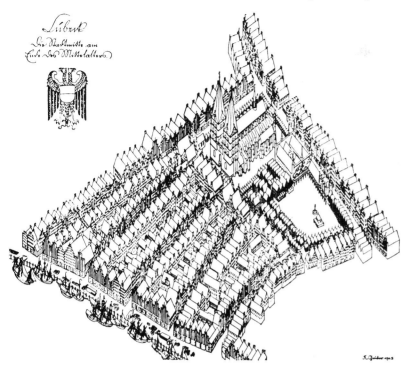

Figs 467–8 Lübeck, the capital of the Hanseatic League. Aerial view and reconstruction of the central area containing the market place.

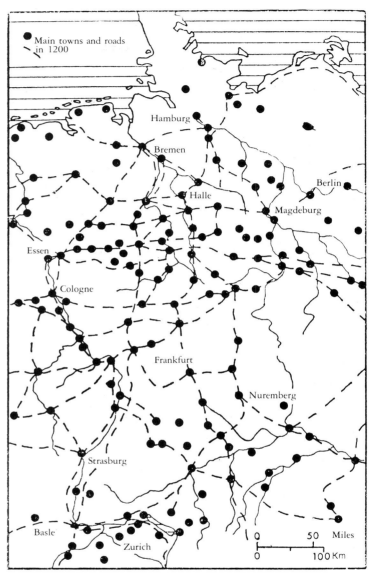

Fig. 469 The network of roads joining up the cities of Germany at the start of the thirteenth century.

Unlike the Greek city, however, it did not grant equal rights to its rural inhabitants; it remained a closed city, whose economic and political activities could equally well be on an international scale as on a national one, but whose politics were oriented to coincide with the restricted interests of the urban population. This population, however, was not a homogeneous one, which could take communal decisions like those taken in the democratic cities of Greece. The ruling class, represented in the councils, gradually expanded, but it never grew to include the manual workers, and when the latter attempted to seize power in Italy during the economic crisis in the second part of the fourteenth century, they were routed and the government fell into the hands of groups of aristocratic families, or sometimes a single family: the *comune*, a relatively democratic institution, had become a *signoria* (seigneury).

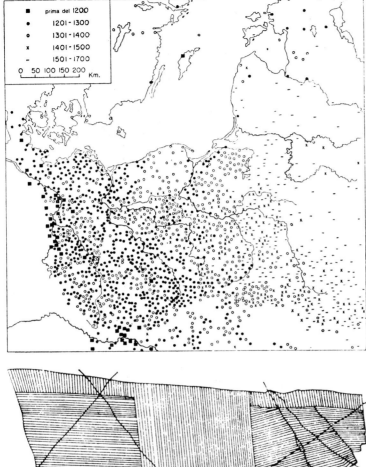

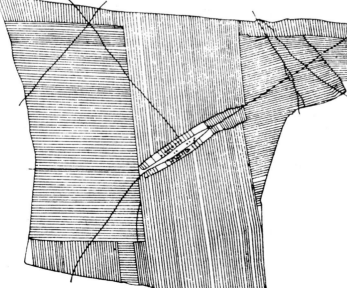

2. *The colonisation of the countryside*

The growth of the cities meant that the rural areas began to change at an ever increasing rate. The mercantile cities imported foodstuffs and raw materials, while at the same time exporting industrial and commercial goods, and the countryside, because of the reciprocal nature of this trade and because of the growth in population, was forced to raise its levels of agricultural production by putting new land under cultivation and by using the existent land more efficiently.

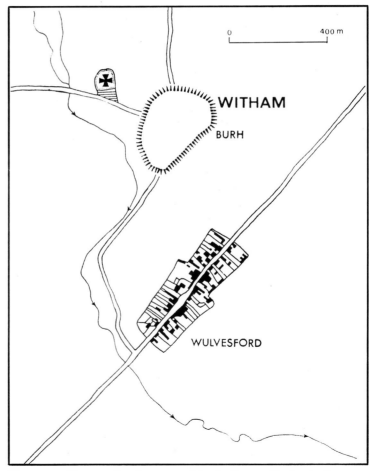

Figs 470–1   European colonisation on the eastern bank of the Elbe: map showing the concentration of settlements, and plan of a planned village, surrounded by its farming land.

Fig. 472   Two medieval communities in Essex: the Anglo-Saxon *burh* of Witham, with its church protecting a small market, and the late medieval town of Wulvesford, built along a Roman road.

The old manorial system, based on the idea of economic self-sufficiency, was not able to cope with this new state of affairs and it began to disintegrate; until that time the villages had only produced enough food for themselves, as well as producing all their own equipment. The manorial villages now found themselves employing a growing number of freedmen, who came from outside the district, and the feudal lords began to establish new settlements for them on land that had not already been reclaimed for agricultural purposes.

Although these new towns were founded by the feudal lords, they were not organised along traditional lines: they guaranteed the individual freedom of the workers, they had self-government and were administered by a magistrate who was almost always elected by the inhabitants themselves. Also, despite the fact that they remained subject to feudal law, both politically and juridically, they copied the municipal organisation of the city-state.

Other new towns were founded on the fringes of Europe for a variety of economic and political reasons:

1. The *bastides* of southern France, erected by the English and French barons and kings during the Hundred Years War;
2. The *poblaciones* of Spain, built in the regions captured by the Christians from the Moors;
3. The settlements founded in eastern Germany in the areas captured from the Slavs by the Teutonic Knights (Fig. 470).

The development of the city-state and the foundation of new towns in country areas was brought to a halt in the mid-fourteenth century by an abrupt decline in population levels, and by the resultant slowing down of economic activity. This drop in population was caused by the Black Death, and particularly by the Great Plague of 1348–9, whose effects were felt in every aspect of city life.

Figs 473–4   Growth of the town of Hereford. In the tenth century the houses were built around a wide road, which contains a number of temporary structures; surrounding them were the common agricultural and grazing lands. In the twelfth century the houses grew larger, and a stockade was built around the inhabited areas; the grazing land, now partially occupied by a church and a castle, was extended to the other side of the river, while a bridge took the place of the old ford.

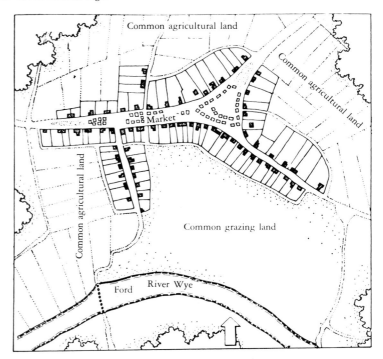

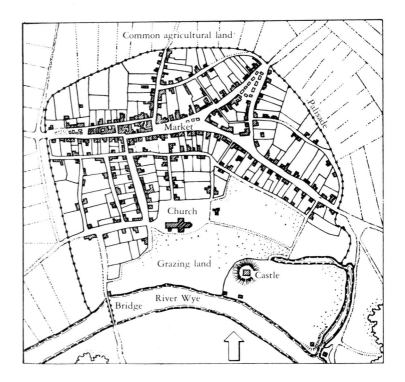

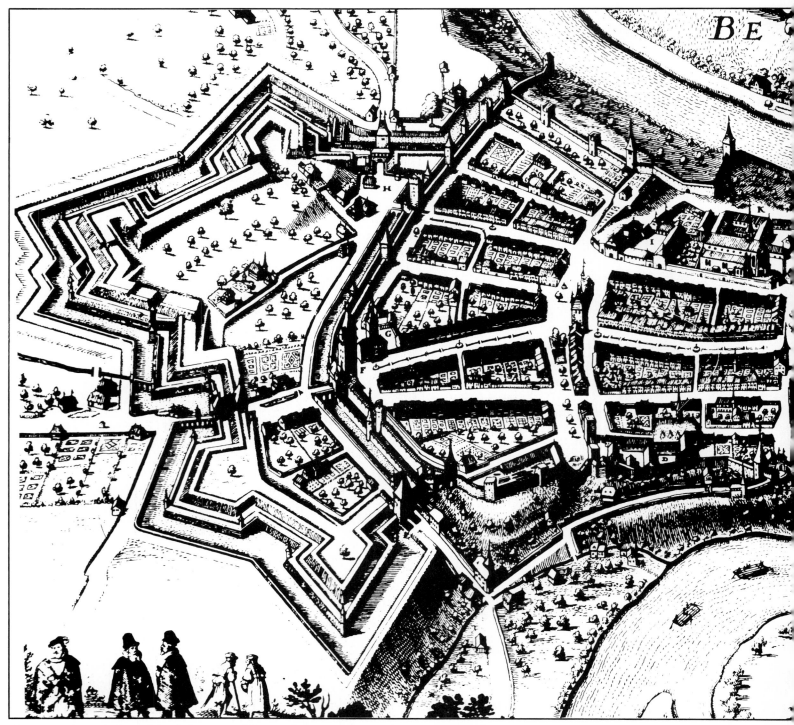

Fig. 475   General view of the Swiss town of Berne, from an engraving by M. Merian (1654).

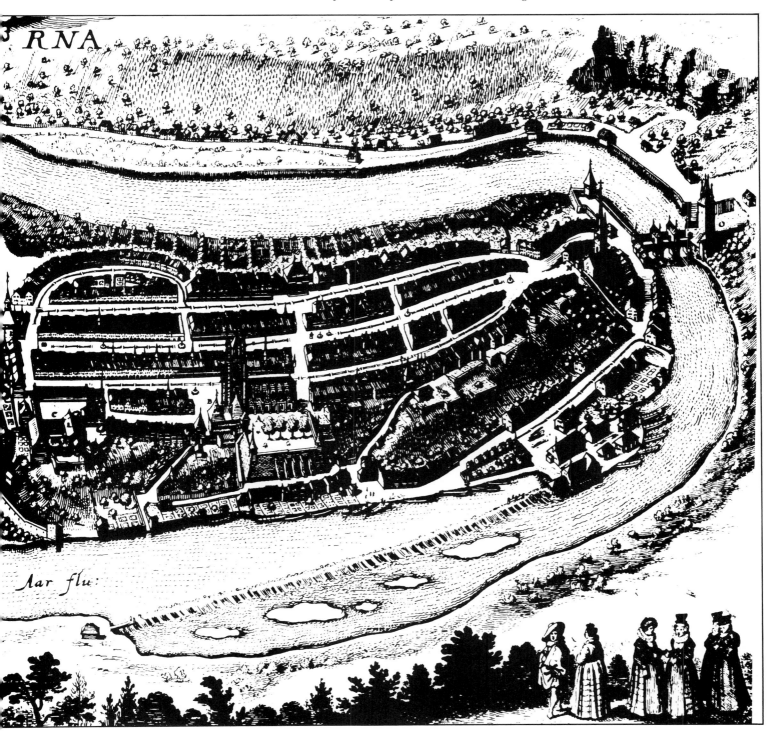

RNA

Aar flu:

Fig. 476   Relief model of the city of Ypres in Flanders; the two squares are dominated by the cathedral and the Hall of the Clothmakers' Guild.

Fig. 477 View of the central square in Bremen (the *Markt*): on the left, the merchants' palace, on the right, the municipal offices, in the background, the guildhalls. From an engraving by M. Merian (1653).

Figs 478–9   The medieval townscape, as seen in two paintings by Ambrogio Lorenzetti and Simone Martini, now in Siena.

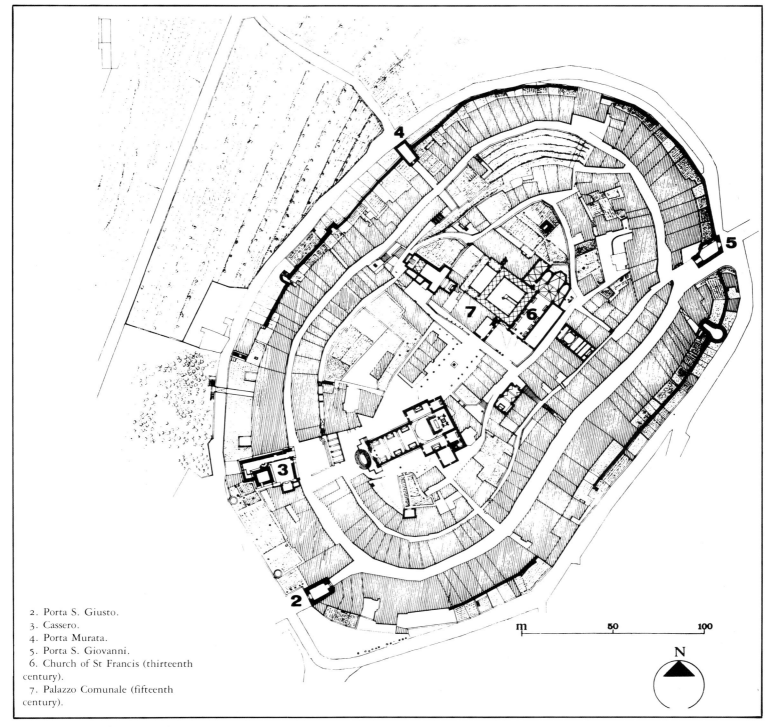

2. Porta S. Giusto.
3. Cassero.
4. Porta Murata.
5. Porta S. Giovanni.
6. Church of St Francis (thirteenth century).
7. Palazzo Comunale (fifteenth century).

Fig. 480   Plan of the city of Lucignano in Val di Chiana.

Figs 481–2   Aerial view and plan of the city of San Gimignano in Tuscany.

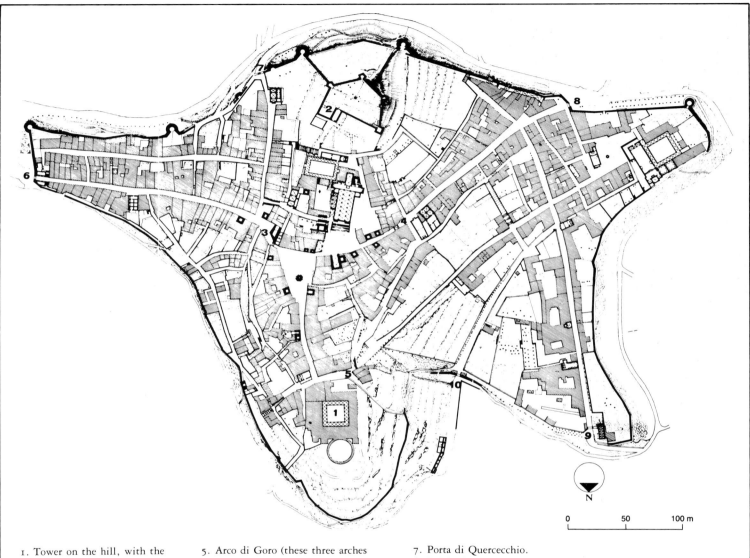

1. Tower on the hill, with the Bishop's Palace.
2. Rocca.
3. Becci Arch.
4. St Matthew's Arch.

5. Arco di Goro (these three arches form part of the original tenth-century walls).
6. St John's Gate.

7. Porta di Quercecchio.
8. St Matthew's Gate.
9. St Jacob's Gate.
10. Porta delle Fonti.

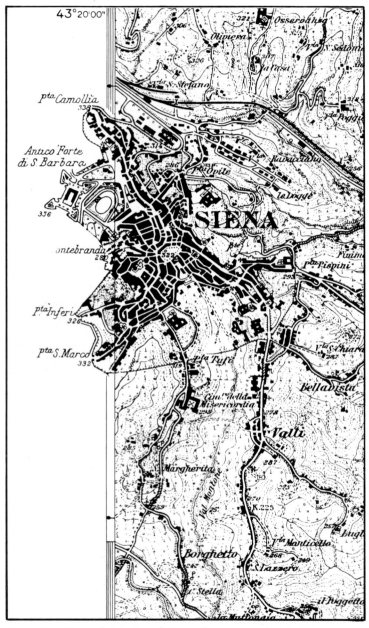

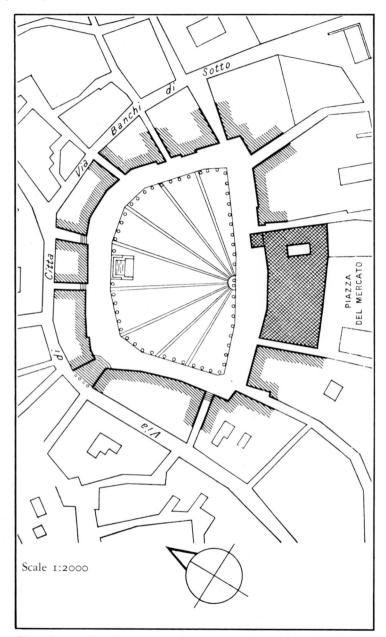

Fig. 483   Plan of the city of Siena, from a map by the Istituto
Geografico Militare (scale of 1:25,000).

Figs 484–5   The Piazza del Campo in Siena, showing the Palazzo
Comunale.

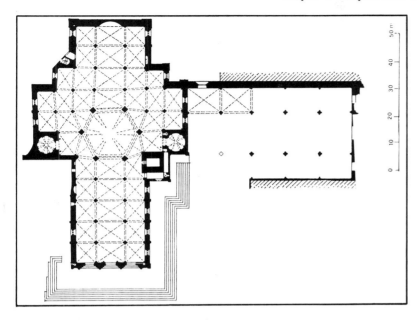

Figs 486–8 Siena. Aerial view of the city centre with the Piazza del Campo and the Piazza del Duomo: aerial view and plan of the cathedral, and the unfinished outline of the planned mid-fourteenth-century enlargement.

Fig. 489   A medieval street in Siena, flanked by houses of five or six storeys.

The very nature of medieval culture, which tended not to establish formal models like classical culture, means that it is impossible to generalise about the form taken by cities during the Middle Ages. Medieval towns and cities came in all shapes and sizes, adapting themselves freely to every geographical and economic circumstance, as has already been noted.

There are, however, universal characteristics, which can be related to the political and economic ones that have been mentioned previously.

1. Medieval towns had a street system that was only marginally less regular than that found in their Arab counterparts. Their streets were, however, laid out in such a way that people would always be able to tell approximately where they were, and also have a general idea of what the particular district or town was like. They varied considerably in size, ranging from full-scale streets to narrow alleyways, and the intervening squares were not just self-contained open spaces: they were closely integrated with the streets which ran into them. Only the lesser streets were intended to act purely as thoroughfares: all the other ones were designed to be used as places to stop, to conduct business or for holding meetings. The houses, almost always built on several floors, faced out on to the public area, and their façades were an important factor in determining the character of the street or square that they overlooked (Fig. 491).

Thus the public and private areas did not form contiguous yet separate areas, as in the cities of antiquity: there was a single common public area, composed of many different elements, which spread throughout the city and provided the setting for all buildings, both public and private, together with whatever internal space they contained, whether courtyards or gardens.

This new balance between the two types of property was the result of a compromise between public law and private interests. In fact, the municipal statutes laid down comprehensive legislation concerning the relationship between the public and private domains and also concerning the areas in which the two sectors overlapped: the parts of a building projecting over a street, colonnades, or external staircases.

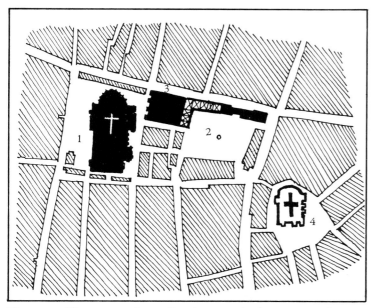

Fig. 490   The centre of a medieval city (Lübeck), showing four characteristic compositional elements: the open space adjoining the main church (1); the market place, containing the Town Hall (2); the main street that runs along the edge of these two squares (3); the open space in front of the secondary church (4).

2. The public areas in the cities had a rather complex layout, due to the fact that they had to accommodate a number of different authorities: the local bishop, the municipal government, the religious orders and the trade guilds. As a result, any city of importance would have more than one centre: a religious centre (with a cathedral and an episcopal palace), a civil centre (with a town hall) and one or more commercial centres with arcades and guildhalls. These areas sometimes overlapped, but the contrast between civil and religious authority, which never existed in antiquity, was always fairly well defined.

Every city was divided into different quarters, each of which had its own character, its own emblem and often its own political organisation. During the thirteenth century, when the cities were growing at a very fast rate, a number of secondary centres sprang up on the outskirts: they were the establishments of the new religious orders — the Franciscans, the Dominicans, the Servites — together with their churches and surrounding squares.

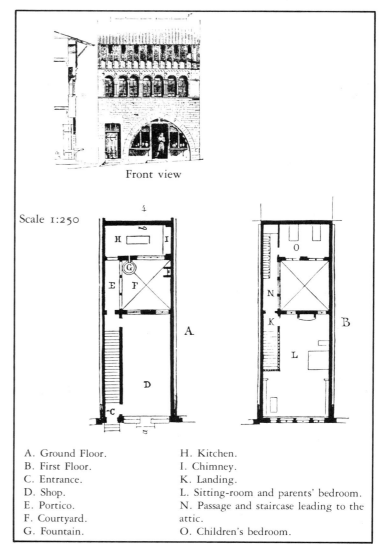

A. Ground Floor.
B. First Floor.
C. Entrance.
D. Shop.
E. Portico.
F. Courtyard.
G. Fountain.

H. Kitchen.
I. Chimney.
K. Landing.
L. Sitting-room and parents' bedroom.
N. Passage and staircase leading to the attic.
O. Children's bedroom.

Fig. 491   A medieval house at Cluny in France.

Fig. 492   Orvieto Cathedral, which soars above the surrounding rooftops.

3. Medieval cities were privileged political entities, with the city bourgeoisie representing only a small part of the total population, which grew rapidly and continuously from the beginning of the eleventh century up until the mid-fourteenth century. The laws were formulated for the benefit of the people concentrated within the city walls: the city centre, where the well-to-do people lived, was the most sought-after area, while the poorer sections of the community lived in the outer districts. The tallest structures were at the centre — the towers of the municipal palace, the campanile, the cathedral spire — and they represented the city's highest points, as well as providing an additional unifying and three-dimensional element.

Every city had to have a surrounding wall to defend it from the outside world, and each time it grew, its walls had to be correspondingly increased until a series of concentric circles of fortification had been constructed. These walls, which represented by far the largest item of public expenditure, almost always had an irregular and rounded outline, designed to encompass a given area of ground as economically as possible (Fig. 466).

The construction of a new wall was always postponed until there was positively no room left for buildings within the existing walls, which accounts for the density of houses in medieval cities and also for the height of the buildings. Only the great walls built at the end of the thirteenth century and the beginning of the fourteenth century, in cities like Florence, Siena, Bologna, Padua and Ghent, proved to be too extensive during the mid-fourteenth century, when population levels remained static or actually dropped. They ended up by enclosing large areas of green, which were only built over during the nineteenth century (Fig. 493).

4. The medieval cities that we know nowadays owe their

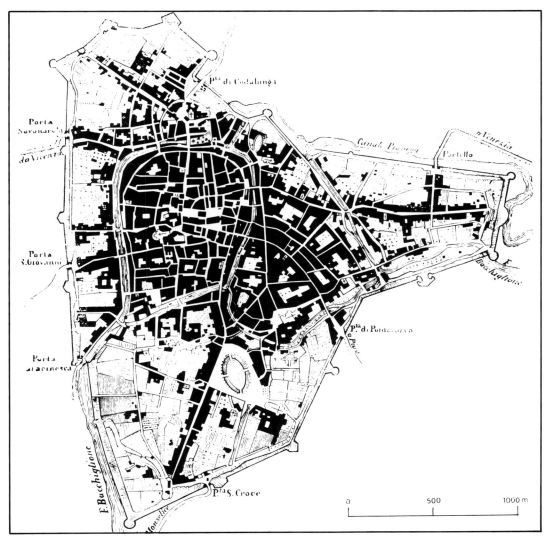

Fig. 493 Map of the city of Padua, showing the final medieval wall, which contains fields and gardens within its perimeter.

present appearance to developments during the period between the fifteenth and seventeenth centuries, when their size and their architecture had already been firmly established.

During preceding centuries, when they were at the height of their development, the cities must have been more disorganised. The most important churches and palaces were still unfinished and covered with scaffolding, and each new addition to the city's architecture added a further dimension to it. Architectural unity was ensured by stylistic coherence, by confidence in the future rather than by memories of the past. The Gothic style of architecture was an international one, and it provided a common link between the construction and embellishment of all the buildings in Europe, from the mid-twelfth century onwards (Figs 494–514).

It is this background that Le Corbusier describes so aptly in his book, written in 1937 and entitled *When the Cathedrals were White*:

When the cathedrals were white, Europe had organised the crafts under the imperative impulse of a quite new, marvellous and exceedingly daring technique the use of which led to unexpected systems of

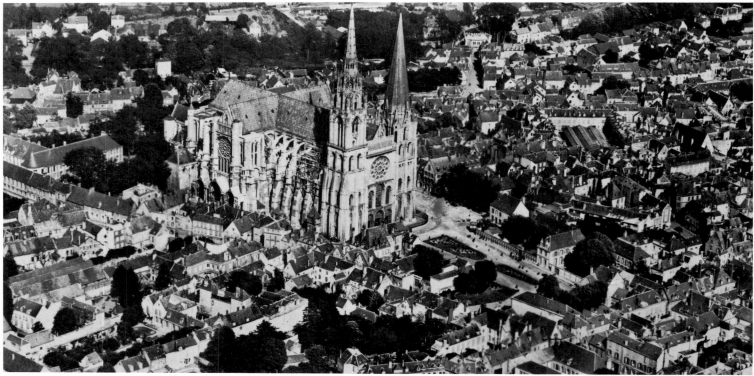

Figs 494–6   Chartres Cathedral,
founded in 1194. Plan and two aerial
views which illustrate how the
cathedral dwarfs the houses around it.

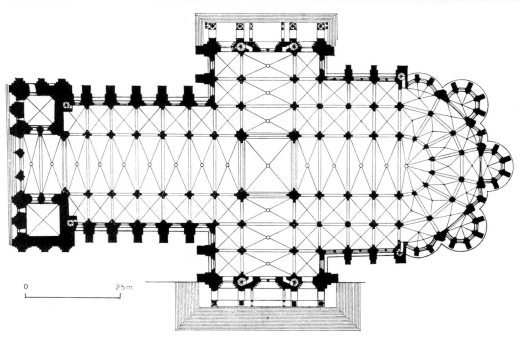

0   25m

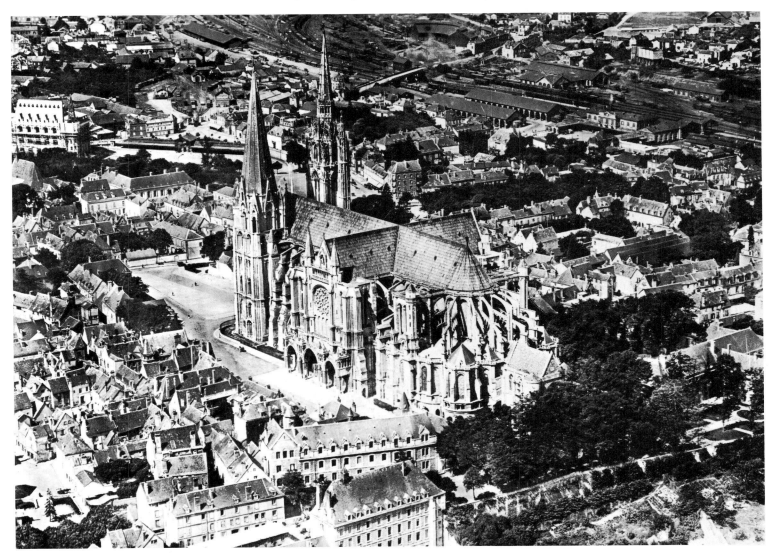

forms — in fact to forms whose spirit disdained the legacy of a thousand years of tradition, not hesitating to thrust civilisation toward an unknown adventure. An international language reigned wherever the white race was, favouring the exchange of ideas and the transfer of culture. An international style had spread from the West to the East and from the North to the South . . .

The cathedrals were white because they were new. The cities were new; they were constructed all at once, in an orderly way, regular, geometric, in accordance with plans . . . Above all the cities and towns encircled by new walls, the skyscrapers of God dominated the countryside. They had made them as high as possible, extraordinarily high. It may seem disproportionate in the ensemble. Not at all, it was an act of optimism, a gesture of courage, a sign of pride, a proof of mastery! . . .

The new world was beginning. White, limpid, joyous, clean, clear and without hesitations, the new world was opening up like a flower among the ruins. They left behind them all recognised ways of doing things; they turned their backs on all that. In a hundred years the marvel was accomplished and Europe was changed.

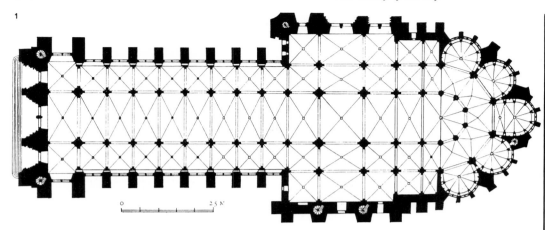

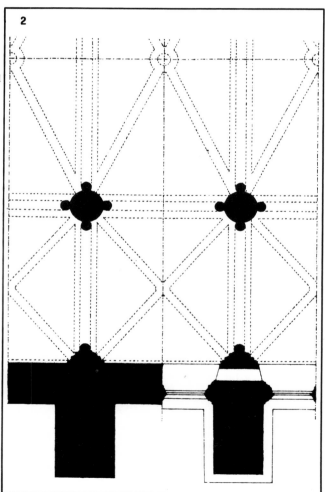

Figs 497–501 The Cathedral of Rheims, founded in 1210.

1. General plan.
2. Plan of two typical spans, at the level of their bases (A–B in the sectional diagram) and at the level of the first windows (C–D in the sectional diagram).
3. Interior view.
4. Cross-section.
5. Exterior view.

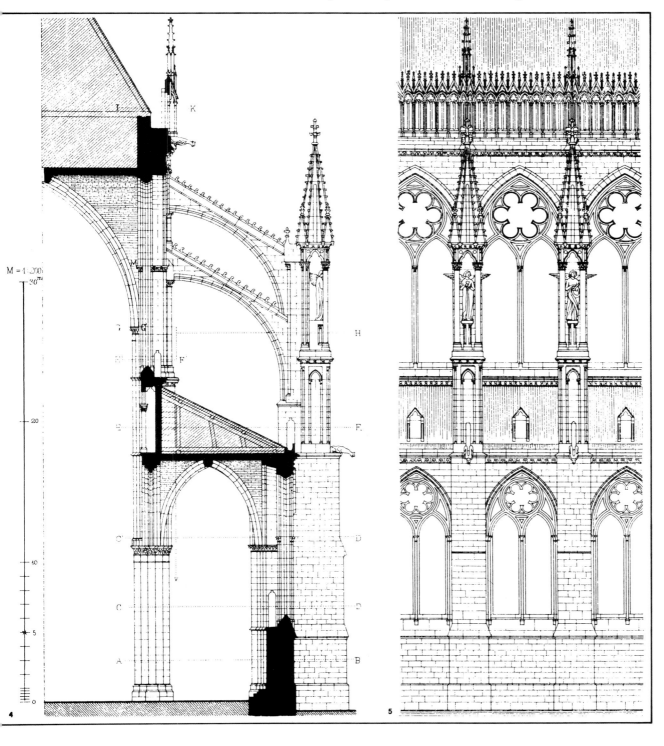

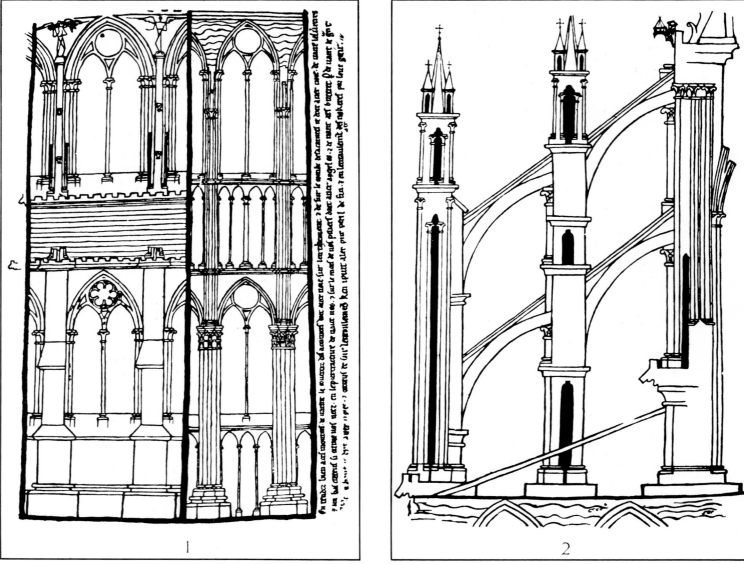

Figs 502–5   Four drawings of the Cathedral of Rheims, taken from the note book of the medieval architect Villard de Bonnecourt (*c.* 1235).

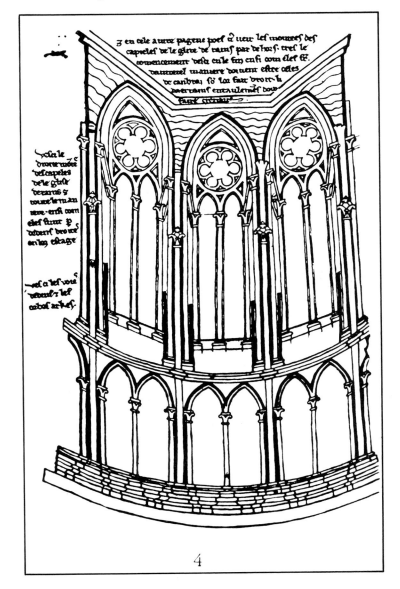

1. Internal and external views of the
three-aisled body of the church.
2. Sectional view of the choir's flying
buttresses.
3, 4. Internal and external views of
the choir.

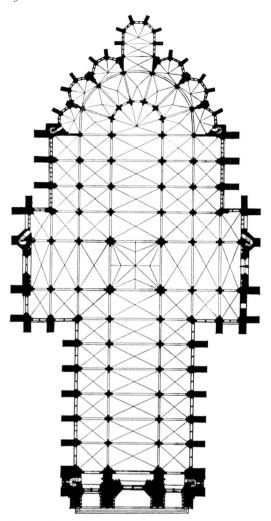

Figs 506–7   Amiens Cathedral,
founded in 1220.
Plan (scale 1:1,000) and interior view.

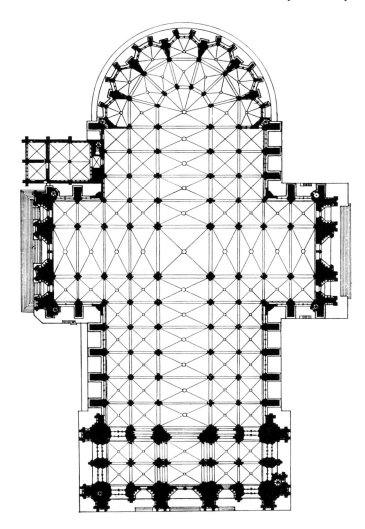

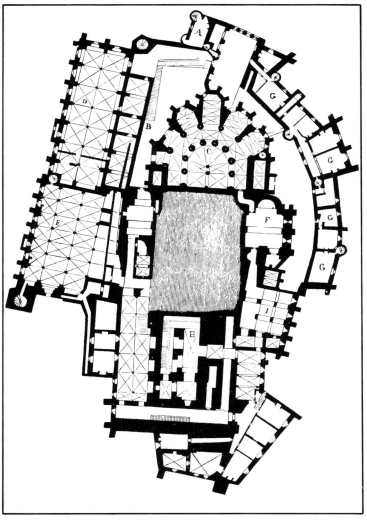

Fig. 508   Plan of Cologne Cathedral, founded in 1248 (scale 1:1,000).

Fig. 509   Plan of the church and the other buildings on the Mont St Michel in France; in this case the Gothic church has been incorporated into a complex of buildings that are both architecturally and proportionally homogenous (scale 1:1,000).

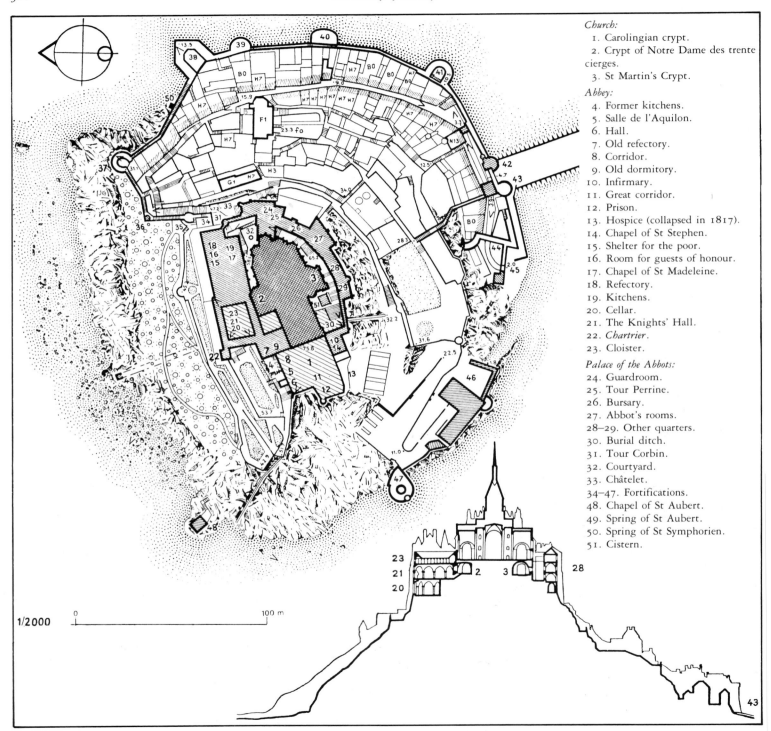

Church:
1. Carolingian crypt.
2. Crypt of Notre Dame des trente cierges.
3. St Martin's Crypt.

Abbey:
4. Former kitchens.
5. Salle de l'Aquilon.
6. Hall.
7. Old refectory.
8. Corridor.
9. Old dormitory.
10. Infirmary.
11. Great corridor.
12. Prison.
13. Hospice (collapsed in 1817).
14. Chapel of St Stephen.
15. Shelter for the poor.
16. Room for guests of honour.
17. Chapel of St Madeleine.
18. Refectory.
19. Kitchens.
20. Cellar.
21. The Knights' Hall.
22. Chartrier.
23. Cloister.

Palace of the Abbots:
24. Guardroom.
25. Tour Perrine.
26. Bursary.
27. Abbot's rooms.
28–29. Other quarters.
30. Burial ditch.
31. Tour Corbin.
32. Courtyard.
33. Châtelet.
34–47. Fortifications.
48. Chapel of St Aubert.
49. Spring of St Aubert.
50. Spring of St Symphorien.
51. Cistern.

1/2000

0   100 m

Figs 510–12   Mont St Michel. Plan and sectional diagram (scale 1:2,000), and a model from the eighteenth century.

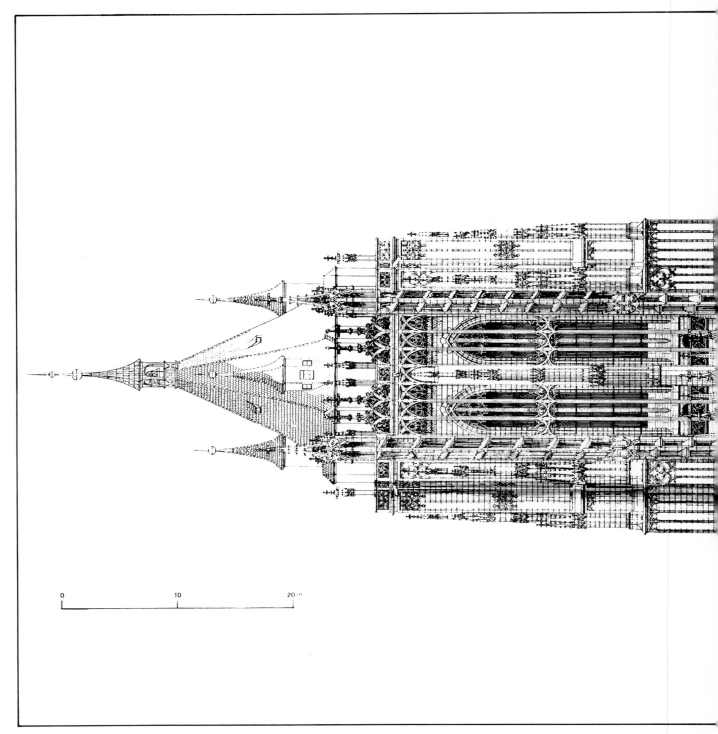

0   10   20 m

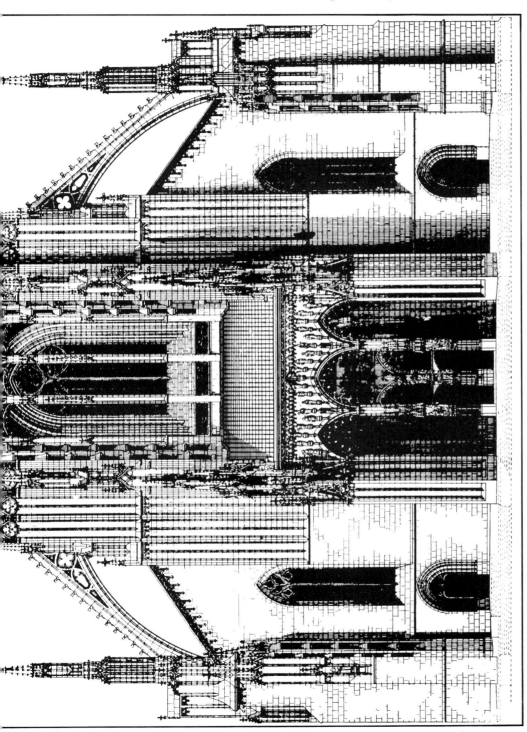

Fig. 513　Façade of Ulm Cathedral in Germany.

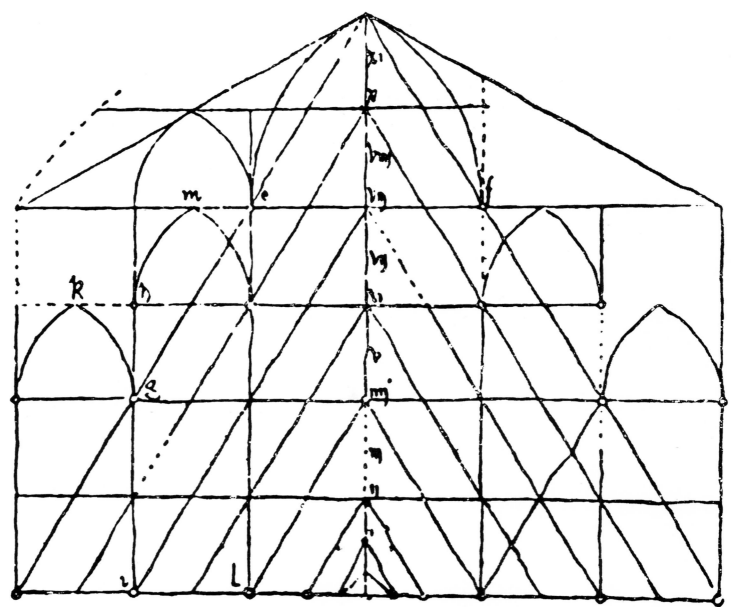

Fig. 514   A drawing by the master architect Stornaloco, showing the proportions of the five aisles of Milan Cathedral (end of the fourteenth century).

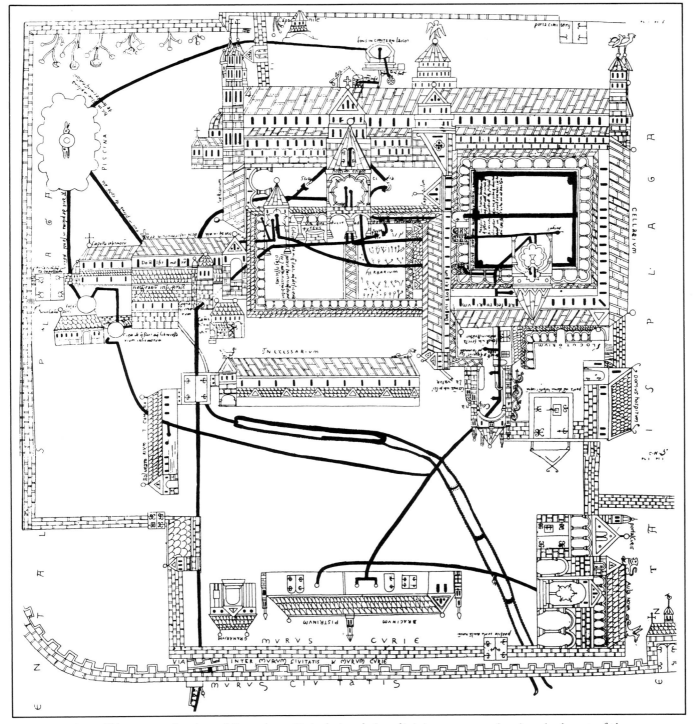

Fig. 515 A twelfth-century drawing of Canterbury Cathedral and the adjoining convent, showing the layout of the water supply and the drainage system.

The three prime characteristics — continuity, complexity, concentration — have survived the passing of time and they still define the basic nature of the European city; the fourth, however, which could be called the capacity for self-renewal, did not survive the crisis in the second half of the fourteenth century. The most important creative moment had passed; from there on the cities looked back before taking any new decisions.

In order to understand the nature of the cities of antiquity, all that is necessary is a full description of a few leading cities: Athens, Rome, Byzantium, for example. In the Middle Ages, however, there were no supercities, only a large number of medium-sized ones, a dozen of which achieved roughly the same size: between 300 and 600 hectares in area and between 50,000 and 150,000 inhabitants.

The principal cities of the late Middle Ages, together with the area enclosed by their last set of walls, were as follows:

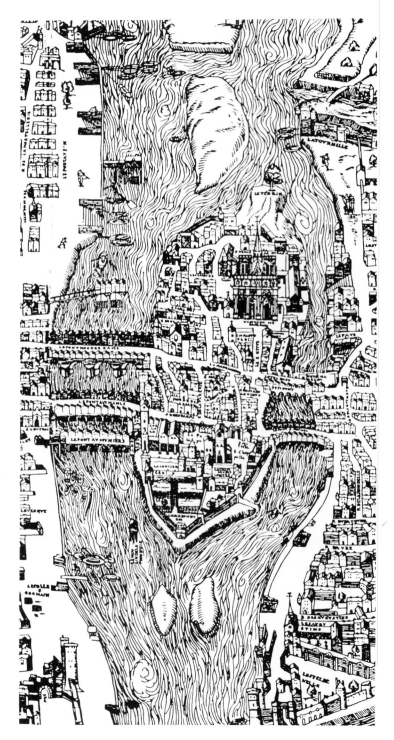

		circa
Venice (the city and its related islands)	600 hectares
Milan (within the fifteenth-century *Mura Viscontee*)	580 hectares
Ghent (within the fourteenth-century walls)	570 hectares
Cologne (within the walls of 1180)	510 hectares
Florence (within the walls of 1284)	480 hectares
Padua (within the fifteenth-century Venetian walls)	450 hectares
Paris (within the walls of Charles V from 1370)	440 hectares
Brussels (within the walls of 1357)	415 hectares
Bologna (within the thirteenth-century walls)	400 hectares
Louvain (within the walls of 1357)	395 hectares
Verona (within the fourteenth-century *Mura Scaligere*)	380 hectares
Bruges (within the walls of 1297)	360 hectares
Piacenza (within the fourteenth-century walls)	290 hectares
Tirlemont (within the fourteenth-century walls)	250 hectares
Naples (within the fifteenth-century Aragonese walls)	200 hectares
Pisa (within the twelfth-century walls)	200 hectares
Barcelona (within the walls of 1350)	200 hectares
Siena (within the fourteenth-century walls)	180 hectares
Lübeck (within the thirteenth-century walls)	180 hectares
London (within the Roman walls, restored during the Middle Ages)	160 hectares
Nuremberg (within the walls of 1320)	160 hectares
Malines (within the fourteenth-century walls)	160 hectares
Frankfurt-am-Main (within the walls of 1333)	150 hectares
Avignon (within the walls of 1356)	140 hectares

Population figures are uncertain, and it is not possible

Figs 516–17   Medieval Paris: the Île de la Cité with Notre Dame Cathedral, and a general plan of the city. The walls of Philip Augustus (1180–1210), centred on the island, can be clearly distinguished, as can the extensions made on the right bank by Charles V (1370). The engravings date from the sixteenth century.

to deduce them from the surface areas of the cities, as building densities varied very considerably. The most populous cities (Milan and Paris) may possibly have reached a total of 200,000 inhabitants, while Venice may have had 150,000 inhabitants, Florence, 100,000, Ghent and Bruges, 80,000 and Siena, 50,000. None of them ever grew larger than the Arab capitals in Europe (Palermo with a population of 300,000 and Cordoba with more than half a million) and they never came anywhere near the totals achieved by the great metropoles of the Near East, such as Constantinople and Baghdad, both of which passed the million mark.

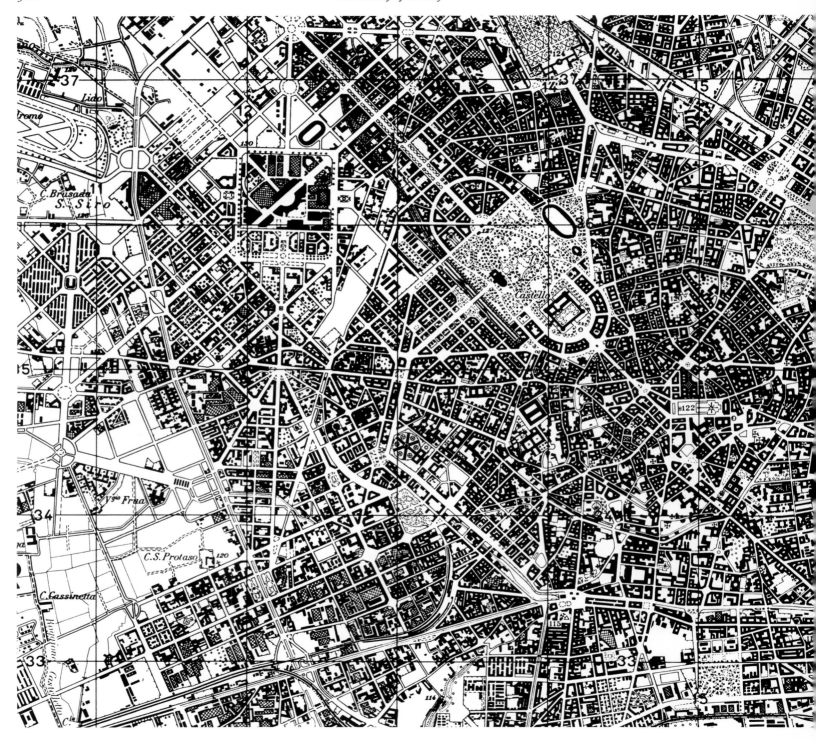

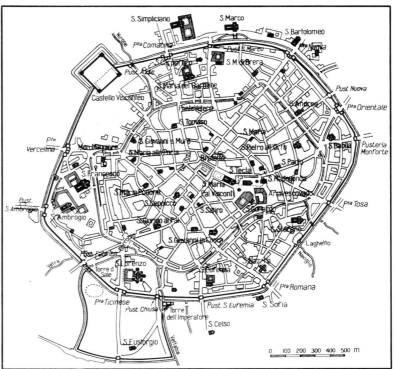

Figs 518–19   Plan of Milan during the mid-fourteenth century, contained within the twelfth-century walls, which were rebuilt after the Battle of Legnano (1176). Left: a map of the modern city, on the same scale (1:25,000), by the Istituto Geografico Militare; in the centre, the first city walls (the *Mura dei Navigli*) can be clearly seen, as can the second set of walls (the *Mura Viscontee*), later reinforced by the Spaniards in the mid-sixteenth century.

Fig. 520   Map of the Lagoon of Venice during the sixteenth century; in the middle of the water is the city of Venice, surrounded by smaller islands.

In a book as general as this, it is not possible to describe each city in the preceding list; we shall therefore limit ourselves to five cities (Venice, Bruges, Bologna, Nuremberg, Florence). Although not the most important, they are best suited to illustrate the variety of city that existed in the Middle Ages. One is a great maritime emporium situated between West and East, one is a Flemish seaport, one is a city in the Po valley that grew up around a Roman nucleus, one is a mercantile and manufacturing city in central Germany, and the last one is an industrial and banking city in central Italy.

VENICE

Venice is an exceptional city even today, and so it was during the Middle Ages, thanks to its extraordinary geographical position and its unique historical development.

In order to escape from the barbarians who were pouring into Italy through the Julian Alps, the inhabitants of the Venetian plain sought refuge in the lagoons between the mouths of the Po and the Tagliamento, which offered an environment that was protected from both land and sea. As a result, several settlements sprang up on the islands, and the most important of these became Venice, which was situated in the middle of the largest lagoon (between the mouths of the Brenta and Piave) and had easy access to the open sea via a natural canal.

Venice was able to escape domination by the kingdoms on the mainland, but it remained formally subject to Constantinople, which enabled it to act as a commercial intermediary between West and East, and also allowed it to develop on liberal political lines without coming into conflict with any princes or feudal nobles, as other cities had.

The shape of the city was already established at the end of the eleventh century, and it remained virtually unchanged in successive maps, from the earliest, dated 1346, which was a precisely planned layout unlike the normal symbolic city views of the Middle Ages (Figs 522–3), right up to the modern ones of today (Figs 570–1).

Venice is an urbanised lagoon, situated at the point where several natural waterways converge and flow into the open sea, passing through openings in the thin strips of land known as Lidos. One of these waterways — the Grand Canal — passes through the whole city in an exaggerated S shape.

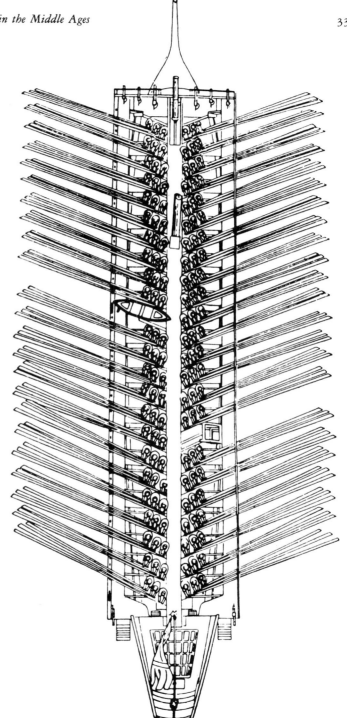

Fig. 521   Drawing of a Venetian galley with three banks of oars (scale 1:200).

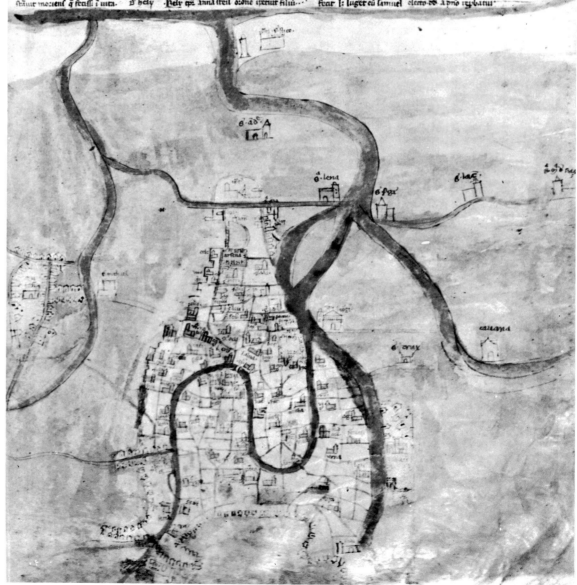

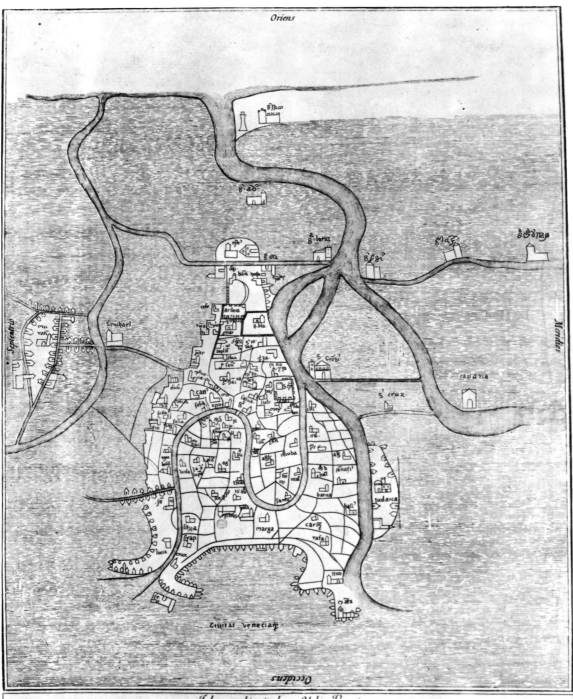

Figs 522–3 The earliest map of the city of Venice, from a 1348 codex, and a copy engraved in 1780. The map charts the course of the navigable channels in the lagoon: the Giudecca canal and St Mark's basin, where the Grand Canal meets the sea after passing through the length of the city.

Fig. 524   A map of Venice from the eighteenth century.

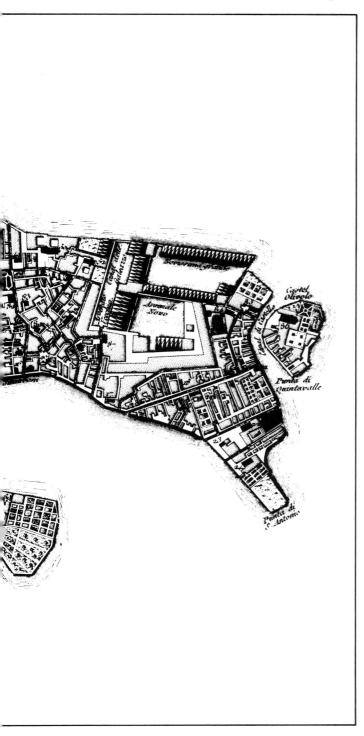

At the mouth of the Grand Canal stood St Mark's (the political centre of the city) and half way along was the Rialto (the commercial centre), where the one bridge that crossed it was to be found. The two centres were very close to each other as the crow flies, and they are both within the *sistiere* of St Mark (one of the six wards into which the city was divided), which was the most populous and earliest inhabited area of Venice. The network of secondary canals, used for the transportation of both goods and people, spread throughout the city, whose density and compactness resembled that of Middle Eastern towns. There were also a number of secondary centres, focused on the parochial churches and the open spaces, called *campi*, where the water cisterns, accessible by means of wells, were sited, while the great State shipyard (the Arsenal), in which the Venetian fleet was built, was situated in the district nearest the sea. The city rose up from the waters of the lagoon, with its distinctive dolphin shape, but its own shape was governed by the configuration of its invisible foundations, as can be seen in the fourteenth-century map (Fig. 522). Even its most important buildings had already gained their final shape between the end of the eleventh century and the beginning of the twelfth.

St Mark's Cathedral (whose ground plan was copied from the Church of the Holy Apostles in Constantinople) was built between 1060 and 1094; the two Rialto markets, on the banks of the Grand Canal, were laid out at the end of the eleventh century and joined by a pontoon bridge; the Doge's Palace was rebuilt in stone, following the fire of 1105, while the administrative division of the city into *confini* and *contrade* was carried out in 1083.

Venice's prosperity increased throughout the twelfth century, and at the beginning of the thirteenth century the political and architectural structure of the city had already been formed. Doge Sebastiano Ziani (1172–8) dismantled the fortifications round the Doge's Palace and opened up the L-shaped piazza between the palace and the cathedral, on to which the loggias of the new buildings faced: it was here that the solemn meeting between Barbarossa and Pope Alexander III took place in 1177. The mathematician Nicolo Barattieri erected two columns of St Mark and St Theodore at the point where St Mark's Square meets the lagoon, and he also designed the second Rialto Bridge, in

Fig. 525   The building of the Tower of Babel, as depicted in a thirteenth-century mosaic in St Mark's.

Figs 526–7   The second Rialto Bridge, built of wood, with a movable central section to enable ships to pass through. A detail from the perspective view of Venice by Jacopo de' Barbari, and as seen in a painting by Carpaccio.

wood, with a movable central section through which ships could sail (Figs 526–7). Doge Enrico Dandolo (1192–1205) led the Fourth Crusade, whose object was the conquest of Constantinople, and brought back a large number of trophies, including the four bronze horses that now adorn the façade of St Mark's. The constitutional ordinances of the Republic were laid down between 1207 and 1220, and finally ratified in 1297, with the laws known as the *Serrata del Maggior Consiglio*. The city became increasingly prosperous and even more firmly established; towards the middle of the century the mendicant orders gained a foothold in the outskirts of the city, and in about 1330, the Dominicans and Franciscans built the great unadorned churches of SS John and Paul, and Santa Maria Gloriosa dei Frari (Figs 566–8). In 1294 minting first began of the gold ducat, which was to remain legal tender right up until 1797 (Figs 536–7).

At this point, what Le Corbusier calls 'a magnificently functional machine' had been completed, based on the maintenance of a strict balance between land and water. Later on 'the "artists" arrived; but everything was already under control, slotted into the environment, the result of

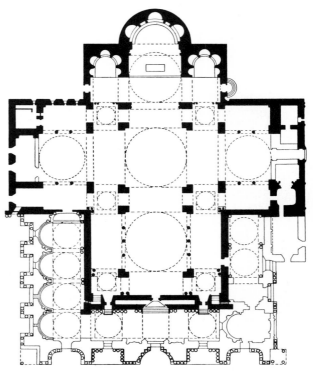

Figs 529–31   A ground plan of St Mark's, on a scale of 1:800.
The façade, in a painting by Gentile Bellini and a contemporary
photograph.

Fig. 528   The monumental centre of Venice, between the Rialto
(with the third, stone bridge, built in 1592) and St Mark's, as seen
in an eighteenth-century view.

everyone's collaboration'.

St Mark's Cathedral, inaugurated in 1094, was further
embellished during the next three centuries with a spectacular array of mosaics, sculptures and metalwork (Figs
529–40). The Doge's Palace was gradually redesigned in
the Gothic manner from 1340 until the end of the fifteenth
century, and St Mark's Square was laid out in the first half of
the sixteenth century by Mauro Codussi, Sansovino and
Sanmicheli. The third Rialto Bridge, in stone, was completed by Antonio da Ponte in 1592, while Palladio (who
became director of public works in Venice between 1570
and 1580) built his two great churches of San Giorgio and
del Redentore on the strips of land just across the water from
St Mark's. And in 1631 Longhena built the Church of Maria
della Salute at the mouth of the Grand Canal (Fig. 544) to
celebrate the passing of a plague epidemic.

Fig. 532   The roof of St Mark's, as seen from the campanile. The five cupolas are made even more imposing by their covering of wood overlaid with lead, which emphasises their outline.

Fig. 533   The interior of one of the cupolas of St Mark's, decorated with a thirteenth-century mosaic.

Figs 534–5   The Pala d'Oro in St Mark's, completed in the fourteenth century using much older materials (from the twelfth and thirteenth centuries), some of which originated in Constantinople.

Figs 536–7   The Venetian gold ducat, minted from 1294 onwards. (Twice life-size.)

Fig. 538　A twelfth-century inlaid marble slab from St Mark's.

Fig. 539   An aerial view of St Mark's sandwiched between its surrounding buildings.

Fig. 540 An aerial photograph of St Mark's Square, showing the Doge's Palace and the cathedral.

Fig. 541   Venice and its lagoon, from a sixteenth-century engraving. The shape of the lagoon has been simplified in order to emphasise the city and its buildings. However, the artist has shown the difference between the rough waters of the sea and the calm waters of the lagoon, populated by many different types of ship. The lesser centres of Murano (above) and Chioggia (below) can also be clearly seen.

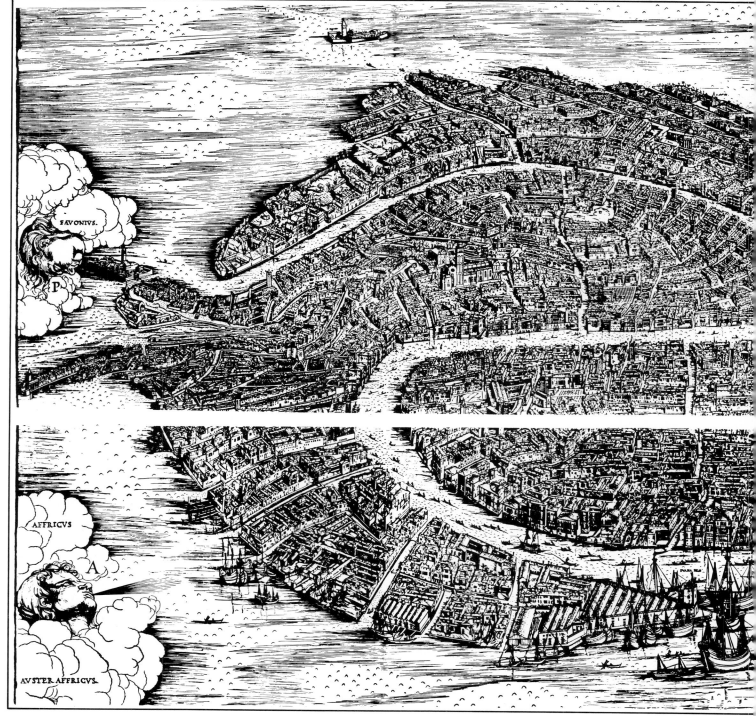

Fig. 542   Jacopo de' Barbari's great panorama of Venice, engraved in 1500.

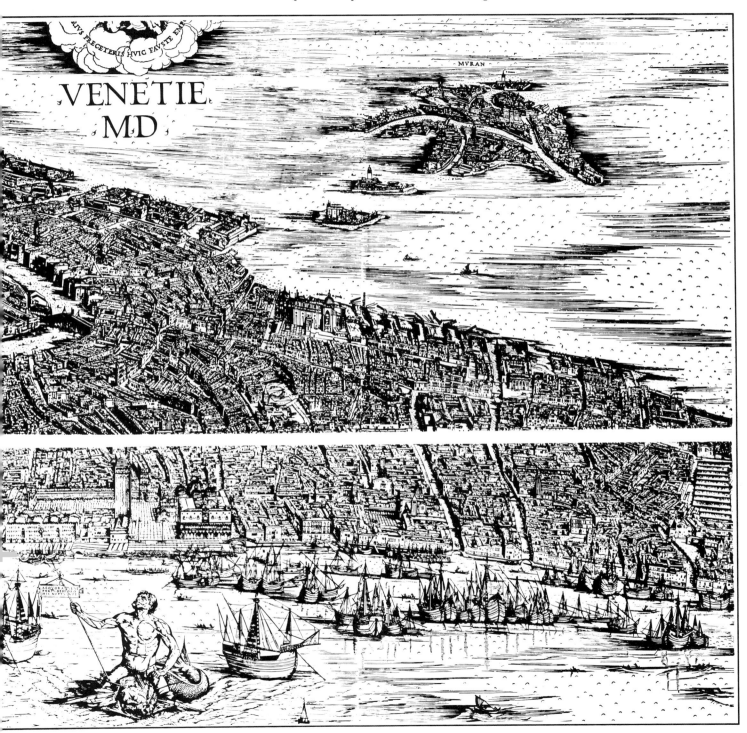

Fig. 543   The Arsenal at Venice (the city's official shipyard), as seen in a detail from Jacopo de' Barbari's engraving.

In the meantime, the engineers of the Republic were working to maintain the lagoon, on which the life of the city depended: they diverted the river mouths that led into the lagoon to prevent it silting up; they dug out new canals to ease the passage of ships and to ensure that the waters were not stagnant in the potentially malarial areas; they reinforced the sandy strips of the Lidos, which lay between the lagoon and the open sea, with *murazzi*, so as to protect the city from the tides.

Although this unique city, fragile yet enduring, was based on a compact design of eastern origin, which resembled that of Byzantine and Arab cities rather than European ones, its alien quality was tempered by some of the most outstanding examples of Gothic and Renaissance architecture. It was also immortalised and adorned by the works of countless artists.

In the second half of the fifteenth century, Venice became the meeting point of the mainstreams of European painting. In 1475, for example, Antonello da Messina and Giovanni Bellini met in the city, while in 1495 Albrecht Dürer arrived there from Germany. Venice became the centre of technical experimentation and artistic innovation: painting in oils, the use of large-scale canvases, typography, engraving by means of copper plates, all originated there. The two Bellinis and Carpaccio painted scenes from the city (Figs 527, 530), and in 1500 Jacopo de' Barbari engraved his great, six-leaf, perspective map, which shows Venice from the south, set in its great expanse of lagoon (Figs 542–3), while Aldo Manuzio printed the most perfect books of the Renaissance. Later on, during the sixteenth century, there was the painting of Giorgione, Titian and Veronese: a tradition that influenced European art for a further three centuries.

This great machine was unbalanced only by the technological transformations of the nineteenth and twentieth centuries. In 1795 Venice ceased to be a sovereign city and fell under the domination of the French, the Austrians and finally the Italians.

Under the French, St Mark's Square was completed by the erection of new buildings along the southern and western sides. The cemetery was laid out on San Michele, and the public gardens inaugurated at Sant'Elena.

Fig. 544 The entrance to the Grand Canal from St Mark's basin, showing the Church of Santa Maria della Salute.

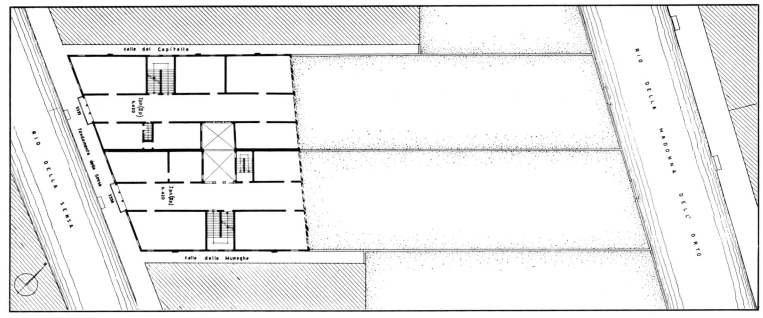

Figs 545–55   Two types of Venetian house. Houses built on long thin plots, with a
garden at the rear leading down to the canal. Right: houses without gardens, built on small
corner plots with no direct access to the canals. The shape of all these houses is determined
by their relationship to the streets and waterways.

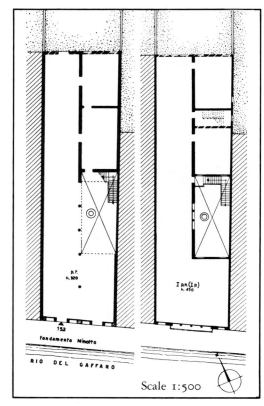

Scale 1:500

Scale 1:1000

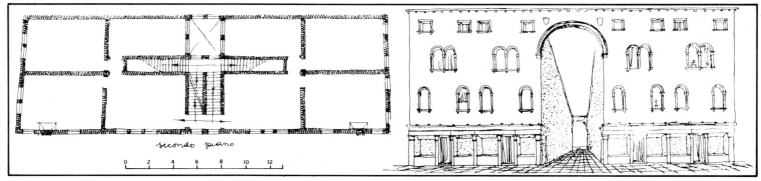

secondo piano

Figs 556–8   The district surrounding the Campo di Santa Marina. The two sketches show a perspective view and a plan of the houses built around the Calle Larga.

Figs 559–60   Two views of the Grand Canal and the Rialto Bridge.

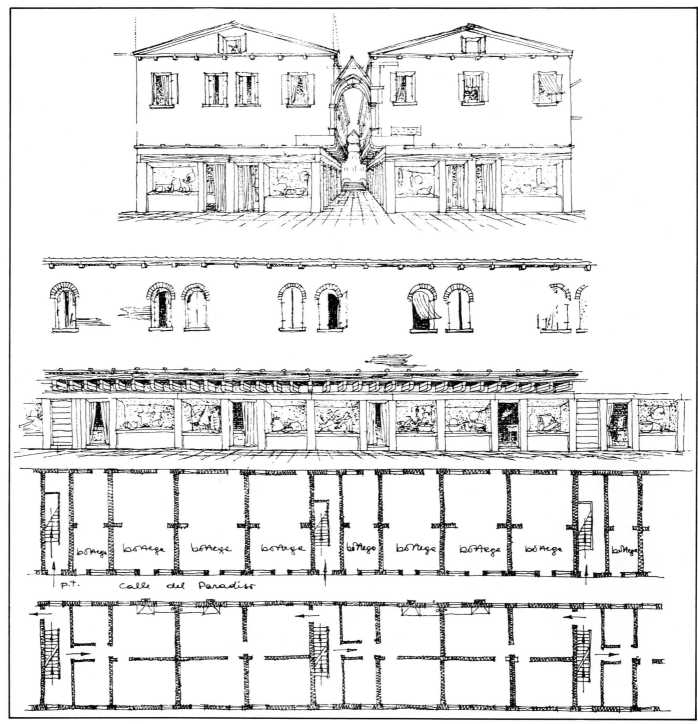

Figs 561–3 Fourteenth century terraced houses between the Calle del Paradiso and the Salizzada S. Lio (*salizzada* is the name given to paved streets).

Fig. 564   An aerial view of part of Venice, showing the open space of the Campo San Polo; in the background is the Church of Santa Maria Gloriosa dei Frari.

Fig. 505   A district of Venice, between the Rio Santa Caterina, the Rio Priuli and the Rio San Felice.

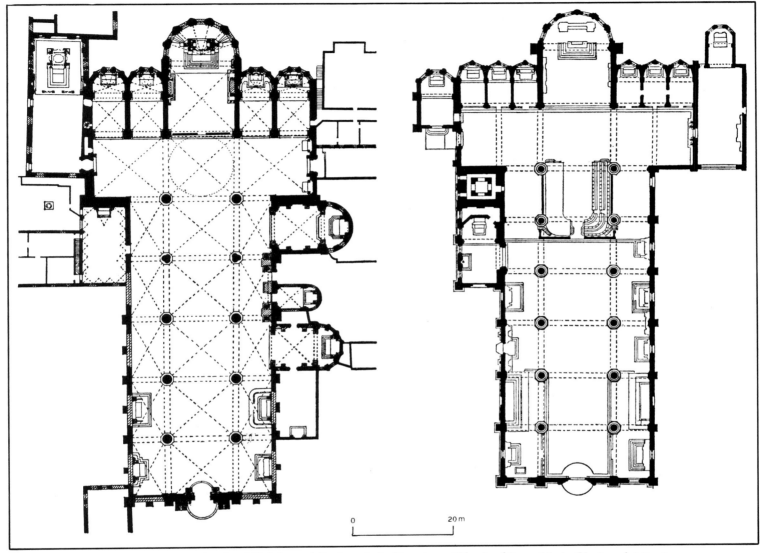

Fig. 566   Plans of the Dominican Church of SS John and Paul, and the Franciscan Church of Santa Maria Gloriosa dei Frari.

Figs 567–8   Aerial views of SS John and Paul and of Santa Maria dei Frari showing surrounding buildings.

Fig. 569 An engraved tablet from the sixteenth century, now in the Correr Museum in Venice.

Translation: *The city of the Veneti, founded by the grace of divine Providence in the middle of the waters, surrounded by the waters, is defended by the waters rather than by a wall. Whosoever, therefore, does harm to the public waters in any way whatsoever, shall be adjudged an enemy of the fatherland. And he will receive no less a punishment than the man who violates the sacred walls of the fatherland. The law established by this edict shall last for ever.*

Under the Austrians, gas lighting was introduced and the aqueduct constructed. Venice was also linked by rail to the mainland for the first time, and a bridge, $3\frac{1}{2}$ kilometres long, was built for this purpose, as well as a station at Santa Lucia, at the head of the Grand Canal (Fig. 570).

After the Italian occupation (1866), a modern port was built — with docks for large tonnage vessels and railway tracks running along the quayside — in the area between Santa Lucia and San Niccolo. The first cars also reached the city, along a bridge that was constructed parallel to the first one, and an arrival area with two large multi-storey car parks was completed in 1932. The Grand Canal, with its two new bridges at the Accademia and the railway station, began to be filled with *vaporettos*, which took the place of the buses and trams used in mainland towns and cities, and in order to facilitate their passage a new canal was opened (the Rio Nuovo), cutting across the upper corner of the Grand Canal. In the meantime, there was also a new seaside resort springing up on the Lido, and an industrial zone developing at Marghera, around which have grown the mainland suburbs that now contain twice as many people as the original island nucleus.

All these innovations have radically altered the lagoon environment: more frequent and higher tides are flooding the city, the fumes from the factories are eating away the marble and destroying the paintings, and the new, deeper canals designed for large cargo vessels have changed the currents in the lagoon. The population of the old city, which reached 180,000 in the 1950s, is rapidly shrinking and has now almost halved, but an attempt is finally being made to restore the city and assist its ailing economy, in order to save a cultural heritage that is of interest to the whole world. It is an attempt to preserve a living city, together with its monuments, its houses and its inhabitants, so as to enable the old machine to function in harmony with the technology and needs of the modern world.

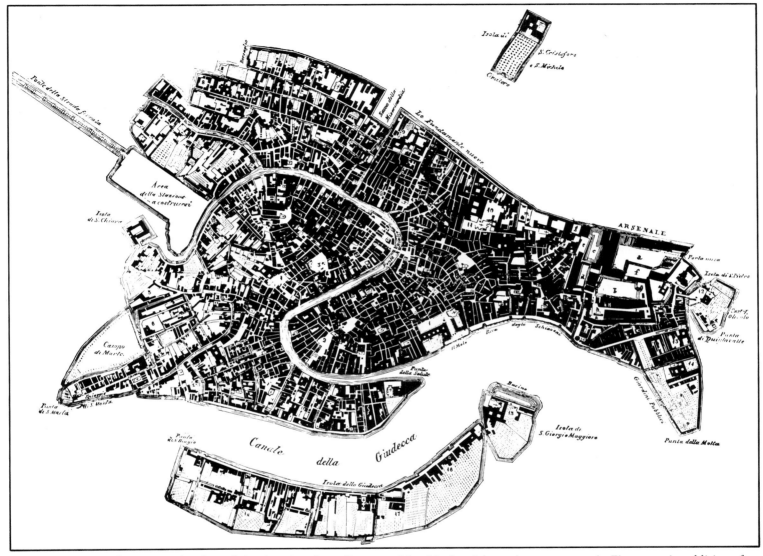

Fig. 570   A plan of Venice at the time of the Austrian siege. Compare this with the eighteenth-century map in Fig. 524: the addition of the public gardens on the outskirts (lower right) can be clearly seen, as can the new Campo Marte (lower left), the railway station under construction (upper left) and the cemetery on the island of San Michele.

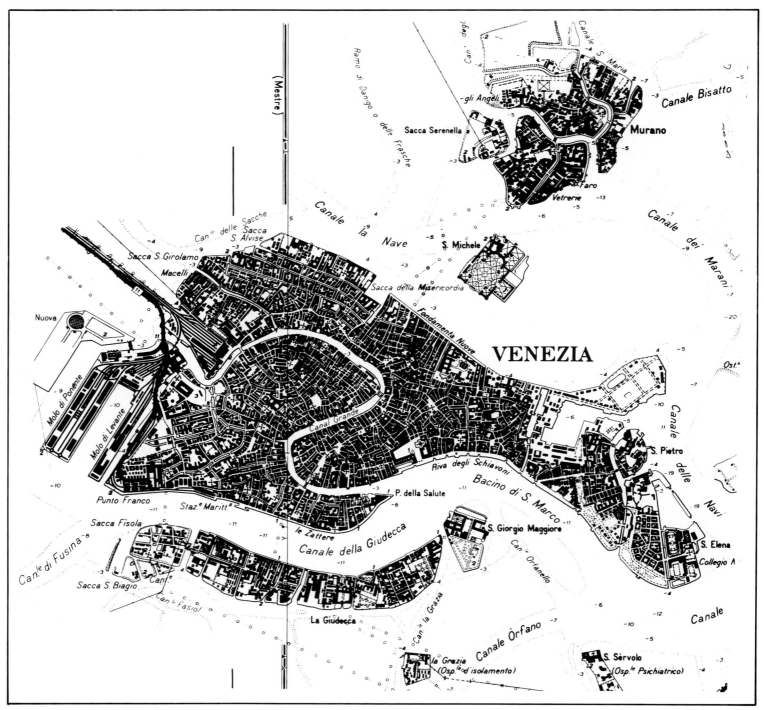

Fig. 571   Plan of modern-day Venice, on a scale of 1:25,000, from a map by the Istituto Geografico Militare. Note the modern additions to the west of the city.

Fig. 572   Aerial view of Venice, showing the lagoon and the open sea.

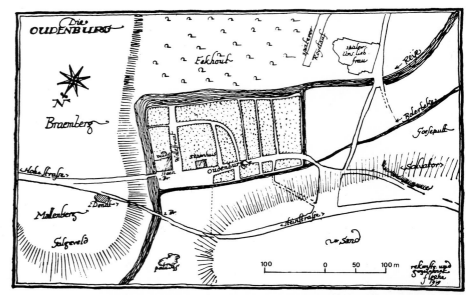

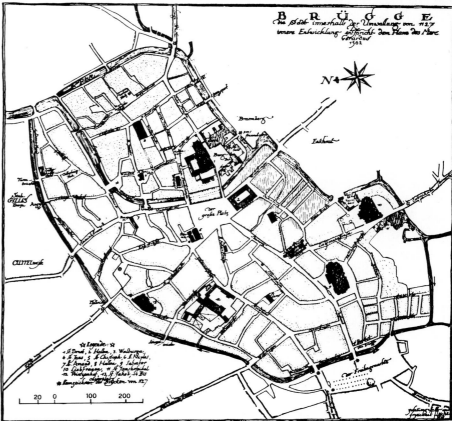

Fig. 573   Bruges. Plans of the
original nucleus and of the second set
of walls.

BRUGES

Bruges, the largest mercantile city in northern Europe, developed round a fortified area castle, later called Oudeburg (old city), which had been founded by the counts of Flanders along the River Reye at the end of the ninth century. Its situation made it eminently suitable for trading activities, as the river flowed into the sea via a long inlet that penetrated deep into the land. In fact, next to the palace of the Counts and the Church of St Donatian a small settlement grew up, which was surrounded by a wall in 915 and held its first fair in 957. A few hundred metres to the west, other small communities developed around the Church of St Sauveur and the Church of Notre Dame, which became independent parishes at the end of the eleventh century. These first beginnings of the city grew up on the areas of high ground that rose from the flat, sandy plain, and were surrounded by marshy land (Fig. 573).

In the eleventh century the population grew rapidly and Bruges became a free city, having succeeded in wresting the right to govern itself with its own magistrature from the local feudal seigneur. It was also during this period that a second wall was built, encompassing an area of roughly 86 hectares and a population of 10,000 people (Fig. 573).

In 1134, a violent storm changed the shape of the coast, gouging out a wide and deep gulf (the Zwin), at the top of the old sea inlet. The merchants of Bruges were quick to take advantage of this new natural harbour, which was situated scarcely a mile from the city: they built an outer port, Damme, and constructed a canal to join it to the Reye and the city. This meant that the large trading ships could anchor at Damme, while smaller craft took their cargoes into the heart of Bruges.

The city, which was nominally subjected to the Counts of Flanders, but powerful enough to stand up to the great rulers of the day, continued to grow throughout the thirteenth century and became the main North Sea port of Europe. Trading agreements with the cities of the Hanseatic League — Hamburg, Bremen and Lübeck — were established in 1252, and relations with England, which supplied the wool for her textile industry, although for a

Fig. 574 A three-masted trading schooner, of the type used in the North Sea at the end of the fifteenth century.

long time strained, were finally regularised in 1274 by the Treaty of Montreuil. In fact, in 1224, the English king (Henry II) decreed that Bruges was to be the sole port of entry for the country's wool exports to the Continent, and in 1227, the first Genoese trading ships appeared in the city, later to be followed by those of Venice. Trade between Italy and the countries of northern Europe was generally conducted by sea during this period, mainly because the cities of Champagne, where the great trading fairs took place, had lost their independence and, from 1284 onwards, formed part of the Royal French dominions.

Fig. 575   An aerial view of the city of Bruges; in the foreground, to the left, can be seen the old castle precincts.

The city was soon expanding at a very fast rate, and the third wall, started in 1297 on the orders of Philip the Fair of France, enclosed an area of almost 400 hectares. During this period Bruges became involved in the struggles between the rulers of France and Flanders, and in 1305 a treaty was signed between the two sides that compelled the city to dismantle its fortifications, and it remained without defences from 1328 to 1338. The walls were, however, subsequently rebuilt, and stayed intact until 1782, when the Emperor Joseph II ordered them to be pulled down.

The administration resided in the Old Halle, inside the Oudeburg, but the life of the city revolved around the Main Square, situated immediately outside the Oudeburg precincts, beyond the Reye. Between these two centres, which straddled the river, the impressive New Halle was erected at the end of the thirteenth century; it was also called the Waterhalle, because boats could enter inside it and be loaded or unloaded under cover. This extraordinary building was unfortunately demolished at the end of the eighteenth century, and on its site there now stands the nineteenth-century palace of the provincial government. Between 1377 and 1420 an impressive new town hall was built on the southern side of the Main Square, with a belfry tower, some 100 metres in height, which became the visual focal point of the whole city (Fig. 576).

During the second half of the thirteenth century, the two main churches, those of St Sauveur and Notre Dame, were rebuilt in the Gothic manner, while the mendicant orders established themselves, as usual, on the outskirts of the city: the Dominicans in 1234, the Franciscans in 1240, the Carmelites in 1266, and the Augustinians in 1276. The municipal hospital of St John, founded in 1188, was also considerably enlarged.

On the western fringes of the city, where the modern railway station is situated, there was a vast uncovered area where the traditional Friday fair took place. It was one of the largest squares of the Middle Ages, partly planted with trees and flanked by a navigable canal.

Fig. 576 The market place with its late fourteenth-century belfry tower.

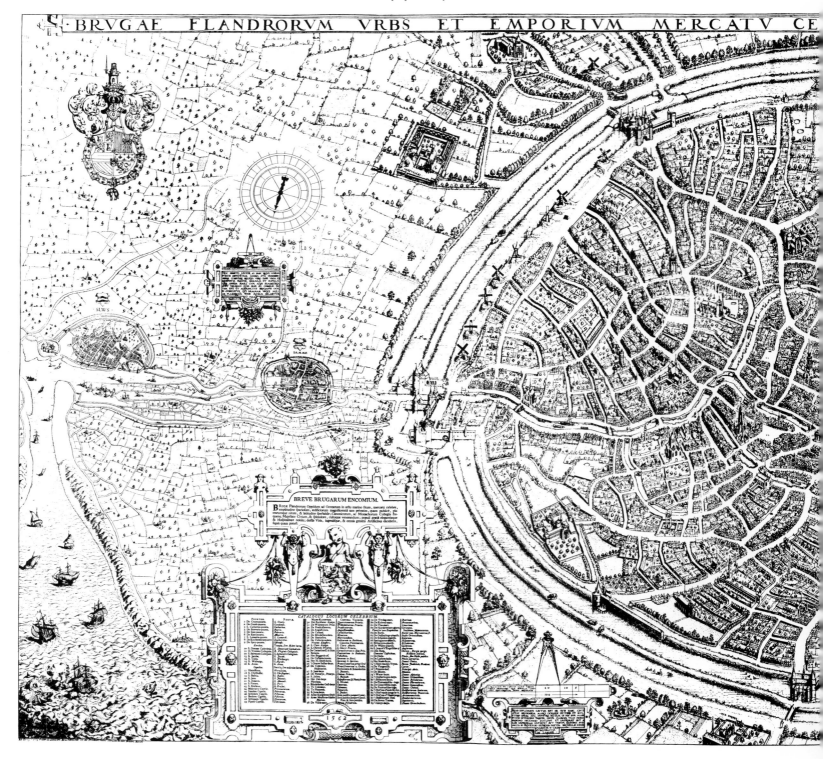

BRE · AN · A · CHR · NAT · CIƆ · IƆ · LXII ·

Fig. 577 The great perspective map
of Bruges published in 1562.

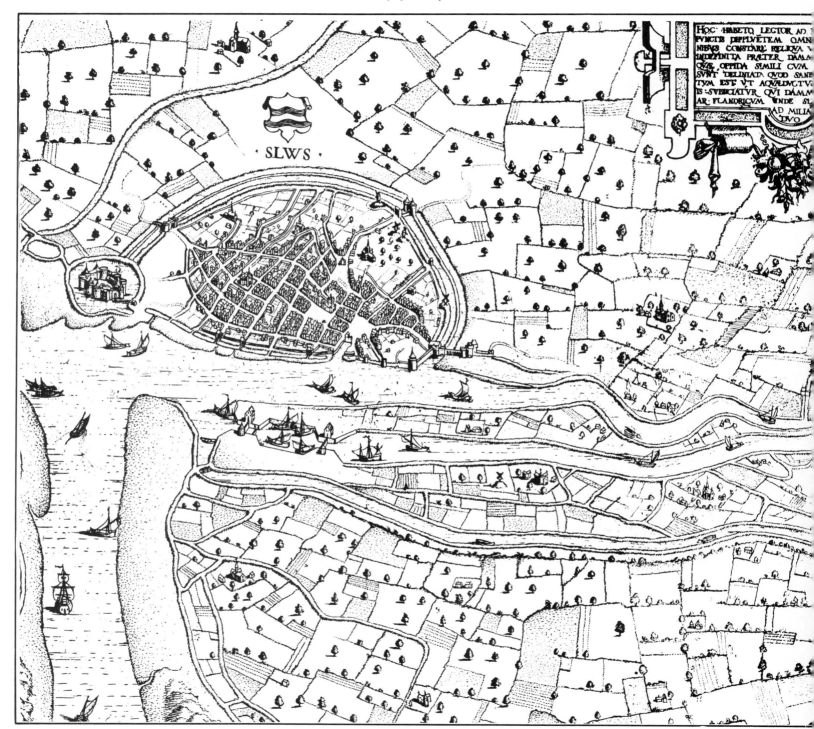

Fig. 578   Details of the preceding map, showing the two outer ports of Bruges, Sluys and Damme.

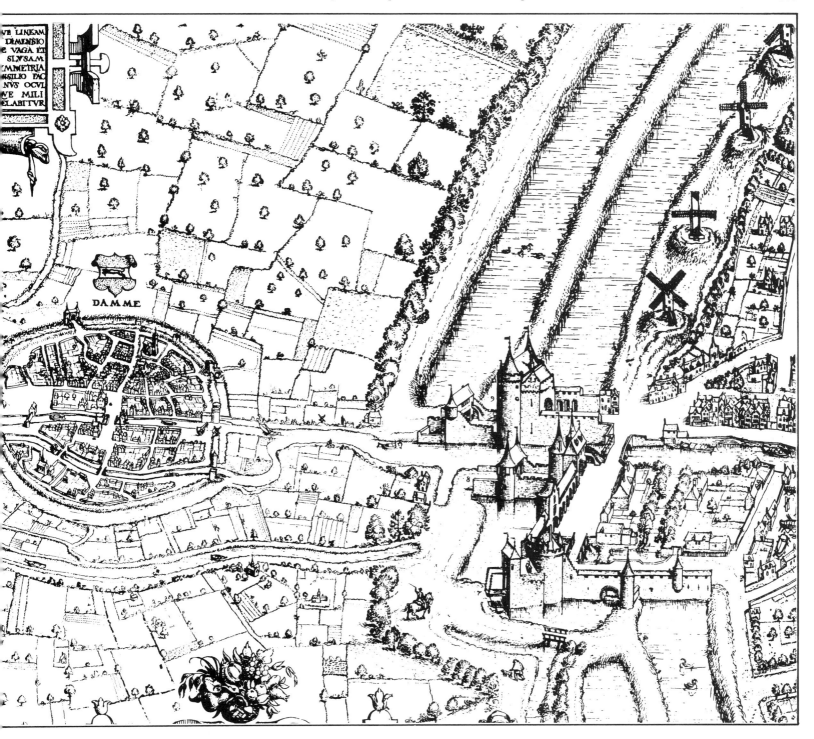

DAMME

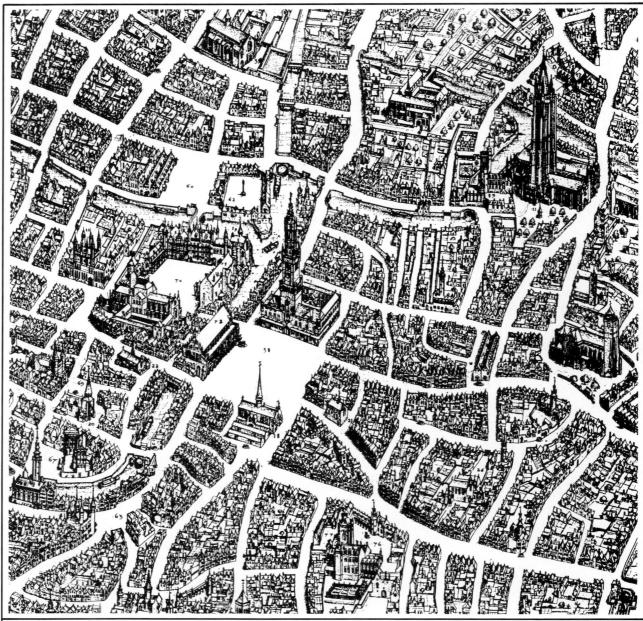

11. Cathedral of Notre Dame.	58. Fish market.	72. Waterhalle.
12. Church of St Sauveur.	60. Grain market.	75. Prison.
18. Chapel of St Christopher.	62. Leather market.	76. Prince's Hall.
20. Chapel of St John.	63. Bourse.	77. Mint.
21. Chapel of St Amanda.	70. Castle, with the Town Hall and	88. So-called 'Castle of the Seven
22. Chapel of St Peter.	Chancellery.	Turrets'.
26. Chapel of the Painters.	71. Halle.	

Fig. 579   Detail of the 1562 panoramic map, showing the heart of the city: the castle, the market place and the two main churches.

Fig. 580   The interior of the Cathedral of Notre Dame at Bruges.

During the closing decades of the thirteenth century, a third of the city's income was devoted to public works: the building of walls, the paving of streets, the provision of water. Private building was governed by a series of regulations: only tiled roofs were allowed (to minimise the risk of fire), but the municipality contributed a third of the cost. The owners of houses which were demolished in order to widen the streets were recompensed, but they were not allowed to demolish any building on their own initiative, and, if this occurred, they were obliged to rebuild within the space of four months.

Bruges continued to flourish throughout the fourteenth and fifteenth centuries. A number of important private houses were built during this period, amongst which are the House of the Portinari (1451), the House of the Hanseatic Merchants (1478), and the House of the Van Beurs Family, where the merchants used to gather to discuss business matters (Fig. 588): it was the first *bourse* of the type later founded in the other cities of Europe. In the rich bourgeois environment of Bruges, the greatest Flemish painters of the

Figs 581–4   Bruges. The houses at the southern side of the market
place; the Marshal's Gate; aerial views of two streets at the centre of
the city.

Fig. 585   An old photograph of the Quai du Rosaire.

Fig. 586   An old photograph of the basin within the castle, showing the tower of the Halle.

Fig. 587   The canal which joins Bruges and Damme, as it is today.

Fig. 588 The Bourse at Bruges, showing the houses of the Florentine and Genoese merchants.

Fig. 589   The Palace of Justice within the castle precincts at Bruges.

Fig. 590 *The Madonna with Chancellor Rolin* by Jan van Eyck, now in the Louvre in Paris.

fifteenth century flourished: Jan van Eyck, for example, who died in 1441, and Hans Memling, who lived in the city from 1465 until his death in 1494. In St John's Hospital there are still works by Memling, which were commissioned by the rich citizens of Bruges: the triptych of the marriage of St Catherine of Alexandria (1479), the triptych of the Adoration of the Magi (1479), the triptych showing the Lamentation of the Dead Christ (1480) and the Reliquary of St Ursula (1489) (Figs 592–8).

The port of Bruges still remained the most important maritime trading centre of Europe; but the Germans, English and Italians were joined in the fourteenth century by the Spaniards and Portuguese, who had begun exploring the spice routes of the southern Atlantic. The Zwin, however, was gradually silting up, and the outer port had to be moved even further away, from Damme to Sluys. In 1378 work began on excavating a new and more direct canal from Damme to the sea, but immediately afterwards it was interrupted by the outbreak of civil war and the link between Bruges and the sea became less and less safe. From the fifteenth century onwards, goods had to be transported overland from Sluys to Bruges, which meant a rise in costs. Finally, in 1460, even the port of Sluys became inaccessible

Fig. 591   The great wooden crane at Bruges, as seen in a fifteenth-century miniature.

Figs 592–8 The reliquary of St Ursula, painted by Hans Memling, in St John's Hospital. The reliquary itself and the six panels showing scenes from the saint's life.

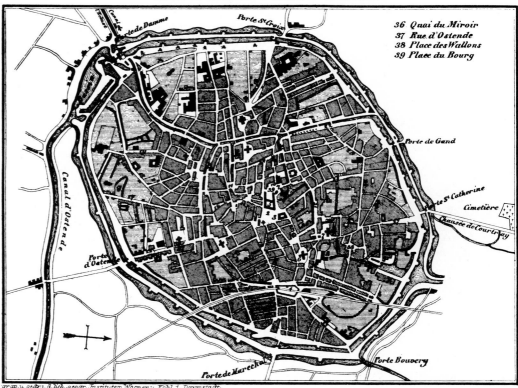

BRUGES . BRÜGGE.

36 *Quai du Miroir*
37 *Rue d'Ostende*
38 *Place des Wallons*
39 *Place du Bourg*

Fig. 599   Map of Bruges during the first half of the nineteenth century, showing the railway line that cuts through the lower half of the city.

to large ships, but by this time the importance of the market at Bruges, founded on the privileges granted by the great trading powers, was being threatened by competition from other cities, who instead guaranteed the merchants freedom of commerce.

In 1488 the Emperor Maximilian invited the foreign merchants to transfer their business from Bruges to Antwerp, and from this moment on Antwerp became the new maritime trading centre of Europe, and Bruges gradually turned into a quiet provincial city. The great panoramic map of Marc Gerards, engraved in 1562, gives a detailed view of the city — complete with its Gothic monuments and its areas of fifteenth- and sixteenth-century houses —

which at the time had failed to fill all the space enclosed within the fourteenth-century walls (Figs 577–9). A census taken in 1580 lists 8,129 buildings, and the population hovered between 30,000 and 35,000 from the sixteenth to the eighteenth century.

Bruges has remained substantially unchanged right up to the present day and it still continues to be a peaceful city isolated from the commercial mainstream. A few suburbs have grown up outside the walls and a new seaport was built in 1914 at Zeebrugge on the present coastline, but the city's main preoccupation nowadays lies in the administration and restoration of its ancient architectural heritage and in finding ways to adapt it to modern life without destroying it.

Fig. 600 Aerial view of modern Bruges, with its new outlying districts. Above, right: the old canal to Damme. Left: the modern canal leading to the new seaport of Zeebrugge.

Fig. 601 A fifteenth-century miniature, from the manuscript containing the statutes of the Drapers' Guild. City Museum, Bologna.

Fig. 602   The earliest view of Bologna, which dates from the sixteenth century.

BOLOGNA

The site of the present city has been inhabited since the earliest days of antiquity, and it was chosen by the Romans for a colony which they founded in 189 BC. The first wave of settlers was composed of 3,000 families, four-fifths of whom settled in the countryside, with the remainder establishing themselves in the central area. Later the town grew and became one of the largest in northern Italy, covering an area of between 50 and 80 hectares and harbouring several tens of thousands of inhabitants, whose water supply came from the Setta valley by means of an aqueduct and an underground channel, 17 kilometres in length.

After the fall of the Empire the town gradually sank into decay, and it was in this ruined state that St Ambrose saw it in the fifth century. Only the eastern part of the town, which was the newest and most solidly-built section, was protected by the first set of walls, possibly erected during the time of Theodoric at the start of the sixth century (Fig. 603). These narrow walls had four gates and enclosed the area that was later to form the centre of the medieval city, containing the cathedral, the Palazzo Comunale, the Basilica of San Petronio, and the Palace of King Enzo, built around the rectangular Piazza Maggiore, whose dimensions coincide with those of one square in the geometrical layout of the original Roman city. Immediately outside the eastern gate (the Porta Ravegnana, where nowadays the two leaning towers stand) the Lombards established an independent settlement with its own semi-circular walls.

The population began to grow, as in the rest of Europe, between the end of the tenth century and the beginning of the eleventh. In 1069 the cathedral, which hitherto had stood outside the walls, was moved to its present site within them, and 1088 marked the foundation of Bologna's famous

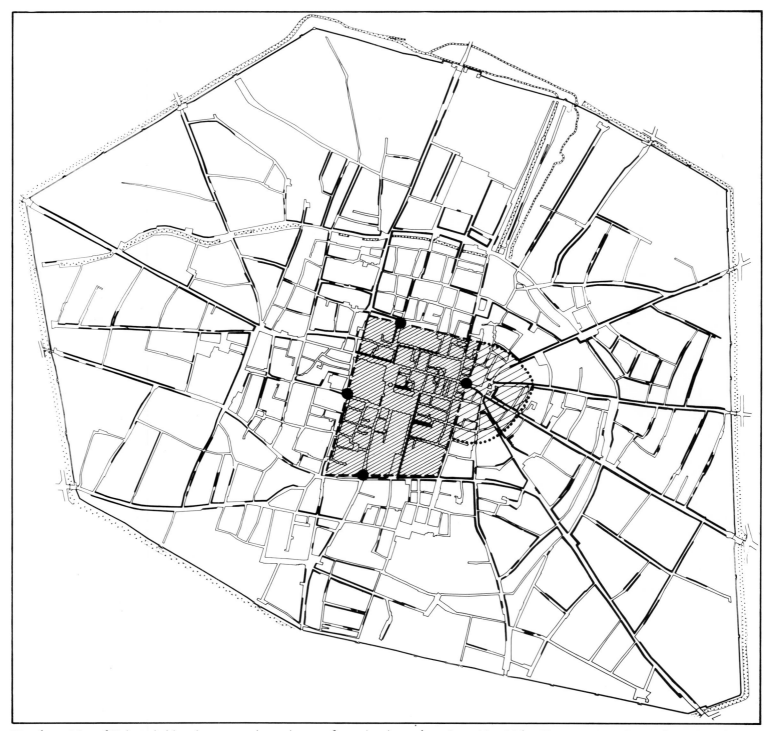

Fig. 603 Map of Bologna's historic centre prior to its transformation in modern times (the thicker lines represent the arcades, which formed a continuous network throughout the city); also shown are the earliest set of walls, with its four gates, and the peripheral Lombard settlement.

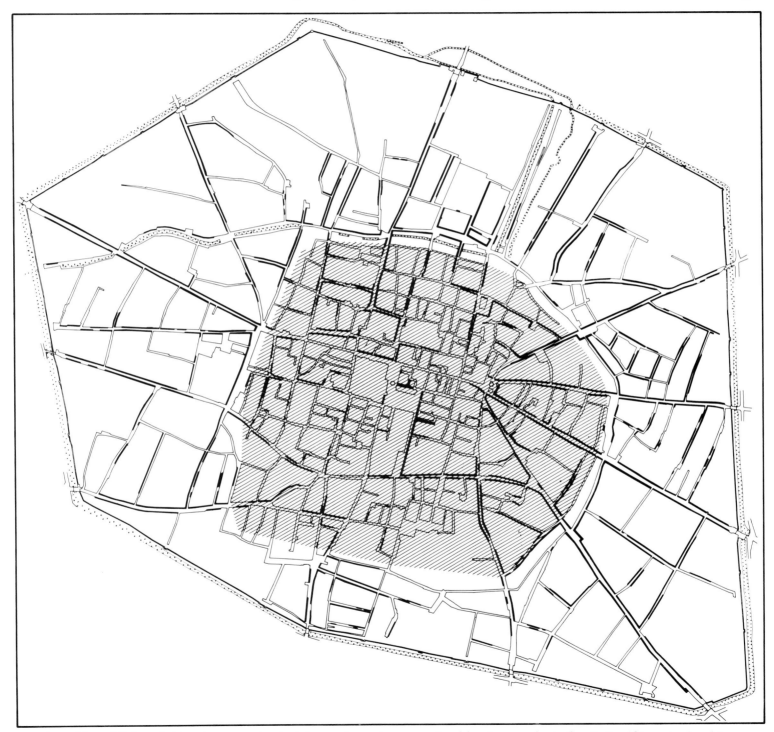

Fig. 604 Map of Bologna's historic centre; the shaded part shows the area enclosed by the second set of walls (twelfth century), whose outline can still be traced in the modern streets.

Figs 605–6 The tomb of St
Dominic in Bologna. A detail
of one of the statuettes on the
front of the tomb (San Petronio
holding a model of the city),
sculpted by Michelangelo in
1495.

university, the oldest in Europe, in which was kept a section of the Codex Justinianus, brought there from Ravenna. After 1115, the year in which the Countess Mathilda of Canossa died, the Commune of Bologna was established and the two towns (the Latin one and the Lombard one) were joined together in a single unit. In the twelfth century a second set of walls was built, concentric to the two earlier ones, which surrounded, for the first time, the whole area of the ancient Roman town, as well as the new settlements that had sprung up to the south and east, some 120 hectares in all (Fig. 604).

This city continued to expand throughout the thirteenth century. In 1201 the Commune established its headquarters in the centre of the city, on the western side of the Piazza Maggiore, and in 1246 a new municipal palace began to be erected on the southern side of the square, in which King Enzo, son of Frederick II, was imprisoned in 1249. Bologna began to spread out in all directions beyond the walls, and the mendicant orders soon established themselves in these new suburbs: the Dominicans to the south, in the monastery where St Dominic himself died and was buried in 1221, and the Franciscans to the west, where they built a church in the Gothic style between 1236 and 1250. In these peripheral churches many major works of art are to be found: in the Church of St Dominic is the sarcophagus containing the body of the saint, a monument that contains work by Italy's greatest sculptors — Nicola Pisano, Arnolfo di Cambio, Niccolo dell'Arca and the young Michelangelo (Figs 605–6) — while the Church of St Francis possesses an altar by the Delle Masegne brothers (1388–92) (Fig. 607). In order to defend this greatly enlarged city a third set of walls was built, which enclosed an area of roughly 400 hectares.

Fig. 607 The marble altar-piece from the great altar of the Church of St Francis, by Antonello and Pier Paolo delle Masegne (1388–92).

Scale 1:1000

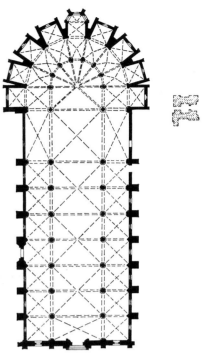

Figs 608–9   Interior and layout of the
Church of St Francis in Bologna
(begun in 1236).

Figs 610–11   Aerial views of the Church of St Dominic and the Church of St Francis in Bologna, showing the surrounding areas.

Fig. 612   Aerial view of the Church of San Petronio in Bologna, started in 1390.

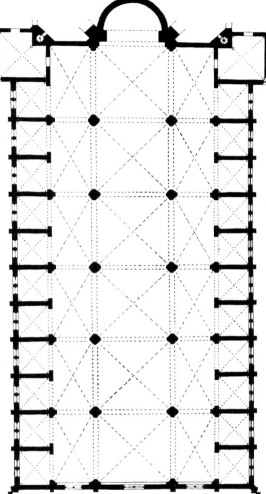

Scale 1:1000

Figs 613–14 Interior view and layout of the Church of San Petronio in Bologna. The modern church consists of the front part of a much larger structure, which was never completed; behind the apse can be seen the points where the wings were to join the octagonal centre.

The economic crisis during the second half of the fourteenth century resulted in a weakening of the city's institutions and Bologna was conquered by the Visconti family
from Milan and then by the Papacy. In 1377 the Commune
and the Holy See came to an agreement, which ensured the
city's administrative autonomy (the so-called 'Government
of the Six Hundred'), an event that triggered off a vast
programme of public works: in 1370 the reconstruction of
the Palazzo Comunale was started, in 1380 the third walls
were completed, and in 1390 work began on an enormous
new church, of San Petronio, which was never to be completed (Figs 612–14).

At the beginning of the fifteenth century Jacopo della
Quercia was commissioned to decorate the main door of San
Petronio with its famous marble reliefs, one of the master-
pieces of the early Renaissance.

It was also during the fifteenth century that the Ben-
tivoglio family emerged from the city's ruling body and
seized power, taking over the government of the city without altering its physical appearance, which by now was
complete. The family's great palace, built by Florentine
architects, was completely destroyed in 1505, when Pope
Julian II reconquered the city, and all that remains of it
today is a pile of rubble. The Papal government, which
continued uninterrupted until the nineteenth century, gave
Bologna a special status, and it became a sort of secondary
capital of the Papal States. Michelangelo, who had already
worked on the tomb of St Dominic as a young man, made a
bronze statue of Pope Julian II, which was destroyed during
a popular uprising in 1511, and in later years Vignola
altered the appearance of the Piazza Maggiore by building
the Palazzo dei Banchi on its eastern side, next to which St
Charles Borromeo built the new university, the Palazzo
dell'Archiginnasio.

The city, which had 50,000 inhabitants at the end of
the fifteenth century, now had the same layout that it was to
retain right up until the unification of Italy. Let us then
examine the city's appearance, as seen in a map of 1582
(Fig. 615).

The shape of the medieval city recalled that of the
Roman town and the roads that converged in it. In the
centre the colonial chequerboard layout is clearly recognisable; the *decumanus maximus* was the Via Emilia (its course

Fig. 615 Panoramic map of Bologna during the second half of the sixteenth century. At the centre can be seen the two towers of the Porta Ravegnana (F, G) and the Piazza Maggiore (M) with San Petronio (B) and the University (E).

within the town seems slightly crooked compared to the stretches outside, and this results from the fact that it was laid out shortly after the colony's founding). The roads emerged from the two exit gates and then spread out in the shape of a fan, a feature that had a decisive effect on the way the medieval suburbs developed. These radiating roads were intersected by the third set of walls, and their length depended on the importance of the settlements surrounding them. The city was thus able to develop without encountering any natural obstacles, and its shape illustrates, almost diagrammatically, the pressures exerted by its internal development, which resulted from the commercial exchanges between the city and the surrounding countryside. If one looks at a map of Italy, from Roman times to the modern day, it becomes clear that Bologna stands at the meeting point of the Po plain and the peninsula, and its whole nature reflects this important function.

The areas between the streets were left as wide open spaces, which were either used for agriculture or kept as gardens. The city's expansion during the last century, however, has resulted in some of these spaces being built over, but others still remain empty. The blocks of buildings in the city, between the second and third sets of walls, were very large; around the edge of each one there was a line of

Almost all the streets of Bologna were originally surrounded by arcades; a civil ordinance decreed that their height should not be less than 7 Bolognese feet (2.66 metres), so that people could also pass through them on horseback. The medieval arcades were often wooden, but they were replaced in subsequent centuries by ones made of stone. The earliest views of the city also show a large number of towers, which belonged to the residences of the noble families and are normally found within the first set of medieval walls (Fig. 602). Almost all of these towers have been either truncated or destroyed completely, except for the two by the Porta Ravegnana, which form one of the city's principal landmarks. In the northern part of the city there were originally several canals, which were used either for the transport of merchandise or to drive watermills, but nearly all of these have since been covered over (Fig. 620).

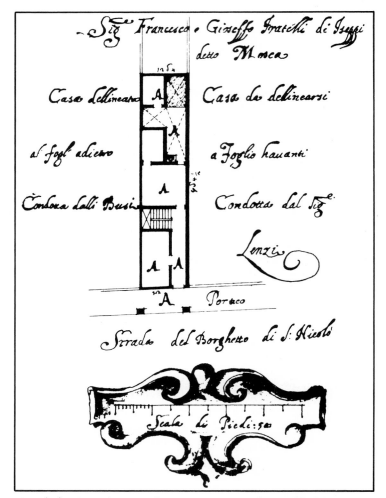

Fig. 616   One of a line of houses on the outskirts of Bologna, as shown in a cadastral drawing from the eighteenth century.

houses joined to each other, often of the same width, varying from 10 Bolognese feet (3.80 metres) to 16 Bolognese feet (6 metres), and built in series by the great landowners of the time — monasteries, guilds, families of the nobility — who rented them out to the artisans and workers. Each house had a vegetable garden, and all the gardens together would form a patch of green at the centre of each block (Figs 616–18).

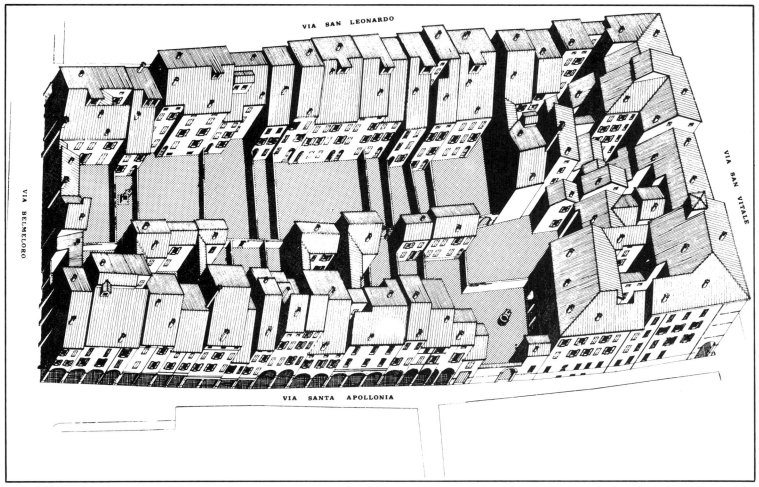

VIA SAN LEONARDO

VIA BELMELORO

VIA SAN VITALE

VIA SANTA APOLLONIA

Fig. 617   A block of buildings on the outskirts of Bologna, showing the terraced houses built round its perimeter and the vegetable gardens in the centre.

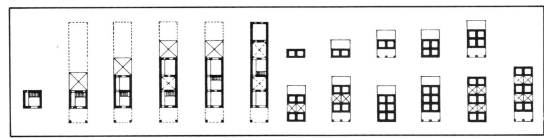

Fig. 618   Plans of the main types of terraced houses in Bologna.

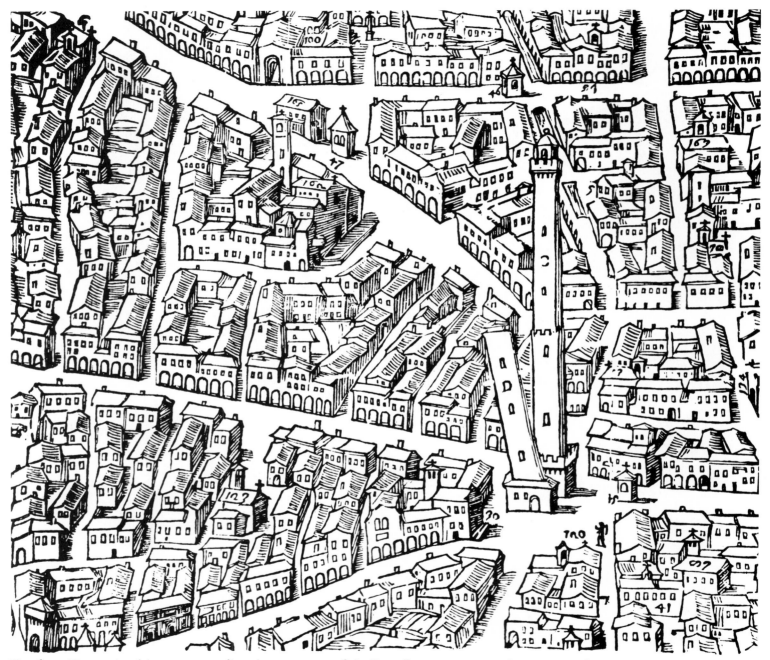

Fig. 619   The porticoed houses surrounding the two towers of the Porta Ravegnana, as seen in a seventeenth-century view.

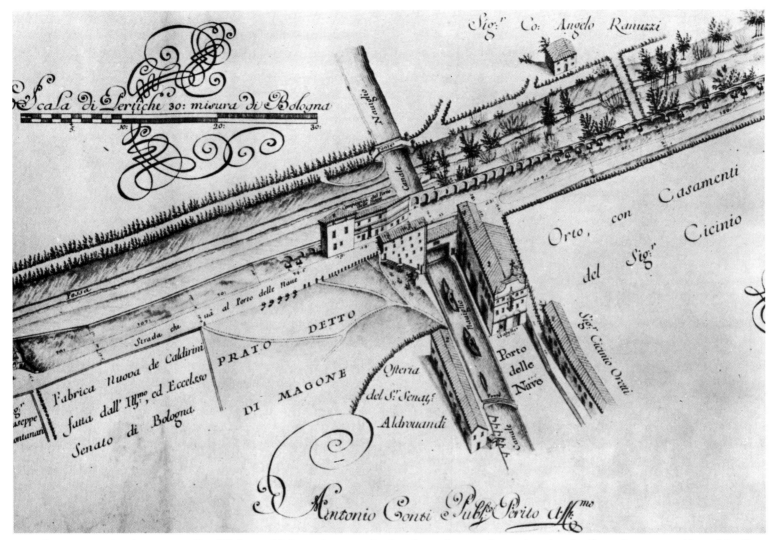

Fig. 620　A gate in the outer walls of Bologna (eighteenth century); also shown is a canal entering the city from the countryside and leading to a port within the walls.

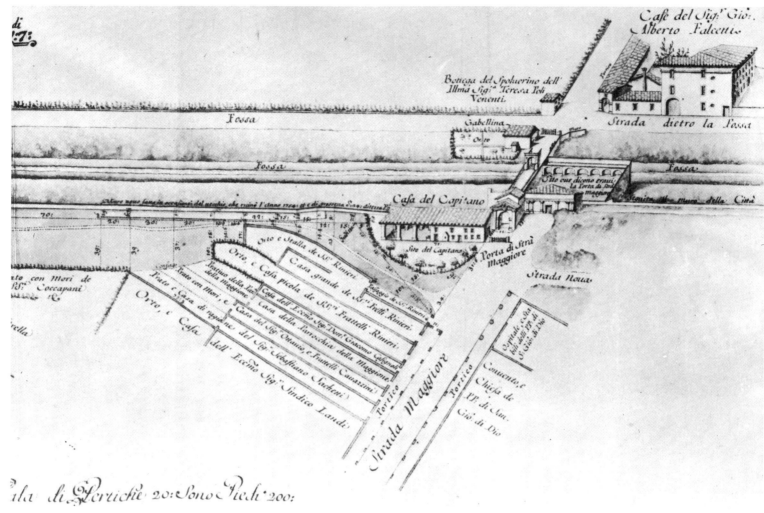

Figs 621–3   Three other gates in the outer walls of Bologna during the eighteenth century.

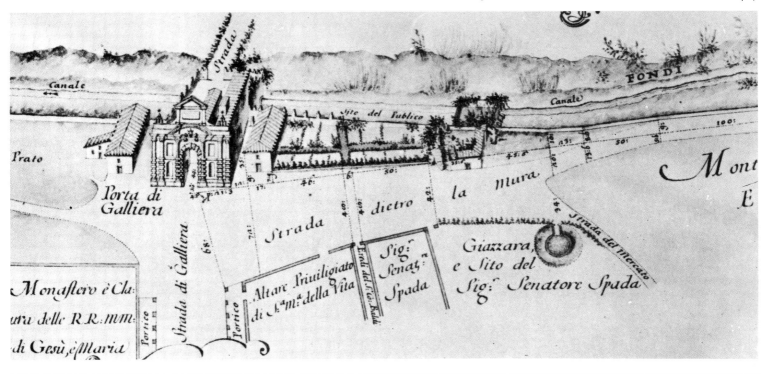

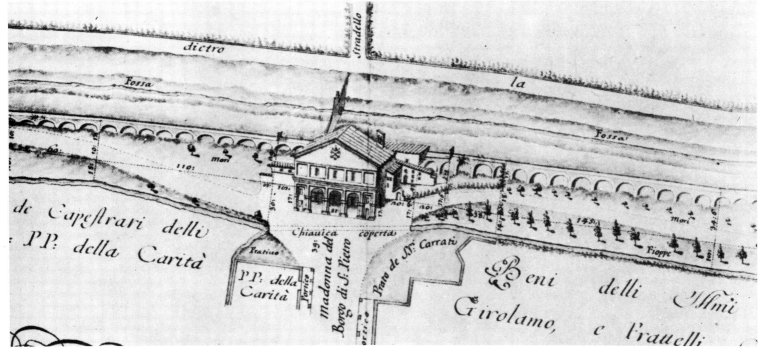

Fig. 624   Aerial view of the historic centre of Bologna. The axis of the Via Emilia can be clearly distinguished, as can the radiating streets of the Middle Ages. In the centre are the two towers of the Porta Ravegnana and the Piazza Maggiore with the Palazzo Comunale and the Church of San Petronio.

After 1859 Bologna began to develop outside the walls; when the Italian railway system was built in the last century, and when the network of autostrades was constructed during this century, the city was once more chosen as one of the main meeting points. The outer suburbs of the city have spread northwards because there are hills blocking development to the south. These suburbs, which as yet have not formed themselves into a unified scheme, have been divided up by great thoroughfares into much larger scale sections than the subdivision of the past.

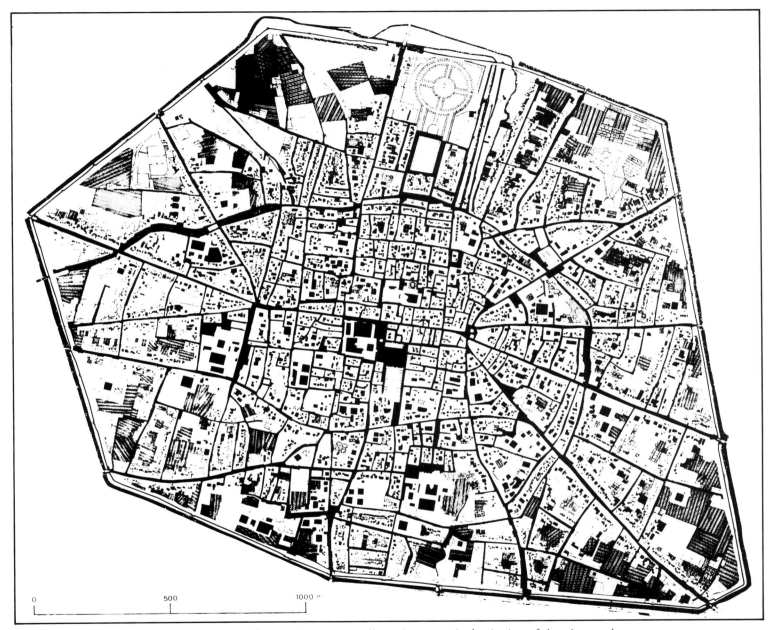

0   500   1000 m

Fig. 625   The centre of Bologna within the fourteenth-century walls, as it was at the beginning of the nineteenth century.

Fig. 626   The seal of the city of
Nuremberg, used from 1368 until
1808.

Fig. 627   Seating plan of the
Nuremberg city assembly, as seen in
an engraving from 1677.

Fig. 628 View of Nuremberg and its rural surroundings, in a painting on vellum from 1516.

NUREMBERG

This city was founded in 1040 by the Emperor Henry III at the meeting-point of the lines of communication between Franconia, Bavaria, Swabia and Bohemia.

The site chosen lies in the valley of the River Pegnitz, dominated by a hill on which a castle was built. The first area of settlement was between the hill and the river, around the market which thereafter became the focal point of the city's life.

In the twelfth century Frederick I founded another town on the other side of the river, which took the name of Lorenzerstadt after the Church of St Lorenz. The marshy area surrounding the River Pegnitz separated the two settlements, each of which possessed its own set of walls: it was not until 1320 that the two walls were linked and a single unit formed, known as Altstadt (the old city).

In the meantime, however, other secondary settlements were springing up to the south and east, where the ground was flatter, and in the second half of the fourteenth century the walls were extended to incorporate these suburbs into the main city. These new walls were one of the most elaborate military structures of the late Middle Ages and they comprised two parallel walls, reinforced by a series of towers, with a large outer ditch. In this way the city reached its maximum size, with a population of some 20,000

§ NVREMBERGA §

Fig. 629 The city of Nuremberg, as depicted in a sixteenth-century engraving.

Fig. 630   A watercolour view of Nuremberg by Albrecht Dürer.

inhabitants and a land area of 160 hectares. The centre of the
city was rebuilt, starting in 1348; the hovels of the oldest
part of the Altstadt were torn down, and the space was
cleared to make way for the new market place. It was during
this period that the main public buildings were constructed, buildings that are amongst the most important
examples of late Gothic German architecture: the Church of
Our Lady in the market place (1355), a simple square
structure covered by a wooden roof borne on nine vaulted
sections of equal height (Figs 631–3); the new choir of the
Church of St Sebald (1361); the famous fountain in the
market place (1385) (Figs 641–2). Other notable decorative
additions were made in the fifteenth century: the new choir
of the Church of St Lorenz (1439) and the resting place of
the Holy Sacrament in the interior of the same church. The
town hall, begun in the 1300s, was repeatedly enlarged
during the sixteenth and seventeenth centuries, but with
remarkable stylistic continuity (Figs 635–40).

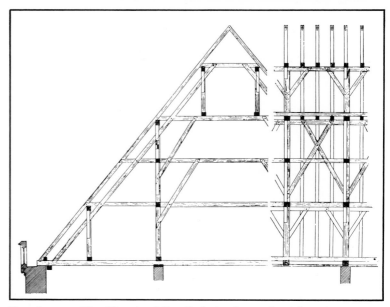

Figs 631–3   The Church of Our Lady in the market place at
Nuremberg; sectional view of the wooden roof construction,
exterior view and ground plan.

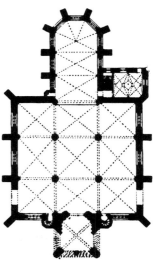

Fig. 634   Detail of the parochial house of St Sebald in Nuremberg.

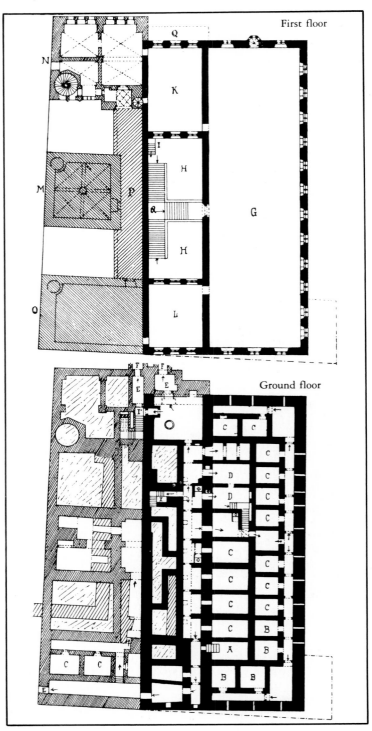

First floor

Ground floor

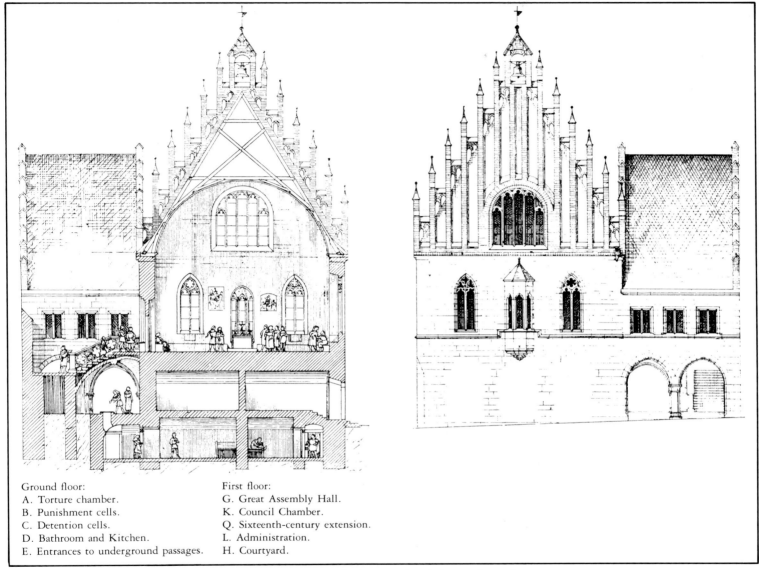

Ground floor:
A. Torture chamber.
B. Punishment cells.
C. Detention cells.
D. Bathroom and Kitchen.
E. Entrances to underground passages.

First floor:
G. Great Assembly Hall.
K. Council Chamber.
Q. Sixteenth-century extension.
L. Administration.
H. Courtyard.

Figs 635–8 Nuremberg's fourteenth-century town hall: ground plans, sectional view and exterior.

Figs 639–40   Details of the spiral staircase in
Nuremberg's town hall, on a scale of 1:50.

Figs 641–2 The fountain in the market place: diagram on a scale of 1:100 and a coloured drawing by Georg Pener, a pupil of Dürer (*c.* 1540).

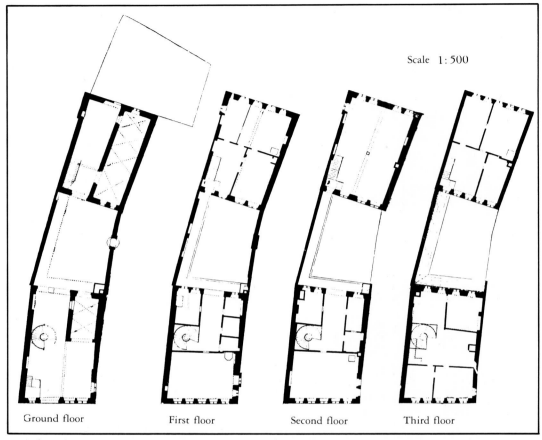

Scale 1 : 500

| Ground floor | First floor | Second floor | Third floor |

Figs 643–6   Plans of a merchant's house (7 Bergstrasse).

1. Entrance.
2. Shop.
3. Courtyard.
4. Workshop (added later).
5. Bedrooms.
6. Reception room.
7. Lavatory.

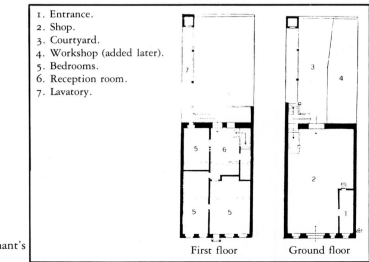

Figs 647–8   Plans of a merchant's
house in Dürerplatz.

First floor   Ground floor

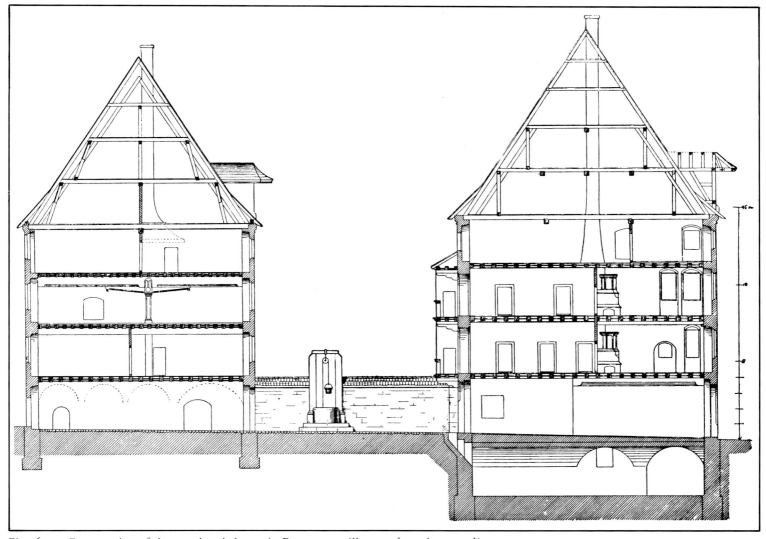

Fig. 649   Cross-section of the merchant's house in Bergstrasse, illustrated on the preceding page.

Fig. 650   Dürer's house in Nuremberg.

Fig. 651 The courtyard of the Heilsbronner house, from an eighteenth-century engraving.

Fig. 652   A section of the River Pegnitz, which flows through Nuremberg.

Fig. 653   Another view of the River Pegnitz at Nuremberg.

Fig. 654 View of the centre of Nuremberg, looking from the Church of St Lorenz towards the castle.

Fig. 655   View of the market place in Nuremberg.

Fig. 656   The public baths in
Nuremberg, from an engraving by
Albrecht Dürer.

Fig. 657   *The Adoration of the Magi* by Dürer, in the Uffizi Gallery, Florence.

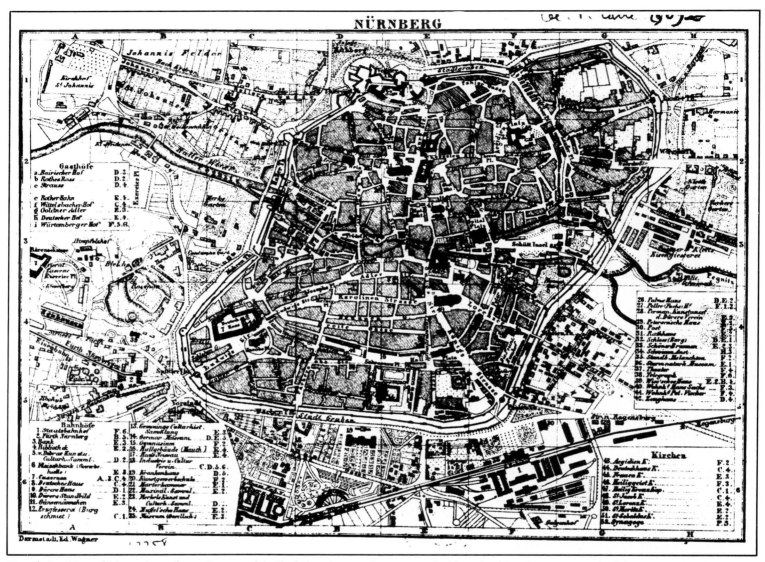

Fig. 658   Map of Nuremberg from the second half of the nineteenth century, showing the historic centre enclosed by the double walls, and the first external suburbs.

Fig. 659　A Nazi rally at Nuremberg.

Fig. 660　The Nuremberg War Crimes Tribunal in session.

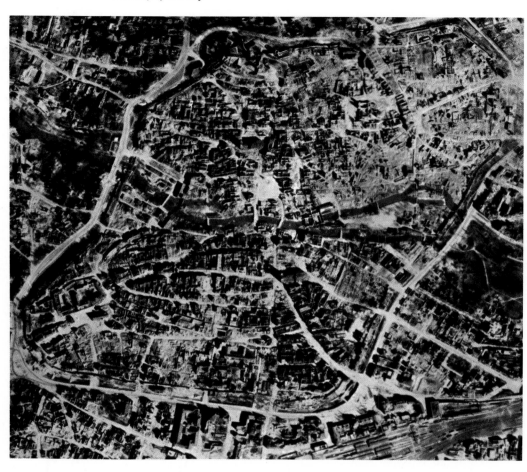

Fig. 661   An aerial photograph of the
centre of Nuremberg, showing the
devastation that occurred during the
Second World War.

In the late Middle Ages and in the Renaissance period
all overland commercial traffic between northern Europe,
Bavaria and the Alpine passes was obliged to pass through
Nuremberg and the city became one of the wealthiest in
Germany. Its government was controlled by the rich mercantile families, and later by bankers, such as the Welsers,
whose business interests stretched throughout the known
world. As is to be expected, the arts flourished in this
prosperous environment, and Nuremberg became the home
of the foremost sculptors of the time — Veit Stoss and the
Vischer family — and of the most illustrious German
painters, amongst whom was Albrecht Dürer. It later
became one of the foremost centres for metalworking, printing and cartography, as well as being the home of Hans

Sachs and the *meistersingers*, who contributed so much to the
development of the German literary tradition. The great
patrician houses, with their main building facing the street
and secondary ones grouped around an internal courtyard
(Figs 643–51), bear witness to the great prosperity of the
urban middle classes in the two hundred years between the
mid-fourteenth century and the Reformation.

After the religious wars Nuremberg continued to be the
capital of a small independent principality, but it was
subsequently absorbed into the kingdom of Bavaria. The
city that had grown up in the late Middle Ages was not
changed by any major alterations in later years: only the
fortifications were reinforced by new external bastions, to
keep pace with new military techniques. During the

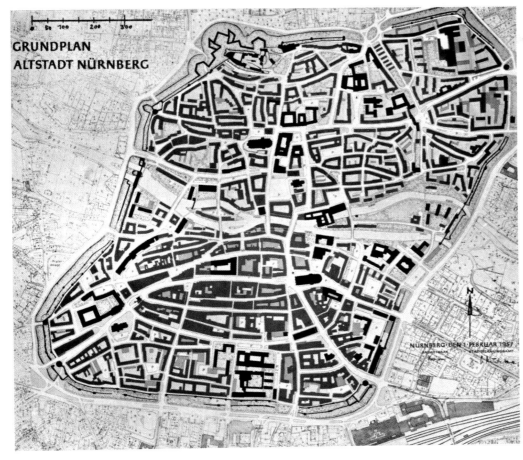

GRUNDPLAN
ALTSTADT NÜRNBERG

Fig. 662   The reconstruction plan for
the historic centre of Nuremberg.

nineteenth and twentieth centuries, however, the city's favourable geographical position led to a fairly conspicuous growth in its population, and the small medieval city became the centre of a large urban conglomeration whose inhabitants numbered some 420,000 at the outbreak of World War II. The Nazi regime organised a great annual rally in the city, and had a special stadium erected for the event, with tiered terraces (Fig. 659).

During the war Nuremberg was devastated by bombing: of the city's 125,000 houses, 57,000 were completely destroyed, 55,000 suffered some form of damage and only 13,000 survived intact. The historical city centre was almost totally destroyed (Fig. 661), and it was against the background of this destruction that the leaders of the Nazi

regime were tried at the famous Nuremberg War Trials during 1945/46 (Fig. 660).

Post-war reconstruction work has tried to respect the traditional nature of the historical city (Fig. 662), but a great many of the old houses have been supplanted by modern buildings. The monuments, however, have all been restored with minute attention to detail, using original drawings where possible.

The memory of the original medieval city has been entrusted to pre-war photographs (Figs 650–5), while the modern panorama of the city reveals an uneasy mixture of ancient and modern buildings, standing alongside each other in precarious harmony (Fig. 664).

Fig. 663   A 1958 map
of the city of Nuremberg.

Fig. 664   A modern aerial view of Nuremberg's historic centre, showing the old restored buildings and the new ones; at the centre is the market place.

Figs 665–6   The Florentine gold florin (twice life-size).

Fig. 667   The Marzocco, emblem of the city of Florence, on the tower of the Palazzo del Capitano del Popolo (The Bargello). In the background can be seen the Cathedral of Santa Maria del Fiore.

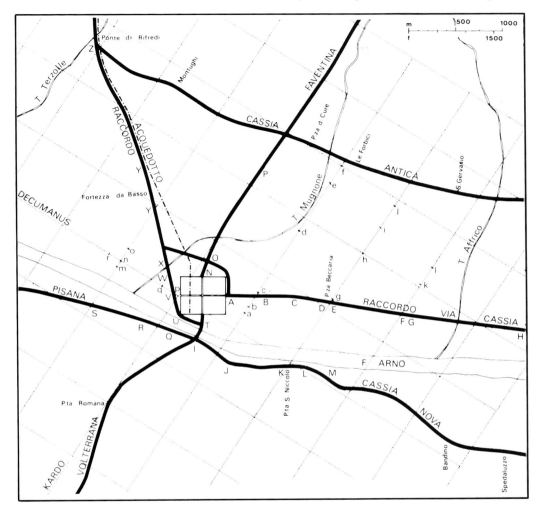

Fig. 668 The Roman colony of Florentia. The dotted lines show the outline of the *centuriatio* in the surrounding countryside.

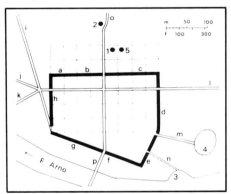

Fig. 669 The second set of walls, dating from Carolingian times.

FLORENCE

The Roman colony of Florentia, much smaller and less important than Bologna, was founded in 59 BC at the point where the Arno and the Mugnone meet.

The *centuriatio* in the surrounding plain ran, as usual, parallel to the river, with *centuriae* 2,400 feet (*c.* 700 metres) long. The town, on the other hand, was a small square, whose position was determined by the cardinal points of the compass, and its western gate coincided with the *umbilicus*, where the *cardo maximus* and the *decumanus maximus* met. It subsequently expanded and achieved a rectangular shape, covering an area of 20 hectares and sheltering a population of 10,000, and the Emperor Hadrian, besides straightening the course of the Via Cassia, also had a bridge built over the Arno, a short distance below the modern Ponte Vecchio (Fig. 668).

After the fall of the Empire the town was subject to the depredations of invading armies on several occasions. The Byzantines transformed it into a military encampment surrounded by trenches, enclosing the centre within a set of walls that gave protection to the remaining thousand or so inhabitants. Under the Lombards Florence continued to be of secondary importance (the capital of the duchy was Lucca, situated on the Via Francigena that joined Rome to northern Italy through the Cisa Pass); it may well have been

Fig. 674   The emblems of the Florentine guilds.

Major guilds:

1. Merchants or Di Calimala.
2. Judges and Notaries.
3. Exchange.
4. Wool.
5. Silk or Por Santa Maria.
6. Physicians and Apothecaries.
7. Vair preparers and Furriers.

Minor guilds:

8. Armourers and Swordmakers.
9. Locksmiths.
10. Shoemakers.
11. Harness Makers.
12. Leather Workers and Tanners.

13. Dressers and Second-hand Dealers.
14. Smiths.
15. Masters in stone and wood.
16. Carpenters.
17. Bakers.
18. Butchers.
19. Vintners.
20. Oil Makers.
21. Hoteliers.

Companies:

22. Compagnia del Bigallo.
23. Compagnia della Misericordia.
24. The emblem of the Opera del Duomo.

Fig. 675   View of Florence in a fifteenth-century illustration from the Divina Commedia.

the Arno was rebuilt after the floods of 1178 (it is now known as the Ponte Vecchio or Old Bridge). The Commune statutes also laid down the precise relationship that was to exist between public and private spaces, regulating the streets and placing limits on the height and projection of the houses.

In the thirteenth century the city embarked on a period of even more rapid development; its population increased from 50,000 to 100,000 and it became one of the most important economic centres of Europe, particularly in the fields of banking and woollen textiles.

The beginning of the century saw the formation of trade guilds for the various branches of commerce and industry; from the old Merchants Guild grew the Exchange Guild (1206), the Wool Guild (1212), the Silk or Por Santa Maria Guild (1218) and the others that came to be known as Major Guilds. The poorer trades organised Minor Guilds, which lacked the same degree of privileges as the major ones. During this time the stability of the Commune was periodically threatened by the conflicts between Guelphs and Ghibellines (victory by the Guelphs and government by the *primo popolo* in 1250; return of the Ghibellines after Montaperti in 1260; new Guelph government, dominated by powerful merchants, in 1267). Each change of government resulted in the destruction of the houses belonging to the losing side, and the centre of Florence became dotted with ruins, but the magistrature continued to exercise strict control over the city's development by means of a series of regulations and ordinances.

A further three bridges were built over the Arno: the Ponte alla Carraia (1218), the Ponte alle Grazie (1237) and the Ponte di Santa Trinita (1252). In the outskirts of the city, and in the new suburbs, the mendicant orders began to establish themselves: the Dominicans at Santa Maria Novella (1221), the Franciscans at Santa Croce (1226), the Servites at Santissima Annunziata (1248), the Augustinians at Santo Spiritu (1250), and the Carmelites at Santa Maria del Carmine (1268). Their convents became the focal points of the surrounding quarters, with the squares in which they stood being planned and constructed under the auspices of the municipal authorities. In addition, these religious orders, and other private and public bodies, constructed a large number of hospitals, so that Florence in the fourteenth

Fig. 676 View of the Via del Proconsolo, with the tower of the Palazzo del Capitano del Popolo (The Bargello).

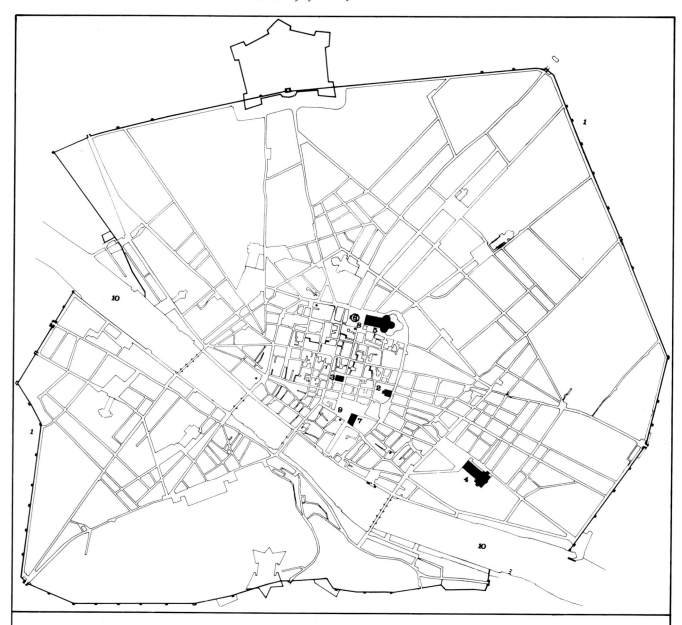

1. The fifth set of walls (1284).
2. The re-structuring of the Badia (1285–1310).
3. Or San Michele (1290).
4. Santa Croce (1295).
5. The founding of the Cathedral of Santa Maria del Fiore (1296).
6. The completion of the external decoration of the Baptistery.

7. The Palazzo dei Priori (Palazzo Vecchio) (1299–1310).
8. The laying-out of the Cathedral Square.
9. The laying-out of the Piazza della Signoria.
Other works attributed to Arnolfo are indicated by a black dot: the Churches of Santa Maria Maggiore, San Remigio and Santa Trinita, the Loggia del Bigallo and the Loggia della Signoria.

Fig. 677   The works undertaken in Florence under the supervision of Arnolfo da Cambio.

century possessed some thousand sick-beds. The Commune, however, was responsible for the inauguration of new streets (the Via Maggio, for example, which links up with the Ponte Santa Trinita), the paving of public areas and the maintenance of the river banks. In 1255 work began on building the Palazzo del Capitano del Popolo (The Bargello), whose tower dominated the whole of the city centre; since 1250 the towers of private houses had been restricted to a maximum height of 50 ells (*c.* 29 metres).

During the last twenty years of the thirteenth century, while the Judicial Ordinances of 1293 were being drawn up, the civic administration embarked on a series of public works that radically altered the physical appearance of the city. The adviser in all these works was Arnolfo da Cambio, who can also be regarded as the man responsible for this exercise in town planning, even though we have no way of knowing exactly how the various decisions were reached. Amongst those to be consulted were the city's magistrates and local officials, the religious orders, the guilds and the administrative bodies representing every commercial and social group in the city (Figs 677–84).

In 1284 it was decided to build a fifth set of walls, with a circumference of $8\frac{1}{2}$ kilometres and an internal area of approximately 480 hectares; it comprised an internal road of 16 ells, a wall of $3\frac{1}{2}$ ells, a 35-ell wide ditch and an outside road of $13\frac{1}{2}$ ells, making altogether a total of 68 ells (*c.* 41 metres), with 73 turrets, each of which had a height of 40 ells (*c.* 23 metres). The whole project was finally completed, at enormous cost, in 1333.

In 1285 the Church of St Reparata was demolished in order to build a great new cathedral dedicated to Santa Maria del Fiore opposite the Baptistery. Thirteen years later, in 1298, work was begun on the new Palazzo dei Priori (nowadays known as the Palazzo Vecchio). And so, on the edge of the first set of walls, two new centres developed — one religious and one political — and two new squares were opened up: the Piazza del Duomo (Cathedral Square), formed by pulling down an old palace opposite the Baptistery, and the Piazza della Signoria, on the site of the houses of the Uberto family, which had been destroyed following the defeat of the Ghibellines. The two centres were joined by the Via dei Calzaioli, which was subsequently widened in the fourteenth century, and half way along it, in 1290, Arnolfo built the loggia of the cornmarket, the modern Or San Michele. 1287 was the year in which the Lungarno was built along the right bank of the river, while in 1294 the meadow of Ognissanti became a public thoroughfare, and in 1292 the district and parish boundaries of the newly laid-out city were fixed.

At the same time as the city's government was establishing a new administrative layout, both in the centre and in the outskirts, the building programme was being renewed with the same spirit of openmindedness and daring. The centres of each district grew in size as the city expanded. In 1278 the new Church of Santa Maria Novella was built at right angles to the earlier one, and a special commission was set up in 1288 to plan the new square surrounding it and to establish its precise dimensions. In 1295 Arnolfo made plans for the new Church of Santa Croce, which was built in the following century and decorated by the greatest Florentine artists of the day, among them Giotto (Fig. 694). At this moment Florence was the most important cultural centre in Italy: Giotto painted at Assisi, Padua and Rome, and Dante wrote his *Divine Comedy* in exile.

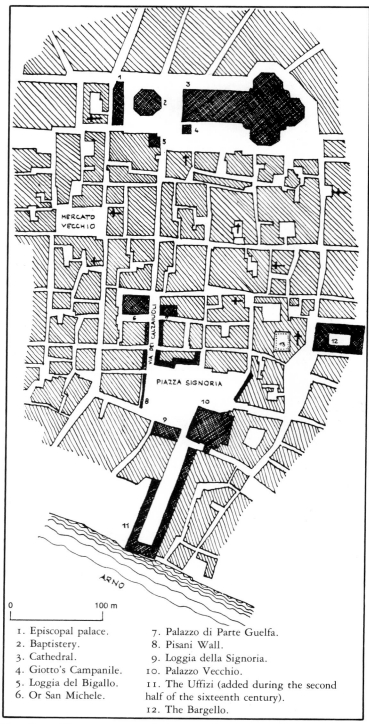

1. Episcopal palace.
2. Baptistery.
3. Cathedral.
4. Giotto's Campanile.
5. Loggia del Bigallo.
6. Or San Michele.
7. Palazzo di Parte Guelfa.
8. Pisani Wall.
9. Loggia della Signoria.
10. Palazzo Vecchio.
11. The Uffizi (added during the second half of the sixteenth century).
12. The Bargello.

Fig. 679   The new centre of Florence, following the work done by Arnolfo.

Fig. 680   An aerial view of Florence, looking from the Piazza della Signoria towards the Cathedral.

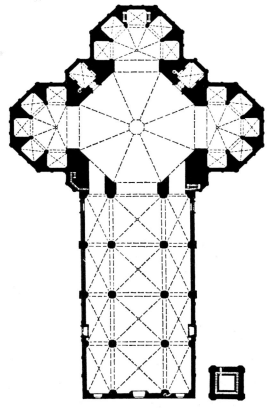

Scale 1:1500

Figs 681–3   The Cathedral of Santa
Maria del Fiore, built between 1296
and 1436; founded by Arnolfo, it was
enlarged during the late fourteenth
century. The Campanile was designed
by Giotto, while the dome was built
by Brunelleschi in the first quarter of
the fifteenth century.

Fig. 684   The Cathedral of Santa Maria del Fiore, as seen in a late fourteenth-century painting in Santa Maria Novella.

Fig. 685   Aerial view of Santa Croce, showing the church and the convent.

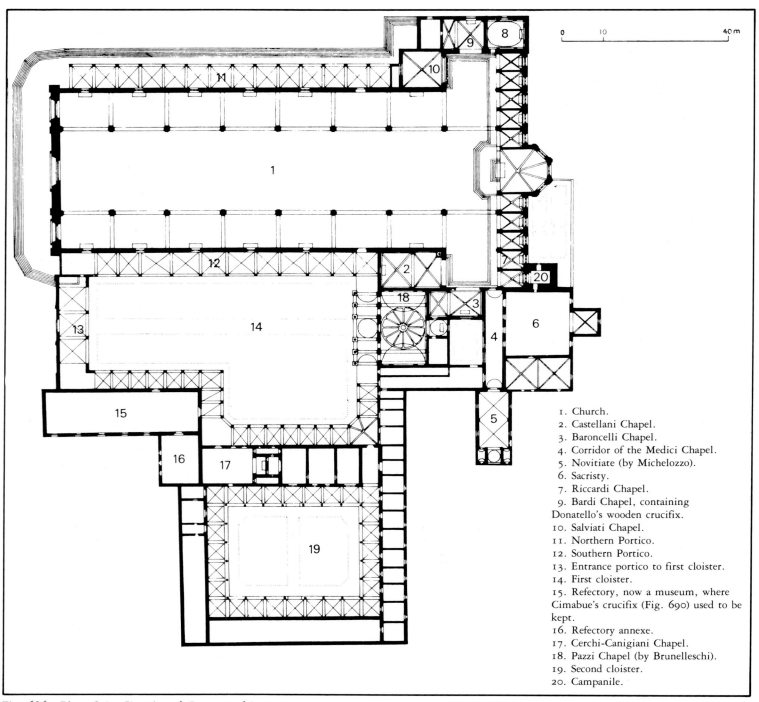

1. Church.
2. Castellani Chapel.
3. Baroncelli Chapel.
4. Corridor of the Medici Chapel.
5. Novitiate (by Michelozzo).
6. Sacristy.
7. Riccardi Chapel.
9. Bardi Chapel, containing Donatello's wooden crucifix.
10. Salviati Chapel.
11. Northern Portico.
12. Southern Portico.
13. Entrance portico to first cloister.
14. First cloister.
15. Refectory, now a museum, where Cimabue's crucifix (Fig. 690) used to be kept.
16. Refectory annexe.
17. Cerchi-Canigiani Chapel.
18. Pazzi Chapel (by Brunelleschi).
19. Second cloister.
20. Campanile.

Fig. 686   Plan of the Church and Convent of Santa Croce.

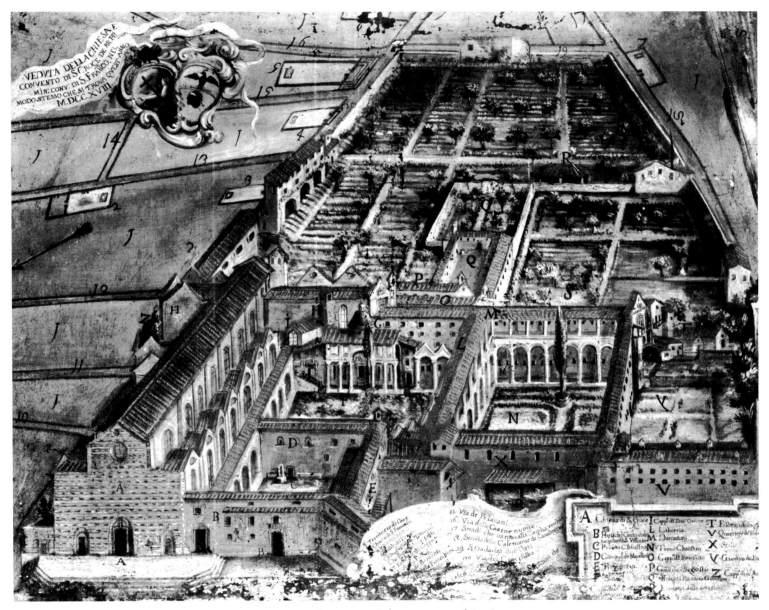

Fig. 687   The complex of buildings around Santa Croce, from a 1718 fresco preserved in the convent.

Fig. 688   The interior of Santa Croce
looking from the entrance.

Fig. 689   The interior of Santa Croce,
looking from the altar.

Fig. 690   Cimabue's crucifix, preserved in the refectory and damaged by floods in 1966.

Scala 1:2500

Fig. 691   Map of the district around Santa Croce. Note the houses to the left which follow the outline of the old Roman amphitheatre; immediately below the church is the modern building housing the Biblioteca Nazionale; to the right, the mainly modern buildings stretching out towards the ring roads.

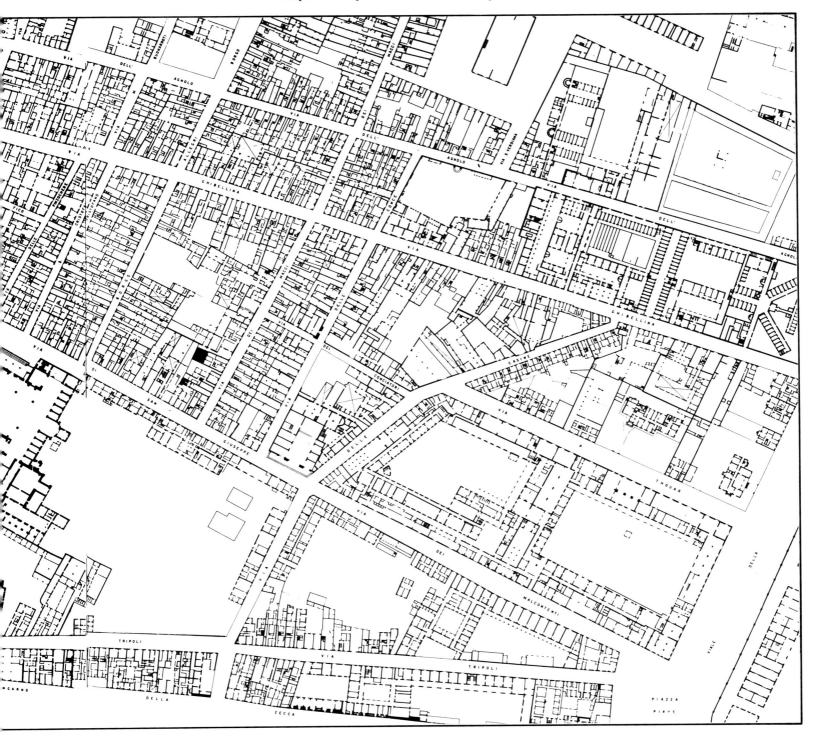

Figs 692–3   Two pictures of the Santa Croce quarter: aerial view from the Piazza della Signoria, looking towards the church, and a view from the tower of the Palazzo Vecchio, showing the hills in the distant background (above right can be seen the Church of San Miniato al Monte).

Fig. 694   A detail of Giotto's frescoes in the Bardi Chapel at Santa Croce.

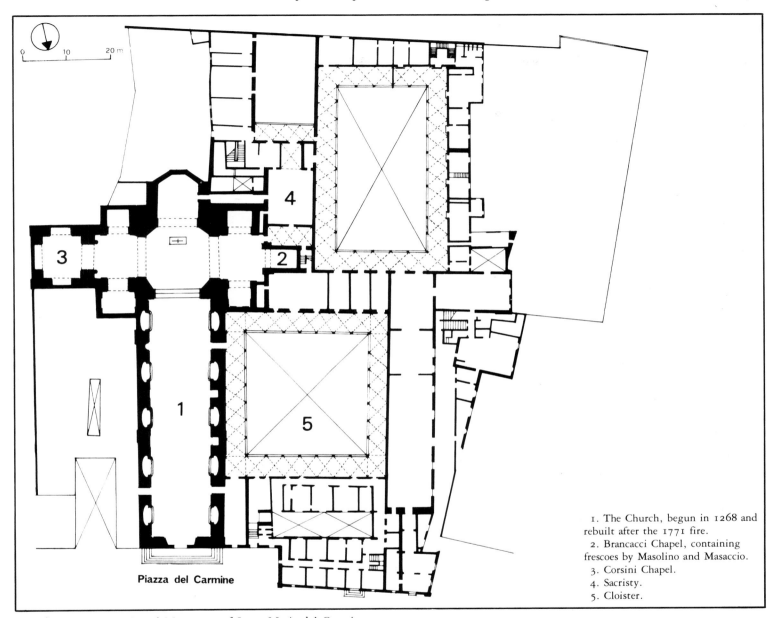

0 10 20 m

Piazza del Carmine

1. The Church, begun in 1268 and rebuilt after the 1771 fire.
2. Brancacci Chapel, containing frescoes by Masolino and Masaccio.
3. Corsini Chapel.
4. Sacristy.
5. Cloister.

Fig. 695   The Church and Monastery of Santa Maria del Carmine.

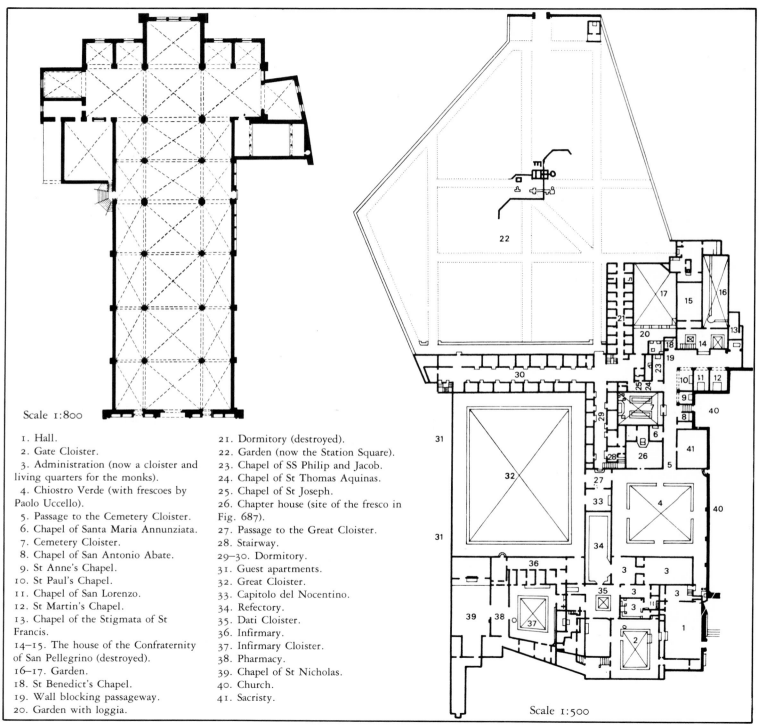

Scale 1:800

1. Hall.
2. Gate Cloister.
3. Administration (now a cloister and living quarters for the monks).
4. Chiostro Verde (with frescoes by Paolo Uccello).
5. Passage to the Cemetery Cloister.
6. Chapel of Santa Maria Annunziata.
7. Cemetery Cloister.
8. Chapel of San Antonio Abate.
9. St Anne's Chapel.
10. St Paul's Chapel.
11. Chapel of San Lorenzo.
12. St Martin's Chapel.
13. Chapel of the Stigmata of St Francis.
14–15. The house of the Confraternity of San Pellegrino (destroyed).
16–17. Garden.
18. St Benedict's Chapel.
19. Wall blocking passageway.
20. Garden with loggia.

21. Dormitory (destroyed).
22. Garden (now the Station Square).
23. Chapel of SS Philip and Jacob.
24. Chapel of St Thomas Aquinas.
25. Chapel of St Joseph.
26. Chapter house (site of the fresco in Fig. 687).
27. Passage to the Great Cloister.
28. Stairway.
29–30. Dormitory.
31. Guest apartments.
32. Great Cloister.
33. Capitolo del Nocentino.
34. Refectory.
35. Dati Cloister.
36. Infirmary.
37. Infirmary Cloister.
38. Pharmacy.
39. Chapel of St Nicholas.
40. Church.
41. Sacristy.

Scale 1:500

Figs 696–8   Plan of the Convent of Santa Maria Novella in 1902, before the opening of the square by the railway station; ground plan of the church and an aerial view of the complex.

Fig. 699 Aerial view of the Ponte Vecchio.

Fig. 700   Fifteenth-century painting, showing a panoramic view of Florence.

After this period of exceptional inventiveness and activity, Florence had all the makings of a great city. All that remained to be done was to continue along the lines of Arnolfo and add the final finishing touches to the city's new appearance. The outbreaks of plague, the most serious of which occurred in 1348 and is described by Boccaccio in the *Decameron*, resulted in a decrease in population, while the economic crisis in Europe had a serious effect on the city's economy. It was against this background that the social unrest of the second half of the fourteenth century developed, culminating in the Ciompi Revolt of 1378. The victorious aristocratic faction governed the city peacefully for two generations, until the time of the Medicis, and it

took upon itself to conclude, or rather realise, the plans envisaged in the thirteenth century. The artists who were commissioned for this purpose — Orcagna, Talenti, Ghiberti and, later, Brunelleschi, Donatello, Masaccio and Paolo Uccello — are those responsible for the city's final appearance. Brunelleschi's dome became the focal point of the whole city, as can be seen in views from the early fifteenth century (Figs 700, 703), but the artists also contributed something of universal value: they suggested a whole new cultural system, which was to transform artistic theory and practice throughout the whole world during the next four centuries.

This new movement — the Renaissance — will be dealt

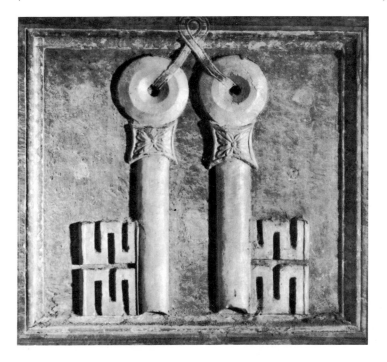

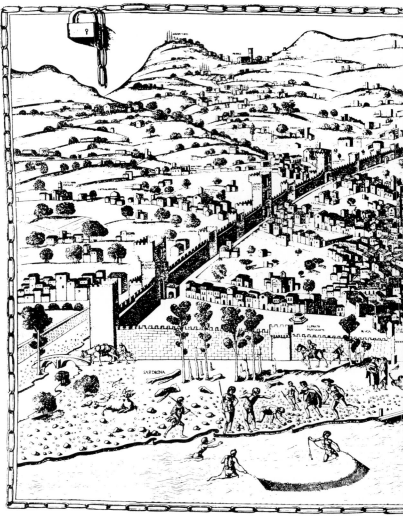

Fig. 703   A view of Florence, engraved between 1471 and 1482. The perimeter of the fifth set of walls takes the form of a circle, while the Cathedral, with its dome by Brunelleschi, occupies the centre of the scene.

Figs 701–2   The emblems of two of the six districts of Florence: Porta San Pietro (with the keys) and Porta del Duomo (with the model of the Baptistery).

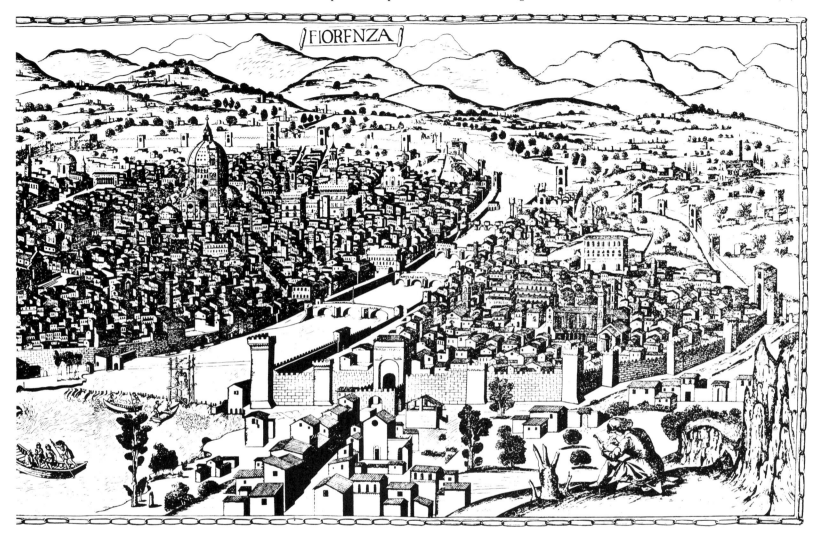

Fig. 704   A detail of the engraving on the preceding page, showing the houses round the Porta San Frediano.

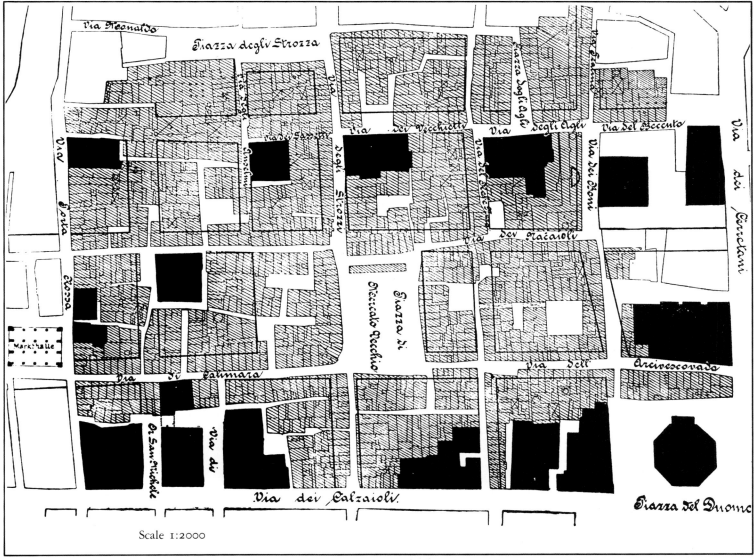

Fig. 705   The old market area, demolished at the end of the nineteenth century to make way for the Piazza Repubblica. All the shaded buildings have been destroyed; the ones in black, considered to be monuments, have been preserved.

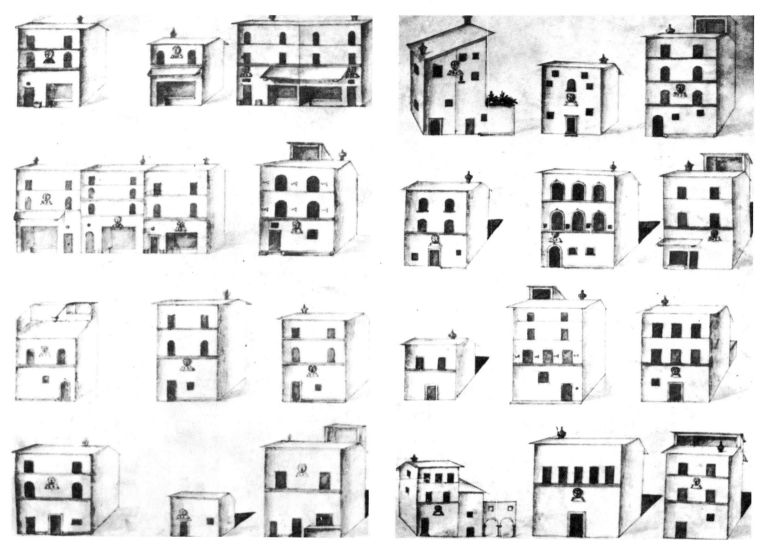

Figs 706–7   Florentine houses, as they appear in cadastral schedules of the eighteenth century.

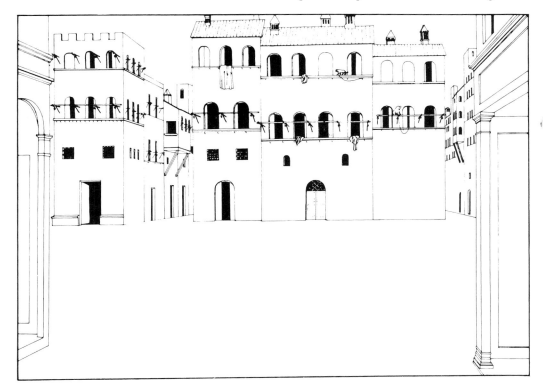

Figs 708–9 Pictures of Florentine houses: in the fourteenth-century Baldovinetti manuscript, and in the background of an early fifteenth-century wall-painting by Masaccio and Masalino at Santa Maria del Carmine.

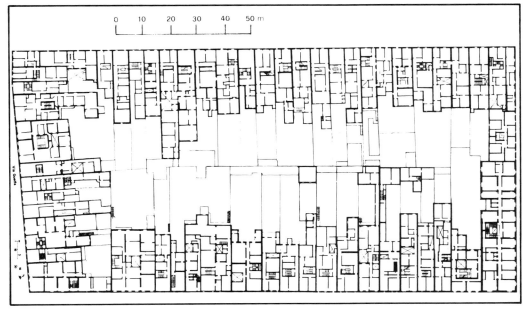

Fig. 710 Map of a block of buildings between the fourth and fifth set of walls, showing the terraced houses round the perimeter and the vegetable gardens in the centre (cf. the group of buildings in Bologna in Fig. 617).

Fig. 711   The emblem of the Wool Guild; a terracotta by the Della Robbias.

Fig. 712   The art of building.

with properly in the next chapter, but in the meantime let us consider the way in which artistic work was organised in medieval cities, in order to understand the nature and full extent of the subsequent transformation.

In the Middle Ages no distinction was drawn between art and any other profession, and artists were classified according to the materials they used. Building workers, the so-called Masters in Stone and Wood, formed one of the median guilds, which was incorporated into the major guilds after the Ordinances of 1293; the men who provided the lesser items, the Locksmiths and Carpenters, belonged to the minor guilds. In 1316 painters were included in the Guild of Physicians and Apothecaries, one of the major

guilds, because it was from these men that they bought their pigments; sculptors, if they worked in stone, were treated as building workers, but if they worked in metal, they were included with the goldsmiths of Por Santa Maria, another of the major guilds.

In this way, painters and metal sculptors already held a privileged position within the guild system. However, the most illustrious of them possessed a degree of personal prestige that raised them above the guilds, and often they were chosen by their city's government to act as high-level consultants and overseers for projects being carried out by the local workforce. Arnolfo, for example, was a sculptor, but he was consulted in connection with building works of

Fig. 713   Sculpture.

Fig. 714   Painting (three panels at the base of Giotto's campanile).

all kinds, and Giotto, who was a painter, was asked to design the campanile of Florence's cathedral. In fact, it was believed that any sculptor or painter, skilled in modelling or drawing visual forms, was able to deal in any formal medium, even on the scale of designing buildings or laying out whole cities. By the same token, the great humanist writers — Coluccio Salutati, Leonardo Bruni — were summoned to be chancellors of the Commune and decide official policy and act as ambassadors to other powers.

The artists of the Renaissance were the heirs of these latter men, not of the medieval specialists, locked in their guilds and restricted to knowledge of one sphere.

The contribution made by these citizen experts — from

Arnolfo to Brunelleschi — explains the excellence and inventiveness of Florentine life from the end of the thirteenth century onwards; the whole nature of their city, the subject of universal admiration, depended equally on the individual genius of these men and the collective organisation within which they worked. But the result of their labours was to bring crisis to this collective organisation, and the artists of the Renaissance, from Alberti onwards, became international experts, who gave their advice to anyone who sought it; they did make other notable contributions, but nobody was ever again able to envisage and shape a city in the same way as had been done during the Middle Ages.

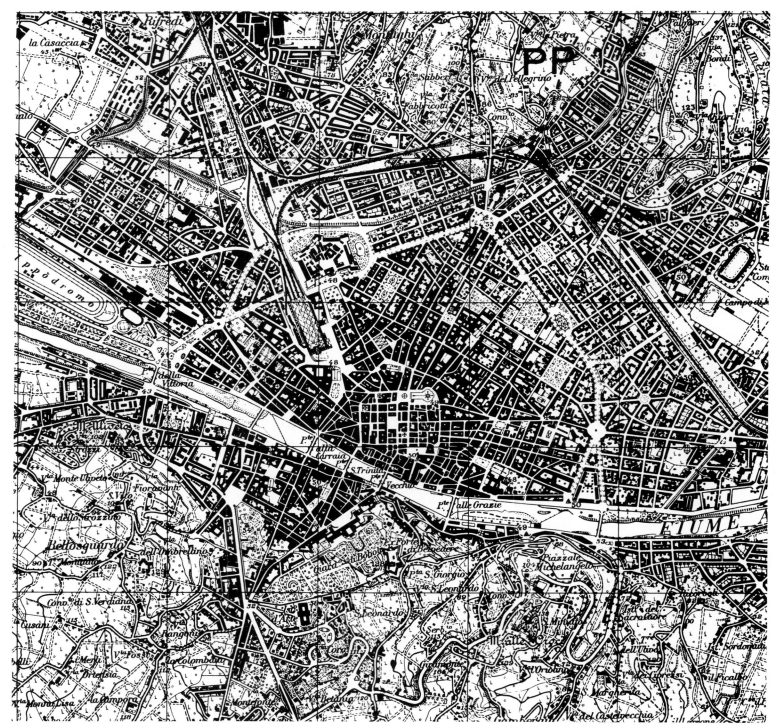

Fig. 715 Map of present-day Florence, from the Istituto Geografico Militare (scale 1:25,000).

Fig. 716   Aerial view of Florence from the east.

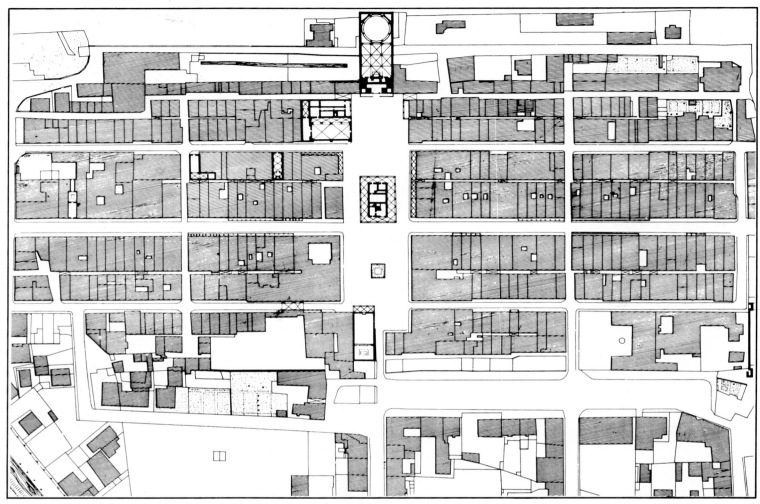

Fig. 717 Plan of the township of San Giovanni Valdarno, founded by the Florentines at the end of the thirteenth century (possibly after a plan by Arnolfo da Cambio).

Fig. 718   View of a fortified city painted by Ambrogio Lorenzetti.

THE NEW CITIES OF THE MIDDLE AGES

Venice, Bruges, Bologna and Florence were all examples of great cities that had been founded in antiquity or during the early Middle Ages, and which had been repeatedly changed in the late Middle Ages. It is impossible to describe them without taking into account this continuous process of evolution, and their complex forms reflect each successive stage in their development.

On the other hand, there were also many lesser towns which were founded during the late Middle Ages and often retained the same layout as when they were first conceived.

These towns come in every possible shape and size, and scholars have tried to categorise them under various headings: linear, circular, radiocentric, chequerboard. They have not, however, been able to find a constant reason for why certain layouts were chosen for some towns and not for others. Each town is a special case; either it developed as a result of a whole series of decisions, or it grew out of one initial decision. There are no hard and fast rules, but there is an infinite variety of circumstantial factors which must be taken into consideration: the nature of the terrain, local tradition, even religion. Any one of these could have been the deciding factor.

The people who founded cities — the kings, feudal barons, abbots or even the governments of city-states — were also the owners of the land on which they stood. They therefore had the power to decide the shape of individual cities down to the last detail: not only the streets, squares and fortifications, but also the way in which the land was to be divided up amongst future inhabitants. It meant that the balance between public and private areas, which in existent cities was obtained with difficulty and had to be constantly readjusted, could be calculated in advance.

In many small medieval townships, whether they were geometrically laid out like some of the French *bastides*, or irregularly, like the market towns of eastern Germany, the cadastral divisions formed a perfect and integral pattern, as in the Hippodamian cities of antiquity (Figs 727, 730, 738–41, 748–57).

In the following figures we show a number of these towns. The majority were founded between the end of the twelfth century and the mid-fourteenth century, with hardly any of them dating from a later period. The mysterious art of designing a town, unlike that of designing a building, was forgotten before it could be theorised in drawings and in books.

Fig. 719   The new towns (*bastides*), founded by the English in Périgord.

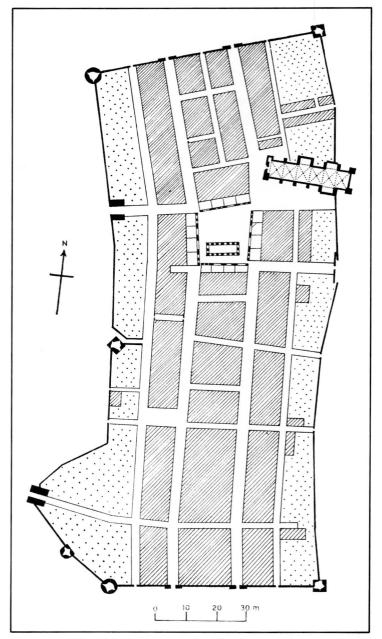

Fig. 720   One of the towns contained in the preceding map: Beaumont du Périgord, founded in 1272 by Luke de Thenney for the King of England.

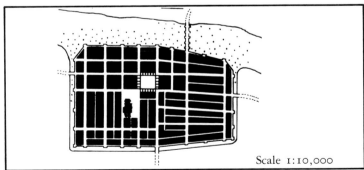

Scale 1:10,000

Figs 721–2 Villeneuve-sur-Lot in Gascony, founded in 1264 by Alphonse de Poitiers for the King of France. Emblem of the city and plan.

Fig. 723 Sainte-Foy-la-Grande on the Garonne, also founded by Alphonse de Poitiers in 1255. Aerial view of the modern city, showing the medieval street grid.

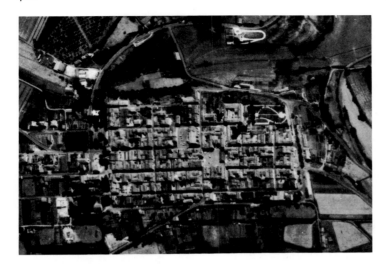

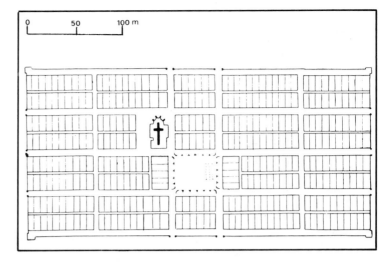

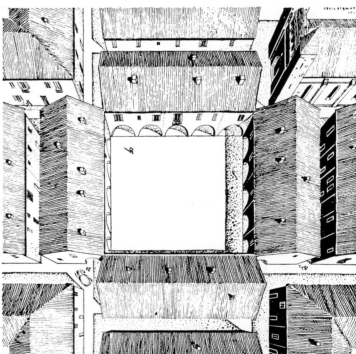

Figs 724–8 Monpazier in Périgord (see Fig. 719), founded in
1284 by Jean de Grailly for Edward I. Aerial photograph, map,
details of the church and the market place.

Figs 729–31   Aigues Mortes at the mouth of the
Rhône, founded by the French king, St Louis IX, in
1246. Aerial view, map and detail of the external
fortifications.

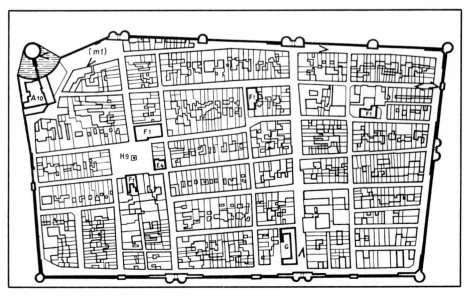

Section

Southern prospect

Plan A–B

Plan B–B

0   5   10   20 m

Figs 732–6 Aigues Mortes. The Tour de Constance, which defends the north-western corner of the city (the one facing inland). Cross-section, external view, two plans at levels A–A and B–B, and a view of the hall on the ground floor, showing the great fireplace and the windows, which gradually reduce in size until they are merely slits in the outer wall.

Fig. 737   View of Aigues Mortes from the Tour de Constance. The
city, which had 15,000 inhabitants during the Middle Ages and now
has less than 5,000, has preserved its original shape perfectly.

1. Cologne.
2. Mirande.
3. Barcelonne du Gers.
4. Beaumont de Lomagne.

0   50   100 m

Figs 738–41   Plans of four French *bastides*, founded by Eustache de Beaumarchais at the end of the thirteenth century.

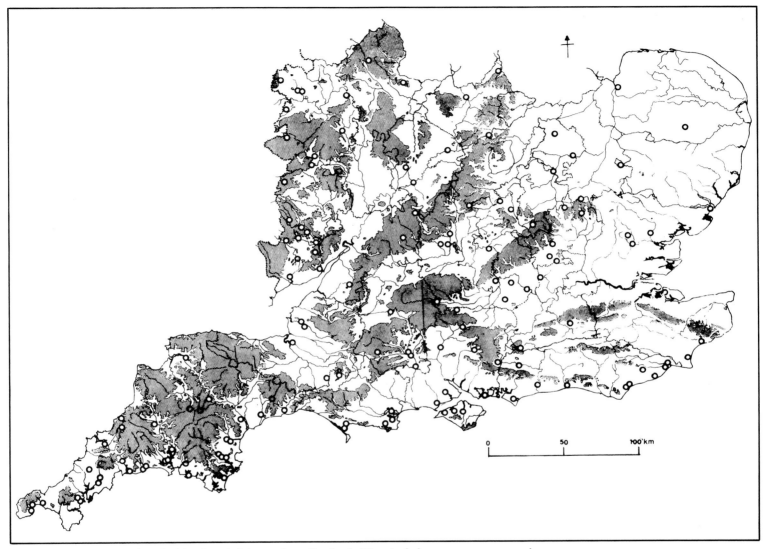

Fig. 742 The new medieval cities founded in southern England. The shaded areas represent woods.

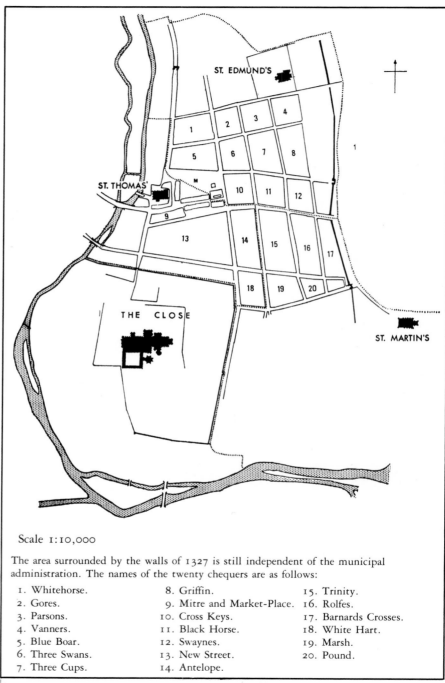

Scale 1:10,000

The area surrounded by the walls of 1327 is still independent of the municipal administration. The names of the twenty chequers are as follows:

1. Whitehorse.	8. Griffin.	15. Trinity.
2. Gores.	9. Mitre and Market-Place.	16. Rolfes.
3. Parsons.	10. Cross Keys.	17. Barnards Crosses.
4. Vanners.	11. Black Horse.	18. White Hart.
5. Blue Boar.	12. Swaynes.	19. Marsh.
6. Three Swans.	13. New Street.	20. Pound.
7. Three Cups.	14. Antelope.	

Figs 743–4   New Sarum (Salisbury) in Wiltshire, founded in 1219. The twenty groups of buildings of the medieval city, the four churches, the most famous of which is the cathedral (founded in 1220), and the market place (M). To the left is the Cathedral Close, still preserved in the modern city.

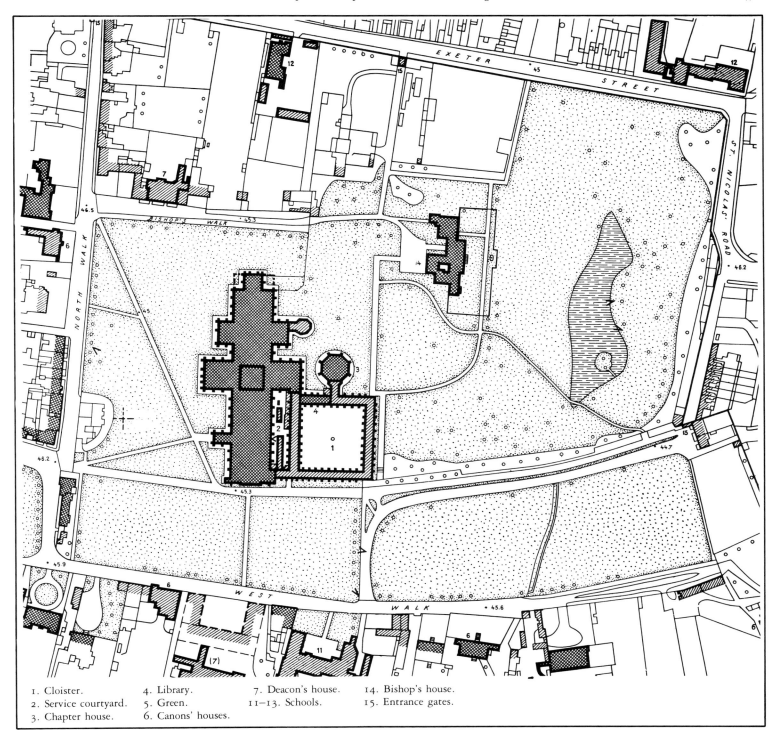

1. Cloister.
2. Service courtyard.
3. Chapter house.
4. Library.
5. Green.
6. Canons' houses.
7. Deacon's house.
11–13. Schools.
14. Bishop's house.
15. Entrance gates.

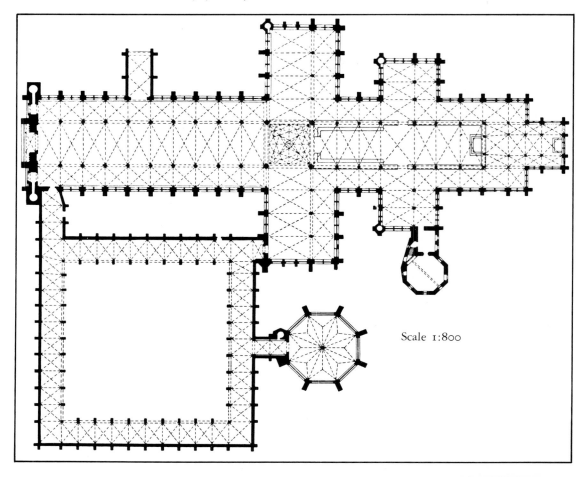

Scale 1:800

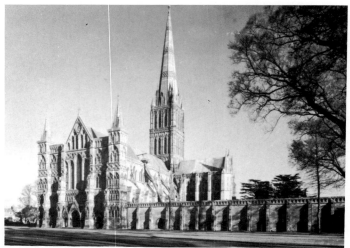

Figs 745–7   Plan, exterior view and aerial view of the cathedral in
Salisbury.

1. Budweis.
2. Novy Jicin.
3. Klattau.
4. Wodnian.
5. Morawska Trebova.
6. Domazlice.
7. Iglau.
8. Unicov.
9. Kolin.
10. Pilsen.

Figs 748–57   Ten medieval cities in Czechoslovakia.

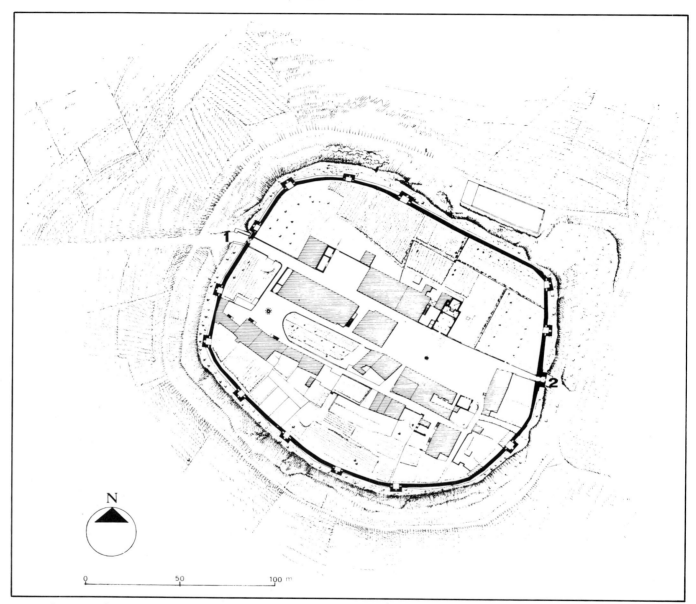

Fig. 758 Plan of Monteriggioni erected in the early thirteenth century by the Sienese, at the northern edge of their territory, in order to defend it from the Florentines.

Fig. 759   Aerial view of Monteriggioni. The town, which has retained its isolation, still possesses its original shape.

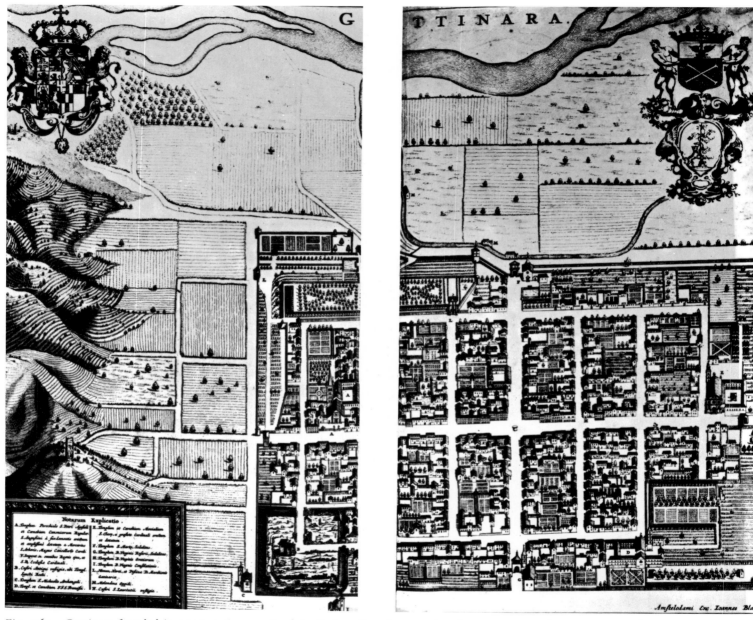

Fig. 760 Garrinara founded in 1242 at the mouth of the Sesia valley. A map taken from a seventeenth-century engraving.

Figs 761–2 Gattinara. Two views of the porticoed central square.

Fig. 763   The medieval universe, with its seven concentric skies, supported by the Eternal Father. A fourteenth-century painting by Piero di Puccio in the Camposanto in Siena.

7
Renaissance art

During the first decades of the fifteenth century, certain Florentine artists — architects, sculptors and painters — discovered a new way of designing buildings, of painting and of sculpting, which changed the whole nature of art and its relationship with other human activities.

We have already explained in the preceding chapter the historical conditions under which this change occurred. The economic development of Florence had been disrupted by the crisis during the fourteenth century, while the social classes that had participated in the formation of the 'Commune' had come into conflict with each other, and the group of aristocratic families, which had seized power in the late 1370s, continued to rule the city for the next fifty years. The city's layout, which had been established at the end of the thirteenth century under the guidance of Arnolfo da Cambio, was more than large enough for a Florence whose population had declined and finally stabilised; all that needed to be done now was to put the finishing touches. There was no necessity for the artists to design new buildings, merely to perfect and refine those already existing.

Although the new generation of artists at the beginning of the fifteenth century — Ghiberti, Donatello, Paolo Uccello, Masaccio — completed the works of preceding generations (the Cathedral, the Baptistery, the great convent churches on the outskirts, the Palazzo Vecchio), their contributions came to be valued in their own right. They embodied a radically new concept, that of universal validity, which was subsequently adopted by the whole of the civilised world as an alternative to the medieval tradition.

At the same time, their professional status was being modified; they were already high-level specialists, no longer dependent on the old medieval guilds, but tied to their patrons by bonds of mutual trust. They now became independent agents, divorced from the main body of citizens, capable of working wherever they were summoned (Brunelleschi was sent to Ferrara and Mantua in 1434, while Paolo Uccello worked in Venice between 1425 and 1430). In fact, the new art was no longer exclusively Florentine, but Italian and universal, just like the poetry and prose of the great fourteenth-century writers, Dante, Petrarch and Boccaccio.

Let us now consider the various innovations that were introduced.

In architecture, a new method of working was established by Filippo Brunelleschi (1377–1446), which can be summarised as follows:

1. The primary duty of the architect was to detail in advance, by means of drawings and models, the precise appearance of the work to be executed. In addition, all major decisions were to be made before construction work began, which meant that the work could be divided into distinct stages: its projection and its completion. The architect was concerned with the project, and he was no longer part of the workforce involved in the actual physical completion of the project.

2. When drawing up his plans, the architect had to

consider the various elements that would affect his project's final appearance, in this logical order:

(a) its proportional characteristics, i.e. the aesthetic relationship between the constituent elements and the whole, independent of the actual linear measurements;

(b) its metrical characteristics, i.e. the final dimensions;

(c) its physical characteristics, i.e. the materials to be used, their natural configurations, their colour, durability, etc.

The concern with proportional elements safeguarded the continuity between the projection of a work and its completion. Although the preliminary drawings only showed miniature versions of the final work, they still gave a very good overall impression of its completed appearance. All that then remained to be done was to decide on its measurements (the scale of enlargement between the model and the actual building) and what materials to use in its construction.

3. The individual elements in a building — pillars, pediments, arches, pilasters, doors, windows — all had to be of a certain type, corresponding to those used in classical antiquity and modelled on ancient examples (this meant Roman ones, which were the only ones known at this time). It was permissible for certain minor modifications to be made to the basic type, but their original source of inspiration had to be clearly recognisable and easily understood within the classical context. This meant that greater attention could be paid to the whole unified ensemble, and it became easier to appreciate the overall effect of a single building or a whole complex of buildings.

In this way, architecture began to achieve a new significance: it acquired an intellectual discipline and a cultural dignity that distinguished it from straightforward mechanical work and made it more like the liberal arts of science and literature.

Brunelleschi upheld this new concept of architecture as a personal statement, which was in direct conflict with the traditional views still held by his patrons, by those responsible for the execution of his work and even by the artists who collaborated with him in the decoration of his buildings. He had to face almost insuperable difficulties, and he was hardly ever able to carry out his project in exactly the same way as he had envisaged. Only two of his works — the dome of Florence Cathedral and the Old Sacristy of San Lorenzo — were properly and regularly financed (by the Wool Guild and the Medici family), which enabled them to be completed under his direction. The others — San Lorenzo, Santo Spiritu, the Pazzi Chapel in Santa Croce, the rotunda of Santa Maria degli Angeli — were slowly and sporadically worked on during the long economic crisis caused by Florence's continual wars, and work was not properly resumed until 1440. As a result, the buildings were still unfinished when Brunelleschi died in 1446, and his original plans were subsequently altered by the men who completed them.

Nevertheless, his ideas gradually came to be accepted, both in Italy and the rest of Europe, because later events proved their validity and their worth. Brunelleschi had founded a type of architecture based on human reason and the prestige of Italy's classical past, which, although applicable to every type of building, both public and private, was based on simple, repeated shapes, that were easily comprehensible. European society, whose sphere of influence spread throughout the world during the fifteenth and sixteenth centuries, adopted this architectural form because of its logical geometricality and its decorative qualities, and ended up by regarding it as the only possible style of architecture.

Bearing these facts in mind, let us take a closer look at Brunelleschi's main works in Florence:

The dome of the Cathedral of Santa Maria del Fiore is his most famous and remarkable work, marking the end of the great public works of the Middle Ages and the advent of the new style of architecture. It thus provided the finishing touch to the building founded by Arnolfo at the close of the thirteenth century, and became the visual focus of the entire city. In fifteenth-century views of the city (Figs 700, 703), Florence appears like the flower from which it took its name (its original Latin name Florentia is ultimately derived from *flor*, meaning flower): the last set of walls, simplified into a circular shape, was the corolla; the dome was the pistil. Brunelleschi invented the means to build it, as well as giving its exterior the simplicity and grandeur needed to fulfil its role as an artistic addition to the landscape.

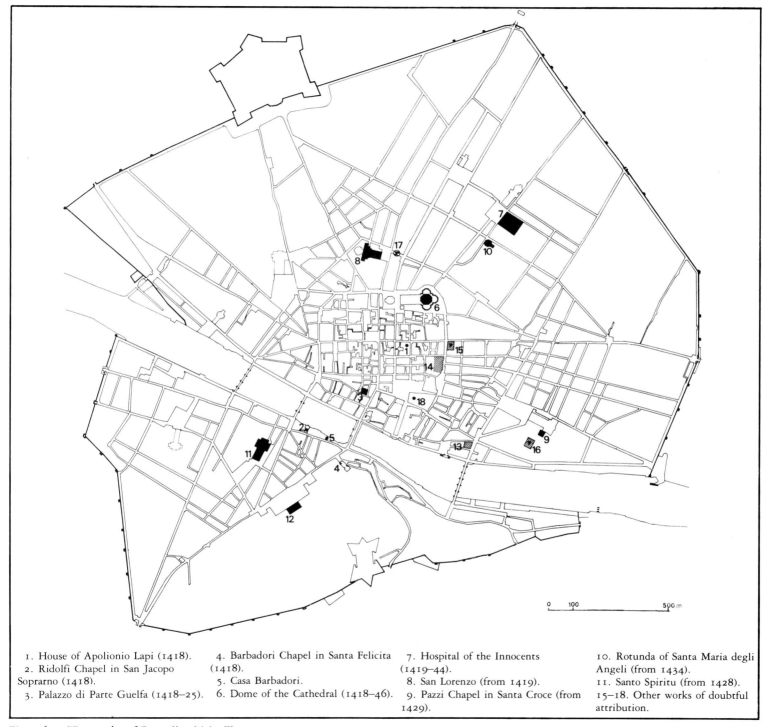

Fig. 764   The works of Brunelleschi in Florence.

1. House of Apolionio Lapi (1418).
2. Ridolfi Chapel in San Jacopo Soprarno (1418).
3. Palazzo di Parte Guelfa (1418–25).
4. Barbadori Chapel in Santa Felicita (1418).
5. Casa Barbadori.
6. Dome of the Cathedral (1418–46).
7. Hospital of the Innocents (1419–44).
8. San Lorenzo (from 1419).
9. Pazzi Chapel in Santa Croce (from 1429).
10. Rotunda of Santa Maria degli Angeli (from 1434).
11. Santo Spiritu (from 1428).
15–18. Other works of doubtful attribution.

Figs 765–6   The dome of Santa Maria
del Fiore by Brunelleschi, as seen from
the roofs of the houses to the south of
the Cathedral, and a sectional view,
which illustrates its relationship with
the main body of the church
(illustrated in Chapter 6).

Fig. 767   A view of Florence, dominated by Brunelleschi's dome, from San Miniato.

The dome, in fact, takes the form of a vaulted octagon, which shows the orientation of the church underneath: two of the sides are parallel to the cathedral's longitudinal walls, while two are at right angles to them, and the other four are set at an angle of 45 degrees. Its eight faces are covered in red terracotta tiles, and the ridges between them are deline-ated by eight white marble ribs. As a result, the dome can be clearly seen from many kilometres away, when the church itself and the other buildings of the city are a blurred and indistinct mass; its simple geometrical form rears up into the sky and provides a reference point for the whole of Florence and the surrounding countryside (Figs 765–72).

Fig. 768   A view of Florence from the Piazzale Michelangelo; behind the dome can be seen the hills of Fiesole.

Fig. 769   The Cathedral of Santa Maria del Fiore, with Giotto's Campanile and Brunelleschi's dome, seen from Or San Michele.

Figs 770–1   The wooden model of the dome's lantern, preserved in the Museo dell'Opera del Duomo, and the completed version.

Fig. 772   The interior of the dome of Santa Maria del Fiore, decorated with late sixteenth-century frescoes.

Figs 773–4   The two panels by Ghiberti and Brunelleschi, submitted in the competition in 1401 to decide who should be given the commission for the third door of the Baptistery in Florence.

Brunelleschi's other works, woven into the existing medieval fabric of the city, are lesser buildings, but extremely important as models for later architects. San Lorenzo and Santo Spiritu are both churches with three aisles, similar to those of the mendicant orders, such as Santa Maria Novella and Santa Croce. All their characteristics — the proportions of their ground plan, the levels of their front elevations — were rationally worked out, using typical classically-derived elements like pillars, pediments and arches, instead of the pilasters and vaults of Gothic architecture. The Old Sacristy of San Lorenzo and the Pazzi Chapel in Santa Croce were small, centrally-placed buildings, based on medieval models, but restructured by the inclusion of such new elements as pillars and arches. Within this framework other refinements were introduced (for example paintings and sculptures), which became works of art in their own right, independent of the surrounding architecture (Figs 775–89).

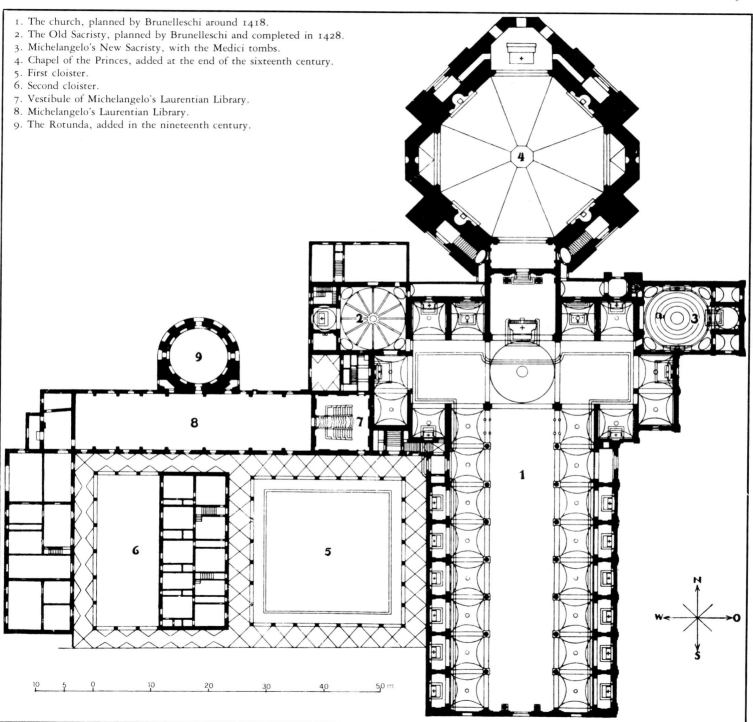

1. The church, planned by Brunelleschi around 1418.
2. The Old Sacristy, planned by Brunelleschi and completed in 1428.
3. Michelangelo's New Sacristy, with the Medici tombs.
4. Chapel of the Princes, added at the end of the sixteenth century.
5. First cloister.
6. Second cloister.
7. Vestibule of Michelangelo's Laurentian Library.
8. Michelangelo's Laurentian Library.
9. The Rotunda, added in the nineteenth century.

Fig. 775   Plan of the monumental cloister of San Lorenzo in Florence.

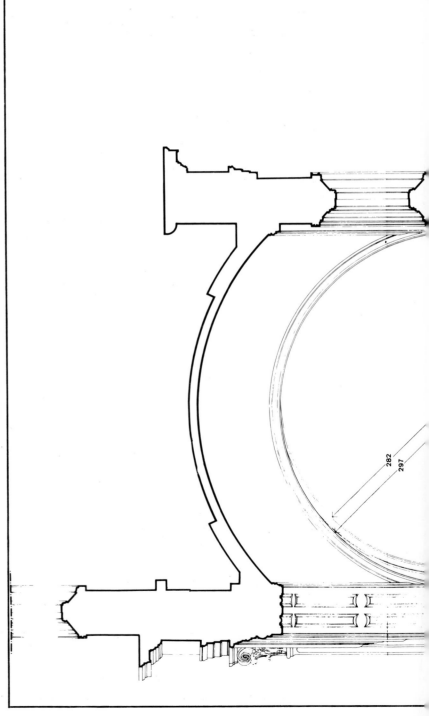

Figs 776–7   Detail of one of the capitals and, section of
one of the side-aisles of San Lorenzo (scale 1:50). The placing
of all the other elements was governed by the rules of
architectural order.

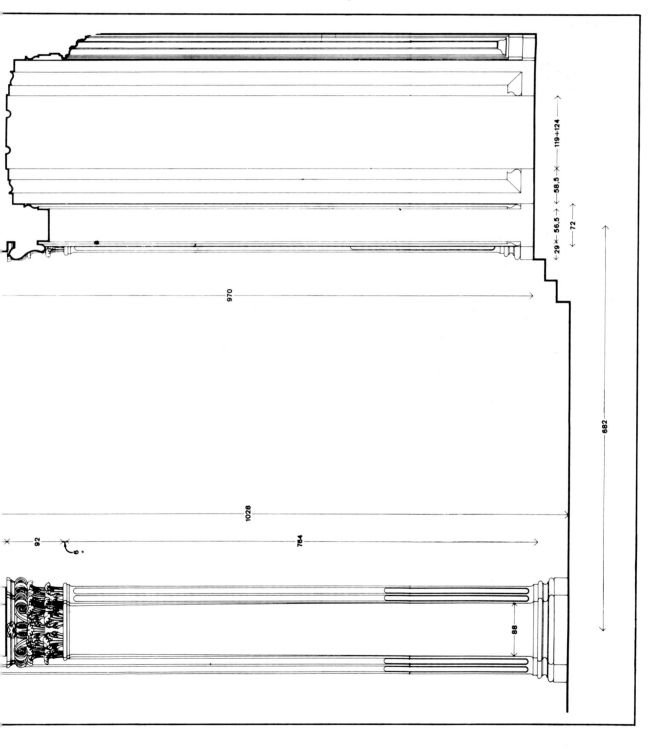

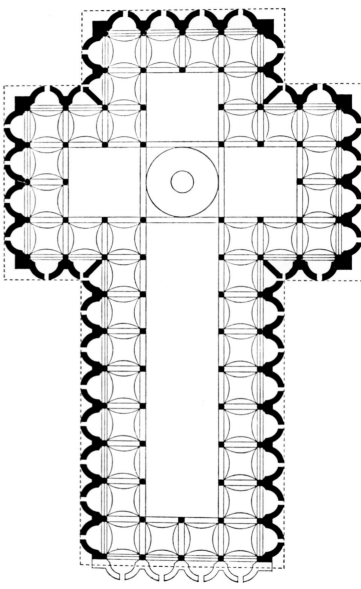

Fig. 780   Plan of Santo Spiritu, as originally conceived by Brunelleschi (scale 1:500).

Figs 778–9   Interior views of San Lorenzo and Santo Spiritu, looking up the aisle.

Fig. 781   Sectional view of one of the spans of Santo Spiritu, showing the arrangement of the walls, the vaults and the pillars.

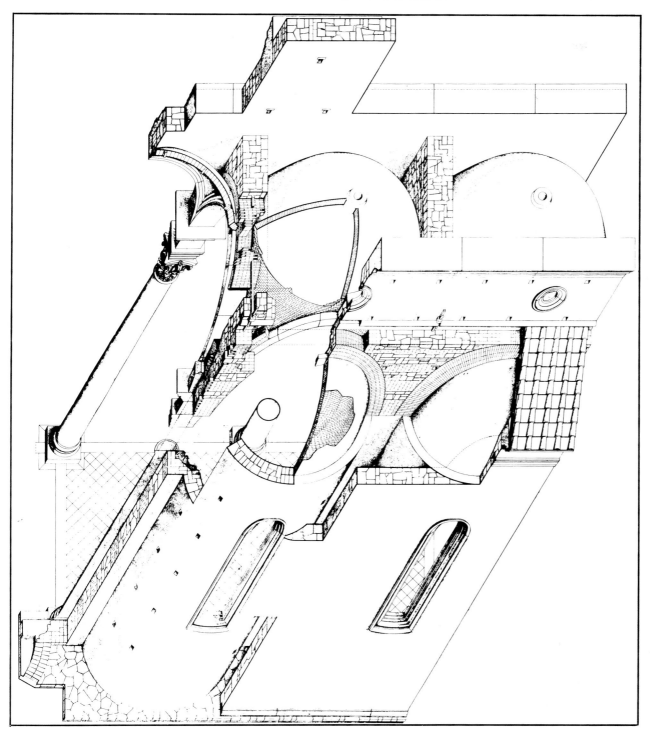

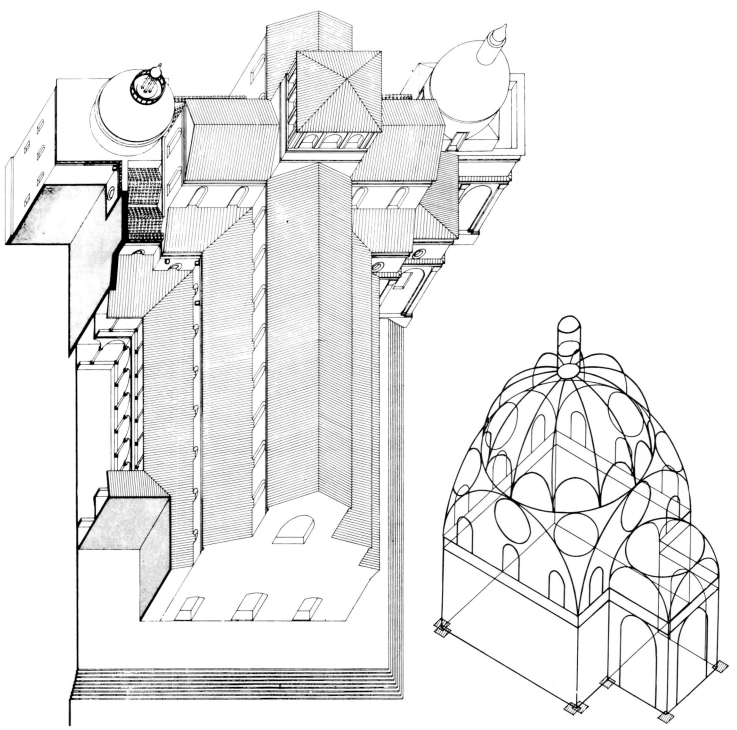

Fig. 782   Sectional view of the Church of San Lorenzo and the Old
Sacristy.

Fig. 783   Diagram of the internal architectonic elements of the
Old Sacristy: arches, cornices, pilasters.

Fig. 784   Interior of the Old Sacristy.

Fig. 785   The dome over the main area of the Old Sacristy, with Donatello's stucco tondoes.

Fig. 786   The dome over the secondary area of the Old Sacristy.

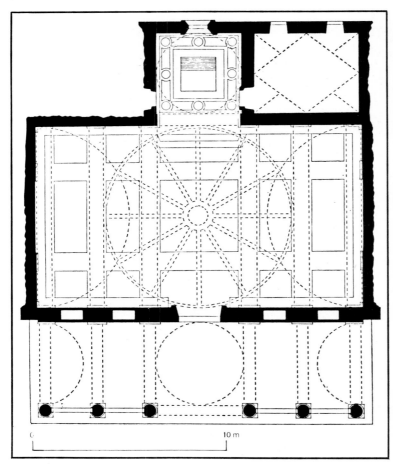

Fig. 787   Plan of Brunelleschi's Pazzi Chapel, in the first cloister of
Santa Croce in Florence (scale 1:200). A general plan of the complex
is shown in Chapter 6.

Fig. 788   The dome of the Pazzi Chapel, showing the terracotta
tondoes which may be the work of Brunelleschi himself.

Fig. 789   Interior view of the Pazzi Chapel. The raised area on which the pilasters stand was designed to solve the problem of the difference in level between the two parts. It also serves as a dais when the chapel is used as the convent's chapter house.

Fig. 790 The central part of the façade of the Pitti Palace in Florence, which corresponds to Brunelleschi's projection.

Sculptures and paintings reproduced objects from the natural world. In some cases this representation became a scientifically exact operation, in which the objects' characteristics were classified in the same way as in architectural works:

I) proportional characteristics

II) metrical characteristics

III) physical characteristics (in this case, primarily colour).

A sculpture, for example, could reproduce the essential aspects of an object, even if it only respected its proportional characteristics and ignored the metrical ones (a statue could be created either on a larger or smaller scale than the original) and the physical ones (it could be made of marble or bronze, which have a completely different grain and colour from the model).

On the other hand, in order to reproduce a three-dimensional object on a two-dimensional surface a geometrical calculation is needed to effect the transition. In modern-day schools the various techniques to achieve this are still taught: linear projections, foreshortening, perspective and axonometry.

This period also saw the establishment of the rules of perspective, the most complicated geometrical method, but also the most familiar, because it gives a similar image to the one formed by the human eye. Writers in former days credited Brunelleschi with the introduction of the rules of perspective. It was he who painted two small panels depicting the Baptistery and the Piazza della Signoria, and built a device that obliged people to view them from a fixed point, in order to compare the picture with the reality.

This historically and culturally significant geometrical construction derived from the classification of elemental characteristics mentioned above. In fact, perspective directly represents only the proportional characteristics of objects (their shape and reciprocal position); it represents indirectly their real dimensions only if the scene includes

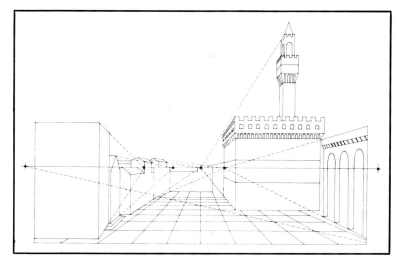

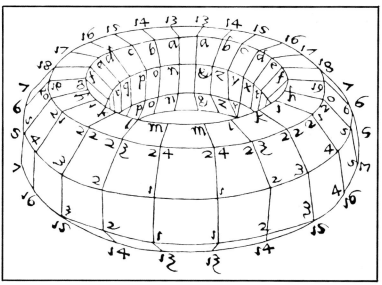

Fig. 791 Above, reconstruction of the second panel (showing a view of the Piazza della Signoria) designed by Brunelleschi to demonstrate the rules of perspective. Below, a complicated geometrical structure (the *mazzocchio*), drawn in perspective by Paolo Uccello.

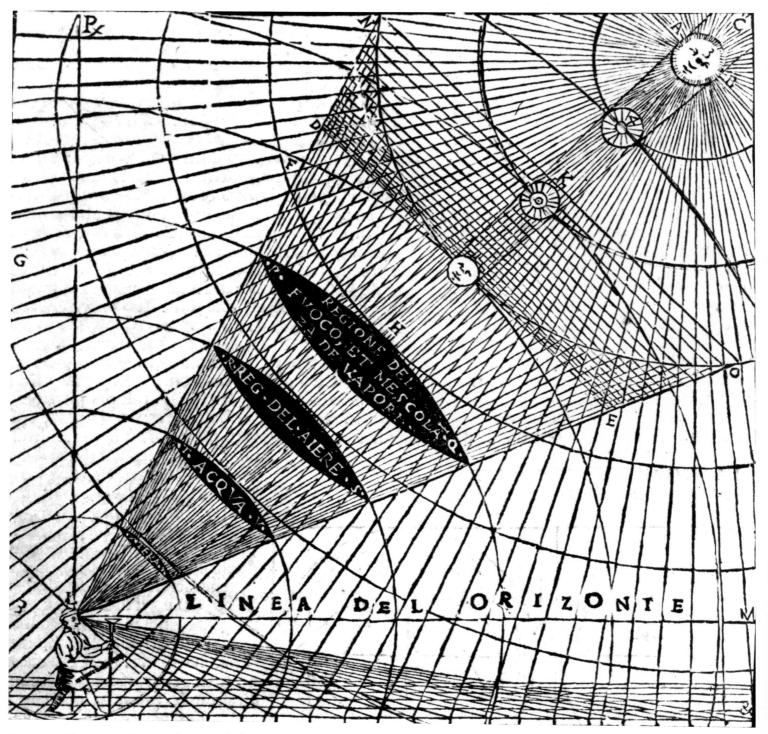

Fig. 792   The perspective area that extends from the human eye into the whole universe. A drawing by Gianbattista Caporali, contained in the 1536 edition of Vitruvius' treatise on perspective.

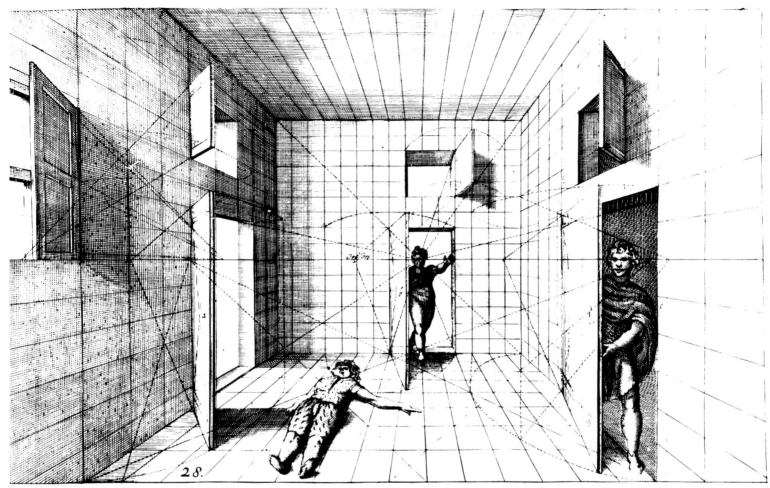

Fig. 793   An illustration from the 1560 treatise on perspective by De Vries.

Fig. 794   Two perspective bronze reliefs, from Donatello's altar in the basilica of Sant'Antonio in Padua.

Fig. 795   Donatello's equestrian statue of Gattamelata, in front of the basilica of Sant'Antonio in Padua.

something whose sizes we already know (a person, for example); it can, however, reproduce an object's colour and its other physical characteristics, using different methods of painting for the surfaces surrounding it.

Nevertheless, the use of colour can complicate physical representation. The colours of an object are never uniform; they are modified by light, shadow, reflection and by atmospheric conditions, which alter its appearance, depending on whether it is seen from far away or close to. The artists of the fifteenth and sixteenth centuries gradually learned how to reproduce these effects, and they widened the scope of painting, which became, to a certain extent, the universal means of representing the visible world.

During the fifteenth century a number of new inventions increased the potential applications of painting: large-scale canvases, which allowed whole series of paintings to be executed in an artist's studio, oil paints, and the engraving of metal plates, which made it possible to reproduce large numbers of copies of a single drawing.

Let us now consider briefly some of the main exponents of Renaissance painting and sculpture.

During the 1430s, a group of Brunelleschi's fellow artists began to adopt his techniques of perspective:

Donatello (1386–1466) used the medium of sculpture to explore the visible world, almost in competition with painting. To achieve a more painterly effect he experimented with all sorts of materials (metals, different types of stone, stucco, terracotta) and techniques (sculpture in the round, which preserved the original proportions of the model, and panels in which relief was diminished or reduced to the minimum — the so-called *rilievo stiacciato* — with a feeling of depth being preserved by the use of perspective, Figs 794–5).

Masaccio (1401–28) was one of the first artists to use an architectonic background in his paintings, adhering strictly to the rules of perspective (Figs 796–7), but he used the new representational methods primarily to give a three-dimensional quality to his human figures. Man was presented as the most important element in art, and by revealing an inner world in his image, a new, emotional dimension was added to painting.

Both Donatello and Masaccio used perspective as a means of seeing the world through new eyes. The eagerness

Figs 796–7 Masaccio's *Trinity* in the Church of Santa Maria Novella in Florence. The *sinopia* (the preparatory drawing done on the wall) and the finished fresco.

(1475–1564), Raphael (1483–1520) — enjoyed an unprecedented degree of social prestige: they were treated as advance, the limitless world that was to be crossed by the explorers of the sixteenth century and studied by the scholars of the seventeenth.

Figs 800–1   *The Holy Family* by Michelangelo, now in the Uffizi Gallery in Florence. *The Madonna of the Chair* by Raphael, now in the Pitti Palace in Florence.

medieval cities and towns. They comp... ...
programmes left unfinished in the fourteenth century or
embarked on new schemes, which almost invariably turned
out to be overambitious and impracticable.

We have already dealt with Florence, where the fifteenth-century buildings were inserted harmoniously into an environment that had been planned at the end of the thirteenth century. Let us now consider some other Italian cities, in which the Renaissance additions were more significant and where the whole new complexes of buildings were introduced.

PIENZA

In 1459, Pope Pius II visited his native town of Corsignano near Siena, and decided to rebuild it as a temporal residence for himself and his entourage.

One of the Pope's followers was Alberti, and Pius II undoubtedly would have followed his advice in deciding on the building programme and also in choosing men to carry out the plans. The small medieval town (covering an area of roughly 6 hectares) stood on the top of a hill, and its main street, which had a gentle bend in it about half way along, followed the main line of the ridge. It was at this point, where the street curved slightly, that Pius II decided to construct a group of monumental buildings: the Piccolomini Palace (on the site of the house in which he had been born), the Cathedral, the Palazzo Pubblico and the Palace of Cardinal Borgia (which later became the Episcopal Palace). The Cathedral stands at the point where the curve is at its most pronounced, while the other buildings are aligned with the two diverging branches of the street. As a result, the square in front of the Cathedral is in the form of a trapezium, and the front of the church is framed by the angled façades of the two palaces, while on each side can be seen the panorama of the valley beyond (Figs 807–8).

The Cathedral has three aisles, all of the same height (it follows the same plan as the German Gothic churches which Pius II had seen in his travels), and its interior lacks any form of decoration, except for the paintings commissioned from the most famous Sienese artists of the day: Sano di Pietro, Sassetta, Giovanni di Paolo and Matteo di Giovanni. The Piccolomini Palace is a square block with a central courtyard, but the whole southern facade is taken up by a loggia, which looks towards the gardens and allows the visitor to enjoy the whole panorama of the valley, with Mount Amiata in the background.

Around this central monumental complex other secondary buildings were constructed: the Cardinals erected their small palaces along the two branches of the main street, while the Pope had built, in the far north-eastern corner of the town, a block of twelve identical two-storey terraced houses for the poorest inhabitants, and a small square was cleared behind the Palazzo Pubblico for use as a market place so that the main square of the town would remain free from the inconvenience of stalls and booths. In this way the whole of the small town became arranged in a hierarchical way around the Cathedral and the Papal Palace. Its principal buildings were distinguished by their greater architectural regularity and not by their size (authority was not expressed by material superiority, but by cultural prestige). However, this regularity, which is less apparent in the secondary buildings, disappeared completely in the buildings of the common people, which fitted into the closely woven fabric of the medieval township with no difficulty at all. In this way a harmonious combination of old and new was achieved: although the new cultural movement respected the traditional environment, it also refashioned it, in a purely qualitative way, with the products of its superior intellectual discipline.

Fig. 804   The emblem of Pius II Piccolomini, from his palace in Pienza.

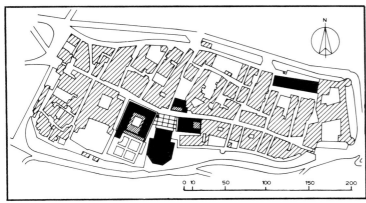

Figs 805–6   Pienza. A view of the town from the valley of the River Orcia, and a map of its layout; in black, the buildings that form its monumental centre (the Palazzo Piccolomini, the Palazzo Pubblico, the Palazzo Borgia, the Cathedral) and a block of terraced houses for the poor.

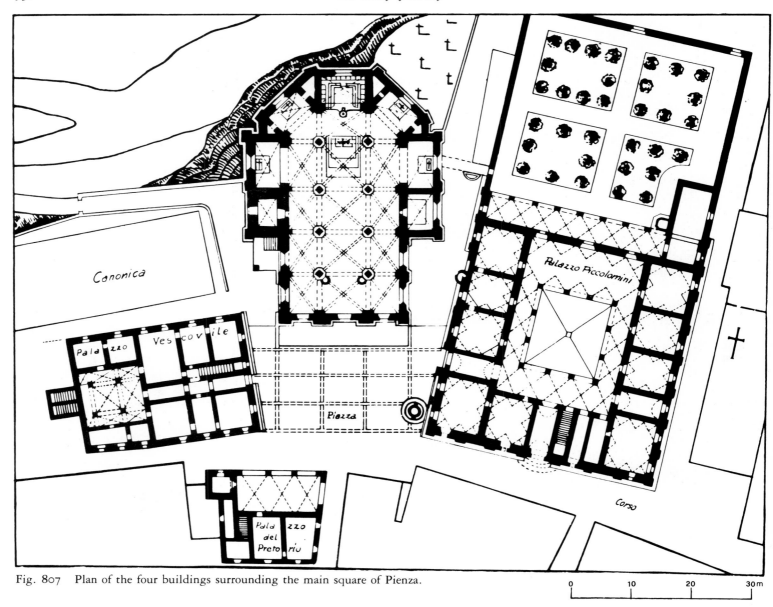

Fig. 807   Plan of the four buildings surrounding the main square of Pienza.

0   10   20   30m

Fig. 808   View of Pienza's main square from the tower of the Palazzo Pubblico; the brick pavement, with its linear stone divisions, emphasises the inclination of the lateral buildings.

The man who planned these new buildings is not mentioned by name in any documents, but it was almost certainly Bernardo Rosselino, one of the foremost Florentine architects of the day (in 1461 he had been appointed foreman of Santa Maria del Fiore). Pius II closely followed the progress of the work, taking the most important decisions himself, as he explains in his *Commentaries*, and the principal monuments were completed in a very short space of time, between 1459 and 1462. In March 1462 the town was renamed Pienza, and for brief periods it played host to the Papal court, until Pius II's sudden death in 1464.

No other changes were made in later years, and Pius II's town reverted to being a quiet country backwater. The equilibrium achieved for a brief moment in this first example of Renaissance town planning was never destroyed by later additions, and it can still be appreciated in the proportions of the streets and buildings, even though the life for which Pienza had been designed disappeared many centuries ago.

Figs 809–10   Pienza. The architectonic composition of the façade of the Palazzo Piccolomini. A detail of the interior of the
Cathedral, with the painting commissioned by Pius II from the Sienese artist Matteo di Giovanni.

Figs 811–12 The obverse and reverse of the painting by Piero della Francesca, which shows the portrait of Federico da Montefeltro and allegorical scene of his triumph (Uffizi Gallery, Florence).

URBINO

Pius II reigned between 1458 and 1464, and had only five years in which to build and live in Pienza. On the other hand, Federico da Montefeltro — the highly successful condottieri chief of the Italian League, which was set up in 1454 — was lord of Urbino from 1444 to 1482 and the only Renaissance prince to have the time and the financial resources to really transform his city, by means of a whole series of architectural undertakings.

Urbino is a small city of 40 hectares, built on two hills. Its centre, which contains the Church of St Francis, lies between the two hills, and from there the main street leads up to the Porta Lavagine, through which passes the road to Rimini and the plains of Romagna. On the top of the southern hill stands the castle of the Montefeltro family, and it was next to this that Federico began to lay out a new rectilinear building, using a group of lesser known local and Tuscan artists.

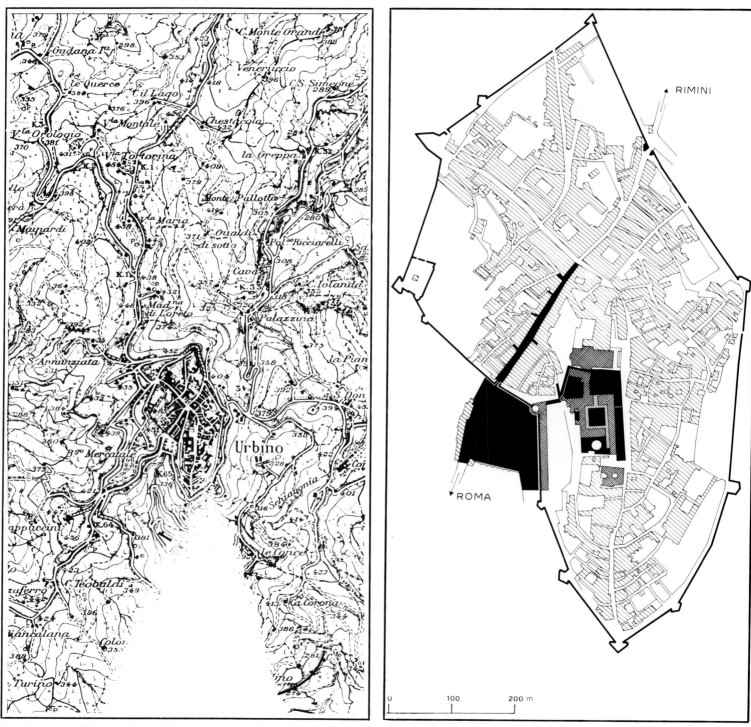

Figs 813–14   Urbino. Map of the city's surroundings by the Istituto Geografico Militare (scale 1:25,000). Plan of the city, showing the open spaces laid out by Federico (in black) and the buildings that made up the complex of the Ducal Palace (shaded).

Fig. 815   Aerial view of Urbino from the south; in the foreground, the Piazza del Mercatale and the Ducal Palace.

Fig. 816   An ideal city, as envisaged in a painting in the Ducal Palace in Urbino.

Towards 1465 this building was incorporated into a new complex, which, although centred on a porticoed courtyard, spread out towards the neighbouring city and countryside, transforming its whole surroundings.

The side of the new palace that faced towards the traditional centre of the town was built in a rough Z shape, thereby leaving enough space for a square, in which the new Cathedral was later built. The part facing towards the valley, on the other hand, was broken up by a series of open-ended buildings that overlooked the surrounding countryside and formed an extraordinary second façade, which seemed to reach out into the endless, hilly landscape as it sloped gently down to the Metauro river.

In the centre were the private apartments of the Duke and his family, with three superimposed loggias, which were flanked by two towers (the so-called *torricini*); to the right are the hanging gardens, enclosed by a wall with windows that frame the vista of the hills opposite, while to the left are two more terraces, in the largest of which (the so-called Cortile del Pasquino) a rotunda was to be built to contain the tombs of the Montefeltro family. From the two towers that flank the central block one descends to the foot of the palace; from there, by means of a circular ramp, which is also negotiable on horseback, one reaches the stables — built half-way up — and a large man-made square (the

Mercatale), formed by filling in the bottom of the valley.

This square, the starting point of the road to Rome, formed the main entrance to the city; it possessed a monumental gateway and also a street that led straight into the area between the two hills, and thence to the upper entrance of the palace. The result of this was that the city's whole orientation was changed: it no longer looked to the Porta Lavagine (i.e. towards Rimini and the Po valley), but to the Porta Valbona (i.e. towards Rome, the seat of Federico's new political interests). The Palace overlooked this thoroughfare (Fig. 826), maintaining its links with both the town and the outside world.

These additions, which were more complex and more exacting than those at Pienza, still managed to achieve the same harmonious effect. A balance between the city and the palace has been carefully sustained: the palace provides the city with both a centre and a monumental façade, but its dimensions do not differ too greatly from those of the other buildings. It is divided into a number of different structural components, each of which possessed, individually rather than as a whole, the ideal geometrical regularity demanded in the visual arts of the day. In this way, the new architecture enhanced the dignity of the town, without destroying its continuity (Figs 813–20).

It is still not certain exactly who was responsible for the

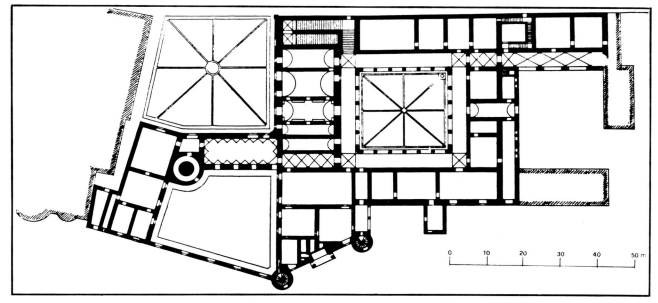

Figs 817–18   Aerial view and ground-plan of the Ducal Palace in Urbino.

Fig. 819   The skyline of Urbino, seen from the south.

Fig. 820   A view of Urbino, in a fresco in the Galleria delle Carte Geografiche in the Vatican.

Fig. 821 Piero della Francesca's *Flagellation* in the Ducal Palace in Urbino.

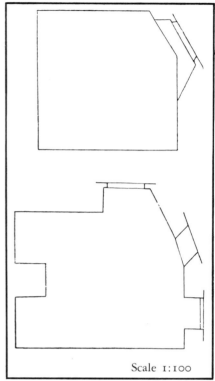

Scale 1:100

Figs 822–5 Federico's study in the Ducal Palace in Urbino: towards the back of the room; view towards the external loggia; ground-plan and plan as far as the height of the upper window.

The adornment of this small room is a product of the collaboration of many artists, but the general plan may well be the work of the young Bramante. The marquetry designs are the work of Francesco di Giorgio or Sandro Botticelli, the panels were made in the workshop of Baccio Pontelli, and the ceiling was built by Giuliano da Maiano. Above the frieze there was formerly a series of portraits of illustrious men, painted by Justus of Ghent and Pedro Berruguete.

Fig. 828   An astronomic instrument; a detail from the marquetry
work in the Duke's study in the Palace at Urbino.

whole new layout; Luciano Laurana and Francesco di Giorgio are recorded as having been employed as architects, and with them, as sculptors, painters and decorators, the foremost Italian artists of the day: Baccio Pontelli, Giuliano da Maiano, Melozzo da Forli, Paolo Uccello, Sandro Botticelli, Giovani Santi (the father of Raphael) and perhaps the young Bramante, together with the Flemish painter Justus of Ghent and the Spaniard Pedro Berruguete. Piero della Francesca lived in the city for a long time (from where he completed, possibly in 1450, his small painting of *The Flagellation*, which recalls the assassination of Federico's predecessor), and it may be that it was he who inspired the more exceptional architectural and decorative features. We do know, however, that Federico himself followed the work of the architects and artists very closely, and that his opinions played an important part in influencing their decisions.

In many cases, the skills of different craftsmen were as closely interwoven as during the Middle Ages. A person who wanted a commission done could call on the services of many different artists, hiring and dismissing them at will; Berruguete, for example, was called on to repaint some of the details on Piero della Francesca's Montefeltro altarpiece. Even the preparation of something as small as Federico's study (Figs 822–6) became as complicated as the building of the whole Ducal Palace.

The court of the Montefeltro family also became a great centre of literary and scientific learning; the Florentine librarian Vespasiano da Bisticci organised the palace's famous library, in which were preserved original Greek and Latin manuscripts, as well as specially-commissioned transcriptions of both modern and ancient works. Piero della Francesca and Francesco di Giorgio dedicated their treatises to Federico, while the mathematicians Luca Pacioli and Paul van Middelburg were employed as tutors for Guidobaldo, Federico's son. Both Bramante and Raphael frequented the court before leaving at the end of the fifteenth century, and it was in the Ducal Palace that Baldassarre wrote the *Cortegiano*.

In this way Urbino became the home of a unique group of specialists, and after the death of Federico these men were summoned to the great cities of Venice, Milan and Rome, where they contributed to the formation of a new international culture during the sixteenth century.

Fig. 829   A detail of the stucco decoration on the ceiling of one of the rooms in the Ducal Palace in Urbino.

FERRARA

Ferrara was the capital of the domain of the Este family and was situated on either side of the Po, at the crossing point between Emilia and the territory of the Venetians. After hostilities had ceased following the Peace of Lodi in 1454, Ferrara became one of Italy's richest and most advanced cities, and its court played host to some of the most important literary figures of the Italian Renaissance, particularly poets: Boiardo, for example, who wrote *Orlando Innamorato* at the end of the fifteenth century, Ariosto, who published *Orlando Furioso* in 1516, and later on, Tasso, who composed *Aminta* and *Gerusalemme Liberata* for the Este family. From 1486 onwards the city organised a series of famous theatrical spectacles, and in 1531 Europe's first fixed theatre was opened there; Ferrara also harboured several famous artists towards the middle of the fifteenth century — Pisanello, Mantegna, Piero della Francesca, Roger van der Weyden — who contributed towards the development of the Ferrarese school of painting (Cosimo Tura, Francesco del Cossa, Ercole Roberti).

During this period it became necessary to add two new quarters to the original medieval city, which were laid out according to the new rules of architecture:

— the *addizione di Borso*, completed by Duke Borso in 1451;

— the *addizione erculea*, planned by Duke Ercole I in 1492 and built by his successors over a period of years during the sixteenth century (Fig. 830).

The first addition covered a long, thin area of reclaimed land on the banks of a tributary of the Po, and it consisted of a single straight street and a number of other ones that crossed it and joined up with those already existing in neighbouring quarters.

The second addition was a properly planned extension to the city, whose surface area it more than doubled (from 200 to 430 hectares). The medieval town had been bounded

Fig. 830   Plan of the city of Ferrara at the end of the sixteenth century. In black, the streets of the *addizione di Borso* (below right) and the *addizione erculea* (above); the dotted areas show the pleasure parks of the Este family — Belfiore (top right-hand corner) and Belvedere (on the island, bottom left).

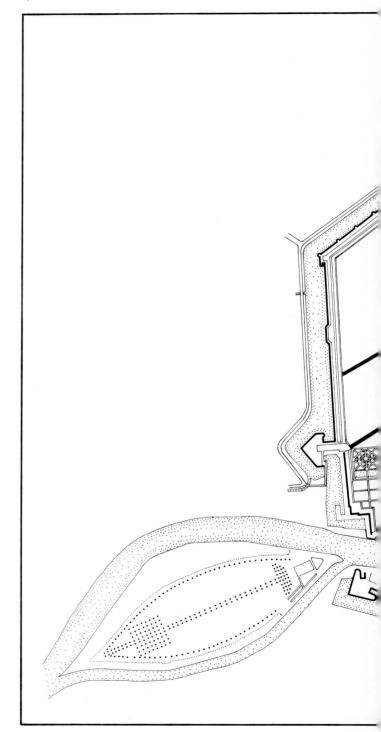

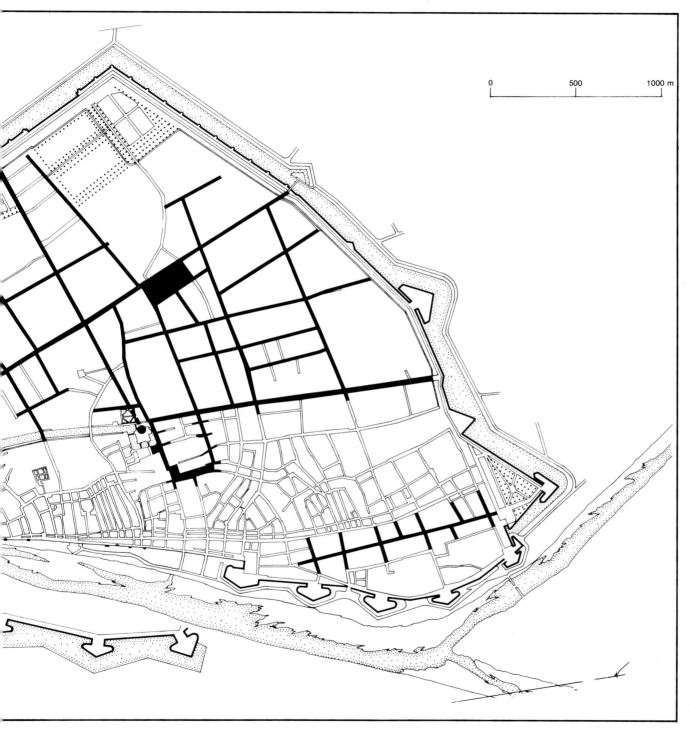

Fig. 831   Ferrara. The Arco del Cavallo with the equestrian statue of Niccolo III of Este.

to the north by a wall and a canal, interrupted at the centre by the Castello Estense. Beyond this boundary a new set of walls was erected, designed to be able to resist artillery attacks, and the vast intervening area was divided up by a series of streets, which did not form a regular grid, but which were designed to fit in with the streets of the medieval part of the city. The two main streets — the old one (Corso Ercole I) that led from the Estes' castle to the Castello di Belfiore and the new one (Corso Porta Po and Corso Porta Mare) that joined the Porta Po to the Porta Mare — met almost at right angles, like the *cardo* and *decumanus* of ancient cities described by Vitruvius. Along this second street a new rectangular square was opened up, the Piazza Ariostea, measuring 120 by 200 metres, which was to have been the centre of the new quarter (Fig. 834). The Este family's court architect, Biagio Rossetti, oversaw the building of the walls and also erected several monumental works along the new streets, which included the palaces built at the point where the two new streets met: the Palazzo dei Diamanti, the Palazzo Prosperi-Sacrati and the Palazzo Turchi-di Bagno.

These works gave Ferrara a modern aspect that was unparalleled in Europe. But the population and prosperity of city did not continue to grow at the same pace; building activities slowed down and the vast *addizione erculea* remained partially empty. At the close of the sixteenth century Ferrara was annexed as part of the Papal States and became a city of secondary importance, with much of the territory contained within the walls of Ercole I reverting to countryside. The city has only resumed its development during the present century, and the streets that were planned in Renaissance times are now used to determine the extent of modern building frontages. Thus the new city envisaged during the fifteenth century is gradually being transformed into an ordinary, peaceful suburban area (Figs 835–6).

In Ferrara the city's planned transformation was split into two stages, and whereas the walls and streets were laid out, the actual buildings were never completed in time. As a result, Ercole I's intervention did not produce a new city, but a two-dimensional plan which could be finished at any time in the future and in a variety of different ways. In the case of Pienza and Urbino the new artistic movement had

Fig. 832   *The Triumph of Venus*, a fresco by Francesco del Cossa in the Palazzo di Schifanoia in Ferrara.

Figs 833–4   Two sections of the
addizione erculea: a street — the Via
Mortara — and the Piazza Ariostea,
intended to be the centre of the new
city.

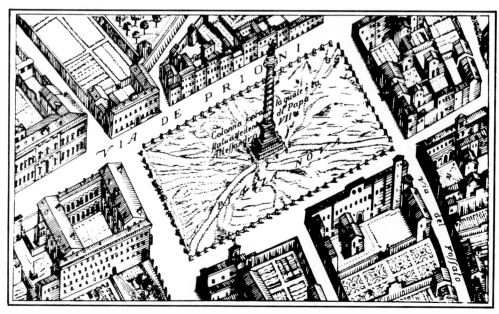

Fig. 835   Perspective view of Ferrara, from the end of the sixteenth century.

been introduced into small towns, and it had the confidence to transform them into modern cities by means of a series of high quality architectural interventions. At Ferrara, on the other hand, this movement, which had become more ambitious and more demanding, tried for the first time to plan the growth of a major city, and made a sharp distinction between the two types of urban environment. In fact, the aim was to build a new city next to an old one, but there was a failure to maintain a coherent relationship between the planning of the city and its architectural realisation. A new method, which distinguished between the planning of a town and the construction of its buildings, had been experimented with, but without a full understanding of the opportunities and pitfalls inherent in it.

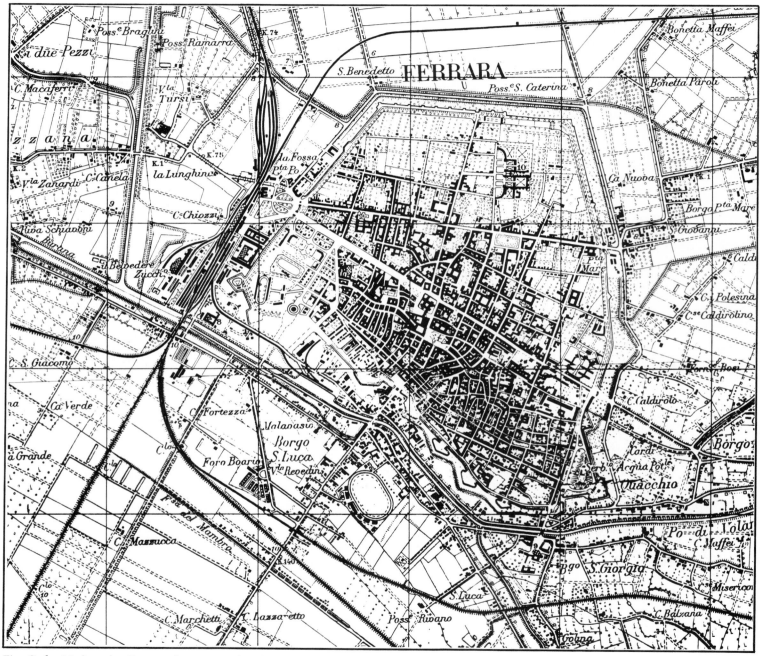

Fig. 836   Modern-day Ferrara, from a map by the Istituto Geografico Militare (scale 1:25,000).

Fig. 837 Castiglione d'Olona. A fresco by **Masolino de Panicale**, showing a view of Rome at the beginning of the fifteenth century. In the centre is the Pantheon, while above left are the Vatican and St Peter's.

ROME

In the mid-fifteenth century, when Florence, Venice and Naples were already fully-fledged cities, Rome was still a small and insignificant town, neglected and impoverished due to the long absence of the Popes.

Its landscape was dominated by the ruins of the ancient metropolis and the great churches of the early Christian era, while the population (less than 40,000 inhabitants) was centred on the two areas of level ground situated on either side of the river — the Campo Marzio and Trastevere — and occupied only a small part of the territory enclosed within the Aurelian Walls (more than 1,300 hectares).

The Popes returned to Rome in 1420, but they did not assume full control over the city until 1453 (after the failure of Stefano Porcari's conspiracy). Pope Nicholas V (1447–55) established the Papal administration's plan of action: to rebuild the imperial city and transform it into a modern city under Papal authority. To this end he planned to repair those amenities that were still usable (bridges, streets, walls, aqueducts), to adapt the monuments of antiquity to new functions (Hadrian's Mausoleum became a fortress, the Pantheon became a church, the Capitol became the seat of the municipal administration), to restore the Christian basilicas and also to build near St Peter's, on the Vatican hill, the citadel of the Papal court. This new Rome, with the dual prestige of being both the successor to imperial Rome and also home of the Apostolic See, was destined to become once more the principal city of the modern world.

However, the political and economic resources of the Papacy were totally inadequate for this undertaking. Rome continued to be a secondary city throughout the fifteenth century, dependent on other larger and more prosperous cities (Florence and the courts of northern Italy). Pope Sixtus IV (1471–84) was responsible for the rebuilding of San Pietro in Montorio, San Pietro in Vincoli and the Church of the Holy Apostles. He also put the Ponte Sisto back into working order, restored the Capitol and placed on its façade the bronze figure of a she-wolf, to which a contemporary sculptor added the twins. Apart from those schemes, he built the new churches of Santa Maria del Popolo, San Agostino, Santa Maria della Pace and the

Bel videre

C

Palatium pape

B

A

D

I

K

Tiberis fl.

T

Q

Fig. 838 A view of Rome at
the end of the fifteenth century, when it was still
dominated by the ruins of
antiquity.

Palazzo della Cancelleria, as well as making a few cautious inroads into the densely-packed medieval quarter by straightening the three streets leading to the Ponte San Angelo. In his architectural works he employed artists of secondary stature, such as Baccio Pontelli, but to paint the frescoes in the Sistine Chapel he summoned from Florence the best artists of the day (Botticelli, Perugino, Ghirlandaio, Pinturicchio, Signorelli and others), but he was unable to persuade them to settle in Rome.

Building activities increased towards the end of the century, in preparation for the Holy Year of 1500. This period also saw the arrival in Rome of the first famous architect, Donato Bramante (1444–1514), who left Milan after the overthrow of the Sforzas in 1499; he did not receive any major commissions, but even in his first limited works — the courtyard of Santa Maria della Pace and the *tempietto*

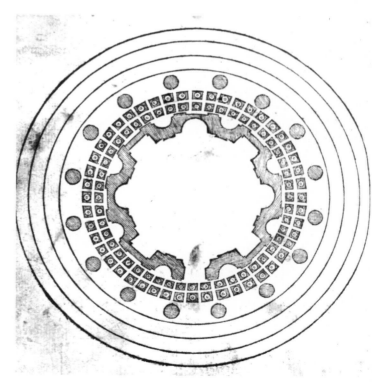

Figs 839–40   The Sistine Chapel in the Vatican, as it was in the fifteenth century and as it is now.

Figs 841–2   Bramante's *tempietto* in San Pietro in Montorio. Plan (from Serlio's treatise) and a view from the courtyard entrance.

Fig. 843   View of the courtyard of San Pietro in Montorio from the campanile, showing Bramante's *tempietto*.

in San Pietro in Montorio — he showed a new and rigid classicism, which openly begged comparisons with the monuments of antiquity (Figs 841–3).

In 1503 Julian II, the nephew of Sixtus IV, was elected Pope. The new Pontiff was a very politically ambitious man and a friend of the Italian and German bankers who financed the Holy See's building projects. He was not only fully prepared to carry out Pope Nicholas's plans, but also able to summon the most important artists of the time to Rome. He managed to persuade Giuliano da Sangallo to come from Florence, and, later, Michelangelo and Raphael, the two most illustrious artists of the new generation.

Michelangelo's first commission was to sculpt Julian II's tomb, which was to be placed in St Peter's, but then the Pope suddenly decided to rebuild the whole church along the lines suggested by Bramante, concentrating all available resources on this project. Michelangelo and Raphael were entrusted with the task of painting two series of frescoes on the ceiling of the Sistine Chapel and the Stanze in the Vatican to illustrate the world's cultural patrimony, both religious and humanistic, in a way which would provide a definitive synthesis of its two component elements (Figs 848–50).

Bramante and his assistants — Perruzi, Antonio da Sangallo, Raphael — planned the monuments of the new Rome on the same gigantic scale as those of its classical predecessor. The new St Peter's, which was an enormous, centrally-planned basilica, was crowned by a cupola as large as the Pantheon (Figs 845–7); the new Vatican Palace, which was to have possessed a massive porticoed façade overlooking the city, was like the Settizonio (a fragment of this façade can be seen in the three-storeyed loggias of the Cortile of San Damaso); and there was the scheme to join the Vatican Palace with the Belvedere by means of a stepped cortile, more than 300 metres long and arranged like a single perspective element.

The squalid, tangled mass of the medieval city was unhesitatingly cut into to make way for straight streets and new, regular buildings (here, as in Ferrara, the contrast between the medieval fabric and the modern city was appreciated, but the piecemeal development of the Middle Ages was destroyed by the superimposition of regular planning). Near the banks of the Tiber two rectilinear streets

Fig. 844   The Via Giulia in Rome, as seen from the entrance to San Giovanni dei Fiorentini.

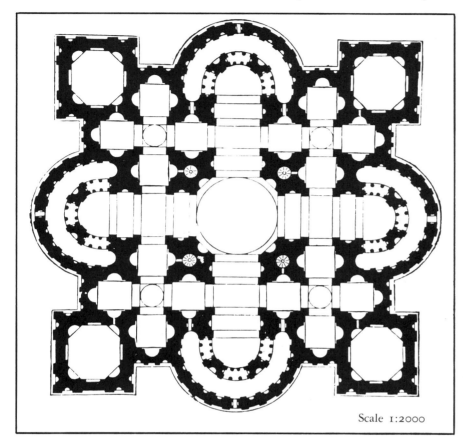

Scale 1:2000

Figs 845–7 The new St Peter's planned by Bramante; plan (from Serlio's treatise) and two contemporary exterior views.

Fig. 848 The ceiling of the Sistine Chapel, painted by Michelangelo.

Fig. 849   Raphael's fresco, *The School of Athens*, in the Stanza della Segnatura in the Vatican.

Fig. 850   Raphael's fresco, *Disputà*, in the Stanza della Segnatura in the Vatican.

were opened — the Via della Lungara and the Via Giulia (on which Bramante began to build the vast Palazzo dei Tribunali) — and on the edge of the city the ancient Roman Via Flaminia was restored and a new system planned of three straight streets (the Via del Corso, Via Ripetta and Via del Babuino), which converged at the city's northern entrance, the Porta del Popolo.

This ambitious programme was modified and interrupted by several decisive events — political, cultural and religious — which took place during the early 1500s. In 1513 Pope Julian died, and his death was shortly followed by Bramante's in the following year. The new Pope, Leo X, a member of the Medici family, divided his interests between Florence and Rome, a city whose cultural life was dominated by the figure of Raphael. The latter controlled a vast network of craftsmen and became involved in a large number of different projects at the same time: he continued building and laying out the city, he supervised the rescue of ancient inscriptions and works of art, he painted, both frescoes and easel pictures, he laid on theatrical spectaculars and even provided the Papal chancellery with calligraphic models. This practice of working in many fields, which contrasts with the individualism of the other artists and writers of the time, seemed destined to finally produce a coherent and easily recognisable modern style. Raphael, however, died in 1520 at the age of thirty-seven, and during the same period the political and cultural equilibrium was suddenly changed. In 1519 Charles V was elected emperor; in 1520 Martin Luther was excommunicated, an act which made a split between the Catholic Church and the Protestants inevitable; in 1521 Leo X died, and his successors became increasingly concerned with defending the independence of Rome in the face of the emperor's growing power. Rome and the Vatican were occupied by the armies of Charles V in 1527, which sacked the city in the same way as the barbarians had done in earlier years.

After the 'sack of Rome' all that could be done was to repair the damage and try to conclude, as well as possible, the schemes that had been started during the opening decades of the century. Michelangelo, now an old man, was commissioned by Pope Paul III (1534–50) to give the Papal city its final shape: he drew up the architectural plans for the Capitol (Figs 852–4), he arranged the gates of the city,

Fig. 851 The Rondanini Pietà, Michelangelo's last work.

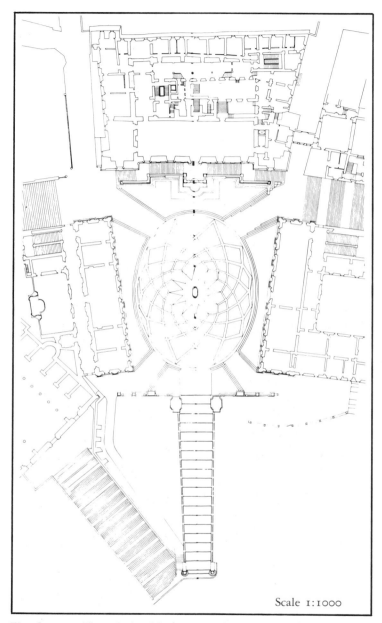

Scale 1:1000

Figs 852–4 The relationship between the Capitol and the city, as
it was before the demolitions of the Fascist era. The layout of the
Capitol, arranged by Michelangelo.

Figs 855–8   The new St Peter's, laid out by Michelangelo. Aerial view of the church from the west. General view of the Vatican at the end of the sixteenth century, after the erection of the obelisk, but prior to the work of Bernini and Maderno. View of the present façade from the Castel Sant'Angelo, which more or less reproduces the façade of Michelangelo. Plan of the church according to Michelangelo's plans (cf. Figs 845–6).

simplified the plan of St Peter's and designed a dome for it which towered over the surrounding areas (Figs 855–9). At the same time he completed the frescoes in the Sistine Chapel by painting *The Last Judgement* (Fig. 860). Whereas in his painting and his sculpture he broke with the idealised classical concept of balance, in his architectural work he realised his obligation to restore a sense of harmony and balance to the incomplete works with whose conclusion he had been entrusted.

DVM·RECTAS·AD·TEMPLA·VIAS·SANCTISSIMA·PANDIT
IPSE·SIBI·SIXTVS·PANDIT·AD·ASTRA·VIAM

Fig. 861   A fresco in the Vatican Library, showing the streets planned by Sixtus V in the hills on the left bank of the Tiber.

The exemplary ideals of the early sixteenth century now formed the basis of a true cultural tradition. They had not completely transformed the city's appearance, nor had they succeeded in resolving the civil and moral conflicts of a totally new world; they continued, however, to provide a series of model examples for the art and *mores* of society, which were to be respected the world over for a long time to come. Rome had become the 'city museum' of European culture, to which people came in order to study the sources of both ancient and modern classicism.

During succeeding centuries the physical shape of the city gradually began to crystallise. In the late 1500s Sixtus V (1585–90) tried to extend the inhabited area of the city as far as the Aurelian Walls by laying out a further series of rectilinear streets on the hills of the left bank (Figs 861–4). Rome, however, whose inhabitants numbered some 100,000 during this period, did not grow enough to fill this area, and it was left to the artists of the baroque era to add the finishing touches to this heterogeneous cityscape, in which the ruins of antiquity, the buildings of the Middle Ages and the monuments of the Renaissance all existed side by side.

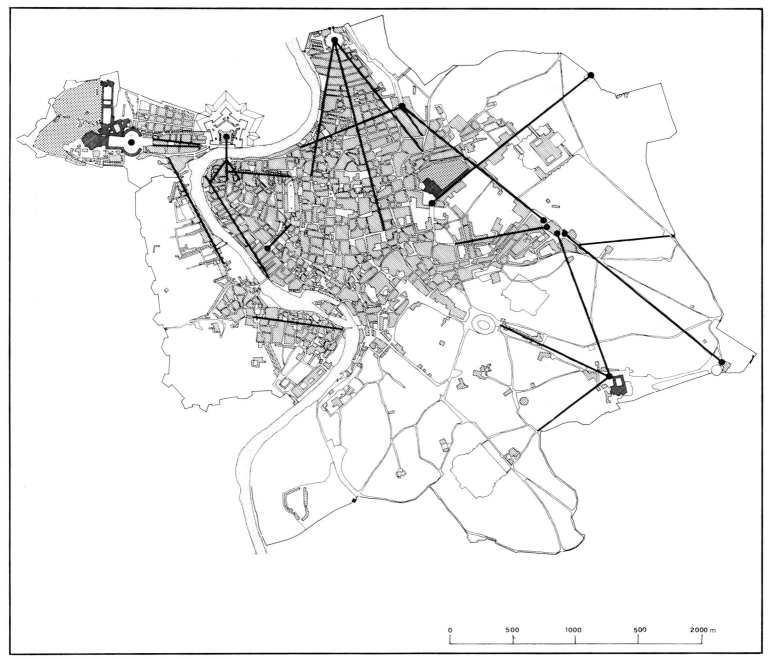

Fig. 862 Eighteenth-century map of Rome, showing the ancient streets that were still in use and also those opened by the Popes during the fifteenth and sixteenth centuries.

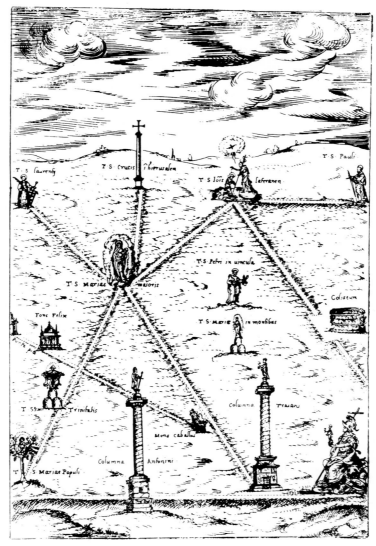

Figs 863–4   Rome. Plan of the new streets between the
monuments of the left bank, from a drawing of 1588; map of the
city in 1602, following the schemes of Sixtus V.

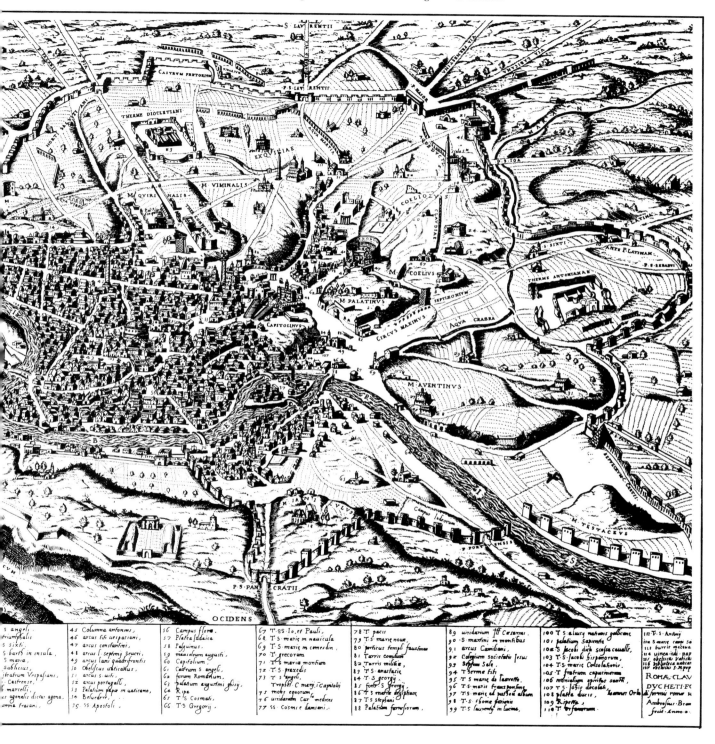

s angeli,	45 Columna antonini,	56 Campus flora.	67 T SS Io, et Pauli,	78 T pacis	89 uiridarium ſſſ Ceſerini	100 T S aluisy naheni galleane	111 V S Antoni
triumphalis	46 arcus fili uespasiani,	57 Platea ſdaica	68 T S marię in nauicula	79 T S marię noue	90 S martini in montibus	101 palatium Sapientie	112 S marie campi ſa
s sixti,	47 arcus constantini,	58 Pasquinus.	69 T S marię in comesdin	80 porticus templi fauſtine	91 arcus Camilani,	102 S Jacobi dicti scolſa cauallr,	113 turris meerena
S barſſ in insula,	48 arcus f septimy Seueri,	59 mausoleum augusti,	70 T grecorum	81 Turris cumlibani	92 Colegium societatis Jesus	103 T S Jacobi hispanorum,	114 uinea-nili-pap
S marię,	49 arcus Jani quadrifrontis,	60 Capitolium	71 T S marię montium	82 Turris milície,	93 Stephani Sole	104 T S marie Consolationir.	115 obeliscus Vaticci
Sublicius,	50 Obeliscus uaticanus,	61 Castrum S angeli,	72 T S praxedis	83 T S anaſtaſie	94 T Serme fili	105 T fratrum capucinorum	116 obeliscus nabuc
fratrum Vespasiani,	51 arcus s uiti,	62 forum Romanum,	73 T S angeli,	84 T S georgij	95 T S marię da ſauretto.	106 monialium spiritus santi	117 obeliscus S M pop
Castrenſe,	52 arcus portugalli,	63 palatium augustini ghisy	Trophři C marij, i Capitolij	85 fons S georgy	96 T S marię transtonſine	107 T S Jobis ascolah,	
marcelli,	53 Palatium pape in uaticano,	64 Ripa	75 mons equorum la	86 T S marię ediptiace	97 T S marię et puſſeu altium	108 platta ducis,	ROMÆ CLAV
us agonelis dicitur agona,	54 Beluederre,	65 T S Cosmati,	76 uiridarum Carlo medices	87 T S ſtephani	98 T S ſbone fericnis	Joannes Orb	DVCHETI FO
mna fraſani.	55 SS Apostoli.	66 T S Gregorij.	77 SS Cosme e damiani.	88 Palatium ſorreſcorum	99 T S laurentij in lucine,	109 Riperta,	Ambroſius Bra
						110 T orſorrorum	frciit Anno .1.

Lorenzo Bernini (1598–1680) was a great architect in that he realised that the vastness of the classical ruins and of Bramante's monumental works had to coexist with the small-scale houses and districts of the common people. As a result, the idea of building a new Rome along the same grandiose lines as the ancient one was finally abandoned, and the contrast between the courtly and the mundane, which could obviously not be totally eliminated, became a characteristic feature of the city. In this spirit Bernini solved the problem of how to make St Peter's blend in with the city by planning the beautiful St Peter's Square: a large open space, whose shape was influenced by the unevenness of the terrain and which was partially screened by an open colonnade that revealed the surrounding districts and a panorama of the city. The scenario led gradually from the poor houses of the Borghi to the façade of the church (behind which loomed the great dome) and then into the interior, right up to the baldachin that occupied the vast space under the dome and, finally, to the bronze *gloria* at the end of the apse (Figs 865–71).

In this way the face of modern Rome became fixed: a city that did not try to relive its past, but acted as guardian of its ancient remains, having learned to live alongside these reminders of a bygone age in a perfectly natural way. The imbalance between life in the modern city and these memorials to the past served to remind people of the way in which time destroys everything; it revealed the emptiness of the myth of the Eternal City and provided an appropriate setting for the spiritual powers of the Roman Catholic Church.

The city retained this appearance up until the last century. Since then, however, the piecemeal development that followed Rome's assumption of the role of Italian capital and an emotive nostalgia for the grandeur of the ancient city have both played their part in destroying the balance of this extraordinary urban phenomenon. The ruins have become isolated and even the monumental ensemble of St Peter's has become the background for an ordinary main street. And yet the city's original appearance — a combination of the monumental and the mundane — can still be seen in many districts that have been spared from demolition, and it continues to resist the excesses of modern development.

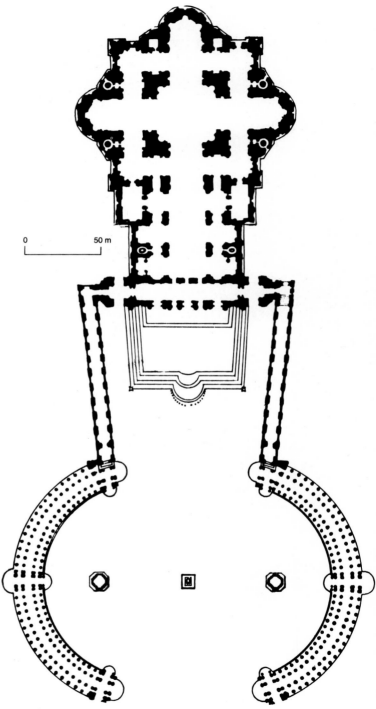

0   50 m

Fig. 865   Plan of St Peter's Square in Rome.

Fig. 866   Photograph of St Peter's Square, taken from a balloon at the beginning of the century, before the demolition work of 1935.

Fig. 866   Plan of St Peter's and its square, from Letarouilly's book, published in the early nineteenth century.

Fig. 869   The interior of St Peter's, showing the decorative scheme of Bernini.

Fig. 870   St Peter's Square, as seen from the roofs of the surrounding houses at the beginning of this century.

Fig. 871   Panoramic view of St Peter's Square and the Borgo district, prior to the demolition carried out to make way for the Via della Conciliazione.

Fig. 872   The three streets that converge on the Piazza del Popolo
in Rome.

Fig. 873   Plan of the ground floor of one of the blocks between
the Via del Babuino and Via Margutta (recognisable in the aerial
photo, above); the upper floors were let out as flats. Scale 1:1,000.

A. Entrance.
B. Shop.
C. Courtyard.
L. Washroom.
P. Concierge.
R. Garage.
S. Stable.

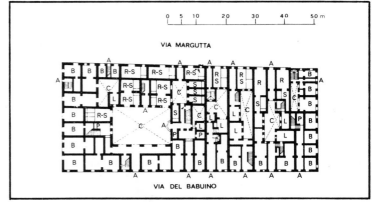

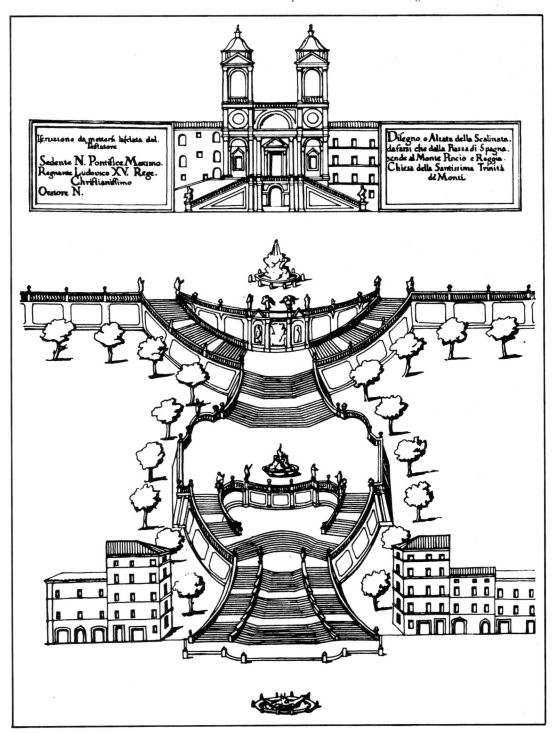

Fig. 874 The eighteenth-century steps (The Spanish Steps) between Trinità dei Monti and the Piazza di Spagna as shown in a contemporary drawing.

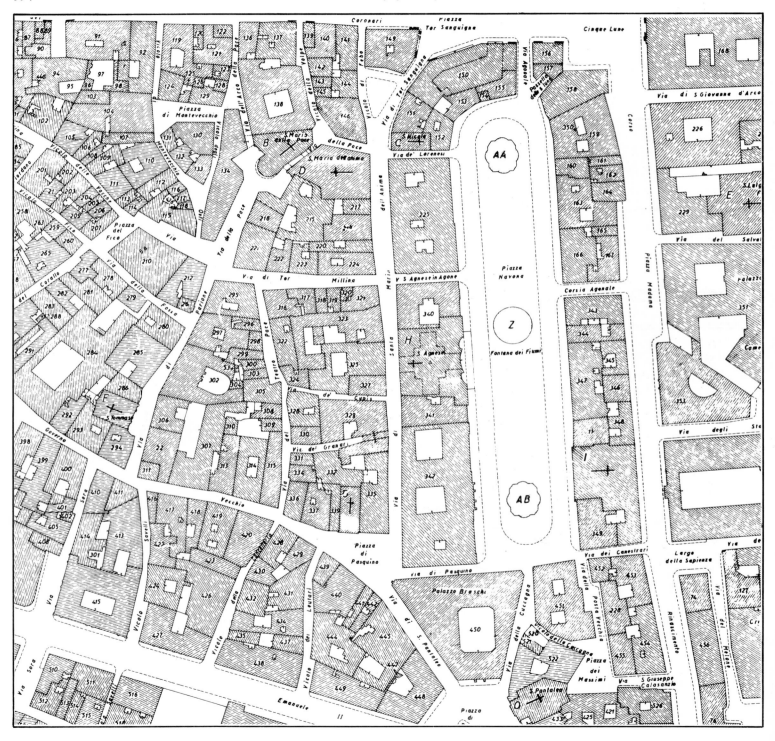

Figs 875–6   The district around the Piazza Navona, the historic centre of Rome: a cadastral map (reduced to a scale of 1:2,000) and an aerial photograph. The shape of the Piazza Navona reproduces that of Domitian's stadium; around it can be seen the winding streets of the medieval city, with its tall, narrow houses — the largest blocks represent palaces, with their regular-shaped courtyards. The two rectilinear streets, below (the Corso Emanuele) and right (the Corso Rinascimento), have been opened within the last hundred years.

Fig. 877   Aerial view of the centre of present-day Rome.

Fig. 878   Aerial view of the Villa Doria-Pamphili, beyond the western walls of the city.

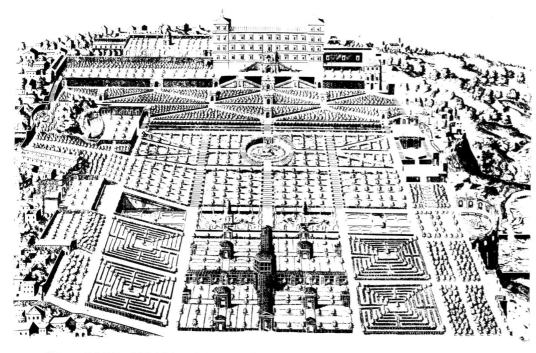

Fig. 879 Panorama of the Villa d'Este at Tivoli, near Rome.

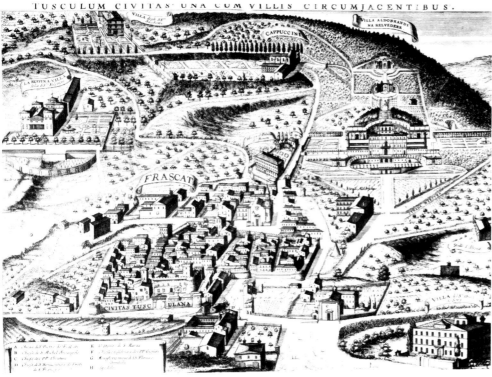

Fig. 880 Panorama of Frascati, showing the sixteenth- and seventeenth-century villas of the nobility.

The villas built between the second half of the sixteenth century and the first half of the seventeenth in the environs of Rome and the other Italian capitals, are limited and regular architectural projects, in direct contrast with the limitless countryside and the irregularity of the small medieval towns.

At Bagnaia — the example shown in the following pages — the combined environment is composed of three elements: the old, walled medieval quarter, the later enlargement with three rectilinear streets that join the old town to the villa, and the grounds of the villa, dominated by a symmetrical axis that ends in the densely wooded hill. Renaissance architecture was only capable of achieving a partial transformation of the existent environment.

Figs 881–3   (Here and overleaf) The village of Bagnaia, near Viterbo, with the Villa Lante built by Vignola in the late sixteenth cadastral map (scale 1:4,000) and two aerial views.

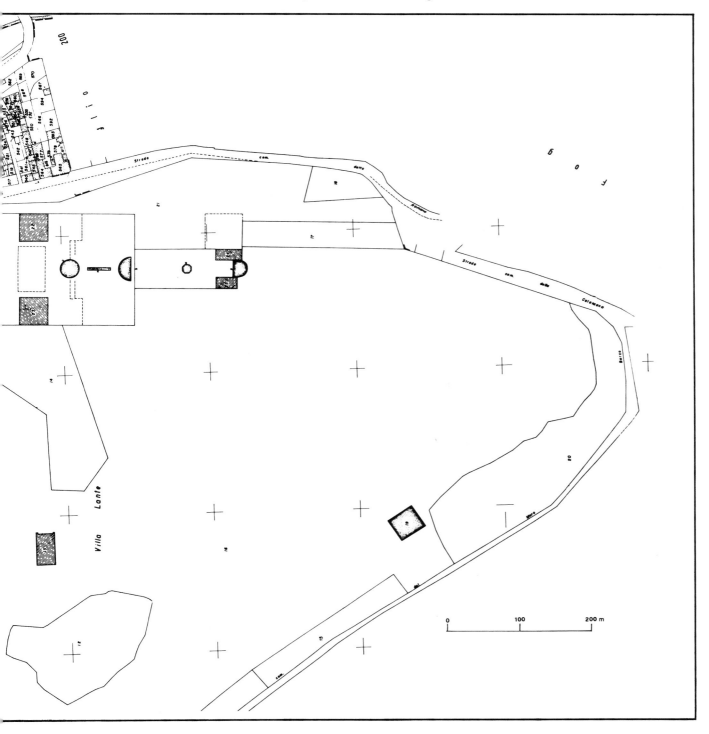

Fig. 884   A view of the Scheldt estuary and the port of Antwerp, from a sixteenth-century engraving.

9
European colonisation

The Renaissance period marked the beginning of the worldwide expansion of European civilisation. The towns and buildings that were completed overseas were on the whole much more important than those of the mother countries. Europe already possessed the cities and territorial layouts of the Middle Ages, which fulfilled the needs of Renaissance society and were only partly modified. In the rest of the world, however, the European invaders and merchants found vast open spaces, in which they were able to embark on large-scale urbanising and colonising projects.

In these spaces, which were much larger than those in Europe, the resources available were not commensurate with the opportunities presented. In Europe specialists of the highest calibre were employed but were unable to complete any major projects, whereas in the colonies there was scope for vast undertakings but the necessary skills were unavailable and the only materials at hand were the by-products of the European experience. The result was that, given the overall picture of Renaissance civilisation, there was no coming together of quality and quantity. The qualitative merits of the new cultural models became lost in the conflicts of Europe and were never able to spread properly throughout the world.

Yet the high quality of the models (examined in the two preceding chapters) and the low quality of their application (which will be dealt with in this chapter) are two closely related aspects of a single cultural system. In order to begin to explain how the second developed from the first, we must consider the nature of the European maritime cities from which the colonists set off on their voyages: Antwerp, which took the place of Bruges as the great entrepôt of central Europe; Lisbon and Seville, the Atlantic ports of Portugal and Spain; and Genoa, which after its alliance with Charles V became the Spanish empire's most important naval base.

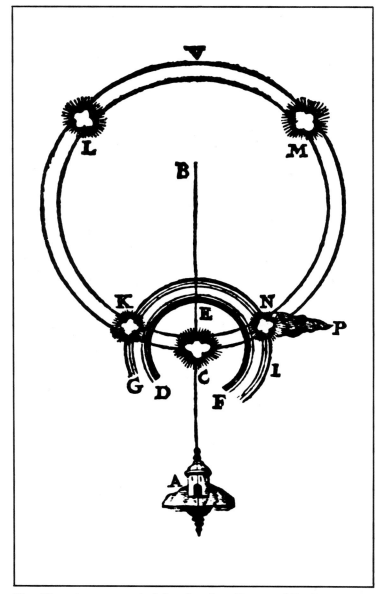

Fig. 885　An astronomical drawing from Descartes' *De Meteoris*.

Fig. 886 The port of Antwerp, as seen in a drawing by Albrecht Dürer.

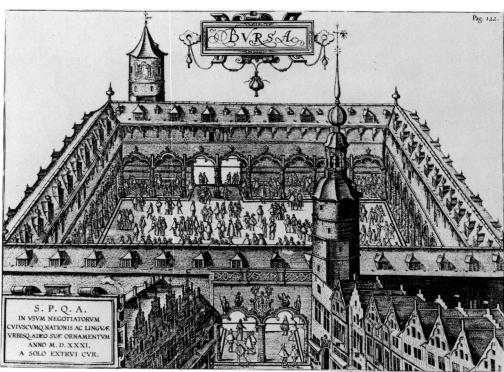

Fig. 887 The Bourse at Antwerp, from a sixteenth-century engraving.

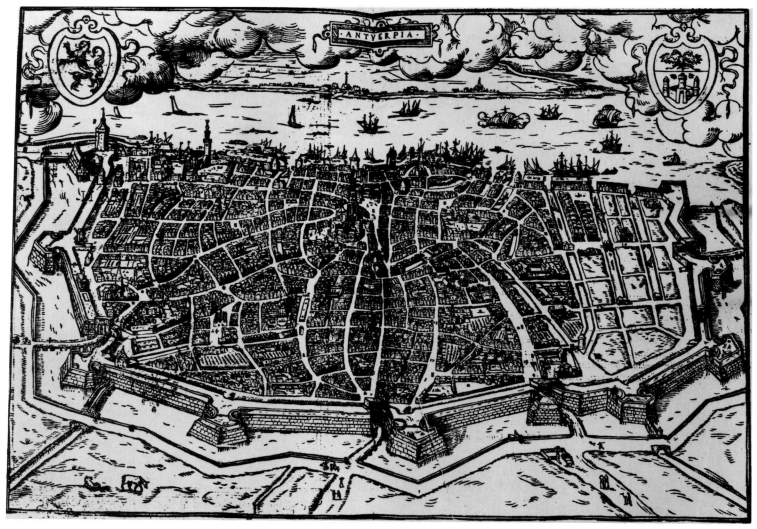

Fig. 888 General view of Antwerp in the second half of the sixteenth century, its period of greatest development: the city did not spread beyond the walls until the second half of the nineteenth century. Right, the new extension to the city, planned on the grid system in 1548.

Fig. 889   The centre of Antwerp, with its Renaissance Town Hall (1561–6), burnt down by the Spanish in 1576. After the Spanish conquest (1599) the Dutch blockaded the mouth of the Scheldt, rendering the port useless.

Figs. 890–1 Seville and Lisbon, the two main Atlantic ports of Spain and Portugal. On the lowest hill in Lisbon can be seen the new district of Barrio Alto, laid out on the chequerboard system in 1513.

Fig. 892   A view of Genoa in 1573, showing the new walls built in 1537.

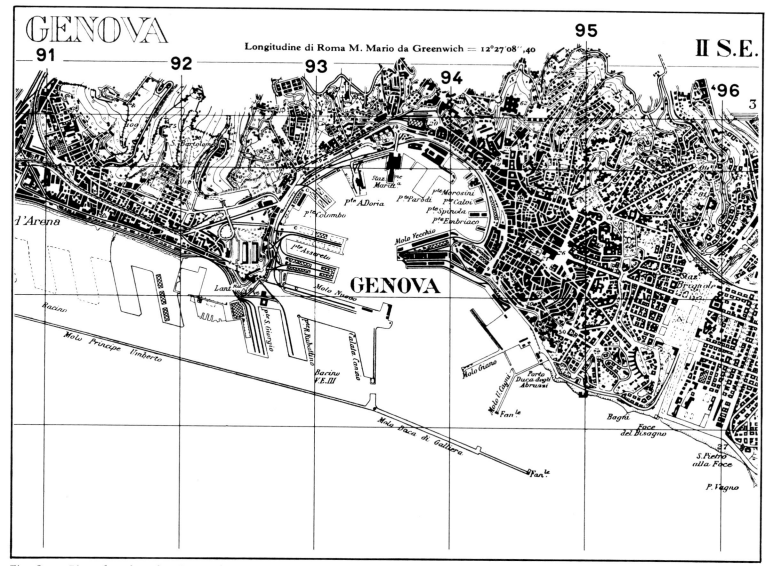

Fig. 893   Plan of modern-day Genoa, from a map by the Istituto Geografico Militare (scale 1:25,000).

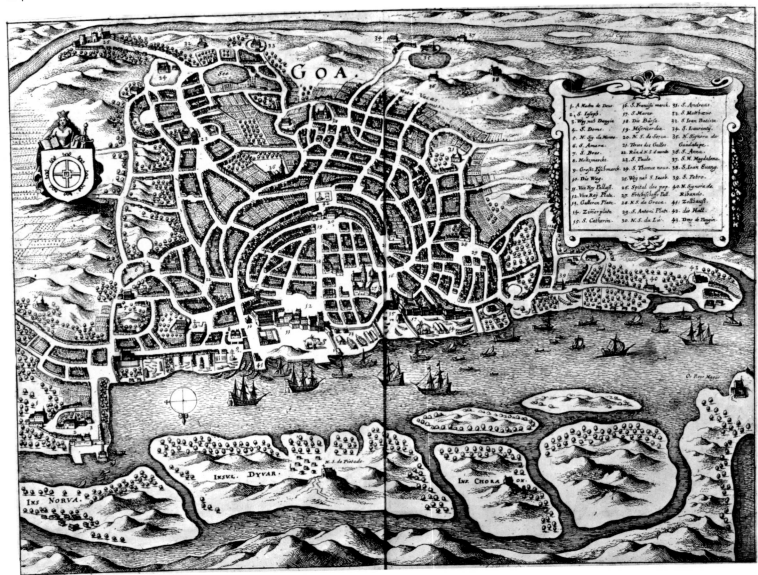

Fig. 897   Plan of Goa, the capital of the Portuguese possessions in India.

In these prosperous and much-visited cities the new cultural ideas were received at first hand, but they were diluted by a tendency towards schematicism, both technological and mercantile, which was a common feature of developments outside Italy. Illustrations of this tendency can be seen in the way in which the cities were divided up (Figs 888, 891, 895) and in the utilitarianism of the buildings (Figs 887, 889).

Overseas exploration during the sixteenth century was the exclusive domain of the Spanish and Portuguese, and it was only during the next century that the other powers of the Atlantic seaboard intervened: France, England and Holland.

In 1494 Pope Alexander VI established the demarcation line between the zones reserved for Spanish and Portuguese colonisation: the meridian that lies 270 leagues west of the Azores. The Portuguese tried for many years to find a sea route to the Orient, and by 1498 Vasco da Gama had reached India by sailing round the southern tip of Africa. In 1492 Christopher Columbus reached America on a voyage of discovery that had been financed by the Spanish.

The Portuguese found either poor and inhospitable lands in their hemisphere (Brazil and southern Africa) or, as was the case in the East, densely populated and warlike countries that they were unable to conquer. As a result, they only founded a series of naval bases to protect their overseas trade, and were unable to conduct a proper full-scale colonising programme. The Spaniards, on the other hand, found in their zone territories that were ideally suited to colonisation: the plateaux of central and southern America, with the indigenous empires that were both rich and highly developed, but incapable of offering any real resistance to the European invaders.

Cortes in Mexico and Pizarro in Peru both occupied several large local cities — Tenochtitlan, which later became Mexico City (Figs 901–6), and Cuzco (Figs 909–10) and transformed them in accordance with the needs of the Spanish settlers. Throughout the continent, however, they destroyed the native settlements which were scattered over the countryside, and forced the population to settle in new, densely-built cities, similar to those of the central Spanish plateau.

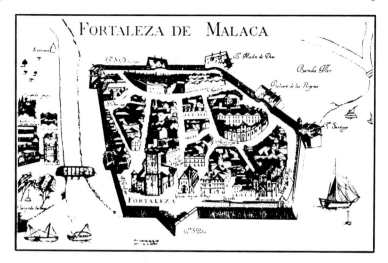

Figs 898–9 Two Portuguese colonial outposts: Malacca in the Far East, and Rio de Janeiro in Brazil, as seen in seventeenth-century engravings.

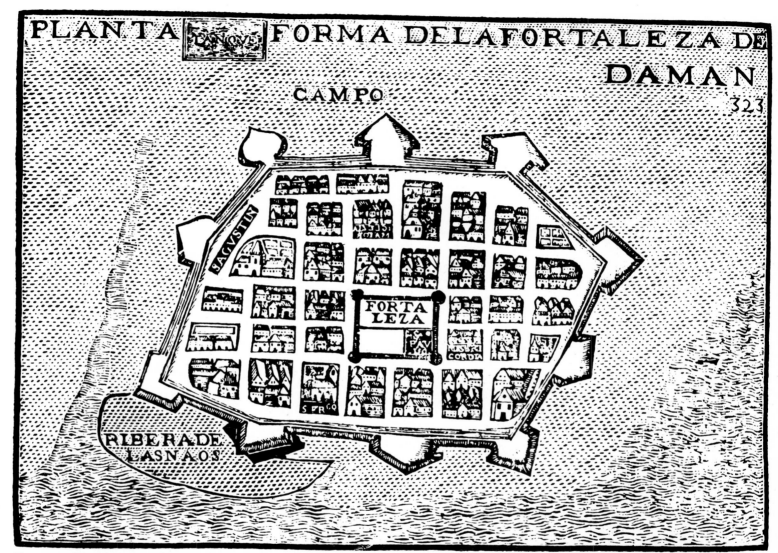

Fig. 900   The Portuguese fortress of Daman, in India.

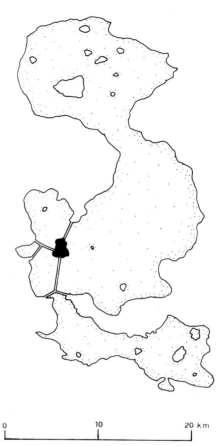

Figs 901–2 The city of Tenochtitlan, capital of the Aztec empire, built on an island in Lake Texcoco; an engraving that forms part of the account of the *Conquistador Anonimo*.

Fig. 903   The main square (Zócalo) of Mexico City, the capital built by the Spaniards on the site of Tenochtitlan. It was one of the largest squares built during the sixteenth century, measuring some 250 metres across, and corresponded to the square that had existed in front of the main temple of the old Aztec city.

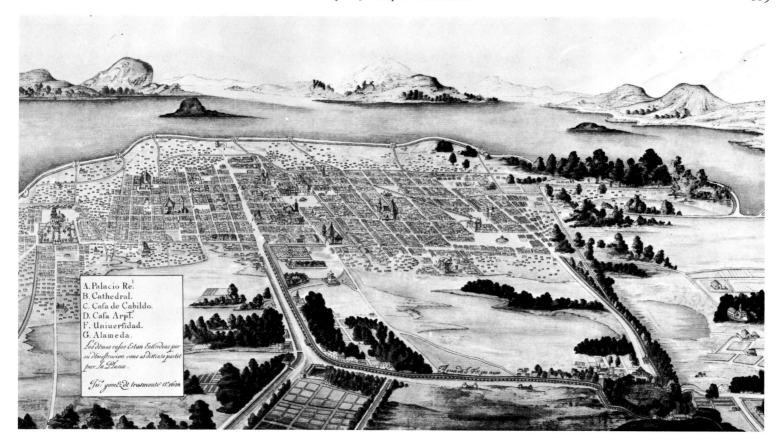

A. Palacio Re.¹
B. Cathedral.
C. Cafa de Cabildo.
D. Cafa Arp¹.
F. Uniuerfidad.
G. Alameda.

Fig. 904   Views of Mexico City in 1628 and 1905. The lake has been partially drained and the city is now linked to the land.

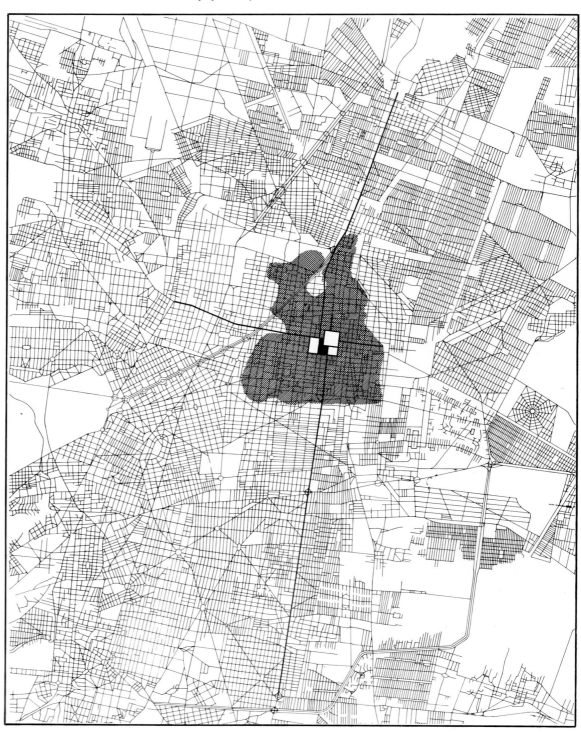

Figs 905–6 The outlines of the
Aztec and Spanish cities, as seen
against the background of a
map of modern Mexico City.

Fig. 907   The holy city of Teotihuacan, near Mexico City, with its ruined pyramids.

Fig. 908 The Mexican town of Cholula. To the left can be seen the remains of an Aztec pyramid, and to the right the reticular layout of the Spanish city, a great deal of which still remains empty, due to the fact that the city failed to develop at the anticipated rate.

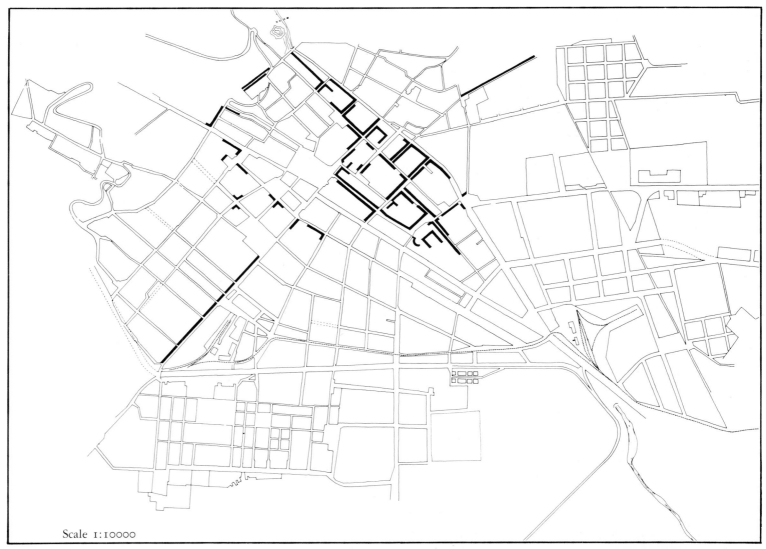

Scale 1:10000

Fig. 909   Cuzco, the imperial capital of the Incas; the heavy lines denote the surviving sections of the original pre-Spanish walls, in the context of the modern city's layout.

The new cities followed a single plan: a chequerboard pattern of rectilinear streets, containing series of isolated blocks, almost invariably square. At the centre of the city, either cancelling out or reducing the size of a few blocks, was the main square on to which the principal buildings of the city faced: the church, the town hall, and the houses of the merchants and richest colonists.

In Mexico, where a large population had to be converted

to Christianity, the churches were built with an extensive courtyard (the *atrio*) in front, while a sort of secondary chapel (the *capilla de indios*) was erected at the side of their façades and used to conduct open-air masses on feast days (Fig. 916).

This model was imposed by the authorities in the early years of the conquest and was codified in a law introduced by Philip II in 1573: it was, in fact, the first town-planning

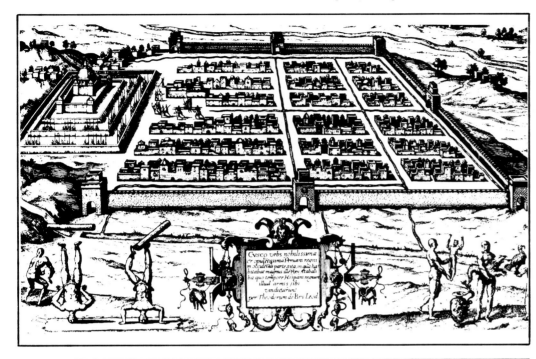

Fig. 910 A rather fanciful European engraving of the city of Cuzco in the sixteenth century.

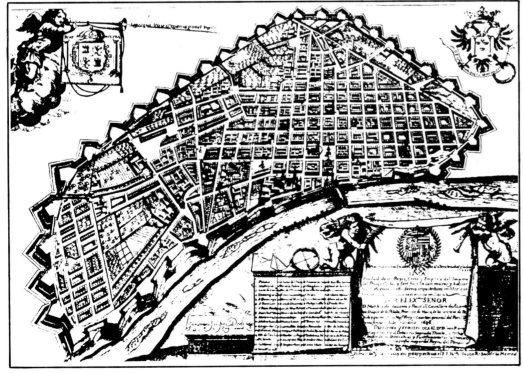

Fig. 911 An eighteenth-century map of Lima, the Peruvian capital built by the Spanish near the coast. Because of its vulnerable position, the city was surrounded by a protective wall.

Figs 912–14   Illustrations in a Spanish chronicle from the end of the sixteenth century, which shows various forms of maltreatment being practised on the natives.

law of the modern era. Its most significant clauses were as follows:

Upon arrival in the locality where the new settlement is to be founded (it is our wish that this should be an unencumbered locality, and occupiable without giving offence to the Indians, and with their agreement) its layout, with squares, streets and building lots should be outlined on the ground by means of cords and pegs, starting from the main square from which the streets should run towards the gates and the principal cross-country roads, and leaving enough open space, so that the city having to grow may extend continually in the same fashion . . . The central square should be at the centre of the city, of oblong shape, with the length at least one and a half times the width, since this is the best proportion for festivals in which horses are used, and for other celebrations . . . The size of the square shall be proportionate to the number of inhabitants, bearing in mind that the cities of the Indies, being new, are subject to growth; and indeed it is our intention that they shall grow. For this reason the square shall be planned in relation to

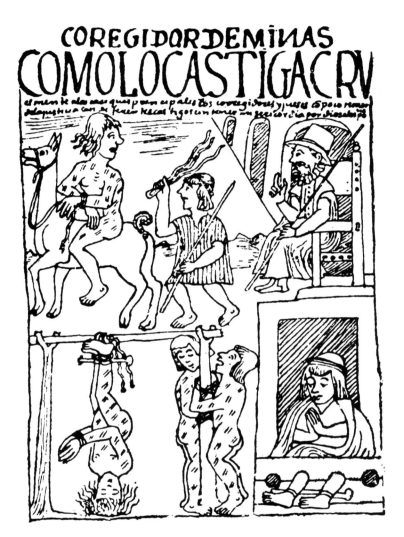

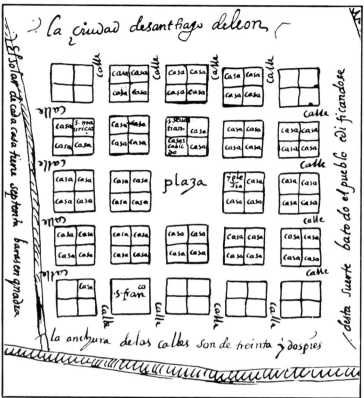

Fig. 915 Plan of the original layout of Santiago de Leon, the modern Caracas.

the possible growth of the city. It should not be less than 200 feet wide and 300 feet long, nor wider than 500 feet or longer than 800 feet. A well-proportioned square of medium size shall be 600 feet long and 400 feet wide.

The four main streets lead out of the square, one from the middle point of each side, and two from each corner. The four corners should be aligned with the four cardinal points, because in this way the streets leading out of the square will not be exposed directly to the four principal winds. The whole square and the four main streets that radiate from it shall be provided with porticoes, because these are of great convenience to the persons who gather there for the purpose of commerce . . .

The eight streets that converge on the square at the four corners should be unimpeded by the porticoes of the square. These porticoes should finish at the corners, so that the pavements of the streets may be aligned with those of the square. The streets shall be broad in cold areas, narrow in hot ones; but for the purpose of defence, where horses are used, it will be agreed that they should be broad . . .

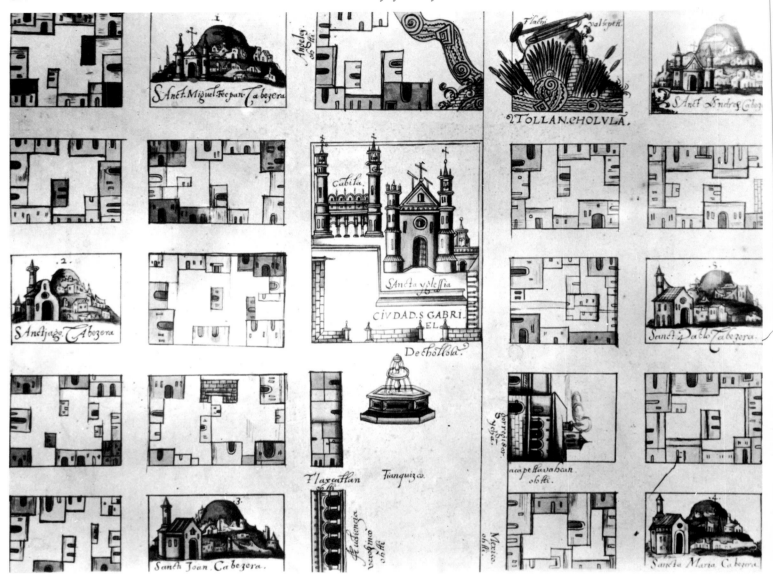

Fig. 916   A map of the centre of Cholula in Mexico (1581); the largest block, at the centre, contains the church, the *atrio* and the *capilla de indios*.

In the cities of the interior the church should not stand on the perimeter of the square, but at such a distance as to appear free, separate from the other buildings so that it may be seen on every side; in this way it will appear more handsome and more imposing. It should be built above the level of the ground, so that the people must climb a series of steps to gain entrance to it . . . The hospital of the poor where the ill are not contagious shall be built on the northern side, so that it faces south . . . The building plots around the main square should not be granted to private people, but reserved for the church, the royal and municipal buildings, the shops and residences of the merchants, which should be the first to be built . . .

The remaining plots shall be distributed by lot to those colonists who are entitled to build around the main square. The unassigned plots should be reserved for those colonists who will be able to come later, or for disposition according to our wishes.

Fig. 917　The central part of an eighteenth-century map of the city of Quito in Ecuador; the four squares were formed by leaving four sections of the chequerboard free of buildings.

These rules were derived from both medieval tradition (the new towns founded during the thirteenth century and the first half of the fourteenth century — the French *bastides* and the Spanish *poblaciones* — which were spread throughout the European countryside) and from the culture of the Renaissance: from the treatises of Vitruvius, Alberti and others, and from the new spirit of geometrical regularity, which had by then become a common practice and a basic technical prerequisite.

In practical terms, the combination of these factors produced a new type of city, with several original features that can be categorised as follows:

1. The first thing to be established upon the foundation of a city was not a three-dimensional organism, but a *traza* (a two-dimensional, regulatory plan, as in Ferrara). In fact, it was not planned to erect the buildings within a short time of each other, or virtually simultaneously, as in the Middle Ages; the building plots were allocated to owners who built

Fig. 918   Map of the Mexican city of Guadalajara.

Fig. 919   An aerial photograph of Guadalajara, showing the main square (nos 2, 3, 4 in the preceding map).

Figs 920–1   Typical scenes from a Spanish colonial city: the façade of a church in which the classical architectural elements have been freely interpreted by local craftsmen, and a street flanked by single-storey houses.

how and when they wanted. In American cities the squares and streets were sometimes pointlessly grandiose, whereas the buildings were squat and unimpressive, with the houses almost always having only one floor (Figs 921–3).

2. The cities had to be able to grow, and it was impossible to know how large they would become; in order to cope with this, the chequerboard plan could be expanded in all directions, whenever new blocks needed to be added. The external boundaries of the cities were always temporary, also because they had no need for walls or moats (it was not until the seventeenth century that the cities nearest the coast were fortified to protect them from pirates). The sharp contrast between city and countryside, so evident in Europe and particularly in Spain, became far less marked, both because of the changeability of the boundaries and because of the abundance of open spaces within the cities. Colonial houses often had a private courtyard, while the city itself possessed the large open area formed by the main square and the *atrio*.

Fig. 922   A street in Mérida, Venezuela, which is still flanked by single-storey colonial houses.

Fig. 923 The same street in Mérida where the colonial houses have been replaced by modern buildings which still retain the old proportions

Figs 924–5   Two examples of
eighteenth-century decorations in
Mexico: a stuccoed dome in Puebla,
and the façade of a church in Tlaxcala.

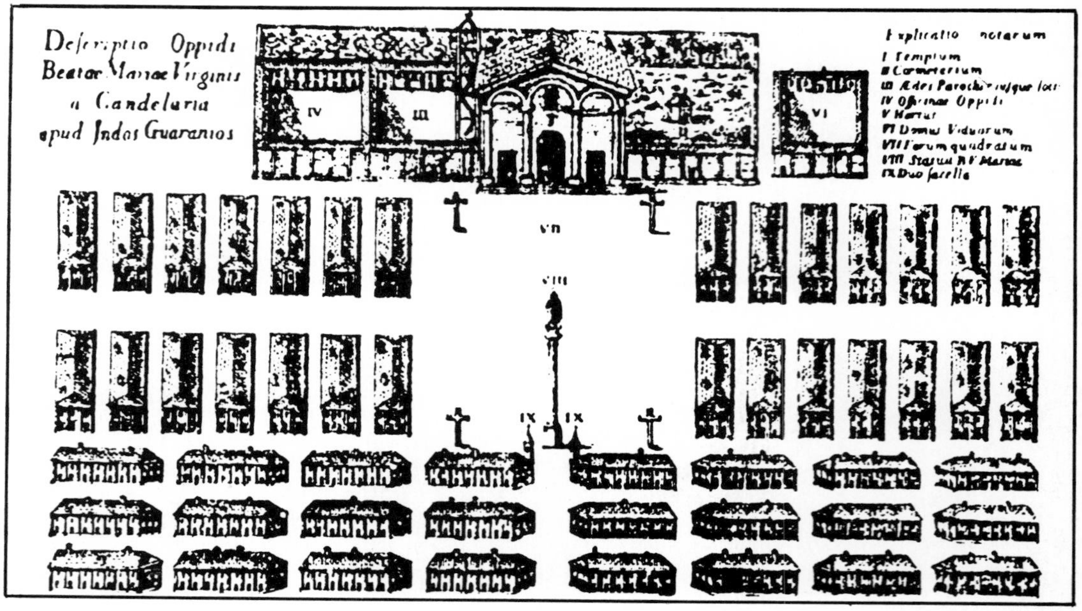

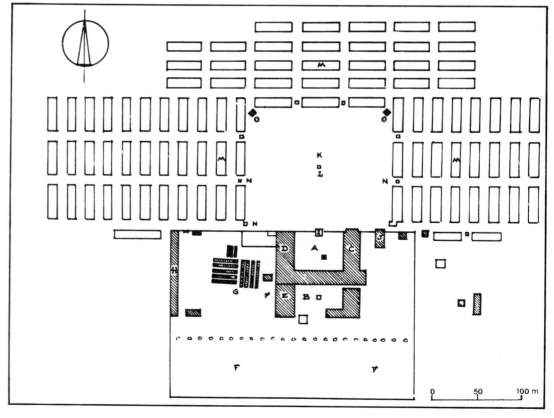

Fig. 926   The town of Candelaria, founded in 1627 by the Jesuits in the interior of Paraguay, as seen in an eighteenth-century engraving.

Fig. 927   Plan of another Jesuit town, San José in Chiquitos, Bolivia.

A. College.
B. Patio.
C. Church.
D. Residence of the Jesuits.
E. Refectory.
F. Gardens.
G. Dryers.
H. Workshops.
I. Tower.
J. Mortuary chapel.
K. Great Cross.
L. Square.
M. Indian houses.
N. Crosses.
O. Chapels.

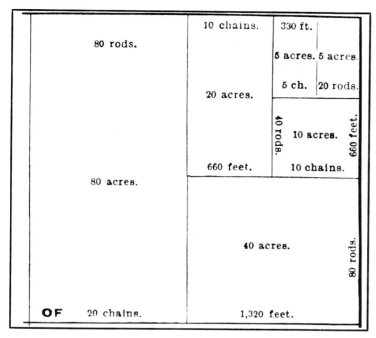

Fig. 928   A section of the territorial grid established by Thomas Jefferson in the United States in 1785.

3. The uniformity of the chequerboard plan — often decided on paper by bureaucrats in Spain — prevented the city from adapting to its natural environment. For this reason the cities of Latin America had a more straightforward appearance than their medieval European counterparts, which made use of much more varied layouts that were decided *in situ*. In addition, the uncertainty of future development gave the cities a precarious, unplanned appearance: some cities, which initially consisted of a few dozen blocks, grew into large conurbations without ever changing their basic plan. The original layout established in the sixteenth century could still be used for the city's development in the nineteenth century and even right up to the present day; in fact, in many respects it resembled modern town planning schemes.

The cities of colonial America were the most important examples of sixteenth-century town planning. The lack of imagination that they showed, when compared with the refinement and inventiveness of European artistic culture, illustrates the way in which ability and opportunity no longer coincided. In Europe the greatest minds of the time found themselves unable to realise their plans, while third-rate technicians who emigrated to America were given the

chance to plan and complete entire cities. And yet they both had the same goal: to bring order to the urban environment in accordance with the new principles of symmetry and geometrical regularity. By imposing these basic tenets, the Europeans were able to assert their dominance in every part of the world.

The chequerboard model, conceived by the Spaniards during the sixteenth century to lay out the new towns of Central and South America, was later adopted by the English and the French during the seventeenth and eighteenth centuries for their North American colonies. The new scientific school of thought viewed this grid system as being universally applicable, on any scale whatsoever: for the laying out of cities, the subdivision of agricultural land, or even for planning a new state. In 1785 Thomas Jefferson, one of the founders of the Unites States, established a reticular system based on meridians and parallels, which was designed to be used in the colonisation of the West (each section consisted of 16 square miles, which could be subdivided into 2, 4, 8, 16, 32 or 64 smaller areas). And thus the geometrical pattern, on which the urban and rural landscape of the New World would be planned (Figs 929–43) became firmly established.

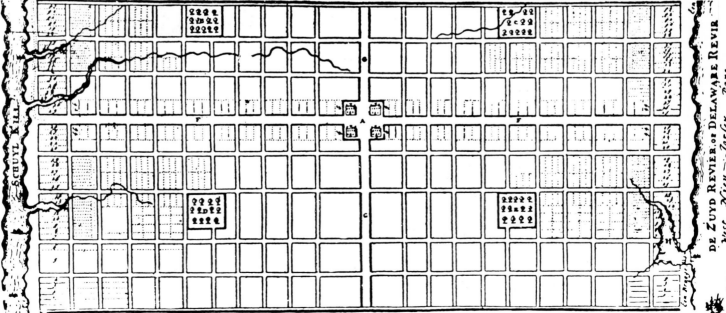

Figs 929–30   The colonisation of North America. The first pioneer settlement at San Francisco; the plan of the city of Philadelphia, outlined by William Penn in 1682.

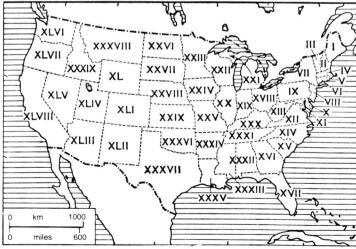

Figs 931–2   The building of Savannah, Georgia, in 1724; the forty-eight stages of the Union (before the inclusion of Hawaii and Alaska).

Figs. 933–6   (Four succeeding pages) The town plan of New York, laid out by the municipal authorities in 1811. It consists of a grid, with avenues (numbered 1 to 11) running lengthwise and streets (numbered 1 to 155) running crosswise; the avenues are wider than the streets, but the whole system maintains strict geometrical regularity despite the uneven terrain of Manhattan Island.

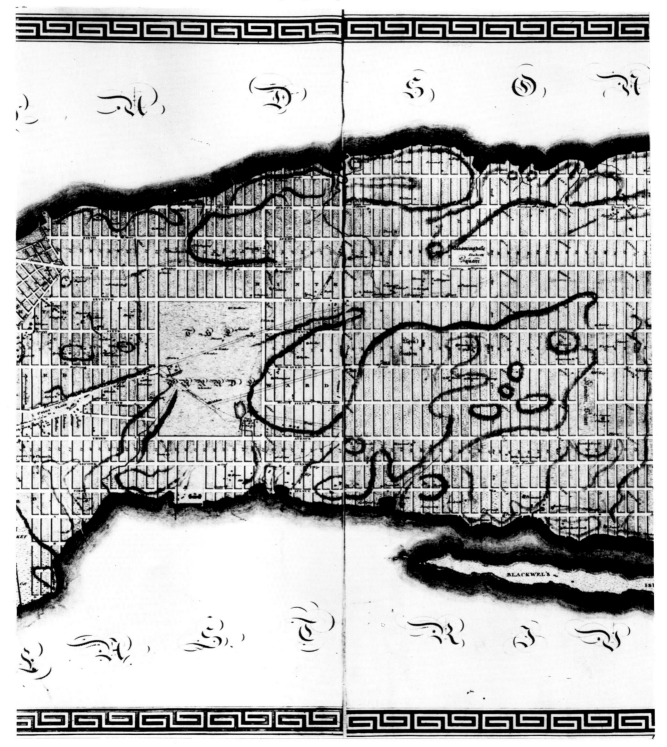

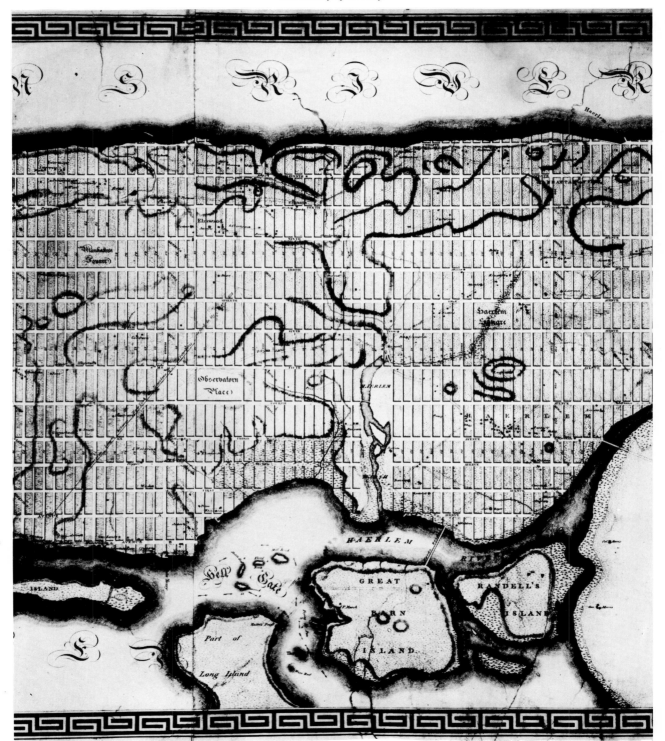

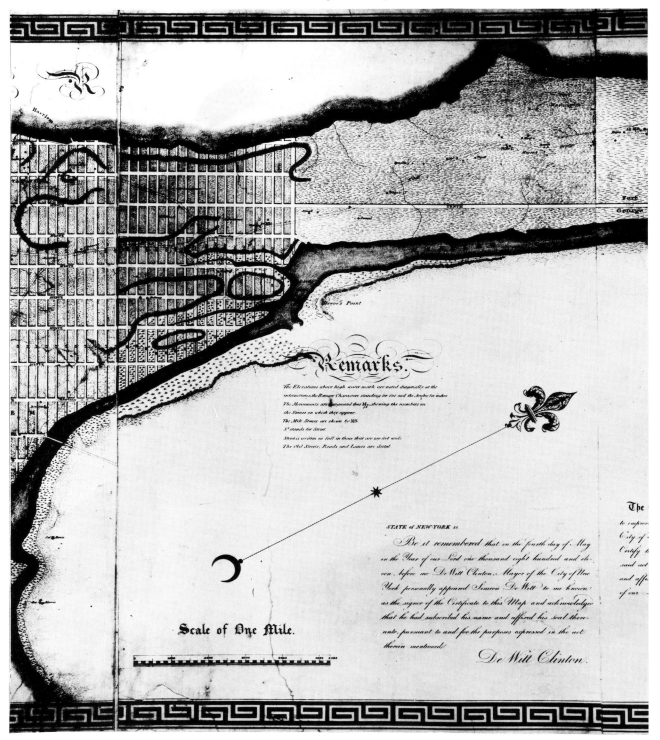

Remarks.

The Elevations above high water mark are noted diagonally at the
intersections, the Roman Characters standing for feet and the Arabic for inches
The Monuments are designated thus M, shewing the numbers on
the Stones on which they appear
The Mile Stones are shown by MS
St stands for Street
Street is written in full in those that are too feet wide
The Old Streets, Roads and Lanes are dotted

Scale of One Mile.

STATE of NEW-YORK ss

Be it remembered that on the fourth day of May
in the Year of our Lord one thousand eight hundred and ele-
ven, before me DeWitt Clinton, Mayor of the City of New
York personally appeared Simeon DeWitt to me known
as the signer of the Certificate to this Map and acknowledged
that he had subscribed his name and affixed his seal there-
unto, pursuant to and for the purposes expressed in the act
therein mentioned

De Witt Clinton

BROADWAY, NEW-YORK.

Figs 937–8   Two nineteenth-century views of New York: a section of Broadway and a panoramic view of the port.

Fig. 939   A section of New York at the end of the nineteenth century: the main landmarks, from left to right, are the Public Library, St Patrick's Cathedral and Grand Central Station.

Figs. 940–1   New York. A general
view of the city and a map of the central
area; some of the blocks in the 1811
plan have been rebuilt and filled with
skyscrapers of 100 floors and more.

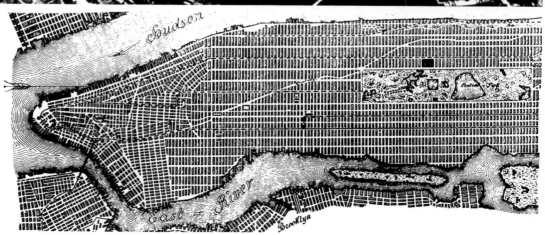

Fig. 942   New York. A view of the district containing the Empire State Building.

Fig. 943   A bird's eye view of Chicago, published at the time of the 1893 Exhibition. In 1832, the city had only been a small stronghold in territory that had yet to be colonised, as can be seen in the small vignette in the bottom right-hand corner of the map.

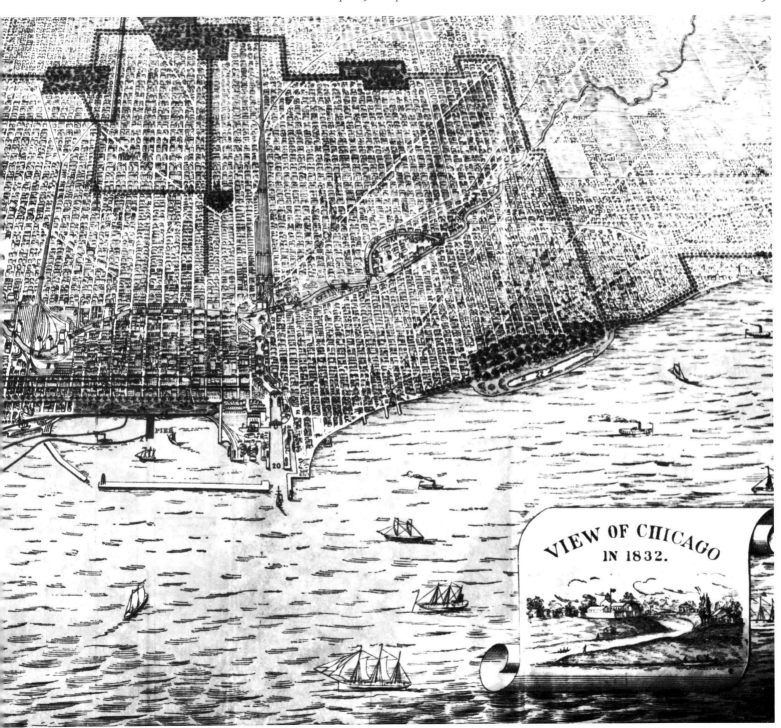

VIEW OF CHICAGO
IN 1832.

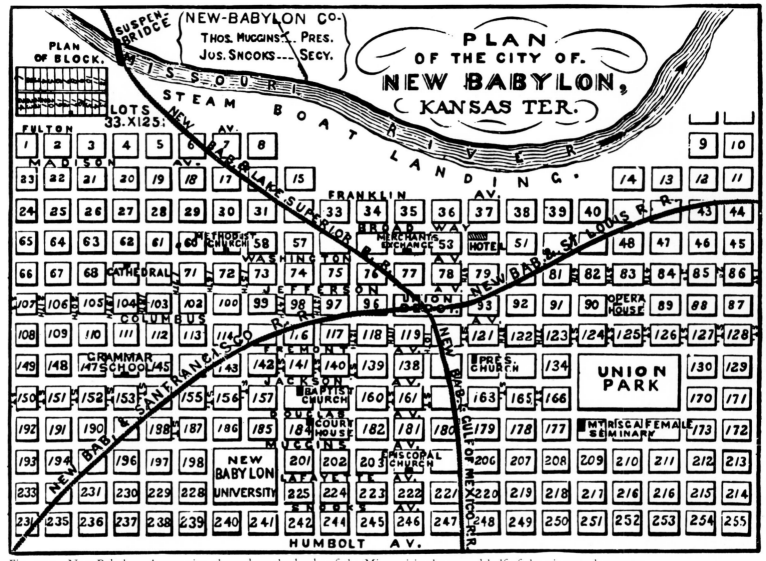

Fig. 944   New Babylon. A new city planned on the banks of the Missouri in the second half of the nineteenth century.

10
The capitals of baroque Europe

The economic crisis in the opening decades of the seventeenth century, the crisis undergone by the ruling classes of the Renaissance and the formation of modern techniques of scientific research brought about a change in the way that cities were planned and built.

The new ruling classes — kings with their courtiers and advisers, the *nouveaux riches* (whether nobles or commoners), the new clerics of the Reformation or Counter-Reformation — no longer had the same ambitions or skills where artistic matters were concerned. At the same time, art ceased to be a means of knowing and controlling the physical environment by the study of its constituent elements; the true nature of things was no longer judged by external beauty: it became something that could be ascertained by scientific research. Art became the study of subjective and emotional qualities; its function was to restrain collective feelings, or provide expression for those of the individual, and it wavered between conformism and evasion or protest.

Let us then study the new forms of art that emerged during the period, starting from the great centres of production and consumption: the capital cities of Europe. We will first examine the French capital, which became the new cultural model of the world.

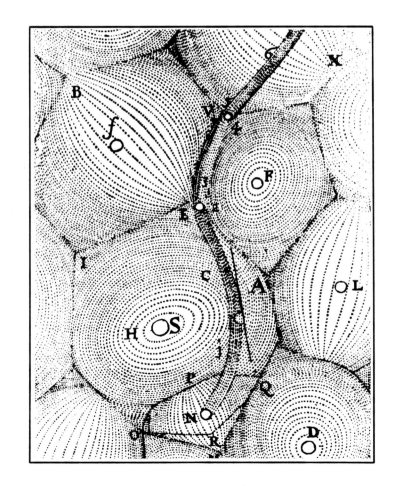

Fig. 945   An illustration from *Principles of Philosophy* by Descartes: the vortices of material particles.

Fig. 946 A map of Paris in 1609; the city is still contained within the medieval walls, and its three districts — the *cité*, the *ville* and the *université* — can be clearly seen (cf. Fig. 517).

PARIS

In Chapter 4 we referred briefly to the layout of medieval Paris, which was already one of the most important cities in Europe.

The city during the Middle Ages was divided into three sections:

— the *cité*, on the island where the Gauls had founded their first village;
— the *université* on the left bank of the Seine, where the Romans had built the colony of Lutetia, and where Abelard and his colleagues had founded their famous school in the early twelfth century;
— the *ville* on the right bank, where the commercial corporations and the municipal government resided.

The three sections were contained within the walls built by Charles V in 1370, and their total area came to 440 hectares, containing a population of approximately 100,000 people (Fig. 946).

The French kings during the Renaissance normally lived in one of the cities of the Loire, but took up residence in Paris in 1528, when Francis I began to rebuild the old Louvre on the right bank. In the sixteenth century Paris developed even more, spreading beyond its walls and reaching a population that may have been as high as between 200,000 and 300,000, but the wars of religion and the siege by Henry IV, which lasted from 1589 to 1594, caused extensive damage to the city, and the new king found himself master of a devastated and depopulated capital.

Over the next fifteen years, until his death in 1610, Henry IV pushed ahead with a programme of public works that no longer consisted of a disjointed series of personal initiatives: it formed part of a carefully planned economic system and depended for its realisation on an established organisation of official bodies (Sully, the minister of finance, was also superintendent of building works and director of highway projects).

A notable part of these public works was concentrated in Paris, so as to accentuate the capital's importance. The main

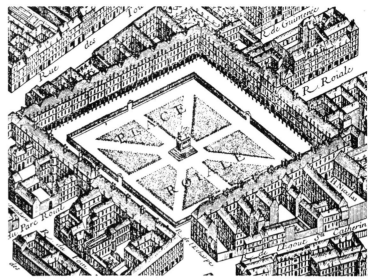

Fig. 947   The Place Royale dedicated to Louis XIII, now known as the Place des Vosges (above left in the preceding map).

projects planned at the start of the seventeenth century were as follows:

— the enlargement of the walls of Charles V on the right bank, in order to include the new western suburbs as far as the Tuileries Gardens;
— the reorganisation of the street system and the overhaul of such utilities as the aqueduct and the sewers;
— the opening up of new, geometrically-shaped squares, surrounded by houses of uniform architecture: the square Place Royale on the right bank (Fig. 947), the triangular Place Dauphine at the far end of the Île de la Cité (Figs 948–50), and the semi-circular Place de la France, which was planned for the high ground by the Temple, but never executed;
— the enlargement of the Palais du Louvre, achieved by joining the medieval château to the sixteenth-century Palais des Tuileries and demolishing the area in between. This project, which was partially completed by Louis XIII and Louis XIV, was finally concluded by Napoleon III in the nineteenth century;

Figs 948–9   Paris, the Place Dauphine; internal view and plan.

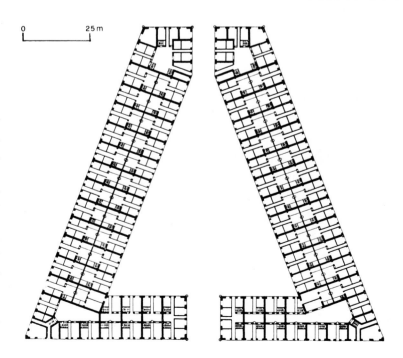

— the building of a new palace on the outskirts of the
city at St Germain-en-Laye, which took the form of a
château set in a terraced garden, in imitation of the Italian
gardens of the sixteenth century (Fig. 952).

After 1610 and up until the start of Louis XIV's reign
(1661), the organisation created by Henry IV continued to
function, but it lacked any kind of decisive political will.
The city of Paris expanded rapidly, and during the second
half of the century its population numbered 400,000, but
Louis XIII, Richelieu and Mazarin were involved in a series
of wars and were unable to maintain a proper public building programme. As a result, the initiative was taken up by
private businessmen, who completed entire *quartiers* on the
Île St Louis (Fig. 951) and on the right bank.

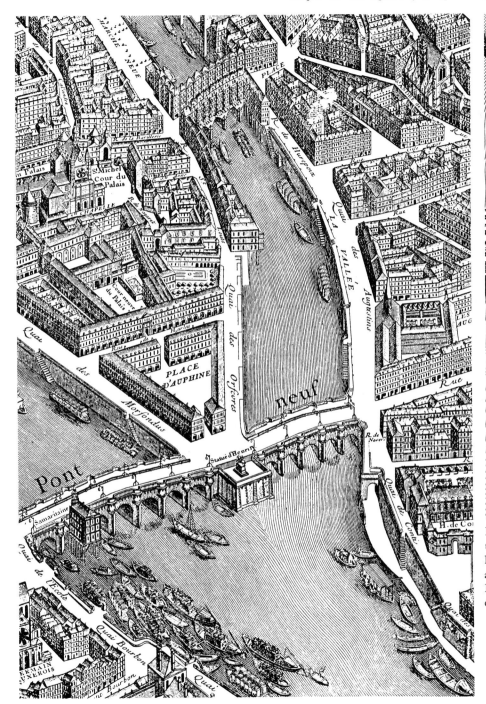

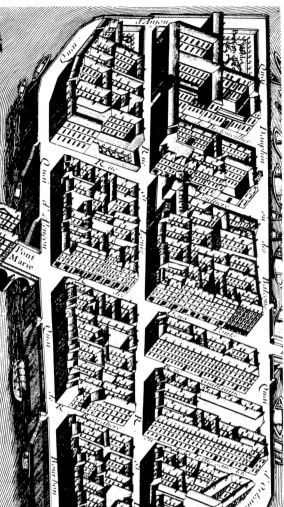

Figs 950–1 Paris, the layout of the
tip of the Île de la Cité, with the Place
Dauphine and the Pont Neuf, and the
architectural division of the Île St
Louis, completed during the first half
of the seventeenth century.

Meanwhile, the new literary and artistic culture of France's Golden Age was developing: Mansart in architecture, Poussin in painting, Corneille in literature and Descartes in philosophy, all laid the foundations of the new Age of Reason, both in France and in the rest of Europe. This new cultural movement paved the way for a more rigorous control over the natural and artificial environment, and it enabled several projects to be completed, in the latter part of the century, on a scale that would previously have been unthinkable. The first of these was the Château of Vaux le Vicomte (Figs 954–8) near Paris, built between 1656 and 1660 by Mazarin's extremely wealthy finance minister, Fouquet. The garden was laid out by Le Nôtre (1613–1700), the architect was Le Vau (1612–70) and Le Brun (1619–90) was responsible for its decoration.

The Château was not built on a site with a panoramic view, like Italian villas or the Château at St Germain; it stood in a gentle depression, surrounded by the woods of the Seine valley, but its grounds included all the land visible from the main building, and these were transformed into a series of interrelating geometrical vistas. The Italian gardens were created on a scale that was directly related to the dimensions of the house and their carefully planned vistas never measured more than 200 or 300 metres, even when they led into the limitless expanses of the natural countryside. The garden as a whole, however, which was one of the first so-called French gardens, took the form of an entire landscape, whose symmetry and regularity stretched as far as the line of the horizon. The first symmetrical axis ran from the Château at an angle to the valley, across a series of terraces, and ended at a fountain on the slope opposite; the second one was formed by a rectilinear canal that flowed along the bottom of the valley and which had been created by channelling the waters of a small river. These two visual elements measured more than a kilometre in length, and the whole park, from the entrance way to the paths that radiated out into the woods, was $3\frac{1}{2}$ kilometres long. From far off, the buildings became part of the chiaroscuro scenario, like the massed trees and the glassy waters; but as one approached them along the pathways they gradually began to assume their true proportions, and, seen from close to,

0   500   1000 m

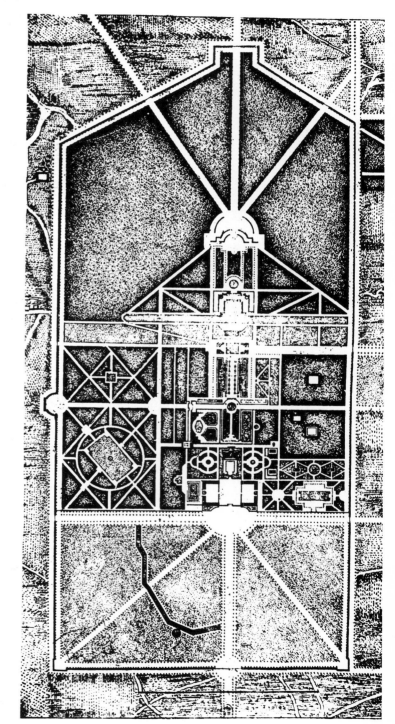

Figs 954–5 Map and aerial view of the park at Vaux le Vicomte.

Fig. 956   Aerial view of the park and Château of Vaux le Vicomte.

the full richness of their decorations was finally revealed. Every one of these elements — from the rural surroundings to the intricate ornamentation — was part of a carefully-planned series, and a vast collective organisation, consisting of a large number of specialists and a lesser number of coordinators, was needed to ensure the success of such a venture.

In the mid-seventeenth century it was possible for a private individual like Fouquet to employ a team of experts on that scale, but in later years only the king was able to maintain and develop such complex organisations. In 1661 Fouquet invited the king and his court to join him in the celebrations for the opening of his château; there was a banquet cooked by the great Vatel, a ballet written by Molière, for which Lully had composed the music, and a firework display. Three weeks later the hapless Fouquet was arrested on the king's orders, and his team of artists passed into the service of Louis XIV, becoming part of the public

Fig. 957   A bedroom in the Château
of Vaux le Vicomte.

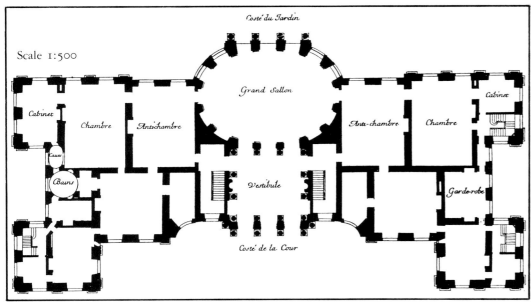

Fig. 958   Ground plan of the Château
of Vaux le Vicomte.

Fig. 959   Portrait of Louis XIV, the Sun King.

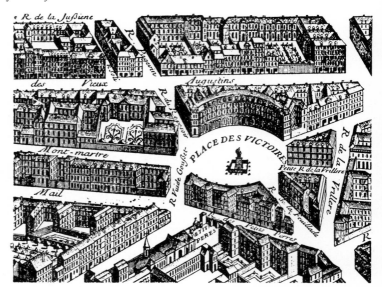

organisation under the control of the new superintendent, Colbert. The king was an enthusiastic advocate of new architectural projects, to which he devoted unprecedented sums of money, and during his lengthy reign (1661–1715) he completed a series of major building works in Paris and its environs, whose style was imitated by every monarch in Europe.

In Paris, however, the Sun King lacked the resources to effect any major transformation of the old parts of the city, but he did succeed in making several important modifications:

— the inclusion of a number of architectural elements within the existing framework: the rearrangement of the Louvre, for which he even consulted the old Bernini (Fig. 963), the Place des Victoires (Fig. 960), the Place Vendôme (Fig 961) and the Palais des Invalides (Figs 964–5);

Figs 960–1   The two squares built by Louis XIV: the Place des Victoires and the Place Vendôme.

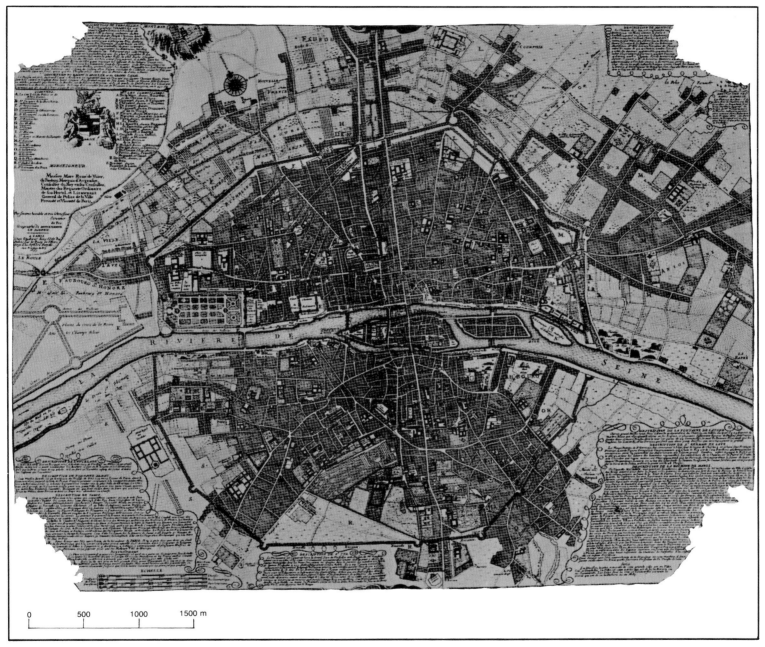

Fig. 962   Map of Paris in 1697, showing the planned tree-lined avenues (*boulevards*) encircling the city.

Fig. 963   The eastern façade of the Louvre, completed by Perrault for Louis XIV.

— the formation of new suburbs, which were uncon-nected with each other and blended in with the countryside. In fact, the old fortifications were dismantled and in their place a number of tree-lined avenues (*boulevards*) were laid out. This temporary boundary enclosed an area of almost 1,200 hectares, but the city was already beginning to spread even further out. Paris had become an open city: a scattered series of built-up areas interspersed with areas of green, with a population of approximately 500,000.

The land around the city, which was completely free of other buildings, could be effectively transformed in accord-ance with the new laws of symmetry and regularity, and the king, together with the other great figures of the day, began to take up residence in the country. Louis XIV moved his

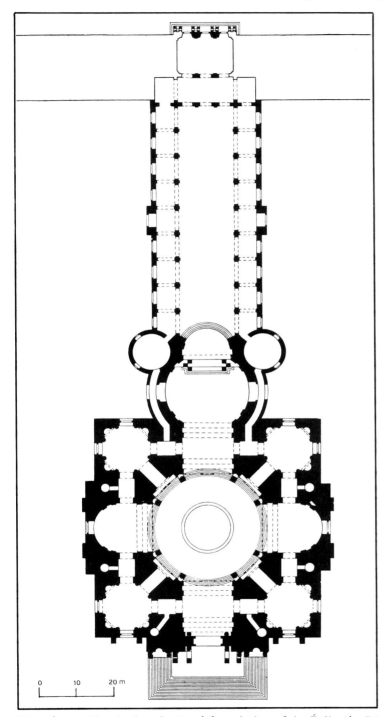

Figs 964–5   Plan (scale 1:800) and frontal view of the Église du Dôme (the Church of the Invalides) built by Hardouin-Mansart.

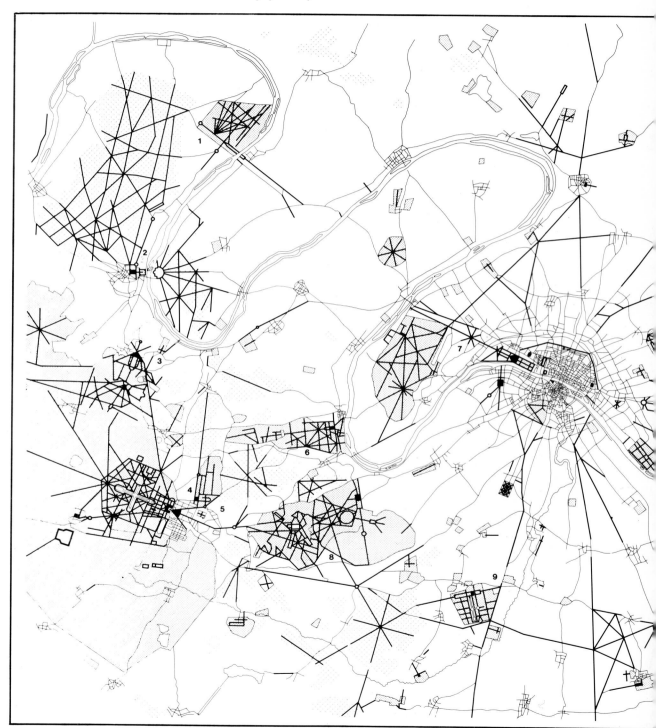

court from the Louvre to his new palace in Versailles, which gradually grew into a kind of second capital.

In Fig. 966 it can be seen that Versailles covered almost the same amount of territory as Paris. It was not a city, however; it was a vast park in which were sited — as subordinate elements — the buildings necessary to maintain the smooth running of the royal court. Here the Sun King was able to create a perfectly regulated, but uninhabited, environment; he was able to bring order to hills, trees and waterways, but not houses.

Le Nôtre laid out the gardens in an area of flat marshland, surrounded by low hills. At the far end he had a canal excavated in the shape of a cross, whose vertical arm, $1\frac{1}{2}$ kilometres long, was aligned with the central axis of the château and can be seen from the central terrace as a straight line receding into the distance. This rectilinear strip of water, which reflects the setting sun, draws the eye inexorably towards the hills some 3 kilometres away; from this point there radiate ten roads, which fan out into the dense, surrounding woods. In front of the château the old access roads were rearranged into a system of three avenues, around which developed the new town that contained the houses of the court officials (Fig. 967).

Le Vau and Hardouin-Mansart were responsible for the design of the new château. Louis XIII's old hunting lodge was enlarged in several stages and it finally developed into a vast building, more than 500 metres long, which separated the park from the town (Figs 968–9). Le Brun was entrusted with the decoration of its interior, whose most spectacular element is the Hall of Mirrors (the *Galerie des Glaces*) situated on the first floor, at the centre of the side overlooking the park. Le Nôtre's carefully planned scenario is reflected in the mirrors, so that architecture and landscape, interior decoration and external infinity, all become fused into a single, dazzling spectacle (Fig. 970).

Fig. 966   Plan of the environs of Paris during the mid-eighteenth century. The thin lines denote the medieval road system, the thick lines are the rectilinear avenues of the seventeenth and eighteenth centuries, and the dotted areas are parkland.

1. Houses; 2. St Germain; 3. Marly; 4. Versailles; 5. Clagny; 6. St Cloud; 7. Bois de Boulogne; 8. Meudon; 9. Sceaux; 10. Vincennes; 11. Ivry; 12. St Maur; 13. Gros Bois.

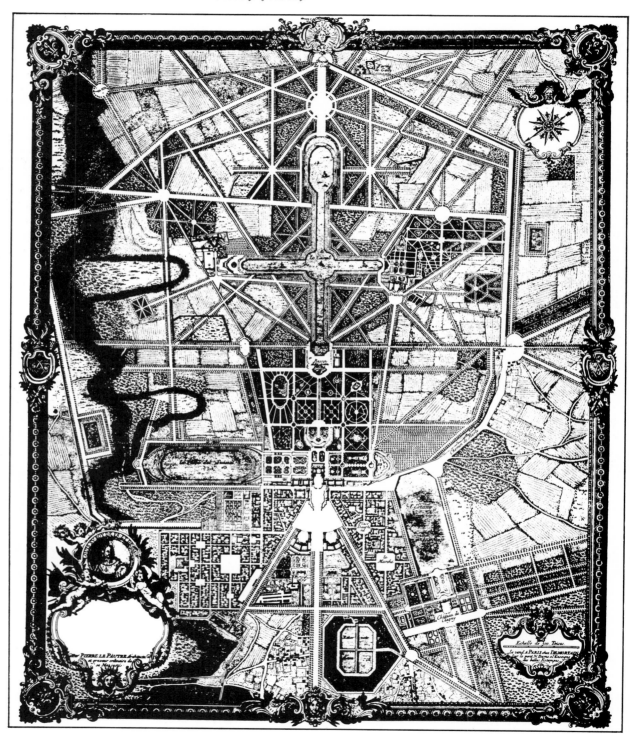

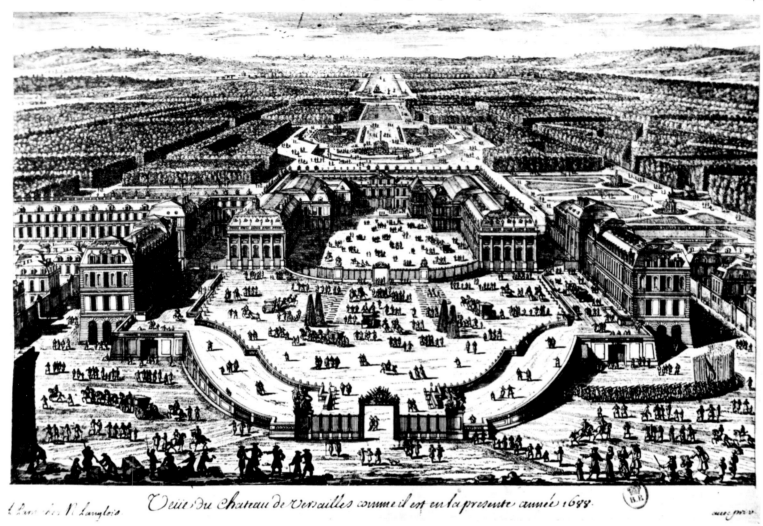

l Pars de N. Langlois *Veüe du Chateau de Versailles comme il est en la presente anneé 1688* *cum priv.*

Figs 967–8   Plan and bird's eye view of the park and Château of Versailles at the end of Louis XIV's reign. The park is the dominant feature, more important than even the town built between the three entrance avenues. Compare this with Bagnaia (Figs 881–3).

Fig. 969   Aerial view of the Château of Versailles. In the foreground is the park, in the background the town.

Versailles and Paris were two complementary environments, and they both revealed the possibilities and the limitations of absolute power between the seventeenth and eighteenth centuries. The stylistic and administrative resources needed to restructure an entire landscape had been developed, but without any of the restrictions on size that had been inherent in the Italian tradition. The transforma-

tion, however, was only achieved in isolated sections, and even then it was confined to the wide open spaces of the countryside and did not include any densely populated urban areas. The result was a mosaic of parks and monumental buildings, which has yet to be shaped into a single coherent entity.

Fig. 970 The *Galerie des Glaces* (Hall of Mirrors) by Hardouin-Mansart, situated at the centre of the façade overlooking the park in the Palace of Versailles.

Fig. 971   The façade of Versailles, as seen from the terraces of the Orangery.

Fig. 972   Versailles. The Latona Basin and the avenue leading towards the central canal, which forms the park's axis.

Figs 973–4   Two decorative elements at Versailles: a garden urn and a door-panel bearing the symbol of the Sun King.

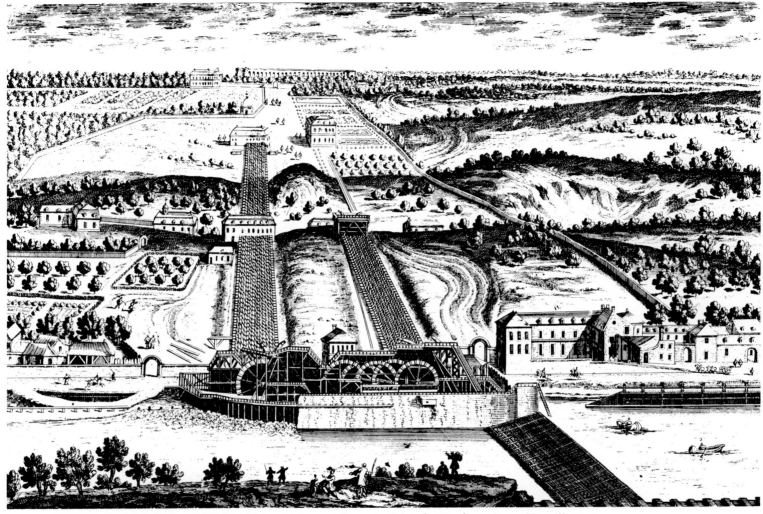

Fig. 975 The hydraulic machine at Marly which raised water from the Seine for the fountains at Versailles.

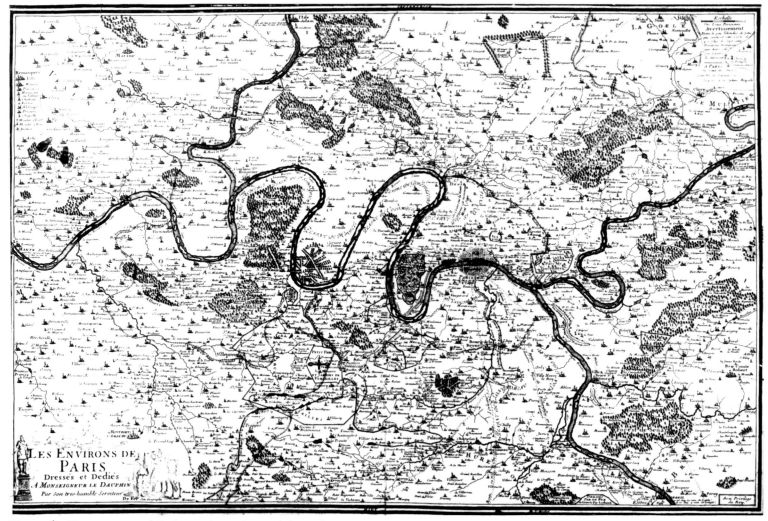

Fig. 976   The area around Paris, as shown in an eighteenth-century map.

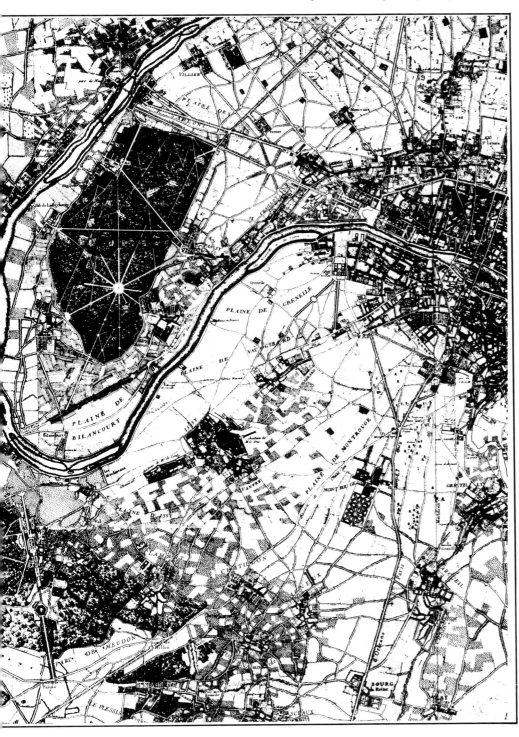

Fig. 977 Mid-eighteenth-century
map of the area between Paris and
Versailles.

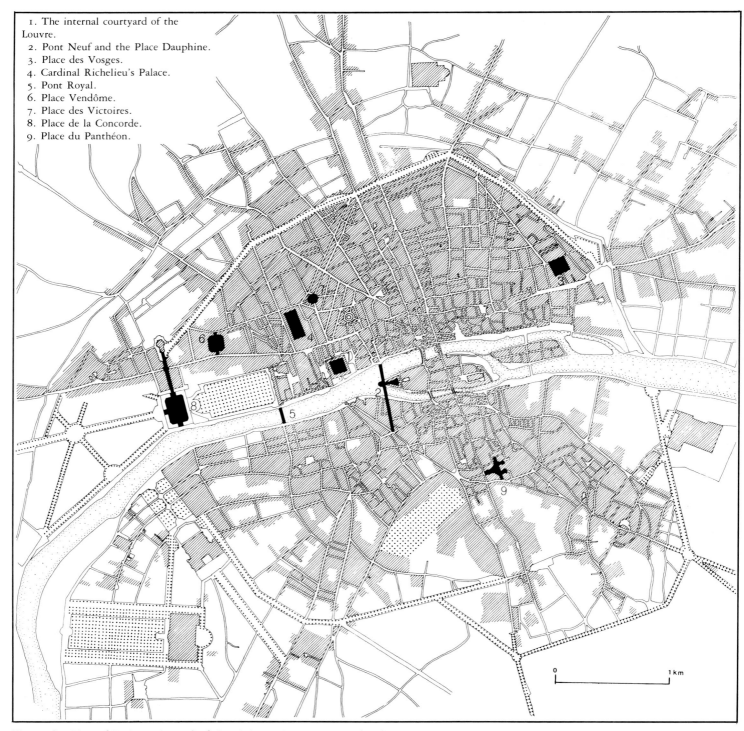

1. The internal courtyard of the Louvre.
2. Pont Neuf and the Place Dauphine.
3. Place des Vosges.
4. Cardinal Richelieu's Palace.
5. Pont Royal.
6. Place Vendôme.
7. Place des Victoires.
8. Place de la Concorde.
9. Place du Panthéon.

Fig. 978   Plan of Paris at the end of the eighteenth century; the black areas show the monarchy's principal architectural undertakings:

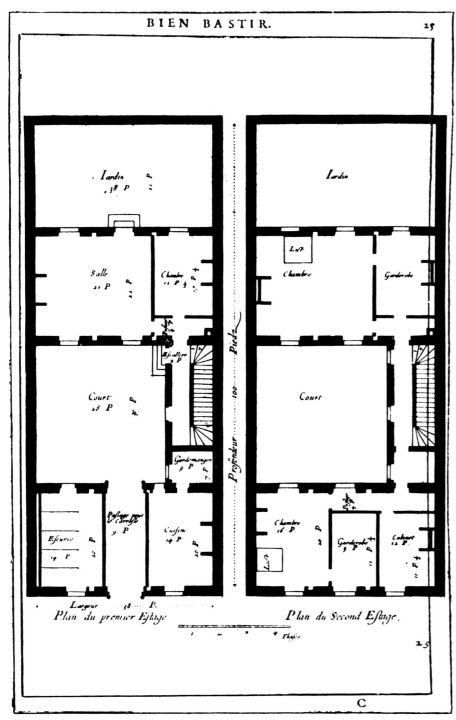

Fig. 979   Plans of a two-storey bourgeois town house, from a seventeenth-century French treatise.

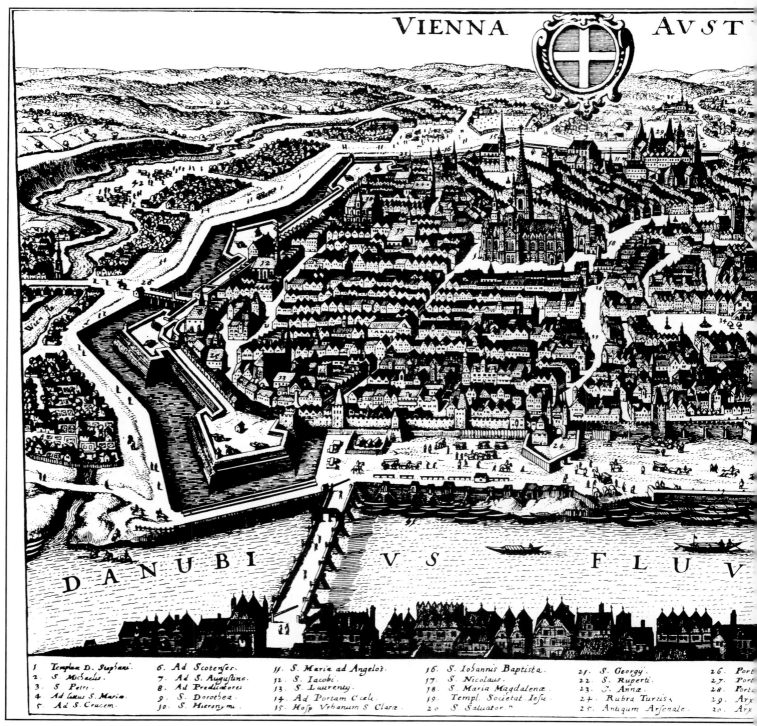

VIENNA   AVST

DANVBI   VS   FLVV

1 Templum D. Stephani.	6. Ad Scotenses.	11. S. Maria ad Angelos.	16. S. Iobannis Baptista.	21. S. Georgÿ.	26. Port
2. S. Michaelis.	7. Ad S. Augustine.	12. S. Iacobi.	17. S. Nicolaus.	22. S. Ruperti.	27. Port
3. S. Petri.	8. Ad Predicatores	13. S. Laurentÿ.	18. S. Maria Magdalenæ.	23. S. Anna.	28. Porta
4. Ad Laeus S. Maria.	9. S. Dorothea.	14. Ad Portam Cæli.	19. Templ. Societat. Iesu.	24. Rubra Turcis	29. Arx
5. Ad S. Crucem.	10. S. Hieronymi.	15. Hosp Vrbanum S Claræ.	20 S Saluator	25. Antiquum Arsenale.	30. Arx

Fig. 980   Mid-seventeenth-century view of Vienna, showing the medieval walls.

31. Vniuersitas.   36. Hernalst.   41. Ad Scapbos Psisut
32. Domus Senatorum Cui   37. Pons Altus.   42. Forum Boarur
33. Arsenale.   38. Locus Sanitatis.
34. Domus Pretoria   39. Domus Pri
25. Capucino   40. Equile Cesareum

Of the other capitals of Europe, let us consider: Vienna, capital of the Austro-Hungarian Empire; Turin and Naples, the capitals of the two most important Italian states of the period; Amsterdam, the principal city of the Low Countries; and London, which became the most important commercial centre of eighteenth-century Europe.

VIENNA

The Hapsburg dynasty became established in Vienna in 1683, following the decisive defeat of the Turks at the Battle of Kahlenberg. The old city, still enclosed within its medieval walls, became an internal fortress, and was surrounded by a strip of land, some 500 metres wide, which was completely free of building. Beyond this there developed the new city, containing the suburbs and residences of the most illustrious personalities of the time: the Belvedere (Fig. 987), the home of the victorious general Prince Eugène of Savoy, the Schwarzenberg Palace and the Lichtenstein Palace. In the early eighteenth century a second set of walls was built, also surrounded by a strip of empty land, this time 200 metres wide. The total area of the city was now 1,800 hectares, excluding the Prater Park, which was situated between two branches of the Danube, and its population at the end of the eighteenth century had reached 200,000 (Figs 981, 984).

The Emperor resided in the royal palace in the old city, the Hofburg (Fig. 985), but in 1690 work began on building a new residence outside the city, similar to Versailles. This was the Palace of Schönbrunn (Figs 982–3), whose grounds occupied a hill overlooking the city, immediately outside the walls.

The imperial architect, from 1690 to 1723, was Fischer von Erlach (1656–1723), who planned the city's new monumental buildings in a consciously grandiose and complex style: buildings such as the new Hofburg Palace, the Library and the Church of St Charles Borromeo (Figs 988–9).

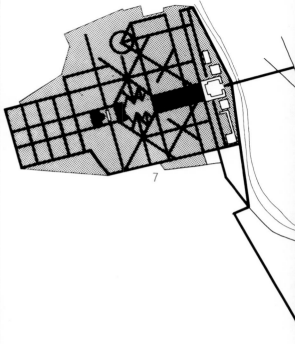

7

Figs 981–3   Map of Vienna at the end of the eighteenth century,
showing the baroque additions; two views, taken on the central axis
of the palace, looking towards the main building and towards the
park.

1. The area of free ground (Glacis)
surrounding the walls of the old city.
2. Lichtenstein Palace.
3. Belvedere Palace.
4. Schwarzenberg Palace.
5. Prater Park.
6. Schloss Hof Castle.
7. Schönbrunn Palace.

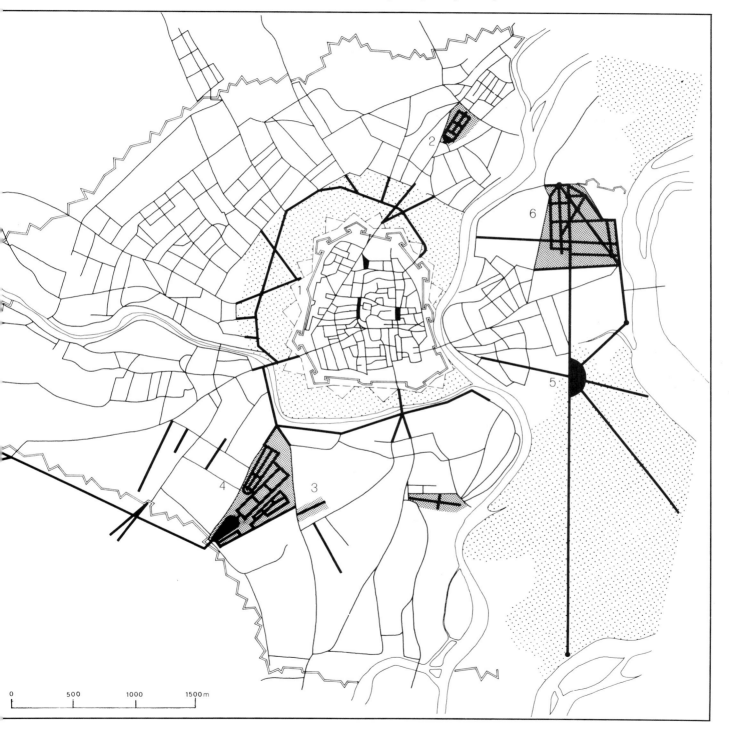

Fig. 984   Panoramic view of Vienna during the eighteenth century.

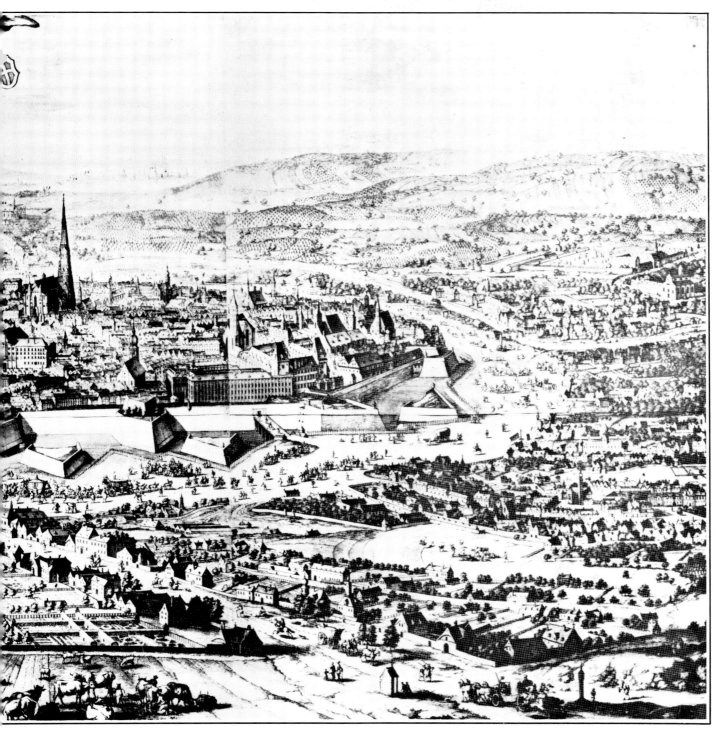

Fig. 985   Model of the old city of Vienna; in the foreground is the Imperial Palace (Hofburg).

Cavallerizza Coperta della Reale Corte di Vienna ridotta in Sala per Comando di S. M. la Regina d'Ungheria e di Boemia in occasione delle Nozze della Serenissima Arciduchessa Mariaii con il Serenissimo Principe Carlo di Lorena, esposta in Veduta piu da una parte, e Senza le Lumiere appese in mezzo.

3

J. G. Bibiena & C. M. Archit. Theatr. Prim. Inv. et del   *A. A. Pfeffel & C. M. Chalcogr. sculp. Inven. A. P.*

Fig. 986   The riding school in the Imperial Palace in Vienna.

Fig. 987   The Belvedere Gardens and
a panoramic view of Vienna during the
eighteenth century.

Figs 988–9   Ground plan and external
view of the Church of St Charles
Borromeo in Vienna, by Fischer von
Erlach.

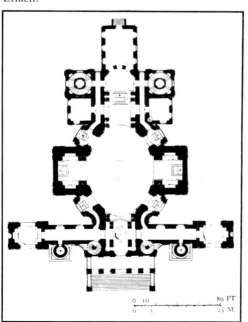

TURIN

Turin, the capital of the duchy of Savoy, at the beginning of the seventeenth century still possessed its old Roman chequerboard nucleus, to which had been added a pentagonal fortress (1).

As Savoy increased in importance, the city was enlarged three times, but it still remained a fortified stronghold, at the mercy of passing French, Spanish and Austrian armies, and as a result it always had to have a strong set of walls.

The first enlargment was planned by Carlo di Castellamonte in 1620 for Duke Charles Emmanuel I; the city reached 100 hectares, with a population of 25,000 inhabitants (2).

The second enlargement was designed by the latter's son, Amedeo di Castellamonte, in 1673, at the end of Charles Emmanuel II's reign; the city now had an area of 160 hectares and a population of 40,000. In addition, the medieval castle became isolated in the middle of a large square, where the city's administrative centre developed (3).

The third extension was laid out in 1714 by Filippo Juvarra for Victor Amedeus II, and it increased the city's area to 180 hectares, while its population grew to 60,000 (4).

The new districts were always arranged along the old Roman lines, but the distances between the streets were varied and the chequerboard design was made less monotonous by the inclusion of squares; the only exception was the Via Po, which was the straightened version of an old road that led down to the river and which cut diagonally across the grid of the second enlargement. As in the great squares of Paris, the façades of the buildings in Turin's most important streets and squares were all the same.

Into the regular layout of the city Guarino Guarini introduced his imaginative architectural works: the Chapel of the Holy Shroud, the Church of San Lorenzo (Figs 996–7) and the Carignano Palace. On the outskirts Juvarra built the Basilica di Superga (Fig. 998) and the Villa Reale di Stupinigi, joined to the city by a long, straight avenue (Figs 999–1003).

Figs 990–3   Turin; the city at the end of the sixteenth century, and its three successive enlargements (1620, 1673 and 1714).

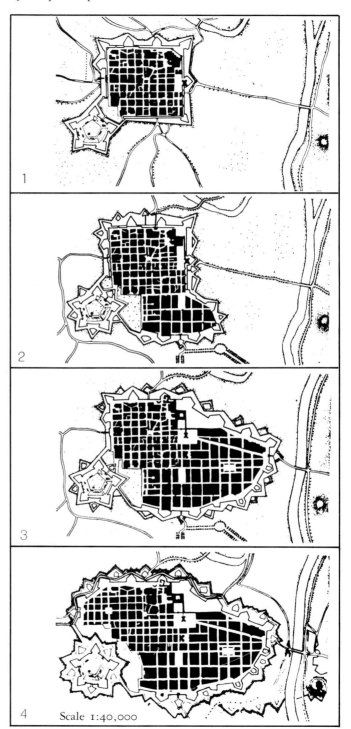

Scale 1:40,000

Figs 994–5   Turin; view of one of its streets and plan of the city
in the eighteenth century.

Fig. 999   Aerial view of the Villa Reale di Stupinigi, built by Juvarra in 1729.

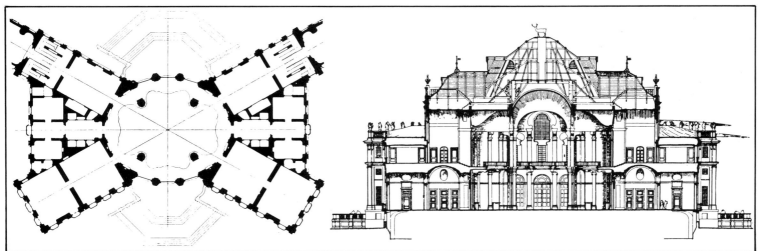

Figs 1000–3 Stupinigi. Aerial view, internal view, plan, and cross-section of the central hall.

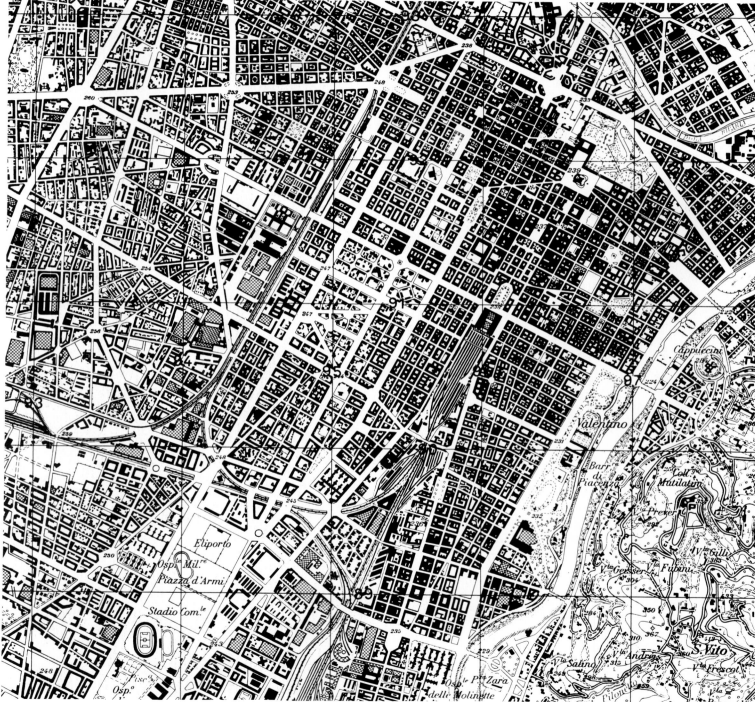

Fig. 1004   Map of the centre of Turin, from a map by the Istituto Geografico Militare (scale 1:25,000).

NAPLES

Naples, capital of the Spanish viceroy, became Italy's most populous city during the seventeenth century. Its medieval centre still retained the Graeco-Roman chequerboard layout, while the new districts were dominated by the straight streets of the sixteenth century, like the Via Toledo, for example.

During the eighteenth century the southern part of the kingdom became an independent state and the new king, Charles of Bourbon (1734–59), tried to rearrange the layout of this great city, which already possessed 300,000 inhabitants: he modernised the harbour, reorganised the suburban street system and erected a number of new public buildings, such as the Tribunale della Salute, and the Albergo dei Poveri, a hostel for poor people, designed to house 8,000 people in a single vast block, more than 600 metres long.

On the outskirts of the city Charles built the Villa di Capodimonte in 1743, and in 1752 he began work on the Palace of Caserta, designed by the famous Vanvitelli; the approach avenue, the oval piazza, the vast palace buildings and the park, which is set into the hill, together form a gigantic monumental ensemble unique in all Italy (Figs 1008–9). Nevertheless, these grandiose additions were unable to bring about a lasting transformation: the city and its surrounding territory remained disorganised and ungovernable, while the population continued to increase.

Fig. 1005 A nineteenth-century photograph of one of the streets in central Naples.

Fig. 1006   A detail from an eighteenth-century map of Naples, showing the Spanish quarter beyond the Via Toledo, the Certosa di San Martino and the Castello Sant'Elmo.

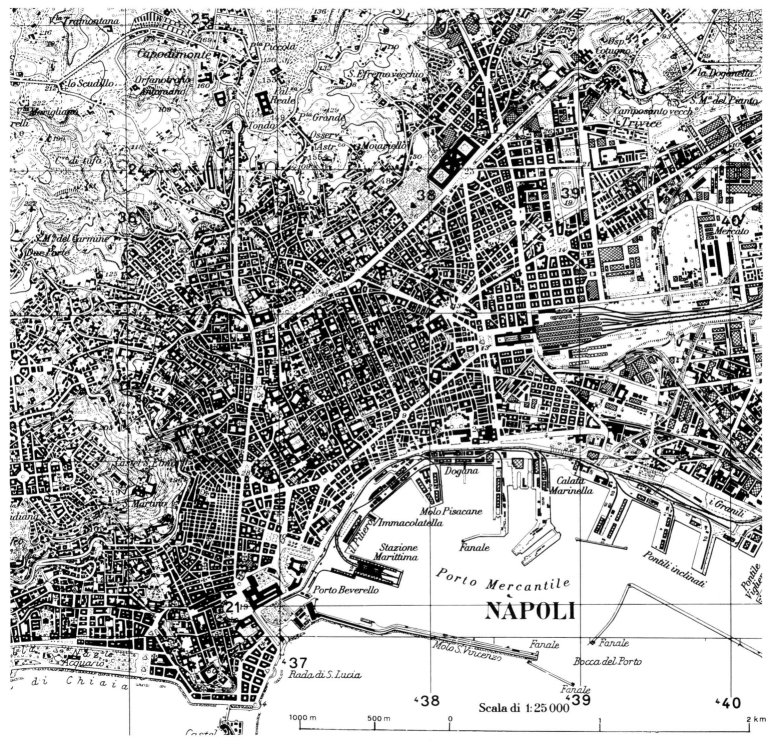

Fig. 1007   Plan of the centre of Naples, from a map by the Istituto Geografico Militare (scale 1:25,000); the large building at the top is the Albergo dei Poveri.

Figs 1008–9   Caserta. Aerial view of the royal palace, and a map of the town from a map by the Istituto Geografico Militare (scale 1:25,000).

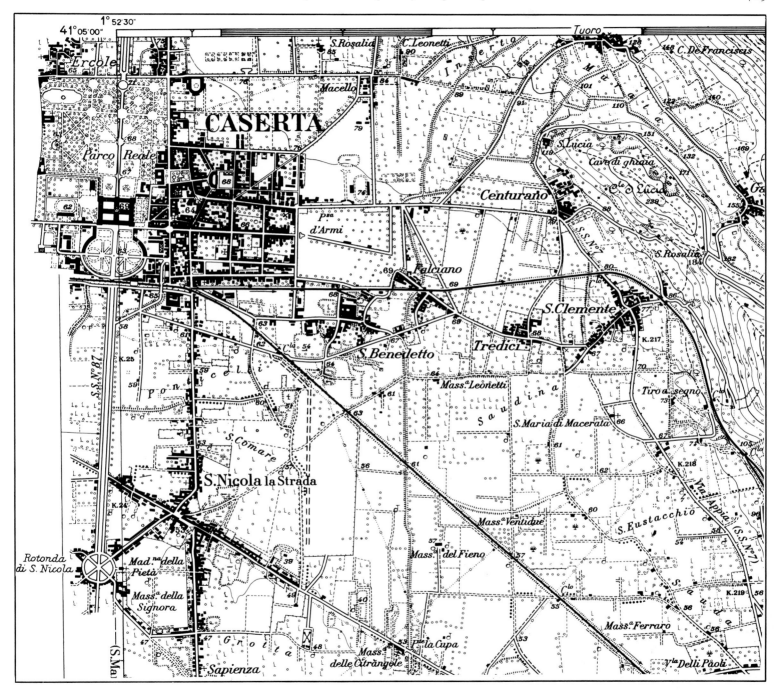

Fig. 1010   Aerial view of a section of Dutch countryside, showing the irrigation canals and the windmill used to raise the water.

AMSTERDAM

The cities so far examined were the products of the absolut-ism that dominated the countries of Europe, both large and small, but the Dutch cities and towns were still being governed like the city-states of the Middle Ages. Political power was wielded by the commercial middle classes and each large city was an independent republic, with its own laws and institutions, even if it belonged to a confederation designed to protect common economic, commercial and military interests.

By preserving this extraordinary political system, the cities of the Low Countries were able to defend themselves from the great powers of Europe, while at the same time becoming extremely prosperous and developing their own brand of anti-monumental, middle-class culture. All one has to do is think of the philosophy of Spinoza, the scientific work of Huygens, the painting of Rembrandt.

Amsterdam, the most important city, became the mer-cantile and banking centre of Europe, and its growth was determined by a number of different factors: the contribu-

Fig. 1011   Detail of a portrait of an old woman by Rembrandt.

tions made by science and the latest technology, its medieval methods of administration, and the Renaissance cultural ideas of visual harmony.

By the first half of the sixteenth century Amsterdam was already a medium-sized port, with a population of some 40,000 inhabitants. In 1578 it was conquered by William the Silent, and immediately afterwards it entered its first period of expansion: the walls of 1481 were demolished, and the surrounding ditch was turned into a canal within the city. In 1593 a new set of outer walls was built in accordance with the latest ideas of military technology (Figs 1012–15).

However, the city continued to grow, and at the beginning of the seventeenth century an ambitious expansion was planned, whereby it was decided to excavate three more concentric canals, which would start out from the westernmost point of the city and gradually be joined up to the eastern district, where it was intended to provide a public park and also enlarge the naval dockyards. This plan was approved by the city government in 1607, and was carried out during the course of the century. The government expropriated the land, built the canals and then sold the building plots to private individuals for housing, thereby recovering their expenses. These private house owners were obliged to conform to a series of detailed building regulations, which laid down the nature of the buildings as well as the duties of their owners (Figs 1016–23).

Each canal was 25 metres wide, which meant that there were four lanes, approximately 6 metres across, for medium-sized ships: one for traffic going in both directions and two for ships that had tied up. On both sides of the canal there were quays for loading and unloading, 11 metres wide and planted with elms, while between each pair of canals there were two rows of building plots, approximately 50 metres deep. Between the backs of the houses there had to be an area of clear ground of at least 48 metres, equivalent to two strips of garden, each of 24 metres. The innermost canal (the Heeren canal) was $3\frac{1}{2}$ kilometres long, the middle one (the Keizers canal) was 4 kilometres long, and the outer one (the Prinsen canal) measured $4\frac{1}{2}$ kilometres; there were some 25 kilometres of quayside and there was enough space for 4,000 ships altogether to be moored in the city at the same time.

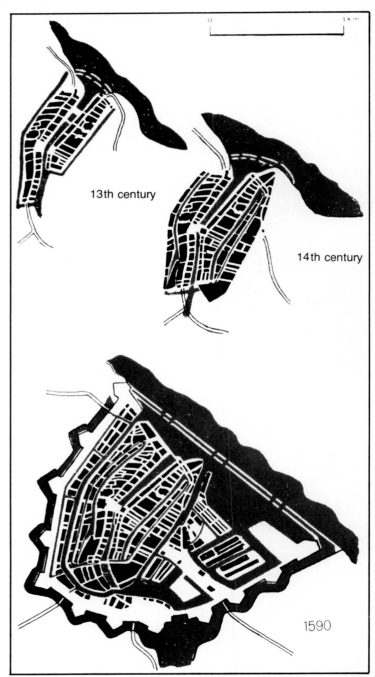

Figs 1012–15   Amsterdam: plans of the city during the Middle Ages and in 1590; a relief map from 1544.

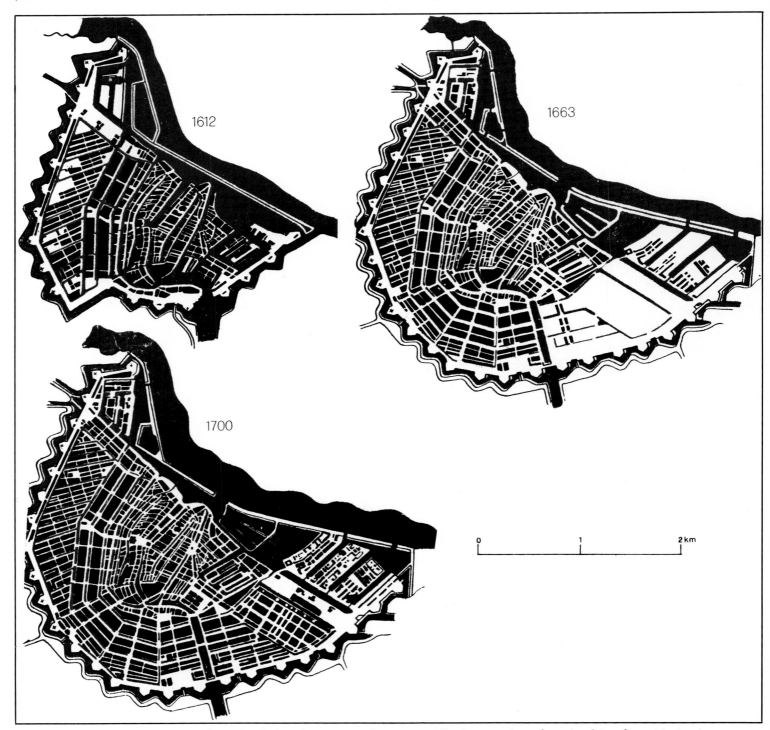

Figs 1016–18   Amsterdam. Plans of the city during the seventeenth century while the new plans, formulated in 1607 with the three concentric canals, were being carried out.

| 11 | 25 | 11 | 102 | 11 | 25 | 11 |

Figs 1019–21 Aerial view of central Amsterdam; the façades of a row of houses along the seventeenth-century canals; cross-section between two canals, showing the measurements of the waterways, the quays and the two building plots.

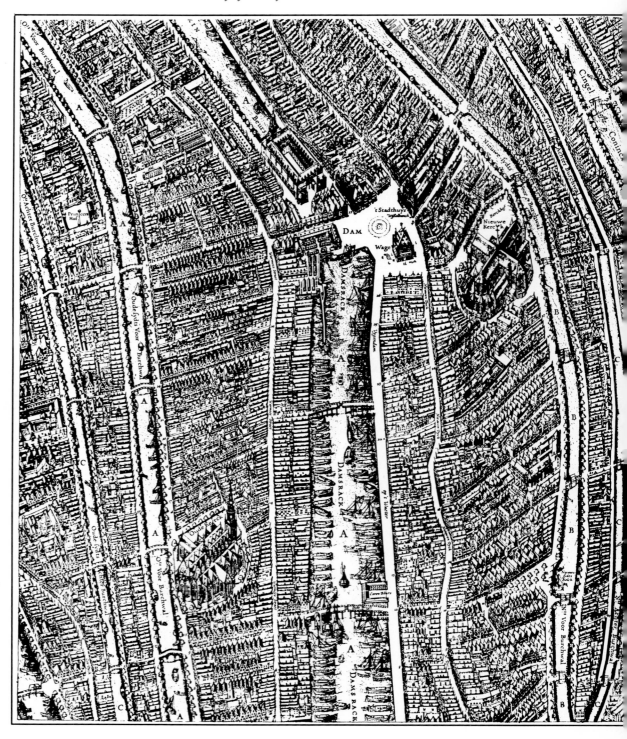

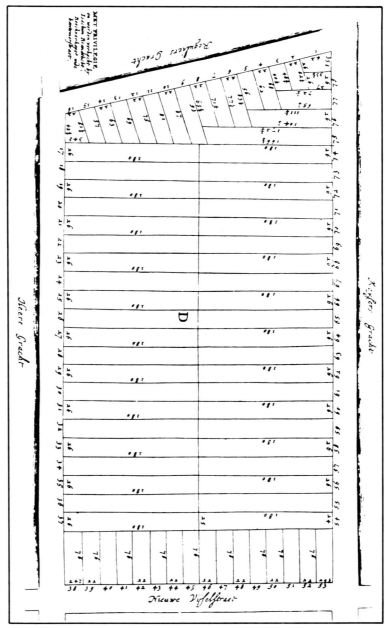

Figs 1022–3   Amsterdam; detail from a relief map of 1663, and the plan of the plots of land between two canals.

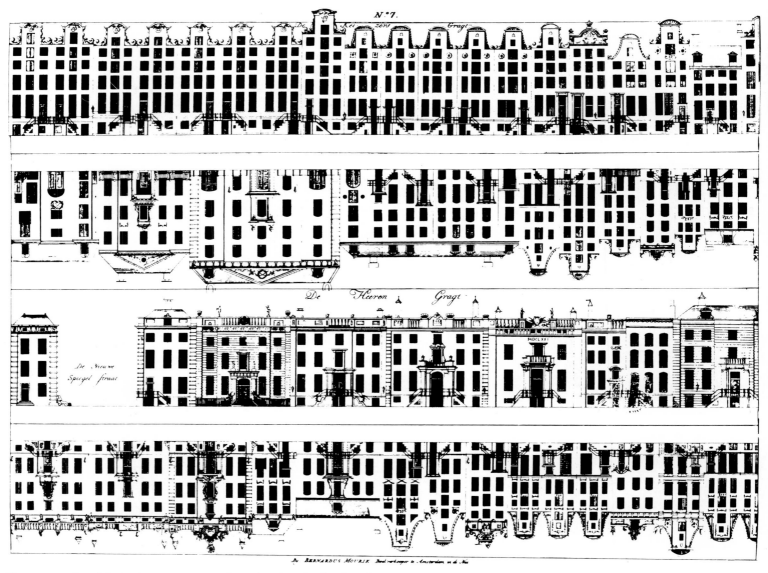

Fig. 1024   An eighteenth-century engraving, showing the façades of houses lining the Heeren canal.

Unlike the earliest canals, the seventeenth-century ones were laid out in a series of straight-sided sections, in order to make the building plots more regular. The houses were almost always of the same width, but their façades were unalike, a feature that produced an extraordinary architectural effect, completely different from the monumental layouts of French classicism, but just as impressive. It was not possible to look at one stretch of the canal in a single sweeping panorama, and if looked at sideways on, the view became obstructed by the leaves of the elm trees and the sails of the boats. The canals had to be enjoyed as a series of individual vignettes, limited by the distance between the two sets of buildings, which was always less than 50 metres (as in medieval squares). Only by advancing along the canals could a true idea of their complexity and their vast scale be gained (Figs 1024–6).

Amsterdam was a city, not an uninhabited theatrical set; the canals were a vital part of everyday life, and the buildings on either side were houses and places of work which belonged to the whole community, not to an absolute monarch. By the end of the seventeenth century the new city, laid out according to the strictest rules, had an area of 650 hectares — as great as the most important medieval cities examined in Chapter 6 — and a population of 200,000 inhabitants. It illustrated the viability of the medieval rules of town planning, which had established a working relationship between public authority and private initiative, even during a period of absolutism and scientific progress. For a long time Amsterdam continued to be the most modern city in Europe, and it has proved to be a source of considerable inspiration for town planners during the nineteenth and twentieth centuries.

In Chapter 14 we will examine recent developments in the city, but the seventeenth-century nucleus still provides its historical and contemporary heart, even though Amsterdam now has a population of one million.

Figs 1025–6   Two photographs of typical houses by an Amsterdam canal, taken from the opposite bank.

LONDON

During the medieval and Renaissance periods London consisted of two districts: the City, which covered virtually the same area as the Roman city and was England's most important commercial centre, and Westminster, the country's administrative centre, which contained the Houses of Parliament and Westminster Abbey. There was only one bridge across the Thames to link the main part of the city to its southern suburbs: London Bridge, which was flanked on each side by a row of houses, like the Ponte Vecchio in Florence.

From the seventeenth century onwards London developed as an 'open city', because it was free from the threat of military attack. A number of suburbs sprang up around the City, following the outline of existent country roads, but in 1666 the whole central area — most of the City and half of the new western district — was destroyed in the Great Fire. This destruction provided a chance to rebuild the city along organised lines, and the principal architects of the time, amongst whom was Christopher Wren (1632–1723), presented King Charles II with a series of plans (Figs 1028–31). The monarchy, however, which had only just been restored after the end of the Protectorate, lacked both the authority and the financial means to embark on such a project. When the debris had been cleared away, the former owners reclaimed their land, and the government was only able to widen the main streets and introduce legislation to control the height of any new buildings (Fig. 1032). St Paul's Cathedral and a number of lesser churches were, however, rebuilt according to the plans of Wren and his followers (Figs 1033–4).

After the exile of James II and the introduction of a constitutional monarchy under William and Mary, England rapidly became the most important economic force in Europe. London took the place of Amsterdam as the world centre for trade and finance, and it finally grew into the largest city in Europe. By the second half of the eighteenth century it was already larger than Paris, and by the end of the century it had become the first Western city to have a population of one million.

This extraordinary growth did not take place within an organised municipal plan, as in Amsterdam, nor was it

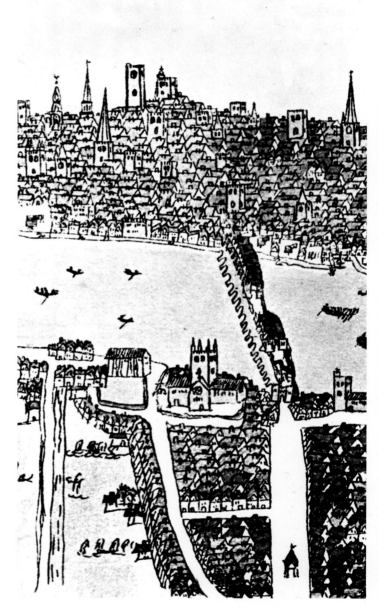

Fig. 1027   Detail of a sixteenth-century view of London, showing London Bridge with its two rows of houses.

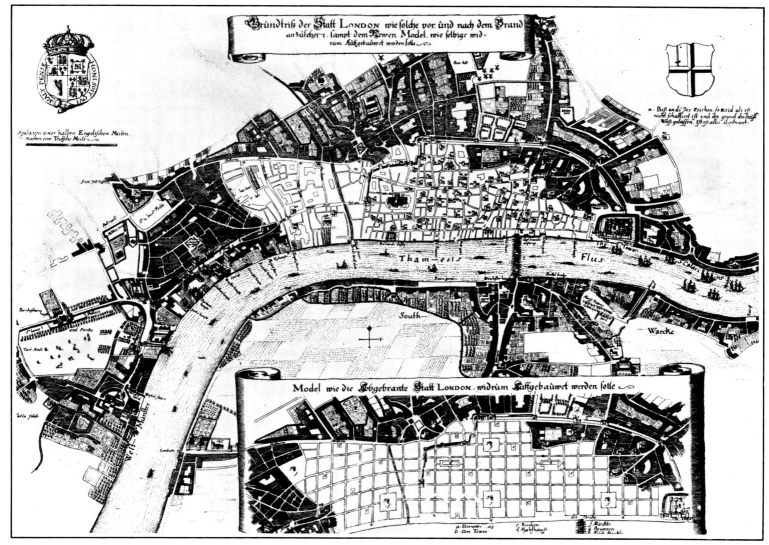

Fig. 1028 Map of London, showing the destruction wrought by the Great Fire in 1666 and a plan for the area's reconstruction by Robert Hooke.

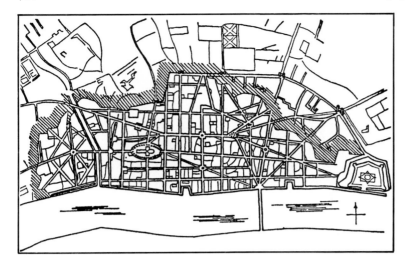

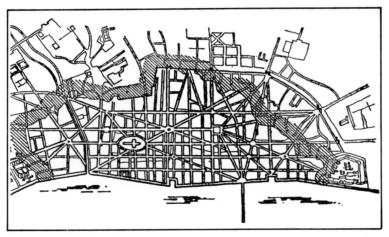

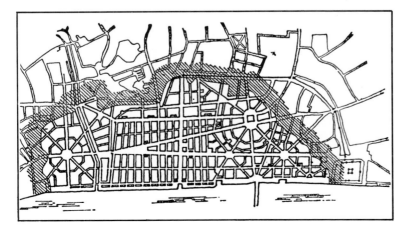

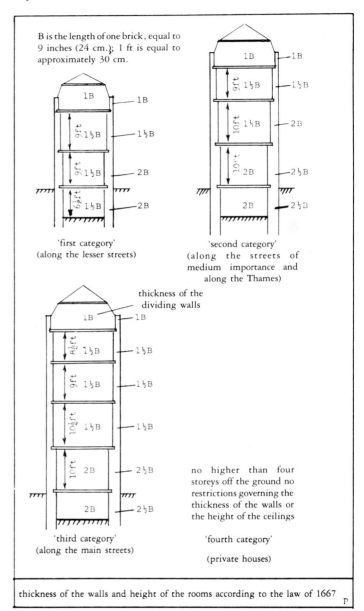

B is the length of one brick, equal to 9 inches (24 cm.); 1 ft is equal to approximately 30 cm.

'first category'
(along the lesser streets)

'second category'
(along the streets of medium importance and along the Thames)

thickness of the dividing walls

'third category'
(along the main streets)

no higher than four storeys off the ground no restrictions governing the thickness of the walls or the height of the ceilings

'fourth category'
(private houses)

thickness of the walls and height of the rooms according to the law of 1667

Figs 1029–32   London: the plans for the rebuilding of the city centre after the Great Fire, as proposed by Evelyn (the first two) and Wren (the third); the regulations governing the reconstruction of houses, as laid down by the law of 1667.

Fig. 1033   St Paul's Cathedral, in the City of London.

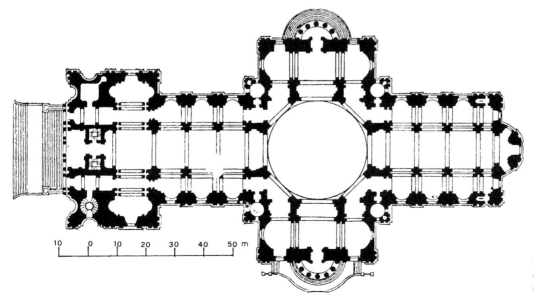

Fig. 1034   Plan of St Paul's, as laid out by Sir Christopher Wren after the Great Fire of 1666.

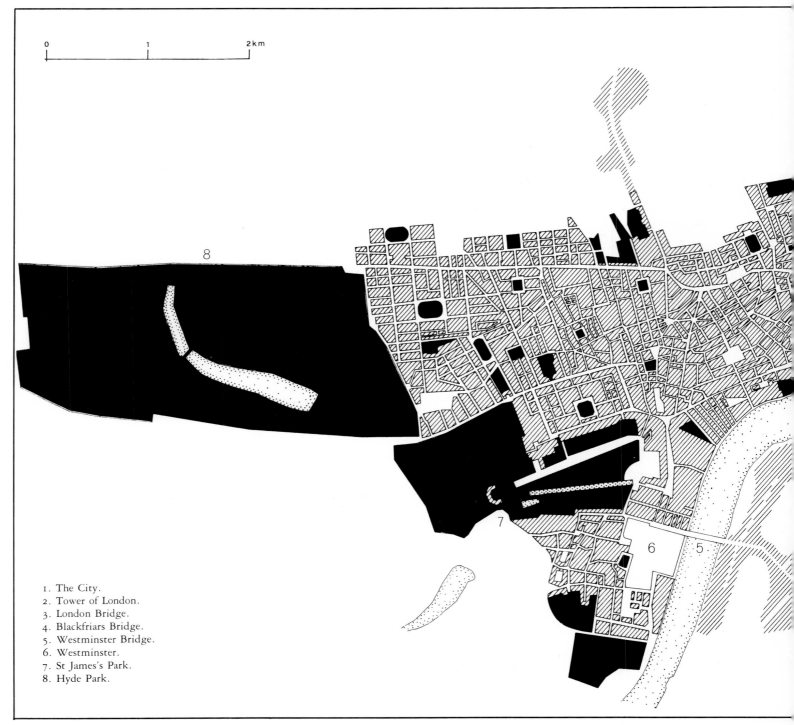

0   1   2km

8

1. The City.
2. Tower of London.
3. London Bridge.
4. Blackfriars Bridge.
5. Westminster Bridge.
6. Westminster.
7. St James's Park.
8. Hyde Park.

Fig. 1035   Plan of the outer areas of London at the close of the eighteenth century; the black denotes the areas of green.

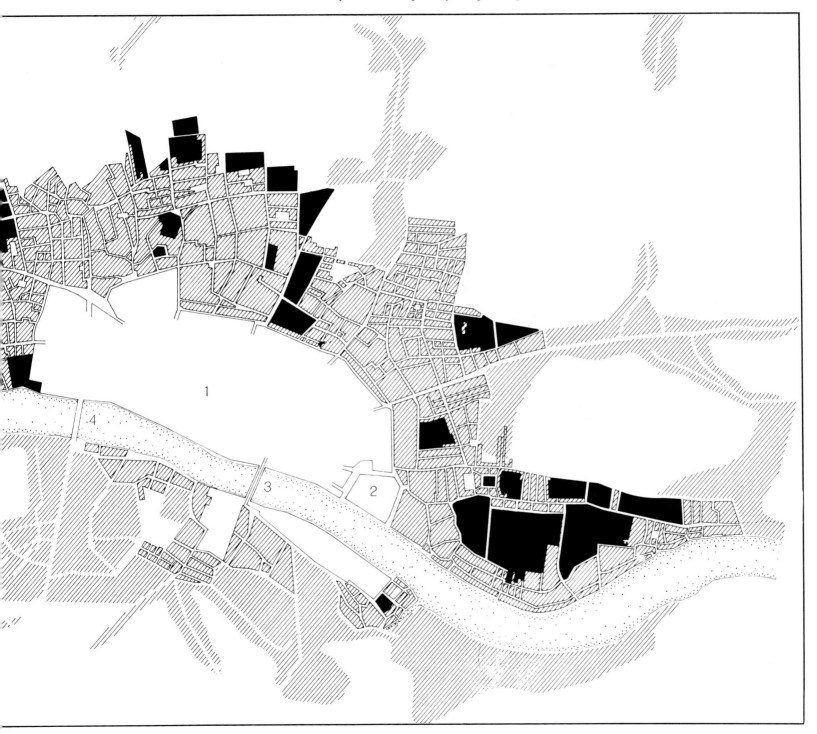

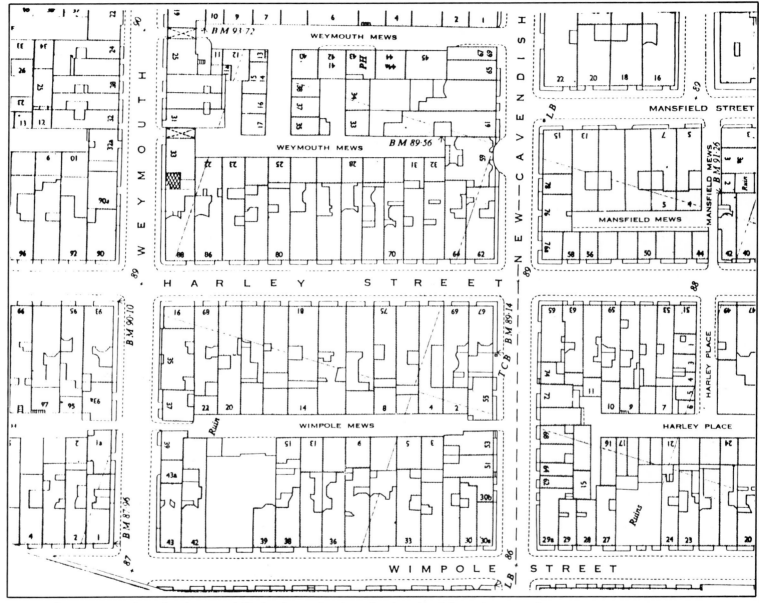

Fig. 1036   A section of the district around Harley Street, London, showing the eighteenth-century layout.

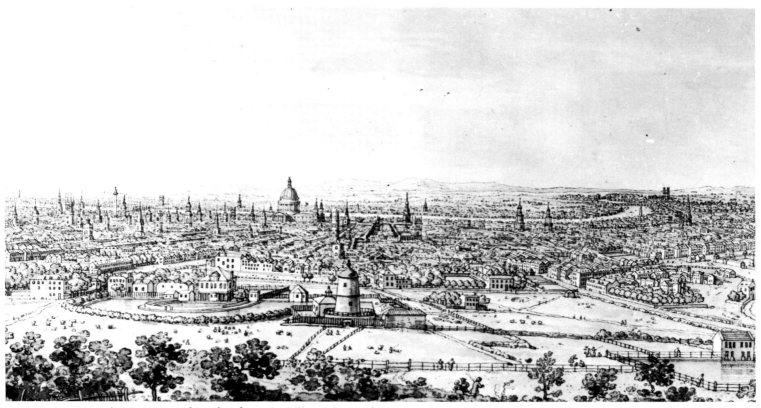

Fig. 1037   A view by Canaletto of London from the hills to the north.

affected by the monumental schemes of the monarchy, as in Paris. London became a mosaic of small enterprises — building ventures promoted by individual landowners — alternating with frequent squares and gardens, both private and public.

Some of these enterprises were elegant and well balanced architectural compositions, consisting of streets or squares flanked by houses of a single style grouped round a communal garden (Fig. 1042). However the repetition of such features produced a new and disconcerting form of urban environment: a vast, incoherent sprawl, which spread in all directions and gradually petered out into the countryside without ever reaching a definite boundary.

In 1726 Daniel Defoe called it a 'monstrous city' and asked, 'Where should one place a boundary line or confining ditch?' A hundred years later, Heinrich Heine arrived in London from Germany and wrote, 'I expected great palaces and saw only ordinary houses. But it is precisely their uniformity and their incalculable numbers that leave such an overwhelming impression.'

In fact, London was the first great middle-class city, whose shape no longer depended on state intervention or the buildings of a small ruling class, but on the countless small contributions of private enterprises. The wealthy English aristocracy built their palaces and great country houses outside the cities (Figs 1043–7), while their town houses blended into the existing framework of buildings (Figs 1038–41). The narrow, twisting streets, however, were already filled with vast numbers of pedestrians and vehicles, even before the advent of the motor-car.

London in the eighteenth century already showed the characteristic problems of the modern city, and these were accentuated as a result of the Industrial Revolution.

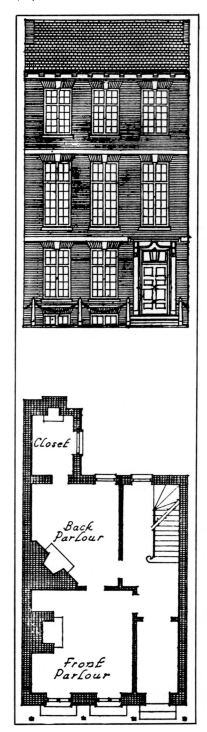

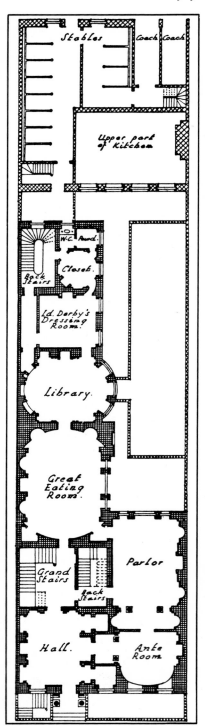

Figs 1038–41	London. Façade and plan of a middle-class house in the late seventeenth century; plan of Lord Derby's house in Grosvenor Square; façade of a late eighteenth-century house in Baker Street, built in accordance with the rules formulated in 1774.

Fig. 1042   Aerial view of Grosvenor Square and its surrounding district.

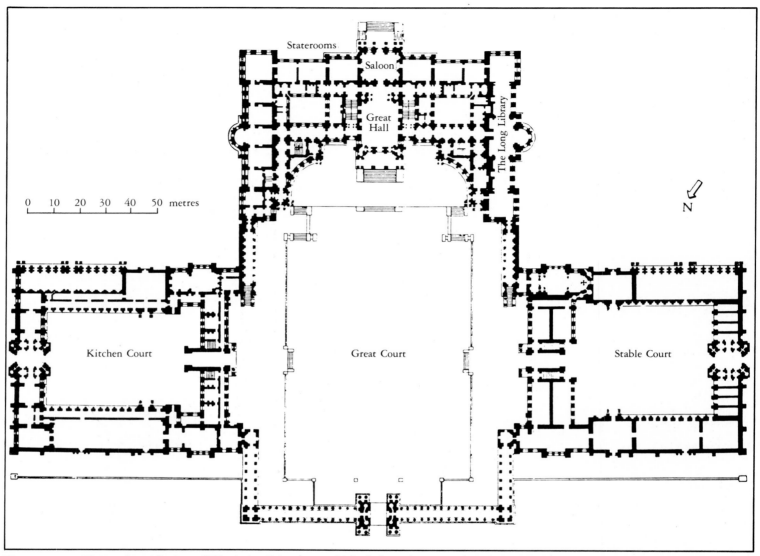

Figs 1043–4   Plan and aerial view of Blenheim Palace, near Oxford, built by the Duke of Marlborough in 1704. The grounds were laid out in the late eighteenth century.

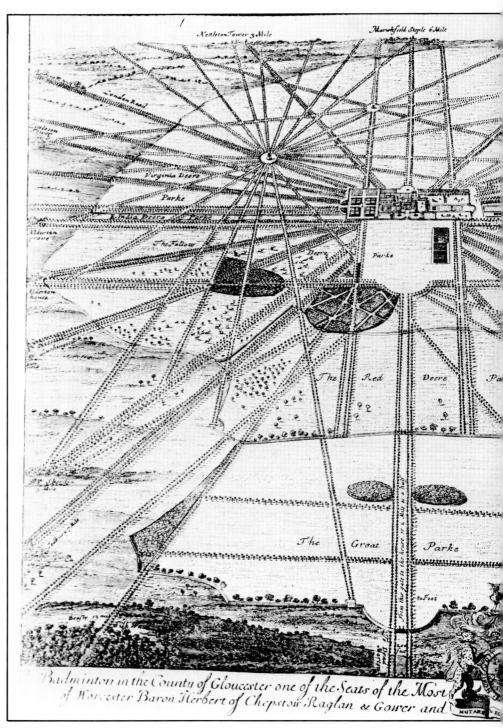

Fig. 1045 View of the grounds of Badminton House, as seen in an early eighteenth-century engraving.

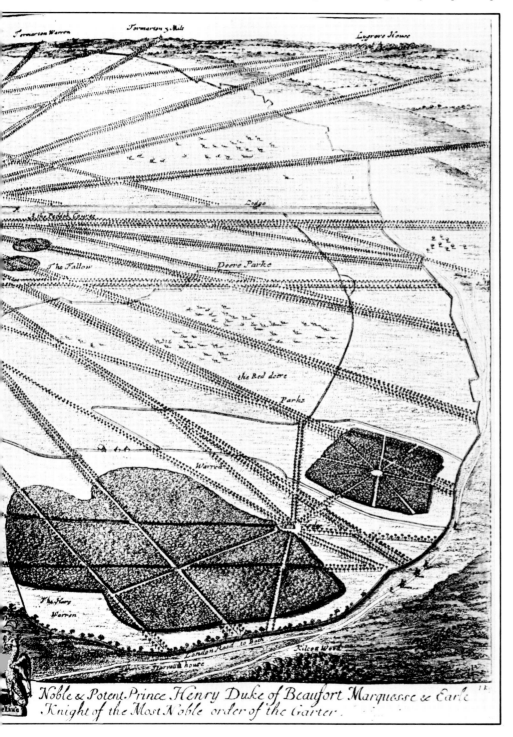

Tormarton Warren   Tormarton y Mill   Lygrove House

Lodge

I the Rideit Corse

The Fallow   Deere Parke

the Red deere

Parke

Warren

The Hary
Warren

London Road to Bath   Kilcot Wood
Tarvells house

*Noble & Potent. Prince. Henry Duke of Beaufort Marquesse & Earle
Knight of the Most Noble order of the Garter.*

Figs 1046–7 Views of the grounds of Stourhead in Wiltshire, laid out in the mid-eighteenth century: one of the principal examples of the 'English Garden', free from geometrical regularity and carefully designed to blend in with the countryside.

Fig. 1048　The arrival of industry in the English countryside: the ironworks at Coalbrookdale, in a painting from 1775.

11
The setting of the Industrial Revolution

From the mid-eighteenth century onwards, the Industrial Revolution began to change the course of history, first in England and then in the rest of the world.

In the Introduction, the Industrial Revolution was referred to in relation to the other great turning-points of human history: the agricultural revolution of Neolithic times and the urban revolution of the Bronze Age. It now remains to describe the effects that it had on the physical environment, and in order to achieve this let us make a brief résumé of the principal factors that affected the basic nature of urban and rural areas:

1. The increase in population, which resulted from the fact that, for the first time, the birth rate exceeded the level of deaths: in England the birth rate remained almost constant at around 37 per thousand, while the level of deaths decreased from 35 per thousand, towards the mid-eighteenth century, to 20 per thousand, towards the mid-nineteenth century.

The population of England rose from seven million in 1760 to fourteen million in 1830, and the average life expectancy rose from roughly thirty-five years to fifty years and more; also, due to a fall in infant mortality rates, the percentage of young people in the population increased. This meant that the balance between the generations was broken, and it was no longer just a question of one generation taking over from the preceding one; each generation now found itself facing a new situation, with new problems to come to terms with.

2. The increase in goods and services produced by agriculture, industry and tertiary activities, due to technological advances and economic expansion. The growth in population combined with a growth in production produced a spiral effect: the increased population needed more goods and services, which in turn produced a further rise in population figures, while the introduction of better and more numerous goods and services raised society's living standards and led to demands for still more varied and abundant goods and services.

3. The redistribution of population, following the increase in the number of inhabitants and the changes in production. Tied agricultural workers became wage-earners, or industrial workers, and moved to the areas that contained the energy sources needed for the new factories: near waterways and, after the invention of the steam engine, near coal deposits. The factories tended to be concentrated around the towns, which meant that the urban areas grew much faster than the rest of the country, because they not only housed the natural increase in population, but also the influx of people from the land.

Manchester, which in 1760 had 12,000 inhabitants, had a population of 400,000 in the mid-nineteenth century, while London, which already had one million inhabitants by the end of the eighteenth century, in 1851 had one and a half million, a figure that surpassed the levels achieved by any other city up to that time.

4. The development in communications: the turnpikes,

built with methods elaborated by Telford and Macadam; navigable canals, which were constructed in England from 1760 onwards; railways, which were introduced in 1825 and spread rapidly throughout England and the rest of the world; and steamships, which took the place of sailing ships during the period.

These new methods of communication introduced an era of unparalleled mobility: all manner of goods, however heavy, could be transported to where they were needed, and people of all classes could travel widely, or even live in one place and work in another, commuting daily or weekly.

5. The speed and open-ended nature of these transformations, which took place in a matter of decades (within the space of a lifetime) and did not lead to a new period of equilibrium, merely acted as the forerunners of other, even more rapid and far-reaching transformations.

No problem ever found a permanent solution and no system was capable of lasting indefinitely: it only lasted for a period whose duration people had to learn to calculate in advance. Buildings were no longer considered as permanent features of the landscape, but as provisional and replaceable

structures. In this way, it became possible to regard building land as an asset in its own right, the value of which was determined by its situation, its scarcity and whether it was subject to any rules or regulations.

6. The new trends in political thought, which tended to undermine the traditional forms of public control over the environment (town-planning schemes, building restrictions) were regarded as relics of a bygone age. At the same time they not only refused to accept as inevitable a decline in the environment, but also had the confidence to rectify faults by means of a concerted plan of action.

The economists of the time preached a doctrine of limiting public intervention in all aspects of society's life, including that of the urban sector. Adam Smith advised governments to sell land in public ownership in order to pay their debts. This advice was welcomed by the ruling classes, who had a vested interest in encouraging the freedom of private enterprise in the housing sector; in that way they could make money out of the chaos of the cities without having to suffer the consequences. However, some of the physical drawbacks of the environment (traffic congestion,

Fig. 1049   Thomas Telford's suspension bridge over the Conway strait (the Menai Bridge), built in 1826. A contemporary engraving.

Fig. 1050   The new industrial landscape of the towns, as seen in an engraving by A. W. Pugin, from 1841.

squalor, filth) made the lives of the lower classes unbearable and even threatened, to a certain degree, the quality of life of the other sections of society. For this reason the most enlightened members of the ruling classes, and also the representatives of the lower orders (the radicals and socialists) proposed new interventions by public authorities, either to deal with the worst cases one by one, or to start from scratch, by building whole new districts on the basis of pure theory.

During the first half of the nineteenth century there seemed to be so much wrong with the great industrial towns that people doubted whether it was possible to remedy their defects. The difference between reality and ideal theory seemed irreconcilable. For this reason we shall divide our examination into two parts, describing in this chapter:

1. The reality: the urban environment and the first attempts at improving it by stages;

2. The alternative to this reality: visualised in books and put into practice in exceptional instances, far from the existing cities.

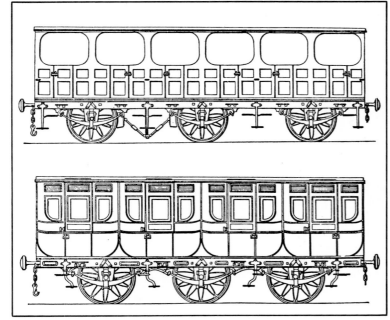

Figs 1051–3   The London–Birmingham railway under construction in 1836; the first- and second-class carriages used by the Great Western Railway in 1839; *The Third Class Carriage*, a painting by Honoré Daumier.

Fig. 1054   An external and internal view of King's Cross Station, London, built in 1850.

Fig. 1055   An allegorical engraving by George Cruikshank, from 1829. *London going out of Town — or — The March of Bricks and Mortar.*

Fig. 1056   Another allegorical engraving, by Robert Seymour, from 1850: *Heaven and Earth: 'Oh! it's very well to Live on the Taxes — but the devil to pay them!'*.

Figs 1057–9   A fashionable district of Paris: the Rue de Rivoli,
started by Napoleon I and completed during the first half of the
nineteenth century. All the houses have an identical façade,
designed by the architects Percier and Fontaine, which were later
imposed by law on subsequent buildings.

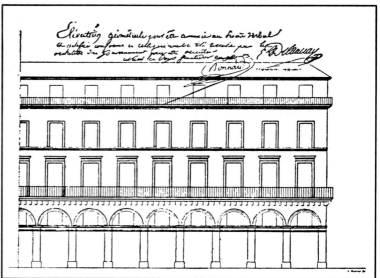

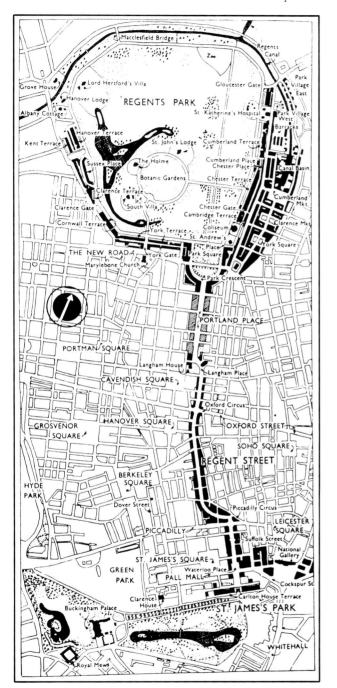

Figs 1060–3   A fashionable district of London: the layout of Regent's Park, planned by John Nash in 1813 and carried out between 1820 and 1830. The engravings show two sections of Regent Street, the curve leading into Piccadilly Circus and the straight line of Portland Place. Below, child labour in the mines of England during the same period.

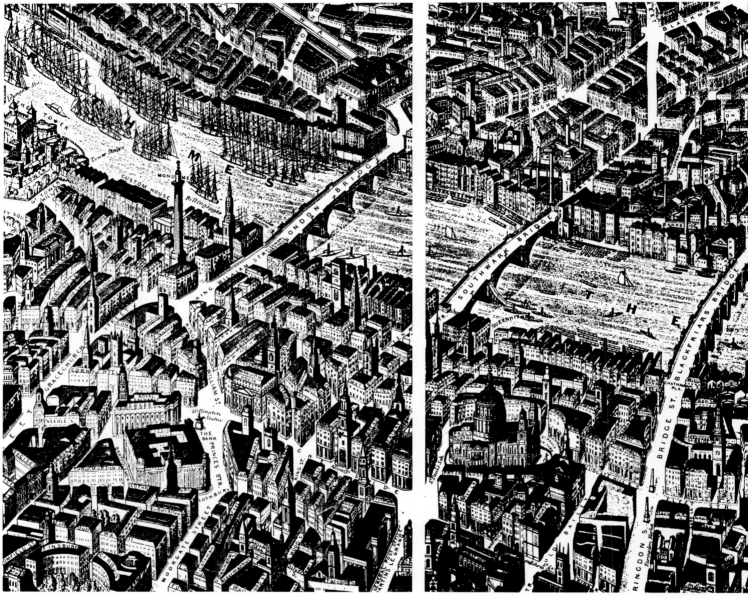

Figs 1064–7   A view of central London, published in 1851 by Banks and Co.; the monuments, houses and offices are all mixed up indiscriminately.

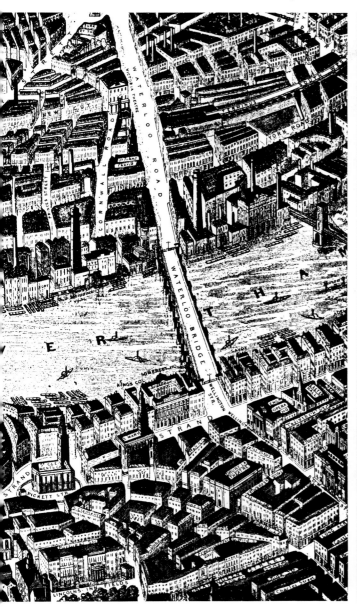

Fig. 1068   A poor district in London, situated amongst railway viaducts, from an engraving by Gustave Doré (1872).

Fig. 1069   A street scene in a poor part of London (Dudley Street), from an engraving by Gustave Doré (1872).

Fig. 1070   The industrial city of Middlesborough, in a photograph taken earlier this century.

Fig. 1071   A modern English industrial town (Colne Valley).

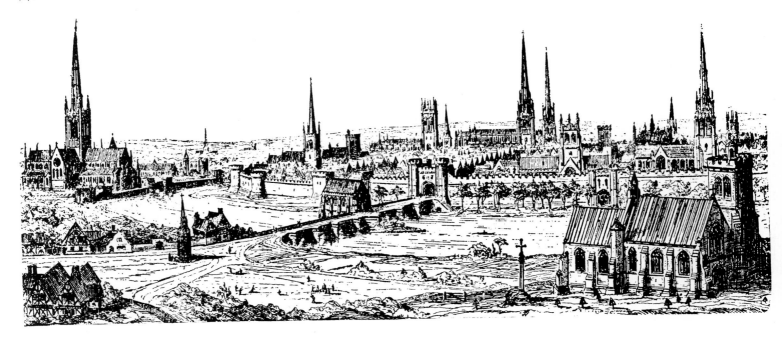

Figs 1072–3   *A Christian city in 1440 and in 1840*; two engravings by Pugin.

Fig. 1074 A group of English factories, sketched by the German architect Schinkel in his travel diary about 1830.

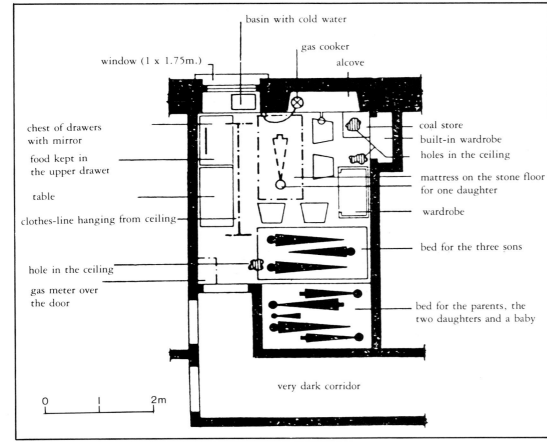

basin with cold water

gas cooker

alcove

window (1 x 1.75m.)

chest of drawers
with mirror

food kept in
the upper drawer

table

clothes-line hanging from ceiling

hole in the ceiling

gas meter over
the door

coal store

built-in wardrobe

holes in the ceiling

mattress on the stone floor
for one daughter

wardrobe

bed for the three sons

bed for the parents, the
two daughters and a baby

very dark corridor

0   2m

Fig 1075 An artisan's dwelling for nine people, discovered in Glasgow in 1948.

Fig. 1076 The poor of
London; a cartoon from an
1859 edition of *Punch*.

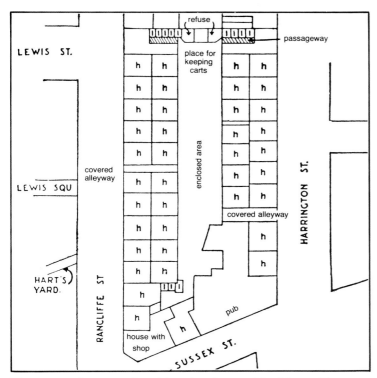

Fig. 1077 A group of working-class houses (h) with outside lavatories (l), in Nottingham, discovered by a commission of enquiry in 1845.

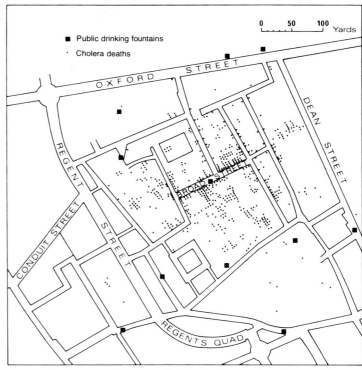

Fig. 1078 A map of cholera deaths in the London district of Soho during September 1854, drawn up by Dr John Snow.

Fig. 1079 The slums of Paradise Row, London, in 1853.

Fig. 1080   The conditions described by Engels in 1845, which still exist on the fringes of some modern cities.

I

The extremely rapid growth of cities during the industrial era transformed the existing urban nuclei (which became the centres of the new towns and cities) and also brought about the construction of new peripheral areas.

The nucleus already had its own shape, determined either during the Middle Ages or in subsequent centuries, and it contained the principal monuments — churches, palaces — which often still dominated the new landscape. But this nucleus would clearly not be large enough to cope with a vast new influx of people: the streets were too narrow to deal with increased traffic, while the houses were too small and compact to provide accommodation with any degree of comfort for a greatly increased number of inhabitants. As a result, the better-off members of society gradually began to abandon the city centres and set up house in the outskirts, and the old houses rapidly developed into overcrowded slums which contained the poor and the new arrivals from the countryside. At the same time, many of the historical buildings of the old city — the houses of the nobility, the convents — were abandoned as a result of the changes in the city's social composition and divided up into makeshift lodgings. The green areas within the old districts — the gardens behind the terraced houses, the grounds of the houses of the nobility, the kitchen gardens — were used to build houses and industrial workshops on.

The effects of these changes began to accumulate and worsen towards the mid-nineteenth century. Engels wrote a classic description of the centre of Manchester, published in 1845, as follows:

Here even the better streets . . . are narrow and tortuous. The houses are dirty, old and tumble-down. The side streets have been built in a disgraceful fashion . . . This is a remnant of the old Manchester of the days before the town became industrialised. The original inhabitants and their children have left for better houses in other districts, while the houses . . . which no longer satisfied them, were left to a tribe of workers containing a strong Irish element. Here one is really and truly in a district which is quite obviously given over entirely to the working classes, because even the shopkeepers and the publicans . . . make no effort to give their establishments a semblance of cleanliness. The condition of this street may be deplorable, but it is by no means as bad as the alleys and courts which lie behind it, and which can be approached only by covered passages so narrow that two people cannot pass. Anyone who has never visited these courts and alleys can have no

idea of the fantastic way in which the houses have been packed together in disorderly confusion in impudent defiance of all reasonable principles of town planning. And the fault lies not merely in the survival of old property from earlier periods of Manchester's history. Only in quite modern times has the policy of cramming as many houses as possible on to such a space as was not utilised in earlier periods reached its climax. The result is that today not an inch of space remains between the houses and any further building is now physically impossible. To prove my point I reproduce a small section of a plan of Manchester. It is by no means the worst slum in Manchester and it does not cover one-tenth of the area of Manchester.

This sketch will be sufficient to illustrate the crazy layout of the whole district lying near the river. There is a very sharp drop of some 15 to 30 feet down to the south bank . . . at this point. As many as three rows of houses have generally been squeezed on to this precipitous slope.

(F. Engels, *The Condition of the Working Class in England*, translated by W. O. Henderson and W. H Chaloner, Oxford 1971.)

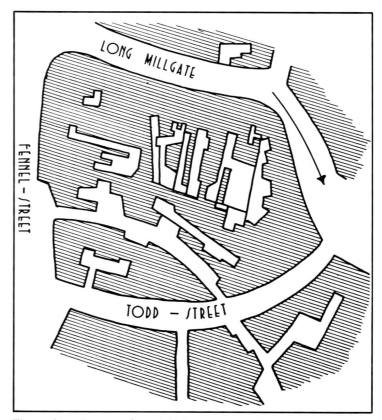

Fig. 1081   An area of central Manchester.

The outskirts of the cities were not planned additions like those of the Middle Ages or the baroque era, but open spaces in which a large number of unrelated private building projects were erected: luxury housing, houses for the poor, factories, warehouses and technical installations. At a certain stage these buildings would unite into a single entity, but not as the result of any conscious attempt at planning.

In the new industrial districts the architectural and social unity of the old cities disappeared completely. People, both as individuals and as members of a particular social class, did not wish to integrate within the city; the classes tended to settle in different areas, in upper, middle or lower-class districts, with very little overlap between them. Houses standing in their own grounds, once the exclusive domain of the kings and noble families, now became accessible (albeit on a reduced scale) to the upper-middle and middle classes, and the degree of separation of the houses became the most important symbol of the residents' social status: the rich had houses with large gardens, while the poor lived much closer together, either in terraced houses or tenement blocks.

The illustrations (Figs 1057–80) show examples of rich and poor districts. The quality of housing reached scarcely tolerable levels for the poorest members of society either because of the lack of building regulations, or because they had fallen into disuse.

Groups of speculators were responsible for building these houses, either a few at a time or in vast complexes, and their sole aim was to make as much profit as possible. The workman, sometimes receiving barely subsistence level wages, had to surrender part of his income in rent, while the landlord, who often built his houses as small as possible and using the cheapest forms of building material, had to try and cover the cost of construction and also make a profit. It was this clash of interests that determined the nature of many houses and the appearance of many working-class neighbourhoods.

Nevertheless, a workman's house of the type mentioned above could well be better than the hut in which he and his family had lived in the countryside: it had brick walls instead of wooden ones, and a tiled roof instead of a thatched one, but its furniture and its services would be equally primitive and inadequate. The hut, however, would have had a lot of space round it, in which refuse could be disposed of, and a lot of activities — the raising of livestock, the passage of pedestrians and carts, even children's games — could take place in the open air. However, the concentration of large numbers of houses in a restricted environment made refuse disposal a problem and also prevented a lot of open-air activities from taking place. Open sewers ran down the streets, garbage accumulated, and the same areas were used as thoroughfares for pedestrians and wheeled traffic, for animals to wander about in, and for the children to play in. In addition, the poorest districts were almost invariably situated in the least pleasant positions, close to the industrial zones and the railways and far away from areas of green. The factories filled the houses with fumes and noise, poisoned the waterways and also attracted a lot of extra traffic.

Engels described the industrial outskirts of Manchester as follows:

The New Town . . . on the other side of the Old Town, is situated on the clayey soil of the rising ground between the River Irk and St George's Road. This district does not give one the impression that it is part of a big city. The New Town is composed of single rows of houses and groups of streets which might be small villages, lying on bare clayey soil which does not produce even a blade of grass. The houses — or rather the cottages — are in a disgraceful state because they are never repaired. They are filthy and beneath them are to be found damp, dirty cellar dwellings; the unpaved alleys lack any form of drainage. The district is infested with small herds of pigs; some of them are penned up in little courts and sties, while others wander freely on the neighbouring hillside. The lanes in this district are so filthy that it is only in very dry weather that one can reach it without sinking ankle-deep at every step . . . We have seen how, in the Old Town, there has been no systematic planning and that the siting of the houses has been purely fortuitous. Builders who erected new houses put them up without regard to the situation of older neighbouring property. The tiny gaps which exist between the houses are called 'courts' for want of a more appropriate name. There is more evidence of planning in the rather newer parts of the Old Town, as well as in other working-class districts which date from the first stages of the Industrial Revolution. Here the spaces between the blocks of dwellings consist of regular — generally square — courts, from which there is access to the streets by a covered passage. (This may be seen from the accompanying diagram). From the point of view of the health of the workers cooped up in these dwellings, this type of regular layout with wholly inadequate ventilation, is even worse than the unplanned streets of the Old Town. The air simply cannot escape and it is only up the chimneys of the houses — when fires happen to be burning — that any draught is provided to help the foul air from the courts to escape . . .

Subsequently another method of constructing workers' houses was introduced, but this has never become universal. Workers' cottages are now hardly ever built singly, but always in larger numbers — a dozen or even sixty at a time. A single contractor will build one or two whole streets at a time. The way in which these houses are built is illustrated by the accompanying diagram.

The cottages which face the street . . . are of a somewhat superior character . . . and are fortunate enough to have a back door and a little backyard. The highest rents are charged for these cottages. Behind the back wall of these yards there is a narrow alley called a back street, which is enclosed at both ends. Access to this back street is either through a little entry or a covered passage. The cottages which have their front doors looking out on to the back street . . . pay the lowest rent and are indeed the most neglected. They have a party wall in common with the third row of cottages which face the street . . . This third row of cottages . . . pay a lower rent than the first class of cottages . . . but a higher rent than the middle row . . . This method of construction ensures that the first row of cottages . . . is well ventilated. The ventilation of the cottages in the third row . . . is at any rate no worse than that to be found in the houses built on the older plan . . . On the other hand the middle row of cottages . . . is just as badly ventilated as the older houses with front doors looking out on to courts. And the back streets of the newer houses are just as disgustingly filthy as the newer courts. The contractors prefer the newer layout, not only because it economises space, but because it gives them an opportunity of successfully exploiting the better paid workers who can pay higher rents for cottages which have front doors facing the street . . .

. . . This method of construction is adopted partly in order to save materials, partly because the builders . . . are not prepared to sacrifice any part of their profits, and partly owing to the system of short leases . . . When unemployment is rife during periods of bad trade whole rows of cottages often stand empty and in such circumstances they soon become virtually uninhabitable.

The most disgusting spot of all is one which lies on the Manchester side of the river. It is situated to the south-west of Oxford Road and is called Little Ireland. It lies in a fairly deep natural depression on a bend of the river and is completely surrounded by tall factories or high banks and embankments covered with buildings. Here lie two groups of about two hundred cottages, most of which are built on the back-to-back principle. Some four thousand people, mostly Irish, inhabit this slum. The cottages are very small, old and dirty, while the streets are uneven, partly unpaved, not properly drained and full of ruts. Heaps of refuse, offal and sickening filth are everywhere interspersed with pools of stagnant liquid. The atmosphere is polluted by the stench and is darkened by the thick smoke of a dozen factory chimneys. A horde of ragged women and children swarm about the streets and they are just as dirty as the pigs which wallow happily on the heaps of garbage and in the pools of filth.

(F. Engels, *op. cit.*)

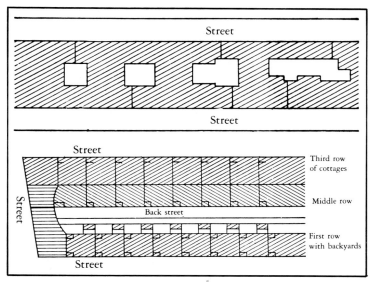

Figs 1082–3   Details of new housing in Manchester, from sketches in Engels' book.

This chaotic and uninhabitable environment, which we shall call the 'liberal' city, was the result of the unregulated and uncoordinated superimposition of countless public and private developments. Individual freedom, demanded as a pre-condition for the expansion of the industrial economy, turned out to be incapable of exercising proper control over the urban and housing developments that were the direct results of this expansion. The lower classes were the ones to suffer most from the unpleasant conditions of life in the industrial cities, but even the rich were unable to escape them completely. Towards 1830 cholera spread into Europe from Asia, and epidemics soon broke out in the major cities, obliging the authorities to take action to improve sanitary arrangements; this involved a contravention of the basic principle of *laissez-faire*, which had been proclaimed in theory and stubbornly defended in practice during the first part of the century.

Fig. 1084 · A 'village of harmony and cooperation', as envisaged by Owen in a drawing from 1817.

In England a group of officials and political radicals sponsored a series of enquiries into living conditions in the cities (published in 1842, 1844 and 1845, and used by Engels in his book on the plight of the English working classes). The worst aspects of housing and living conditions in working-class areas were brought to the notice of the public, who reacted by demanding that the government take action. It was, however, to take many years of heated debate before the first law concerning public health was passed in the summer of 1848.

In France, during the July Monarchy, the enquiries into the living conditions of working men were conducted by opposition groups, both Socialist and Catholic, but it was not until after the 1848 Revolution that the Second Republic approved a public health law in 1850.

These two laws, together with those subsequently passed in Italy (1865) and other European countries, were made use of in the second part of the nineteenth century to administer the 'post-liberal' city, a phenomenon that will be discussed in the next chapter.

2

During the difficult post-war period from 1815 onwards, a number of revolutionary theories were expounded, both in the field of politics and of town planning, which were designed to change the structure of society and also the nature of the community. The old society had produced a rift between the town and the country. The new society was going to produce a new form of carefully planned community, half way between a town and a farm. It would be small enough to be laid out as a cohesive entity, but large enough to support a complete and self-contained economic and cultural life.

Robert Owen (1771–1858), a rich English industrial-

Fig. 1085   The village designed to be built according to Owen's plans in Harmony, Indiana, as seen in an 1825 engraving.

ist, proposed a settlement of some 1,200 people, covering an area of 500 hectares of agricultural land. The houses would be arranged in a square, three sides of which would be taken up by married couples and children of less than three years, while the fourth side would contain the young people's dormitories, the infirmary and guest accommodation. The central area was designated for public buildings: the kitchens of the communal restaurant, schools, a library, a club for adults, and green areas for recreation and sporting activities. Along the external perimeter there would be gardens and a ring road, while further on there would be industrial units, storehouses, a laundry, a brewery, a mill, a brick factory, stables and farm buildings. There were no courts or prisons, because the new society would have no need for such things (Fig. 1084).

This plan was presented between 1817 and 1820 to the English government and also to local authorities, but with-

out success. Owen then tried to put it into practice in North America: in 1825 he bought an area of land in Indiana, on which he intended to build his first model village (Fig. 1085), but it had to fit in with another village already there, and the experiment petered out after a few years.

The French writer Charles Fourier (1772–1837) published his account of a new philosophical and political system during the reign of Louis Philippe. He pinpointed the passions that govern human relationships, and planned a grouping that would serve to activate all these relationships, formed of 1,620 people of different social backgrounds; this group, called the 'Phalanx', would have to occupy an area of one square league (250 hectares) and live in a single building, called the Phalanstère. Fourier described this building in minute detail: it was a monumental omega-shaped palace, like Versailles, with an inner courtyard and a number of lesser courtyards. The ground floor

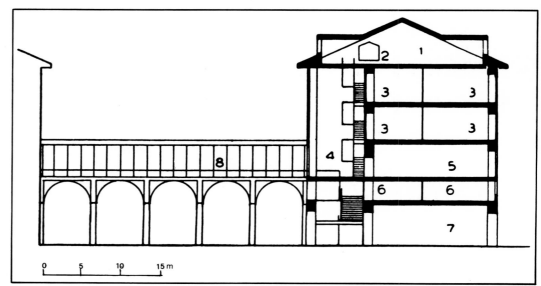

Fig. 1086   Schematic plan of Fourier's Phalanstère, reconstructed from the description given in 1841; the black lines are internal raised walkways.

Fig. 1087   Schematic cross-section of Fourier's Phalanstère.

 1. The attic, containing guest rooms.
 2. Water tank.
 3. Private apartments.
 4. Raised walkway.
 5. Assembly hall.
 6. Mezzanine floor with young people's quarters.
 7. Ground floor with entrances for carriages.
 8. Covered footbridge.

was broken up by a number of entrances for carriages, while the first floor had a system of covered galleries, used for communications between the different areas, instead of streets. The adults' quarters were on the second and third floors, while the children were on the mezzanine floor and guests were housed in the attic (Figs 1086–7).

This concept, however demanding, exercised an extra-ordinary fascination on several countries: there were at least fifty attempts at realising it, in France, Russia, Algeria and America, between 1830 and 1850. Later, during the Sec-ond Empire, an industrialist from Guise, Jean Baptiste Godin, constructed a building for his workforce which, although on a smaller scale than the Phalanstère, was inspired by it; he called it a Familistère, because each family had its own apartment. The main section consisted of three four-storey blocks, and their courtyards, of medium size and covered by glass roofs, acted as internal walkways. The services — schools, a theatre, a laundry, public baths and workshops — were situated in adjoining buildings, and the whole complex stood in a park contained within the bend of

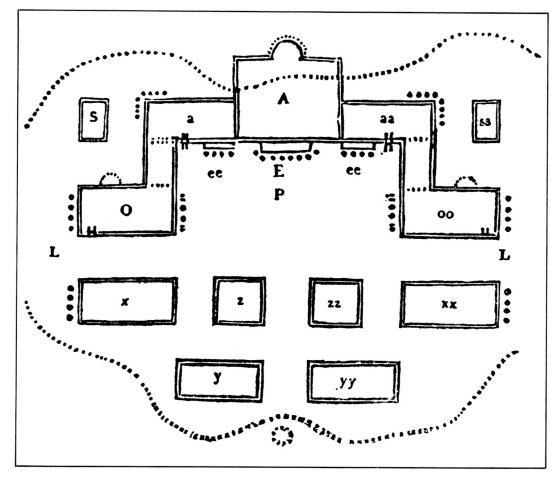

Fig. 1088 The Phalanstère, as interpreted by the American journalist Albert Brisbane.

A, O. Internal gardens.
E. Main entrance.
P. Courtyard.
S, X, Y, Z. Secondary buildings.

a river (Figs 1089–95). After 1880 the factory and the Familistère were run by a workers' co-operative.

These idealised models, impracticable during the first half of the nineteenth century, and overtaken by the political events of the second half, represented the theoretical antithesis of the 'liberal' city. They shifted the emphasis from private initiative to collective responsibility, by endeavouring to bring every or almost every aspect of family and social life into the public sector. They were a direct result of the wave of protest at the intolerable conditions in existent cities, and they sought for the first time to escape from the latter's tyranny by resorting to analysis and rational thinking. They were instruments designed to relieve man of the strains imposed by the traditional urban concept, which hindered political change and favoured vested interests. Their isolated experiments in many ways anticipated the research done by architects in the following century.

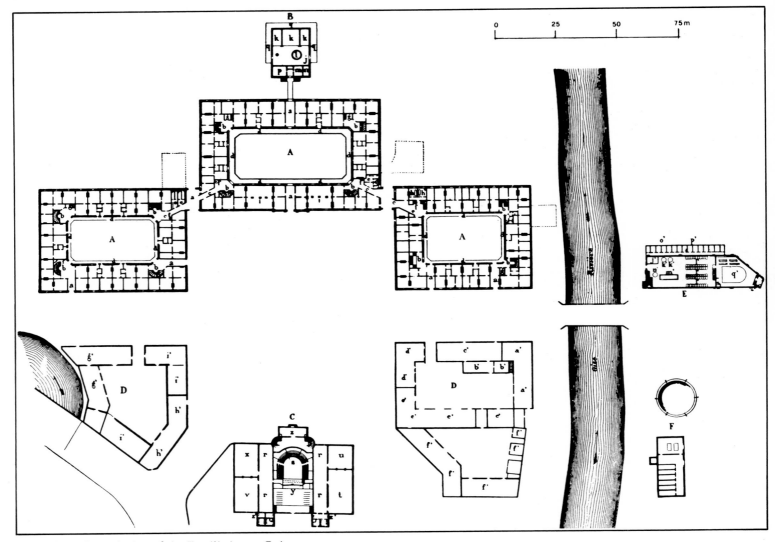

Fig. 1089   General plan of the Familistère at Guise.

A. Main buildings of the Familistère.
B. Children's nursery.
C. School complex with theatre.
D. Secondary buildings (abattoir,
restaurant, café, recreation room,
stables, hen-house, studies and
laboratories).
E. Public baths and covered swimming
pool.
F. Gas installations.

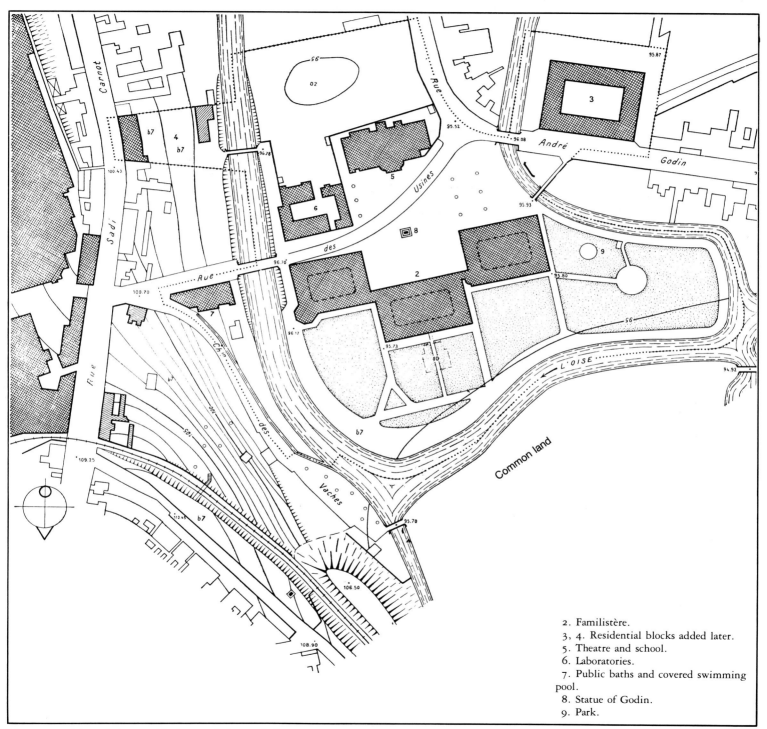

2. Familistère.
3, 4. Residential blocks added later.
5. Theatre and school.
6. Laboratories.
7. Public baths and covered swimming pool.
8. Statue of Godin.
9. Park.

Fig. 1090 Plan of the Familistère at Guise, as it is now.

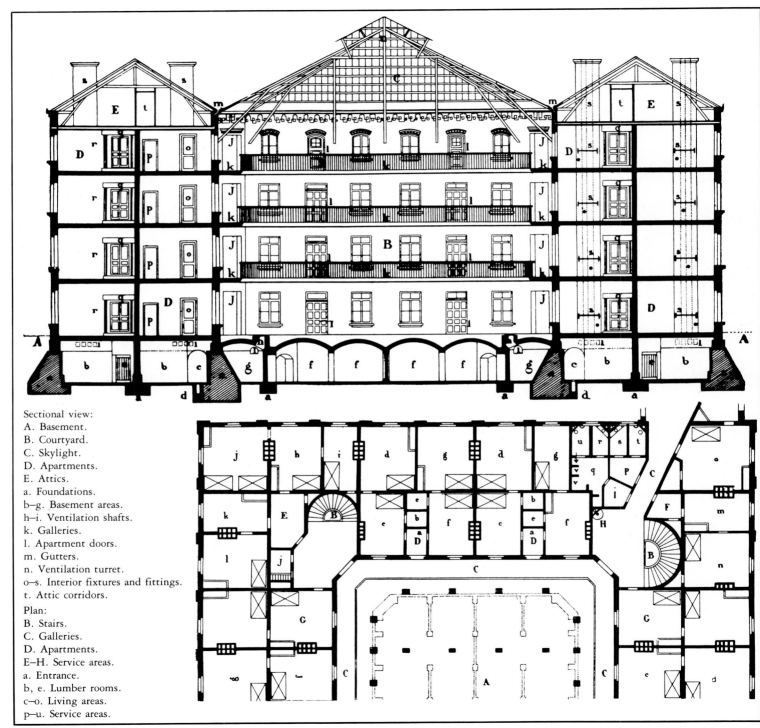

Sectional view:
A. Basement.
B. Courtyard.
C. Skylight.
D. Apartments.
E. Attics.
a. Foundations.
b–g. Basement areas.
h–i. Ventilation shafts.
k. Galleries.
l. Apartment doors.
m. Gutters.
n. Ventilation turret.
o–s. Interior fixtures and fittings.
t. Attic corridors.

Plan:
B. Stairs.
C. Galleries.
D. Apartments.
E–H. Service areas.
a. Entrance.
b, e. Lumber rooms.
c–o. Living areas.
p–u. Service areas.

Figs 1091–2   Cross-section and plan of the central unit of the Familistère.

Fig. 1093   View of the courtyard with its glass roof, as it is now.

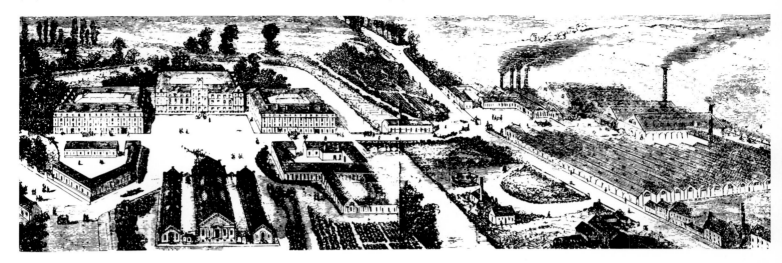

Figs 1094–5   Bird's eye view of the Familistère and interior view of the children's nursery, as shown in engravings published by Godin in 1870.

12
The 'post-liberal' city

The European revolutions of 1848 precipitated a severe crisis in both the movements of the Left, which had tried to seize power but had failed, and the liberal régimes in the early part of the century, which had proved incapable of defending themselves against such a threat.

The leftists lost faith in sectional reforms, including those that had to do with housing and buildings in general, while their scientific socialists (Marx and Engels, who published their *Manifesto of the Communist Party* in 1848) criticised the socialists of the earlier part of the century, amongst whom were Owen and Fourier, for being Utopian. Marx and Engels maintained that the workers had to seize power and, most important of all, assume control over the means of production, thereby enabling changes to be made throughout the system. This was the theory put into practice by Lenin in 1917.

The Rightists, however, who came out on top after the struggles of 1848 — the régime of Napoleon III in France, Bismarck in Germany, and the Conservatives under Disraeli in England — abandoned the old tradition of non-intervention by the State in the private sector. They used the methods formulated during the first part of the century (by the reformers and Utopian socialists) to ensure that the changes in society did not get out of hand.

The victorious middle class established a new urban model, in which the interests of the dominant groups — the entrepreneurs and landlords — were partly coordinated, and the most glaring contradictions caused by the presence of the poorer classes were corrected. Complete freedom of action for private enterprise was limited by the intervention of the State, which established building regulations and carried out public works, but it was still clearly guaranteed within those limitations. Thus the transition from the 'liberal' city to the 'post-liberal' city was achieved.

This new model had an immediate and lasting success: it allowed for the further development of Europe's great cities (particularly Paris), the foundation of colonial cities all over the world, and it still has a determining effect on the nature of modern cities.

Let us briefly list the characteristics of this model, which had many features comparable with those of the cities of today.

1. The public administration and the private sector came to an agreement; both of them recognised the other's domain, and the extent of their respective spheres of influence became precisely established.

Control over the minimum amount of land necessary for a city to function properly was exercised by the administration. This included the space needed for thoroughfares (streets, squares, railways) and utility installations (aqueducts, sewers, and later, gas, electricity, telephones). The private sector was responsible for all the rest, that is the areas of land served by the thoroughfares and utilities, and it was these public amenities that made the land suitable for urban development. If, however, the administration had to provide buildings or open space for the benefit of the public as an alternative to those provided by the private sector (schools, hospitals, gardens), it was obliged to act like any other business proprietor in competition with his rivals. It was as a result of this phenomenon that a distinction came to be made between primary and secondary services.

2. The way in which urban land was used depended on

Figs 1096–7 Two drawings by Le Corbusier: the 'corridor street', and three types of city arranged on the 'corridor street' principle — Paris, New York and Buenos Aires.

the individual owners (private or public), on whom the administration exercised only an indirect influence by means of regulations controlling the size of buildings in relation to the adjacent public areas, and by fixing the relationships between adjoining buildings. The private landlords retained all the profits that they made from the city's expansion, as a result of which the administration was unable to recoup the expenses involved in laying on public services; the money was treated as an irretrievable capital investment and the authorities found themselves in a perpetual state of deficit.

3. The boundaries between the public and private domains — the street frontages — determined the shape of a city.

Buildings could be sited in two ways:

— directly adjoining a street or road. In the city centres, where commerce was the main activity, the most convenient arrangement was a 'corridor street', which acted both as a thoroughfare for traffic and as a means of access to the shops on the ground floors. All the other elements (flats and offices, situated on the upper floors) were obliged to fit into this scheme, which was specifically designed for the benefit of traffic and shops, and endure all the attendant discomforts: noise, lack of air and light, crowds;

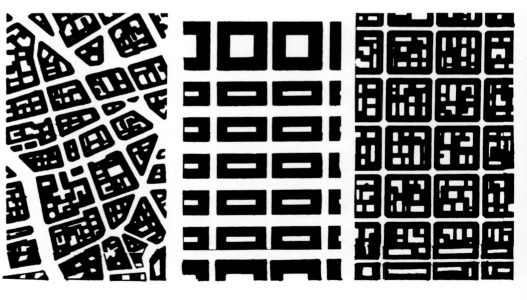

Two instructive designs by Godin, from 1870:
Fig. 1098 The first type of building in nineteenth-century towns: terraced houses.
Fig. 1099 The second type of building in nineteenth-century towns: the semi-detached house.

Figs 1100–2 'A workman's cottage' designed by John Wood Jr and published in 1781.

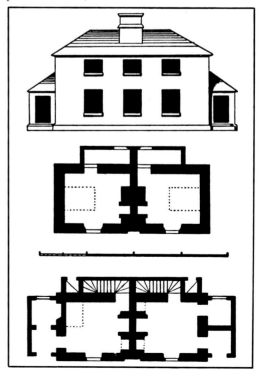

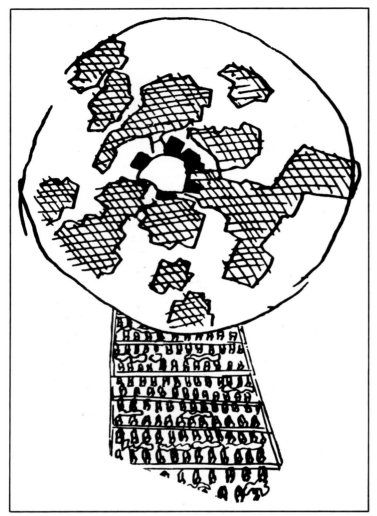

Fig. 1103   A drawing by Le Corbusier, showing the outskirts of a town with large numbers of small houses.

— set back from the road. This arrangement allowed the discomforts mentioned above to be avoided, but it lessened the building density and was only suitable for the outskirts, which were mainly residential. In residential areas the land could be commercially exploited in two almost equally profitable ways: by a low density of expensive housing (the villas of the well-off) or by a high density of cheaper housing (the terraced houses for the lower classes).

Figs 1104–12   Nine different types of suburban villa, from an English manual of 1846.

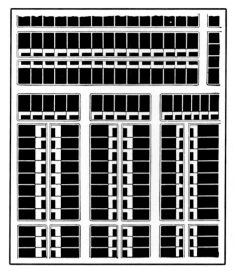

Figs 1113–15   Examples of the
outskirts of English cities, built in
accordance with the 1875 regulations;
a desire to stretch the legal limits to
their maximum led to an obsessive
uniformity in these districts.

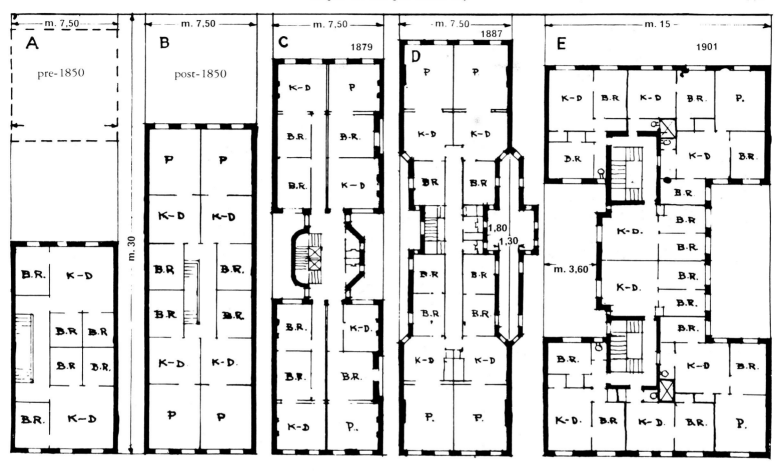

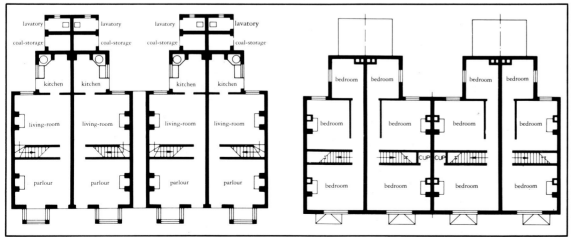

Figs 1116–22 Plans of terraced houses in New York, showing the modifications made by successive regulations during the second part of the nineteenth century. (BR. bedroom; K–D. kitchen-diner; P. parlour.) Plans of English terraced houses, as laid down by the regulations of 1875.

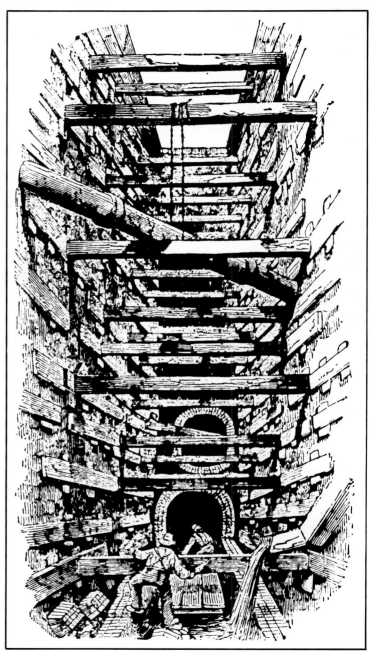

Figs 1123–5   Services in a mid-nineteenth-century city: the cross-section of a Paris street (1853); a bath tub hired for use in the home, in Paris (from an engraving by Gavarni, reproduced in Balzac's *Grande Ville*, 1844); work in progress on the drains in Fleet Street, London (1845).

Fig. 1126 The London Underground Railway from *Universal Illustrated*, 1867.

Fig. 1127 Sectional view of the Thames Embankment, built between 1848 and 1865.

Figs 1128–30 The development of the modern water closet.

A. Bramah's device of 1778: 1. Water tap; 2. Overflow with siphon; 3. Valve; 4. Handle.
B System in use in 1790: 1. Bowl; 2. Handle.
C. System with integral siphon, nineteenth century.

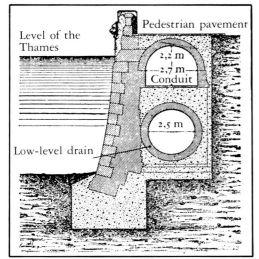

Level of the Thames

Pedestrian pavement

2,2 m
2,7 m
Conduit

2,5 m

Low-level drain

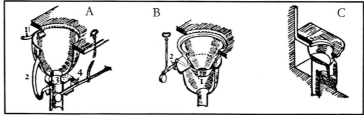

A   B   C

4. The arrangement of the outskirts in this way led to a rise in house prices and made it necessary to preserve a certain number of low-cost dwellings for the poorest sections of society. The district also tended to become increasingly compact and left no space for larger buildings or ones that needed to develop (industrial establishments, warehouses). These elements — vital to the city's functioning, but incompatible with the layout already described — were pushed out into a third concentric zone, suburbia, which was a mixture of city and countryside that spread further and further out as the city developed.

5. Some of the more obvious drawbacks of the 'post-liberal' city — the excessive density of the centre, the absence of low-cost housing — were alleviated by a number of corrective measures: public parks, which provided an artificial slice of the inaccessible countryside, and council houses built with public money, which were either terraced blocks or small houses set back from the road (Figs 1132–6). But these remedies proved inadequate: the overcrowding and the lack of housing either persisted or grew worse.

6. The 'post-liberal' city was superimposed on the earlier city, tending to destroy it. It treated the old streets as 'corridor streets', it eliminated the areas in which land served a dual public and private purpose, but, above all, it treated buildings as expendable, allowing them to be demolished and rebuilt by preserving their original ground area or straightening and realigning them in order to widen the streets. However, this destruction was never total: the principal monuments, and the most characteristic streets and squares were retained, because the formal quality of the new city depended a great deal on them. The old buildings — churches, palaces — were used as models on which the stylistic elements of the new architectural creations were based, and they were preserved within the modern city as in an open air museum, like the paintings and sculptures that are preserved in real museums.

The presence of these old monuments and the stylisation of the new buildings was not enough to compensate

Fig. 1131 'A working class quarter as a hygienist would like', from a Hoepli manual of 1905.

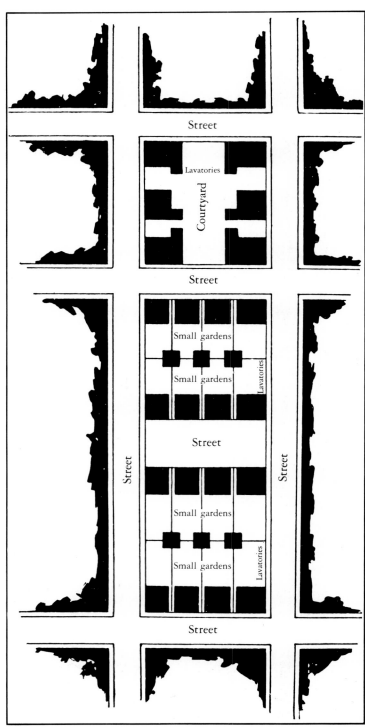

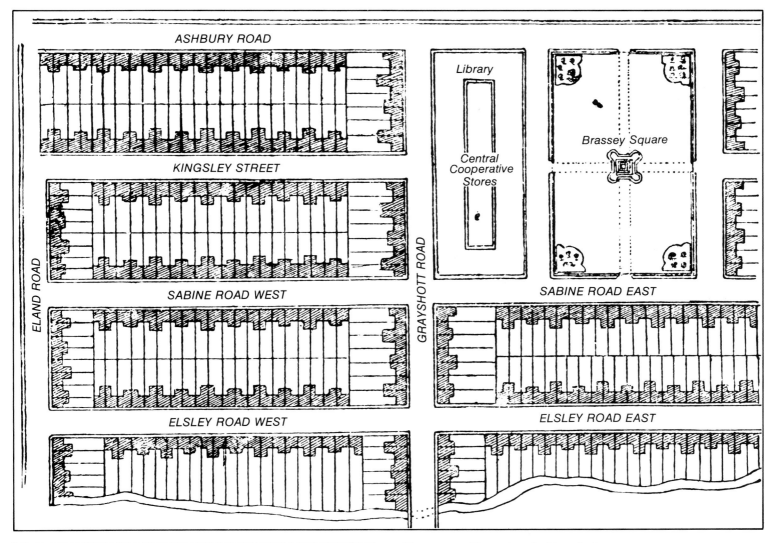

ASHBURY ROAD

KINGSLEY STREET

SABINE ROAD WEST

ELSLEY ROAD WEST

ELAND ROAD

GRAYSHOTT ROAD

Library

Central
Cooperative
Stores

Brassey Square

SABINE ROAD EAST

ELSLEY ROAD EAST

Fig. 1132   The artisans' village built
by the Artisans, Labourers and General
Dwellings Co. in Battersea, London.

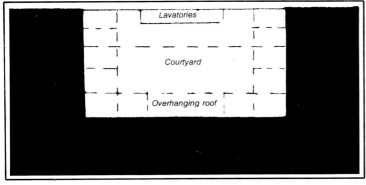

Lavatories

Courtyard

Overhanging roof

Fig. 1133   An elementary school
built along the side of a road,
containing an internal courtyard; from
a Hoepli manual of 1905.

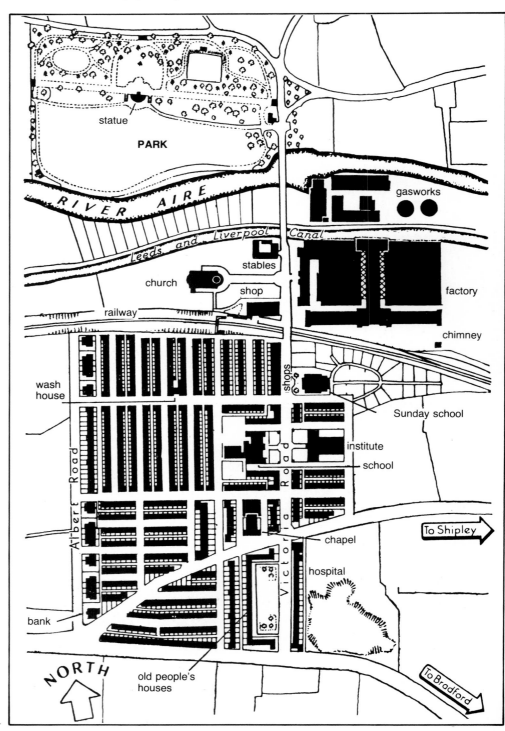

Fig. 1134   Plan of the workmen's
village of Saltaire, founded in 1851.

A. Sitting room.   C. Kitchen.
B. Bedrooms.   WC. Lavatory.

Figs 1135–6   The workmen's houses presented at the 1878 Paris Exhibition; model workmen's dwellings built in Pancras Road, London, in 1848.

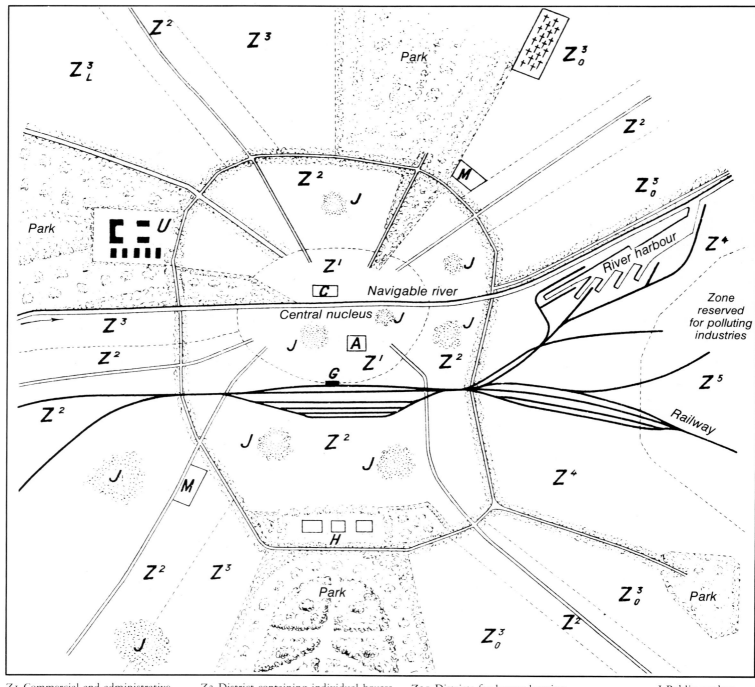

Z1 Commercial and administrative centre (tall, tightly packed buildings)
Z2 District containing houses for multiple occupation
Z3 District containing individual houses
Z4 Industrial zones
Z5 Zones for polluting industries
Z30 Working-class districts
Z31 Districts for luxury housing
G Central station
A Commercial centre (market, stock exchange)
C Civic Centre (town hall, prefecture)
J Public gardens
M Barracks
H Hospital
U University

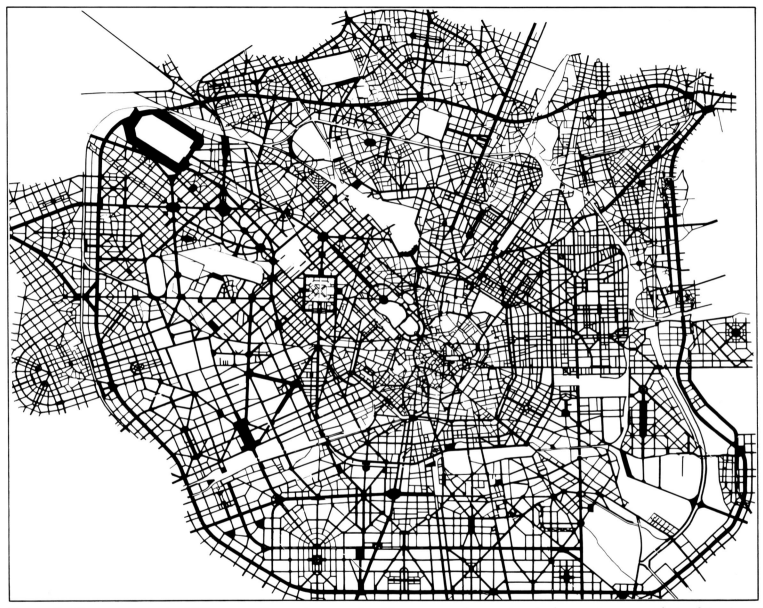

Fig. 1138   The street network of Milan, according to the 1934 plan. The squares and streets have broken up the new outskirts of the city in an attempt to weld them into a single unit.

Fig. 1137   (Facing) Plan of an ideal city, from a French town-planning treatise of 1928, in which the city's fabric is divided into seven zones.

Fig. 1139   A cast iron statue of Andromeda, produced by the Coalbrookdale Company and displayed at the Great Exhibition in London in 1851.

completely for the city's lack of balance. The harshness of the ordinary environment seemed irrevocable; beauty became a rare commodity and works of art were considered to be something out of the ordinary. They were executed and judged by specialists (the artists and art critics), they belonged to a separate world of dealers and collectors, and they were displayed in specific locales (exhibitions and museums). In fact, all the qualities lacking in the man-made environment were concentrated in painting and sculpture, which became the means of experimenting with the harmony that had disappeared from man's everyday surroundings.

7. The specialists needed to ensure the running of a city were compelled to accept a secondary role, dominated by the combined forces of bureaucracy and private ownership. They were not expected to question the decisions that had already been taken, merely to be competent enough to carry them out and capable enough to render them in an acceptable form.

In this way the distinction between technicians and artists, which had begun in the seventeenth century, became even more firmly entrenched. Technicians were supposed to make scientific studies of specific aspects of a project, but not of general problems (for example, calculations involving individual buildings and installations, but not how they should be distributed through a city or particular area of countryside). Artists were called on to deal with the external appearance of a city without discussing its structure because their field of work was deemed to be independent and irrelevant to the needs of everyday life. The technicians' field of choice, therefore, became severely restricted and extremely predictable, while the artists enjoyed greater freedom of choice, but in an unimportant and purely superficial area. Styles derived from earlier monuments and buildings were alternately adopted and dropped for a variety of reasons, some more convincing than others, and, because they were never permanent decisions, they were constantly being rediscussed.

This separation of technical from artistic led to a decline in the integrity, and hence also the formal qualities, of most of the articles in everyday use: works of art were glittering exceptions to the mass of trivial and vulgar objects that industry produced in ever-increasing quantities. Technical

Fig. 1140 *L'Atelier des Batignolles* by Fantin Latour. Standing: Scholderer, Renoir, Zola, Maître, Bazille, Monet. Seated: Manet and Astruc.

Figs 1141–3   Three *objets d'art*
displayed at the Great
Exhibition in London in 1851:
an easy chair, a console table
and mirror, and a piece of lace.

Fig. 1144   Joseph Paxton's Crystal Palace, erected in Hyde Park for the Great Exhibition, from a contemporary engraving.

Fig. 1145   The interior of the Crystal Palace.

Fig. 1146   Another interior view of the Crystal Palace, showing the great vaulted roof built to enclose one of the trees in Hyde Park.

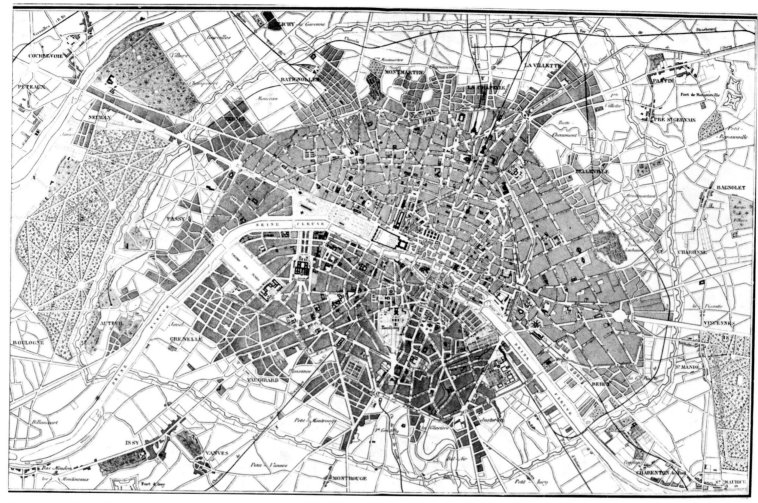

Fig. 1147   Plan of Paris in 1853, before Haussmann had started work.

practicability, cheapness and design were the respon-
sibilities of different departments, and no single person had
control over the end product.

In this situation the interests of the property owners —
parasitical and in direct conflict with the interests of productive capital — were quite clearly privileged. The cities
were designed so as to enable the landlords to obtain the
maximum rents possible. This meant that there was a vast
difference between the centre, as densely built-up as possible, and the less-populous peripheral areas, divided up
into different kinds of neighbourhood, even if the result was
both costly and inefficient. The cities were continually in
danger of grinding to a complete halt, because the public
services — the streets and utilities — were never adequate,
whilst the areas of land in private ownership were being
exploited as much as, or more than the laws allowed. These
technical and economic drawbacks were 'compensated' for
by a decisive political advantage: the people who really
suffered from the difficulties of city life were the poor, and
the city became a vast discriminatory apparatus, which

confirmed the dominion of the strong over the weak. The whole middle class was able to obtain privileges for their particular neighbourhood, if it needed some form of improvement, by taking advantage of this apparatus. By taking care of their interests, the property-owning classes protected the interests of the whole ruling class.

Let us examine the most important example: the transformation of Paris during the Second Empire, from 1851 to 1870.

A series of favourable circumstances — the far-reaching powers of Napoleon III, the extraordinary vision of Baron Haussmann, the presence of a number of highly-skilled technicians, and the existence of two very progressive pieces of legislation (one concerning compulsory purchase orders which was passed in 1840, and the other concerning public health passed in 1850) — combined to produce a comprehensive town-planning scheme within a relatively short space of time. The new Paris not only illustrated the success of the 'post-liberal' system, but also became the recognised model for cities throughout the world, from the mid-nineteenth century on.

The transformation of Paris consisted of:

(a) new streets, which were laid out in the city proper and also in the surrounding area. Old Paris — within the 1785 tax boundaries — had 384 kilometres of street; Haussmann opened a further 95 kilometres, cutting through the medieval quarters in all directions and obliterating 50 kilometres of old streets. This modern network also linked up with the baroque *boulevards*, which it integrated into the system, as well as reaching into the outskirts where Haussmann inaugurated a further 70 kilometres of street;

(b) new primary services: water supply, sewers, gas lighting, and a public transport system of horse-drawn omnibuses;

(c) new secondary services: schools, hospitals, colleges, barracks, prisons, and, above all, public parks — the Bois de Boulogne to the west of the city and the Bois de Vincennes to the east;

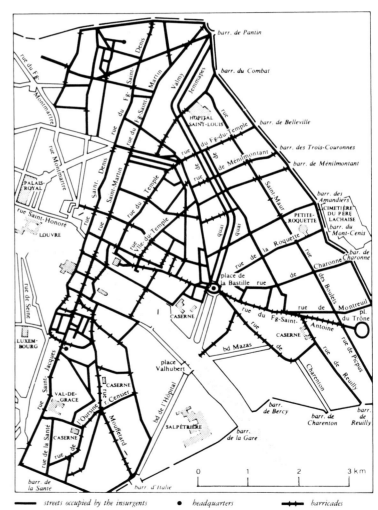

Figs 1148–9   An armed encounter in the Rue Saint-Antoine during the Revolution of 1848; a map of the streets controlled by the insurgents in June 1848.

―― *streets occupied by the insurgents*   ● *headquarters*   ➕ *barricades*

The landlord: 'Good! They're knocking down another house.
I will raise my tenants' rent by 200 francs'.

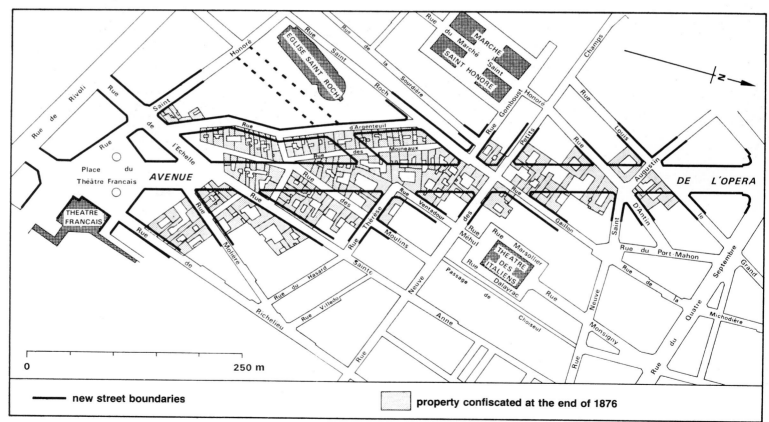

new street boundaries   property confiscated at the end of 1876

Figs 1150–2   The demolition work done by Haussmann in Paris: a cartoon by Daumier, published in 1854; a caricature of Haussmann as a demolition artist; a map of the Avenue de l'Opéra, showing the line of the projected street and the properties expropriated in accordance with the 1850 law.

Fig. 1153 The demolition to make way for the Rue de Rennes (the church on the right is that of Saint-Germain des Prés), as shown in an engraving published in *L'Illustration* in 1868.

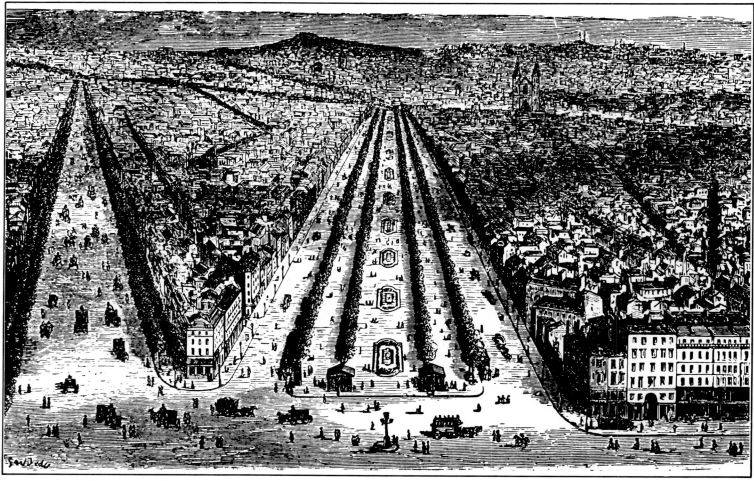

Fig. 1154   Bird's-eye view of the Boulevard Richard Lenoir (1863).

(d) the city's new administrative system: the eighteenth-century tax boundaries were abolished, and a series of outlying *communes* were annexed to the *Commune de Paris* (Paris City Council). In this way the city stretched as far as the outer fortification (an area of 8,750 hectares in all), and became divided into twenty *arondissements*, each of which enjoyed a degree of autonomy.

This programme ended up by costing the city a vast sum of money (2½ billion francs), which was borrowed from banks. During this period the population of Paris almost doubled — from 1,200,000 to 2 million — and the revenue of the Commune de Paris was increased tenfold, which meant that they were able to sustain a deficit and postpone repayment of their debts until a future date.

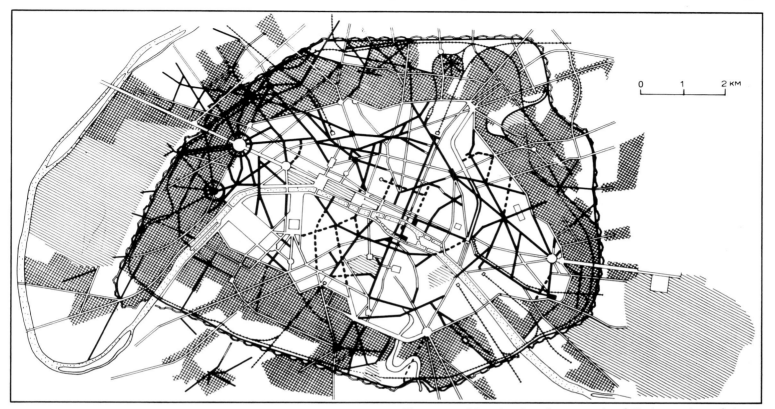

Fig. 1155 Map showing the vast scale of Haussmann's work in Paris. The black lines show the new streets, the cross-hatched areas are the new districts, and the horizontally-shaded areas are the two great parks on the outskirts: the Bois de Boulogne (left) and the Bois de Vincennes (right).

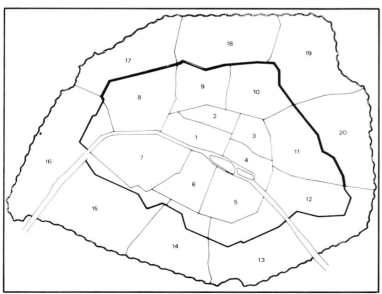

Fig. 1156 The arrangement of Paris into 20 *arondissements*; the black lines denote the old eighteenth-century tax boundaries.

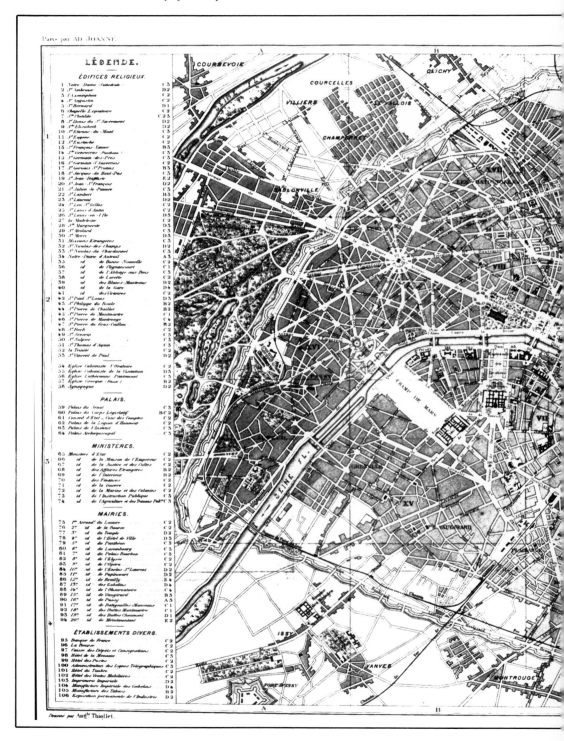

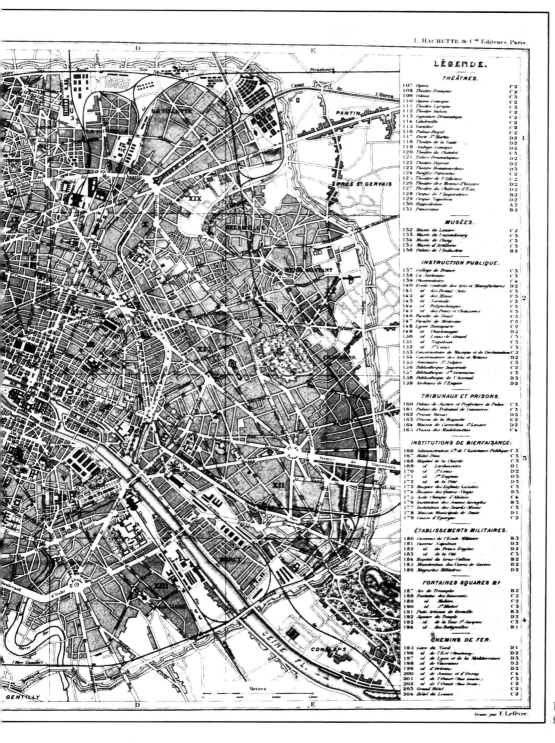

Fig. 1157   An 1873 map of Paris
from the Hachette Guide.

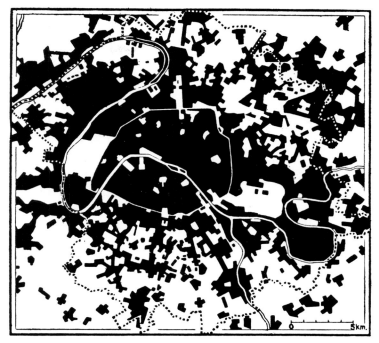

Figs 1158–9   An aerial photograph of central Paris, as it is now;
map of the urbanised areas surrounding Paris (the dotted line shows
the boundary of the Seine *département*).

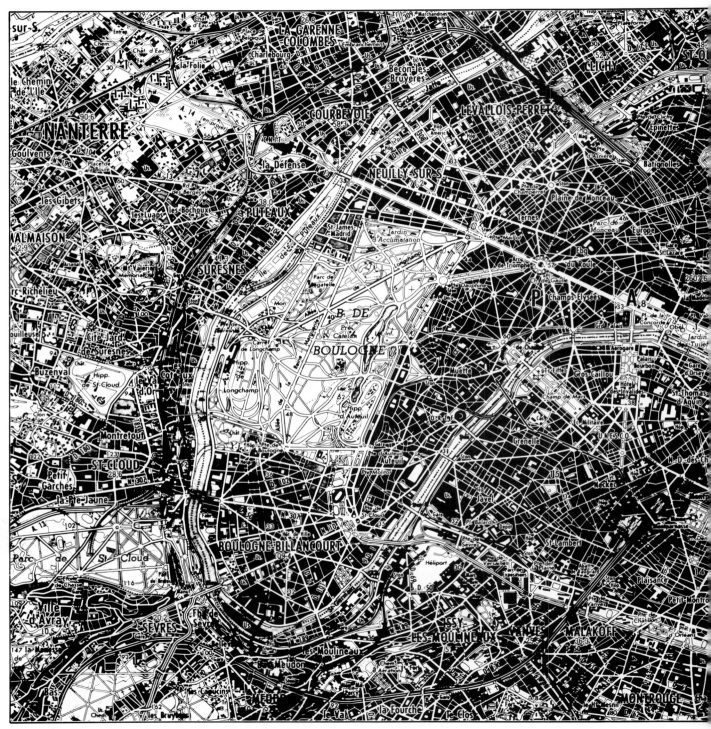

Fig. 1160   Map of Paris by the Istituto Geografico Militare (scale 1:50,000).

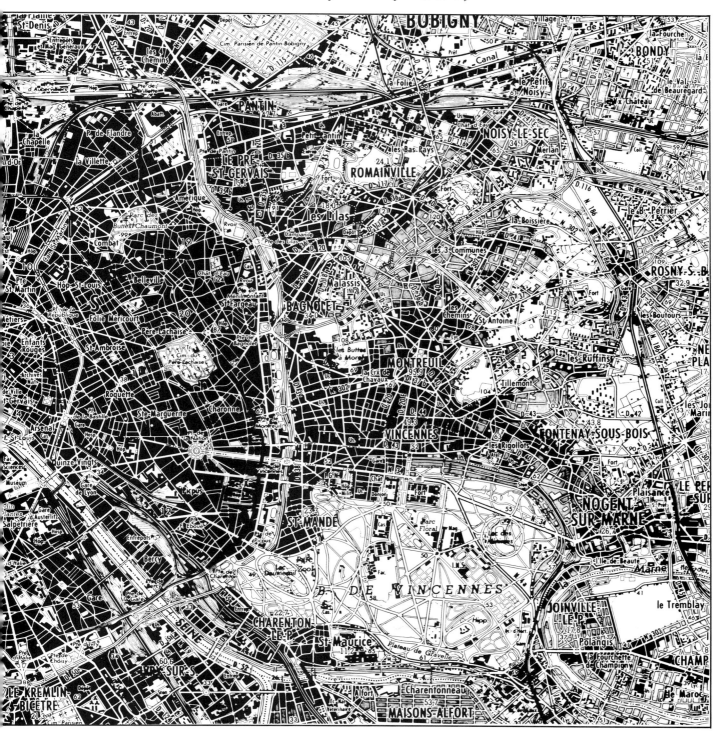

Fig. 1161   Aerial view of Paris, engraved on the occasion of the Exhibition of 1889; in the centre is the Champs Elysées leading towards the Louvre.

Haussmann endeavoured to improve the quality of the new environment by making use of the traditional tools of the town planner. He tried to impose a degree of geometrical regularity and chose some form of monumental structure, either ancient or modern, to provide the focal point of each new street. He enforced the architectural uniformity of the facades overlooking the most important streets and squares, the Place de l'Étoile, for example. But the vast extent of these new open spaces and the amount of traffic that frequented them prevented their being enjoyed as perspective views. The different areas lost their individuality and blended into each other, the façades of the build-

ings became merely a constantly unfolding backcloth, while the street furniture — lamps, kiosks, benches, trees — began to assume a much greater importance. The never-ending ebb and flow of traffic and pedestrians changed the city into a constantly moving spectacle, which was described by realist authors such as Flaubert and Zola and reproduced on canvas by Impressionists like Monet and Pissarro (Figs 1172, 1186, 1187). This was the face of the modern metropolis, where Baudelaire felt alone in the midst of millions of his fellow men; it was an anonymous organisation, which allowed hundreds of thousands of small private units to act independently of each other and in

Fig. 1162   Another aerial view of Paris in 1889; in the centre is again the Champs Elysées, leading from the Place de la Concorde to the Arc de Triomphe.

which people lived their own separate lives. The public and private sectors, which hitherto had always been inter-related, became separated in the bourgeois environment: on one hand there were the houses, workshops, studios and offices, isolated from each other as much as possible and into which it seemed that a person could penetrate only by magic or, as one writer of the time put it, with the help of a devil that could take the roofs off the houses. Even the different forms of entertainment and relaxation acquired a characteristic exclusivity from their small, enclosed surroundings — the theatres and salons — whose size bore no relation to that of the city as a whole. The new Théâtre de l'Opéra in

Paris had only enough seats for 2,200 people, while the city had two million inhabitants; compare this with ancient Athens, where almost the whole population could enter into the Theatre of Dionysos. On the other hand there were the pavements and public streets, where a person was obliged to mingle with his fellow men, but could still retain his anonymity. A single person or group of people could retain their individuality within the labyrinthine confines of the buildings, but they lost all personal identity upon entering into the open street, where crowds of people came into contact with each other, but rarely acknowledged each other's presence.

Figs 1163–4   A typical Parisian
mansion block, built during the time
of Haussmann (from an English
periodical of 1858); the two plans
show the ground floor, used for shops,
and one of the upper floors, containing
three middle-class apartments.

V. Vestibule.
S. Drawing-room.
B. Bedroom.
K. Kitchen.
W. Bathroom.
D. Dining-room.

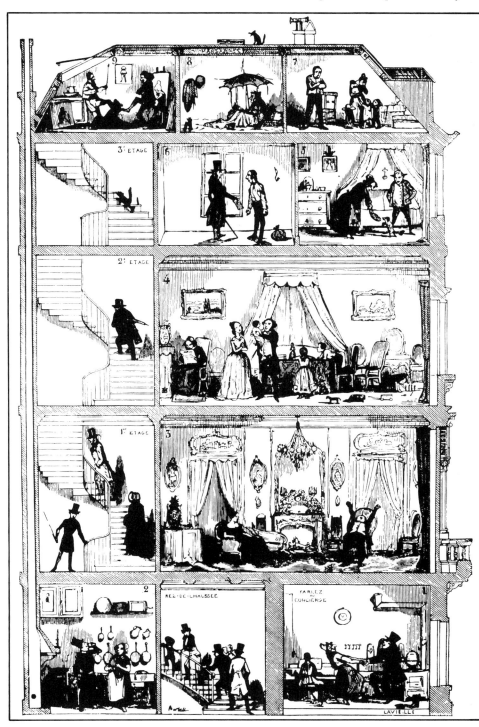

Fig. 1165 A sectional view of a
Parisian mansion block from 1853,
showing the different living conditions
of the tenants on each floor: the
concierge and his family on the ground
floor; the rich, upper-middle-class
couple relaxing on the first floor; the
middle-class family leading a slightly
more cramped life on the second floor;
the *petit bourgeois* on the third floor
(one of them is receiving a visit from
the landlord); the poor, the artists and
the old in the attics; the cat on the
roof.

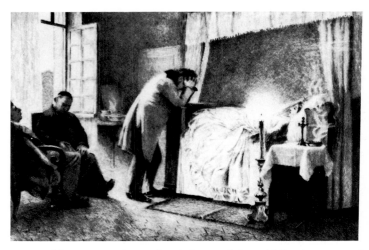

Figs 1166–8   Behind the closed doors of the middle-class town there unrolled all the private trials and tribulations that novelists presented as being the only reality worth writing about. These illustrations show scenes by Fourié for Gustave Flaubert's *Madame Bovary*: Madame Bovary taking her baby in her arms in the house of the wet nurse; Charles Bovary discovering his wife's suicide note; Madame Bovary on her deathbed, surrounded by her weeping husband and the sleeping figures of the priest and Monsieur Canivet.

Two examples of late
nineteenth-century interiors:

Fig. 1169   A morning-room,
designed by Bruce Talbert in 1869.

Fig. 1170   A drawing-room, designed
by Edward Godwin and published in
the catalogue of the furniture dealer,
William Watt, in 1877.

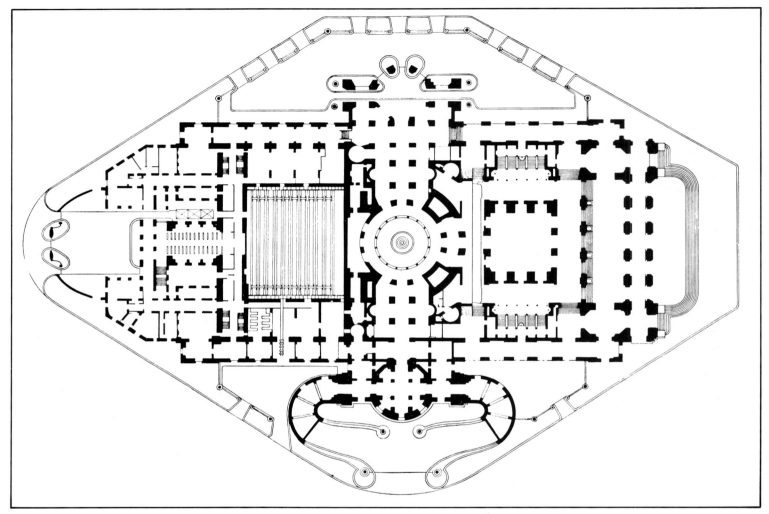

Fig. 1171 Plan of the Opéra in Paris, planned by Charles Garnier and built between 1861 and 1875 (scale 1:1,000).

European society was fascinated and perturbed by this new and contradictory environment. Modern technology had finally produced a new type of city, but instead of solving the old problems, it had revealed other, unexpected ones.

The new city, for all its unpleasantness and inconvenience, became accepted as the universal model, because there were no alternatives: intellectuals merely bewailed the passing of the ancient city, while revolutionary politicians had no interest in hazarding a description of cities in some far-distant future. The various aspects of industrial civilisation finally stood revealed in such a way that an appraisal could be made, and these newly-revealed problems became matters for immediate consideration.

Fig. 1172   View of the Avenue de l'Opéra, in a painting by Camille Pissarro from 1898; in the background can be seen the theatre's façade.

Fig. 1173 Cross-section view of the
Opéra in Paris, from an engraving
published in 1878.

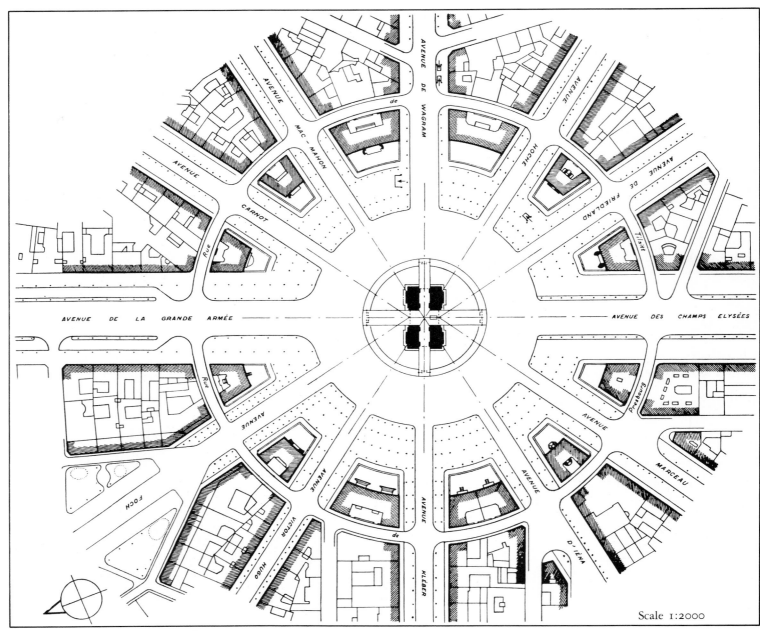

Fig. 1174   Map of the Place de l'Étoile in Paris.

Fig. 1175   Aerial view of the Étoile and the surrounding district.

Fig. 1176   Avenue des Champs Elysées.

Fig. 1177   Avenue de Wagram.

Fig. 1178   Avenue Foch.

Fig. 1179   Avenue d'Iéna.

(These four photographs were taken from the top of the Arc de Triomphe.)

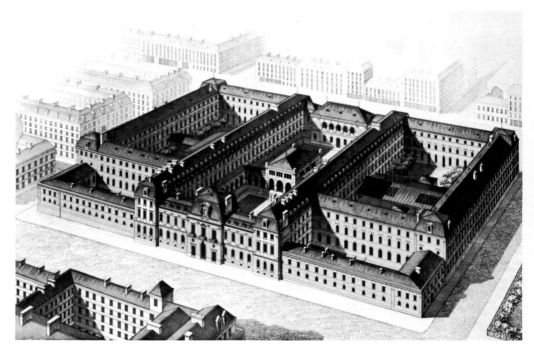

Two public buildings in Paris, built along the street front:

Fig. 1180   Collège Rollin (1877).

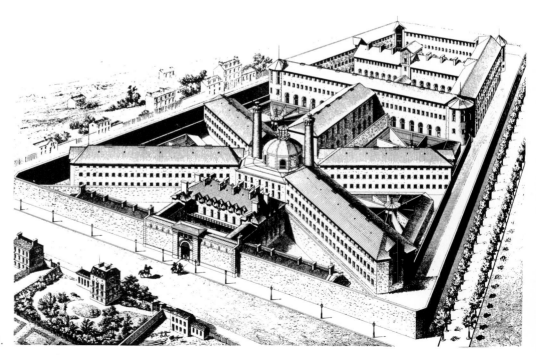

Fig. 1181   The Santé prison (1864).

Fig. 1182   A Parisian public building, set back from the street in the shape of a number of detached blocks: the Old People's Home of Sainte-Perine (1861). The two principal building models of the 'post-liberal' city also had a determining influence on the nature of public buildings.

Fig. 1183 The many faces of the open street in Paris (Saint-Lazare). The shop windows, the advertisements, the kiosks and the lamp posts all combine to provide a setting for the continual flow of pedestrians and traffic.

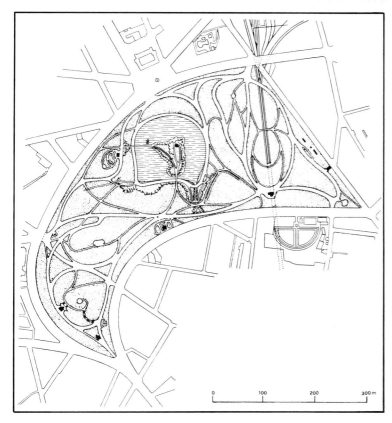

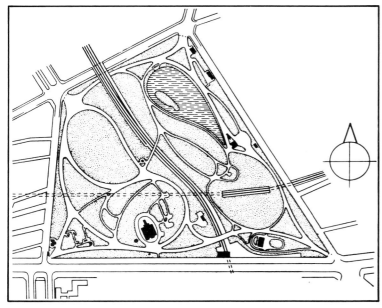

Figs 1184–5   Two public parks inaugurated in Paris during the Second Empire: the Parc des Buttes Chaumont and the Parc de Montsouris.

Fig. 1186 Claude Monet's painting of the Boulevard des Capucines (1873).

Fig. 1187   Claude Monet's painting of the Gare Saint-Lazare (1877).

Three examples of covered areas in Paris:

Fig. 1188   The interior of Les Halles Centrales, planned by Victor Baltard in 1853.

Fig. 1189   The interior of the 1855 Paris Exhibition.

Fig. 1190   The Winter Gardens by the Champs Elysées.

Three street views of Paris:

Fig. 1191   Traffic in the Rue Richelieu, from a 1904 photograph.

Fig. 1192 The Boulevard du
Temple.

Fig. 1193 The Parc Monceau.

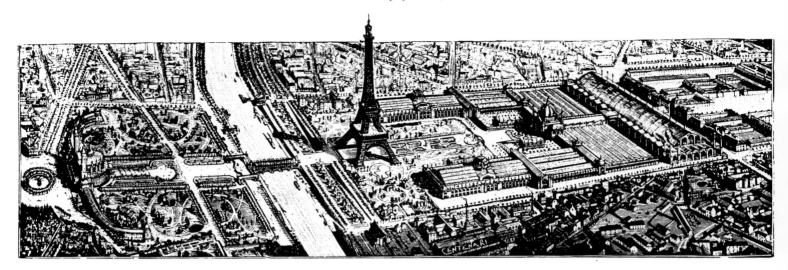

Figs 1194–5   Two major new urban developments in Paris: The layout of the 1889 Paris Exhibition, dominated by the Eiffel Tower;
Les Halles Centrales.

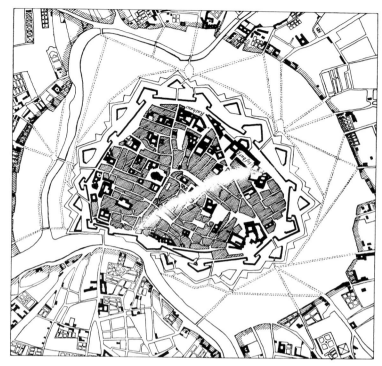

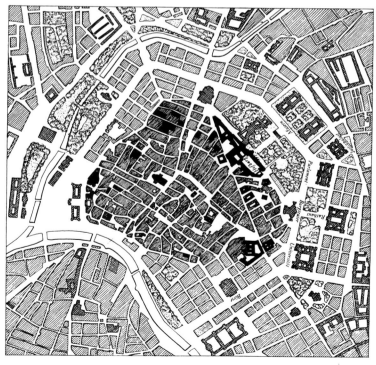

Let us now consider other cities during the second half of the nineteenth century.

No European city was so radically and comprehensively transformed as Paris, and the old shape of the other cities was a major factor in deciding their modern appearance: Vienna (Figs 1196–9), for example, where the area of clear ground between the medieval town and the baroque outskirts was built over from 1857 onwards; Florence (Fig. 1200), which became the new capital of Italy in 1864; and Barcelona (Fig. 1201), which was enlarged on the basis of a plan formulated in 1859.

New colonial cities (Figs 1202–15), however, could be created in strict accordance with the latest town-planning practices. The native towns were either left to one side or demolished because they were totally at variance with European ideas, and as a result they were often unimaginative and monotonous. They did however reveal more clearly the nature of the imported European system.

Towards the end of the century the European system was also able to be superimposed on the cities of North America (Figs 1216–23), where the traditional chequerboard pattern (see Chapter 9) had served its purpose throughout the nineteenth century, but where also the outlying districts of one-family houses were spreading rapidly and the city centres were being rebuilt at an ever-increasing rate. Plans were laid to cut through the chequerboard with a network of broad streets, to insert public parks and to lay out the central areas with great unified architectural precincts. Ultimately, however, it was possible only to make partial modifications, as the rigid, traditional set-up proved extremely difficult to alter.

Fig. 1196 The centre of Vienna during the early 1800s.

Fig. 1197 The centre of Vienna in the late 1800s, after the new layout of the Ring.

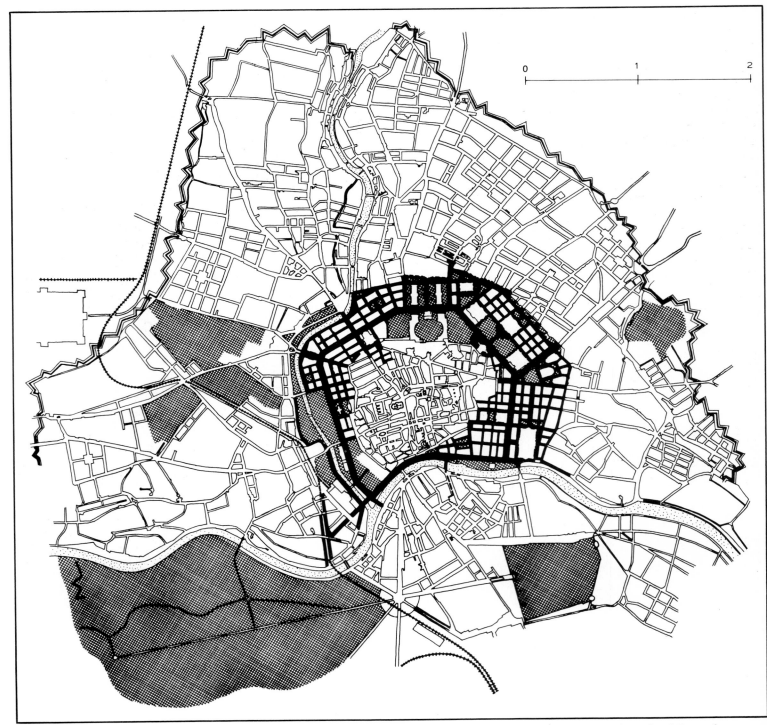

Fig. 1198 The layout of the Ring in Vienna; the black lines are the new streets, the cross-hatched areas are parks and public gardens.

Fig. 1199   Aerial view of the modern city of Vienna (cf. Figs 980–5).

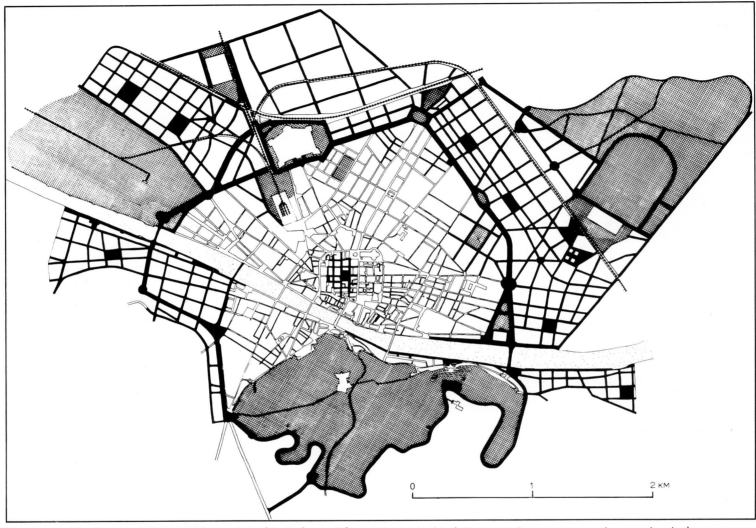

Fig. 1200   The layout of Florence (the capital of Italy from 1864 to 1871): the black lines are the new streets, the cross-hatched areas are parks and gardens. The scale is the same as that of Fig. 1198. Compare this map with those shown in Chapter 6.

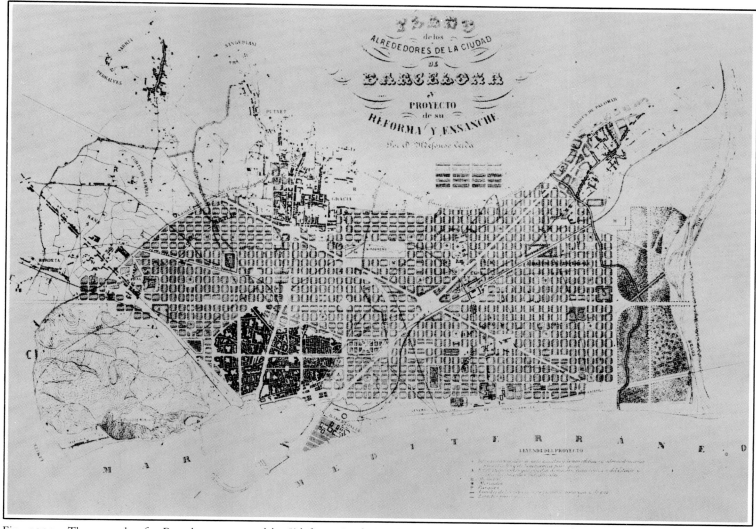

Fig. 1201   The new plan for Barcelona, proposed by Ildefonso Corda in 1859.

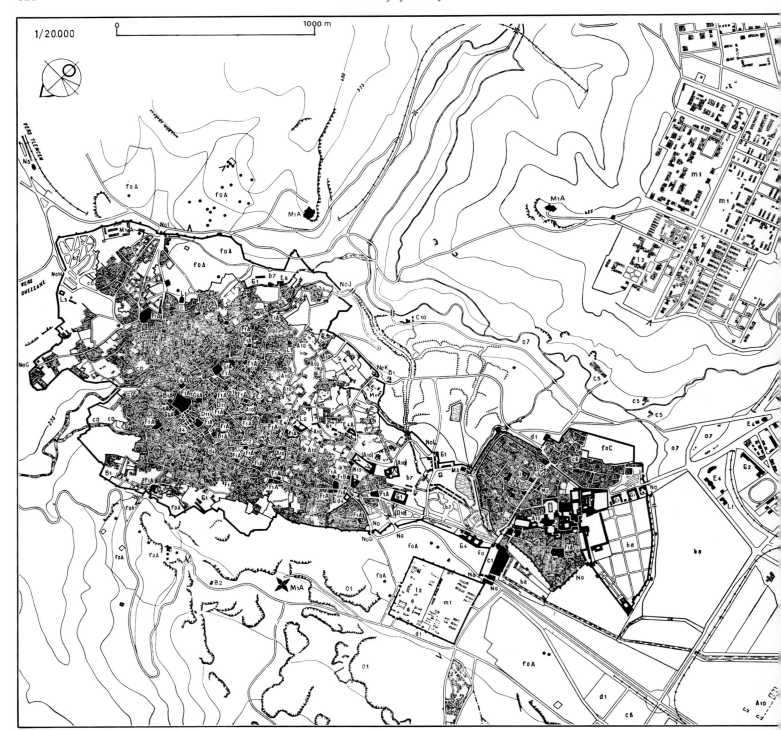

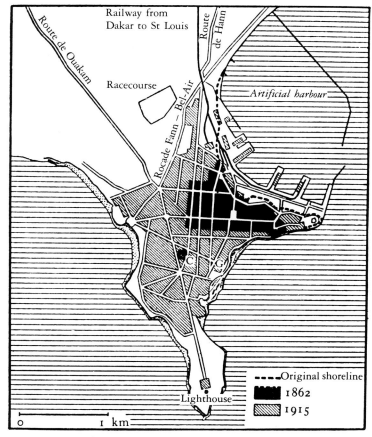

Railway from
Dakar to St Louis

Route de Ouakam

Route
de Hann

Racecourse

Rocade Fann – Bel-Air

Artificial harbour

Original shoreline

1862

1915

Lighthouse

0   1 km

Fig. 1203   Plan of Dakar, the capital of Senegal, laid out by the
French during the Second Empire.

VERS IFRANE

Fig. 1202   Map of Fez in Morocco; the European town was built
next to the Arab one and the two are clearly distinguishable.

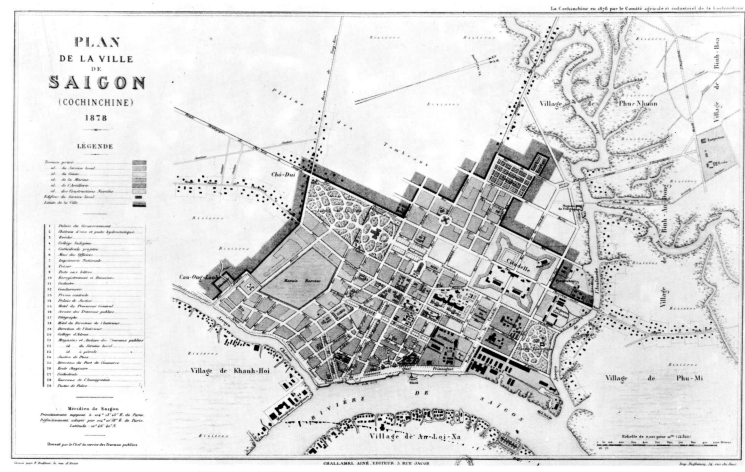

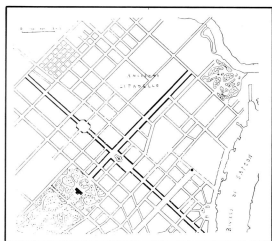

Figs 1204–5   Saigon, the capital of French Indo-China; this city
was also laid out during the Second Empire, on the site of a native
settlement of which no trace remains. Above, a map of the city in
1878, right, a detail of the city centre in 1891. From that time,
up until the end of colonial domination (1975), Saigon grew into a
metropolis of several million people.

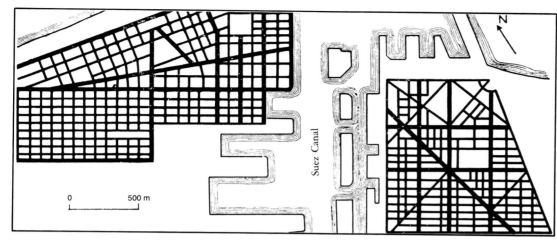

Fig. 1206   The twin towns of Port Said (1859) and Port Fuad (1914), built at the mouth of the Suez Canal.

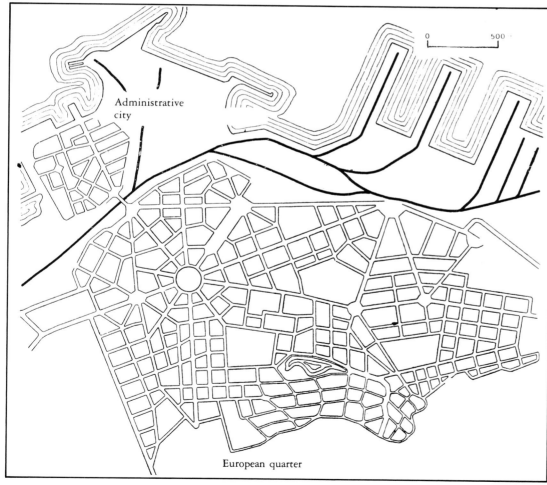

Fig. 1207   The town of Dalny, built in Manchuria around 1890.

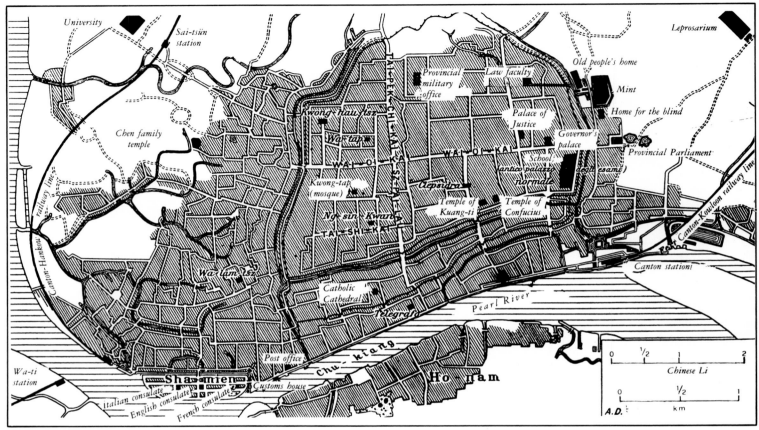

Fig. 1208   Canton, the main port of southern China, which
became an important centre for European merchants who for
centuries had occupied the nearby port of Macao. The Chinese city,
with its walls and chequerboard layout, can be clearly seen, while
in the south and west are the hastily constructed extensions with
their irregular street systems.

Fig. 1209   Peking, the Chinese imperial capital; a map of the
historical centre, showing the principal monuments.

Fig. 1210 Peking; a settlement built close to the fortified walls, as seen in an engraving from the end of the nineteenth century.

Fig. 1211 Peking; an avenue in the present-day city, laid out along European lines, but filled with pedestrians rather than cars.

Fig. 1214   Shanghai; a view of part of the European quarter, on the banks of the Yang Tze river.

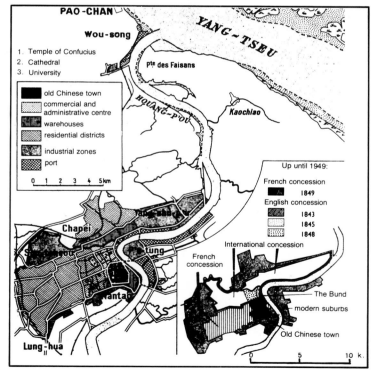

Figs 1212–13   Shanghai; an aerial view showing the English concession at the centre of the photograph, while to the right can be seen part of the Chinese town. Map showing the European concessions.

Fig. 1215   A street scene in Shanghai during the European occupation; the cars mingle freely with the traditional traffic in the 'corridor street'.

Figs 1216–17   The transformation of twentieth-century Chicago (cf. Fig. 943). The commercial centre has been rebuilt, with skyscrapers taking the place of the original houses, while the proliferation of single family houses on the outskirts was originally made possible by the development of the railways and, later, by the rise in private car ownership.

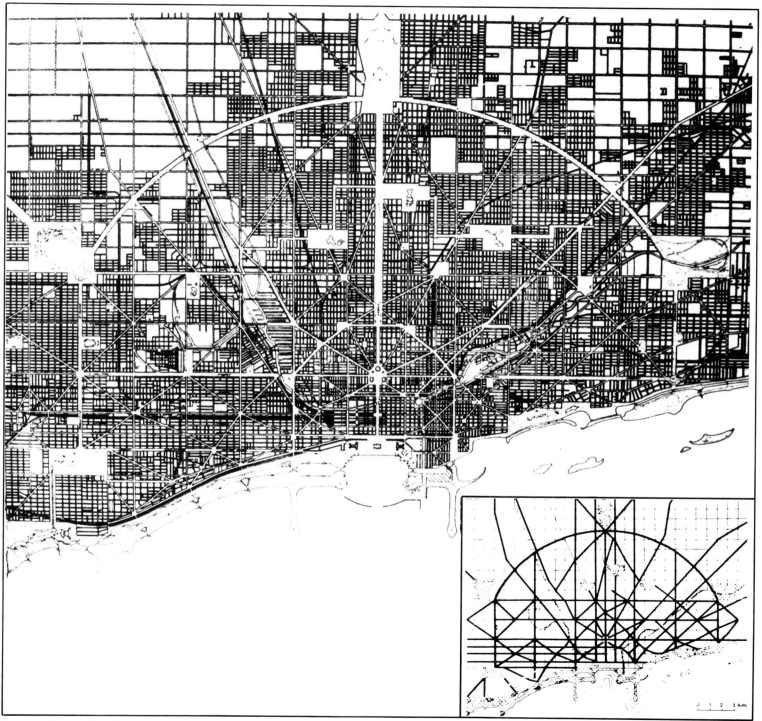

Figs 1218–19   The first attempt to rearrange Chicago during its period of transformation: the plan proposed by Burnham and Bennett in 1912, showing the new network of main streets and roads superimposed on the traditional chequerboard pattern.

Figs 1220–1   The skyscrapers built on the southern tip of Manhattan, from the end of the nineteenth century onwards; their style, whether modern or traditional, does not alter their basic architectural qualities or the effect they have on the cityscape.

Fig. 1222   A residential suburb of Houston, Texas, in which each house belongs to a single family.

Fig. 1223   A new motorway under construction in the heart of Boston.

13
The modern city

Modern architecture involved the search for a new alternative to the traditional urban model and it first began when the artists and the technicians, who had been called on to collaborate in the running of the 'post-liberal' city, became capable of producing a new method of working, free of the former institutional divisions.

The artists, entrusted with the task of finding a new image for the 'post-liberal' city, started by reacting against its ugliness: they began to criticise their surroundings and to attack the methods that had produced them.

The new wave of architects — Horta, Van de Velde, Wagner — were not content with merely borrowing a style from the past; they used the freedom of action that they had been granted to search for a new model, one that was original and not dependent on tradition.

The new free-thinking school of painters began to question the truths of external reality, patiently analysing and dissecting the world about them. The Impressionists — Manet, Monet, Pissarro — strove to isolate form and colour from reality and endow then with new qualities, while the neo-Impressionists — Cézanne, Van Gogh, Gauguin — explored the hidden structure (the linear outline, the volume, the colours) that lay behind the visual exterior. The Fauves and Cubists — Matisse, Picasso, Braque — succeeded in distorting the conventional image of visual reality, thereby putting an end to the age-old function of the painter: that of establishing an immutable rule by which the external world could be recognised and interpreted. In the middle of the century the artists of the avant-garde began to

call into question all the established rules concerning the organisation of the physical environment (the styles derived from past eras and the principle of correspondence between reality and representation) together with all their cultural and formal consequences.

The technicians, working within their restricted and specialised environments, were unable to control the consequences of their work. But they were continually modifying the everyday lives of mankind with ever-increasing speed and effect, making it more and more difficult to impose the traditional forms of control described in the preceding chapter.

The invention of the Bessemer Process in 1856 meant that the use of steel became even more widespread, thereby allowing the manufacture of new machines and new structures of a type never previously seen: large roof spans with no intermediate supports, for example the rotunda at the 1878 Exhibition in Vienna with a diameter of 102 metres, and the Galerie des Machines at the 1889 Exhibition in Paris, which measured 115 by 420 metres (Fig. 1224); suspension bridges of ever greater lengths ranging from the 488 metre long Brooklyn Bridge of 1873, to the Washington Bridge over the Hudson, built in 1928 and measuring 1,050 metres in length; and higher and higher skyscrapers, from the early twenty to thirty storey buildings in Chicago erected at the end of the nineteenth century, to those built in New York in the opening decades of this century with 100 or more floors (Figs 1226–7). The invention of the dynamo in 1869 allowed electricity to be used as a driving

Figs 1224–5   The Galerie des Machines at the 1889 Paris Exhibition: a comprehensive display of the machinery of the day from all over the world. A contemporary caricature of Gustave Eiffel, who built the 300 metre high tower for the 1889 Exhibition (see also Fig. 1194).

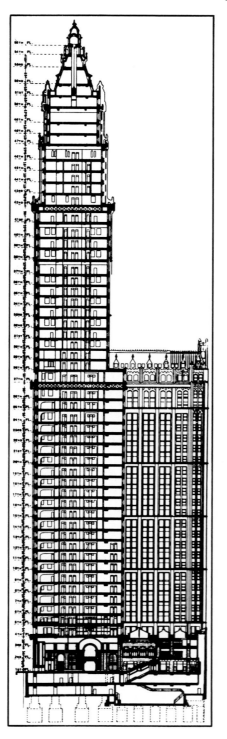

Figs 1226–7   Two American steel-frame buildings: the Woolworth Building in New York (1910), and the Leiter Building in Chicago (1885).

force and made endless applications possible: the telephone in 1876, the electric light in 1879 and the lift in 1887. The invention of the internal combustion engine in 1885 enabled petroleum to be used to propel ships, cars and, later, aeroplanes.

The new methods of construction made it increasingly difficult to make a separate decision about a building's external appearance: whether it should be designed along traditional lines or in accordance with the latest ideas of avant-garde architecture. Also, the greatly increased amounts of traffic and the new urban services — gas, electricity, telephone, trams, underground railways — had to be crammed into the inadequate public areas of the 'post-liberal' city, at a time when cities were expanding more and more rapidly. London had achieved a population of 4 million inhabitants at the end of the nineteenth century, and cities throughout the world were growing at the same rate as those in Europe.

These changes placed severe strains on the traditional methods of running a city and led to popular demands for a renewal of the urban environment.

Fig. 1228　A landscape by Piet Mondrian (1912).

A few works by the neo-Plastic group:
Fig. 1229   A beach carriage, built by Gerrit Rietveld in 1919.

During the second decade of this century, a period that included World War I, these new trends in art and technology became united in a single movement. The end of painting as a means of reproducing a fixed concept of reality paved the way for a new artistic function: the projection of a different kind of world, independent of traditional models but conforming to the objective researches of technical science.

The artists who had participated during the 1920s in the neo-Plastic movement — Van Doesburg and Mondrian — provided an exact explanation of the nature of this plan to bridge the traditional gap between art and technology.

The environment and man's everyday life are lacking, by virtue of their imperfect state and their barren necessity. And so art becomes a means of escape. In art man seeks the beauty, the harmony, which is lacking or which he pursues vainly in his life and his environment. Beauty and harmony have become irrealisable ideals: placed in art, they have been banished from life and the environment.

Tomorrow, however, the realisation of a plastic equilibrium within the concrete reality of our environment will take the place of works of art. Then there will be no need for paintings and sculptures, because we will be living in a realisation of art. Art is only a substitute for when there is not enough beauty in life; it will vanish as life regains its equilibrium. (Mondrian)

This statement of intent — to restore balance to the man-made environment — abolished the difference between the objective methods of scientific work and the subjective methods of artistic work. 'Art and technology are indivisible, and the pure plastic invention will always conform to practical exigencies, because they are both questions of balance. Our times (the Future!) demand this equilibrium and it can be achieved in only one way' (Mondrian). But the division of the technical side into different sectors and the arbitrary way in which responsibility for the artistic elements was decided, had to be abandoned. The new wave of architects accepted the objective, experimental and collective methods of modern scientific research, but they wanted to remain free of domination by institutionalised authority and they were already on their guard against the use of science and technology as a means of obtaining power. This indeed happened, with tragic consequences, in later years.

Fig. 1230   An abstract painting by
Piet Mondrian (1928).

Figs 1231–2   The Schroeder House,
built by Rietveld in 1924, and a
model of the Rosenberg House,
planned by Van Doesburg and Van
Eesteren in 1923.

Fig. 1233 Gino Severini.
Composition with mechanical objects.

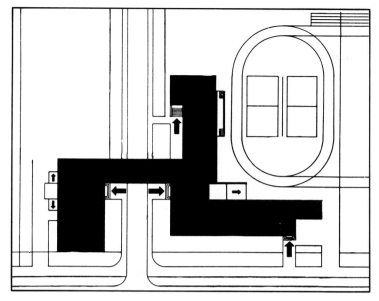

Figs 1234–5   Plan and aerial view of the Bauhaus building at Dessau, built by Walter Gropius in 1926.

Fig. 1236   The emblem of the Bauhaus, during the 1919–21 period.

The greatest names of modern architecture — Walter Gropius (1883–1969), Mies van der Rohe (1886–1969), Le Corbusier (1887–1965) — were the first men to try and put this method into practice in the field of building and town planning. From 1919 to 1928 Gropius ran a special school, the Bauhaus, in which the teachers were some of the best modern artists (Klee, Kandinsky, Schlemmer) and where the students learned how to design the whole range of objects that make up the modern environment, from furniture to whole urban districts (Figs 1234–6, 1271–80). Mies van der Rohe designed buildings that were extremely simple and acted as models for other architects, and he also supervised some important public works, one of which was an experimental district at Stuttgart, for which modern architects from all over the world were invited to design the buildings (Figs 1237–50). Le Corbusier worked in Paris as a freelance architect, but he was able to see only a few of his projects realised: a certain number of private houses (Figs 1252–9) and also some minor public buildings. His plans for more ambitious projects (the headquarters of the League of Nations in Geneva, the Palace of the Soviets in Moscow and later the UN Headquarters in New York) were either turned down or completed by other people independently (Figs 1251, 1260–1).

Figs 1237–9   Two photo-montages and a plan of the steel and
glass skyscraper planned by Ludwig Mies van der Rohe in 1921.

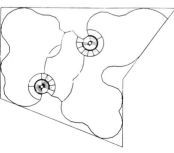

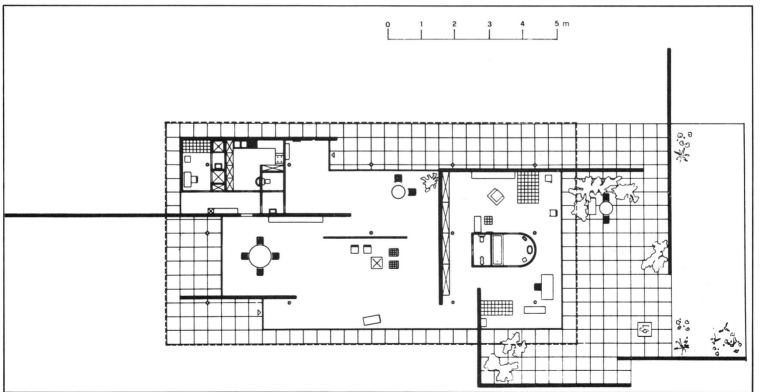

Figs 1240–2   Two interior views and the ground plan of Mies van der Rohe's experimental house, completed for the 1931 Berlin Architectural Exhibition.

Figs 1243–4   Crown Hall on the campus of Chicago's Illinois
Institute of Technology, completed by Mies van der Rohe in 1955.

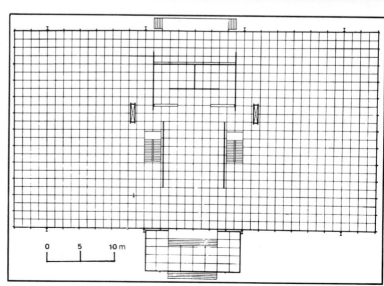

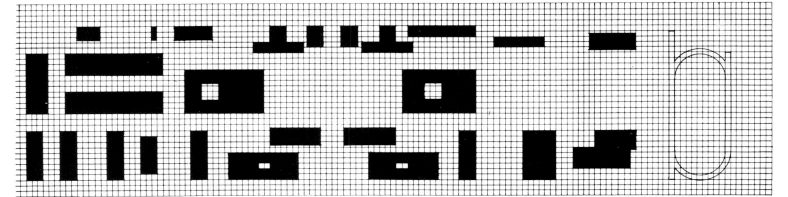

Figs 1245–6 The campus in Chicago; an aerial view, showing the city centre in the background, and a general plan.

Figs 1247–50 The Weissenhof
complex, completed at Stuttgart in
1927 for an exhibition of the German
Werkbund, arranged by Mies van der
Rohe. A contemporary aerial
photograph, the general layout, and a
view and plan of Mies van der Rohe's
house (1).

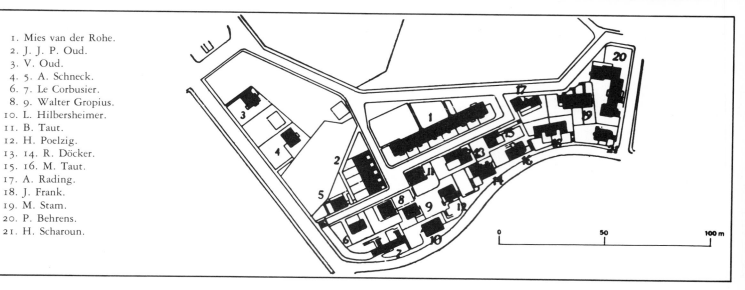

   1. Mies van der Rohe.
   2. J. J. P. Oud.
   3. V. Oud.
   4. 5. A. Schneck.
   6. 7. Le Corbusier.
   8. 9. Walter Gropius.
  10. L. Hilbersheimer.
  11. B. Taut.
  12. H. Poelzig.
  13. 14. R. Döcker.
  15. 16. M. Taut.
  17. A. Rading.
  18. J. Frank.
  19. M. Stam.
  20. P. Behrens.
  21. H. Scharoun.

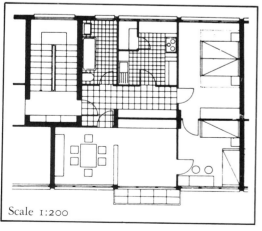

Scale 1:200

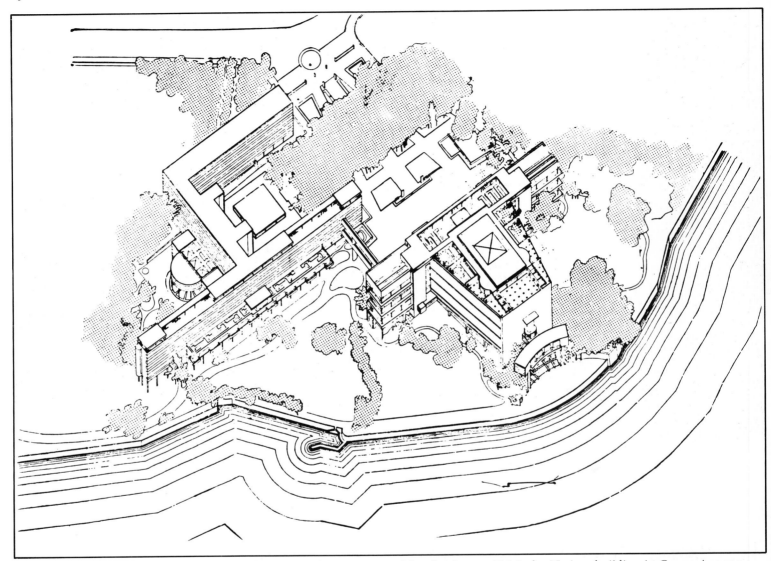

Fig. 1251   Aerial view of Le Corbusier's plan, submitted to the competition for the new Palais des Nations building in Geneva in 1927.

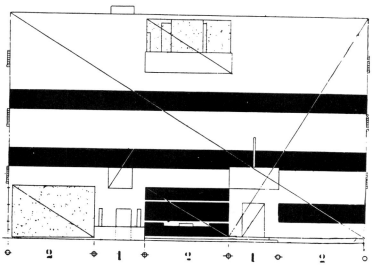

Figs 1252–3   The Villa Stein, built by Le Corbusier at Garches near Paris in 1926. Photograph and drawing of the façade, showing the geometrical lines that govern the proportions of the filled spaces (in white) and the empty ones (in black).

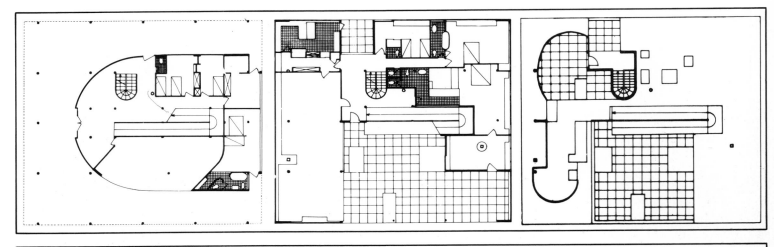

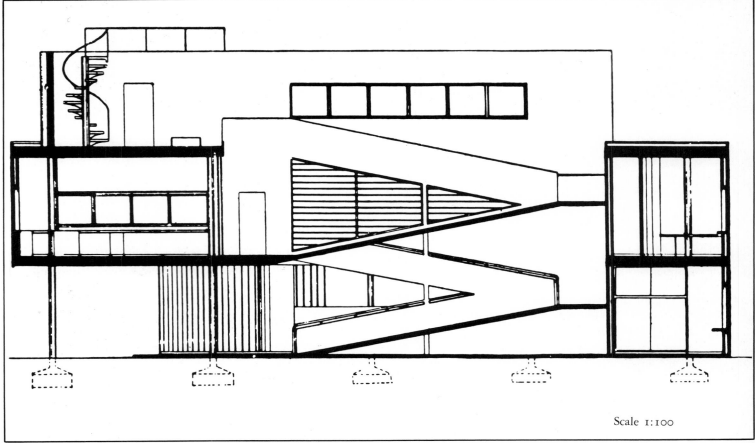

Scale 1:100

Figs 1254–9   The Villa Savoie, built by Le Corbusier at Poissy near Paris in 1930. Ground plans, sectional view and two photographs taken in 1957 (the villa has now been restored by the state).

Figs 1260–1   The glass palace of the United Nations in New
York, built by Harrison and Abramowitz between 1948 and 1950,
on the basis of a sketch by Le Corbusier in 1946.

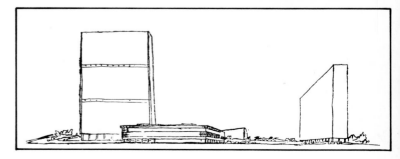

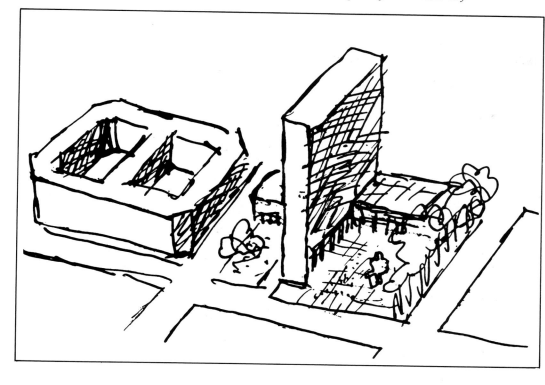

Fig. 1262 A design by Le Corbusier for the Ministry of Education in Rio de Janeiro, executed between 1937 and 1943.

Against this difficult background the modern architects were prepared to present themselves as artists of the avant-garde, because in that way society would give them more leeway. In fact they were embarking on a process of collective research, working together on the same problems and offering comparable solutions, which were collated and perfected over the years. We will now describe the main aspects of this common research programme, which continued for the next fifty years and is still in progress today.

1. An analysis of the activities taking place in the modern city.

The idea of the city as an integral entity did not prevent a rigorous process of analysis to isolate its constituent elements, that is the combination of activities that dominated urban life; Le Corbusier listed four of these:

— living
— working
— cultivating the body and the mind
— moving about

In the 'post-liberal' city the privileged activities were those concerned with production, together with the tertiary functions (commerce and movement); all the others were more or less ignored. This system of priorities was criticised, and another was established, in which:

— housing, where people spent the greater part of their days, became the most important element in the city; but housing was considered to be inseparable from the services that formed its immediate complement (the 'extensions of the home' as Le Corbusier put it);

— productive activities (agriculture, industry, commerce) were all placed on an equal footing, and they determined the three basic types of human establishment;

— 'the scattered farm' in the countryside
— 'the linear industrial city'
— 'the radiocentric trading city' (Fig. 1263);

— recreational activities were up-graded, so that they required their own special open spaces, spread throughout the city — the areas of green for games or sport at the foot of the houses, neighbourhood parks, municipal parks, national parks. These green areas, which in the middle-class

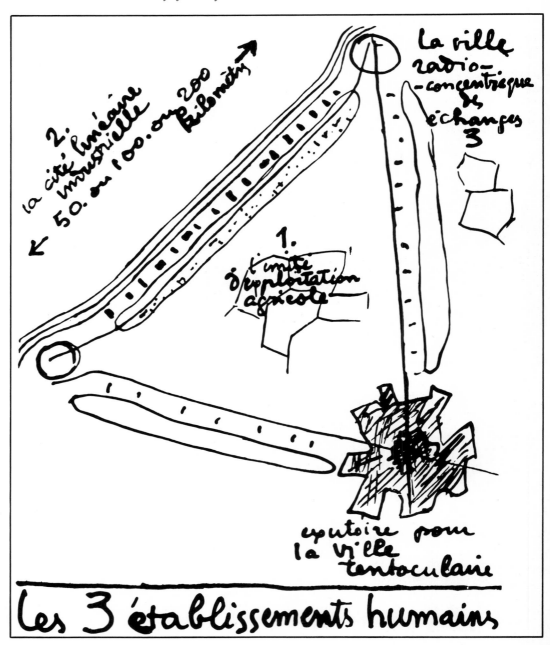

Fig. 1263   The three human
settlements: a drawing by Le Corbusier
in 1947.

1. 'The unit of agricultural exploitation'
2. 'The linear industrial city'
3. 'The radiocentric trading city'
These three settlements were designed to
take the place of today's tentacular city,
which mixes up the three functions and
hinders their development.

cities were isolated patches in the densely built-up environment, were to form a single stretch of land, in which all the other elements of the city would be distributed. The city would thus become a park equipped to deal with all the activities of urban life (Figs 1264–9);

— the traditional means of moving about in the city were categorised according to the method of transport and the needs of the other activities, in order of their importance. The 'corridor street', with its pavements for pedestrians and its carriageway where all types of vehicle intermingled, was to be supplanted by a system of separate streets for pedestrians, bicycles and slow and fast vehicles, which would be liberally provided through the length and breadth of the 'park-city'.

This new urban structure was intended to overcome the traditional dualism of the town and the country, and also its natural consequence: the appropriation of urban land by private individuals for financial gain. From the very beginning, modern architects criticised the combination of public interest and private ownership that formed the basis of the bourgeois city, and they clearly indicated the alternative: the transfer of all urban land into public ownership.

Fig. 1264 The fabric of the modern city, designed to replace that of the traditional city: a plan by Le Corbusier for the rehabilitation of an area of slums in Paris (1936).

Fig. 1265 The new landscape of the modern city, showing the trees and grass in the foreground; a drawing by Le Corbusier.

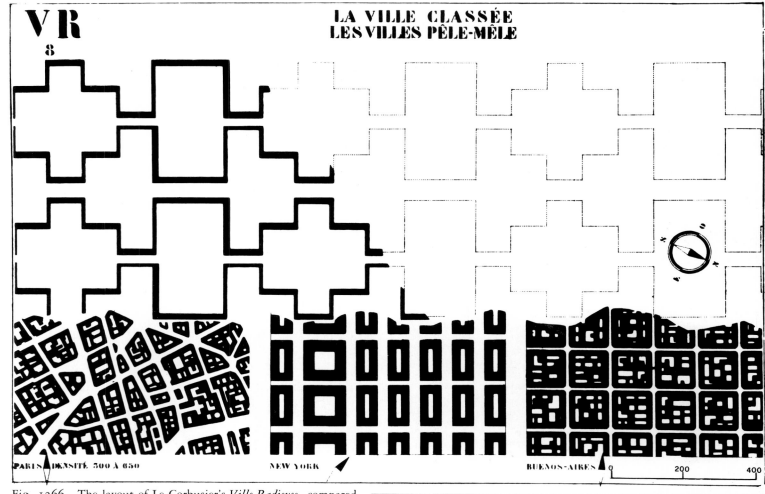

Fig. 1266   The layout of Le Corbusier's *Ville Radieuse*, compared
with those of Paris, New York and Buenos Aires (cf. Fig. 1097).

Fig. 1267   Sectional view of one of the buildings of the *La Ville
Radieuse*. Each home faces directly on to greenery and the sky; the
roads for vehicles are elevated so as not to hamper the free passage
of pedestrians.

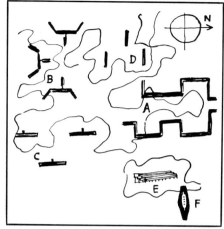

Figs 1268–9 Two further designs by Le Corbusier: the landscape of the modern city, governed by the course of the sun; the various types of building, spread out in the areas of green, which go to make up the modern city.

A. Residential blocks, joined together to form a kind of Greek key pattern.
B. Residential or office blocks, in the shape of a claw.
C, D. Linear buildings, running from east to west or north to south.
E. Stepped buildings.
F. Office skyscrapers, made wider in the middle in order to accommodate the central lifts.

2. Defining the minimum number of elements needed for each urban function.

The principle of working from the particular to the general forms part of the traditional scientific process, and it was accepted in architectural research from the beginning, both as a corrective measure and as a way of ensuring control over each stage of a project. Every structure should be broken down into its basic elements, and then rebuilt by reassembling these elements in a new and rational way.

The research work done by the painters had demonstrated the possibility of using this method to destroy the traditional concept of shape and form, by starting again from scratch and revealing a whole new visual world. The architects learned to start their plans by first considering the fundamental constructive elements (the materials, the methods of construction), which they combined freely, according to the particular needs (technical, economic, psychological) of the time. This process could obviously not be gone through from the start on every occasion: certain combinations were needed which could be used to solve a particular problem that recurred and which would also lend themselves to association with other more complex combinations.

Such combinations are often encountered in our daily lives: the union of an ink-filled tube, a writing point, a case and a cap produces a ballpoint pen, thereby solving a specific problem: how to write by hand on a sheet of paper. The union of an internal mechanism, an external plate and a metal shaft produces a handle, which solves the problem of how to open a door. But the handle, together with the frame, the hinges and the panel form a complete door; the door, together with windows, walls, a floor, a ceiling and furniture forms a room, which can be used for sleeping, eating, studying etc.; a number of rooms make a house, a number of houses form a district, a number of districts make a city, and so on.

If the problem is a simple one (opening and shutting) the object can have a constant form, with few variations: if, however, the problem is a more complex one (sleeping, studying) the object may come in many forms, with numerous variations. In order to design a room for sleeping there is no need to redesign the door, whose opening and shutting function remains constant; the door can be the same for a

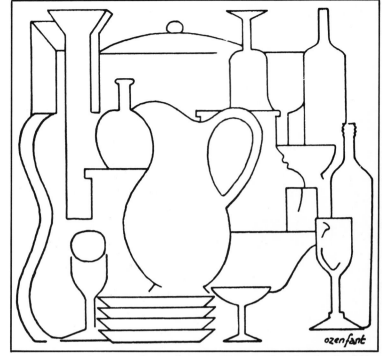

Fig. 1270   A group of everyday utensils, in a drawing by Amédée Ozenfant (1925).

large number of rooms, and need only be changed when there is a specific problem to be confronted, for example, the provision of greater security for a house or other building from the outside, the sound-proofing of a particular room.

The scientific method allows these kinds of problems to be tackled logically, and also pinpoints the smallest number of functional elements needed for a particular object, that is the simplest combination that will solve a specific problem and remain constant even when it forms part of other, more complicated combinations.

This research was immediately successful when applied to the simplest objects, whose function was to solve a well defined problem. Indeed, from the very beginning modern architects redesigned the whole range of accessories that play a major part in everyday life — chairs, tables, beds, crockery, glassware, lamps — and some of the prototype models that they have developed have been used ever since (Figs 1270–80).

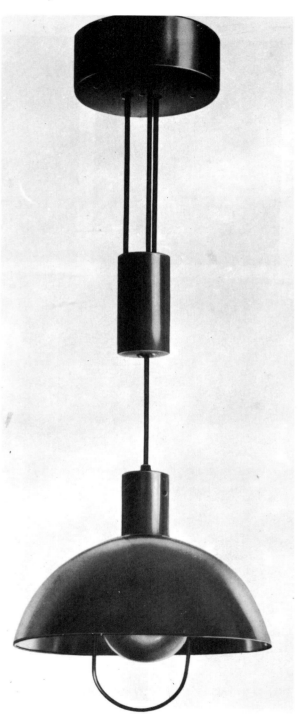

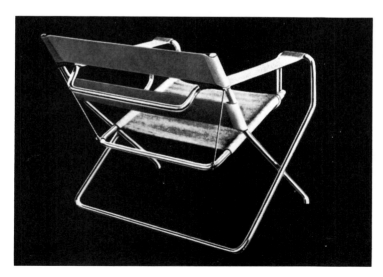

Figs 1271–3   Three metal objects designed by the Bauhaus in Dessau: two lamps by Marianne Brandt and a folding chair by Marcel Breuer (1924–5).

Fig. 1274　A bentwood relaxing chair, designed by Marcel Breuer in 1936 for the English company of Isokon.

Fig. 1275 The chassis of the Adler automobile, designed by Gropius in 1930.

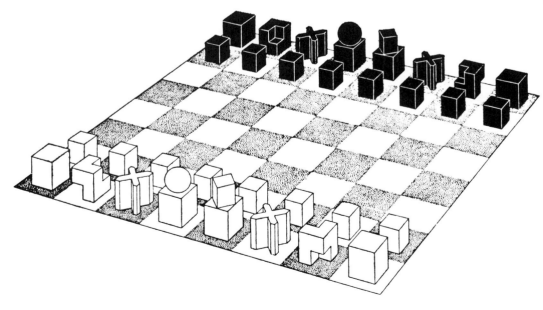

Fig. 1276 A chess set designed by Joseph Hartwig in the Bauhaus in 1924.

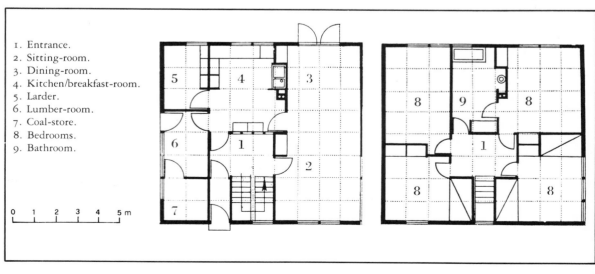

1. Entrance.
2. Sitting-room.
3. Dining-room.
4. Kitchen/breakfast-room.
5. Larder.
6. Lumber-room.
7. Coal-store.
8. Bedrooms.
9. Bathroom.

0 1 2 3 4 5 m

Figs 1277–80   Two interior views and plans of Gropius' prefabricated houses in the Weissenhof exhibition at Stuttgart (see Fig. 1247), its contents including the metal furniture, lamps and crockery designed in the Bauhaus during the preceding years.

This research, however, did not recognise traditional limitations: it progressed beyond the design of individual utensils and implements into the realms of composite work, formed from a combination of the various design elements. Its principal goal was the definition of the basic functional elements corresponding to the four urban activities already mentioned: living, working, cultivating the body and the mind, moving about. Because living was considered to be the prime function, the smallest habitable unit — the home — became the basic element of the new city.

By treating the home — and not the building — as the starting point for the reorganisation of the city, it became possible to criticise and reject the characteristic buildings of the bourgeois city: the mansion blocks with their street frontage and the small villas set back from the road. These buildings depended on the relationship between private

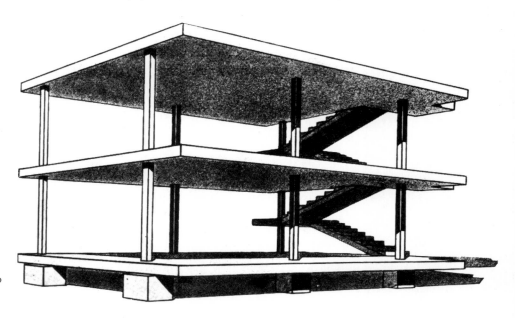

Fig. 1281   The reinforced concrete structural framework of the Domino houses, planned by Le Corbusier in 1918.

property and the public areas, and they became important because the 'post-liberal' city was based on precisely that relationship, as we have already seen. The home, on the other hand, is the element that most concerns the inhabitants of a town or city, and the acceptance of the home as the starting point for modern architecture involved the restructuring of the urban environment to satisfy the needs of the inhabitants, not the interests of officialdom and landlords.

Therefore, modern architectural research involved:

— the first ever detailed analysis of the internal structure of houses, and of the relationship between their component elements (the rooms), and an examination of the principal variations in their distribution;

— the establishment of rules to govern the grouping of homes in accordance with the needs of their occupants, that is by considering the relationship of the houses with each other and also with the public services. The houses and different types of services — schools, hospitals, shops, playing fields, entertainment centres, pedestrian walkways, streets — together went to make up a neighbourhood, the principal unit of the modern city.

3. Research into the ways in which the functional elements could be most effectively combined requires the definitive structuring of the modern urban complex.

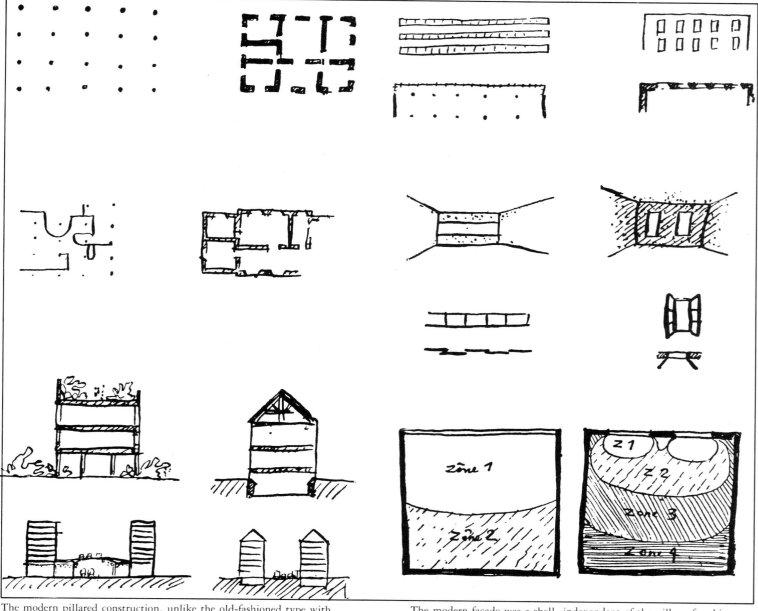

The modern pillared construction, unlike the old-fashioned type with supporting walls, allowed the basic layout to be freely adapted, the building to be raised off the ground and the roof to be substituted for a terrace with a garden. In this way twice the ground area of the building could be recovered for use as a green area or for traffic.

The modern façade was a shell, independent of the pillars; for this reason the windows could be a continuous strip stretching the whole length of a wall, thereby providing much more light for the interior. The old façade, on the other hand, had windows cut out of the supporting wall, which meant that they had to be smaller and spaced farther apart.

Figs 1282–5   A series of sketches by Le Corbusier, illustrating the five points of the new architecture: the free plan, the free façade, the house raised off the ground by means of *pilotis*, the roof garden, the elongated window.

Scale 1:200

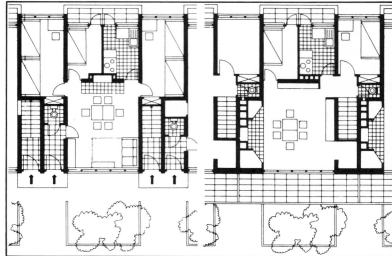

Figs 1286–91 A distict with terraced houses completed by
J. J. P. Oud near Rotterdam in 1924. Photographs, general layout
and plan of two types of home.

Scale 1:1000

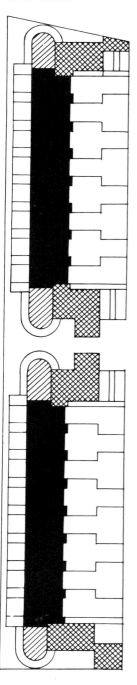

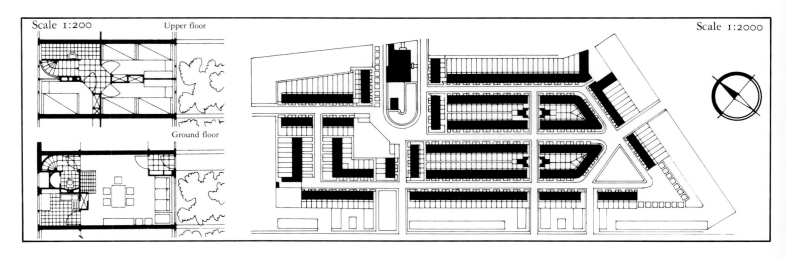

Scale 1:200   Upper floor

Ground floor

Scale 1:2000

Figs 1292–6   Another neighbourhood with terraced houses by J. J. P. Oud in Rotterdam in 1925. Photographs, plan of the most common type of house and general layout.

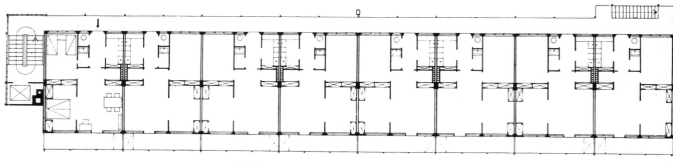

Figs 1297–1300 The first tower
blocks with balconies, built in
Rotterdam by Brunkmann, van der
Vlugt and Maaskant: the Bergpolder
(1934) and the Plaslaan (1938). View
and plans on a scale of 1:300.

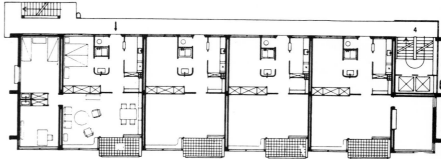

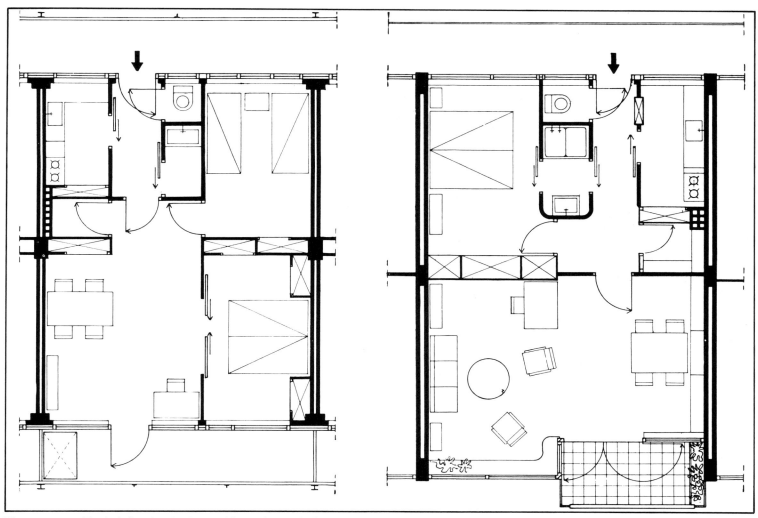

Figs 1301–2   Typical flats in the Bergpolder and the Plaslaan (scale 1:100).

In the traditional home the functions of the
rooms are distributed haphazardly; the
paths of daytime activities (the dotted
lines) and of night-time activities (the
unbroken lines) cross each other in a
completely random way.

In the modern home the functions of
the various rooms are arranged into two
separate zones, one for daytime activities
and one for the night-time; their paths no
longer cross.

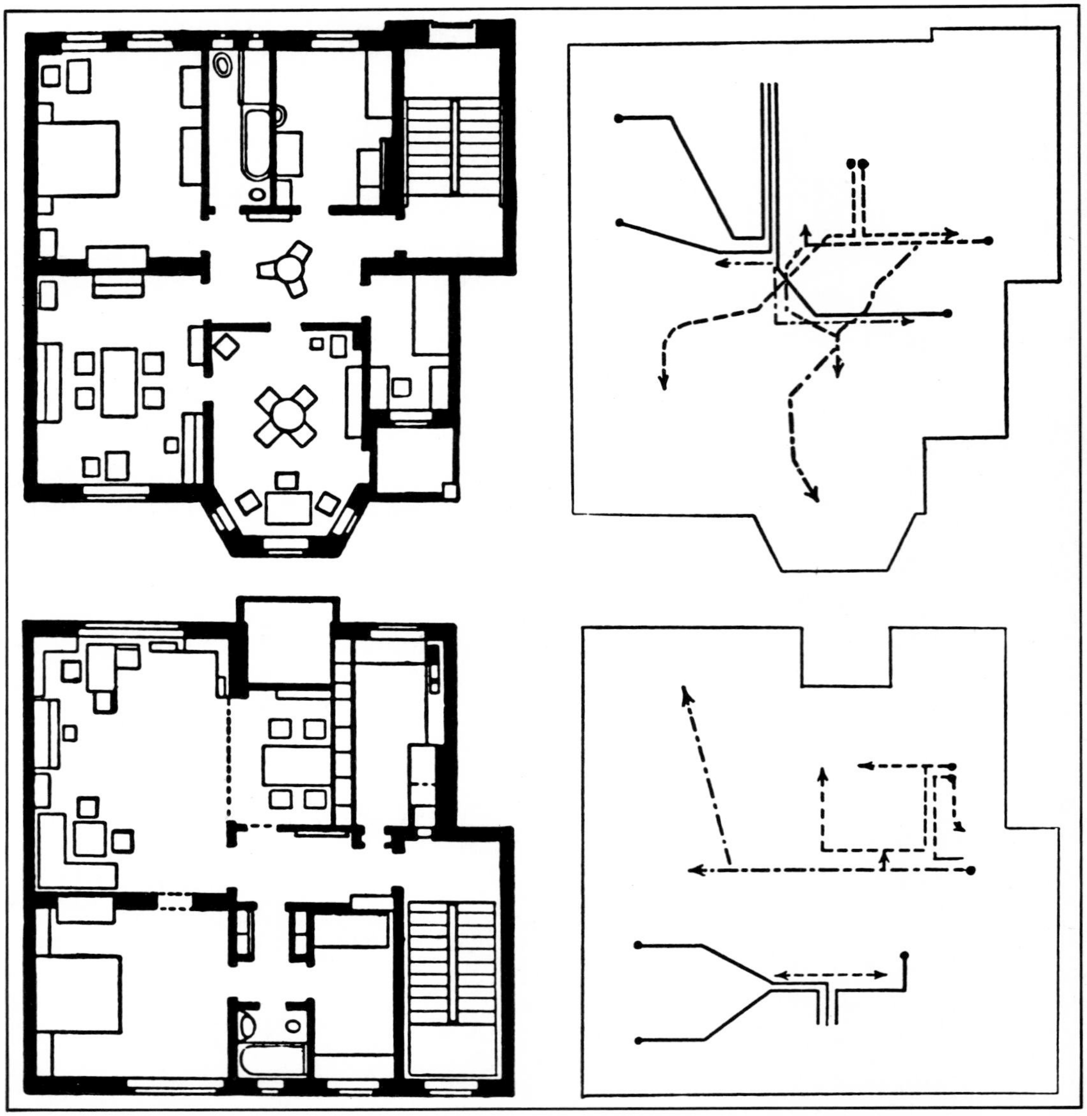

Figs 1303–6   A traditional home and
a modern one, as analysed in a
publication by Alexander Klein for a
German research institute in 1928.

Experiments with various possible internal layouts for homes could not be conducted without also considering how they should be arranged in relation to each other. For this reason research into housing was carried out not only on the scale of single units, but of whole neighbourhoods, and it led to the introduction of a new kind of functional element. This comprises a certain number of residential units and a certain number of services: the so-called *unité d'habitation* (residential unit).

The smallest unit — containing approximately 300–400 homes, a nursery school, shops selling essential goods, and recreation areas for adults and children — would become the smallest basic urban unit (like single buildings in the traditional city). A certain number of these complexes, grouped together, would form a larger unit, containing a greater number of homes and enjoying a wider range of services. For example, three primary units of the size already mentioned would form a secondary unit, with roughly 1,000 to 1,200 homes, three nursery schools, an elementary school, a more comprehensive range of shops, and a larger area for sport and recreation.

In this way a precise relationship could be established between all the city's components (the various types of services, the recreation areas, the streets and roads, the parking lots, and even the factories) and the housing, and the urban structure could be truly subordinated to the residential sector, in accordance with the original hypothesis.

Le Corbusier's concept of the *unités d'habitation*, which formed a continual gradation from the smallest unit to the largest and ultimately to the whole city, allowed architectural control to be extended on a much larger scale. In fact, the city's shape could be extremely varied, but it would be derived from a limited number of combinations and different ways of joining buildings to each other, whose technical and visual consequences would already be known. The traditional city or town was composed of large numbers of small plots, each occupied by independent buildings; their combinations were potentially too numerous to be anticipated or controlled and their closely serried ranks ultimately

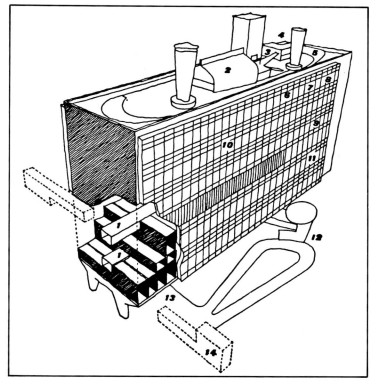

Fig. 1307   Le Corbusier's Unité d'Habitation at Marseilles, built in 1951.

1. *Rues intérieures*.
2. Gymnasium.
3. Café and solarium.
4. Restaurant.
5. Play sculptures.
6. Health centre.
7. Crèche.
8. Nursery school.
9. Club.
10. Workshops and meeting room for the young.
11. Laundry.
12. Entrance and porter's lodge.
13. Garages.
14. Typical duplex flat (see Figs 1310–12).

created an impression of monotony. The modern city, however, could be formed from much larger units, each planned as a single architectural entity, and also the relationship between these units could be planned in advance, which meant that the overall effect could be both varied and co-ordinated at the same time.

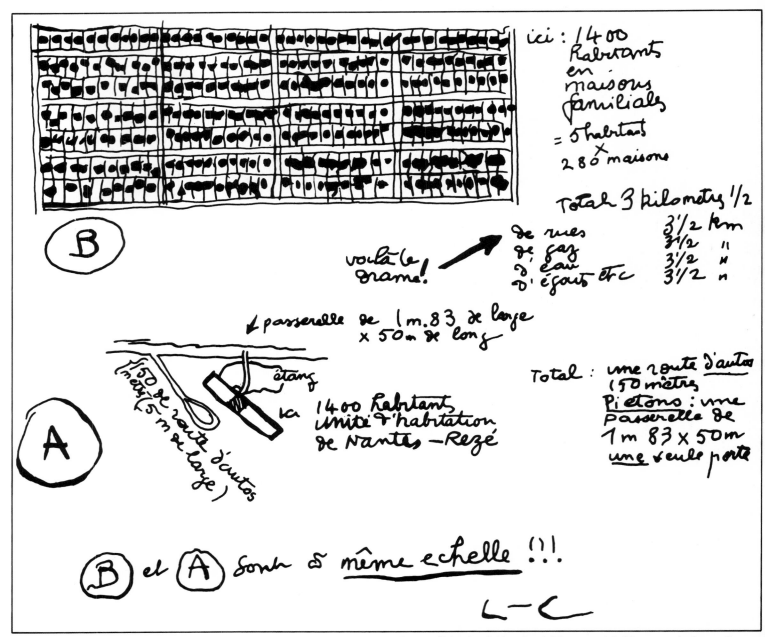

Fig. 1308 Le Corbusier's rationalisation of the suitability of his *unité d'habitation*.

In a traditional neighbourhood (B), 1,400 inhabitants need 280 small houses (5 people in each). To gain access to these houses, 3½ kilometres of road is needed, as well as 3½ kilometres of gas pipes, water pipes and drainpipes: that is the problem!

In an *unité d'habitation*, all that is needed is a road for cars, 5 metres wide and 150 metres long, and a raised pedestrian walkway, 1.83 metres wide and 50 metres long, which passes over a stretch of water.

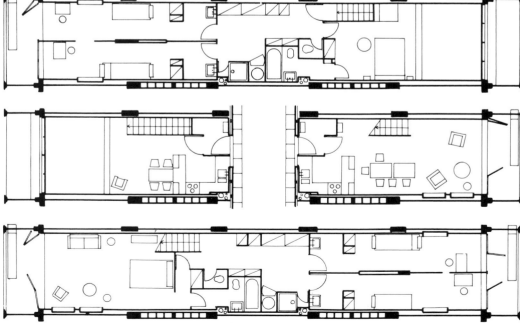

Figs 1309–12 General view and
plans of the different types of flats in
the Marseilles Unité d'Habitation,
designed for 1,400 inhabitants.

Fig. 1313   A group of *unités d'habitation*, set in a park, which could form a neighbourhood or a whole town; design by Le Corbusier for Nemours (1934).

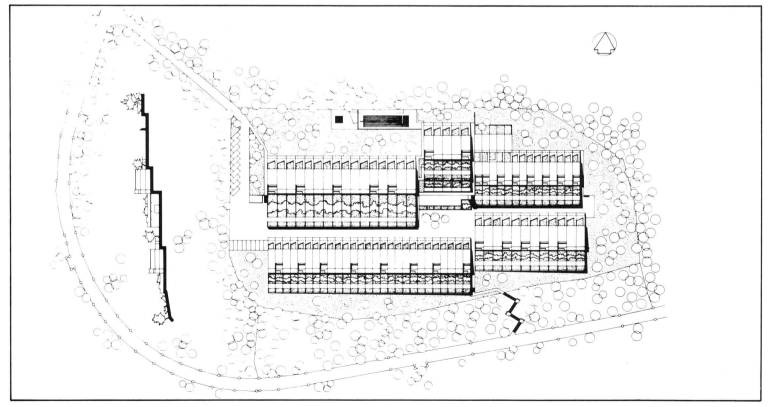

Figs 1314–15 Aerial view and layout of a horizontal residential unit, comprising 74 terraced homes: the Siedlung Halen near Berne, planned in Atelier 5 in 1963.

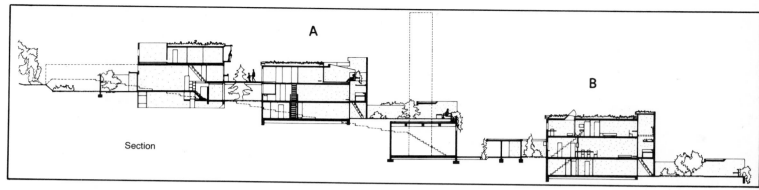

Section

Key (for the two
types of building):

1. Entrance.
2. Store-room.
3. Sitting-room.
4. Balcony.
5. Bedrooms.
6. Garden.
7. Cellar.

Section E
Plan of house
Type A

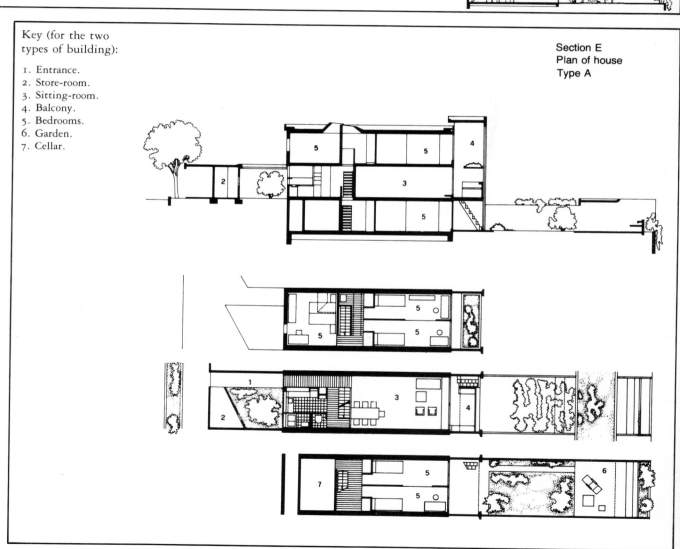

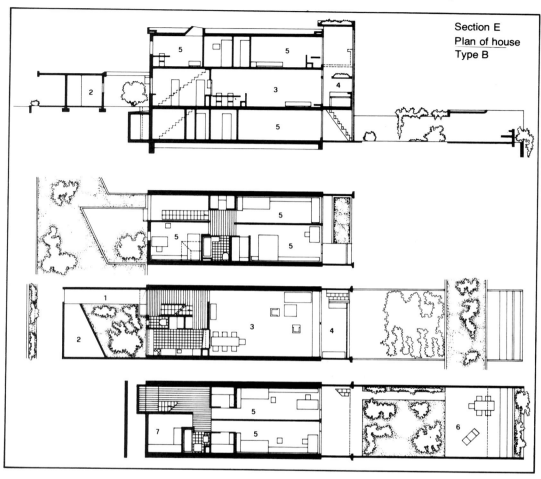

Section E
Plan of house
Type B

Figs 1316–25 Cross-sections and plans of the main types of buildings in the Siedlung Halen. The ground sloping down towards the river has been terraced, allowing houses to be built on three storeys, in which the entrance and the day rooms are on the first floor; in this way there are two separate groups of bedrooms, one on the ground floor, leading onto the garden, and one on the second floor.

The photograph shows the balcony of the sitting-room with the pierced screen copied from Le Corbusier.

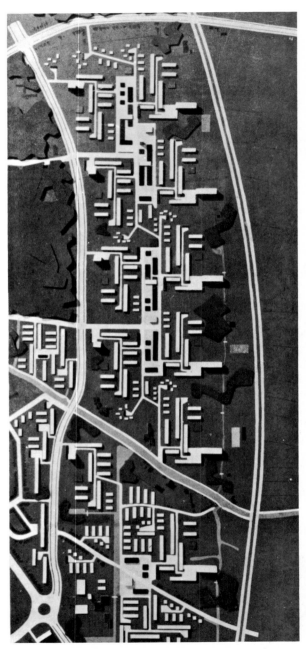

Fig. 1326   The scheme for expanding Leeuwarden,
planned by Bakema and van den Broek in 1958. The
different types of buildings form a series of repeated
combinations: the mixed residential unit.

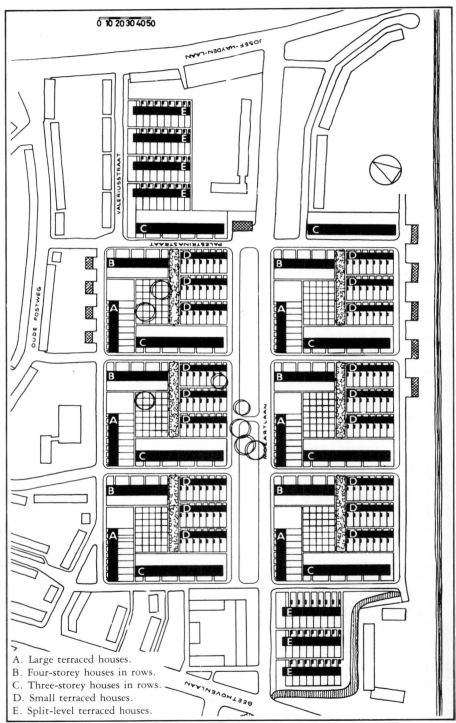

A. Large terraced houses.
B. Four-storey houses in rows.
C. Three-storey houses in rows.
D. Small terraced houses.
E. Split-level terraced houses.

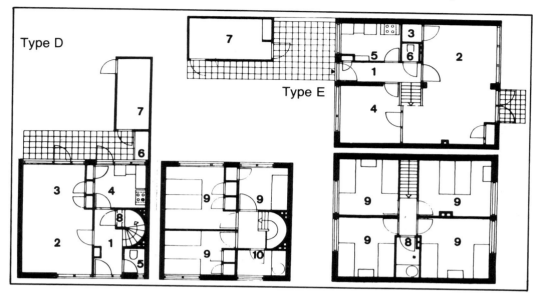

Type D

Type E

1. Entrance.
2–7. Day-rooms.
8. Wash-basin.
9. Bedrooms.
10. Bathroom.

Figs 1327–32   The Klein Driene district at Hengelo, completed by Gakema and van den Broek between 1956 and 1958.

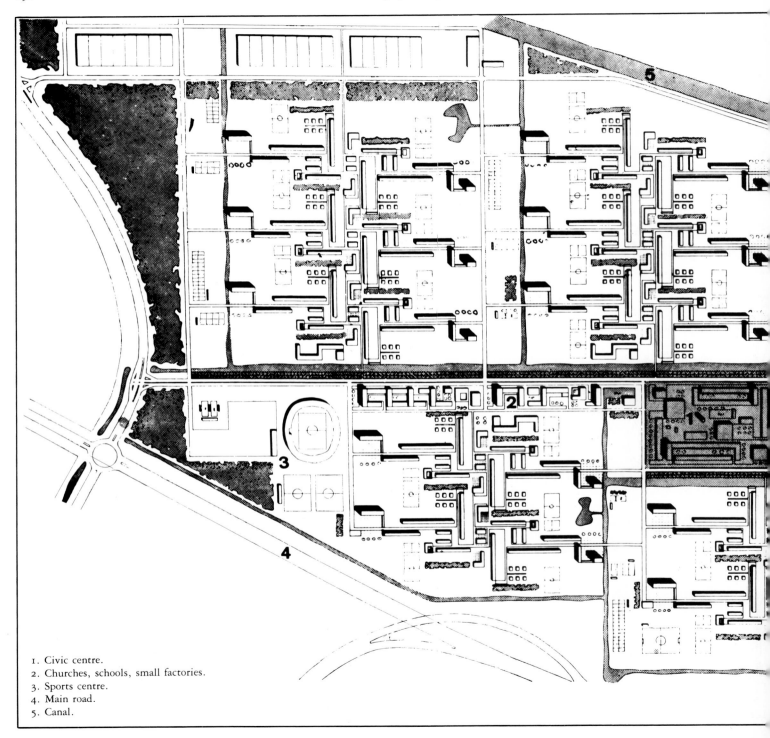

1. Civic centre.
2. Churches, schools, small factories.
3. Sports centre.
4. Main road.
5. Canal.

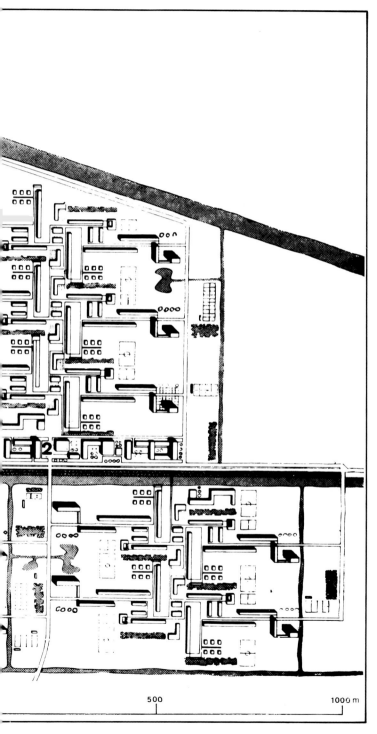

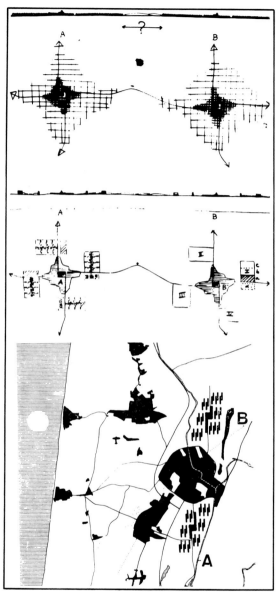

Figs 1333–6   The development for the Noord-Kennemerland district in
Holland, proposed by Bakema and van den Broek in 1959. The old
villages (A and B) are surrounded by tightly-packed outlying districts,
which tend to occupy all the land between each other. In place of this
uncontrolled expansion, the planners suggested a series of residential units
with a fixed shape and dimensions, which would respect the balance
between the countryside and the built-up areas. A certain number of the
units would be grouped together to form a larger district with a more
comprehensive range of public services.

500   1000 m

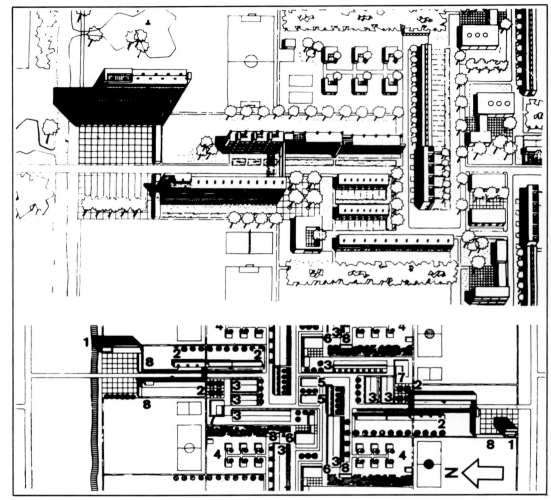

Figs 1337–8   Plan for the
development of Noord-Kennemerland.
Plan of a residential unit for 1,900
people and a three-dimensional aerial
drawing of part of the unit.

1. Fifteen-storey residential block.
2. Houses on three or six floors, with
one-level and duplex flats.
3. One-family terraced houses.
4. Detached one-family houses.
5. Shops.
6. School.
7. Nursery school.
8. Garage.

Fig. 1339   Panoramic view of the mixed residential unit.

Fig. 1340   View of the central area; in the foreground are the detached houses.

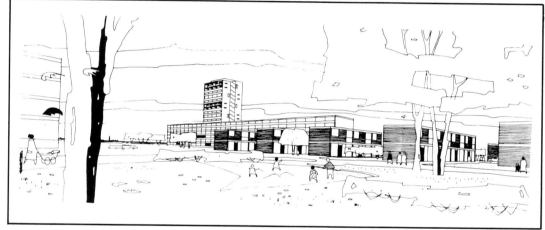

Fig. 1341   View of the central area; in the foreground are the two-storey terraced houses.

Fig. 1342   The inner pedestrian precinct in the town centre.

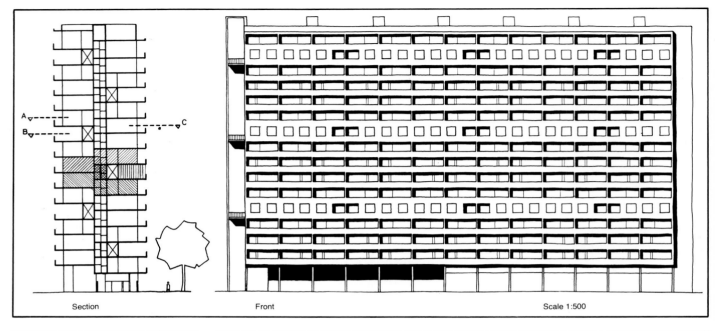

Section   Front   Scale 1:500

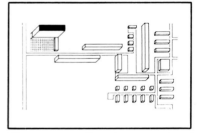

Figs 1343–7 Development plan for
Noord-Kennemerland. Cross-section
front view, and layouts of the
fifteen-storey block.

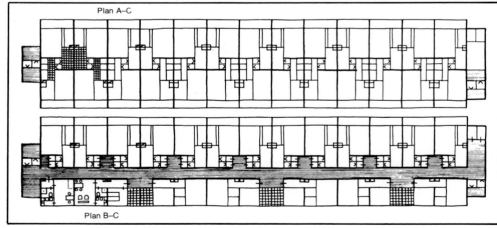

Plan A–C

Plan B–C

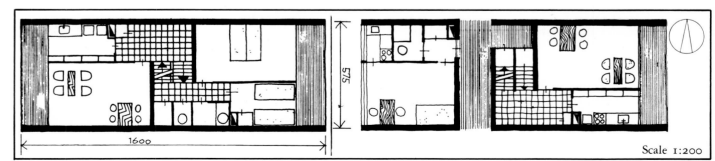

Figs 1348–9 Plans of the structural elements of the fifteen-storey block.

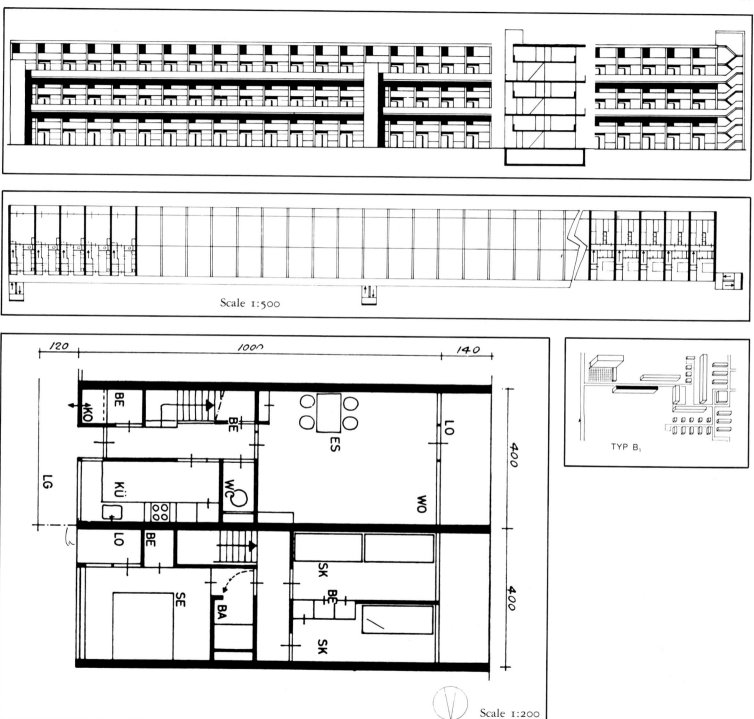

Scale 1:500

Scale 1:200

Figs 1350–4   Front view cross-section and plans of the six-storey block of duplex flats.

Figs 1355–6   The residential units (*supercuadras*) in Brasilia. Each
supercuadra contains 2,500–3,000 inhabitants and four *supercuadras*
form a more complete unit of 10,000–12,000 inhabitants.

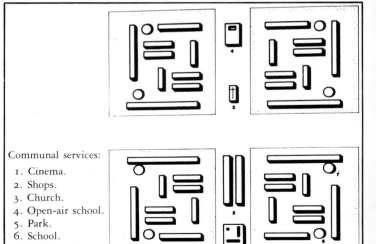

Communal services:
  1. Cinema.
  2. Shops.
  3. Church.
  4. Open-air school.
  5. Park.
  6. School.
  7. Nursery school.

14
The situation today

The results of architectural research have been partly accepted and partly rejected by contemporary society.

The scientific approach to the problems of the man-made environment has become part of scientific culture, vital to the development of modern society. But these problems have been purposely removed from the realms of scientific analysis, because only in this way is it possible to protect the vested financial interests established during the nineteenth century, which not only act as a source of privilege for certain economic groups, but also as an instrument of power for the ruling classes. Indeed, no régime has so far been able to renounce completely the use of this political tool.

For this reason contemporary society has learned to treat the results of this research selectively. Let us now see what has happened in the case of the three points that we have already examined.

As far as the functional activities of the city are concerned, the principle of separating each of them into different zones has been accepted. Since the 1930s, town-planning schemes have distinguished between residential areas, industrial areas, service areas. As a result, there has been a reduction in the inconvenience which derived from their indiscriminate mixing in the traditional city. What has not been accepted, however, is the new system of priorities: the overriding importance of housing, the development of recreational areas so as to form a continuous green space, and the segregation of pedestrians and traffic. Attempts have been made to give towns a more rational layout without altering the dominant role of the tertiary activities (commerce and offices), which produces the consequences that have already been noted: overcrowding in the central area, a loss of housing, and traffic congestion.

The principle of reducing the functional elements in small objects, from everyday utensils to single homes, to their basic minimum, has been accepted because it makes for greater efficiency and lower prices than is possible with traditional models, and at the same time it can also be adapted to fit in with the existing system of mixed private and public ownership. The larger functional elements, and particularly the residential unit, which has provided a new definition of the relationship between homes and services, have been almost totally ignored, because they conflict with the interests of the ruling classes. The units that can be repeated in different combinations, as proposed by Le Corbusier, Candilis, Bakema and van den Broek, have so far only been introduced in exceptional cases: they are acknowledged as admirable pieces of architecture, but not as a means of transforming the general structure of the city.

In the bourgeois city, as has already been noted, the authorities did build some public housing to provide an alternative to the private sector, which offered no cheap houses for the lowest income groups. After World War I public building programmes became increasingly important, and they provided the best opportunities for putting into practice the findings of modern architectural research because the authorities were starting out with completely empty areas of land, which later had to be divided up between houses, services and roads. The public building schemes in Germany, Holland and Scandinavia were indeed the first practical demonstrations of the new urban environment, as proposed by modern architects. These projects can continue to be merely isolated examples or they can develop so as to transform the whole man-made environment, depending on the success, or lack of it, shown by modern architectural techniques. In some countries — England, Holland, Denmark, Sweden, France — the authorities have accepted the criteria of modern architecture, and public sector intervention has developed into an alternative to the traditional means of building and running a city. It has not eliminated the machinery of the bourgeois city, which still continues to be quantitatively greater, but it has succeeded in providing a concrete example of an alternative city, by testing the theoretical propositions of research and gradually improving on them.

It is, therefore, pointless to treat the latest revolutionary architectural concepts as though they were previews of some soon to be completed city. On the contrary, the sole function of the majority of these schemes, which are purposely futuristic, is to forget or hide the difficulties of dismantling the institutions of the 'post-liberal' city which still dominate the contemporary scene.

It would be more appropriate to ask ourselves the question: to what degree has modern architectural research changed our everyday environment?

We will first describe the two best examples of cities in which this change has been partially successful — Amsterdam and London. We will then try to compare these two examples with the overall situation, and we will see the dramatic problems that have been caused throughout the world by economic growth and the attendant rise in urban population levels.

AMSTERDAM

This Dutch city, dealt with at length in Chapter 10, reached its period of maximum prosperity at the end of the

Fig. 1357   The historical centre of Amsterdam, as it is today, surrounded by the new peripheral districts (cf. Figs 1012–18).

seventeenth century, while the 1607 plans to extend it were still being completed. From then on, this magnificent city ceased to grow and the port slowly lost its importance, as the Zuider Zee, the stretch of inland water on which it was situated, began to silt up.

In 1875 a canal was dug, which connected the city directly with the North Sea. Amsterdam immediately began to start growing again; the old walls were turned into a belt of gardens, and around them grew up an area of second-rate neighbourhoods, arranged on the chequerboard system; the railway was built right along the harbour front and the station was placed at the centre of the seventeenth-century fan-shaped layout, thereby separating the city from the Zuider Zee.

In 1901 the first Dutch town-planning laws were passed, which decreed that all cities with a population of more than 10,000 should draw up general development plans, to be brought up to date every ten years. The State provided finance for local authorities to buy up land and to pay for public works, and it also gave money to building cooperatives to provide houses for ordinary people. In 1896 the municipal authorities in Amsterdam decided not to

Figs 1358–9 The scheme for the Amsterdam South extension, planned by H. P. Berlage in 1917. The houses are grouped in great elongated rectangles, measuring approximately 50 by 200 metres.

make any further sales of land, but merely to rent it out, which meant that from that point on urban development could be controlled to fit in with the public programme.

In 1902 Berlage, the most important Dutch architect of the early twentieth century, was asked to provide plans for extending Amsterdam southwards, and these were carried out over the next thirty years (Figs 1358–9).

In 1928 a new, independent town-planning section was opened in the public works department in Amsterdam, which was capable of putting into practice the research work

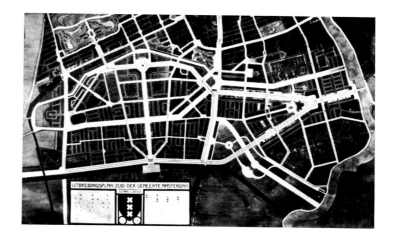

Fig. 1360   The town-planning scheme for Amsterdam in 1935.
The cross-hatched areas are the new districts, the black areas are the
new green zones.

done by modern Dutch architects.

Into this office there entered a member of the neo-Plastic group, Cornelius van Eesteren, who supervised the preparation of an overall plan for the city, applying, for the first time, the findings of the first ten years of architectural research.

In fact, the new plan for Amsterdam involved three innovatory features:

1. The first step to be taken, with the help of specialists, was to make a number of scientific surveys, which allowed the planners to know roughly how the population would grow until the year 2000 and what its needs would be. It was calculated that when the plan was finally approved the city's population would stand at 650,000 and that it would subsequently increase to 960,000. During this period it was planned to build:

84,300 new homes for the extra 310,000 inhabitants, taking into account the fact that the average family would drop from 3.74 people to 3.37;

13,460 new homes to take the place of those that would have to be demolished because of their unsuitability;

12,000 new dwellings to take the place of those pulled down in the central area to make way for offices and shops; a total of some 110,000 homes in all, which were to be added to those already existing.

2. The outskirts of the city were divided into districts containing roughly 10,000 houses (35,000 inhabitants), provided with all the necessary services and separated by strips of green. The authorities decided to begin work on the districts one at a time, and only when an individual decision had been taken was the particular plan drawn up, so that it could incorporate the latest developments.

3. Continual control was exercised over the execution of the plan, to prevent the freedom accorded to the planners of the buildings from destroying the overall unity of the scheme. Each district was divided into small units, which were the individual responsibility of a number of architect supervisors who had the task of approving every single building project and who worked in collaboration with the permanent commission presided over by van Eesteren.

The overall plan for Amsterdam was approved in 1935 and completed during the next thirty years, so that it can now be assessed as a completed project.

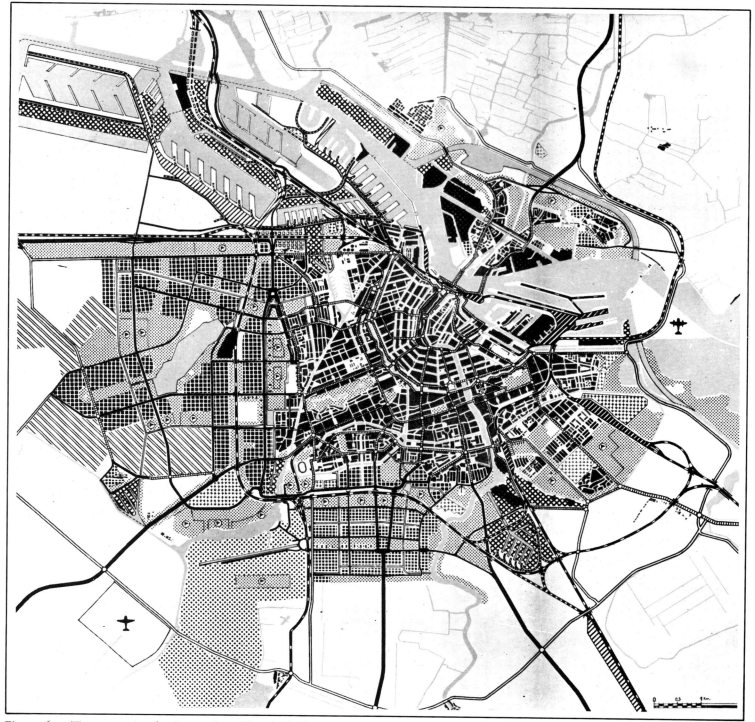

Fig. 1361   The 1935 plan for Amsterdam. The checked areas are the new districts, the dotted areas are open spaces, the crossed areas are industrial zones, and the diagonally hatched areas are for horticulture.

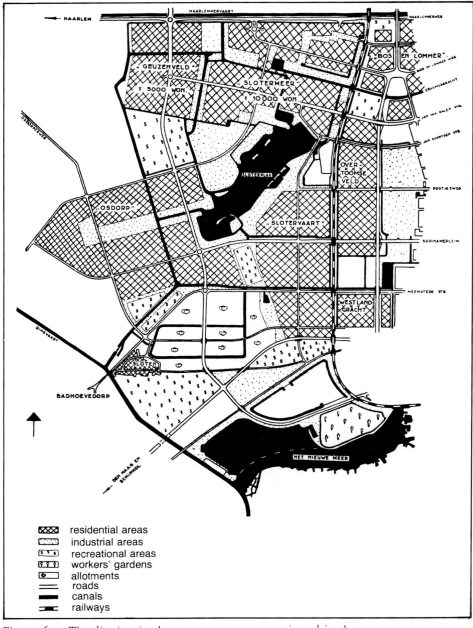

residential areas
industrial areas
recreational areas
workers' gardens
allotments
roads
canals
railways

Fig. 1362   The districts in the western sector, as envisaged in the
1935 plan for Amsterdam.

Fig. 1363   The western sector during its completion; every area of
land was consolidated and had services laid on by the public
authorities before being built on.

Fig. 1364   Aerial view of the Slotervaart district of Amsterdam.

Fig. 1365   Aerial view of the Bosch en Lommer district of Amsterdam.

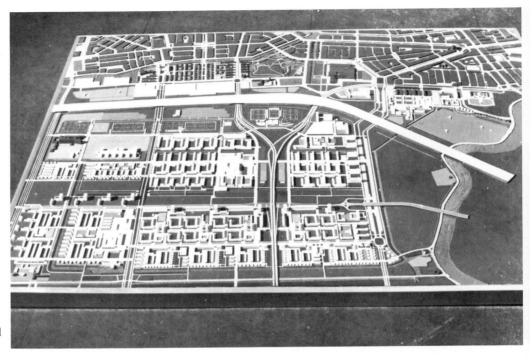

Fig. 1366   Model of the Buitenveld
district of Amsterdam.

Fig. 1367   Model of the Osdorp
district of Amsterdam.

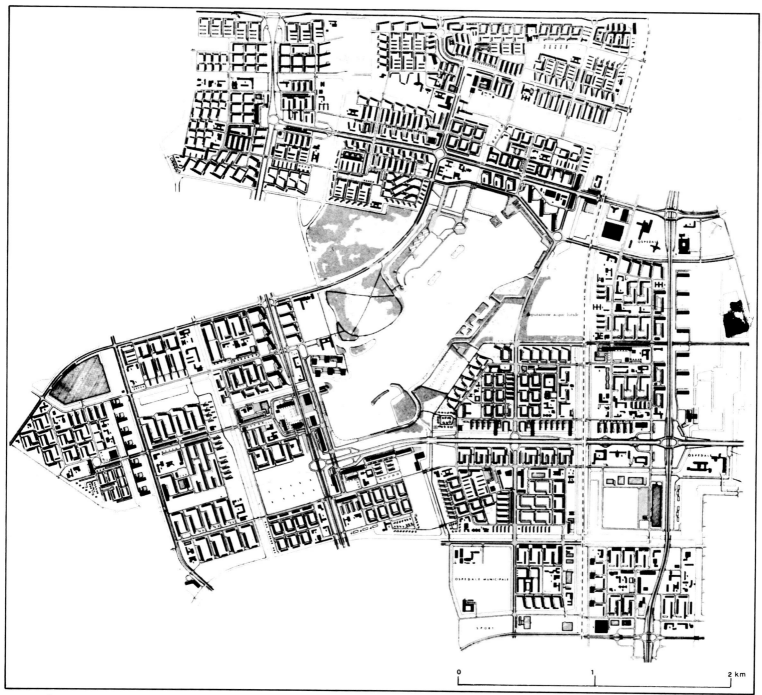

Fig. 1368   The western sector, after the completion of work.

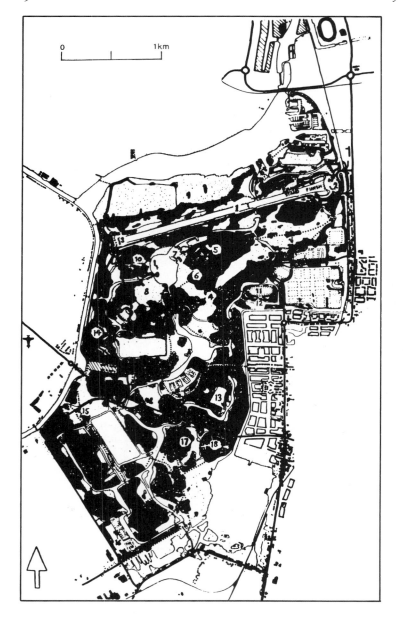

Figs 1369–70   Plan of the wood to the south east of Amsterdam.

 1. Boating lake.
 2. Area for keeping boats.
 3. Aquatic sports centre.
 4. Hill.
 5. Ornamental garden.
 6. Maze.
 7. Children's playground.
 8. Adults' recreation area.
 9. Area reserved for water sports.
10. Open-air theatre.
11. Hurdle track.
12. Riding track.
13. Solarium.
14. Sanctuary for migratory birds.
15. Farm.
16. Youth hostel with camping site.
17. Zoo.
18. Nursery.

Fig. 1371   Aerial view of Amsterdam's historic centre (cf. Figs 1019–26).

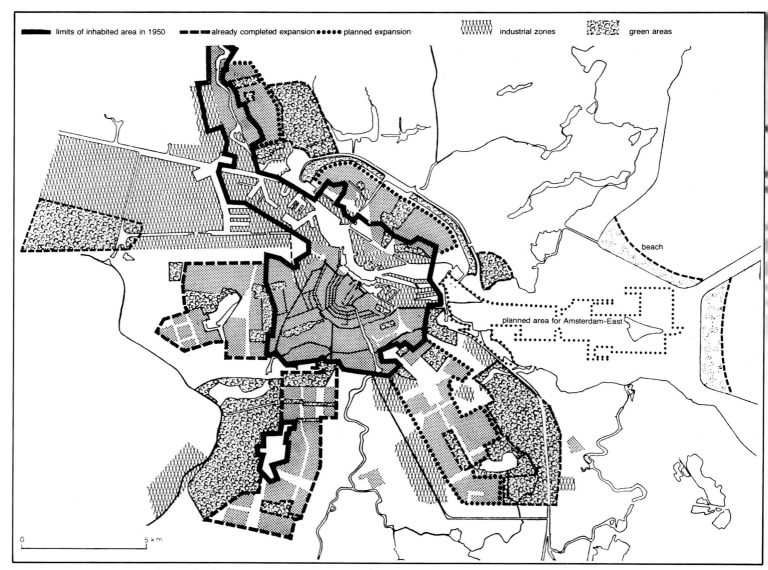

limits of inhabited area in 1950   ▪▪▪already completed expansion ●●●● planned expansion   industrial zones   green areas

beach

planned area for Amsterdam-East

0   5 km

Fig. 1372   The new plan for Amsterdam, proposed during the 1960s.

Most of the new districts are situated to the west of the city, in such a way that they are connected either to the old city centre and the harbour or to the factories in the north, which have been built along the canal leading to the open sea. They are grouped round an artificial lake, the Sloterplas, which means that they have a large recreational centre, with uninterrupted views stretching for one or two kilometres. The oldest districts (Bosch en Lommer, begun in 1936) are made up of traditional four-storey houses, grouped into closes, open and half-open blocks. Newer districts, begun in the post-war period, have a more varied appearance, with individual houses on one or two floors, medium-sized houses with four or five storeys and tower blocks with twelve storeys.

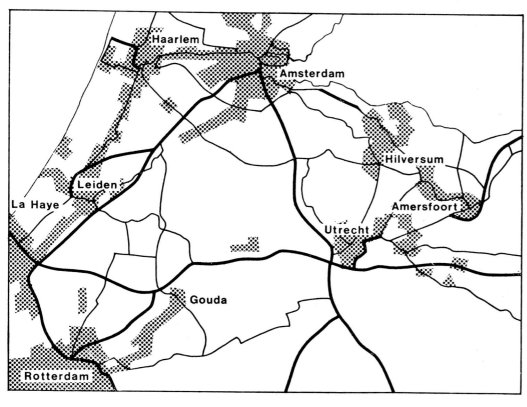

Fig. 1373 The ring of towns and cities that form the Randstad in central Holland.

Every neighbourhood has great expanses of green, for use as recreation areas by children, young people and adults. But the scheme also provided for a municipal park of some 900 hectares (like the Bois de Boulogne in Paris), created artificially in a sandy area to the south-west of the city (Figs 1369–70).

This park contains all kinds of sporting and recreational facilities, such as a canal two kilometres in length for boating competitions, an open-air theatre and two protected areas for migratory birds and deer, and it was completed with the help of a large number of specialists: botanists, zoologists, health and educational experts.

The old town — the medieval heart with its three seventeenth-century canals — has been retained as the centre of the new city, which now has four times as many people as the old one; the streets are jammed with traffic, and many buildings have been altered. Nevertheless, the authorities have tried to preserve its traditional character, by subsidising the restoration of the old houses and by turning the main shopping streets, which form a long thoroughfare of roughly $1\frac{1}{2}$ kilometres, into pedestrian precincts.

The city, however, has developed at a faster rate than anticipated in the 1935 plan. In 1958 Amsterdam's population reached 870,000, and it was decided not to allow any further expansion within the municipal boundaries. In future, all development would take place in the surrounding districts to the north and south, but not to the west, so as to preserve a green belt between Amsterdam and Haarlem. Thus a new plan was drawn up, which encompassed a much greater area around the city, and in 1968 it was decided to build a metropolitan railway system, running underground in the old town and above ground in the suburbs.

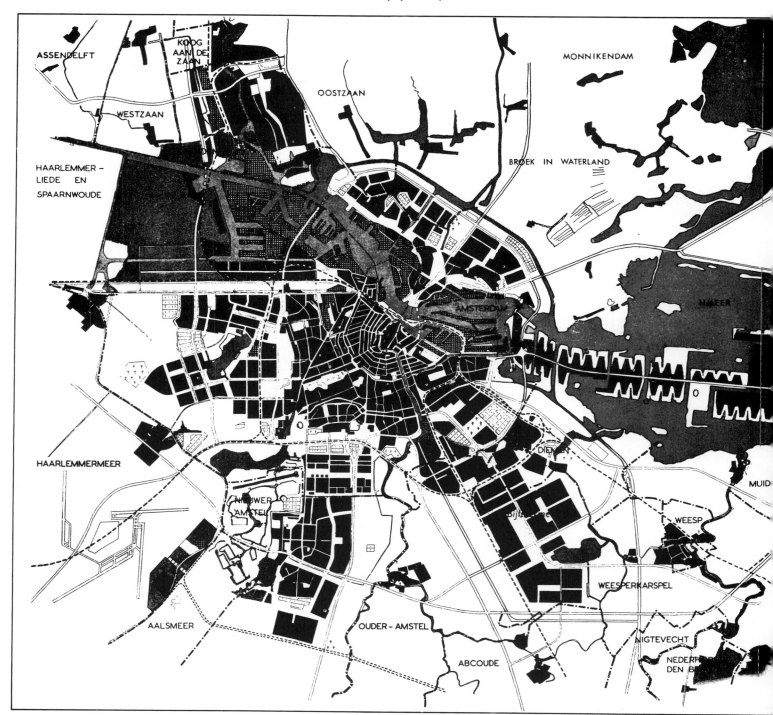

Fig. 1374   Plan of Amsterdam and its outlying districts, containing Bakema and van den Broek's scheme for the eastern sector.

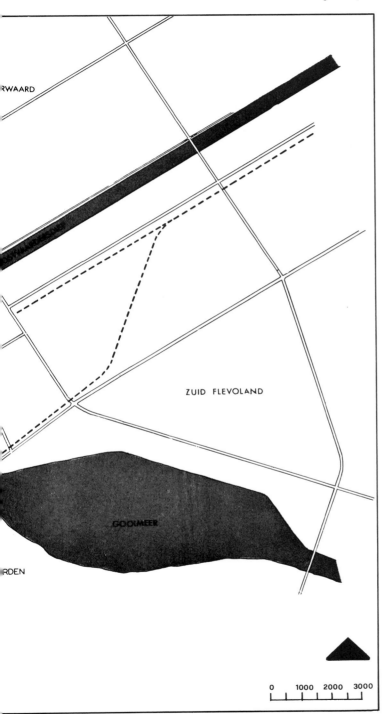

RWAARD

ZUID FLEVOLAND

GOOIMEER

RDEN

0 1000 2000 3000

The enlargement of the city, however, has spotlighted the mistakes that were made in planning the new districts. Although they were carefully designed, with plenty of open spaces and ample public services, they still form a densely built-up area, which has lost touch with the countryside and, particularly, with the water (even the harbour area is separated from the city by the railway line). And so, despite what the planners intended, not every building in the new districts has an equally favourable position: there are some houses, in the front rows, that look straight out on to the parks, but there are others occupying the second rows. In addition, the road and street system has proved to be unnecessarily complicated, and there are too many points at which it cuts across the pedestrian footways between the houses, the various amenities and the parks. Nor, however simple it may be, is the way in which the houses are distributed justified by any precise functional need, and on occasion it becomes merely an abstract design, creating unnecessary differences for no logical reason.

In order to demonstrate the possibility of a decisive change of direction, the architects Bakema and van den Broek in 1965 presented a scheme for enlarging Amsterdam towards the east, on the stretch of water that still remained between the city and the reclaimed land in the Zuider Zee (Figs 1374–86).

This project involved building, on a series of artificial islands, a linear city of 350,000 inhabitants, with a branch of the metropolitan railway and a motorway running through the middle. The new city would be formed of thirty-five residential units, each housing 10,000 people and situated $1\frac{1}{2}$ kilometres from each other, at right angles to the main rail and road route. Each unit would be divided into three zones: the central one, where the railway and motorway passed through, and in which the highest density of housing and offices would be sited, and the two lateral ones, with buildings of medium height surrounding a system of raised walkways on various levels (the parking areas would be below, and the schools, churches, auditoriums and other services would be above). All three zones would face the recreation area that separated the units from each other: an inlet with gardens and playgrounds, with at least 300 metres between one block and the next.

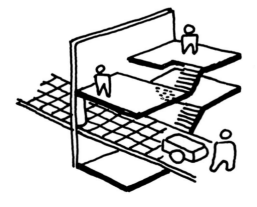

A unit of 10,000 people would have to be planned and completed as a great unitary composition: therefore, the balance between the public planners and private enterprise, which had been tried and tested during the preceding thirty years, would have had to be modified and transferred to a larger scale. The Amsterdam authorities, who during the 1930s had been the first people to accept the early findings of modern architectural research (the analysis of urban functional activities and the definition of the basic functional elements), were not yet ready to accept the latest products of research, i.e. the new modes of arranging the functional elements. For that reason, this project had to be presented as a private proposal: as an exercise in technical feasibility, which was not, however, realisable in the conditions prevailing at the time within the Dutch administration.

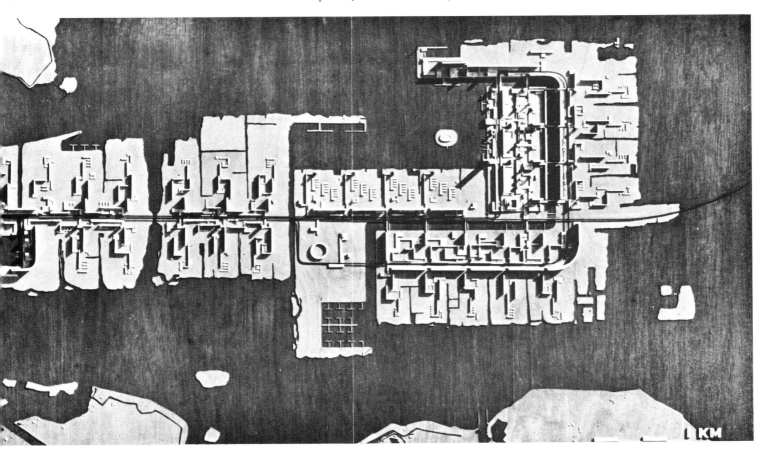

Figs 1375–7   Model of the scheme for Amsterdam's eastern sector; details of the relationship between the buildings and the lines of communication, based on a system of split levels.

1. Tower blocks.
2. Blocks of medium height.
3. Monorail station.
4. Street for local traffic.
5. Monorail.
6. Motorway.

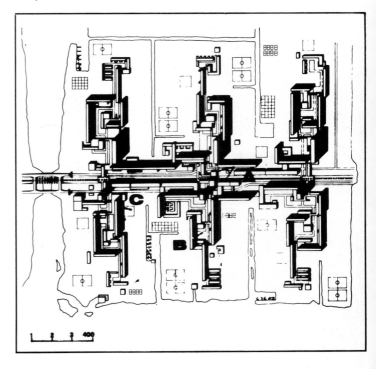

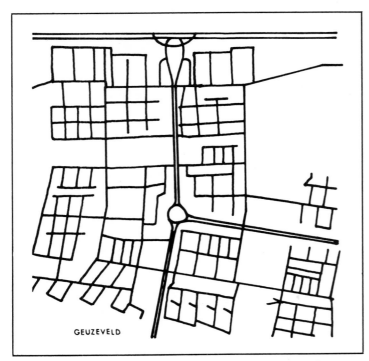

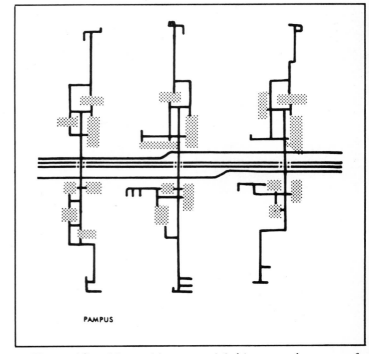

Figs 1378–81 Comparison between a district of Amsterdam's western sector (Geuzeveld), with roughly 30,000 inhabitants, and a group of three residential units in Amsterdam-East, each with 10,000 inhabitants. Above, the distribution of the buildings, below, the street network.

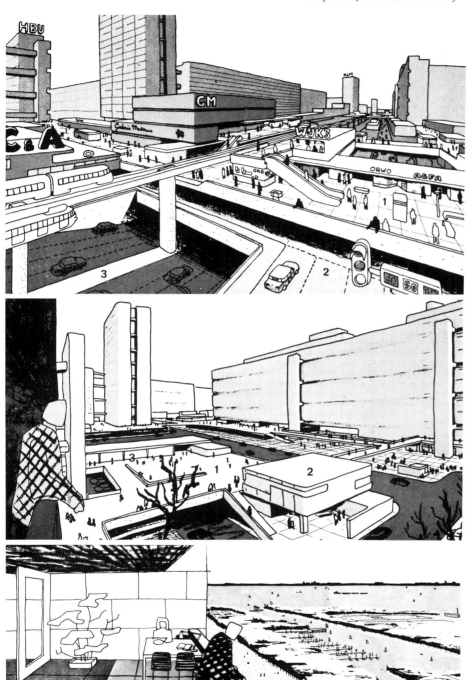

The three environments that make up Amsterdam-East (see Fig. 1379):

Fig. 1382 The environment in which the inhabitants meet (A), along the central spine. The pedestrians circulate on level 1, slow traffic on level 2, and fast traffic on level 3.

Fig. 1383 The environment in which the districts meet (B), in the enclosed space between the unit's houses, above and below the central spine. The pedestrians move in a series of raised walkways, which lead to meeting places 1, shops 2, and schools 3.

Fig. 1384 The recreational environment (C), in the clear spaces between adjoining units. A single person, from his home, can look on to environment B or environment C.

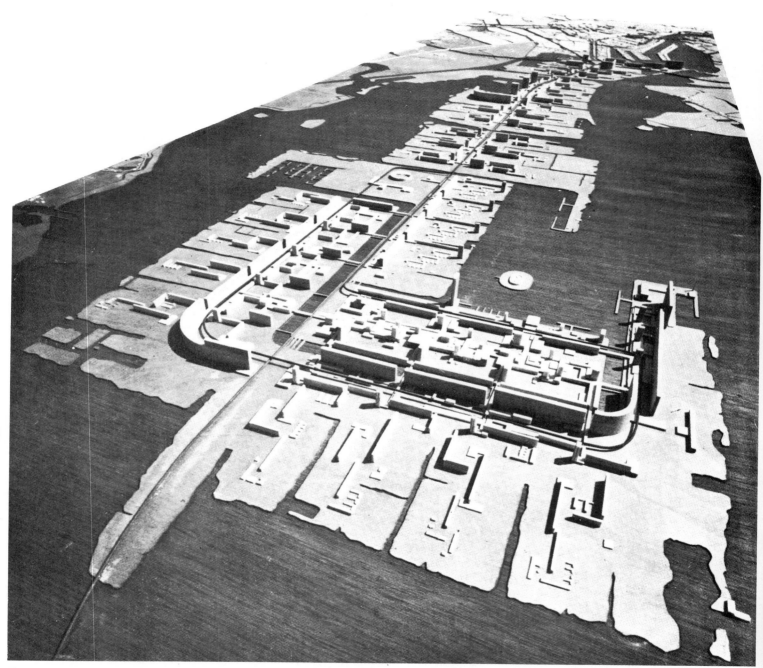

Fig. 1385 View of the model, looking from the lagoon towards the centre of the city.

Fig. 1386   Model of one of the
residential units.

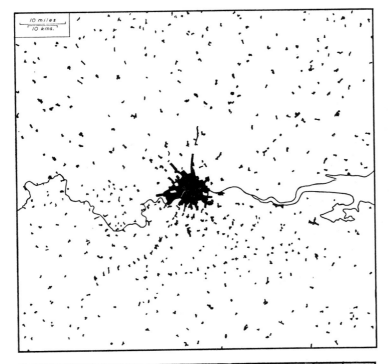

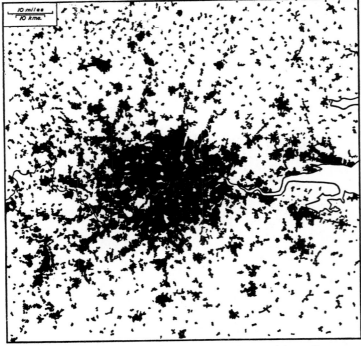

Figs 1387–8   The London urban area, in 1830 and in 1960.

LONDON AND THE NEW TOWNS OF ENGLAND

At the beginning of the nineteenth century London was the world's largest city and already had a million inhabitants. In 1851, the year of the Great Exhibition in the Crystal Palace, it had 2½ million, while in 1901 it reached the figure of 4½ million and covered almost the whole of the county of London, which had been set up in 1888 (30,000 hectares). There were, however, a further two million people living beyond the city boundaries, and these contributed to form a vast conglomeration, whose population in 1901 was 6½ million, in 1921 7½ million, and in 1939, on the eve of the outbreak of World War II, almost 9 million.

This extraordinary concentration of houses, streets and services seemed, on the one hand, disastrous and ungovernable, and on the other, capable of producing the most wonderful technical advances. In 1805 Pall Mall was the first street in the world to have gas lighting; the Crystal Palace, site of the Great Exhibition in 1851, was the largest building ever erected — it was precisely 1,851 feet long (550 metres) and covered an area of 7½ hectares. In 1863 work began on the Underground Railway, between 1848 and 1865 the two embankments along the Thames, between the City and Westminster, were completed, and in 1894 the new Tower Bridge, with its two movable central sections to allow the passage of tall ships, was opened. The City, which in 1861 still had 110,000 inhabitants, by 1911 only had 20,000, and it became a specialised centre, composed almost totally of offices, shops, workshops and public buildings; it also became the most important economic and financial centre in the world.

The control of this enormous city lay in the hands of more than 300 local authorities, which in 1855 were united into a single body. The measures that they took, however, were both limited and incomplete: attempts were made to break up the uniform mass of the new outer areas by means of more public parks — Regent's Park (1830), Victoria Park (1845), Finsbury Park (1869) — and provisions were made for the clearance of the worst slums, with the powers granted by the laws of 1868, 1875 and 1890.

As well as the intervention of public bodies, action was also taken by a number of private groups: the society for the improvement of workers' housing, founded in 1854; the

Fig. 1389 London traffic;
an engraving by Gustave
Doré from 1872.

Fig. 1390 A mid-nineteenth-century
map of London.

1814, before the advent of the railways.

1864, following the completion of Regent's Park (cf. Fig. 1060).

Figs 1391–4 The development of one of London's districts (in the north west, towards Hampstead).

1914, after the absorption of Hampstead Village.

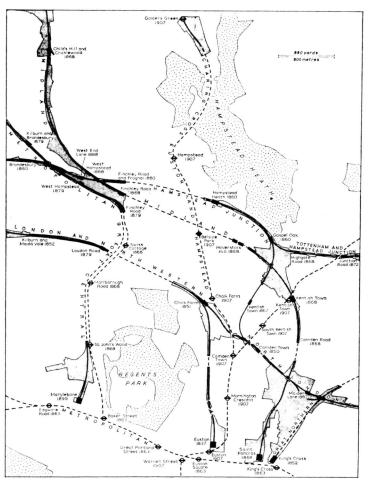

The area's railway network in 1914.

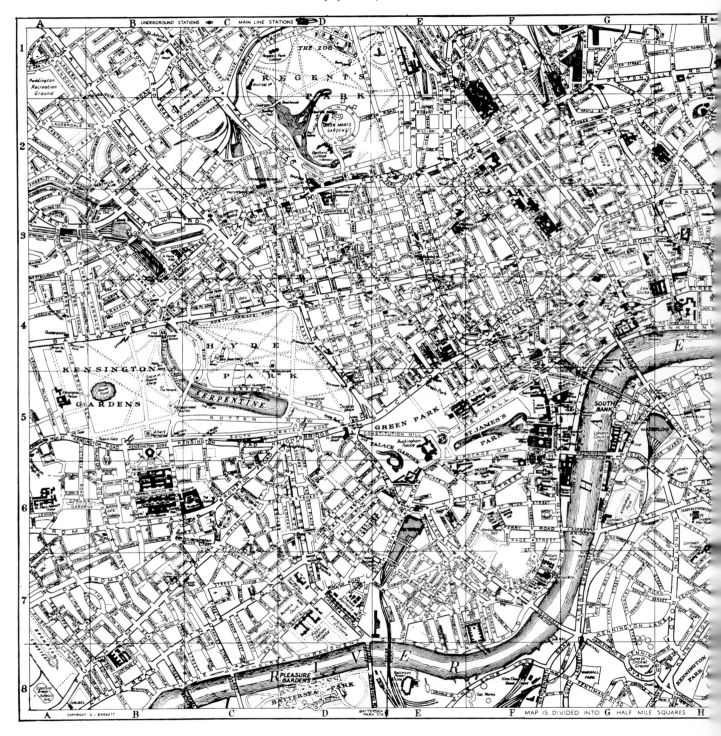

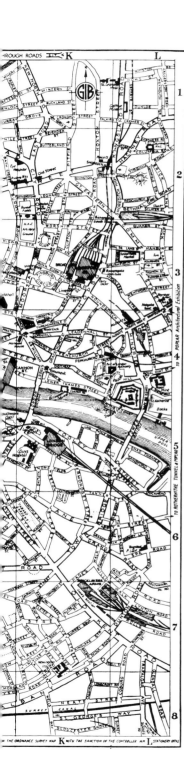

Figs 1395–6   Map and aerial view of central London as it is today (cf. Figs 1028, 1035).

building activities started by Octavia Hill, with the help of John Ruskin, in 1865; the founding of the Garden City Association by Howard in 1899, which resulted in the formation of two new cities in the vicinity of London — Letchworth, in 1902, and Welwyn, in 1919 (Figs 1397–9). These initiatives had an important cultural significance, but they had little effect in actually modifying the development of the vast urban sprawl.

Large-scale public intervention, in order to regulate to some extent the growth of England's cities, only became possible in the 1930s when attempts were made to tackle the effects of the 1929 crisis, and it was realised that the distribution of the country's economic activities — agriculture, industry, commerce and public utilities — needed to be reorganised.

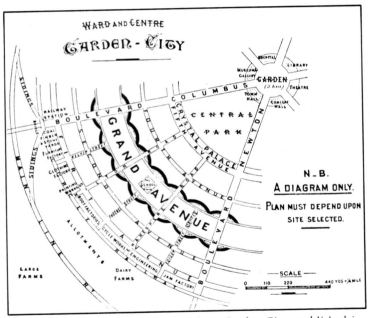

Fig. 1397   The schematic theory of the Garden City, published in Howard's book of 1899. In the centre is a park, surrounded by a 'crystal palace', which contains the town's public buildings: the town hall, a theatre, a library, a museum. Next are the residential districts and the schools, while the outer rings contain the factories, farm land, the railway station and links with the main roads.

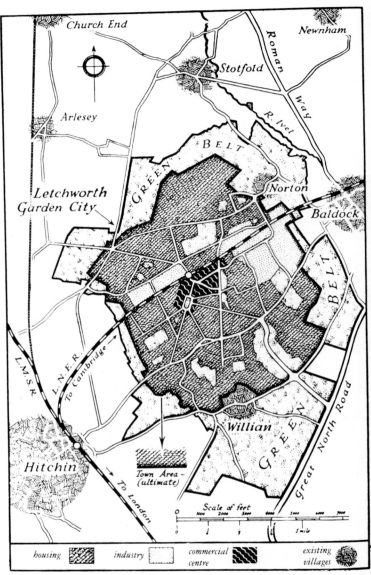

Fig. 1398   Map of Letchworth, the first Garden City, founded in 1902.

Fig. 1399   Aerial view of Letchworth.

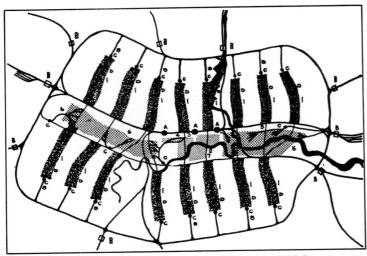

Fig. 1400   The plan for London proposed by the MARS group.

1. Residential districts.
2. Commercial and administrative
centre (The City).
3. Political centre (Westminster).
4. Commercial centre with underground
railway link.
5. Cultural centre and park.
6–8. Industrial zones.
A. Passenger railway stations.
B, C. Goods stations.
D. Markets.

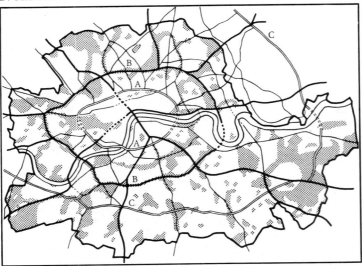

Fig. 1401   The 1944 planning scheme for London. A, B and C are
the three concentric ring roads; the dotted areas are parks.

The royal commission set up in 1937 to study the
distribution of the country's population and industry, published its findings in 1940, and it severely criticised the way
in which both elements were concentrated round the great
cities. London was the most extreme example of this, and a
law was passed in 1938, which blocked any further expansion of the city, prohibiting any more building beyond the
boundaries already reached and establishing a surrounding
area of undeveloped land called the Green Belt.

In the summer of 1940 a large part of the city was
destroyed by German bombing, and discussions began as to
how to rebuild it. In 1942, the modern English architects of
the day, the MARS group, put forward a plan that would
have broken up London's mass into two rows of districts,
alternating with areas of green (Fig. 1400), but in 1944 the
County Council decided on a more traditional plan,
designed by two well-known experts, Abercrombie and
Forshaw (Figs 1401–4).

This plan divided London into three zones:

1. the inner zone, that is the county of London and the
most densely built-up areas adjoining it, containing a population of about 5 million people in an area of 55,000
hectares; this density was considered to be excessive and a
drop of 400,000 inhabitants was foreseen;

2. the suburban zone, in which a further 3 million
people lived in an area of 58,000 hectares; this density was
considered to be satisfactory and no changes in the population were planned;

3. the outer zone, which included the Green Belt and
the surrounding areas up to a 60–80 kilometre radius from
the city centre. This was to be the site of future expansion,
which would take two forms: the enlargement of smaller
existent towns, and the founding of new towns.

The post-war Labour government, which came to power
in 1945, passed two important pieces of legislation: one, in
1946, which concerned the setting up of New Towns, and
the other, in 1947, which established new criteria for town
planning.

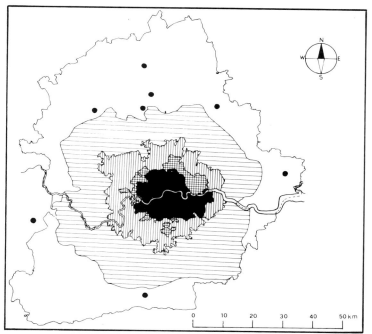

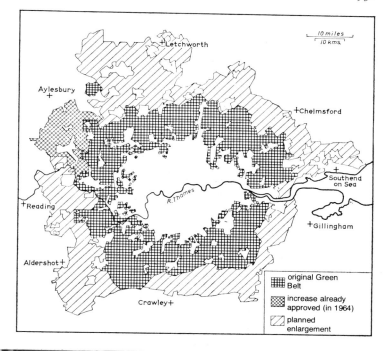

Fig. 1402   The concentric zones of the 1944 plan for London. Working outwards: the county of London (in black), the inner zone, the suburban zone, the Green Belt and the outer zone, in which it was planned to build New Towns.

Fig. 1403   The areas of Green Belt in 1964.

Fig. 1404   The 1944 plan for London, being shown to the public in the early post-war period.

Figs 1405–6   Two cartoons from a book published shortly after the end of the war: the soldier, having thrown off his uniform, starts work on the rebuilding of London, using the reports and plans formulated during wartime.

It was against this background that the decision was taken to build fourteen New Towns: eight in the outer zone of London:

Stevenage	begun in 1946 for 60,000 inhabitants
Hemel Hempstead	1947	65,000
Crawley	1947	62,000
Harlow	1947	60,000
Hatfield	1948	26,000
Welwyn (an expansion of the Garden City)	1948	42,000
Basildon	1949	86,000
Bracknell	1949	25,000

six elsewhere in Britain:

Newton Aycliffe	begun in 1947 for 15,000 inhabitants
East Kilbride	1947	50,000
Glenrothes	1948	32,000
Peterlee	1948	25,000
Cwmbran	1949	45,000
Corby	1950	55,000

These New Towns had much in common with the Garden Cities of the early part of this century: they were not much larger than the size predicted by Howard (35,000), they had relatively low population densities, and the houses were, for the most part, single family units with gardens. They were not closely packed, but consisted of a series of individual elements separated by large expanses of green: the residential neighbourhoods, each of which contained 10,000 inhabitants, with two primary schools and other community services (nursery schools, shops); the industrial areas, which were sited near the railway lines; and the main town centre, where the offices and main commercial services were to be found. The main roads and some of the more important services, such as the schools of higher education, were included in the green areas. This disjointed layout favoured piecemeal development, as well as making subsequent additions easier, but it also produced an environment which was too spread out and came in for a good deal of criticism during the 1950s.

In later towns, attempts were made to correct this planning defect: the average population of residential districts was reduced from 10,000 to 5,000 and less, while the overall size of the towns was increased to 100,000 inhabitants, and later to as many as 250,000. The resulting urban

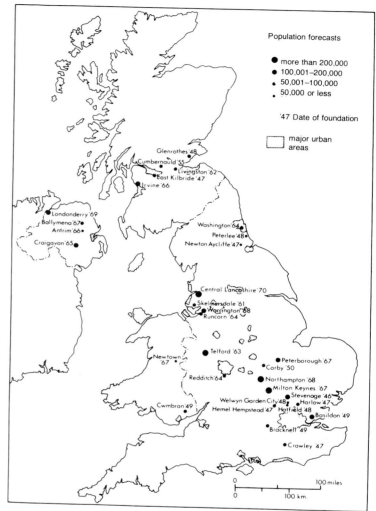

Fig. 1407   A map showing the distribution of New Towns in England up to 1975.

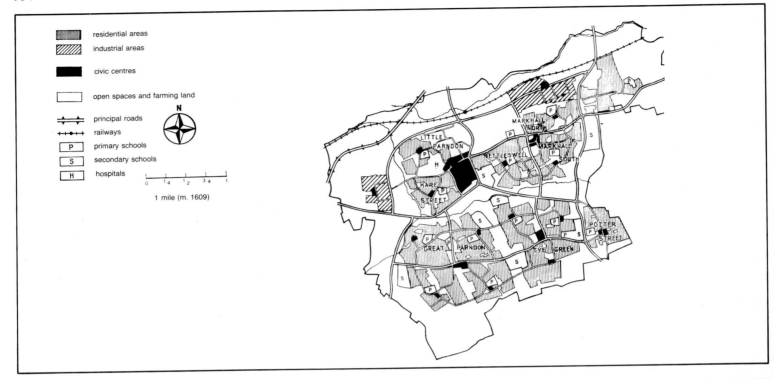

Fig. 1408   Plan of Harlow New Town, as proposed by Frederick Gibberd in 1947–8.

In Harlow, every district of 10,000 inhabitants is formed of three or four smaller units, each with an elementary school and its own centre. This means that every zone of the town is in immediate contact with some form of green space, fingers of which penetrate into every part of the town. The intermediary schools are situated in these spaces. There are also two small industrial areas near the railway.

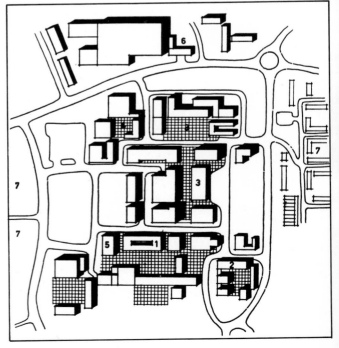

Fig. 1409   Plan of Harlow's commercial centre.

1. Civic centre.
2. Offices.
3. Shops.
4. Entertainment complex.
5. Church.
6. Fire station.
7. Houses.

Fig. 1410 Aerial view of a section of Harlow, showing a tower block and a group of terraced houses.

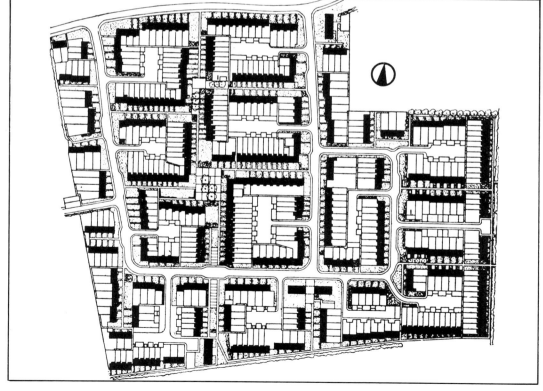

Fig. 1411 Plan of a residential district of Harlow, with terraced housing. Private gardens are in white; the dotted sections are the communal areas of green, in which there is a continuous network of pedestrian walkways.

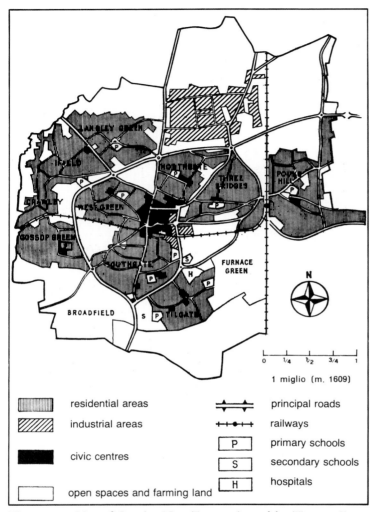

residential areas   principal roads

industrial areas   railways

civic centres   P   primary schools

    S   secondary schools

open spaces and farming land   H   hospitals

Fig. 1412   Map of Crawley New Town, planned by Thomas Sharp between 1946 and 1950.

GOSSOP GREEN

Figs 1413–15   Plans of three residential districts in Crawley. Crawley has a more compact layout. Each district of about 5,000 inhabitants forms an individual unit; the school normally stands at its centre and also acts as a community centre. An existent village has been transformed into a primary commercial centre. Industry is confined to a single area.

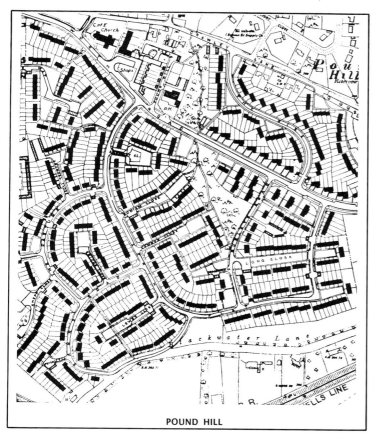

POUND HILL

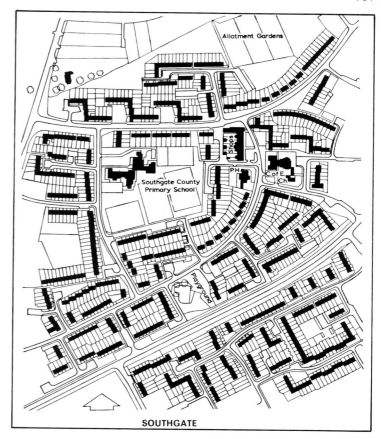

SOUTHGATE

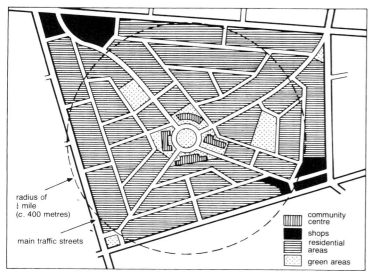

radius of
¼ mile
(*c.* 400 metres)

main traffic streets

community centre

shops

residential areas

green areas

Fig. 1416 The principle of the neighbourhood unit, adopted as the basis for the layout of early English New Towns.

Fig. 1417 Stevenage, one of the New Towns founded in the 1940s. From top to bottom: a residential neighbourhood, the commercial centre, and an industrial zone.

Fig. 1418 Cumbernauld, founded in the 1950s: the residential districts are distributed in a ring round the commercial centre (work on which had hardly begun when this photograph was taken); the industrial zones are further away, on the town's outskirts.

Cumbernauld, planned ten years later than the post-war New Towns, took account of the rise in motorised traffice and has two completely separate areas: one for pedestrians and one for cars and lorries. The network of streets for wheeled traffic is so arranged that all its crossroads have flyovers or underpasses, and it enters directly beneath the town centre. The whole town has become more compact: it has only one centre, which can be reached on foot from every district, while the industrial zones are situated on the outskirts.

Fig. 1419   The system of streets and pedestrian walkways in
Cumbernauld.

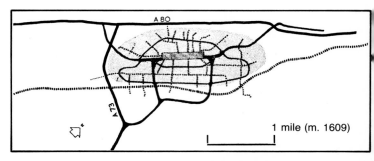

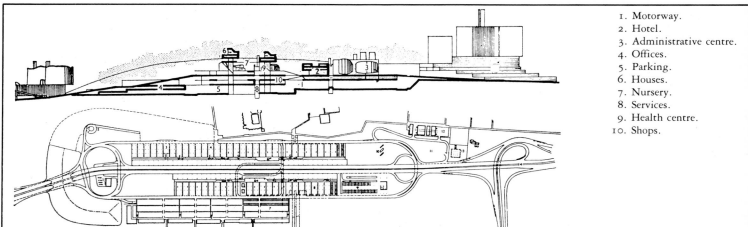

1. Motorway.
2. Hotel.
3. Administrative centre.
4. Offices.
5. Parking.
6. Houses.
7. Nursery.
8. Services.
9. Health centre.
10. Shops.

Figs 1420–1   The commercial heart of Cumbernauld, directly linked to the main network of roads.

structure was more compact and more logical, and it also partially rejected the integration of those districts built in the green areas.

Let us now examine, in chronological order, the most important of the New Towns built during the last twenty years:

Cumbernauld	planned in 1956 for	70,000 inhabitants
Hook (never built)	1960	100,000
Runcorn	1964	100,000
Milton Keynes	1970	250,000

As yet, it is not possible to assess these towns as completed works: they are attempts at establishing a new form of urban environment for the future, by eliminating the

defects of the traditional town.

Hugh Wilson, the man responsible for planning Cumbernauld, has declared, 'The New Towns should be considered as town-planning laboratories, in which the ideas for restructuring existent cities can be developed.' For the moment these new types of town are the exception rather than the rule, even in England, and for precisely that reason they have become very different from existing towns and cities: they highlight the changes that would need to be made to the latter, but only in future years will we be able to see what effects this exemplary demonstration has had.

While experimenting with these new forms of town, the English authorities were also taking action within the

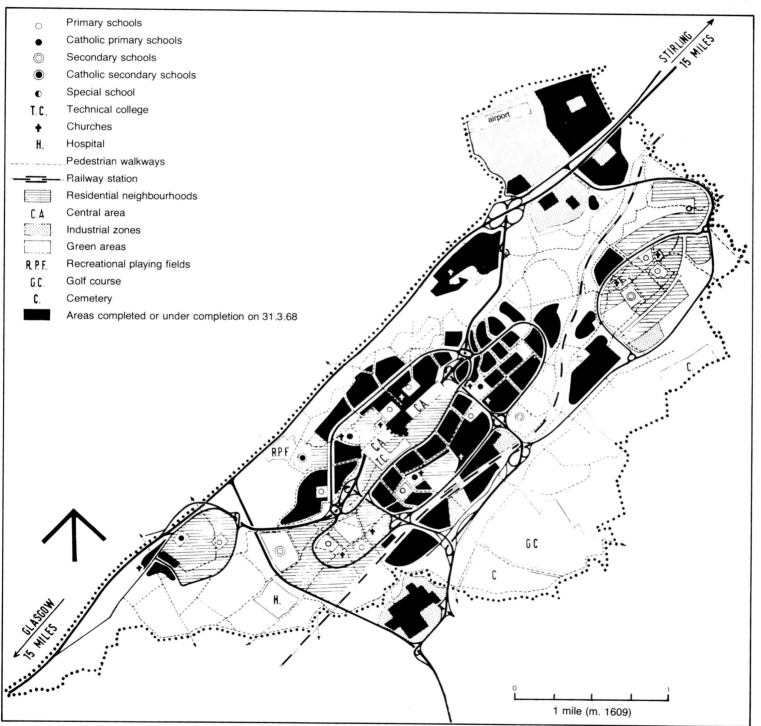

Primary schools

Catholic primary schools

Secondary schools

Catholic secondary schools

Special school

T.C. Technical college

Churches

H. Hospital

Pedestrian walkways

Railway station

Residential neighbourhoods

C.A Central area

Industrial zones

Green areas

R.P.F. Recreational playing fields

G.C. Golf course

C. Cemetery

Areas completed or under completion on 31.3.68

Fig. 1422 Map of Cumbernauld New Town, planned by Hugh Wilson between 1958 and 1960.

Figs 1423–4   The network of streets and pedestrian walkways in Hook New Town; the dark areas are green spaces.

Hook was a New Town for 100,000 people, planned by London County Council in 1960 on behalf of Hampshire County Council. As in Cumbernauld, traffic and pedestrians were to be segregated and the town planned around a commercial centre. The industrial zones and green areas were to be situated on the town's outskirts.

Fig. 1425 Sectional view of a residential district in Hook. The pedestrian walkways are at ground level in the outer areas and raised nearer the centre.

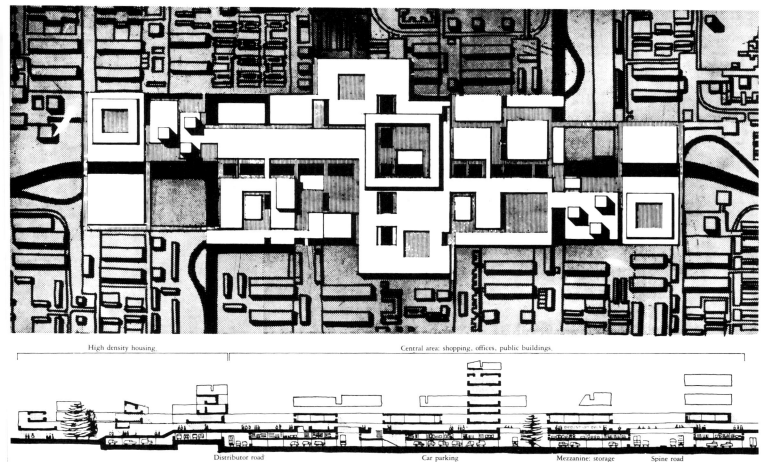

Figs 1426–7 Plan and sectional view of Hook's commercial centre.

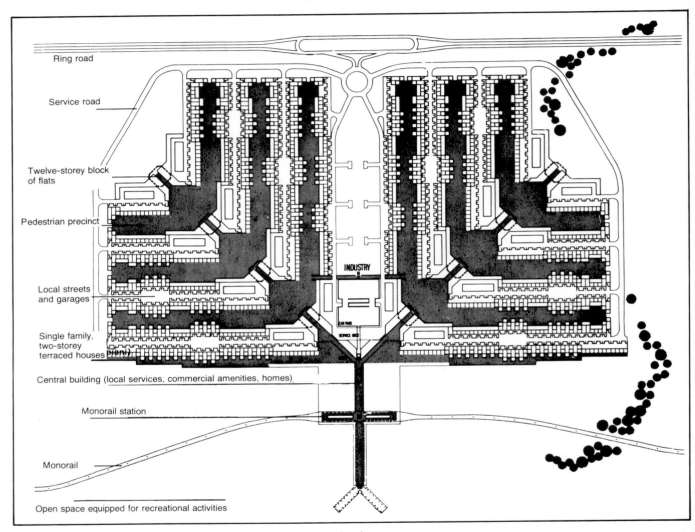

Ring road

Service road

Twelve-storey block
of flats

Pedestrian precinct

Local streets
and garages

Single family,
two-storey
terraced houses

Central building (local services, commercial amenities, homes)

Monorail station

Monorail

Open space equipped for recreational activities

INDUSTRY

Figs 1433–4   Preliminary study for Milton Keynes. Schematic plan
of one of the 47 residential units for 5,000 people and general plan.

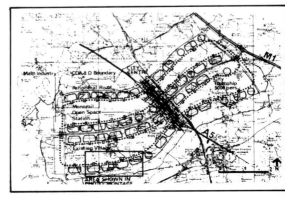

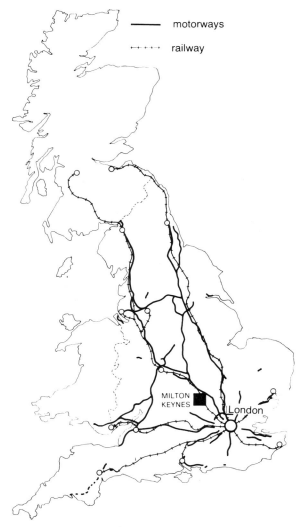

Fig. 1435 The position of Milton Keynes in relation to the main road and rail network.

Milton Keynes is a new city of 250,000 inhabitants, situated to the north west of London, and its size has posed new problems both in its planning and its completion. The preliminary scheme (envisaged by Fred Pooley in 1967) included a network of public transport based on the monorail, independent of the system of streets for pedestrians and traffic. The final plan (1970), however, is based on a chequerboard of dual carriageways, which intersect at intervals of approximately one kilometre. Each square (of about 100 hectares) contains an environmental area in which the homes and services can be arranged with a great deal of freedom.

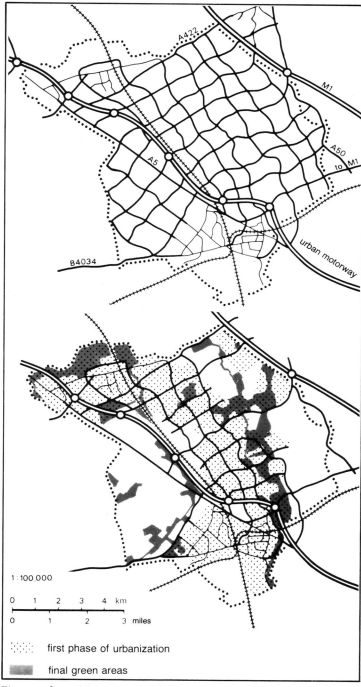

1:100,000

0 1 2 3 4 km

0 1 2 3 miles

first phase of urbanization

final green areas

Figs 1436–7 The network of main roads within the final plan for Milton Keynes. The area to be built during the first ten years (in dots) and the areas of green (in heavy shading).

Fig. 1438   An aerial sketch of part of Milton Keynes, based on the 1970 plan.

Figs 1439–41 Three artists' impressions of Milton Keynes, showing the residential neighbourhoods adjoining the city centre.

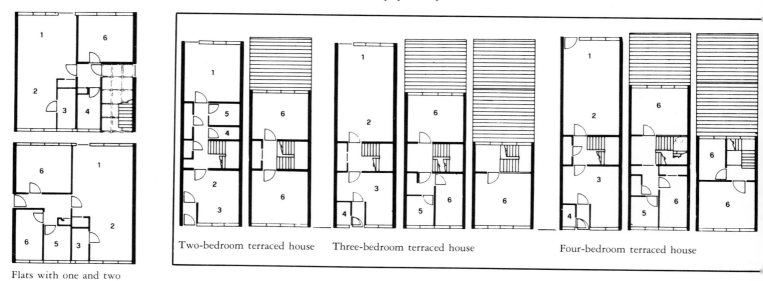

Flats with one and two
bedrooms

Two-bedroom terraced house   Three-bedroom terraced house   Four-bedroom terraced house

Figs 1442–52   Houses in Milton Keynes in the Fullers Slade complex.

Detached three-bedroom house

Detached four-bedroom house

1. Sitting-room. 5. Bathroom.
2. Dining-room. 6. Bedroom.
3. Kitchen. 7. Store-room.
4. Lavatory. 8. Garage.

Figs 1453–7   Houses in Milton Keynes in the Tinker's Bridge 3 complex.

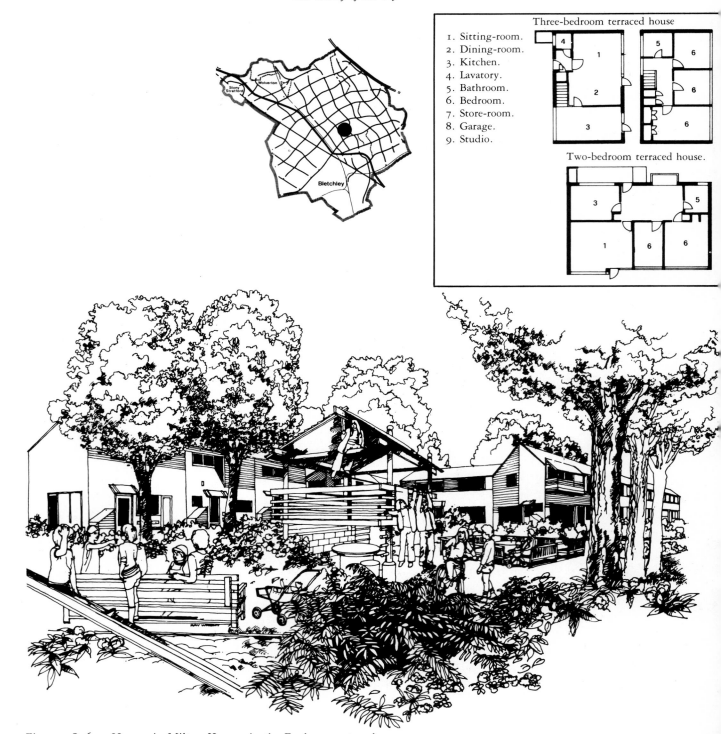

1. Sitting-room.
2. Dining-room.
3. Kitchen.
4. Lavatory.
5. Bathroom.
6. Bedroom.
7. Store-room.
8. Garage.
9. Studio.

Three-bedroom terraced house

Two-bedroom terraced house.

Figs 1458–62   Houses in Milton Keynes in the Eaglestone complex.

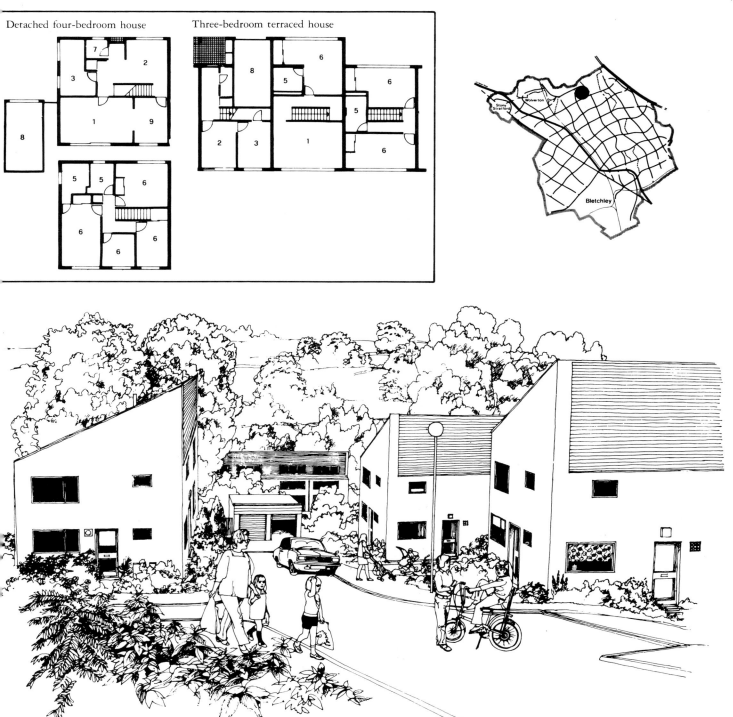

Detached four-bedroom house

Three-bedroom terraced house

Figs 1463–7　Houses in Milton Keynes in the Stantonbury 3 complex.

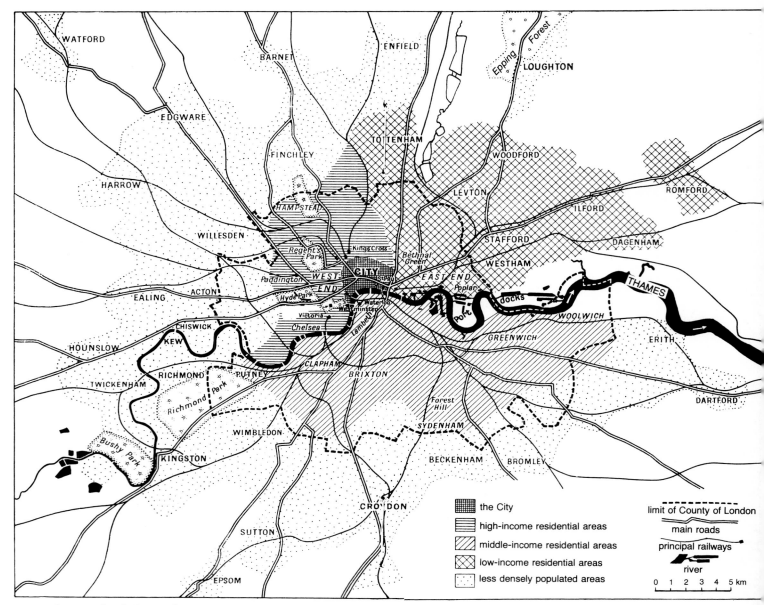

Fig. 1468   London before 1965.

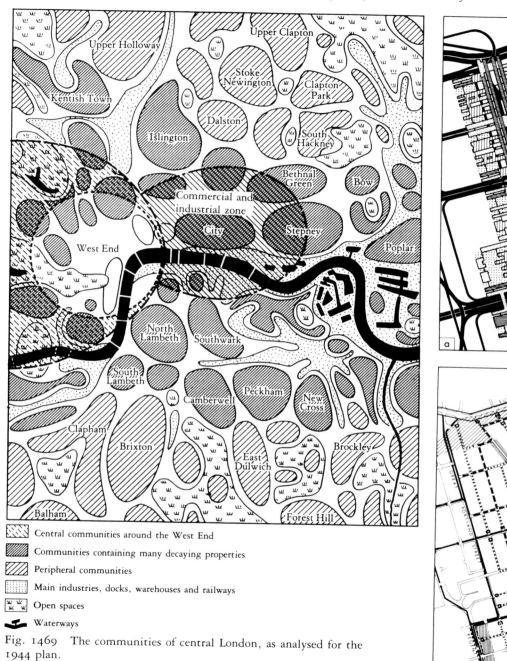

Central communities around the West End

Communities containing many decaying properties

Peripheral communities

Main industries, docks, warehouses and railways

Open spaces

Waterways

Fig. 1469 The communities of central London, as analysed for the 1944 plan.

Figs 1470–1 Two alternative proposals — a maximum (a) and a minimum (b) — for the rebuilding of part of London's West End, contained in Buchanan's report *Traffic in Towns* (1963).

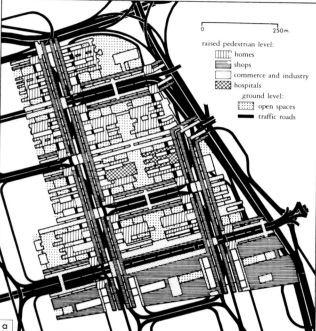

raised pedestrian level:
homes
shops
commerce and industry
hospitals
ground level:
open spaces
traffic roads

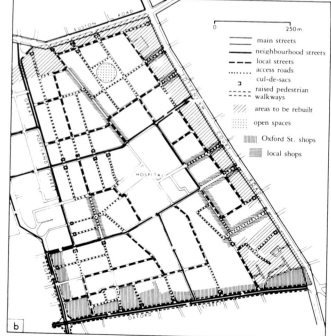

main streets
neighbourhood streets
local streets
access roads
cul-de-sacs
raised pedestrian walkways
areas to be rebuilt
open spaces
Oxford St. shops
local shops

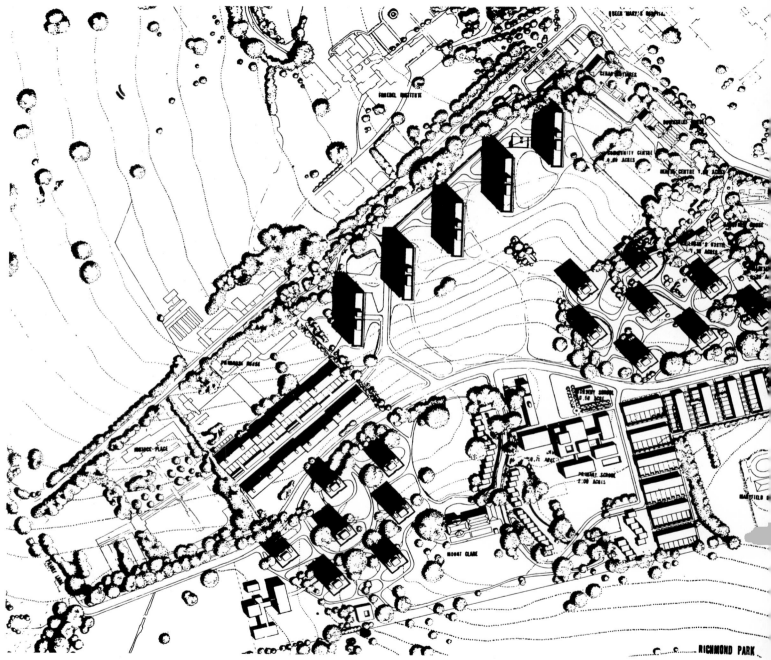

Fig. 1472　General plan for the new district of Roehampton, designed for 13,000 inhabitants, completed by London County Council at the end of the 1950s.

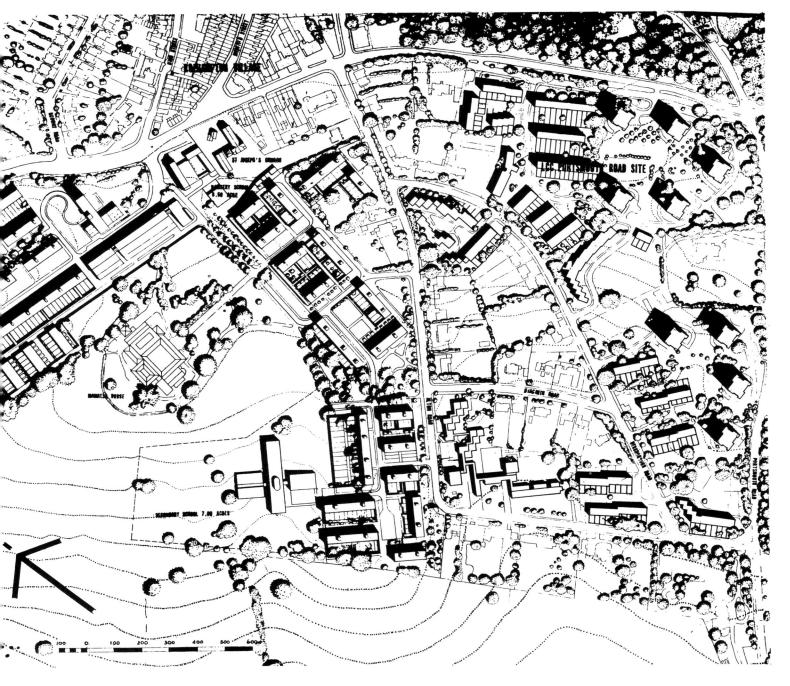

Fig. 1473 A view of the district of
Roehampton in London.

Fig. 1474 Another view of
Roehampton.

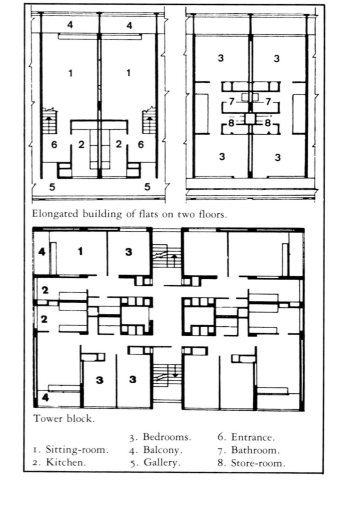

Elongated building of flats on two floors.

Tower block.

1. Sitting-room. 3. Bedrooms. 6. Entrance.
2. Kitchen. 4. Balcony. 7. Bathroom.
  5. Gallery. 8. Store-room.

Figs 1475–80   Different types of buildings in Roehampton.

Fig. 1481   A sitting-room in one of Roehampton's tower blocks, showing the view over London.

Fig. 1482   Children in one of the schools in Roehampton.

Figs 1483–4   Homes for old people and a primary school in Roehampton.

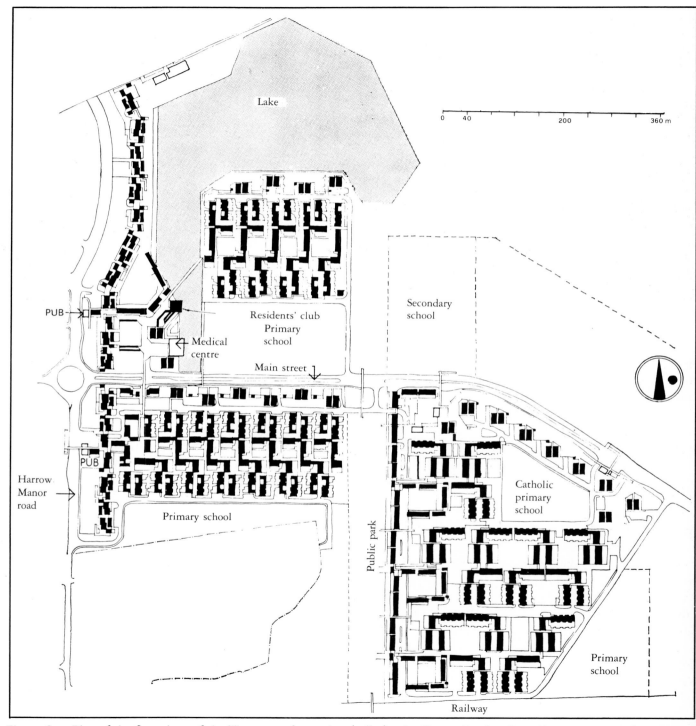

Lake

PUB

Medical
centre

Residents' club
Primary
school

Main street

Secondary
school

Harrow
Manor
road

PUB

Primary school

Public park

Catholic
primary
school

Primary
school

Railway

Fig. 1485   Plan of the first phase of the Thamesmead complex, built by the Greater London Council at the mouth of the Thames

Fig. 1486   Aerial view of Thamesmead.

country's existing towns and cities, trying to adapt them to the new conditions, but within a much more rigid framework. The London County Council built several new suburban developments (Figs 1472–84), as well as some in the heart of the city (Figs 1487–91), and started work on a large district at the mouth of the Thames, whose size was equivalent to that of a new town (Figs 1485–6).

The Ministry of Transport commissioned a report from a group of town-planners, headed by Colin Buchanan, called *Traffic in Towns*, which was published in 1963 and which dealt for the first time with this serious problem in a modern context. It demonstrated that traffic levels could not keep rising without also destroying the urban environment. The aim of town-planners, therefore, should not be to increase traffic as much as possible, but to try and find ways of preserving and enhancing the quality of life in the city's various districts, restricting expenditure on roads to sums immediately available (Figs 1470–1).

Many English towns have begun to follow this advice, and there are various schemes under way to transform town centres so as to enable cars and pedestrians to exist side by side.

In England the results of modern architectural research have been accepted by municipal authorities and applied on a much wider scale than anywhere else in the world. Not only has this produced a marked improvement in the traditional environment, but it has also created a comparative juxtaposition between the environment as it is and as it could be, the consequences of which have begun to have political repercussions. The Labour Party, for example, has proposed the gradual nationalisation of all building land. The vested interests of the 'post-liberal' city have been directly threatened, and the people have seen how their environment can be changed; as a result, the future of the city has become a matter for public debate, even if the outcome of this debate cannot be forecast.

The buildings:

I.   16-storey housing block.
II.   Recreation complex.
III.   4-storey housing block.
IV, V, VI, VII. 6-storey housing blocks.
VIII. 4-storey housing block.
IX.   6-storey housing block.
X.   Building with shops and four floors of flats.
XI.   Community centre.
XII.   Workshops.

The Arabic numerals show the complex's other services:

8.   Pedestrian precinct;
20.   Shops;
24, 39. Green spaces;
26.   Club;
27, 31. Playing fields;
29.   Football ground;
33.   Swimming pool;
36.   Gymnasium;
45.   Site of the future primary school.

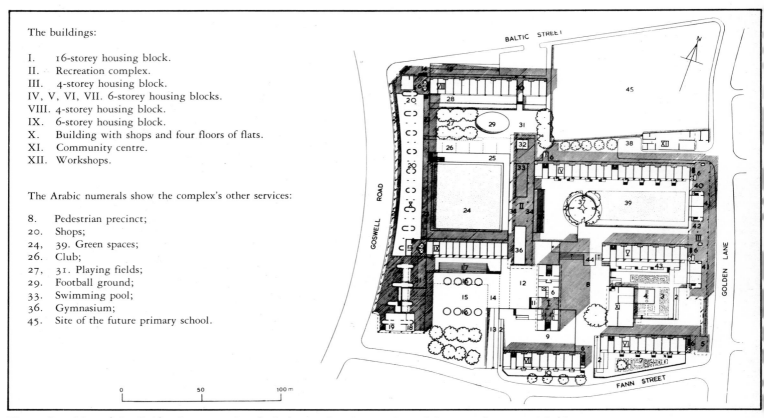

Fig. 1487   Map of the Golden Lane complex, built by London County Council in 1954 for 1,400 inhabitants.

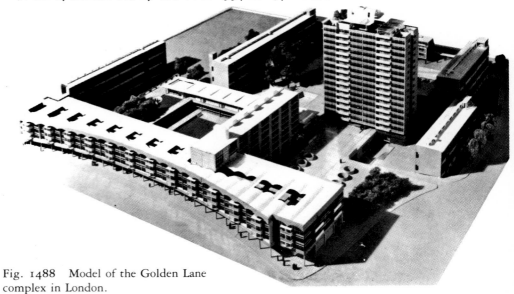

Fig. 1488   Model of the Golden Lane complex in London.

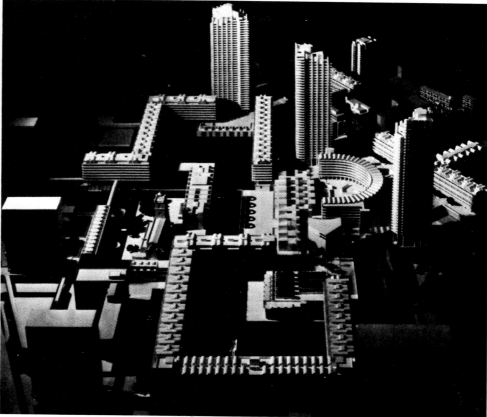

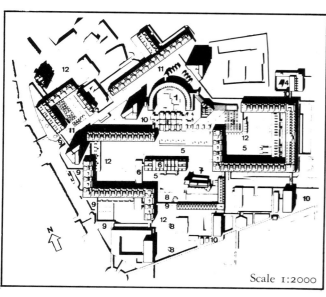

Scale 1:2000

Figs 1489–91 Two views of the
model and plan of the Barbican
complex in the City of London,
completed in 1974 by the Greater
London Council. It includes 2,100
homes for 6,500 people, and a large
number of commercial and recreational
activities.

1–3. Art centre.
4. Office blocks.
5. Ornamental pool.
6. Girls' school.
7. Church.
8. Remains of a Roman wall.
9. Overhead walkway.
10. Raised pedestrian walkway (19 metres).
11. Raised pedestrian walkway (21.5
metres).
12. Green areas.

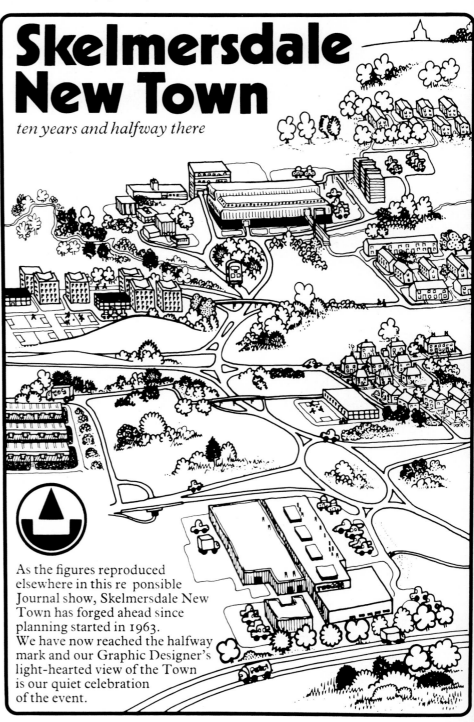

Skelmersdale New Town

ten years and halfway there

As the figures reproduced elsewhere in this re ponsible Journal show, Skelmersdale New Town has forged ahead since planning started in 1963. We have now reached the halfway mark and our Graphic Designer's light-hearted view of the Town is our quiet celebration of the event.

Fig. 1492   Publicity brochure for Skelmersdale New Town, published ten years after its founding; from the magazine *Town and Country Planning*, January 1974.

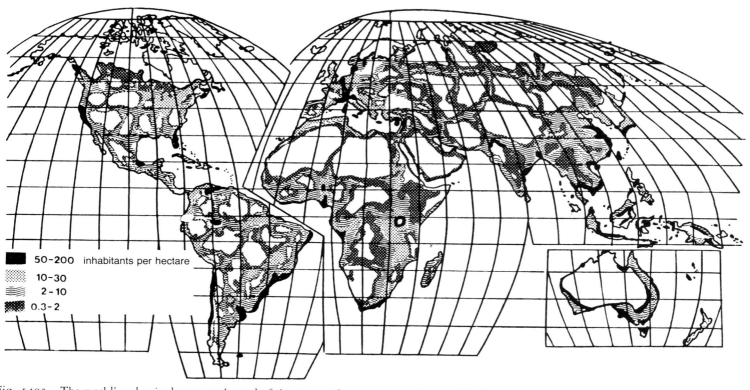

Fig. 1493   The world's urbanised areas at the end of the twenty-first century, as forecast by Constantine Doxiadis.

THE THIRD WORLD AND THE PHENOMENON OF THE 'MARGINAL' SETTLEMENT

In the so-called developed countries of Europe and North America, a confrontation is taking place between the traditional methods of running a city and the proposals set forth by modern research. The result of this confrontation can be either a confirmation of the traditional city, a more or less pronounced improvement, or the fulfilment of the alternatives envisaged by modern architecture. In certain countries the territorial balance is safeguarded by the public planning authorities; urban development is controlled in a reasonable way, and some of the basic elements demanded by theoretical research (reasonably-priced housing, the separation of pedestrians and motor cars, as well as a range of easily accessible amenities) are guaranteed to the majority of citizens.

In the other countries of the world, the towns and cities are developing just as rapidly, if not more so; in 1950, the urban population represented a fifth of the world's total population, now it has risen to almost half, and soon town dwellers will be in the majority. Some experts have tried to predict the shape of the new, world-wide city of the future (Fig. 1493). But this great rise in urban development has taken many different forms. Architect-designed housing, which conforms to certain standards, and properly laid out towns and cities, complete with public services, parks and paved streets, are enjoyed by only part of the world's inhabitants. The other part has no access to such refinements: they live in their own unplanned environment, often directly adjoining regular developments, but completely different from them. They have no legal title to the land that they occupy, their homes are built from whatever materials are available, and the basic amenities are either totally lacking or are laid on subsequently, to a completely

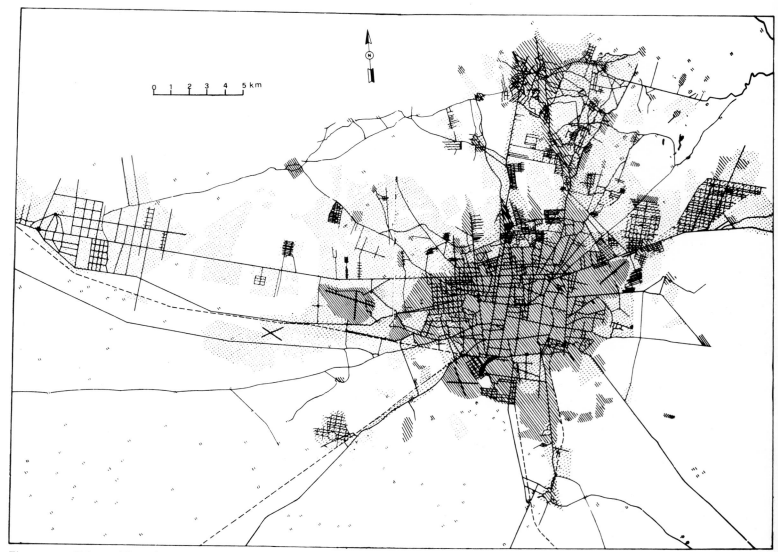

Fig. 1494   Tehran. The urbanised areas (shaded), the partially urbanised areas (broken shading) and the unbuilt areas already prepared for development (in dots), from data supplied in 1960–1.

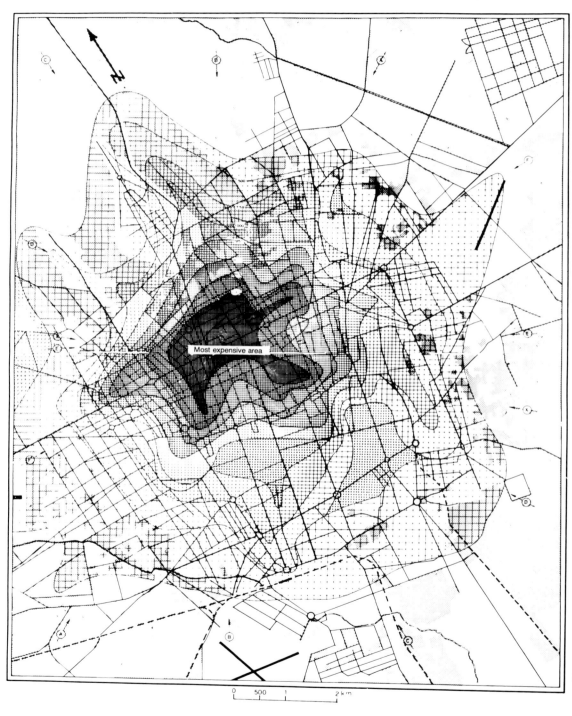

Most expensive area

Fig. 1495 Diagram showing
the prices of building land in
Tehran. The prices vary from
£3.50 to £26.50 per square
metre, but they reach £200 per
square metre along the main
streets. Information from
1960–1.

0   500   1   2 km

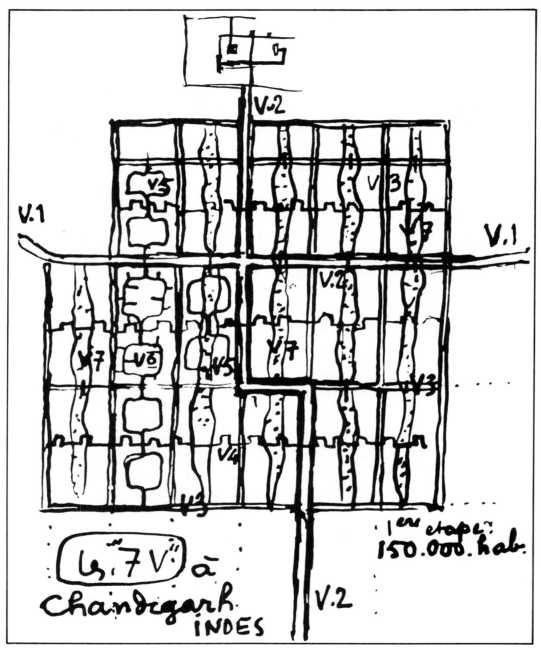

Figs 1496–8 Chandigarh.
General layout, showing the
different categories of roads:
main highways (VI, V2), local
roads (V3), commercial
thoroughfares (V4), streets
leading to the entrances of the
houses (V5, V6), paths leading
through the open spaces of
green between the educational
establishments and the
recreational areas (V7). View
and plan of the Capitol (at the
northernmost edge of the city),
which contains the government
buildings:

1. Parliament.
2. Secretariat.
3. Governor's Palace.
4. Law Courts.
5, 6. The earth sculptures at the
centre of the esplanade.
7. The Open Hand sculpture.

Chandigarh is the new capital of the Indian
Punjab, planned by Le Corbusier and a
team of European and Indian colleagues at
the request of Pandit Nehru in 1951. The
old master planned the city's layout and he
also designed and executed the Capitol, the
most important work of his career. Due to
the exceptional degree of involvement felt
by both those who commissioned it and
those who executed it, this city is the most
significant one so far built in the Third
World since the end of the colonial era.

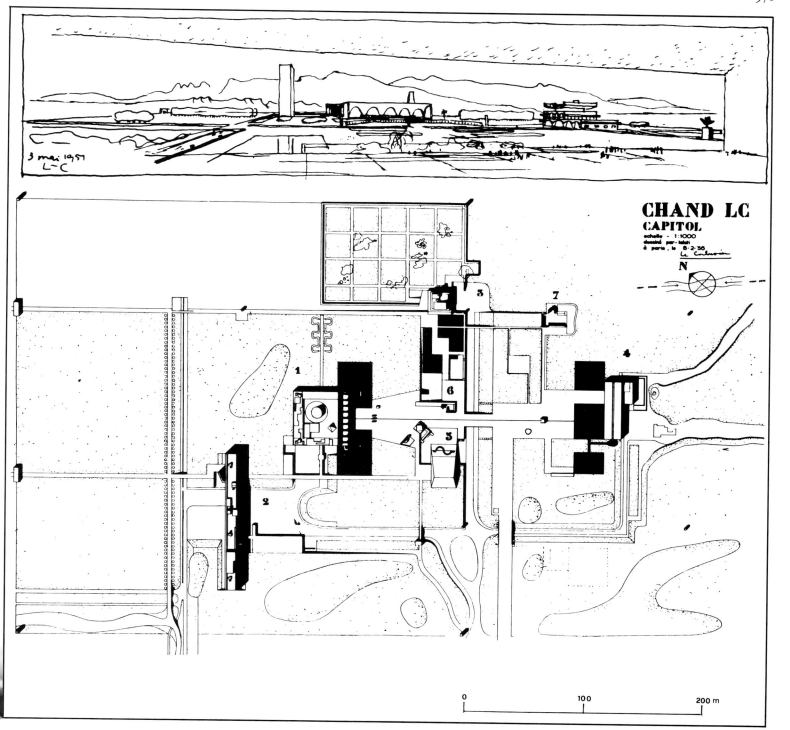

3 mai 1957
L-C

CHAND LC
CAPITOL
echelle - 1:1000
dessiné par- Intuti
à paris, le 8-2-56
Le Corbusier
N

0   100   200 m

Figs 1499–1500   Two views of *La Salle des pas perdus* in the Parliament building: one of Le Corbusier's most extraordinary achievements.

A. Rajendra park
B. Capitol
C. Museum of Knowledge
D. Parliament
E. Secretariat
F. Open Hand
G. Supreme court
H. Polytechnic
I. Engineering
J. Houses for the ministers
K. Houses for the judges
L. Architecture
M. Hospital centre
N. Art school
O. Museum and art gallery
P. Hostels
Q. Faculty
R. University campus
S. Crematorium
T. Bus station
U. Civic/commercial centre
V. Library

1. Lake Bukhna
2. General markets
3. Fruit and cereals
4. Wood
5. Transport goods
6. Railway station
7. Architecture office
8. Tagore theatre
9. Indo-Swiss trading centre
10. Industrial area

Fig. 1501   Plan of the city of Chandigarh, in its final form.

The numbers indicate the different sectors of the city (from 1 to 38).

Fig. 1502   Exterior view of a group of 'marginal' dwellings (Caracas).

different standard from that prevailing in the rest of the city.

These unofficial settlements have been called 'marginal' because they are regarded as a secondary fringe of the 'post-liberal' city; almost every major city in the world has a number of inhabitants who are either homeless or live in conditions of extreme poverty. But in the Third World this 'marginal' definition no longer holds good, because the unplanned settlements often grow faster than the city proper, and already in many countries they provide the majority of the population with somewhere to live.

In the planned areas of the towns and cities modern methods of architecture and urban layout are applied with varying degrees of success, but this helps to create privileged sectors. The techniques become instruments of luxury, a means of improving the living conditions of a minority, who already enjoy a far higher standard of living in any case, and the gap between the privileged few and the rest of the population becomes wider.

Let us take a look at the main evidence.

According to a 1962 United Nations report, half of the people living in Africa, Asia and Latin America either

Fig. 1503   The interior of a 'marginal' home (Lima).

possessed no home at all, or one that was insanitary, over-crowded and inadequate.

An ever-increasing section of this population has drifted from the countryside into the towns. It has been estimated that the population of Asia, Africa and Latin America has grown by 40 per cent during the last fifteen years, while the urban population has doubled (from 750 to 1,500 million). But only a fraction of these people have been absorbed into the planned cities and towns. By far the greater part have gone to swell the shanty towns and illegal settlements, which are growing faster than ever. In Venezuela, for example, 60 per cent of the people live in towns of more than 10,000 inhabitants, and of these, 50 per cent live in so-called 'marginal' settlements; the most ambitious programmes of public intervention have been proposed to try and keep this potentially growing percentage at its present level. Each country has its own name for these unplanned districts: they are called *ranchos* in Venezuela, *barriadas* in Peru, *favelas* in Brazil, *bidonvilles* in French-speaking countries and *ishish* in the Middle East. Where the climate allows it, people do not bother to build homes: in Calcutta, for example, 600,000 people sleep on the streets (Fig. 1504).

Fig. 1504   View of a street in Calcutta.

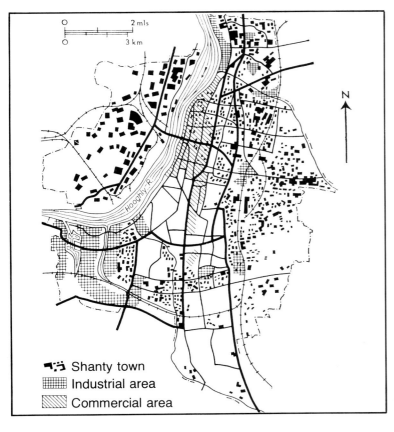

Fig. 1505 Map of Calcutta showing marginal settlements (bustees).

Fig. 1506 The people who live and sleep on the streets of Calcutta.

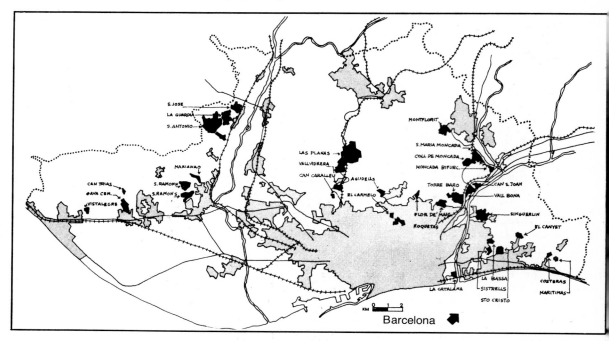

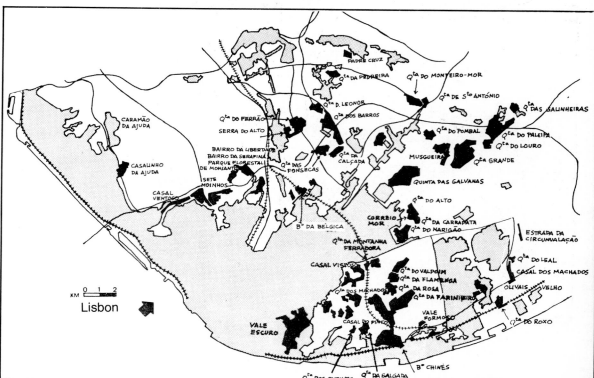

Figs 1507–8 Districts of illegal housing (shown in black) which have sprung up in recent years in Barcelona and Lisbon.

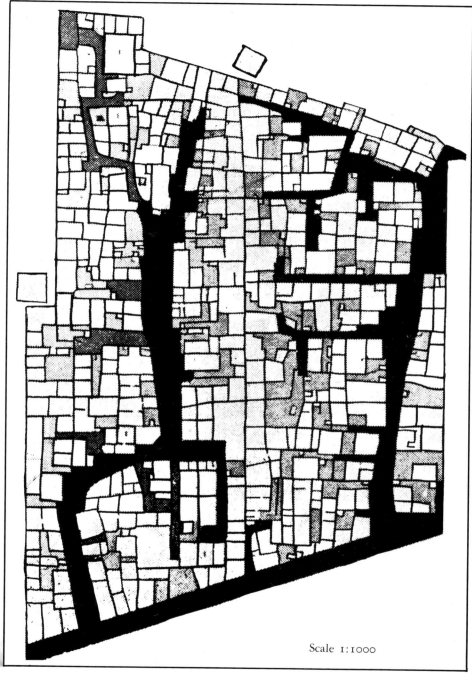

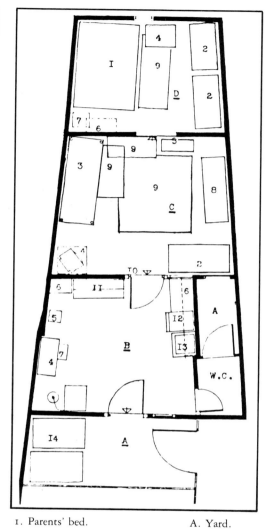

1. Parents' bed.   A. Yard.
2. Children's beds.   B. Kitchen.
3. Bunk beds.   C, D. Rooms.
4. Table.
5. Stove.
6. Shelf.
7. Chair.
8. Wardrobe.
9. Carpets.
10. Curtain.
11. Cupboard.
12. Wash basin.
13. Cement sink under the water taps.
14. Fuel store.

Figs 1509–10   A district of illegal housing in Nanterre, near
Paris; diagrams from 1966. The black parts denote the public areas,
the semi-public areas are in grey and the private areas in pale grey.

Figs 1511–12   Aerial photograph and map of part of the outskirts of Rome (Centocelle); in the foreground is the planned district, while beyond the road is a district of illegal housing, made out of bricks and mortar, and also a small shanty town.

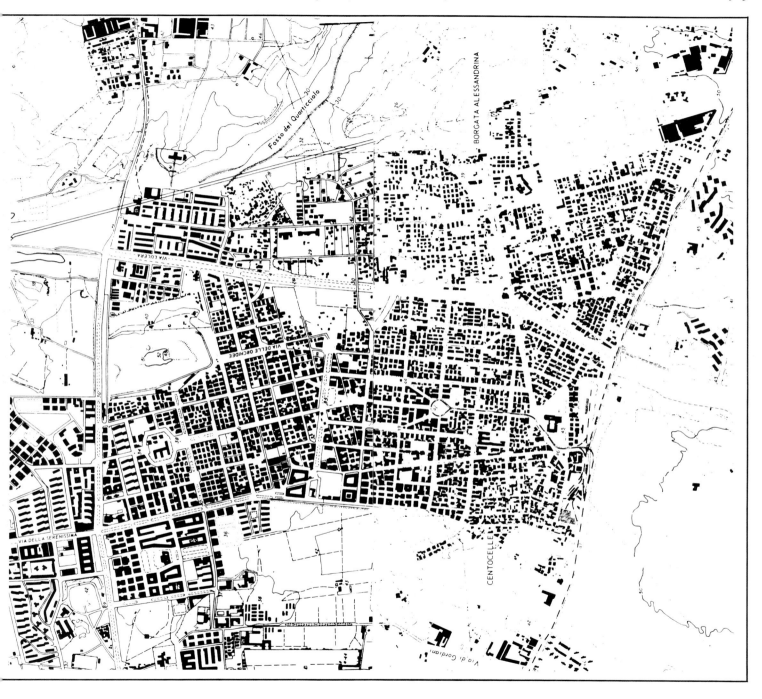

Figs 1513–14   Examples of illegal housing units, erected by small builders
on plots belonging to a large property owner near Rome. All the money
available has been put into building the houses, one floor at a time, and the
public areas remain a wasteland, with no services and no proper layout. The
local council will be obliged to lay on water, electricity and a bus stop.

Fig. 1515 A shanty town in
Rome (Batteria Nomentana), built
along the side of a railway
embankment.

Fig. 1516 Another shanty town in
Rome (Campo Parioli), built on an
unused stretch of public land.

Fig. 1517   A street scene in South America.

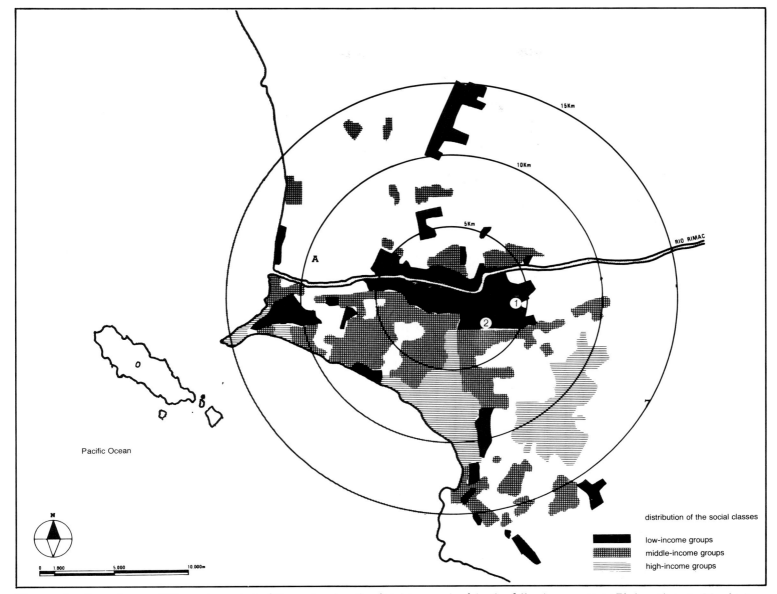

Pacific Ocean

RIO RIMAC

15Km

10Km

5Km

A

distribution of the social classes

low-income groups
middle-income groups
high-income groups

N

0   1,000   5,000   10,000m

Fig. 1518   General map of Lima, the capital of Peru, showing the districts examined in the following pages: 1. El Agustino, 2. Mendocita.

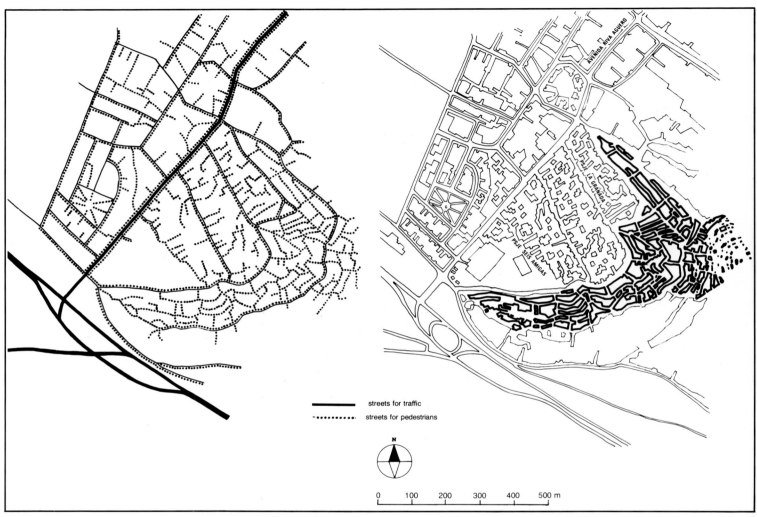

The 'marginal' settlement of El Agustino in Lima:
Fig. 1519   The network of streets for pedestrians and traffic.   Fig 1520   The houses in the hilly part (outlined in black).

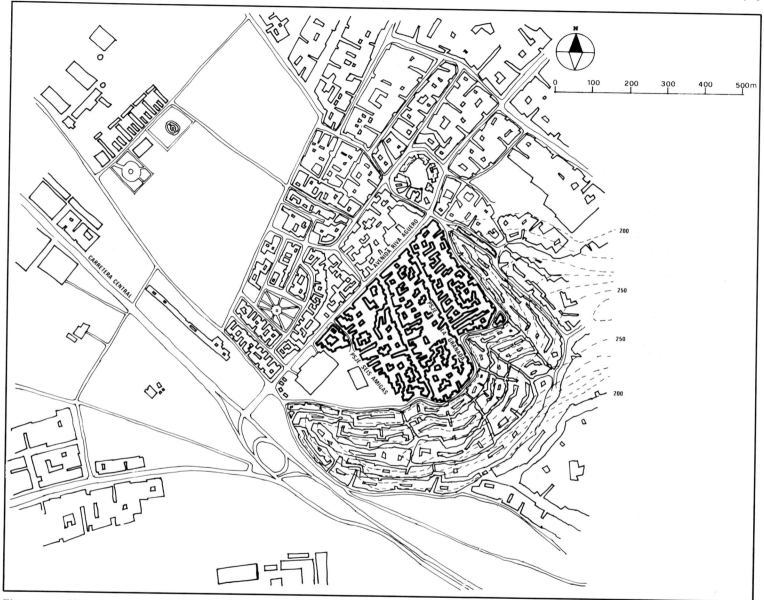

Fig. 1521 The houses on level ground (outlined in black).

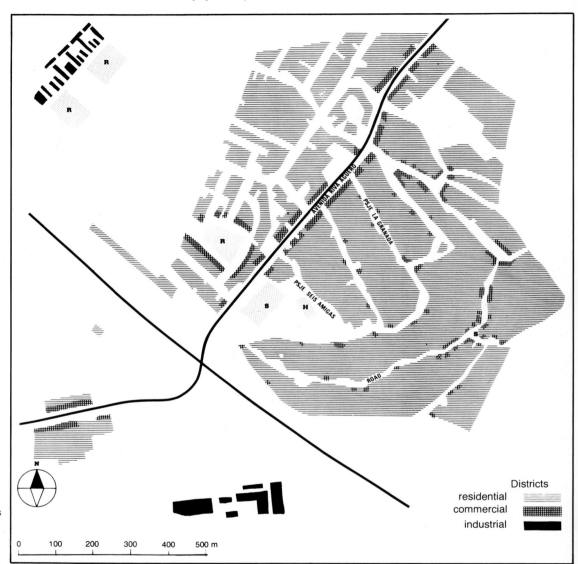

The dotted sections are service areas
R – Recreation
S – School
H – Hospital

Districts
residential
commercial
industrial

Fig. 1522   The distribution of buildings in the El Agustino district of Lima.

Fig. 1523 Aerial photograph of the district.

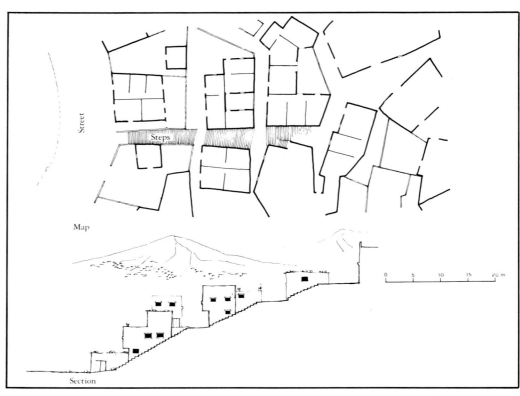

Street

Steps

Map

Section

0   5   10   15   20 m

Figs 1524–5   Plan and section of a group
of houses in the hilly part of El Agustino.

Fig. 1526   Aerial view of the same sector;
the group of children to the right are
looking up at the aeroplane from which
this photograph was taken.

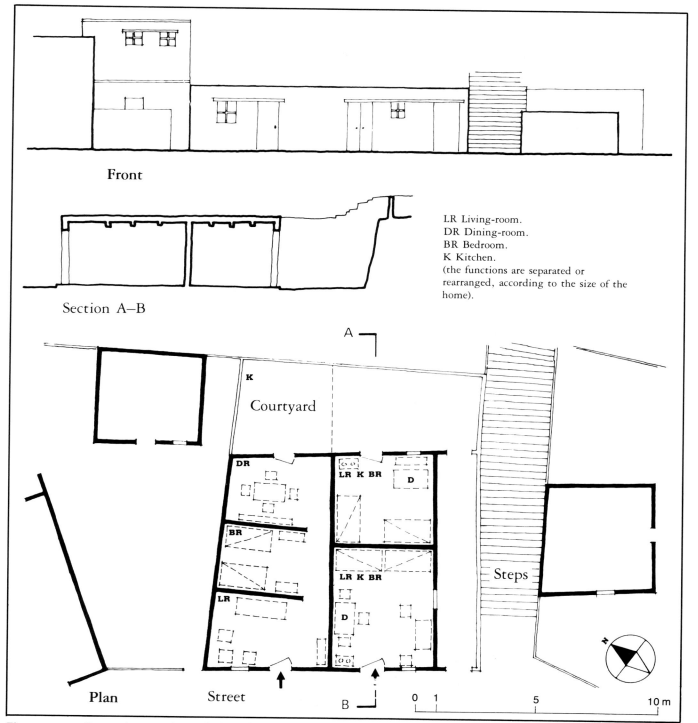

Front

Section A–B

LR Living-room.
DR Dining-room.
BR Bedroom.
K Kitchen.
(the functions are separated or rearranged, according to the size of the home).

Plan   Street

Figs 1527–9   Front view, section and plan of three homes in the hilly part of El Agustino. One home has three rooms, and two have only one room, and they share a communal courtyard.

SECTION   PLAN

Figs 1530–2   Plan and sectional view
of a group of houses in the level part
of El Agustino; view of a street, with
the hilly area in the background.

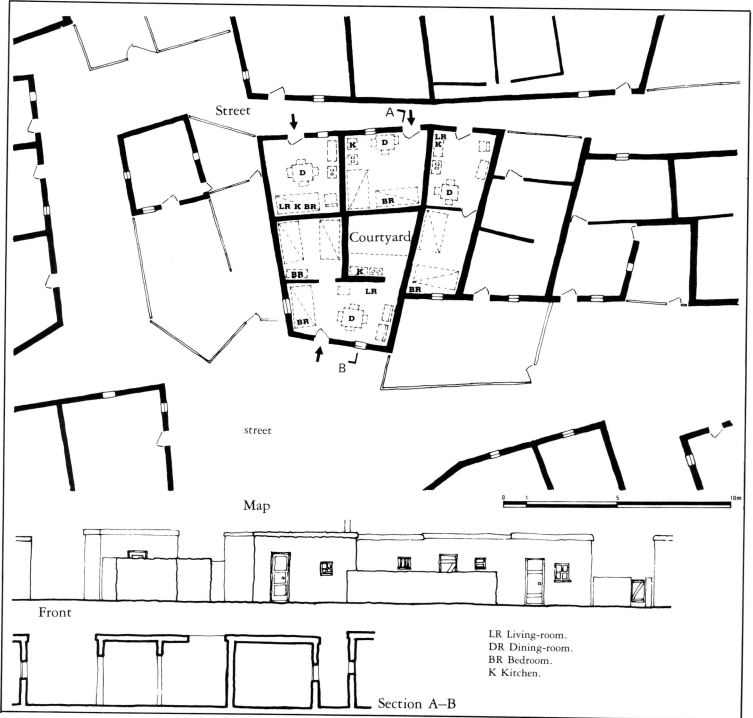

Street

A

B

Courtyard

LR K

K D LR K

D

BR D

BR

BR K

LR

BR

street

Map

0   1   5   10m

Front

LR Living-room.
DR Dining-room.
BR Bedroom.
K Kitchen.

Section A–B

Figs 1533–5   Front view, plan and section, of four homes in the level part of El Agustino. One home with two rooms and a yard, one home with just two rooms and two homes of only one room.

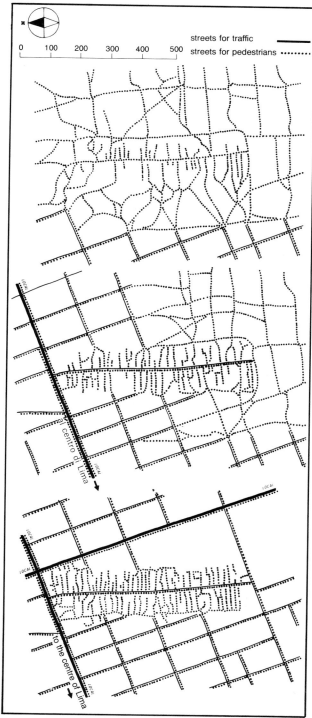

streets for traffic

streets for pedestrians ········

0 100 200 300 400 500

Figs 1536–44 The 'marginal' district of Mendocita in Lima, originally built in the countryside, but later incorporated into the outskirts of the city. Plans of the buildings, of the way in which they were distributed and of the street network (for pedestrians and for traffic), in 1942, 1952, and 1961.

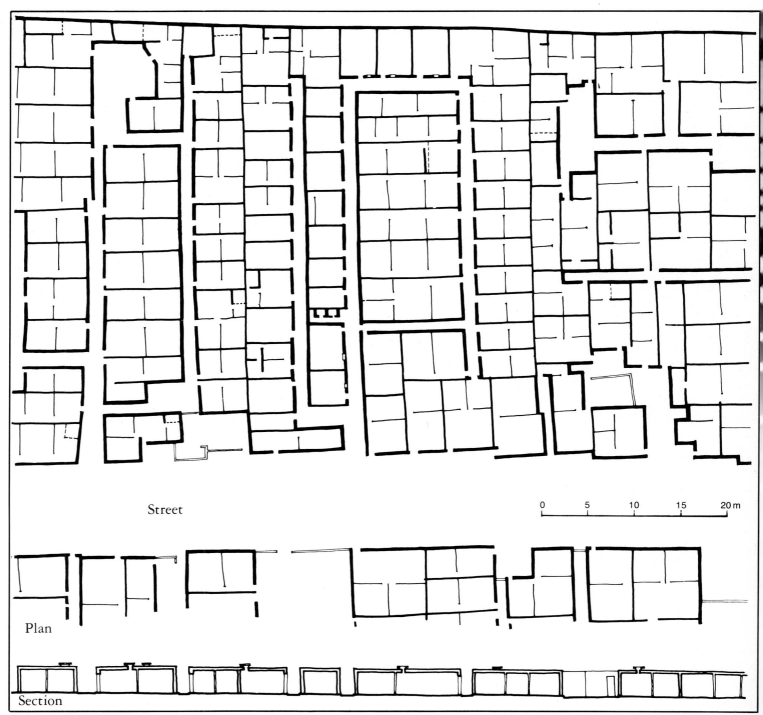

Street

Plan

Section

0   5   10   15   20 m

Figs 1545–6   Plan and sectional view of a group of houses in Mendocita.

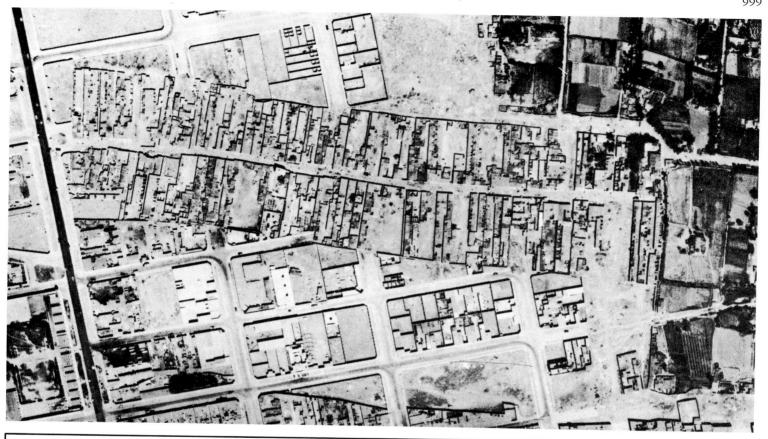

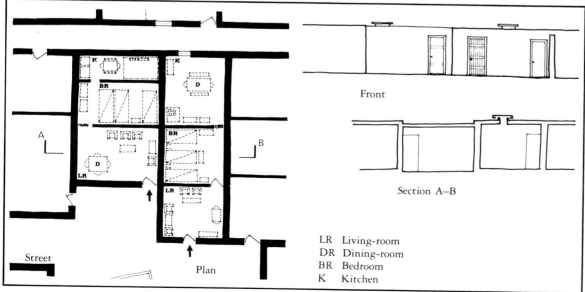

Front

Section A–B

LR Living-room
DR Dining-room
BR Bedroom
K Kitchen

Street

Plan

Figs 1547–50 Aerial view of Mendocita in 1952; plan, front view and section of two 3-bedroom homes.

Fig. 1551 Aerial view of Mendocita in 1961; the layout of the planned city and that of the 'marginal' settlement are in direct conflict with each other.

Fig. 1552   Panoramic view of Caracas in 1974. A city of 2 million inhabitants, about a half of whom live in 'marginal' districts.

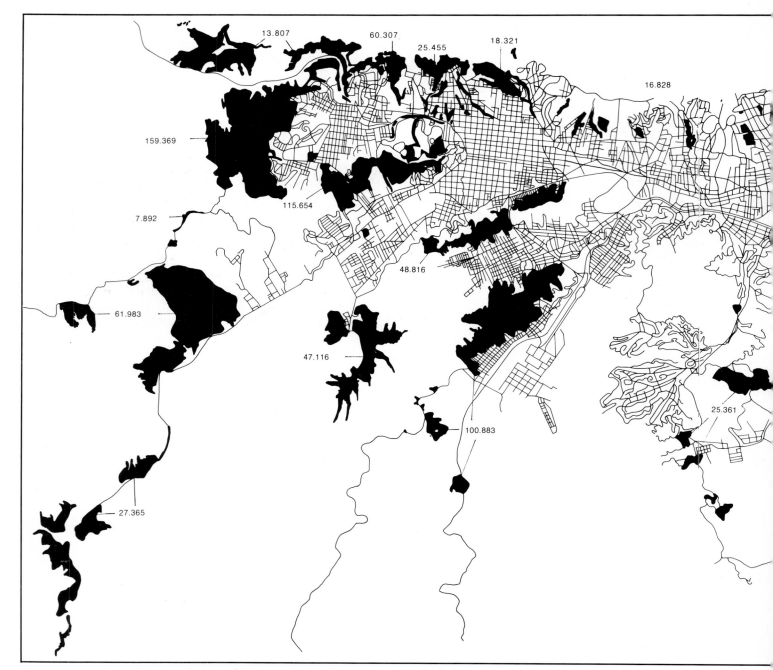

Figs 1553–4   General map and view of Caracas; the black parts are 'marginal' districts, showing the 1971 population figures; the combined figures come to 866,919, from a total population of about 2 million.

Figs 1555–6　Two views of the stepped streets in the San Agustin district of Caracas; each street is composed of cement steps and flanked by open drainage channels.

ig. 1557   A children's 'playground' in the San Agustin district of Caracas.

Fig. 1558   A district of squatters' houses, laid out on the fringes of Lima.

Economic development has not alleviated the situation, has accentuated the difference between the planned and unplanned urban areas. There are even shanty towns in the rich oil-producing countries, such as Kuwait, which has the highest *per capita* income in the world. In the very near future the majority of the world's population will be housed in unplanned settlements; in fact, while the world's total population is doubling every thirty years and the urban population every fifteen years, the 'marginal' urban population is doubling every seven and a half years.

The developed countries of Europe and North America are not completely sheltered from the effects of this rise in population levels. During the past years the number of illegal buildings has increased considerably: in Rome, approximately 800,000 people live in houses built without the necessary permits, and although these buildings are less 'picturesque' than those in Asia and South America, they still form a separate town, as well as being too numerous to be considered a temporary phenomenon.

The formation of unplanned towns next to planned ones, which is the main problem facing the world, means that one has to take a fresh look at the way in which modern architecture has developed over the past fifty years, as well as reassessing its future prospects.

Modern architecture started out as a means of overcoming the social discriminations of the 'post-liberal' city, and of providing all its inhabitants with the benefits of a scientifically planned environment. Its proposals were partially, and tardily, accepted, due to the resistance of the interests and institutions that depended on the administration of the 'post-liberal' city for their existence.

Meanwhile, the properly planned city, whether 'post-liberal' or modern, is no longer within the reach of everybody. The majority of the world's population is crammed into unplanned cities and towns, which resemble, on a much larger scale, the 'liberal' settlements of the early industrial era.

Modern architecture, therefore, now stands at a crossroads: it can content itself with improving the environment of the dominant minority and become the instrument of a new, world-wide discrimination, or it can start to analyse the divisions between the two new types of urban development. It thereby enters into the midst of a political conflict, which not only involves every country in the world, but also international relations as a whole.

This urban dualism results from the policy of declaring illegal the homes and districts built spontaneously by the inhabitants, and of building, instead, great complexes of purpose-built homes along conventional modern lines. The authorities make no attempt to utilise the capacity for spontaneous work of those who want to provide their own housing; instead, they offer woefully inadequate numbers of homes, which are in any case beyond the economic reach of the majority of people, but which are intended to fit in with the buildings inhabited by the rich and can be absorbed into the city designed for them. The homes built in this way are for occupation by employees, workers belonging to recognised trades unions and other registered persons. It is accepted that the homes in the illegal settlements may well become intolerably crowded and insanitary, because the authorities refuse to acknowledge their existence. In that case, the worst defects are corrected by the introduction of basic amenities — water supply, electricity, schools, police stations, and stretches of metalled road to allow free passage for ambulances and army jeeps. These amenities are a pale imitation of those available in the modern sectors, and they serve to underline the differences between the two settlements. They protect the rest of the city from contact with the unofficial districts and they also establish the latter's dependent character. The elements of the planned city — modern houses, paved streets, public services — are simultaneously reserved for an élite minority and imposed as an unattainable model for everyone else. As a result, the division between the two cities becomes an instrument of discrimination and oppression, vital for the social system's stability.

Contemporary Utopian thinkers such as Ivan Illich propose a different policy, which 'should start by defining what it is that people cannot procure by themselves for building a house, and then guarantee everyone a plot of land, a water supply, a certain number of pre-fabricated elements, the necessary tools (from drills to lifting machinery) and a basic minimum loan. In this way, people would be able to build homes that were more lasting, more comfortable and more sanitary, whilst also learning how to deal with new materials and new building techniques.' Some experiments along these lines, as yet on a very limited scale, are being conducted in Peru and other countries, but this means that the whole housing policy, as hitherto described, will have to be reassessed from the 'unplanned' inhabitants' point of view, rather than from that of the 'planned' inhabitants. The city would have to be reorganised, reserving the best sites, instead of the worst ones, for the self-built districts. The communication network would have to be modified to give precedence to pedestrian walkways and a comprehensive public transport system, which, although slower, would take the place of the fast urban motorways designed for use by private motorists.

Modern architecture can be the instrument of the first policy, or the second policy. If the validity of the second policy is accepted, it would be necessary to re-examine what is taking place in the developed countries, and discover to what degree the new building and town-planning schemes are meeting the real needs of the people, or whether they are merely designed to fulfil the exigencies imposed on the people by the need to ensure a continued growth of the industrial machine. This continual architectural escalation can be made accessible to the many or to the few, but it is of no real benefit to either, while at the same time it creates an unbridgeable gap between the developed and the less developed countries. Architectural research, like all scientific research, can be of real service to everyone, or it can foster the dream of a continually improving environment which in reality is the exclusive domain of an increasingly small fraction of the world's total population.

Fig. 1559   An allegorical representation of the alternatives open to modern architecture: *Contemporary disaster or the spatial freedom of the environment?* A drawing by Le Corbusier, made during World War II.

Index of names

Figure numbers are set in italic type

Aachen (Aix-la-Chapelle), *398*
Abercrombie and Forshaw, *930*
Abusir, *77–8*
Aegina, 57, 69
Agra, 272
Agrigentum, 57, 107, *201–4*
Agrippa, *152*, 100, 192
Ahrenburg-Holstein, *3–4*
Aichbühl, *6–7*
Aigues Mortes, *729–37*
Alatri, 209
Alberti, Leon Battista, 530, 799, 629
Alcantara, 207, *321*
Alemtejo, 8
Alexander the Great, 128
Alexandria, *210–11*, 221, 259
Algiers, *413–17*
Amalfi, 287
Amiens, *506–7*
Amsterdam, 706, 708, *1012–26*, 715, *898–900*, *1357–72*, *910–11*, *1374–86*, *913–14*
Antioch, *212*, 259
Antoninus Pius, 147
Antwerp, 386, *884*, 605, *886–9*
Aosta, 221
Arbela, *47*
Arezzo, 140
Argos, 57
Aristotle, 107
Arles, *404*
Arslan Tash, 57
Assisi, 253
Athens, 1) Classical, *56–7*, 69, *71–3*, *123–57*, 95, 98, 100, *170*, 143
　　2) Modern, 100, *171–8*
Augustus Caesar, 140, 231, 145, 147, *251–3*, 176, 194, 203, 207
Avignon, 326

Babylon, 28, *58–63*, 107

Badminton, *1045*
Baghdad, 259, *421–5*, *438–9*, 327
Bagnaia, *881–3*
Bakema and van den Broek, *1326–54*, *897*, *1374–7*, *913*, *1380–6*
Barattieri, Nicolo, 335
Barbari, Jacopo de', *526*, *542–3*, 351
Barcelona, 326, 823, *1201*, *1507*
Basildon, *933*
Bauhaus, *849*, *1234–6*, *1271–3*, *1276–80*
Beaumont du Périgord, *720*
Berlage, H. P., *1358–9*, *899*
Berne, *475*
Bernini, *263*, *584*, *869*, *664*
Blenheim Palace, *1043–4*
Boğazköy (Hattusa), *64–5*
Bologna, *337*, 221, 310, 326, 389, *601–25*, 393, 400, 402, 408, 477
Bolsena, 140
Bonnecourt, Villard de, *502–5*
Boston (USA), *1223*
Bracknell, *933*
Bramante, Donato, 554, 566, *841–3*, 569, *845–7*, 573, 584
Brasilia, *1355–6*
Bremen, *477*, *367*
Bruges, 253, 326, 327, 573, *367* *575–600*, *369*, *375*, *384*, 386, 477
Brunkmann, van der Vlugt and Maaskant, *1297–1300*
Brunneleschi, Filippo, *681–3*, *465*, *703*, *473*, *501–2*, *764–7*, 769, *510*, *774*, 780, *787–8*, *790–1*, *523*, *528*, 530
Brussels, 326
Buchanan, Colin, *1470–1*, *963*
Budingen, *459*
Buenos Aires, *1097*, *1266*

Byzantium, 147, 236 (*see also* Constantinople)

Cadiz, 221
Cairo, 259, 412
Calcutta, 977, *1504–6*
Cameroons, *14–16*
Candelaria, *926*
Candilis, *897*
Canterbury, *515*
Canton, *1208*
Capua, 205, 221
Caracalla, 140, 147, 194, 203
Caracas, *915*, *1502*, *1552–7*
Carthage, 221
Caserta, 701, *1008–9*
Cerveteri, *222–3*, 140
Chandigarh, *1496–1501*
Chartres, 353, *494–6*
Chicago, *943*, *1216–19*
Chiusi, 140
Cholula, *908*, *916*
Claudius, *234–5*, *303*, *325*
Cleisthenes, 71
Cleon, 71
Cluny, *491*
Coalbrookdale, *1048*
Codussi, Mauro, 338
Colne Valley, *1071*
Cologne, 221, *508*, 326
Como, *350–1*
Constantine, 147, 266, 203, 236
Constantinople, 135, 229, 236, *373–95*, 327, 335, *534–5* (*see also* Byzantium)
Corby, *933*
Cordoba, 259, 272, *440–3*, 327
Corinth, 57
Cortuna, 140
Crawley, *935*, *1412–15*
Crete, 57
Cumae, 205
Cumbernauld, *1418–22*, *940*
Cuzco, 615, *909–10*

Cwmbran, *933*
Czechoslovakia, *748–57*

Da Cambio, Arnolfo, 445, *681–3*, *472–3*, *717*
Dakar, *1203*
Dalny, *1207*
Daman, *900*
Damascus, 260, *407–9*
Deir-el-Medina, *82–5*
Delhi, 272
Delos, *158–60*
Delphi, *117–20*
Diocletian, *299–300*, 194, 203, *362–3*, 229
Domitian, 147, *243*, 194, 212
Doxiadis, Constantine, *1493*

East Kilbride, *933*
El Lahun, 80
Engels, Friedrich, *753–4*, *1082–3*, 765
Epidauros, *115–16*

Ferrara, 556, *830–6*, 558, 561, 629
Fez, 259, *1202*
Florence, 214, 221, 310, 326, 327, *665–716*, *437–8*, 443, *445–6*, 477, *501–2*, *764–90*, 505, 510, *530–1*, 564, 823, *1200*
Florida, *13*
Fontaine, *1057–9*
Fourier, Charles, 757, *1086–7*, 765
Frankfurt-am-Main, 326
Frascati, *880*
Fulda, *398*

Garches, *1252–3*
Garnier, Charles, *1171*
Gattinara, *760–2*
Geneva, *849*, *1251*

Genoa, 287, 367, 605, *892–6*
Germanicus, 212
Ghardaia, *430–6*
Ghent, 310, *326–7*
Gibberd, Frederick, *1408*
Gizeh, 66, *69–70*, *72–74*, *39*, *76*
Glasgow, *1075*
Glenrothes, 933
Glotz, G., *59*
Goa, 897
Godin, Jean Baptiste, 758, *1089–95*, *1098–9*
Granada, *447–51*
Gropius, Walter, *1234–5*, 849, *1275*, *1277–80*
Guadalajara (Mexico), *918–19*
Gubbio, 253

Hacilar, *19–20*
Hadrian, 100, 147, 149, *262*, *269–70*, *203*, 212, *329*, 437
Hafaga, *43–4*
Hallstatt, 5
Hamburg, 367
Hardouin-Mansart, Jules, 660, *964–5*, *669*, 970
Harlow, 933, *1408–11*
Harrison and Abramowitz, *1260–1*
Hatfield, 940, *1423–7*
Haussmann, G-E., 787, *1151–5*, 798, *1163–4*
Hemel Hempstead, 933
Hengelo, *1327–32*
Herculaneum, 176, 296
Hereford, *473–4*
Herodes Atticus, 100, *174*, *176–177*
Herodotus, 69
Hill, Octavia, 928
Hippodamus, 71, 107, *179–81*, *184–5*, 128, *276–7*, 220, 409
Honorius, 147, 231
Hook, 940, *1423–7*
Horta, 841
Howard, Ebenezer, 928, *1397*, 933
Houston, *1222*

Illich, Ivan, *1007*
Imola, *336–7*
Isfahan, 272, *454–8*

Jerusalem, 259
Julius Caesar, 143, 177, 192
Justinian, 236

Kairouan, 259
Karnak, 44, *88–92*
Khorsabad, *49–56*
Klein, Alexander, *1303–6*
Kuwait, 1007

Lagash, 24
Lambaesis, *346*
Lauriacum, *349*
Le Corbusier, *123*, 311, *336*, *1096–7*, *1103*, 849, *1251–69*, 861, *1281–5*, 881, *1307–13*, *1325*, 897, *1496–1500*, *1559*
Leeuwarden, *1326*
Leptis Magna, 221
Lesbos, 57
Letchworth Garden City, 928, *1398–9*
Le Vau, Louis, 660, 669
Lima, *911*, *1503*, *1518–51*, *1558*
Limoges, *405*
Ling, Arthur, *1428*
Lisbon, *891*, *1508*
London, 221, 253, 326, 716, *1027–42*, *723*, *1054–5*, *1060–9*, *1078–9*, *1125–7*, *1132*, *1136*, *1144–6*, 920, *1387–96*, 930, *1400–6*, *1468–71*, *1468–91*
Louvain, 326
Lübeck, *467–8*, 490, 326, 367
Lucca, 437
Lucignano, 480
Luxor, 44
Lyons, 209, 221

Malacca, 898
Malines, 326
Manchester, 733, *753–5*, *1081–3*
Marseilles, *1307*, *1309–12*
Marx, Karl, 765
Memphis, 37, 39, 47, 71
Mérida (Spain), 207
Mérida (Venezuela), *922–3*
Mesopotamia, 20, 25, 39
Mexico City, 615, *903–6*
Michelangelo Buonarroti, 531, 800, 569, 573, *851–60*
Middlesbrough, *1070*
Mies van der Rohe, Ludwig, 849, *1237–50*
Milan, 221, 229, *514*, 326, 327, *518–19*, *1138*
Miletus, 107, *184–6*
Milton Keynes, 940, *1433–67*

Minturno, *335*
Misenum, 209
Mondrian, Piet, *1228*, 849, *1230–2*
Montagnola, *12*
Monteriggioni, *758–9*
Montpazier, *724–8*
Mont St Michel, *509–12*
Moscow, 849
Mycenae, 55

Nanterre, 981
Naples, 107, 326, 701, *1005–7*
Nash, John, *1061–2*
Naxos, *107*, *57*
Nemours, *1313*
Nero, 145, *232*, *147*
New Babylon, *944*
New Towns, 930, 933, *1407*, *1416*, 940, (*see also* Basildon, Bracknell, Corby, Crawley, Cumbernauld, Cwmbran, East Kilbride, Glenrothes, Harlow, Hatfield, Hemel Hempstead, Hook, Milton Keynes, Newton Aycliffe, Peterlee, Runcorn, Skelmersdale, Stevenage, Welwyn)
Newton Aycliffe, 933
New York, *933–42*, *1097*, *1116–22*, *1220–1*, 841, *1226*, 849, *1260–1*, *1266*
Nîmes, *324*, 209, *327–8*, 221
Nineveh, *48*, 28
Nippur, *27–9*
Noord-Kennemerland, *1333–54*
Nottingham, *1077*
Nuremburg, 326, 411, *626–64*, *432–3*

Olympia, *110*, *113–14*
Olynthus, 107, *179–83*
Orvieto, *226*, 492
Ostia, 176, *194*, *304–10*
Oud, J. J. P., *1286–96*
Ovid, 140
Owen, Robert, *1084–5*, *756–7*, 765

Padua, 310, *493*, 326, *794–5*
Paestum, *109*, 107, *195–200*, 316
Palermo, 259, 272, *452–3*, 327
Palladio, Andrea, 338
Paris, 221, 253, 326, 327, *516–17*, *946–51*, *655–6*, 664,

960–66, *666*, 672, *976–8*, 765, *1097*, *1123*, *1135*, *1147–65*, 787, 790, *798–9*, *1171–95*, 823, 841, *1224–5*, 849, *1264*, *1266*
Pasargadae, 28
Peking, *1209–11*
Percier, *1057–9*
Pergamum, *213–17*
Pericles, 71, *154*, 98
Périgeux, *401*
Persepolis, 28
Perugia, 140, 253
Peterlee, 933
Philadelphia, 930
Philip of Macedon, 128
Piacenza, 326
Pienza, 536, *804–10*, *539*, *341*
Piraeus, 71, *155*, 100
Pisa, 287, 326
Pisistratus, 69
Pola, 221
Polybius, 345
Pompeii, 107, 176, *276–97*
Pozzuoli, 205
Priene, *187–194*
Puebla, 924

Quito, 917

Ratisbon, 347
Ravenna, 337, 229, *364–72*, *231*, 393
Rheims, *497–505*
Rhodes, 57, 107
Rietveld, Gerrit, *1229*, *1231*
Rimini, 221
Rio de Janeiro, 899, *1262*
Roehampton, *1472–84*
Rome, 1) Classical, 135, *219*, *227–32*, *140–3*, 145, 147, *234–66*, 149, *176–7*, 271, *274–5*, *192*, *297–303*, 194, *311–13*, 205, *319–20*, *325–6*
   2) Renaissance, *837–71*, 564, 566, 569, 573, 577, 580, 584
   3) Modern, *240–1*, 201, 203, *314–15*, 872, *875–7*, *1511–16*
Rosselino, Bernardo, 539
Rotterdam, *1286–1302*
Runcorn, 940, *1428–32*
Ruskin, John, 928

Saigon, *1204–5*

Sainte-Foy-la-Grande, *723*
St Germain-en-Laye, 656, *952*, 660
Salamis, 57, 69
Samos, 57
Salisbury, *743–7*
Saltaire, *1134*
San Francisco, *929*
San Gimignano, *481–2*
San Giovanni Valdarno, *717*
San Giovenale, *11*
San José (Bolivia), *927*
Sanmicheli, 338
San Vittorino, *460–3*
Sansovino, Jacopo, 338
Savannah (USA), *931*
Segovia, *323*, 209
Selinunte, *205–6*
Senlis, *402*
Septimius Severus, 265
Servius Tullius, *142*, 230
Seville, 446, 890
Shanghai, *1212–15*
Sharp, Thomas, *1412*
Shiraz, 40, 259, 272
Siedlung Halen (Berne), *1314–25*
Siena, 253, *483–9*, 310, 326
Silchester, *344*
Skelmersdale, *1492*
Spalato (Split), *362–3*
Sparta, 57
Stevenage, 933, *1417*
Stornaloco, 324
Stourhead, *1046–7*
Stuttgart, 849, *1247–50*, *1277–80*
Sumer, 37
Syracuse, 57, 207

Tacitus, *145*
Tarragona, 209
Tarquinia, 140
Tehran, *1494–5*
Tenochtitlan, 615, *901–3*
Teotihuacan, *907*
Tell Asmar, 30
Tell-el-Amarna, *96–100*
Terracina, 214
Thamesmead, *1485–6*
Thebes, 37, *87–92*
Themistocles, 71, *151*
Theodoric, 389
Theodosius, 229, 236
Theseus, 69
Tiberius, *212*

Timgad, *352–8*
Tirlemont, 326
Tiryns, 55
Titus, *246–50*
Tivoli, 149, *269–70*, 879
Tlaxcala, *925*
Toledo, *444–5*
Tours, *403*
Trajan, *244*, *259–61*, 176, 194, *303*, *321*
Trier, 221, *359–61*
Tripoli, *418*
Tunis, *437*
Turin, 221, 693, *990–1004*

Ukraine, *1*, *17–18*
Ulm, *513*
Ur, 21, *31–8*, *41–2*, 28, 263
Urbino, 541, *813–29*, 544, 554

Van de Velde, 841
Van Doesburg, 846, *1232*
Van Eesteren, Cornelius, *1232*, 900
Val Camonica, *9–10*
Valley of the Kings, *82–5*, *93–4*
Varro, *142*
Vaux-le-Vicomte, 660, *954–8*
Veli, 221, 140
Venice, 236, 287, 326, 520, 331, *522–4*, *335–6*, *525–72*, 351, 367, 477
Verona, 221, 326
Versailles, 272, 669, *967–75*, 672
Vespasian, *147*
Vetulonia, 140
Vienna, *348*, *980–9*, 685, 823, *1196–9*, 841
Villa dei Sette Bassi, *267–8*
Villa di Boscoreale, *338–41*
Villa Doria-Pamphili, *878*
Villeneuve-sur-Lot, *721–2*
Viterbo, 253
Vitruvius, 2, 140, *343*, *792*, *629*
Volsinii, 224
Volterra, 140
Von Erlach, Fischer, 685, *988–9*
Von Klenze, Leone, *173*
Vulci, 140

Welwyn Garden City, *928*
Welwyn, 933
Welzheim, *333*
Wilson, Hugh, 940, *1422*

Witham, *472*
Wood, John Jr., *1100–2*
Wulvesford, *472*

Xanten, *330*

Zeebrugge, 386, 600